ENTERPRISE TRANSFORMATION

ENTERPRISE TRANSFORMATION

Understanding and Enabling Fundamental Change

edited by

William B. Rouse

Tennenbaum Institute
Georgia Institute of Technology

WILEY-INTERSCIENCE

A JOHN WILEY & SONS, INC., PUBLICATION

For general information on our other products and services or for technical support, please contact our
Customer Care Department within the United States at (800) 762-2974, outside the United States at
(317) 572-3993 or fax (317) 572-4002.

Wiley also publishes its books in a variety of electronic formats. Some content that appears in print may
not be available in electronic format. For information about Wiley products, visit our web site at
www.wiley.com.

Library of Congress Cataloging-in-Publication Data is available.

ISBN-13 978-0-471-73681-3
ISBN-10 0-471-73681-3

Printed in the United States of America.

10 9 8 7 6 5 4 3 2 1

TABLE OF CONTENTS

Part III. Transformation Practices

Part IV. Transformation Case Studies

PREFACE

ENTERPRISE TRANSFORMATION

WILLIAM B. ROUSE

Technological invention and market innovation are widely recognized as primary factors in economic growth. This phenomenon is commonly illustrated in terms of new technologies that enable new products, often brought to market by startup companies whose goals include public offerings of their stock. This view is much too narrow and, equally important, very simplistic.

One reason is that many innovations involve processes rather than products. More effective and efficient processes for manufacturing, distributing, and servicing products can result in substantial market innovations. There is no better example than Wal-Mart's revolutionizing the retail market via information technology and associated new business practices.

Another argument for a richer view is the fact that both product and process innovations often originate with established enterprises rather than startups. Realization of the full value of these innovations often requires transformation of these enterprises to design business practices and organizational cultures to better align with the nature of the innovations. UPS provides a great example of such fundamental changes, transforming from a leading package delivery company to a global supply chain management services company.

Such transformations present enormous challenges. This book considers how best to understand and accomplish these fundamental changes. The goal is to document and communicate these best practices to the many enterprises – in both private and public sectors -- in need of transformation. The methods, tools, and practices discussed in this book can foster tremendous economic value. Indeed, Wal-Mart's and UPS's stories, as well as many other case studies provided in this book, offer definitive evidence of the enormous value of transformation.

ORGANIZATION OF THIS BOOK

Enterprise Transformation is organized in four parts. Part 1, "Introduction to Transformation," includes three chapters than provide an introduction and overview of the book, a broad systems-oriented view of transformation, and a more theoretical perspective on the forces that prompt transformation and the nature of how transformation is pursued.

Part 2, "Elements of Transformation," includes eight chapters. Two chapters address the crosscutting issues of transformational leadership, and organizational and cultural change. More functionally oriented chapters focus on manufacturing, logistics, services, R&D, enterprise computing, and quality management. These chapters provide a mixture of transformation principles and case studies of transformation within their domains.

Part 3: "Transformation Practices," includes six chapters. These chapters focus on transformation planning and execution, financing, bankruptcy, tax issues, public relations, and lessons learned from a wide range of transformation experiences. These chapters reflect the collective wisdom of several key players in the business of transformation.

Part 4: "Transformation Case Studies," includes five chapters on Newell Rubbermaid, Reebok, Lockheed Martin, and Interface, as well as consideration of transformation in academia that provides an overview of fundamental change at Georgia Tech. These chapters provide in-depth views of how principles and practices were actually applied and the consequent results.

ORIGINS OF THIS BOOK

My interest in enterprise transformation and motivation for this book grew out of a rich set of experiences working with private and public sector enterprises. Beginning in the late 1980s and continuing now, I have worked with over 100 major corporations and government agencies to address strategy issues that often involved fundamental changes of the enterprise. These changes ranged from pursuit of new markets, to offering significantly different products and services, to adopting new processes for allocating resources.

Most of these changes were much easier to design than they were to deploy and sustain. Conceptualizing transformation was much easier than making it happen. This realization led me to explore past transformations in the transportation, computer, and defense industries. In *Start Where You Are* (Jossey-Bass, 1996), I considered a wide variety of attempts to transform and the great difficulties of making such transitions. My thesis was that transformation failures were due to enterprises not having good assessments of their situations, externally and/or internally.

This led to a deeper look at why assessments tend to be so poor. In *Don't Jump to Solutions* (Jossey-Bass, 1998), I explored organizational delusions that often undermine strategic thinking by management teams as they attempt to address – or avoid addressing – needs for fundamental change. Managers seem to delude themselves regarding what is happening in the marketplace, how well they stand with their customers, and the extent to which their change initiatives are succeeding. Consequently, their plans fail because they are designed for an enterprise that no longer exists, or perhaps never existed.

The research underlying these two books caused me to see the common challenges that every management team must face. In *Essential Challenges of Strategic Management* (Wiley, 2001), I outline the strategic challenges of growth, value, focus, change, future, knowledge, and time and summarize alternative ways of addressing these challenges. Of particular importance, there are many ways to address each challenge and no "silver bullets," except senior management commitment.

The present book, *Enterprise Transformation*, emerged from recognition that a range of material needed to be brought together in one source. Beyond the topics addressed, multiple perspectives are needed. Consequently, the authors of the chapters include many senior executives, numerous top consultants, and a range of academics. These people have led enterprise transformations, supported management teams addressing fundamental change, and researched the best ways to transform functions, organizations, and whole enterprises.

I am indebted to these authors for what I have learned from them, both from their writing and our ongoing interactions. Fundamental change is very difficult and most initiatives are less than fully successful. The authors of the chapters in this book have addressed fundamental change, succeeded in accomplishing such change and, in this book, provide the insights gained and lessons learned.

I am also pleased to acknowledge the assistance of Kristi Kirkland of Georgia Tech who served as managing editor in bringing together and integrating all of the elements of this book.

William B. Rouse
Atlanta, Georgia
October 2005

CONTRIBUTORS

Ray C. Anderson, Founder and Chairman of Interface, Inc., graduated from Georgia Institute of Technology with Highest Honors in 1956 and with a bachelor's degree in industrial engineering. He learned the carpet and textile businesses through 14-plus years at various positions at Deering-Milliken and Callaway Mills, and in 1973, set about founding a company to produce the first free-lay carpet tiles in America -- Interface, Inc. He developed a partnership with Britain's Carpets International Plc. that year and set up operations in LaGrange, Georgia. Ten years later, Interface took over Carpets International. Today, Ray commands the world's largest producer of commercial floorcoverings. Ray received the inaugural **Millennium Award** from Global Green, presented by Mikhail Gorbachev in 1996, and was named co-chairman of the **President's Council on Sustainable Development** in 1997. He was also recognized in 1996 as the Ernst & Young **Entrepreneur of the Year** for the Southeast Region, and as the Georgia Conservancy's **Conservationist of the Year** in 1997. In January 2001, the National Academy of Sciences selected Ray to receive the prestigious **George and Cynthia Mitchell International Prize for Sustainable Development**, the first corporate CEO to be so honored, and in September of that year, the SAM-SPG Award Jury presented the **Sustainability Leadership Award 2001** to Ray in Zurich, Switzerland. The **US Green Building Council** honored Ray with their inaugural green business **Leadership Award** for the private sector in November, 2002. Ray was named a **Senior Fellow and Leading Voice for Green and Sustainable Design** by the Design Futures Council in 2003, and also received the **IIDA Star Award.** In 2004, he was honored with the **National Ethics Advocate Award from The Southern Institute for Business and Professional Ethics**. He holds honorary doctorates from Northland College (public service), LaGrange College (business), N.C. State University (humane letters) and University of Southern Maine (humane letters). His book, Mid-Course Correction, (Chelsea Green, 1998) describes his and Interface's transformation to environmental responsibility.

Paul Aronzon is the Co-Chair of the Financial Restructuring Group of Milbank, Tweed, Hadley & McCloy LLP and is resident in the Firm's Los Angeles office. Mr. Aronzon has had a diverse twenty-plus year practice, having represented domestic and international debtors, financial institutions, lender syndicates, public debt, trade and other creditors, trustees and receivers, committees of creditors and equity securities holders, and entities interested in acquiring overleveraged or otherwise troubled companies or their assets both in and out of court. Mr. Aronzon is a Fellow in the American College of Bankruptcy and a frequent lecturer and author in the fields of bankruptcy and commercial law. He was included in

Turnarounds and Workouts Special Report: Outstanding Bankruptcy Lawyers 2001. Mr. Aronzon is also included in the Best Lawyers in America (Woodward/White) and in the K&A Register of the Leading Bankruptcy and Financial Restructuring Lawyers and Financial Advisors in the United States. He is admitted to practice law in California, Washington, D.C. and New York.

Scott Avila is a managing partner with Corporate Revitalization Partners, LLC an interim and crisis management consulting firm. Serving as an advisor and an interim executive, Mr. Avila has led the organizational transformation of many domestic and international organizations in a wide range of industries. Mr. Avila received his bachelor's degree in Business Administration from California State University at Hayward and his Masters in Business Administration from the University of Southern California. He has earned the designation of Certified Turnaround Professional and is actively involved in numerous professional organizations. Mr. Avila is a frequent speaker on the topics of corporate reorganizations and has served on the board of directors of numerous corporations.

Mark Barbeau is a managing partner of Corporate Revitalization Partners, LLC, an interim and crisis management firm. He has extensive experience in the reorganization of distressed companies as an interim and crisis manager, financial advisor and investor. Since 1990 he has been involved in more than 40 turnaround and restructuring engagements in a wide range of industries. He and partners also invest in distressed companies through privately negotiated transactions and bankruptcy proceedings. He writes and speaks on the subjects of corporate reorganizations and bankruptcy, and has served on several boards of directors. Mark has an MBA from Washington University in St. Louis, and a Bachelor of Journalism from the University of Missouri.

Rahul C. Basole is a Doctoral Candidate and Tennenbaum Fellow in the School of Industrial and Systems Engineering at the Georgia Institute of Technology. Most recently, he was the CEO and VP Research of mobileAnalytics, the Director of Research and Development at MShift, and a Technology Consultant at AMS-CGI. His current research interests include strategic IT management and planning, the business value and impact of IT, and issues related to IS/IT adoption, implementation, and use with a particular focus on mobile information and communication technologies. He holds a B.S. in Industrial and Systems Engineering from Virginia Tech, a M.S. from the University of Michigan, Ann Arbor in Industrial and Operations Engineering, and has completed graduate research in Engineering-Economic Systems and Operations Research at Stanford University.

Dale Belman is a Professor and Associate Director for Graduate Studies in the School of Labor and Industrial Relations at Michigan State University. He is an Associate Director of the Trucking Industry Program, academic chair of the

Construction Industry Council of the Labor and Employment Relations Association, and facilitates the Construction Economics Research Network of the CPWR. His two most recent books, Sailors of the Concrete Sea: The Work and Life of Truck Drivers (Michigan State University Press, 2005) and Trucking in the Age of Information (Ashgate, forthcoming), both address issues of the trucking and the logistics industries.

Kenneth R. Boff, Ph.D., serves as Chief Scientist of the Human Effectiveness Directorate, Air Force Research Laboratory, Wright-Patterson Air Force Base, Ohio. In this position, he has responsibility for the technical direction and quality of a broad multi-disciplinary R&D portfolio encompassing human-engineering of complex systems, training, safety, biotechnology, toxicology, and deployment logistics. He is best known for his work on understanding and remediating problems in the transition of research to applications in the design and acquisition of complex human-systems. Holder of a patent for rapid communication display technology, Boff has authored numerous articles, book chapters and technical papers, and is co-editor of "System Design" (1987), senior editor of the two-volume "Handbook of Perception and Human Performance" (1986), and the four-volume "Engineering Data Compendium: Human Perception and Performance" (1988). Boff actively consults and provides technical liaison with government agencies, international working groups, universities and professional societies. He is founder and technical director of the Department of Defense Human System Information Analysis Center, and founding member and former Chair of the DoD Reliance Human-Systems Interface Technology Panel. Currently, he is serving part-time on the faculty of the Georgia Institute of Technology, School of Industrial and Systems Engineering as an Edinfield Executive in Residence. Until recently, he was the US National Voting Member and Chair for the NATO RTO human factors technology area. In 2003, he received the NATO Scientific Achievement Award. Boff is a Fellow of the Human Factors & Ergonomics Society and the International Ergonomics Association.

Wally Buran is a Senior Partner with The Monitor Group, a global family of professional service firms focused on enhancing client competitiveness, and is The Edenfield Executive in Residence at The Georgia Institute of Technology. He is also a Senior Advisor in The Tennenbaum Institute for Enterprise Transformation, helped establish its initial research agenda and supports its major initiatives. He has consulted and advised clients in a broad range of industries for over 25 years in strategic planning, enterprise transformation, supply chain strategy, SG&A management, business process reengineering, mergers & acquisitions, sales and marketing effectiveness, procurement, and innovation management. Previously, Mr. Buran was CEO of Worldcrest Group, and was a line manager with General Motors, Avon Products and IBM. Currently his research focuses on enterprise transformation, frontier management concepts and shareholder value development.

He serves as an advisor to several private equity firms and lives in Atlanta with his wife and children.

W. Bruce Chew, PhD, is a Global Thought Leader with The Monitor Group based in their Cambridge, Massachusetts office. Dr. Chew's work and research focuses on the bridging of management action and enterprise competitiveness. This work began while he was a professor at the Harvard Business School and has continued with an emphasis on practical application since joining Monitor over a decade ago. He is the co-founder of Monitor's Activities, Processes and Systems Group which focuses on effective *operational* redesign as opposed to organizational design, i.e., the configuration of assets activities, and people to create distinctive capabilities. Currently, major themes in his work include identifying and building advantaged systems of capabilities, managing strategic tensions as a basis for breakthrough strategies, creating industrial solutions and supporting transformation efforts through research, advisory services and executive education. Dr. Chew is an award-winning teacher and journal editor who has been published in the Harvard Business Review, The Sloan Management Review, the papers of the Brookings Institute as well as contributing to other journals, books and periodicals. He lives in Massachusetts and Maine where he enjoys his four children and fishing for striped bass.

Tirthankar Dasgupta is Ph.D. student in the School of Industrials and Systems Engineering at Georgia Institute of Technology, Atlanta, working under the supervision of Prof Jeff Wu. Prior to his Ph.D. work, he was associated with several reputed Industries in India as a Quality Management and Six Sigma Consultant.

Richard A. DeMillo is the Imlay Dean and Distinguished Professor of Computing at the Georgia Institute of Technology. He returned to academia in 2002, after a career as an executive in industry and government. He was Chief Technology Officer for Hewlett-Packard, where he had worldwide responsibility for technology and technology strategy. Prior to joining HP, he was in charge of Information and Computer Sciences Research at Telcordia Technologies (formerly Bellcore) in Morristown, New Jersey, where he oversaw the development of many Internet and web-based innovations. He has also directed the Computer and Computation Research Division of the National Science Foundation. Before joining industry during the height of the internet boom, he was Professor of Computer Sciences and Director of the Software Engineering Research Center at Purdue University. He also held major faculty positions at Georgia Tech where he was the founding Director of the Software Research Center and a visiting professorship at the University of Padua in Padua, Italy. The author of over 100 articles and books, Dr. DeMillo's research has spanned several fundamental areas of computer science and includes fundamental innovation in computer security, software engineering and mathematics. His present research interests are focused on information security and nanotechnology. He is developing hardware-based architectures for trusted computing platforms. He is also working on computing and communication architectures for massively distributed nano-scale components. He is active in many aspects of the IT industry, serving on advisory boards and panels and he is a member of the Boards of Directors for several companies. He is a fellow of the Association for Computing Machinery and The American Association for the Advancement of Science.

Dominie Garcia is a PhD candidate in the Tennenbaum Institute at the Georgia Institute of Technology. Her research interests include triggers and processes of enterprise transformations, as well as outcomes measures of transformations. Her current focus is on measuring the variables of transformation processes. She has worked with the Vice Chairman of AOL Time Warner, and is a co-founder of Emerging Venture Network, an organization focused on matching high-growth potential, minority-led organizations with private equity funding sources. Dominie holds a Bachelors degree in Economics from Vassar College and an MBA from Babson College.

Bill George is former chairman and CEO of Medtronic, the world's leading medical technology company. He is a board member of Goldman Sachs, Target, and Novartis. He has served as an executive-in-residence at Yale University and is currently Professor of Management Practice at Harvard Business School. George has been recognized as "Executive of the Year" by the Academy of Management, "Director of the Year" by the National Association of Corporate Directors, and one of Business Week's "Top 25 Managers." He has been widely quoted in the *New York Times*, *Fortune*, *Face the Nation*, *The News Hour with Jim Lehrer*, and NPR's *All Things Considered*. He is the author of <u>Authentic Leadership: Rediscovering the Secrets to Creating Lasting Value</u> (Jossey-Bass, 2003).

Ralph D. Heath serves as Executive Vice President - Aeronautics, Lockheed Martin Corporation. In this role, he has leadership responsibility for the corporation's military aircraft business activities. With some 28,000 employees and major locations in Fort Worth, Texas; Marietta, Georgia; and Palmdale, California, Lockheed Martin Aeronautics' product lines include combat aircraft, air mobility, advanced development programs, and reconnaissance aircraft. Before assuming responsibility for the business area at the beginning of 2005, Mr. Heath served as LM Aeronautics' Executive Vice President and General Manager for the F/A-22 since 2002, leading the restructure of this $60 billion program and the transition from development to full rate production. From 2000-2002, Mr. Heath was the Chief Operating Officer for the newly formed LM Aeronautics company and led the three heritage companies into the single company that exists today. During the past 20 years he has been a leader in the tremendous growth of LM Aeronautics international business, starting with the formation of TAI Joint Venture Aerospace Company in Turkey. In the 1990s, Mr. Heath successfully led the Business Development organization during the build-up of the largest F-16 backlog in the history of the company.

Steven J. Joffe is a Senior Managing Director with FTI Consulting and primarily provides tax expertise in bankruptcy restructurings and other business transactions. Mr. Joffe is a transactional tax specialist and lawyer with over 28 years of diversified experience in consulting, private industry, law firm practice and government service. Mr. Joffe has extensive experience in the identification of tax issues and the development of tax efficient strategic solutions for restructuring distressed companies, mergers, and the acquisitions and dispositions of assets. Mr. Joffe has co-authored numerous articles on bankruptcy tax and other tax subjects.

Dr. William C. (Bill) Kessler serves as Vice President Advanced Enterprise Initiatives at Lockheed Martin Aeronautics Company. In this position, he provides executive assessment of the company operating concept and capability alignment with the customer's transforming needs. From 2000-2003, He supported the Chief Operating Officer in the restructure and transformation from three heritage companies to one company, LM Aeronautics. This effort involved the development and deployment of the concept of operations, capability architecture design and deployment, and the deployment of company-wide capable processes. From 1997-2000, Bill was Vice President of Enterprise Productivity at the Marietta Company and led the deployment of lean and six sigma across the company. Prior to 1997, Dr Kessler was an Air Force senior executive leading the Air Force manufacturing technology and industrial base assessment programs.

Thomas R. Kreller is a Partner in the Financial Restructuring Group of Milbank, Tweed, Hadley & McCloy LLP and is resident in the Firm's Los Angeles office. Mr. Kreller specializes in bankruptcy and corporate reorganization law and has represented debtors, lenders, equity holders, committees and acquirors in bankruptcy cases, loan restructurings and workouts and out-of-court acquisitions. Mr. Kreller was admitted to the California bar in 1992 following his graduation from the School of Law (J.D. 1992) and Anderson Graduate School of Management (M.B.A. 1992) at the University of California, Los Angeles. Prior to entering the J.D./M.B.A. program at UCLA, Mr. Kreller was a Certified Public Accountant with the Chicago office of Ernst & Young (formerly Ernst & Whinney). Mr. Kreller is a member of the Los Angeles County and American Bar Associations, The State Bar of California and Financial Lawyers Conference.

Leon McGinnis is Gwaltney Professor of Manufacturing Systems at Georgia Tech, where he also serves as Director of the Product Lifecycle Management Center of Excellence, and Associate Director of the Manufacturing Research Center. Professor McGinnis teaches and leads research in the area of discrete event logistics systems, including warehouse and logistics system design, material handling systems design, high-fidelity simulation methodology, and system performance assessment and benchmarking tools. He is a Fellow of the Institute of Industrial Engineering and a recipient of the Reed-Apple Award by the Material Handling Education Foundation.

David A. Perdue is Chairman of the Board and Chief Executive Officer of Dollar General Corporation. Prior to joining the company in April 2003, Mr. Perdue was chairman and CEO of Pillowtex Corporation, a leading home textiles company. He also served as executive vice president of Reebok International Limited and president/CEO of the Reebok Brand. Earlier in his career, Mr. Perdue spent 12 years with Kurt Salmon Associates, an international management consulting firm. Subsequently, he served as vice president and managing director of Asian operations at Sara Lee Corporation in Hong Kong and as senior vice president of operations for Haggar Corporation. Mr. Perdue received both his Bachelor of Science in Industrial Engineering and his Master of Science in Operations Research from the Georgia Institute of Technology. He is a director of Alliant Energy Corporation, is on the Georgia Tech Advisory Board and serves on various philanthropic, industry and community boards.

William B. Rouse is the Executive Director of the university-wide Tennenbaum Institute whose multi-disciplinary portfolio of initiatives focuses on research and education to provide knowledge and skills for enterprise transformation. He is also a faculty member in the College of Computing and the School of Industrial and Systems Engineering. Rouse has written hundreds of articles and book chapters, and has authored many books, including most recently *Essential Challenges of Strategic Management* (Wiley, 2001) and the award-winning *Don't Jump to Solutions* (Jossey-Bass, 1998). He is co-editor of the best-selling *Handbook of Systems Engineering and Management* (Wiley, 1999) and edited the eight-volume series *Human/Technology Interaction in Complex Systems* (Elsevier). Rouse is a member of the National Academy of Engineering, as well as a fellow of the Institute of Electrical and Electronics Engineers, the Institute for Operations Research and Management Science, and the Human Factors and Ergonomics Society. He received his B.S. from the University of Rhode Island, and his S.M. and Ph.D. from the Massachusetts Institute of Technology.

Jerome M. Schwartzman is a tax attorney with extensive experience in US and cross-border transactions, advising private equity investors, corporate strategic investors and financial institutions in connection with mergers & acquisitions, leveraged buyouts, and acquisition and disposition transactional structuring. Mr. Schwartzman also has substantial bankruptcy tax experience and has co-authored numerous articles in that field. Mr. Schwartzman began his tax career in the National Office of the Office of Chief Counsel (IRS) in Washington, DC where he specialized in corporate tax matters and tax controversies.

Joyce Shields serves as a senior leader of the Hay Group and is an Owner of the firm. Hay Group is a worldwide human resources consulting firm with over 60 offices in 30 countries. Her areas of expertise are in leadership development, executive coaching, human resource planning and development, change management, competency-based systems, selection and retention, and HR reengineering. Dr. Shields has consulted with a large number Fortune 500 companies as well as major governmental and non-profit groups and has been widely recognized by professional societies for her contributions to the field of psychology. Dr. Shields holds a Ph.D. in Measurement and Statistics from the University of Maryland, an M.A. in Experimental Psychology from the University of Delaware, and a B.A. in Psychology from the College of William and Mary.

Michael S. Sitrick is Chairman and Chief Executive Officer of Sitrick And Company. A nationally recognized expert in the strategic use of communications, Mr. Sitrick has been the subject of numerous articles and profiles focusing on the results he has achieved for clients. The *Los Angeles Times* called him, "The Wizard of Spin." Forbes called him "The Flack For When You're Under Attack." Since founding Sitrick And Company, he has provided advice and counsel to hundreds of companies, including some of the nation's largest corporations, and to some of our nation's highest profile individuals -- both on routine and extremely sensitive matters. Under his direction, Sitrick And Company has consistently been ranked either the number one or number two strategic public relations firm in the U.S. by leading trade publications. Prior to forming the firm, Mr. Sitrick served as Senior Vice President - Communications for Wickes Companies, Inc. Before joining Wickes, Mr. Sitrick headed Communications and Government Affairs for National Can Corporation, was a Group Supervisor for the Chicago public relations firm Selz, Seabolt and Associates, and served as Assistant Director of Public Information in the Richard J. Daley administration in Chicago. He also did reporting for such publications as the *Washington Star* and *the Baltimore News American,* as well as WSID Radio in Baltimore. Mr. Sitrick is the author of the critically acclaimed book, "*Spin-- How to Turn the Power of the Press to Your Advantage*" published by Regnery, and is a contributing author to the book, "*Turnarounds and Workouts*," published by Dow Jones/Irwin. Mr. Sitrick serves on the Board of Directors of the Turnaround Management Association, the Jewish Television Network and is a member of the Advisory Board of The1939 Club, the largest Holocaust Survivors organization in the U.S. He holds B.S. degrees in Business Administration and Journalism from the University of Maryland, College Park.

Benjamin Schneider is Senior Research Fellow at VALTERA (formerly PRA, Inc.), a human resources consulting firm in suburban Chicago specializing in employee opinion surveys, personnel selection systems, and 360 degree feedback systems. Prior to VALTERA, Ben for many years was the Head of the Industrial and Organizational Psychology program at Maryland where he is now Professor

Emeritus. He has published more than 125 professional journal articles and book chapters, as well as eight books. His most recent books are (with Susan White) *Service Quality: Research Perspectives* (Sage, 2004) and (with D. Brent Smith) *Personality and Organizations* (Erlbaum, 2004). Ben has consulted on service quality issues with numerous companies, recently including Allstate, IBM, Toyota, Giant Eagle, Nextel and Pepsico.

A writer and editor, **Lynn Selhat** started her career as a journalist and later shifted to business and academic writing. Working primarily with professors from INSEAD and The Wharton School, Selhat writes and edits books, business cases, working papers, and academic articles. She is a contributing writer to Knowledge@Wharton, an online business publication with some 400,000 readers. Selhat holds a bachelor's degree in English Literature from Gettysburg College and a master's degree with a concentration in Science and Technical Communication from Drexel University.

William Pierre Sovey is a 1955 graduate of Georgia Institute of Technology with a degree in Industrial Engineering. He attended Harvard Business School's Advanced Management Program in 1977. Mr. Sovey's business career spans 50 years with the last 15 years with Newell Rubbermaid where he served as President and Chief Operating Officer, Vice Chairman and Chief Executive Officer and Chairman of the Board of Directors. He retired as CEO in 1997 and now divides his time between homes in Georgia and Connecticut.

Michael E. Tennenbaum is the founder of the Tennenbaum Institute and Senior Managing Partner of Tennenbaum Capital Partners, Chairman of PEMCO Aviation Group, Chairman of Anacomp, Vice Chairman of Party City Corporation, and former Vice Chairman of Bear Stearns & Co., Inc. A graduate of the Georgia Institute of Technology with a degree in Industrial Engineering, Mr. Tennenbaum received a Masters in Business Administration, with honors, from Harvard University. He is a member of the Board of Associates of Harvard Business School and was a member of its Visiting Committee. In addition, he served as a member of the National Advisory Board of Georgia Tech and as a Trustee of the Georgia Institute of Technology Foundation, Inc., where he was Chairman of its Investment Committee, and he currently is Trustee Emeritus.

L. Beril Toktay is an Associate Professor of Operations Management in the College of Management at the Georgia Institute of Technology. She received her PhD in Operations Research from the Massachusetts Institute of Technology. She holds BS degrees in Industrial Engineering and Mathematics from Boğaziçi University, and an MS degree in Industrial Engineering from Purdue University. Dr. Toktay's recent research focuses on the management of closed-loop supply chains, which are supply chains in which value is recovered from used products via recycling, remanufacturing or repair operations. Dr. Toktay's research in this area has received distinctions such as The Wickham Skinner Award for the Best Unpublished Paper presented at the 2005 POMS conference. She has published in *Management Science* and *Operations Research*. She serves on the Editorial Board of *Manufacturing and Service Operations Management* and *Production and Operations Management*.

Chelsea C. White III holds the Schneider National Chair of Transportation and Logistics in the School of Industrial and Systems Engineering at Georgia Tech, where he is the Director of the Trucking Industry Program (TIP) and the Executive Director of The Logistics Institute (TLI). He serves on the boards of directors for several organizations, including CNF, Inc. His most recent research interests include analyzing the role of real-time information and enabling information technology for improved logistics and, more generally, supply chain productivity and security, with special focus on the U.S. trucking industry. He has recently served as keynote speaker for the U.S.-China Modern Logistics Conference (Beijing, May, 2004). His recent activities include presentations at the Council on Competitiveness and the Brookings Institution, both of which were concerned with the impact of information technology on international freight distribution, security, and productivity.

Professor C.F. Jeff Wu is Coca-Cola Chair Professor of Engineering Statistics in the School of Industrials and Systems Engineering at Georgia Institute of Technology, Atlanta. He is a member of the National Academy of Engineering and a fellow of the American Society for Quality and the American Statistical Association.

CHAPTER 1
INTRODUCTION & OVERVIEW

WILLIAM B. ROUSE

Change is inherent in all enterprises, whether they are companies, government agencies, educational institutions, non-profit associations or perhaps even religions. The forces driving change may have economic, political, social, and/or technological sources. The implications of change may be both positive and negative, with the balance between positive and negative depending on perspectives of the particular types of stakeholder impacted by change.

This book concerns how enterprises can understand and should respond to change – how they can best change themselves in response to both external and internal forces. In particular, this book addresses fundamental change rather than routine business process improvement[1]. As elaborated in later chapters, fundamental change involves more than doing work better. It involves doing work differently and/or doing different work. Consequently, fundamental change is almost always very challenging.

CONTEMPORARY CONTEXT

Enterprise transformation is not a new topic. Indeed, later chapters in this book include many "stories" of transformation over the past 200 years. Nevertheless, several contemporary trends make this topic of particular importance now. Senior executives in both private and public sectors are seriously concerned with how best to respond to these trends.

During the late 1980s and early 1990s, there was a wave of "downsizing" and "rightsizing" as companies tried to reduce costs, in part due to recession and, more importantly, in part due to capacity gluts in several industries such as steel, tires, and automobiles. Jensen (2000) discusses the great difficulties companies had in exiting when they found that their high-cost capacity was no longer competitive[2]. A mixture of denial and dithering wasted huge amounts of capital.

Perhaps the best ongoing example of this phenomenon is the automobile industry (Easterbrook, 2005). This industry can produce many more cars than the world can buy. Thus, financial incentives are often needed to sell cars, which

---

[1] The phrase "business process" is intended to relate to how enterprises conduct business, whether they are in the private, public, or non-profit sectors.
[2] Jensen cites Schumpeter (1976) on capitalism's overall penchant to create and destroy capacity, as well as the enterprises that invest in capacity to satisfy marketplaces.

undermines and often eliminates profits. There is too much capacity. One or more players have to reduce capacity or possibly exit the industry.

Jensen (2000) describes the great difficulty that managers have making such decisions. They often invest good money after bad to avoid addressing such problems. They cannot face the personal pain, increased uncertainty, and sidetracked careers, for themselves, their teams, and their employees. Consequently, they use cash flow to shore up losing businesses rather than investing it where returns are possible and likely.

This may be due, in part, to a lack of information about costs and the enterprise's true competitive position. It also can be due to organizational delusions that undermine managers' abilities to understand what is happening in their markets and their positions in these markets (Rouse, 1998; Economist, 2005). Thus, for one reason or another, managers may be relatively clueless.

However, another strong possibility is that managers understand where they are and have quite reasonable strategies for pursuing change. Their difficulty is that they cannot get their enterprises to implement these strategies. Charan and Colvin (1999) address this possibility and report that 70% of high-profile CEOs that were fired lost their jobs for exactly this reason. Quite simply, they failed to make change happen.

Moving forward to the late 1990s and early 2000s, we find, as Thomas Friedman (2005) argues, that the world is flat. Areas where we once had no equals – R&D, new product development, and graduate education – are now competitive battlegrounds involving China and India. The 1,000,000 engineers produced annually by China, India, and Japan is dwarfing our production of 65,000 engineers each year.

Consequently the playing field has quickly been leveled. Computer and communications technologies have enabled outsourcing and offshoring to countries with high levels of education and relatively low wages (Baskerville, et al., 2005). As business processes increasingly become standardized, this trend will accelerate (Davenport, 2005). Friedman's vignettes and scenarios convincingly illustrate this possibility.

So, change is pervasive in both traditional industries such as automobiles and leading-edge industries like software. Leaders of enterprises must address change creatively and energetically or risk losing their jobs and/or their enterprises. The marketplace will not be patient with "business as usual" and leaders must accept and pursue the challenge of change.

PURSUING TRANSFORMATION

Once managers agree to the premise that business process improvement will be insufficient for long-term success, their next concern is how to move beyond improvement to transformation. It is much more straightforward to try to do work better than it is to do work differently. It is an even bigger challenge to attempt to do different work (Gouillart & Kelly, 1995; Kotter, 1995).

The next two chapters in Part 1 of the book address these issues in some depth as, of course, does the whole book.   At this point, discussion of how transformation can be pursued is limited to a few broad themes.   These include business processes and value streams, outsourcing and offshoring, and redeploying assets.

Business Processes and Value Streams

A business process is the set of activities that an enterprise pursues to achieve particular objectives for specific external or internal customers.   Processes typically cut across business functions such as marketing, finance, and so on. Processes create value by doing work that yields outcomes of benefit to customers. Functions contribute to processes and, thereby, help to create value. Understanding and managing processes are central to business process reengineering (Hammer & Champy, 1993) and lean thinking (Womack & Jones, 1996).

Value streams are those processes that directly provide the benefits sought by customers.   External customers want products and services that provide desired features and functions, as well as high quality at a reasonable price.   Thus, it is common to think in terms of product development and product support as value streams.   As Slywotsky (1996, 1997) demonstrates, these desires tend to evolve and perceptions of value in terms of willingness to pay change, making it necessary to rethink value streams to find "profit zones."

Thus, transformation tends to involve focusing on processes and understanding where and how value is created. Processes and activities that do not create value – either for external or internal customers – should be eliminated. Investments should be targeted at areas where value can be greatly enhanced. Such decisions should be driven by the benefits sought by the marketplace.

Adopting of process-oriented thinking can be transformational in itself. For example, explicit portrayal of decision processes and the use of data to inform these processes can be a transformative step from ad hoc advocacy-based decision making to well-informed collaborative problem solving and decision making (Rouse, 2001, 2002). This not only yields better decisions; it can transform an enterprise's view of itself.

Outsourcing and Offshoring

With a process-oriented view of one's enterprise, it is natural to assess the effectiveness and efficiency of the enterprise's processes. Benchmarking among peer enterprises is common. Various professional associations and other providers conduct periodic benchmarking studies. Thus, for example, we regularly see tabulations of metrics such as labor hours per automobile produced for each car manufacturer or cost per mile flown for each airline.

Benchmarking helps one to know where to improve. Increasingly, it also raises the question of whether or not processes should be outsourced rather than performed internally. In general, enterprises try to retain core competencies and the processes associated with these competencies. For instance, a company might retain R&D, product design, marketing, and sales, and outsource manufacturing, finance, human resources, customer support, and information systems.

Outsourcing can be transformative. However, success depends on dismantling these functions internally and dovetailing the outsourced functions with one's business processes. The idea is to both recoup assets formerly deployed in these functions and create efficient value streams across both internal and external operations. Another important issue concerns value stream risks due to dependence on other enterprises and, in some cases, other economies.

Offshoring typically involves outsourcing to another country, especially of late to China and India. In some sense, offshoring is just a particular flavor of outsourcing. However, the ramifications are more profound for our economy and creation of high-paying jobs. The "best and brightest" from Asia are no longer automatically coming to the U.S. for graduate school and, consequently, they are deploying their knowledge and skills in their home countries. On the long term, companies may have no choice but outsource R&D and software development, for example, to the Asian companies that employ this talent.

Asset Management

Once one understands the enterprise's business processes, has benchmarked their effectiveness and efficiency, and identified outsourcing candidates and providers, the next concern is how best to deploy and manage the enterprise's assets – financial, human, and physical.

Transformation may involve streamlining processes, investing in core processes, outsourcing non-core processes, acquiring key competencies via acquisitions, and/or selling or liquidating assets. As a result assets will be redeployed. Such redeployment requires capturing assets freed by outsourcing, liquidation, and sales. It also involves managing these assets in the context of the "to be" enterprise rather than the "as is" enterprise.

As indicated earlier, the decision-making processes associated with asset deployment and management are also candidates for transformation. Data-driven decision making can change the ways that an enterprise thinks of itself and its context. Indeed, addressing many aspects of transformation can be enhanced by well-designed and well-informed decision processes.

TRANSFORMATION ARCHETYPES

Later chapters outline the nuances of enterprise transformation. This section describes, quite simply, three broad archetypes that necessarily gloss over the nuances. These archetypes are illustrated with over twenty examples of well-known transformations. These illustrations provide compelling evidence of the pervasive and necessary nature of enterprise transformation across the economy. This book is focused on how best to transform, to maximize success amidst a plethora of false starts and failures.

Transformed Value Propositions

This archetype includes enterprises that transform their business models and market offerings. Transformation requires that they dismantle old ways of doing things and adopt new ways. The extent of the dismantling required influences both the scope of transformation, investment required, and the likelihood of success. Illustrations of this archetype include (in alphabetical order):

- The U.S. Department of Defense is in the process of adopting effects-based planning of military operations and capabilities-based acquisition of military systems. This enables, for example, DoD to purchase airlift capabilities rather than airplanes. Once this transformation is accomplished, the defense industry will necessarily have changed profoundly.

- General Electric transformed from a broad, unfocused conglomerate to a more focused emphasis on leading market positions, revenue growth, and profitability, as well as financial services. The company shrank dramatically initially then achieved strong growth.

- Georgia Tech dramatically changed its market position from being a strong undergraduate educational institution to become a leading research university via streamlined entrepreneurial leadership and substantial investments in human and physical resources. (See Chapter 22.)

- Interface redefined its business model around green practices (i.e., minimal use of non-renewal resources and minimal production of waste) and, consequently, repositioned itself in the carpet industry and more broadly as an exemplar of "doing well by doing good". (See Chapter 21.)

- IBM moved from tabulators to mainframes to networks (servers, PCs, etc.) to technology services via, for example, outsourcing the components of the IBM PC (when such outsourcing was unknown in the computer industry) to selling its PC business to its leading Chinese supplier.

- Motorola moved from battery eliminators to radios to cell phones to satellite networks, the latter with little success. Its successful moves were associated with decisive leadership, committed investments, and technological innovations. Indecisiveness lost Motorola its lead in the cellular market when it stuck with analog technology too long.

- NCR moved from cash registers to applications of computer and communications technologies in retail and banking, revolutionizing the latter with ATMs. Banking was transformed more than NCR, who tried to play in the computing market, was acquired by AT&T, and then spun off to return to its strong roots.

- Reebok innovated in women's sports shoes and apparel, consequently growing to a dominant position. Nike with its sports celebrity orientation took the lead away. Reebok rebounded by focusing on original values, product innovation, and execution. (See Chapter 19.)

- UPS transformed from a successful, one-size fits all, package delivery company to a global supply chain services company via strategic acquisitions, information technology, and focus on people, carefully redesigning the brand to leverage strong roots while creating a new, aggressive market position.

These nine illustrations suggest several variations on the archetype of new value propositions. Some involved strategic acquisitions, e.g., UPS, while others involved strategic divestitures, e.g., GE. Other involved changing the game played, e.g., Georgia Tech, while others involved changing the rules of the game, e.g., Interface. All of these illustrations required fundamental change, pursued by strong leadership with committed investments. Transforming an existing enterprise involves dismantling the "as is" enterprise to create the "to be" enterprise, while also keeping the enterprise running, keeping customers satisfied, and yielding acceptable financial results. This archetype results in many more failures than successes.

Transformation Via Acquisitions & Mergers

Another transformation archetype involves enterprises that transform the companies they acquire. The examples shown below are but a few of the large number of companies transformed in this manner. The chapters on "Transformation Practices" provide a wealth of other examples.

- Newell Rubbermaid continually acquired and "Newellized" scores of home products companies focusing on process efficiency and management competency, enabling low costs and prices. Their acquisitions were transformed to high-value companies within this retail domain. (See Chapter 18.)

- DRS Technologies continually acquired and rationalized defense electronics companies taking advantage of weakened companies in depressed markets. Good management practices, especially strong financial controls, enabled transforming weak independent companies to strong members of the DRS defense conglomerate.

- Lockheed Martin merged three aircraft companies into one (Lockheed Martin Aeronautics) due to reduced customer demand that prompted consolidation. Three strong corporate cultures of former competitors were transformed into an integrated aeronautics company and leader in military aviation. (See Chapter 20).

- Tennenbaum Capital acquire dominant positions in disparate companies – for example, Pemco Aviation (aviation), Anacomp (information technology), and Party City (retail) – and installed strong management teams, reengineered business processes, and exacting accountability to create highly competitive, profitable businesses.

Note that this transformation archetype is rather different than the previous archetype. The acquiring company can dictate the business processes and practices of the acquired company. Such dictates often fail, but transforming the new members of the portfolio is quite different from transforming long-standing members of the portfolio. At the very least, the act of acquisition will have gotten people's attention. They will not expect business as usual.

Transformation Via New Value Propositions

There are a wealth of examples of innovative enterprises that forced competitors and suppliers to transform. Typically, the innovating company does not really transform. They develop and perfect the new business model and practices. If they are successful – most ideas fail to become successful innovations – then their competitors and suppliers often have to transform themselves to adopt the innovation. An excellent example is K-Mart and Sears having to adopt Wal-Mart's practices to remain competitive and, more recently, agreeing to merge to remain players in the retail arena.

Note that most of the ten examples listed below (in alphabetical order) involve companies that were started on the basis of the new business model and practices. Thus, by definition, they did not transform in the processes of deploying and refining their models.

- Amazon redefined the retail book market via new business practices supported by information technology, resulting in Amazon being the largest customer of most major publishers.

- CNN redefined news offerings with 24 x 7 news, frequent updates, embedded reporters, and a sense of news happening in one's own living room. As CNN, Fox, and others have refined this model, traditional network news has declined in popularity, as have print newspapers.

- Dell developed and refined build-to-order computer assembly and sales supported by information technology, resulting in dramatically reduced inventory costs and making Dell the leading seller of PCs.

- e-Bay redefined the resale market by leveraging information technology and building an online community that supports and facilitates the selling and buying process, with links to invoicing, payment, and shipping.

- Fedex defined the overnight mail market via new business practices and processes, i.e., central hub with feeder spokes and air delivery, competing at first with fax and more recently with email.

- Home Depot redefined the hardware store industry via a new business model and practices that emphasize a comprehensive selection of materials and tools, as well as in-store advice on use of these materials and tools.

- Nucor resuscitated the U.S. steel industry, for a period, via continuous-casting mini-mills and new business practices that dramatically lowered the cost per ton of steel, and also significantly contributed to roughly 90% of automobile bodies, frames, and engines being recycled into new steel.

- Southwest repositioned discount air travel via new business practices that focused on low costs, timely operations, and upbeat air and cabin crews. AirTran, JetBlue, and other startups copied this model, but the large traditional airlines have had great difficulty transforming themselves to such lean operations.

- Starbucks repositioned coffee via product quality and the experience of its coffee shops, which are now pervasive on city streets and neighborhood strip malls, resulting in their becoming a meeting place, as well as a place to read and do work on one's laptop.

- Wal-Mart redefined the retail industry via new business practices supported by information technology and systematic use of the immense amounts of data collected. Suppliers were, in effect, forced to respond with greatly improved supply chain performance, vendor managed inventories and, in some cases, vendor owned inventories. Competitors were compelled to adopt similar practices.

As noted earlier, these companies built their business models and practices from the ground up. They did not have to transform. However, the successes of their innovations have been a tremendous driving force in other companies' transformation initiatives and, as such, have played a pervasive role in the global economy.

Summary

The three transformation archetypes outlined in this section provide a course view of important distinctions among types of transformation initiatives. Transformation of an existing large enterprise is probably the greatest challenge, at least in terms of understanding and implementing fundamental change. Transformation via acquisitions and mergers is rife with difficulties and risks – and many such transformations fail – but they rarely cause the demise of the acquiring company.

Our economy depends on new companies developing and refining new business models and practices. These companies do not have to transform because there is no status quo to dismantle. However, the innovations these companies bring to the marketplace are very important drivers of transformation in existing companies and, thereby, essential ingredients in economic growth.

OVERVIEW OF BOOK

Table 1 summarizes the organization and topics of the chapters in this book. Note that while chapters are placed in particular sections, their content often also addresses other sections. Thus, for example, every chapter has some case study aspects to its contents. Similarly, many chapters reference methods and tools employed in the areas discussed by the chapters.

Introduction to Transformation

The purpose of this section is to define transformation and provide in-depth knowledge of the topic from both empirical and theoretical perspectives. This begins, of course, with this first chapter.

Chapter 2, "Enterprises As Systems," considers the fundamental nature of enterprises. This exploration begins with discussion of the work of enterprises, with emphasis on challenges rather than routine operations. This reflects a desire to support enterprises as they address essential challenges. Situations where enterprise transformation is needed to successfully deal with challenges are then discussed. The nature of enterprise transformation is discussed in terms of ends, means, and scope, as well as perspectives, approaches, and solutions. This leads to elaboration of a portfolio of important research issues that suggests a wealth of potential means for supporting people in enterprises to accomplish the work of these enterprises.

Chapter 3, "A Theory of Enterprise Transformation," outlines a theory of enterprise transformation to guide research on the fundamental questions raised in Chapter 2. The theory focuses on why and how transformation happens, as well as ways in which transformation is addressed and pursued in terms of work processes and the architecture of these processes. The nature and influence of management decision making – for better or worse -- are considered. A variety of industry and corporate vignettes are used to illustrate the theory. The portfolio of research initiatives presented in Chapter 2 are discussed in terms of how they can advance the proposed theory, while also enhancing practices of enterprise transformation.

Chapter	Section	Topic
1	Introduction	Introduction & Overview
2		Enterprises As Systems
3		A Theory of Enterprise Transformation
4	Elements of Transformation	Transformational Leadership
5		Organizational Culture and Change
6		Manufacturing and Enterprise Transformation
7		Transformation in the Logistics Industry
8		Services Management
9		Value Centered R&D
10		Six Sigma Quality
11		Enterprise Computing
12	Transformation Practices	Turnaround Planning and Execution
13		Financing in Crises
14		Bankruptcy
15		Tax Issues in Crises
16		Public Relations in Crises
17		Lessons From Practice
18	Case Studies	Newell Rubbermaid
19		The Transformation of Reebok
20		Lockheed Martin
21		Interface
22		Transformation in Academia

TABLE 1. Organization and Topics of Chapters

Elements of Transformation

Chapter 4, "Transformational Leadership," argues that, for all the promise that new ideas and systems have to transform business, transforming an enterprise comes down to one thing: *leadership*. This chapter contrasts transactional and transformational leadership. Discussion focuses on mission and values, vision, strategies, organizational building, systems and processes, and measurement.

Chapter 5, "Organizational and Culture Change" presents a framework and approach to organizational change. The importance of culture and leadership in transforming organizations is emphasized. Experiences and practices within the Hay Group that lead to successful organizational transformation are provided as illustrative examples of each of the phases of the change process. The focus is primarily on the "how to" aspects of organizational transformation with examples of specific tools and techniques.

Chapter 6, "Manufacturing and Enterprise Transformation," observes that manufacturing enterprises were dramatically different at the end of the twentieth century than at the opening of the century. Understanding the nature of these changes, and their enablers, provides a basis for anticipating or even planning future transformations. A number of examples of twentieth century transformative innovations and changes are described. A framework for describing the manufacturing enterprise is presented and used to generalize the nature of the transformations observed. Some conjectures are given on the future of manufacturing enterprise transformation.

Chapter 7, "Transformation in the Logistics Industry," notes that the logistics industry has fundamentally changed over several decades. This transformation has, in part, been driven by regulatory changes, including economic, coordinative, and social regulations. Customers have also driven transformation via lean manufacturing, disintermediation, the Internet, outsourcing, expanded services, offshoring, and information technology. Consumers of logistics services have benefited substantially from these changes. In contrast, employees of the companies providing these services have not always benefited from the transformation of this industry.

Chapter 8, "Services Management," describes how marketing, operations management (OM) and human resources management (HR) have confronted issues of managing firms in service industries. This includes discussion of marketing's conceptualization of service quality (especially the intangible nature of services), how OM has seen the importance of customer contact as a key issue in the design of service delivery processes, and how HR has revealed the linkage between internal organizational processes as experienced by employees and customer experiences and satisfaction. Several contingencies are identified that relate to when service quality is likely to have maximum payoffs for organizations (high intangibility, high customer contact, service that requires people to cooperate to get the job done), including a set of issues requiring simultaneous attention by management for organizations wishing to achieve service quality excellence.

Chapter 9, "Value-Centered R&D," observes that the management of R&D organizations has received considerable attention in terms of the nature of the flow from research to development to deployed technology, as well as planning and managing this flow. R&D strategies, innovation funnels, and multi-stage decision processes, to name just a few constructs, have been articulated and elaborated. This chapter builds on this foundation to consider the nature of the value created by this process. An options-based approach is advocated for economic valuation of the products of R&D. Adoption and implementation of this approach is outlined in terms of ten principles for characterizing, assessing, and managing value.

Chapter 10, "Enterprise IT and Transformation," argues that today's enterprises are using information technology (IT) in virtually all aspects of their business. IT enables enterprises to provide seamless access to corporate data; streamline existing and create new business processes; design, improve, and deliver new products and services; and communicate and collaborate with customers, suppliers and other organizations across the globe. As enterprises undergo transformation of various kinds, IT can become a driving or inhibiting force to successful change. This chapter highlights some of the current enterprise IT trends, presents the fundamental drivers of the information economy, and suggests some basic architectural IT principles that can facilitate a smooth transformational process. The successes and failures resulting from appropriately, and lack of, implementing these principles are illustrated in numerous examples and case studies throughout the chapter. The chapter concludes by introducing a novel concept of enterprise IT and transformational maturity and offering some practical guidelines.

Chapter 11, "Six Sigma Quality," notes that the Six Sigma philosophy, pioneered by Motorola and popularized by GE, has spread like a wildfire across the corporate world during the last decade. This chapter discusses what Six Sigma means as a metric, a philosophy and as a company-wide approach for Quality Management. The road map, organizational structure and training necessary for successful deployment of Six Sigma are discussed. A case study based on an Indian manufacturing company illustrates a typical Six Sigma project leading to financial benefits.

Transformation Practices

Chapter 12, "Turnaround Planning and Execution," argues that the process of transforming an enterprise can be broken down into clear and logical steps. An honest assessment must be made of the situation and organization. The management team must provide leadership, and focus the organization on the problems at hand. Management must encourage prompt decision-making with the best information available, and communicate effectively both inside and outside the company. This chapter outlines four stages of enterprise transformation and discusses the elements of each stage, including key issues and success factors.

Chapter 13, "Financing in a Crisis," observes that enterprise transformation often emerges from crises, particularly crises that threaten the financial survival of the enterprise. In such crises, cash control is often the primary, near-term goal. This chapter first considers the objectives in such crises – operate or liquidate. Selecting a capital structure, formulating a negotiating strategy, considering bankruptcy, and necessary characteristics of leaders are then discussed. Several examples of financial turnarounds are used to illustrate key points.

Chapter 14, "Transformation and the Chapter 11 Reorganization Process," notes that the choice of any particular restructuring strategy will be driven by the nature of the problem or problems requiring repair. One of the more drastic restructuring alternatives that a distressed company may consider is the filing of a bankruptcy case under chapter 11 of the Bankruptcy Code. While a chapter 11 filing is a dramatic step that can shake an enterprise to its core, the Bankruptcy Code recognizes that fact and, in response, affords a troubled business significant protections and powerful tools designed to facilitate management's efforts to repair the problems and right the business. The major protections and tools available to management in chapter 11, and how specific protections and tools can be used to assist in enterprise transformation efforts, are described in this chapter. A broader overview of the chapter 11 environment and process, including a discussion of some of the more significant risks and burdens of chapter 11, provides meaningful context for consideration of the transformation opportunities available through the chapter 11 reorganization process.

Chapter 15, "Tax Issues in Crises," stresses the importance of managing taxes to the success of a business, and indicates that this is even truer for companies in crisis. The tax consequences of restructuring are addressed. Restructuring in bankruptcy versus out of bankruptcy is discussed. These issues are considered from the perspectives of several key stakeholders. General limitations on the use of net operating losses and taxes on pre-bankruptcy operations, as well as partnership bankruptcies, are discussed.

Chapter 16, "Public Relations In Crises," addresses communications in times of crises. Several principles are outlined and illustrated. These principles include telling the truth, organizing the facts, focusing of messages, using irrefutable sources of facts, taking control of communications, getting help for communicating, and maintaining consistent messages. Extensive vignettes and case studies are used to illustrate these principles.

Chapter 17, "Lessons from the Transformation Front" defines enterprise transformation in terms of two types of transformation: playing the game better (Type I) and playing by different rules (Type II). These two types of transformation are compared and contrasted. Type I transformations are centered on *focus* and *performance*; they are built on breakthroughs in control. Type II transformations are centered on *capabilities* and *advantage*; they are built on breakthroughs in integration. Lessons from successful transformations are also discussed, particularly the concept of pivot points and the notion of fatal moves. Finally, the relationship of enterprise transformation to strategy is considered.

Transformation Case Studies

Chapter 18, "Newell Rubbermaid," chronicles the formation and evolution of the Newell Company from 1902 to 2000. Changes of the retail marketplace in that period are discussed and Newell's adaptations are explained. The lessons learned from almost 80 acquisitions in the 1967-2000 period are summarized. The experience base gained from these acquisitions led to the construct of "Newellization," which is introduced and elaborated.

Chapter 19, "The Transformation of Reebok," indicates that corporate transformation can take many forms and be instigated by a diverse set of forces. In the case of Reebok, a prolonged period of losing to the competition and not foreseeing market changes precipitated the need for major change. David Perdue, one of the leading executives during the transformation, tells the story of how the company was able to pull itself out of danger, and reorient itself both internally and externally. Reebok, for at least the second time in its history, was able to reinvent important aspects of the footwear business while at the same time infusing its corporate culture with renewed energy and focus.

Chapter 20, "Lockheed Martin Aeronautics Restructuring and Transformation," discusses the formation of Lockheed Martin Aeronautics Company (LM Aero) in January 2000 from three existing Lockheed Martin business units. The restructuring and transformation were necessary to re-establish a viable aeronautics company for customers, shareholders and employees. The approach was to set clear intents, support the deployment of operating capability to meet those intents, and then to execute to achieve the outcomes desired. The outcomes to date, as compared to the transformation intents, are impressive. This chapter chronicles the key elements of the restructuring and transformation that led to successful outcomes. The chapter also addresses a more formal, structured approach to transformation based on the lessons learned from the large-scale transformation of LM Aero.

Chapter 21, "Doing Well by Doing Good: Interface's Vision of Becoming the First Industrial Company in the World to Attain Environmental Sustainability," addresses one of the most challenging transformations a company can undertake -- transforming towards sustainability. The raw materials used in production are often not recyclable, technologies to close the loop are often not available, and most importantly, legislation and market economics are not strong enough reasons to completely overhaul the way the company designs, manufactures and distributes its products. Consequently, there seldom is a pressing need to undertake such a transformation. Interface Inc. is one company that initiated such a transformation ten years ago, and has made significant progress towards its goal of being not only sustainable, but also restorative. This chapter traces the company's journey, analyzes this transformation in the context of John Kotter's eight steps on leading change (Kotter, 1995), and discusses key challenges and learnings of interest to top-level managers who wish to lead such a transformation in their own organization.

Chapter 22, "Transformation in Academia," observes that the globalization of university-based engineering education and research is associated with the creation of national and international "brands" by leading research universities. Such branding is reflected in rankings of universities and their programs. High brand visibility appears to lead to high rankings and vice versa. This chapter explores this phenomenon for university-based engineering programs. Attributes associated with ranking systems are discussed and universities' abilities to influence these attributes are considered. Both moving up in the rankings and sustaining highly ranked positions are discussed. These issues are addressed both in general and for the specific case of Georgia Tech. Three fundamental conclusions are reached: research and education continue to be the key to universities achieving world class status and economic development for key stakeholders; size provides universities with the resources and abilities to pursue strategies that lead to increasing recognition; and vision and leadership both attract resources and enable the focus needed to achieve the highest levels of recognition.

REFERENCES

Baskerville, R., Mathiassen, L., Pries-Heje, J., & Degross, J. (Eds.).(2005). Business agility and information technology diffusion. New York: Springer.

Charan, R., & Colvin, G. (1999, June 21). Why CEOs fail. Fortune, 68-78.

Davenport, T.H. (2005). The coming commoditization of processes." Harvard Business Review, 83 (6), 100-108.

Easterbrook,G. (2005). What's bad for GM ... New York Times, June 12, pp 1 and 3.

Economist, (2005). A question of management. The Economist, June 11, p. 74.

Friedman, T.L. (2005). The world is flat: A brief history of the 21st century. New York: Farrar, Straus and Giroux.

Gouillart, F.J., & Kelly, J.N. (1995). Transforming the organization. New York: McGraw-Hill.

Hammer, M., & Champy, J. (1993). Reengineering the corporation: A manifesto for business revolution. New York: Harper Business.

Jensen, M. C. (2000). A theory of the firm: Governance, residual claims, and organizational forms. Cambridge, MA: Harvard University Press.

Kotter, J.P. (1995). Leading change: Why transformation efforts fail. Harvard Business Review, 73 (2), 59-67.

Rouse, W.B. (1998). Don't jump to solutions: Thirteen delusions that undermine strategic thinking. San Francisco, CA: Jossey-Bass.

Rouse, W.B. (2001). Essential Challenges of Strategic Management. New York: Wiley.

Rouse, W.B. (2002). Need to know: Information, knowledge and decision making. IEEE Transactions on Systems, Man, and Cybernetics – Part C, 32 (4), 282-292.

Schumpeter, J. A. (1976). Capitalism, Socialism and Democracy. New York: Harper & Row.

Slywotsky, A.J. (1996). Value migration: How to think several moves ahead of the competition. Boston, MA: Harvard Business School Press.

Slywotsky, A.J., & Morrison, D.J. (1997). The profit zone: How strategic business design will lead you to tomorrow's profits. New York: Times Books.

Womack, J.P., & Jones, D.T. (1996). Lean thinking: Banish waste and create wealth in your corporation. New York: Simon & Schuster.

CHAPTER 2
ENTERPRISES AS SYSTEMS[*]

WILLIAM B. ROUSE

ABSTRACT

The nature of enterprises as systems is considered. This exploration begins with discussion of the work of enterprises, with emphasis on challenges rather than routine operations. This reflects a desire to support enterprises as they address essential challenges. Situations where enterprise transformation is needed to successfully deal with challenges are then discussed. The nature of enterprise transformation is discussed in terms of ends, means, and scope, as well as perspectives, approaches, and solutions. This leads to elaboration of a portfolio of important research issues that suggests a wealth of potential means for supporting people in enterprises to accomplish the work of these enterprises.

INTRODUCTION

When members of the technology community talk about systems, they often are thinking of airplanes, process plants, factories, transportation networks, and command and control systems, to name just a few typical domains. Within these domains, concerns often focus on the effectiveness, efficiency, and safety of these systems. Pursuit of these issues may cause one to take great interest in the operators, maintainers, and perhaps designers of these systems. Consequently, in the past several decades, an enormous amount has been learned about how to support design and operation of such systems, e.g., see Sheridan (1974, 1992, 2002), Rasmussen (1986, 1994), Sage (1992, 1995), and Sage & Rouse (1999).

These types of systems are certainly very important. However, their importance to our economies and societies should be kept in perspective. There are thousands of commercial airplanes and hundreds of nuclear power plants, for example, and many thousands of people involved in their operations. In contrast, a much more ubiquitous type of system is the enterprise. An enterprise is a goal-directed organization of resources -- human, information, financial, and physical – and activities, usually of significant operational scope, complication, risk, and

---

[*]This chapter is based on an article titled "Enterprises as Systems: Essential Challenges and Approaches to Transformation," that appeared in **Systems Engineering**, Vol. 8, No.2, 2005.

duration. Enterprises can range from corporations, to supply chains, to markets, to governments, to economies[1].

If we consider this full range, there are millions of enterprises and billions of people involved in these systems. Despite their prevalence, enterprises are seldom considered to be systems. Instead, the focus is on engineering or manufacturing, or perhaps finance or sales, or maybe human resources. One might pursue optimal designs of products, processes, supply chains, etc. Or perhaps one might be concerned with managing the uncertainties of revenues and costs. This emphasis on maximizing, or minimizing, one attribute in isolation from others is sometimes termed suboptimization. One makes sure to get one thing "right" but, in the process, ignores everything else[2].

However, computer and communications technologies are leading to everything becoming more integrated – everything connects to everything. We decrease our potential success when we try to design and manage functions within the enterprise independently of each other. The interactions are important, indeed essential to fully leveraging the enterprise's assets – human, information, financial, and physical – to the greatest benefit for all stakeholders. This requires that we look at the whole enterprise as a system, rather than as a collection of functions connected solely by information systems and shared parking lots.

This chapter addresses the nature of enterprises as systems[3]. This exploration begins with consideration of the work of enterprises, with emphasis on strategic challenges rather than routine operations. This reflects a desire to support enterprises as they address essential challenges. We then discuss those situations where enterprise transformation is needed to successfully deal with these challenges. The nature of enterprise transformation is discussed in terms of ends, means, and scope, as well as perspectives, approaches, and solutions. This leads to elaboration of important research issues whose pursuit is central to both understanding and enabling transformation. The portfolio of research issues outlined suggests many potential means for supporting people in enterprises to accomplish the work of these enterprises.

ESSENTIAL CHALLENGES

What do enterprises do? There are lots of meetings, much typing and filing, and many things are lifted and stacked. There are innumerable tasks and activities. It

---

[1] Supply chains can be viewed as extended enterprises linking upstream and downstream providers and consumers of raw materials, components, products, services, and so on. Markets can be viewed as further extensions, often involving several supply chains.

[2] "Systems of systems" where component systems have goals and priorities that are not fully aligned with enterprise goals and priorities appear to be more prone to such suboptimization (Sage & Cuppan, 2001).

[3] It is important to distinguish enterprise systems from enterprises as systems. For example, ERP (Enterprise Resource Planning) systems are often referred to as enterprise systems. ERP can certainly be important to enterprises as systems, but they are by no means synonymous. Interestingly, if ERP architecting and integration are based on a view of the enterprise as a system, then many of the difficulties encountered with ERP initiatives might be mitigated (Economist, 1999).

is important that this work be productive, safe, and rewarding. However, we cannot approach enterprise as systems at this level.

We need to begin with the work of the enterprise as a system, rather than the jobs, tasks, and activities of the many people that work in the enterprise. To an extent, we need to conduct a work domain analysis of an enterprise (Rasmussen, et al., 1994; Vicente, 1999). This analysis should begin with consideration of the goals and objectives of the work of enterprises.

Goals and objectives might be considered in terms of revenues, profits, market share, etc. for the private sector, and budgets, constituencies served, and so on for the public sector. However, this level of analysis tends to be idiosyncratic. Instead, we should begin with the recognition that all enterprises face similar strategic challenges – shown below -- that must be appropriately understood and addressed for enterprises to succeed (Rouse, 2001).

- Growth: Increasing Impact, Perhaps in Saturated/Declining "Markets"

- Value: Enhancing Relationships of Processes to Benefits & Costs

- Focus: Pursuing Opportunities & Avoiding Diversions

- Change: Competing Creatively While Maintaining Continuity

- Future: Investing in Inherently Unpredictable Outcomes

- Knowledge: Transforming Information to Insights to Programs

- Time: Carefully Allocating the Organization's Scarcest Resource

There is a variety of ways of approaching these challenges (Collins & Porras, 1994; Collins, 2001; Rouse, 2001). Despite the pronouncements of a plethora of management gurus, there is no "silver bullet" that handles all these challenges. Strategic management involves understanding which challenges are central and adopting a reasonable approach among the many possibilities.

As shown in Figure 1, *growth* has to be the goal. Growth can be cast in terms of economic, behavioral, and/or social impacts, or possibly in terms of improved quality, service, and responsiveness. The key point is that growth is a must – the only alternative is decline. Enterprise stasis is not a stable state. Hence, growth must be pursued or decline is assured.

It should be emphasized that share price, earnings per share, revenues, market share, and so on reflects just one perspective on growth. Impact can be measured in many ways. Enterprises can improve the quality of their offerings, the benefits of their services for their constituencies, and/or the influence of their activities and communications without necessarily growing financially or in terms of staff and facilities. Indeed, in some situations, growth of impacts may have to be pursued while such human, financial, and physical resources are declining.

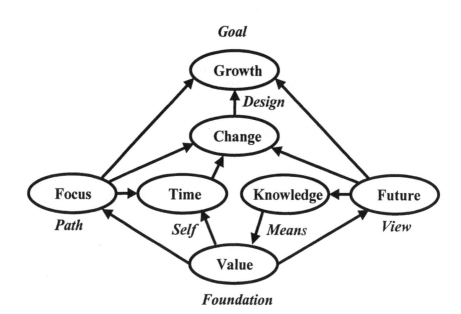

FIGURE 1. Relationships Among Challenges

There are, admittedly, situations where graceful decline may be the appropriate goal. In such cases, the enterprise transformation of interest might be from providing value to providing nothing, perhaps in the sense of doing no harm in the process. Ideally, one might like to assure a "soft landing" for the enterprise's stakeholders. This unusual, though not improbable, case involves many concerns beyond pursuit of negative growth, e.g., liability and tax implications of ceasing operations, which are beyond the scope of this chapter.

Value provides the foundation for growth. Understanding the nature of value, its evolution or migration, and the consequent growth opportunities are critical elements of this challenge (Slywotsky, 1996, 1997). One then, of course, must devise a value proposition and associated business processes to secure this growth. Understanding and enhancing the value streams that provide value to constituencies are keys to successful growth (Womack & Jones, 1996).

Focus provides the path to growth. Pursuit of opportunities and avoidance of diversions can be quite difficult (Rouse, 1998), particularly in the presence of significant organizational learning disabilities (Senge, 1990), or when the organization is trapped in single-loop learning (Argyris & Schon, 1978). Equally difficult is *change* in terms of designing the enterprise to pursue this path (Rouse,

1993). Both focus and change can create enormous organizational and cultural change problems (Collins & Porras, 1994; Collins, 2001). Strong leadership is crucial during such transitions (Charan & Colvin, 1999; Bennis & O'Toole, 2000; Rouse, 2001).

The nature of the *future*, especially the long-term future, exacerbates the difficulties of focus and change. Not only are the magnitudes and timing of investment returns uncertain – the very nature of the returns is uncertain (Burke, 1996). Further, most large enterprises have difficulty taking advantage of new ideas, even when they are due to their original investments (Christensen, 1997).

The uncertainties and risks associated with an enterprise's view of the future create needs for hedges against downsides, while still being focused on the upsides. Option-based thinking can provide the needed balance between these two perspectives (Luenberger, 1997; Amram & Kulatilaka, 1999; Boer, 1999, 2002). Options provide ways for addressing an enterprise's future, contingent opportunities and needs (Rouse & Boff, 2004).

Knowledge is the means by which enterprises increasingly address these challenges. It can be quite difficult to transform data, information, and knowledge into programs of action and results (Whiting, 1999; Zack, 1999). This involves both understanding the roles of information and knowledge in problem solving and decision making in different domains (Rouse, 2002), as well as the ways in which archival knowledge and people with knowledge can meet these needs (Cook & Brown, 1999; Brown & Duguid, 2000).

Time is an overarching challenge for leaders of enterprises. To a great extent, leaders define themselves by how they spend their time (Rouse, 1994, 2001). Transformational leadership involves devoting personal time to those things that will create lasting value (Kouzes & Posner, 1987; George, 2003). Time is the scarcest of leaders' resources, much more than financial and physical resources. Nevertheless, leaders often report being trapped by urgent but unimportant demands for their time (Covey, 1989; Miller & Morris, 1999). This is a classic challenge for senior management (Oncken & Wass, 1974; Mintzberg, 1975).

Considering the nature of the above challenges, what do executives or teams of executives do? One might imagine that they spend time creating models, analyzing tradeoffs, and attempting to optimize allocations of resources. However, the fact is that executives and managers spend their time reacting to their environments, negotiating compromises, and "satisficing" much more than optimizing (Mintzberg, 1975; Simon, 1957, 1969). In general, they have to consider and balance the perceptions, concerns, and desires of the many stakeholders in their enterprises.

To understand and support these executives, we need to adopt a similar human-centered philosophy (Rouse, 1991, 1992, 1993). Understanding and supporting the interests of an enterprise's diverse stakeholders – and finding the "sweet spot" among the many competing interests – is a central aspect of discerning the work of the enterprise as a system and creating mechanisms to enhance this work.

ENTERPRISE TRANSFORMATION

There is a wide variety of ways to address the essential challenges just outlined (Collins & Porras, 1994; Collins, 2001; Rouse, 2001). Process improvements and other incremental changes may be sufficient for a particular enterprise's challenges. However, in some cases, addressing these strategic challenges may involve enterprise transformation, i.e., fundamental changes in terms of relationships to markets, product and service offerings, market perceptions, and/or cost pressures (Hammer & Champy, 1993). Understanding and supporting transformation are critical to enhancing enterprises as systems.

A framework for understanding the nature of transformation is shown in Figure 2. The goal or ends pursued via transformation tends to significantly differentiate initiatives. The approach or means adopted for transformation pursuits relates to both the goals pursued and the nature and competencies of the enterprise. The ends and means, as well as extent of integration of the enterprise, influence the scope of transformation.

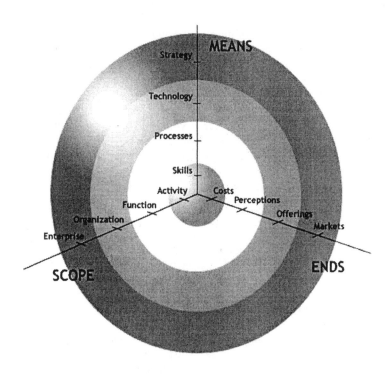

FIGURE 2. Transformation Framework

The ends of transformation can range from greater cost efficiencies, to enhanced market perceptions, to new product and service offerings, to fundamental changes of markets. The means can range from upgrading people's skills, to redesigning business practices, to significant infusions of technology, to fundamental changes of strategy. The scope of transformation can range from work activities, to business functions, to overall organizations, to the enterprise as a whole.

We have found this framework to provide a useful categorization of a broad range of case studies of enterprise transformation. Considering transformation of markets, Amazon leveraged IT to redefine book buying, while Wal-Mart leveraged IT to redefine the retail industry. Illustrations of transformation of offerings include CNN redefining news delivery, Motorola moving from battery eliminators to radios to cell phones, UPS transforming from solely package delivery to being a provider of integrated supply chain management services, and IBM moving from an emphasis on selling computer products to providing integrated technology services. Examples of transformation of perceptions include Dell repositioning computer buying and Starbucks repositioning coffee buying. The many instances of transforming business operations include Lockheed Martin merging three aircraft companies and Newell resuscitating numerous home products companies.

The costs and risks of transformation increase as the endeavor moves farther from the center in Figure 2. Initiatives focused on the center (in green) will typically involve well-known and mature methods and tools from industrial engineering and operations management. In contrast, initiatives towards the perimeter (in red) will often require substantial changes of products, services, channels, etc., as well as associated large investments.

It is important to note that successful transformations in the outer band of Figure 1 are likely to require significant investments in the inner bands also. In general, any level of transformation requires consideration of all subordinate levels. Thus, for example, successfully changing the market's perceptions of an enterprise's offerings is likely to also require enhanced operational excellence to underpin the new image being sought. As another illustration, significant changes of strategies often require new processes for decision making, e.g., for R&D investments (Roussel, Saad & Erickson, 1999; Matheson & Matheson, 1998; Miller & Morris, 1999; Rouse & Boff, 2004).

Perspectives on Transformation

There are basically four alternative perspectives that tend to underlie perceived needs for transformation:

- Market and/or technology opportunities – the lure of greater success prompts transformation initiatives

- Market and/or technology <u>threats</u> – the danger of anticipated failure prompts transformation initiatives

- <u>Competitors'</u> initiatives – others' transformation initiatives prompt recognition that transformation is necessary to continued success

- Enterprise <u>crises</u> – steadily declining market performance, cash flow problems, etc. prompt recognition that transformation is necessary to survive

The perspectives driven by external opportunities and threats often allow pursuing transformation long before it is forced on management, increasing the chances of having resources to invest in these pursuits, leveraging internal strengths and mitigating internal weaknesses. In contrast, the perspectives driven by external competitors' initiatives and internally-caused crises typically lead to the need for transformation being recognized much later and, consequently, often forced on management by corporate parents, equity markets, or other investors. Such reactive perspectives on transformation often lead to failures.

Approaches to Transformation

Transformation initiatives driven by external opportunities and threats tend to adopt strategy-oriented approaches such as:

- Markets Targeted, e.g., pursuing global markets such as emerging markets, or pursuing vertical markets such as aerospace and defense

- Market Channels Employed, e.g., adding web-based sales of products and services such as automobiles, consumer electronics, and computers

- Value Proposition, e.g., moving from selling unbundled products and services to providing integrated solutions for information technology management

- Offerings Provided, e.g., changing the products and services provided, perhaps by private labeling of outsourced products and focusing on support services

On the other hand, transformation initiatives driven by competitors' initiatives and internal crises tend to adopt operations-oriented approaches including:

- Supply Chain Restructuring, e.g., simplifying supply chains, negotiating just-in-time relationships, developing collaborative information systems

- Outsourcing & Offshoring, e.g., contracting out manufacturing, information technology support; employing low-wage, high-skill labor from other countries

- Process Standardization, e.g., enterprise-wide standardization of processes for product and process development, R&D, finance, personnel, etc.

- Process Reengineering, e.g., identification, design, and deployment of value-driven processes; identification and elimination of non-value creating activities

- Web-Enabled Processes, e.g., online, self-support systems for customer relationship management, inventory management, etc.

It is essential to note, however, that no significant transformation initiative can rely solely on either of these sets of approaches. Strategy-oriented initiatives must eventually pay serious attention to operations. Similarly, operations-oriented initiatives must at least validate existing strategies or run the risk of becoming very good at something they should not be doing at all.

Recognitions of perspectives and adoption of appropriate approaches should be determined by a clear understanding of the current and emerging situations faced by the enterprise (Rouse, 1996). Delusions about the current situation can completely undermine strategic thinking about opportunities, threats, competitors, and crises (Rouse, 1998). Consequently, the approaches adopted may not match the underlying needs of the enterprise.

Enterprise Solutions

Many approaches to transformation, especially those that are operations-oriented, are pursued in the context of information technology "solutions" such as:

- Enterprise Resource Planning (ERP)

- Customer Relationship Management (CRM)

- Supply Chain Management (SCM)

- Sales Force Automation (SFA)

The large investments required to deploy these types of solutions need to be understood in the context of how they help enterprises to address essential challenges and, in many cases, fundamentally transform. "Installing" these solutions is only a beginning, as many enterprises have discovered after the fact (Economist, 1999).

The architecting of such enterprise information systems should reflect the enterprise as a system, or system of systems (Sage & Cuppan, 2001). Integration across the component systems should consider the primary value streams of the enterprise (Rouse & Boff, 2001, 2003). Particular attention should be paid to how information and knowledge are shared and support creation and execution of programs of action that enhance value (Rouse, 2001, 2002).

Ideally, these types of enterprise solutions are viewed as just a piece of the transformation puzzle, albeit a large one. Addressing and resolving the people and organizational issues associated with these solutions are often the thorniest part of the road to success. Understanding work processes, both as they are and should be, is usually central. Training and aiding of personnel – at all levels – also tends to be very important, as does alignment of incentives and rewards with new processes.

RESEARCH ISSUES

The essential challenges of strategic management, as well as the overarching challenge of enterprise transformation, suggest a large number of research issues. Figure 3 portrays several broad categories of issues. A number of initiatives within these categories are described below.

Best Practices

As noted earlier, there is a wealth of practices available with which to address the essential challenges as well as enterprise transformation (Collins & Porras, 1994; Collins, 2001; Rouse, 2001). An important research issue concerns the extent to which any of these practices can be declared "best" practices, at least for specific types of situations and enterprises with particular characteristics. Quite frankly, many published practices tend to be reasonable and good ideas that are reported to have worked someplace at least once[4].

To declare a practice as "best," we need to measure the benefits of employing the practice relative to alternative practices. Addressing the challenges, as well as transformational approaches to the challenges, tends to take quite a bit of time, and measuring the benefits takes even longer. As the medical profession knows well, it is very difficult to conduct studies over many years and maintain support and commitment, as well as control.

---

[4] Of course, it can be quite reasonable to proceed with a good, but less than best practice, perhaps because it is important to act immediately. Nevertheless, it important to understand how well practices work and why some practices might work much better than others.

FIGURE 3. Research Issues in Enterprise Transformation

This reality has led us to focus on what enterprises have done in the past and the consequences of these initiatives. We are using a database of the yearly and quarterly reports of all public companies worldwide, as well as major analysts' projections and assessments of these companies' performance, over the past 20-30 years. We are sleuthing what transformation initiatives these companies undertook and the subsequent benefits of these undertakings, including the time frame within which benefits typically emerge.

As we have discussed this research with various senior executives, in both private and public sectors, several have asked that we not limit ourselves to just best practices. They have indicated keen interest in worst practices. Specifically, they would like to know what types of transformation practices have never worked in any measurable manner. They expect that this will eliminate many candidate approaches.

This points up the need to understand the whole distribution of practices, not just the tails of best and worst. Such understanding will enable understanding of the internal and external factors that influence the success of practices, e.g., role of leadership, nature of industry, and state of economy. Thus, the notion of best practices is clearly a multi-dimensional construct rather than a one size fits all "silver bullet."

This research on best – and worst – practices will tell us what really has worked, including the conditions under which it worked. Also very important is the fact that this research is providing deep grounding on current practices and experiences implementing these practices. This grounding provides a foundation for looking further out. We are particularly interested in the 3-5 year time horizon to be able to understand the opportunities, threats, problems, and issues likely to affect enterprises just beyond their current planning horizon. The following subsections consider this time horizon and beyond. This is a perfect place for enterprise-oriented research to focus.

Methods & Tools

To pursue science-based engineering approaches to understanding, designing, and managing enterprises as systems, we need methods and tools. Fortunately, there is a wide variety of systems-oriented concepts, principles, methods, and tools with which one can pursue the essential challenges and, if necessary, transform the enterprise (Sage & Rouse, 1999; Rouse, 2001). In fact, the wealth of alternatives poses the problem of understanding how all these approaches fit together or, at least, where one or the other applies.

For example, when is Total Quality Management, Six Sigma, Business Process Reengineering, or Lean Transformation the best approach? At a methodological level, when should one employ models based on queuing networks, system dynamics, Petri nets, or agent-based simulation? We are in the process of trying to make sense of the many alternatives and provide guidelines – and guidance – for what to use where.

More fundamentally, we are concerned with formal modeling of enterprises. One needs to understand both the "as is" and "to be" enterprise and the nature of the transformations for getting from one to the other. This is difficult because we need to determine how alternative representations interact with the range of mathematical machinery that can be brought to bear, while also being able to incorporate essential economic, behavioral, and social phenomena.

Beyond the difficulty of formally representing the "as is" and "to be" enterprise, it can be difficult to simply characterize the "as is" enterprise. People within the enterprise often have remarkably little perspective for the business processes to which their activities contribute. They may also be defensive and apprehensive regarding possible changes.

This can be particularly difficult when activities are part of the "overhead" that does not clearly contribute to the value streams of the enterprise. Such activities are likely candidates for being outsourced or eliminated. Even when these activities are required for regulatory reasons, for example, people can be concerned that their jobs are at risk.

At this point, we are working with methods drawn from engineering, computing, and architecture. These three disciplines pursue formal methods for quite different reasons – engineering to represent the physical flows in the system, computing to represent the information flows, and architecture to represent human flows within and among physical spaces. Enterprises, of course, include all these types of flows. We need methods that enable representation and manipulation of these different flows across a set of computationally compatible tools.

These models, methods, and tools are likely to provide the basis for aiding leaders of enterprises in that they will enable making sense of and portraying what is happening in the enterprise, as well as developing and evaluating potential courses of action (Mykityshyn, 2004). A rudimentary example is provided by a suite of tools we developed to address market situation assessment, new product planning, and technology strategy (Rouse & Howard, 1995, Rouse, et al., 2000, Rouse, 2001). This suite integrates multi-stakeholder, multi-attribute models, Quality Function Deployment, technology/market maturity models, production learning curves, option pricing models, and expert systems to address the enterprise challenges of growth and value. These tools draw upon representations from marketing, engineering, manufacturing, finance, operations research, and artificial intelligence.

One of the difficulties in employing these and other method and tools concerns the ability to estimate needed parameters, preferably as probability distributions rather than point estimates. Despite the wealth of data typically collected by many enterprises, it usually requires substantial effort to translate these data into the information and knowledge needed by these methods and tools. This leads us to consideration of information technologies.

Enterprise Technologies

Current and emerging enterprise technologies are both driving and enabling enterprise transformation. Computer and communications technologies are central. Information technology (IT) is a broad description. Most people see IT as the key to transformation. Yet, as just noted, simply "installing" these technologies does not fully address enterprise challenges.

The central concern in this research area is not with what technologies will emerge, but instead with the implications of their adoption if they do emerge. In particular, the focus is on organizational implications and strategy/policy issues associated with these implications (Rouse & Acevedo, 2004). Thus, the issue is not whether it will happen, but the implications if it does happen.

A good example of an emerging technology or capability is knowledge management, including its key enabler -- collaboration technology (Rouse, 2001, 2002; Rouse & Acevedo, 2004). Fully leveraging this technology/capability requires a deep understanding of how knowledge is – and could be – generated and shared in an enterprise, as well as its impact on important metrics of enterprise success. The issue is not so much about how the technology functions as it is about how work currently gets done and could be done with these capabilities (Cook & Brown, 1999; Brown & Duguid, 2000).

Another good illustration of an emerging enterprise technology relates to the area of identity management. How should one authenticate who and what is connected to the enterprise network? The relevant technologies include Public Key Infrastructure (PKI), Common Access Cards (CAC), Biometrics, and Radio Frequency Identification (RFID). Our research is focused on the interoperability, security, and privacy implications of adopting these technologies to provide the needed functionality and performance within various IT systems, i.e., authentication, authorization, confidentiality, integrity, non-repudiation, availability, etc. An additional important issue is the total cost of ownership of such capabilities.

Another area is wireless communications and mobile computing. Basole (2004) addresses the implications for enterprises that entertain these technologies. One implication may be greater reliance on virtual organizations and less use of traditional workspaces. Ashuri (2004) looks at the strategic decision to move towards a balance of virtual and traditional workspaces. The value of both mobile and virtual technologies depends on how they affect work and productivity.

Organizational Simulation

When enterprises entertain major, transformational changes, they typically perform a wealth of feasibility and financial analyses. At some point, they may determine that "it's worth it." However, there still may be reluctance among key stakeholders. The problem is likely to be that economic analyses do not usually address behavioral and social concerns. Spreadsheet models and colorful graphic presentations seldom provide a sense of what the changes will feel like.

Organizational simulation can address these concerns (Rouse & Boff, 2005). Immersive simulations can enable decision makers and other stakeholders to experience the future, act in that future, and have the future react to them. If this is a positive experience, then decision makers can proceed with increased confidence. On the other hand, if problems are encountered, the future can be redesigned before the check is written.

This research draws upon traditional modeling and simulation as well as artificial intelligence, gaming, and entertainment. Our overriding premise is that people are more likely to embrace those futures that they can experience beforehand.   Embracing these futures will, in turn, enable enterprise transformation by mitigating the human and organizational concerns that often undermine transformation initiatives.

It is also useful to note that this element of the research portfolio tends to generate comments of "wow" more often than other elements. The immersive experience tends to be compelling. Of course, that is exactly the point. Enterprise transformation can be strongly facilitated and sustained by compelling experiences of the post-transformation future.

This can be particularly important in environments where some of key stakeholders do not find financial analyses and spreadsheet presentations convincing. For example, the public, politicians, unions, etc. may need to experience infrastructure innovations – new modes of public transportation, for instance – before they will support such initiatives.

Simulation of organizational futures can be particularly useful if it allows for unintended consequences to emerge. This is quite possible when a range of stakeholders "play the game" and react differently than expected to the environment and to each other. In some cases, participants may subvert the game, i.e., work around the rules, and prompt discoveries and insights that possibly lead to innovations in strategy, doctrine, and strategic thinking in general (Rouse & Boff, 2005).

Organizational simulations can offer interactive glimpses of the future, enable the design of operational procedures in parallel with system design, and provide rich, ready-made training environments once systems are deployed. This may result in enterprise transformation being an adventure rather than a dreaded threat. In particular, transformation can perhaps be an adventure that the key stakeholders design and redesign as they experience it.

Investment Valuation

Starting with best practices, we employ methods and tools to design the transformed enterprise, enabled by emerging enterprise technologies, and experienced via organizational simulation. This nevertheless begs the question, "What's it worth?" How should we attach value to the investments needed to transform the enterprise?

Of course, this question has been with us for a long time. We just need to project revenues, costs, and profits (or savings) and discount these time series to get a Net Present Value (NPV). Unfortunately, most of the investment for transformation occurs in the near-term while much of the return from transformation occurs in the long-term. Aggressive discount rates – adopted because of the large uncertainties – will render long-term payoffs near worthless.

This phenomenon also impacts investments in R&D, as well as investments in education, the environment, and so on. The value of any long-term initiatives with upstream investments, downstream returns, and large uncertainties will suffer from discounted cash flow analysis. This raises a question of the fundamental purpose of such investments.

Should an enterprise invest in transformation solely to fix today's problems? For example, should the R&D budget of an enterprise be justified solely on the basis of the likely contributions to today's product and service offerings? The answer clearly is, "No." Investments in R&D should provide the enterprise options for meeting contingent downstream needs, many of which are highly uncertain in nature and impact (Rouse & Boff, 2001, 2003, 2004).

In this area, we are researching alternative option-pricing models for valuation of long-term investments such as R&D, economic development, and transformation. We have conducted numerous case studies and, as a result, influenced many investment decisions. It is clear that options for the future are exactly what most enterprises need. These models and methods enable them to determine what these options are worth.

This research has provided several insights, at least one of which is fundamental. Using NPV for valuation of long-term, highly uncertain transformation initiatives tends to emphasize preservation of investment capital. In contrast, using Net Option Value (NOV) tends to maximize the value gained by the enterprise. In other words, using NPV minimizes risks to the transformation budget, while using NOV maximizes the benefits of transformation. We are in the process of determining how this contrast is affected by the magnitude, timing, and uncertainties associated with these investments.

Organizational Culture & Change

The above initiatives imply substantial changes of processes, practices, technologies, and measures of success. These changes must be pursued in the context of the organizational culture of the enterprise in question. Often this culture is not compatible with what will be needed to successfully transform. A lack of recognition of this mismatch is a fundamental organizational delusion that may enfeeble change initiatives (Rouse, 1998).

As depicted in Figure 3, our concern is not with organizational culture and change in general. The topic is far too immense. Instead, we are interested in culture and change as they relate to the other initiatives. For instance, we have pursued the implications of deploying of new enterprise technologies, e.g., collaboration suites, in terms of interactions with cultural norms of knowledge sharing and online work (Rouse & Acevedo, 2004).

One particularly interesting phenomena concerns enterprises' decisions to pursue transformation rather than, for example, incremental process improvements. A related phenomenon is the emerging recognition that transformational change is at hand despite never having explicitly decided to pursue such a fundamental initiative. Garcia (2004) is researching the antecedents of transformation decisions, including emergent decisions. Specifically, she is concerned with what drives and triggers such decisions and recognitions.

Research Methodology

Pursuit of the broad set of research issues and approaches outlined in this section requires a similarly broad set of research methods. Modeling representations can range from discrete-event to continuous-time models, to a range of network models, to rule-based and statistical models. Different disciplines bring a range of representations to the study of complex systems (Sage & Rouse, 1999; Rouse, 2003).

There is also a range of simulation and computational tools, with differences reflecting the variations of the modeling representations. Unfortunately, it is still rather difficult to move across representations and tools. Thus, hybrid representations such as needed for organizational simulation often must be hand crafted (Rouse & Boff, 2005). Lack of powerful, easy-to-use tools tends to drive up the time, costs, and risks when modeling complex enterprise systems.

Another methodological issue concerns identifying, collecting or accessing, and interpreting data. In many cases, data that one would assume would easily be available has not been captured or has been archived in difficult-to-access forms. Thus, data for benchmarking, model fitting, and validating predictions can be quite expensive to obtain, often prohibitively. Ongoing developments of enterprise information systems should improve this situation, but not without some forethought.

Summary

The research portfolio summarized in Figure 3 constitutes the puzzle pieces of a foundation for understanding and supporting enterprise transformation. We need to understand best practices to move beyond an endless stream of reasonable, yet unproven ideas. Methods and tools are important to increasing the rigor of this work, while also making it more efficient. Emerging enterprise technologies both drive and enable the transformations designed with these methods and tools. Organizational simulation provides a laboratory for enterprise experimentation, as well as furnishes a means to communicate with stakeholders less open to purely analytical arguments. Investment valuation provides new methods and tools for assigning value to transformation initiatives with highly uncertain, long-term returns. Finally, understanding organizational culture and change is essential to successful implementation of any of these ideas.

CONCLUSIONS

Understanding enterprises as systems – or as a system of systems -- is critical to moving beyond piecemeal transformations. This understanding is also important to creating better enterprise systems that can support transformation rather than just incremental improvements of collections of enterprise functions. Overall, the goal is for these huge investments to yield greater returns, sooner.

Fundamental research is necessary to provide a firm foundation for achieving this goal. This research is inherently highly multi-disciplinary and must address somewhat messy, complex problems laced with technological, economic, behavioral, and social issues. The research outlined here can certainly contribute to understanding the apparent complexity of these problems. However, we must also create the means for coping with the complexity of reality if we are to improve this reality.

Understanding enterprises as systems is necessary to facilitating and sustaining enterprise transformation. Previous functionally oriented solutions have resulted in suboptimization and substantially less benefit than possible with more integrated solutions that involve architectures premised on a system of systems perspective. The "macro" perspective advocated here embraces multiple views of the enterprise and, thereby, can take advantage of the concepts, principles, methods, and tools of many disciplines – this strongly reflects both the philosophy and substance of systems engineering and management. The resulting level of integration and interoperability, both theoretically and practically, we believe will prove to be the key to successful enterprise transformation.

REFERENCES

Amram, M., & Kulatilaka, N. (1999). Real options: Managing strategic investment in an uncertain world. Boston: Harvard Business School Press.

Argyris, C., & Schon, D.A. (1978). Organizational learning: A theory of action perspective. Reading, MA: Addison-Wesley.

Ashuri, B. (2004). Framing strategic tradeoffs between traditional and virtual organizations and workspaces. Proceedings of IFAC Symposium on Analysis, Modeling & Evaluation of Human-Machine Systems, September.

Basole, R. (2004). The value and impact of mobile information and communication technologies. Proceedings of IFAC Symposium on Analysis, Modeling & Evaluation of Human-Machine Systems, September.

Bennis, W., & O'Toole, J. (2000, May-June). Don't hire the wrong CEO. Harvard Business Review, 171-176.

Boer, F.P. (1999). The valuation of technology: Business and financial issues in R&D. New York: Wiley.

Boer, F.P. (2002, July-August). Financial management of R&D: 2002. Research Technology Management, 45 (4), 23-35.

Brown, J.S., & Duguid, P. (2000, May-June). Balancing act: How to capture knowledge without killing it. Harvard Business Review, 73-80.

Burke, J. (1996). The pinball effect: How Renaissance water gardens made the carburetor possible and other journeys through knowledge. Boston: Little, Brown.

Charan, R., & Colvin, G. (1999, June 21). Why CEOs fail. Fortune, 68-78.

Christensen, C.M. (1997). The innovator's dilemma: When new technologies cause great firms to fail. Boston: Harvard Business School Press.

Collins, J.C., & Porras, J.I. (1994). Built to last: Successful habits of visionary companies. New York: Harper Business.

Collins, J.C. (2001). Good to great: Why some companies make the leap and others don't. New York: Harper Business.

Cook, S.D.N., & Brown, J.S. (1999). Bridging epistemologies: The generative dance between organizational knowledge and organizational knowing. Organization Science, 10 (4), 381-400.

Covey, S.R. (1989). The seven habits of highly effective people. New York: Simon & Schuster.

Economist, (1999, June 24). ERP RIP? The Economist.

Garcia, D. (2004). Enterprise transformation: Forces and processes of change. Proceedings of IFAC Symposium on Analysis, Modeling & Evaluation of Human-Machine Systems, September.

George, B. (2003). Authentic Leadership: Rediscovering the Secrets to Creating Lasting Value. San Francisco: Jossey-Bass.

Hammer, M., & Champy, J. (1993). Reengineering the corporation: A manifesto for business revolution. New York: Harper Business.

Kouzes, J.M., & Posner, B.Z. (1987). The leadership challenge: How to get extraordinary things done in organizations. San Francisco: Jossey-Bass.

Luenberger, D.G. (1997). Investment science. Oxford, UK: Oxford University Press.

Matheson, D., & Matheson, J. (1998). The smart organization: Creating value through strategic R&D. Boston, MA: Harvard Business School Press.

Miller, W.L., & Morris, L. (1999). Fourth generation R&D: Managing knowledge, technology, and innovation. New York: Wiley.

Mintzberg, H. (1975, July/August). The manager's job: Folklore and fact. Harvard Business Review, 49-61.

Mykityshyn, M. (2004). Enterprise transition/transformation: Conceptual frameworks for understanding nonlinear growth dynamics. Proceedings of IFAC Symposium on Analysis, Modeling & Evaluation of Human-Machine Systems, September.

Oncken, W. Jr., & Wass, D.L. (1974, Nov-Dec). Management time: Who's got the monkey. Harvard Business Review.

Rasmussen, J. (1986). Information Processing and Human-Machine Interaction. New York: Elsevier.

Rasmussen, J., Pejtersen, A.M., & Goodstein, L.P. (1994). Cognitive Systems Engineering. New York: Wiley.

Rouse, W.B. (1991). Design for success: A human-centered approach to designing successful products and systems. New York: Wiley.

Rouse, W.B. (1992). Strategies for innovations: Creating successful products, systems, and organizations. New York: Wiley.

Rouse, W.B. (1993). Catalysts for change: Concepts and principles for enabling innovation. New York: Wiley.

Rouse, W.B. (1994). Best laid plans. Englewood Cliffs, NJ: Prentice-Hall.

Rouse, W.B. (1996) Start where you are: Matching your strategy to your marketplace. San Francisco, CA: Jossey-Bass.

Rouse, W.B. (1998). Don't jump to solutions: Thirteen delusions that undermine strategic thinking. San Francisco, CA: Jossey-Bass.

Rouse, W.B. (2001). Essential Challenges of Strategic Management. New York: Wiley.

Rouse, W.B. (2002). Need to know: Information, knowledge and decision making. IEEE Transactions on Systems, Man, and Cybernetics – Part C, 32 (4), 282-292.

Rouse, W.B. (2003). Engineering complex systems: Implications for research in systems engineering. IEEE Transactions on Systems, Man, and Cybernetics – Part C, 33 (2), 154-156.

Rouse, W.B., & Acevedo, R. (2004). Anticipating Policy Implications of Emerging Information Technologies. Information • Knowledge • Systems Management, 4 (2), 77-93.

Rouse, W.B., & Boff, K.R. (2001). Strategies for value: Quality, productivity, and innovation in R&D/technology organizations. Systems Engineering, 4 (2), 87-106.

Rouse, W.B., & Boff, K.R. (2003). Value streams in science & technology: A case study of value creation and Intelligent Tutoring Systems. Systems Engineering, 6 (2), 76-91.

Rouse, W.B., & Boff, K.R. (2004). Value-centered R&D organizations: Ten principles for characterizing, assessing & managing value. Systems Engineering, 7 (2), 167-185.

Rouse, W.B., & Boff, K.R. (Eds.).(2005). Organizational Simulation: From Modeling and Simulation to Games and Entertainment. New York: Wiley.

Rouse, W.B., & Howard, C.W. (1995). Supporting market-driven change. In D. Burnstein (Ed.), The Digital MBA (pp. 159-184). New York: Osborne McGraw-Hill.

Rouse, W.B., Howard, C.W., Carns, W.E., & Prendergast, E.J. (2000) Technology Investment Advisor: An options-based approach to technology strategy. Information • Knowledge • Systems Management, 2 (1) (2000), 63-81.

Roussel, P.A., Saad, K.N., & Erickson, T.J. (1991). Third generation R&D: Managing the link to corporate strategy. Cambridge, MA: Harvard Business School Press.

Sage, A.P. (1992). Systems engineering. New York: Wiley.

Sage, A.P. (1995). Systems management for information technology and software engineering. New York: Wiley.

Sage, A.P., & Cuppan, C.D., (2001). On the systems engineering and management of systems of systems and federations of systems. Information • Knowledge • Systems Management, 2 (4), 325-345.

Sage, A.P., & Rouse, W.B. (Eds.).(1999). Handbook of systems engineering and management. New York: Wiley.

Senge, P.M. (1990). The fifth discipline: The art and practice of the learning organization. New York: Doubleday/Currency.

Sheridan, T.B. (1992). Telerobotics, Automation, and Human Supervisory Control. Cambridge, MA: MIT Press.

Sheridan, T.B. (2002). Human and Automation: Systems Design and Research Issues. New York: Wiley.

Sheridan, T.B., & Ferrell, W.R. (1974). Man-Machine Systems: Information, Control, and Decision Models of Human Performance. Cambridge, MA: MIT Press.

Simon, H.A. (1957). Models of man: Social and rational. New York: Wiley.

Simon, H.A. (1969). The sciences of the artificial. Cambridge, MA: MIT Press.

Slywotsky, A.J. (1996). Value migration: How to think several moves ahead of the competition. Boston, MA: Harvard Business School Press.

Slywotsky, A.J., & Morrison, D.J. (1997). The profit zone: How strategic business design will lead you to tomorrow's profits. New York: Times Books.

Vicente, K.J. (1999). Cognitive Work Analysis: Toward Safe, Productive, and Healthy Computer-Based Work. Mahwah, NJ: Lawrence Erlbaum Associates.

Whiting, R.   (1999, Nov 22nd). Knowledge Management: Myths and realities. Information Week, 42-54.

Womack, J.P., & Jones, D.T. (1996). Lean thinking: Banish waste and create wealth in your corporation. New York: Simon & Schuster.

Zack, M.H. (1999). Developing a knowledge strategy. California Management Review, 41 (3), Spring, 125-145.

CHAPTER 3

A THEORY OF ENTERPRISE TRANSFORMATION[*]

WILLIAM B. ROUSE

ABSTRACT

The information technology revolution has driven the pace of competition and rapid globalization. Consequently, enterprises increasingly need to consider and pursue fundamental change – transformation – to maintain or gain competitive advantage. This need raises important research issues concerning how transformation is best understood and pursued. This chapter outlines a theory of enterprise transformation to guide research on these issues. The theory focuses on why and how transformation happens, as well as ways in which transformation is addressed and pursued in terms of work processes and the architecture of these processes. A variety of industry and corporate vignettes is used to illustrate the theory. A portfolio of research initiatives are discussed in terms of how they can advance the proposed theory, while also enhancing practices of enterprise transformation.

INTRODUCTION

Enterprise transformation concerns change, not just routine change but fundamental change that substantially alters an organization's relationships with one or more key constituencies, e.g., customers, employees, suppliers, and investors. Transformation can involve new value propositions in terms of products and services, how these offerings are delivered and supported, and/or how the enterprise is organized to provide these offerings. Transformation can also involve old value propositions provided in fundamentally new ways.

Transformation can be contrasted with business process improvement. Adoption of the principles of Total Quality Management (Deming, 1986) has resulted in many enterprises focusing on their business processes and devising means to continually improve these processes. The adoption of TQM may be transformative for an enterprise. However, as judged by the definition of transformation provided here, the ongoing use of TQM subsequent to

---

[*] This chapter is based on an article titled "A Theory of Enterprise Transformation," that appeared in **Systems Engineering**, Vol. 8, No. 4, 2005.

implementation is not transformative. The whole point of TQM is to make continual change a routine undertaking.

Business Process Reengineering (Hammer & Champy, 1993) can be much more transformative. Adoption of BPR has led to much fundamental redesign of business processes. This rethinking followed the guidance "don't automate; obliterate." In this way, both the adoption and implementation of BPR tends to be transformative, although success is, by no means, guaranteed. One can then apply the principles of TQM to continually improve the reengineered business processes.

Rather than routine, transformation tends to be discontinuous, perhaps even abrupt. Change does not occur continually, yielding slow and steady improvements. Instead, substantial changes occur intermittently, hopefully yielding significantly increased returns to the enterprise. Transformation and routine change converge when, as with BPR and TQM, the transformation involves fundamental new ways of pursuing routine change.

This chapter outlines a theory of enterprise transformation. The theory focuses on why and how transformation happens, as well as ways in which transformation is addressed and pursued in terms of work processes and the architecture of these processes. As later discussion elaborates, the theory argues for the following definition:

> *Enterprise transformation is driven by experienced and/or anticipated value deficiencies that result in significantly redesigned and/or new work processes as determined by management's decision making abilities, limitations, and inclinations, all in the context of the social networks of management in particular and the enterprise in general.*

A variety of industry and corporate vignettes are used to illustrate the elements of this theory and definition. A portfolio of research initiatives are discussed in terms of how they can advance the proposed theory, while also enhancing practices of enterprise transformation.

ROLE OF THEORY

The study and pursuit of enterprise transformation is very much a transdisciplinary endeavor. The types of initiatives discussed later in this chapter involve disciplines ranging from artists and architects, to engineers of all types and economists, as well as management, public policy, and so on. The efforts of research teams pursuing these initiatives often begin with intense discussions of the fundamental basis for these pursuits.

In essence, these discussions involve two questions. First, what is the theoretical basis for our research initiatives? Second, how do the emerging results of these efforts contribute to and advance theory? Given the range of disciplines just noted, it is important to understand what is meant by "theory" in the context of our investigations of enterprise transformation.

Are we like Newton or Einstein postulating an axiomatic basis for the universe and working to derive "laws" such as $F = MA$ or $E = MC^2$? Or are we more like Darwin, combing the South Seas for evidence of our origins? For the former, we would formulate mathematical models from which we could deduce system behaviors and then compare those behaviors with observations. Eventually, we would devise theorems and proofs regarding behavioral phenomena such as response, stability, observability, and controllability in our "model worlds" (Rouse, 2003).

For the latter, we would rely on statistical inference to gain an understanding of what affects what, and under what conditions. This choice reflects the complex nature of the world of interest, with a wide range of players, forces, and factors interacting dynamically to slowly yield long-term changes. This complexity precludes creating a model world of sufficient validity to enable reaching defensible conclusions about the real world. Thus, we must experiment in the real world.

The distinction just elaborated contrasts the role of theory in axiomatic and empirical traditions in science and engineering. However, the research initiatives of interest also include participants from art, literature, music, politics, law, and so on. This suggests that we might need to consider the role of theory in the arts and humanities vs. science and engineering (Snow, 1962; Rouse, 2003), as well as the role of theory in legal, political, and social systems (Diesing, 1962).

These elaborations might be overwhelming were it not for the fact that the theory we need is to drive our research rather than explain or motivate change, perhaps of artistic or social nature, for instance. The theory should drive our hypotheses, determine the variables of interest, and specify potentially relevant environmental factors. Research results should confirm or reject our hypotheses, support or refute the effects of variables, and assess the relevance of environmental factors. The rules of statistical inference will govern these evaluations.

Therefore, we are very much like Darwin combing the enterprise seas to gain understanding of the origins and processes of transformation. The theory presented in this chapter is intended to help us determine where to look and what to look for. Specifically, the theory helps us to recognize enterprises of potential interest and the variables of importance to identifying enterprises that have attempted transformation, how they have pursued it, and the consequences of these pursuits. Thus, our theory fits into the empirical tradition. The possibility of an axiomatic theory depends on the relationships and patterns that our empirical studies will unearth.

CONTEXT OF TRANSFORMATION

Enterprise transformation occurs in – and is at least partially driven by -- the external context of the economy and markets. As shown in Figure 1, the economy affects markets that, in turn, affect enterprises. Of course, it is not quite as crisply hierarchical as indicated in that the economy can directly affect enterprises, e.g., via regulation and taxation. The key point is that the nature and extent of transformation are context dependent.

For public sector enterprises, the term "constituency" can replace the term "market." The financially oriented metrics shown in Figure 1 also have to be changed to reflect battles won, diseases cured, etc. This chapter will occasionally draw parallels between private and public sector enterprises; however, full treatment of these parallels is beyond the scope of this chapter.

There is also an internal context of transformation – the "intraprise" in Figure 1. Work assignments are pursued via work processes and yield work products, incurring costs. Values and culture (Davenport, 1999), reward and recognition systems (Flannery, et al., 1996; Weiss & Hartle, 1997), individual and team competencies (Katzenbach & Smith, 1993), and leadership (Kouzes & Posner, 1987; George, 2003) are woven throughout the intraprise. These factors usually have strong impacts on an enterprise's inclinations and abilities to pursue transformation.

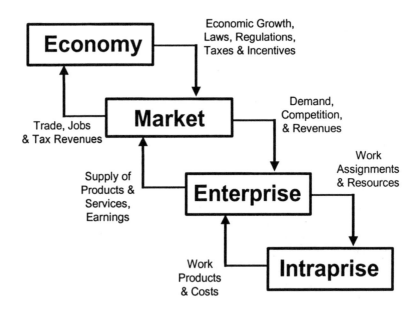

FIGURE 1. Context of Enterprise Transformation

MODELING THE ENTERPRISE

Enterprise transformation occurs in the external context of Figure 1.   The enterprise, with its internal strengths and weaknesses, and external opportunities and threats, operates within this broader external context.   Possibilities for transformation are defined by the relationships between the enterprise and this context.   The model of the enterprise as a system shown in Figure 2 provides a basis for understanding these possibilities.

Relationships among the elements of the enterprise system are as follows. Inputs affect both work processes and enterprise state.   For example, input resources (e.g., people, technology, and investment) affect both how work is done and how well it is done.   As another example, input market conditions (e.g., demand and competition) affect quality and pricing of products and services.

The concept of "state" is central to the theory of enterprise transformation. The state of a system is the set of variables and their values that enable assessing where the system is and projecting where it is going.   We tend to think that financial statements define the state of an enterprise as a system.   However, financial variables are usually insufficient to project the future of an enterprise and a deeper characterization of state is needed (Rouse, 2001). The Balanced Scorecard (Kaplan & Norton, 1996) or, deeper yet, an enterprise-oriented version of the House of Quality (Hauser & Clausing, 1988) are two possibilities.

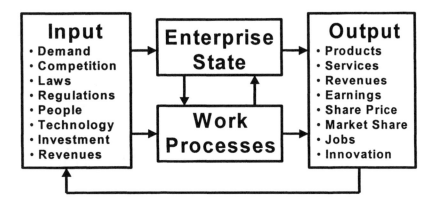

FIGURE 2.   Elements of Enterprise System

Output is derived from the evolving state of the enterprise. For example, revenues can be determined from the numbers of units of products or services sold and the prices of these offerings. Determining profits requires also knowing the costs of providing offerings. Units sold relate, at least in part, to customer satisfaction as determined by product and service functionality, quality, and price, all relative to competing offerings.

The construct of "value" is central to the arguments that follow. The value of the enterprise is traditionally viewed as its market capitalization, i.e., share price times number of outstanding shares. Share price is traditionally conceptualized as the net present value of future enterprise free cash flows, i.e., revenues minus costs. This view of value is often characterized as shareholder value.

From this perspective, state variables such as revenues, costs, quality and price determine value. These variables are themselves determined by both work processes and architectural relationships among processes. Inputs such as investments of resources affect work processes. Coming full circle, the value of projected outputs influences how input resources are attracted and allocated.

Table 1 summarizes several examples of enterprise domains, processes, states, work, and value. It is important to note that value, for example in terms of unit prices, will depend on the competing offerings from other enterprises. Similarly, the importance of any set of military objectives secured depends on the objectives secured by adversaries. Thus, as noted earlier, knowledge of context is essential to understanding enterprises as systems.

Domain	Process	State	Work	Value
Manufacturing	Production	Work in Process	Products	Unit Price Minus Cost
Service	Delivery	People in Queues	Transactions	Customer Satisfaction
R&D	Research	Studies in Progress	Technology Options	Potential of Options
Military	Operations	Positions of Forces	Objectives Secured	Importance of Objectives

TABLE 1. Example Domains, Processes, States, Work & Value

The examples in Table 1 serve to illustrate the multi-faceted nature of value. It could be argued that all of the facets shown in the right column are simply intermediate surrogates for shareholder value; hence, shareholder value is the central construct. On the other hand, it is very difficult to argue that shareholder value, as traditionally defined, is the sole driver of enterprise transformation. For many types of enterprises, shareholder value is the ultimate measure of success, but other forces such as markets, technologies, and the economy often drive change. Examples discussed later illustrate these forces.

Many fundamental changes address value from the perspective of customers and, to a much lesser extent, suppliers and employees. According to Peter Drucker (2001), "The purpose of a business is to create a customer." Thus, for example, while loss of market share and subsequent decreasing stock market valuation can be viewed as end effects in themselves, they also may be seen as symptoms of declining value of products and services as perceived by customers. Clearly, a broader view of value is needed (Slywotsky, 1996; Slywotsky & Morrison, 1997).

A THEORY OF ENTERPRISE TRANSFORMATION

Succinctly, experienced or expected value deficiencies drive enterprise transformation initiatives. Deficiencies are defined relative to both current enterprise states and expected states. Expectations may be based on extrapolation of past enterprise states. They may also be based on perceived opportunities to pursue expanded markets, new constituencies, technologies, etc. Thus, deficiencies may be perceived for both reactive and proactive reasons.

Transformation initiatives involve addressing what work is undertaken by the enterprise and how this work is accomplished. The work of the enterprise ultimately affects the state of the enterprise, which is reflected, in part, in the enterprise's financial statements, Balanced Scorecard assessment, or the equivalent. Other important elements of the enterprise state might include market advantage, brand image, employee and customer satisfaction, and so on. In general, the state of the enterprise does not include variables internal to work processes.

This is due to the fact that we only need state estimates sufficient to enable explaining, predicting, and/or controlling future states of the system. To illustrate, the state of an aircraft is usually defined in terms of its location, speed, attitude, etc., but not the current RPM of its fuel pumps, air flow in the cabin, and electron charge of its LED displays. Similarly, the state of an enterprise does not include current locations of all salespeople, ambient temperatures in each of its factories, the water flow in the rest rooms, etc. Were we not able to define state at a higher level of aggregation and abstraction, the complexity of modeling airplanes or enterprises would be intractable.

Value Deficiencies Drive Transformation

More specifically, enterprise transformation is driven by perceived value deficiencies relative to needs and/or expectations due to:

- Experienced or expected downside losses of value, e.g., declining enterprise revenues and/or profits

- Experienced or expected failures to meet projected or promised upside gains of value, e.g., failures to achieve anticipated enterprise growth

- Desires to achieve new levels of value, e.g., via exploitation of market and/or technological opportunities

In all of these cases, there are often beliefs that change will enable remediation of such value deficiencies. Change can range from business process improvement to more fundamental enterprise transformation.

Work Processes Enable Transformation

In general, there are three broad ways to approach value deficiencies, all of which involve consideration of the work of the enterprise:

- Improve how work is currently performed, e.g., reduce variability

- Perform current work differently, e.g., web-enable customer service

- Perform different work, e.g., outsource manufacturing and focus on service

The first choice is basically business process improvement. As discussed in the Introduction, this choice is less likely to be transformative than the other two choices. The second choice often involves operational changes that can be transformative depending on the scope of changes. The third choice is most likely to result in transforming the enterprise. This depends, however, on how resources are redeployed. Liquidation, in itself, is not necessarily transformative.

The need to focus on work processes is well recognized, e.g., (Hammer & Champy, 1993; Womack & Jones, 1996; Kessler, 2002). Reengineered and lean processes have been goals in many transformative initiatives. Indeed, a focus on processes may, at least initially, require transformation of management's thinking about an enterprise. The extent to which this subsequently transforms the enterprise depends on the extent of changes and success in their implementation.

Transformation can also involve relationships among processes, not just individual work processes in and of themselves. These relationships are often framed in terms of an "architecture." It is common to express architectures in terms of multiple "views." The <u>operational</u> view is a description of the activities, operational elements, and information flows required to support enterprise operations. The <u>technical</u> view is a set of rules defining the interactions and interdependencies of system elements to assure compatibility and satisfaction of requirements. The <u>system</u> view describes the physical connections, locations, key nodes, etc, needed to support enterprise functions (Sage & Lynch, 1998).

Transformation of work processes inherently must affect the operational view of the architecture. Changes of this view are likely to affect the technical and systems views. In contrast, changes of system and/or technical views that do not change operational views do not, by definition, change work processes. Hence, these types of changes may improve processes but do not transform the enterprise.

Bailey and Barley (2004) have argued for a renaissance in the study of work. They chronicle the substantial changes in work – from production workers to knowledge workers – while industrial engineering was abandoning the study of work practices and design. In the context of the theory outlined here, engineering will have to re-embrace work studies to play a central role in enterprise systems research (Rouse, 2004).

Rasmussen and his colleagues (1986, 1994) have pioneered the use of work domain analysis to characterize human roles, jobs, and tasks in complex systems. Building on this foundation, we can characterize the work of the enterprise in terms of the hierarchy of purpose, objectives, functions, tasks, and activities. Transformation of work can be pursued at all levels of this hierarchy.

Changing the tasks and activities of the enterprise, by themselves, relates to business process improvement. In contrast, changing the purpose, objectives, and/or functions of the enterprise is more likely to be transformational. Such changes may, of course, cause tasks and activities to then change. Thus, change at any level in the hierarchy is likely to cause changes at lower levels.

It seems reasonable to hypothesize that the higher the level of transformation, the more difficult, costly, time consuming, and risky the changes will be. For instance, changing the purpose of the enterprise is likely to encounter considerable difficulties, particularly if the extent of the change is substantial. In many cases, e.g., defense conversion, such change has only succeeded when almost all of the employees were replaced (Rouse, 1996).

Ultimately, one could liquidate the enterprise and redeploy its financial and perhaps physical assets in other ventures. However, it is difficult to characterize this as transformation. Thus, there is a point at which the change is sufficiently substantial to conclude that the enterprise has been eliminated rather than transformed.

Allocation of Attention & Resources

Input is also central to the theory of enterprise transformation. As implied by Figure 2, input includes both external variables related to customers, competitors, demand, interest rates, and so on, as well as internal variables such as resources and their allocation among work processes. Transformation involves allocating attention and resources so as to:

- Anticipate and adapt to changes of external variables, i.e., control the enterprise relative to the "road ahead" rather than the road behind

- Cultivate and allocate resources so as to yield future enterprise states with high projected value with acceptable uncertainties and risks

Thus, the ability of an enterprise to redeploy its human, financial, and physical resources is central to the nature and possibility of transformation.

Management Decision Making

Value deficiencies and work processes define the problem of enterprise transformation – one should recognize and/or anticipate deficiencies and then redesign work processes to remediate these deficiencies. To fully understand transformation, however, we need to understand both the problem and the problem solvers. Thus, a characterization of management decision making is central to our overall theory.

Nadler and Tushman (1989) summarize how managers address change, ranging from tuning, to adaptation, to reorientation, to re-creation. They focus on how management addresses the more complex and difficult changes of reorientation and re-creation in terms of diagnosing the problem, formulating a vision, creating a sense of urgency, linking change to core strategic issues, communicating and leading, and broadening the base of leadership, all in the context of a mixture of planning and opportunism that includes redesign of key processes and nurturing of investments as returns emerge over time.

Hollnagel's (1993) contextual control model of cognition has potential for describing how managers address the problems and decisions outlined by Nadler and Tushman. He outlines how the competence of decisions makers, combined with the characteristics of the situation (i.e., number of goals, available plans, mode of execution, and event horizon) combine to determine the chosen mode of control, ranging from scrambled, to opportunistic, to tactical, to strategic. The overarching premise is that strategic control is preferable to scrambled control.

However, Mintzberg's (1975) classic paper, as well as more recent works (Mintzberg, 1998,1999), serves to shatter the myth of the manager as a coolly analytical strategist, completely focused on optimizing shareholder value using leading-edge methods and tools. Simon (1957, 1969) articulates the concept of "satisficing," whereby managers find solutions that are "good enough" rather than optimal. Another important factor is the organizational environment that can be rife with delusions that undermine strategic thinking (Rouse, 1998).

Thus, Nadler and Tushman describe the work of managers addressing transformation, and Hollnagel's model suggests how managers' respond to this work. Mintzberg and Simon's insights provide realistic views of real humans doing this work, often in an organization beset by one or more of Rouse's organizational delusions.

This somewhat skeptical view of management decision making ignores several important aspects of human decision making. Managers' expertise and intuitions (Klein, 2002) and abilities to respond effectively in a blink (Gladwell, 2005) can be key to success, especially in recognizing what is really happening in an enterprise. The effective use of analogical thinking can also be invaluable, although there is the risk of relying on poor analogies (Gavetti & Rivkin, 2005). This can lead to doing the wrong things very well.

Managers' roles as leaders, rather than problem solvers and decision makers, are also central to transformation (George, 2003; Kouzes & Posner, 1987). The leadership styles of managers who are well attuned to business process improvement may prove to be poor matches for situations requiring reorientation and re-creation (Rooke & Torbert, 2005). Thus, the nature of the problem solver can have a substantial impact.

Beyond the individual skills and abilities of managers and management teams, the "social networks" both internal and external to the enterprise can have enormous impacts (Burt, 2000, Granovetter, 2005). An important distinction is between strongly and weakly connected networks. Strongly connected networks result in rapid and efficient information and knowledge sharing among members of these networks. Weakly connected networks have "holes," in many cases between strongly connected subnetworks.

Several researchers (Granovetter, 2005, Mohrman, Tenkasi, & Mohrman, 2003; Tenkasi & Chesmore, 2003) have found that weakly connected networks are better sources of new information and novel ideas. The resulting "big picture" perspective may better inform the nature of transformations pursued. In contrast, strongly connected networks are better at implementing change, at least once sense has been made of the anticipated changes and new meaning has been attached to these changes.

Summarizing, the problem of transformation (i.e., value deficiencies prompting redesign of processes) combines with the nature of the problem solvers addressing transformation, as well as their organizations, to determine whether transformation is addressed, how it is addressed, and how well desired outcomes are achieved. Several theories of human problem solving and decision making, as well as theories of social phenomena, are relevant and useful for elaborating these aspects of the theory of enterprise transformation. The key point is that explanations of any particular instance of transformation will depend on the situation faced by the enterprise, the nature of the particular managers leading the enterprise, and the social structure of the enterprise.

Transformation Processes

How does transformation happen? Transformation processes could be external to the model in Figure 2. However, it would seem that higher levels of transformation expertise would involve incorporation of transformation processes into the work processes in Figure 2. This possibility has been characterized in terms of constructs such as double-loop learning and organizational learning (Argyris & Schon, 1978; Senge, 1990).

Thus, transformation might become integral to normal business practices, perhaps even routine. Of course, this raises the question of the extent to which routine fundamental changes should be considered transformative. It is quite possible that such an evolution of an enterprise would not render changes less fundamental, but would enable much easier implementation of changes.

Summary of Theory

Figure 3 summarizes the theory of transformation outlined in this chapter. Transformation is driven by value deficiencies and involves examining and changing work processes. This examination involves consideration of how changes are likely to affect future states of the enterprise. Potential impacts on enterprise states are assessed in terms of value consequences. Projected consequences can, and should, influence how investments of attention and resources are allocated. The problem solving and decision making abilities of management, as well as the social context, influence how and how well all of this happens.

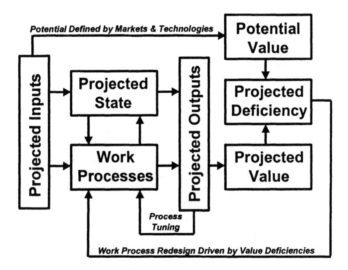

FIGURE 3. Theory of Enterprise Transformation

ENDS, MEANS & SCOPE OF TRANSFORMATION

As indicated in an earlier paper (Rouse, 2005), there is a wide range of ways to pursue transformation. Figure 4 summarizes conclusions drawn from numerous case studies. The ends of transformation can range from greater cost efficiencies, to enhanced market perceptions, to new product and service offerings, to fundamental changes of markets. The means can range from upgrading people's skills, to redesigning business practices, to significant infusions of technology, to fundamental changes of strategy. The scope of transformation can range from work activities, to business functions, to overall organizations, to the enterprise as a whole.

The framework in Figure 4 has provided a useful categorization of a broad range of case studies of enterprise transformation. Considering transformation of markets, Amazon leveraged IT to redefine book buying, while Wal-Mart leveraged IT to redefine the retail industry. In these two instances at least, it can be argued that Amazon and Wal-Mart just grew; they did not transform. Nevertheless, their markets were transformed. The U.S. Department of Defense's effort to move to capabilities-based acquisition (e.g., buying airlift rather than airplanes) has the potential to transform both DoD and its suppliers.

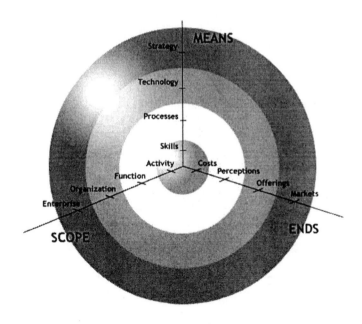

FIGURE 4. Transformation Framework

Illustrations of transformation of offerings include UPS moving from being a package delivery company to a global supply chain management provider, IBM's transition from manufacturing to services, Motorola moving from battery eliminators to radios to cell phones, and CNN redefining news delivery. Examples of transformation of perceptions include Dell repositioning computer buying, Starbucks repositioning coffee purchases, and Victoria's Secret repositioning lingerie buying. The many instances of transforming business operations include Lockheed Martin merging three aircraft companies, Newell Rubbermaid resuscitating numerous home products companies, and Interface adopting green business practices.

The costs and risks of transformation increase as the endeavor moves farther from the center in Figure 4. Initiatives focused on the center (in green) will typically involve well-known and mature methods and tools from industrial engineering and operations management. In contrast, initiatives towards the perimeter (in red) will often require substantial changes of products, services, channels, etc., as well as associated large investments.

It is important to note that successful transformations in the outer band of Figure 4 are likely to require significant investments in the inner bands also. In general, any level of transformation requires consideration of all subordinate levels. Thus, for example, successfully changing the market's perceptions of an enterprise's offerings is likely to also require enhanced operational excellence to underpin the new image being sought. As another illustration, significant changes of strategies often require new processes for decision making, e.g., for R&D investments.

Value Deficiencies Drive Transformation

Elaborating earlier value-centered arguments, there are basically four alternative perspectives that tend to drive needs for transformation:

- Value Opportunities: The lure of greater success via market and/or technology opportunities prompts transformation initiatives

- Value Threats: The danger of anticipated failure due to market and/or technology threats prompts transformation initiatives

- Value Competition: Other players' transformation initiatives prompt recognition that transformation is necessary to continued success

- Value Crises: Steadily declining market performance, cash flow problems, etc. prompt recognition that transformation is necessary to survive

The perspectives driven by external opportunities and threats often allow pursuing transformation long before it is forced on management, increasing the chances of having resources to invest in these pursuits, leveraging internal strengths and mitigating internal weaknesses. In contrast, the perspectives driven by external competitors' initiatives and internally-caused crises typically lead to the need for transformation being recognized much later and, consequently, often forced on management by corporate parents, equity markets, or other investors. Such reactive perspectives on transformation often lead to failures.

Work Processes Enable Transformation

Transformation initiatives driven by external opportunities and threats tend to adopt strategy-oriented approaches such as:

- Markets Targeted, e.g., pursuing global markets such as emerging markets, or pursuing vertical markets such as aerospace and defense

- Market Channels Employed, e.g., adding web-based sales of products and services such as automobiles, consumer electronics, and computers

- Value Proposition, e.g., moving from selling unbundled products and services to providing integrated solutions for information technology management

- Offerings Provided, e.g., changing the products and services provided, perhaps by private labeling of outsourced products and focusing on support services

On the other hand, transformation initiatives driven by competitors' initiatives and internal crises tend to adopt operations-oriented approaches including:

- Supply Chain Restructuring, e.g., simplifying supply chains, negotiating just-in-time relationships, developing collaborative information systems

- Outsourcing & Offshoring, e.g., contracting out manufacturing, information technology support; employing low-wage, high-skill labor from other countries

- Process Standardization, e.g., enterprise-wide standardization of processes for product and process development, R&D, finance, personnel, etc.

- Process Reengineering, e.g., identification, design, and deployment of value-driven processes; identification and elimination of non-value creating activities

- Web-Enabled Processes, e.g., online, self-support systems for customer relationship management, inventory management, etc.

It is essential to note, however, that no significant transformation initiative can rely solely on either of these sets of approaches. Strategy-oriented initiatives must eventually pay serious attention to operations. Similarly, operations-oriented initiatives must at least validate existing strategies or run the risk of becoming very good at something they should not be doing at all.

The above approaches drive reconsideration of work processes. Processes are replaced or redesigned to align with strategy choices. Operational approaches enhance the effectiveness and efficiency of processes. Of course, the possibilities of changing work processes depend greatly on the internal context of transformation. Leadership is the key, but rewards and recognition, competencies, and so on also have strong impacts on success. Social networks enormously affect implementation of change.

Work processes can be enhanced (by acceleration, task improvement, and output improvement); streamlined (by elimination of tasks); eliminated (by outsourcing); and invented (by creation of new processes). An example of acceleration is the use of workflow technology to automate information flow between process steps or tasks. An illustration of task improvement is the use of decision aiding technology to improve human performance on a given process task (e.g., enabling consideration of more options). Output improvement might involve, for example, decreasing process variability. Streamlining could involve transferring tasks to others (e.g., transferring customer service queries to other customers who have addressed similar questions). Elimination involves curtailing processes, e.g., Amazon created online bookstores thus eliminating the need for bookstore-related processes in their business. Invention involves creating new processes, e.g., Dell created innovative build-to-order processes.

ILLUSTRATIONS OF TRANSFORMATION

Enterprise transformation is, by no means, a new phenomenon. The longbow transformed war -- as weapon technology often has -- when the English decimated the French at Agincourt in 1415. The printing press in 1453 led to the "pamphlet wars" and Martin Luther's complaints in 1517 that seeded the transformation known as the Protestant Reformation. History is laced with many stories like this.

This section briefly reviews transformative developments and events in the transportation and computer industries, drawing on a longer work on these industries (Rouse, 1996). Attention then shifts to a range of contemporary stories of change in the telecommunications, retail, entertainment, information, and computing industries. These stories illustrate the range of ongoing transformation throughout the global economy.

Transportation

Before the early 1800s, the dominant forms of transportation -- horse, stagecoach, sailing ship, and so on -- had not changed substantially in centuries. Then, within roughly 100 years, we had steamboats, railroads, automobiles, and aircraft. In the process of moving from stagecoaches and canal boats to jet planes, humankind changed the speed at which it traveled by a factor of 100. Trips that once took days, now take minutes.

Robert Fulton is traditionally credited with the invention of the steamboat. He was fortunate, however, to be able to build on a variety of earlier efforts. For example, several steamboats were demonstrated following James Watt's improvements of the steam engine in 1769. Nevertheless, with Fulton's demonstration in 1807, the steamboat industry blossomed. By 1819, a steamboat had sailed from Savannah, Georgia to Russia. The first all-steam crossing, without the use of supporting sails, occurred in 1827. By the mid 1800s, transatlantic steamboat lines were competing.

The first reported self-propelled steam land vehicle was in the late 1600s and, by the late 1700s, a French-built steam car had been demonstrated in Paris. Soon after, an English built car was demonstrated. John Blenkinsop built the first practical and successful locomotive in Britain in 1812. The beginning of the railway industry is usually reported as starting with George Stephenson who created the Stockton and Darlington Railway in Britain that opened in September 1825. Soon after, it is argued, the railway era really began with the opening of Liverpool and Manchester Railway in Britain in September 1830. By the 1850s, the railroad's effects on the American economy were pervasive. Uniform methods of construction, grading, and bridging emerged. Much of the design of rails, locomotives, coaches, and freight cars was close to what we have today, at least in terms of appearance.

Frenchman Nicolas-Joseph Cugnot designed the first true automobile in 1769. This automobile was a steam-powered tricycle and was capable of 2.25 mph for 20 minutes. Germans Carl Benz and Gottlieb Daimler are credited with the first gasoline-engine automobile in 1885. In the U.S., George Selden filed a patent for the automobile in 1879. Charles and Frank Duryea created an American gas-powered automobile in 1892-93. By 1898, there were 50 automobile companies. Between 1904 and 1908, 241 automobile companies went into business. Interestingly, steam propulsion retained a dominant position for quite some time – at the turn of the century, 40% of U.S. automobiles were powered by steam, 38% by electricity, and 22% by gasoline.

Serious speculation about flight occupied such thinkers as Roger Bacon in the 13th century and Leonardo da Vinci in the 15th century. After a wealth of attempts over several centuries, Orville Wright, in 1903, flew for 12 seconds and landed without damage. In 1914 the Census Bureau listed 16 firms as aircraft manufacturers with combined total output for the year of 49 planes. By 1918, the American aircraft industry was delivering 14,000 aircraft with 175,000 employees.

However, after the signing of the World War I armistice, production dropped to 263 in 1922.

Commercial aviation eventually diminished the dominance of military customers in the aircraft market. Until the late 1950s, over half of the commercial aircraft in the world were built by Douglas Aircraft, having continually built upon the success of the DC-3. However, Boeing quickly moved into jet aircraft, mostly due to military contracts. Using the military KC-135 as a starting point, Boeing introduced the 707 commercial transport in 1958. Douglas was much slower to shift paradigms. Boeing's "bet" on jet aircraft provided the basis for its strong position in commercial aviation today.

The patterns of transformation just outlined for steamboats, trains, automobiles, and airplanes are closely linked to propulsion – steam, internal combustion, and jet engines. Combined with inventions in mechanical systems, aeronautics, and manufacturing – including many, many inventions that never gained broad acceptance – these patterns moved us faster and higher, both literally and economically. In the process, many enterprises were formed, and a few transformed successfully to created the companies we know today.

Computing

The evolution of computer technology and the computer industry took hundreds of years. Frenchman Blaise Pascal built the first mechanical adding machine more than 300 years ago. German Gottfried Wilhelm Liebniz, after seeing Pascal's machine, created the Stepped Reckoner in 1673. Charles Babbage conceived the first digital computer in the 1830s. He envisioned this computer -- the Analytical Engine -- as powered by steam that, as noted in the last section, was "high tech" in the 1830s.

Babbage got his idea for a digital computer from Frenchman Joseph-Marie Jacquard's punch-card programmed looms, developed in the early 1800s. Jacquard's punched card method for controlling looms also influenced American Herman Hollerith who invented a card-based system for tabulating the results of the 1890 census. Hollerith's venture led to what would later become IBM.

During the latter half of the 19th century and first half of the 20th century, IBM, NCR, Burroughs, Remington Rand, and other companies became dominant in the business equipment industry with tabulators (IBM), cash registers (NCR), calculators (Burroughs), and typewriters (Remington). The dominance of these companies in their respective domains set the stage for their becoming primary players in the computer market.

The emergence of digital computing and the process of maturation of the computer industry started with John V. Atansoff of Iowa State who built a prototype of an electromechanical digital computer in 1939. By 1946, John W. Mauchly and J. Presper Eckert at the University of Pennsylvania had completed the Electronic Numerical Integrator and Calculator, ENIAC, which was the first all-purpose, all-electronic digital computer and led to Remington-Rand's UNIVAC. In the same period, John von Neumann's concepts of stored-program computing served as the model for many digital computers.

Remington-Rand had some early success, including selling UNIVAC machines to the Census Bureau, which displaced IBM tabulators. However, IBM eventually beat out Remington-Rand because IBM recognized the tremendous potential of computers and how they had to be marketed. IBM recognized what was likely to happen in the business machines industry and responded by developing a customer-oriented strategy that helped their customers to deal successfully with trends that were affecting them.

In the late 1950s and early 1960s, a whole new segment of the computer market emerged – interactive rather than centralized computing. IBM dismissed and then ignored this segment. They apparently could not imagine that customers would want to do their own computing rather than have IBM support and possibly staff a centralized computing function. Later IBM tried to catch up, but did so poorly. By the late 1960s, Digital Equipment Corporation (DEC) dominated interactive computing with their minicomputers.

By the late 1970s, Apple was putting the finishing touches on the first microcomputer that would spark a new industry. DEC, in a classic business oversight, failed to take interactive computing to the next logical step of personal computing. Apple, exploiting pioneering inventions at Xerox, created the Macintosh in the mid 1980s. The Mac became the industry standard, at least in the sense that its features and benefits were adopted throughout the personal computer industry. Microsoft and Intel were the primary beneficiaries of this innovation.

Microsoft prospered when IBM chose them to create the operating system software -- DOS -- for IBM's personal computer. DOS soon became the industry standard, except for Apple enthusiasts. Microsoft Windows replaced DOS as the standard. With the introduction of Windows, Microsoft was able to create software applications for word processing, spreadsheets, presentations, and databases and now controls these markets.

More recently, of course, the Internet has dominated attention. Microsoft continues to battle with a range of competitors, hoping to transform a variety of inventions into dominant market innovations. The rules of the game have changed substantially as this industry has moved from mainframe to mini to micro and now Internet. Most inventions will not become innovations, but certainly a few will.

The patterns of transformation in computing revolve around power and speed. More and more computing operations, faster and faster, differentiate the mainframe, mini, and micro eras. Increasing user control has also been an element of these patterns, although this has resulted with increasing numbers of layers between users and computation. Further, it has been argued that pervasive networking is only possible with increased centralized management of standards, protocols, etc. Thus, the latest pattern of transformation may inherently borrow from old patterns.

Contemporary Illustrations

We have just skimmed through two centuries of innovations in transportation and computing -- and the formation (and demise) of thousands of enterprises as these industries transformed. Now, let's consider what has happened in the opening few years of this century. A summary of these vignettes is provided in Table 2.

The telecommunications industry has recently provided several compelling stories of transformation, particularly failures to transform. Perhaps the biggest story is AT&T. The company underestimated the opportunities in wireless and then overpaid for McCaw Cellular to catch up and later spun the cellular business off. They attempted to get into computers via NCR and then spun it off. They overpaid for TCI and MediaOne and then spun them off. They also spun off Lucent. They came late to the Internet data market. All of this created a debt crisis. With reduced market cap, AT&T was acquired by SBC, a former Baby Bell. (Economist, 2005, Feb 5).

Lucent, AT&T's progeny, has not fared much better. Adopting a "high tech" image when spun off in 2000, Lucent abandoned the traditional Baby Bell customers for Internet startups who bought on credit. Lucent overdid mergers and overpaid. They delayed developments of optical systems. Of greatest impact, they inflated sales to meet market expectations. When the Internet bubble burst and customers could not repay loans, Lucent's $250 billion market cap in 1999 quickly shrunk by more than 90% (Lowenstein, 2005).

While AT&T and Lucent were stumbling, Nokia was a star of the telecommunications industry. However, by 2003, Nokia was losing market share (35% to 29%) due to stodgy designs of cellphones, unwillingness to adapt to cellular providers, and internal preoccupation with reorganization. They reacted with new phone designs (e.g., cameras, games, and a velvet cell phone!) and market share rebounded. Nevertheless, the company is being pushed down market to maintain growth in an increasingly competitive market. One expert projects they will end up with something like a 22% market share, with Asian competitors the main beneficiaries (Economist, 2005, Feb 12).

The retail industry has been highly competitive for several decades. Procter & Gamble has been one of the stalwarts of this industry. They have maintained their competitive position by boosting innovation, ditching losing brands, buying winning ones and stripping away bureaucracy. However, the consumer goods industry has found itself caught between slowing sales, rising costs, and waning pricing power. The big box retailers now have the pricing power, both via private labels and "trade spending," i.e., requiring suppliers to pay for store promotions, displays, and shelf space. The acquisition of Gillette for $50B followed P&G's acquisition of Clairol for $5B and Wella for $7B. At the same time, P&G sold off numerous brands. China is a rapidly growing P&G market. Nevertheless, whether these changes can sustain P&G's growth remains to be seen (Economist, 2005, Feb 5).

Company	Transformation	Outcome
AT&T	Came late to wireless, computers, and cellular, paying too much to enter.	Facing a debt crisis and reduced market cap, AT&T was acquired by SBC.
Clear Channel	Clear Channel executed a long series of acquisitions, accelerated by the 1996 deregulation.	Cost leadership, combined with bundled selling resulted in their revenues growing over 50%.
IBM	Transformed from mainframe maker to robust provider of integrated hardware, networking, and software solutions.	Earnings and share price rebounded as services business flourished.
Kellogg	Remained committed to its brand strategy but focused on channel needs for consumers' changing concept of breakfast.	Acquired Keebler, resulting in revenue growth of almost 50 % and operating income nearly doubling in 5 year period.
Lucent	Adopting "high tech" image, abandoned Baby Bells, overdid mergers, delayed developments of optical systems, and inflated sales.	When Internet bubble burst and customers could not repay loans, $250 billion market cap in 1999 shrunk to $17 billion by 2005.
Newell Rubbermaid	With a track record of successfully acquiring over 60 companies, acquisition of Rubbermaid seemed like a natural match.	Acquisition dragged Newell down, losing 50% of the value of the investment. Brand strategy of Rubbermaid did not match Newell.
Nokia	New cell phone designs introduced to combat loss of market share.	Market share rebound, but likely temporary due to aggressive competitors.
Procter & Gamble	Acquisition of Gillette, Clairol and Wella while selling off numerous brands.	Outcome uncertain as the "consumer goods industry is caught between slowing sales, rising costs, and waning pricing power."
Siemens	Focused on cost reduction, innovation, growth, and culture change, in part by convincing people that there was a crisis.	Revenue almost doubled, net income more than tripled, and revenue per employee almost doubled over 12 years.
Thomson	Transformed itself from a traditional conglomerate into a focused provider of integrated electronic information to specialty markets.	They sold more than 60 companies and 130 newspapers, and then acquired 200 businesses becoming a leader in electronic databases.

TABLE 2. Contemporary Illustrations of Transformation

Despite fierce competition in the breakfast foods business – including a redefinition of breakfast by time-pressured consumers -- Kellog remained committed to its broad strategy that involved excelling at new product development, broad distribution, and a culture skilled at executing business plans. To sustain this strategy, Kellogg needed a distribution channel for delivering fresh snack-like breakfast foods. They acquired Keebler that also had a brand strategy. Revenue rose by 43% between 1999 and 2003 and operating income nearly doubled (Harding & Rovit, 2004).

Newell had a 30-year track record of successful acquiring over 60 companies in the household products industry. Their success was recognized by the industry's adoption of the concept of "Newellizing" acquisitions. Rubbermaid seemed like a natural match – household products through the same sales channels. However, the acquisition dragged Newell down – losing 50% of the value of the investment. Newell's focus on efficiency and low prices did not match Rubbermaid's brand focus and premium prices (Harding & Rovit, 2004).

Clear Channel and Thomson can illustrate transformation in the entertainment and information sectors, respectively. Clear Channel Communications executed a long series of acquisitions of radio stations, accelerated by the 1996 deregulation, rising to lead the industry with 1200 stations. Focusing on cost leadership involving packaged playlists, central distribution of formats, and shared personnel. They sold bundled advertising and promoted live concerts. Between 1995 and 2003, their revenues grew 55% annually and shareholder return averaged 28% annually (Harding & Rovit, 2004).

From 1997 to 2002, Thomson transformed itself from a traditional conglomerate that included newspapers, travel services, and professional publications into a focused provider of integrated electronic information to specialty markets. They sold more than 60 companies and 130 newspapers. With the proceeds of $6B, they acquired 200 businesses becoming a leader in electronic databases and improving operating margins significantly (Harding & Rovit, 2004).

Large high-technology companies also have to address the challenges of transformation. Following the reunification of Germany, prices in Siemens' markets dropped dramatically, by as much as 50% in 3 years in some businesses. Siemens reacted by focusing on cost reduction, innovation as reflected by patents, growth, and culture change, prompted by the CEO convincing people that there was a crisis. They adopted many of General Electric's ideas, i.e., only staying in businesses where they could be No. 1 or No. 2, GE's people development ideas, and GE's benchmarking practices. Siemens focused on financial markets, alliances, and the internal political and persuasion process. From 1992 to 2004, revenue almost doubled, net income more than tripled, and revenue per employee almost doubled (Stewart & O'Brien, 2005).

By 2002, under the leadership of Louis Gerstner, IBM had been pulled back from the brink, transforming from a mainframe maker into a robust provider of integrated hardware, networking, and software solutions. The new CEO, Samuel Palmisano, continued the company's transformation via a bottom-up reinvention of

IBM's venerable values. The transformed values are: 1) dedication to every client's success, 2) innovation that matters – for our company and for the world and, 3) trust and personal responsibility for all relationships. Processes and practices are now being aligned – or realigned -- with these values (Hemp & Stewart, 2004).

Summarizing these ten vignettes in terms of the theory of enterprise transformation, we can reasonably assert that:

- Increasing shareholder value by mergers and acquisitions sometimes succeeds (Clear Channel, Kellogg and Thompson), sometimes fails (AT&T, Lucent, and Newell), and takes time to evaluate (Procter & Gamble).

- Transformation of the enterprise's value proposition to customers via new product and service offerings is illustrated by the success of IBM, Kellogg, and Thompson and, to a lesser extent, by Nokia.

- Improving productivity via extensive process improvements, as illustrated by IBM and Siemens, can transform an enterprise's value provided to customers, suppliers, and employees and increase shareholder value.

Thus, experienced and/or anticipated value deficiencies drove these transformation initiatives. Process changes were accomplished either organically or via mergers and acquisitions. Success was mixed, as was the case for the many examples from early times.

Conclusions

The need to transform – change in fundamental ways – has long been a central element of the economy and society (Jensen, 2000; Collins, 2001; Collins & Porras, 1994). Many enterprises are started; some flourish. Those that succeed eventually must face the challenges of change; some succeed in transforming, as illustrated by these vignettes. Most enterprises fail to transform. The study of enterprise transformation focuses on understanding the challenges of change and determining what practices help most to address change and successfully transform.

IMPLICATIONS OF THEORY

An enterprise can be described in terms of how the enterprise currently creates the value it is achieving – how it translates inputs to states to work to value. Research in enterprise transformation should, therefore, address one or more of these constructs. Elsewhere (Rouse, 2005), I have argued that such research should include six thrust areas:

- Transformation Methods & Tools
- Emerging Enterprise Technologies
- Organizational Simulation
- Investment Valuation
- Organizational Culture & Change
- Best Practices Research

Table 3 summarizes the relationships among initiatives in these six thrust areas with the state, work, value, and input constructs defined above. This tabulation can enable two important facets of enterprise systems research. First, it can provide a theoretical grounding to research initiatives. Of course, the researchers pursuing these initiatives need to elaborate these theoretical underpinnings much more specifically than presented here. This need will surely result in elaboration and refinement of the basic theory outlined here.

	Enterprise Input	Work Processes	Enterprise State	Enterprise Output
Transformation Methods & Tools	How to represent, manipulate, optimize, and portray input, work, state, output, and value for the past, present, and future of the enterprise.			
Emerging Enterprise Technologies		How emerging enterprise technologies are likely to impact work, state and output, and the strategy/policy implications of these impacts.		
Organizational Simulation		How work processes affect state and the experience of the state of an enterprise.		
Investment Valuation	How investments of financial resources			Affect value generated, e.g., options created
Organizational Culture & Change		How value priorities drive work processes, affect organizational culture and change, and thereby influence state and output.		
Best Practices Research	How past and current approaches to and changes of input, work, state, and output have impacted subsequent enterprise value creation, for better or worse.			

TABLE 3. Relationships of Initiatives to Enterprise Model

The second facet concerns the value of the outcomes of these research initiatives. One certainly can expect these outcomes to directly benefit the stakeholders in these initiatives. Beyond these direct benefits, this research should advance fundamental understanding of the nature of enterprises, how they can and should address change, and the factors that affect success and failure. Providing such advances will require paying careful attention to the constructs of state, work value and input.

It is unlikely that these constructs will soon be codifiable into an axiomatic set of equations – the phenomena of interest are much too complex. Nevertheless, one can gain deeper understanding of the nature of these constructs, how they can and should be changed, and how best to accomplish such changes. Eventually, this may support formulation of a valid model world with axioms, theorems, proofs, etc. Along the way, the fundamental knowledge gained should help enterprises to recognize needs for fundamental change and address such challenges with success.

IMPLICATIONS FOR SYSTEMS ENGINEERING AND MANAGEMENT

System engineering and system management are inherently transdisciplinary in the attempt to find integrated solutions to problems that are of large scale and scope (Sage, 2000). Enterprise transformation involves fundamental change in terms of redesign of the work processes in complex systems. This is clearly transdisciplinary in that success requires involvement of management, computing, and engineering, as well as behavioral and social sciences.

Upon first encountering the topic of enterprise transformation, many people suggest that this must be the province of business schools. However, the functional organization of most business schools mitigates against this possibility. Academic credibility depends on deep expertise in finance, marketing, operations management, organizational behavior, or corporate strategy. Great professional risk can be associated with spreading one's intellectual energy across these areas.

In contrast, systems engineering and management can and must inherently look across functions and view the whole enterprise system. Consider automobile manufacturing as one illustration. The Toyota Production System (TPS) has transformed the automobile industry (Liker, 2004). Interestingly, development and refinement of the TPS represents business process improvement for Toyota but transformation for all the competitors that had to adopt lean production to compete with Toyota, or compete in other markets, e.g., aircraft production (Kessler, 2003). In these cases, TPS could not simply be "installed." These practices affected the whole enterprise and success depended on addressing this breadth.

A more recent innovation in the automobile industry is build-to-order (Holweg & Pil, 2004). If you are Dell, where the company was founded using build-to-order, this is another case of business process improvement. On the other hand, if you are Ford or GM, adopting build-to-order affects the whole enterprise. Manufacturing, supply chains, and distribution have to change, e.g., you do not really need a traditional dealer network any more. You have to look at the whole enterprise, particularly because the overall cost structure changes significantly once you no longer build cars "on spec."

Systems engineering and management have long been strong suits of defense companies. The concepts, principles, methods, and tools have been applied successfully to definition, design, development, and deployment of complex platforms ranging from aircraft to ships to command and control systems. However, the emphasis has shifted recently from platforms to capabilities, e.g., from airplanes to airlift, for instance (Rouse, & Boff, 2001; Rouse & Acevedo, 2004). This requires an airlift enterprise, not just airplanes. Further, the airlift enterprise will be a transformation of current enterprises for selling airplanes and providing cargo capacity as well.

Thus, enterprises and their transformation are central constructs and phenomena in the complex systems addressed by systems engineering and management. The theory outlined in this chapter provides a foundation for thinking about and addressing these challenges. The transdisciplinary perspective inherent in systems engineering and management provide us with an inherent competitive advantage in tackling complex problems.

CONCLUSIONS

This chapter has outlined an initial formulation of an overarching theory of enterprise transformation. This theory is very much a work in progress. A wide range of colleagues from numerous disciplines has offered comments and suggestions on the evolving theory, providing rich evidence of the diversity of perspectives that different disciplines bring to this broad problem area. Indeed, it can reasonably be argued that there are few problems so central to our society and economy as the problem of how complex systems address fundamental changes.

REFERENCES

Argyris, C., & Schon, D.A. (1978). Organizational learning: A theory of action perspective. Reading, MA: Addison-Wesley.

Bailey, D.E., & Barley, S.R. (2004). Return to work: Toward post-industrial engineering. IIE Transactions, in press.

Burt, R.S. (2000). The network structure of social capital. In R.I Sutton & B.M. Staw, Eds., Research in Organizational Behavior (Vol. 22). Greenwich, CT: JAI Press.

Collins, J.C. (2001). Good to great: Why some companies make the leap and others don't. New York: Harper Business.

Collins, J.C., & Porras, J.I. (1994). Built to last: Successful habits of visionary companies. New York: Harper Business.

Davenport, T.O. (1999). Human capital: What it is and why people invest it. San Francisco: Jossey-Bass.

Diesing, P. (1962). Reason in society: Five types of decisions and their social conditions. Urbana, IL: University of Illinois Press.

Deming, W.E. (1986). Out of crisis. Cambridge, MA: MIT Press.

Drucker, P.F. (2001). The essential Drucker: In one volume the best of sixty years of Peter Drucker's essential writing on management. New YorK: HarperBusiness.

Economist, (2005, February 5). The fall of a corporate queen. The Economist, 57-58.

Economist, (2005, February 5). Consumer goods: The rise of the superbrands. The Economist, 63-65.

Economist. (2005, February 12). Nikoa's turnaround: The giant in the palm of your hand. The Economist, 67-69

Flannery, T.P., Hofrichter, D.A., & Platten, P.E. (1996). People, performance, and pay: Dynamic compensation for changing organizations. New York: Free Press.

Gavetti, G. & Rivkin, J.W. (2005). How strategists think: Tapping the power of analogy. Harvard Business Review, 83 (4), 54-63

George, B. (2003). Authentic Leadership: Rediscovering the Secrets to Creating Lasting Value. San Francisco: Jossey-Bass.

Gladwell, M. (2005). Blink: The power of thinking without thinking. Boston: Little, Brown.

Granovetter, M. (2005). The impact of social structure on economic outcomes. Journal of Economic Perspectives, 19 (1), 33-50.

Hammer, M., & Champy, J. (1993). Reengineering the corporation: A manifesto for business revolution. New York: Harper Business.

Harding, D., & Rovit, S. (2004, September). Building deals on bedrock. Harvard Business Review, 121-128.

Hauser, J.R., & Clausing, D. (1988, May-June). The house of quality. Harvard Business Review, 63-73.

Hemp, P., & Stewart, T.A. (2004, December). Leading change when business is good. Harvard Business Review, 60-70.

Hollnagel, E. (1993). Human reliability analysis: Context and control. London: Academic Press.

Holweg, M., & Pil, F.K. (2004). The second century: Reconnecting customer and value chain through build-to-order. Cambridge, MA: MIT Press.

Jensen, M. C. (2000). A theory of the firm: Governance, residual claims, and organizational forms. Cambridge, MA: Harvard University Press.

Kaplan, R.S., & Norton, D.P. (1996, Jan-Feb). Using the balanced scorecard as a strategic management tool. Harvard Business Review, 75-85.

Katzenbach, J.R., & Smith, D.K. (1993). The wisdom of teams: Creating high-performance organizations. Boston, MA: Harvard Business School Press.

Kessler, W.C. (2002). Company transformation: A case study of Lockheed Martin Aeronautics Company. Information • Knowledge • Systems *Management*, 3 (1), 5-14.

Klein, G. (2002). Intuition at work: Why developing your gut instincts will make you better at what you do. New York: Currency.

Kouzes, J.M., & Posner, B.Z. (1987). The leadership challenge: How to get extraordinary things done in organizations. San Francisco: Jossey-Bass.

Liker, J.K. (2004). The Toyota way: 14 management principles from the world's greatest manufacturer. New York: McGraw-Hill.

Lowenstein, R. (2005, February). How Lucent lost it: The telecommunications manufacturer was a Potemkin village. Technology Review, 78-80.

Mintzberg, H. (1975, July/August). The manager's job: Folklore and fact. Harvard Business Review, 49-61.

Mintzberg, H., Ahlstrand, B., & Lampel, J. (1998). Strategy safari: A guided tour through the wilds of strategic management. New York: Free Press.

Mintzberg, H. & Lampel, J. (1999, Spring). Reflecting on the strategy process. Sloan Management Review, 21-30.

Mohrman, S.A., Tenkasi, R.V., & Mohrman, A.M. Jr. (2003). The role of networks in fundamental organizational change. Journal of Applied Behavioral Science, 39, (3), 301-323.

Nadler, D.A., & Tushman, M.L. (1989). Organizational frame bending: Principles for managing reorientation. Academy of Management Executive, 3 (3), 194-204.

Rasmussen, J. (1986). Information Processing and Human-Machine Interaction. New York: Elsevier.

Rasmussen, J., Pejtersen, A.M., & Goodstein, L.P. (1994). Cognitive Systems Engineering. New York: Wiley.

Rooke, D., & Torbert, W.R. (2005). Seven transformations of leadership. Harvard Business Review, 83 (4), 66-76.

Rouse, W.B. (1996). Start where you are: Matching your strategy to your marketplace. San Francisco: Jossey-Bass.

Rouse, W.B. (1998). Don't jump to solutions: Thirteen delusions that undermine strategic thinking. San Francisco, CA: Jossey-Bass.

Rouse, W.B. (2001). Essential Challenges of Strategic Management. New York: Wiley.

Rouse, W.B. (2003). Invention and innovation in technology and art. In B. B. Borys and C. Wittenberg, Eds., From Muscles to Music. Kassel, Germany: University of Kassel Press.

Rouse, W.B. (2003). Engineering complex systems: Implications for research in systems engineering. IEEE Transactions on Systems, Man, and Cybernetics, 33 (2), 154-156.

Rouse, W.B. (2004). Embracing the enterprise. Industrial Engineer, March, 31-35.

Rouse, W.B. (2005). Enterprises as systems: Essential challenges and enterprise transformation. Systems Engineering, 8 (2), 138-150.

Rouse, W.B., & Acevedo, R. (2004). Anticipating policy implications of emerging information technologies. Information • Knowledge • Systems Management, 4 (2), 77-93.

Rouse, W.B., & Boff, K.R. (2001). Impacts of next-generation concepts of military operations on human effectiveness. Information • Knowledge • Systems Management, 2 (4), 347-357.

Sage, A. P. (2000). "Transdisciplinarity perspectives in systems engineering and management," in M. A. Somerville and D. Rapport, Eds. Transdisciplinarity: Recreating Integrated Knowledge (pp. 158-169). Oxford, UK: EOLSS Publishers.

Sage, A.P., & Lynch, C.L. (1998). Systems integration and architecting: An overview of principles, practices, and perspectives. Systems Engineering, 1 (3), 176-227.

Senge, P.M. (1990). The fifth discipline: The art and practice of the learning organization. New York: Doubleday/Currency.

Simon, H.A. (1957). Models of man: Social and rational. New York: Wiley.

Simon, H.A. (1969). The sciences of the artificial. Cambridge, MA: MIT Press.

Slywotsky, A.J. (1996). Value migration: How to think several moves ahead of the competition. Boston, MA: Harvard Business School Press.

Slywotsky, A.J., & Morrison, D.J. (1997). The profit zone: How strategic business design will lead you to tomorrow's profits. New York: Times Books.

Snow, C.P (1962). Two Cultures: Cambridge, UK: Cambridge University Press.

Stewart, T.A., & O'Brien, L. (2005, February). Transforming an industrial giant. Harvard Business Review, 115-122.

Tenkasi, R.V., & Chesmore, M.C. (2003). Social networks and planned organizational change. Journal of Applied Behavioral Science, 39, (3), 281-300.

Weiss, T.B., & Hartle, F. (1997). Reengineering performance management: Breakthroughs in achieving strategy through people. Boca Raton, FL: St. Lucie Press

Womack, J.P., & Jones, D.T. (1996). Lean thinking: Banish waste and create wealth in your corporation. New York: Simon & Schuster.

CHAPTER 4

TRANSFORMATIONAL LEADERSHIP

WILLIAM GEORGE

ABSTRACT

For all the promise that new ideas and systems have to transform business, transforming an enterprise comes down to one thing: *leadership*. This chapter contrasts transactional and transformational leadership. Discussion focuses on mission and values, vision, strategies, organizational building, systems and processes, and measurement.

INTRODUCTION

Transactional Leaders and Transformational Leaders

Just as enterprises cannot transform themselves, systems don't run businesses – people do. Transforming an enterprise, as IBM, Xerox, General Electric, Procter & Gamble, and Novartis have done, requires *transformational leadership*, something that is in scarce supply in most organizations. For the past decade or more, we have venerated the *transactional leader*, the dealmaker who can acquire huge companies, put them together, take out tens of thousands of jobs, and then move on. But this is *not* transformational leadership.

Regrettably, many of these transactional leaders claim victory as they leave to their successors the difficult task of transforming the enterprise *after* they have rendered it much weaker than ever before. Just look at the so-called "game changing" transactions carried out by Mike Armstrong at AT&T in spending more than $100 billion for cable companies, only to sell them for a $30 billion loss. Or Ed Brennan's remaking of Sears into a "financial supermarket" by acquiring Dean Witter, Coldwell Banker, the Discover Card, Western Auto, and expanding All-State Insurance, only to spin them off years later, leaving Sears retail business in a non-competitive state. Look at Carly Fiorina's five-year tenure at Hewlett-Packard, and examine closely the mess she left for her successor after the controversial Compaq merger. AT&T and Sears, two great American icons of the 20th century, no longer exist as independent companies, and the new leadership of HP is trying desperately to restore the company to its former greatness.

The Rise of "The Gamesman"

William H. Whyte (1901) wrote "The Organization Man" to describe the man (and they were mostly men in those days) who joined an organization in his early twenties, retired in his mid-sixties, worked hard and did his job, but never rocked the boat. His goal was to make incremental improvements in the efficiency of the business and to get ahead by getting along with his colleagues until he reached the top. Steadiness and predictability were his watchwords.

Michael Maccoby's ground-breaking book, "The Gamesman," changed all that (Maccoby, 1977). He described a new kind of leader he labeled "the gamesman," a transactional leader that "plays the game, doing whatever it takes to win." Between 1977 and 2000 the "game" for CEOs changed dramatically. Instead of being judged for their vision, strategies, and ability to transform companies and industries through their leadership, the criteria for evaluating CEOs shifted to their ability to produce immediate results. With lots of help from the media, Wall Street compressed the time frame for measurement from three to six *years* to three to six *months*.

The criterion for success shifted from growth in revenues and earnings to meeting the expectations of security analysts – to the nearest penny – for this quarter and the succeeding seven quarters. As trading volumes increased tenfold, the holding period for stocks dropped from five years to six months. CEOs that missed expectations, even by a penny, could literally see their shares change hands overnight and their stock drop 30-40% or more. Some witnessed declines exceeding 90%. No wonder CEOs could not afford to ignore the short-term market and still keep their jobs!

Many CEOs figured out how to play this game and were rewarded handsomely for succeeding at it. Knowing they could not affect transformation strategies in such a short time frame, they elected to get earnings up by cutting people, expenses and investments. This produced near-term earnings increases with the consequences not being seen for three to five years. Their reward? CEO compensation increased tenfold in the 1990s, while the real salaries of their employees remained flat.

What's wrong with this picture? The problems arose when many of these gamesmen began to stretch the rules well beyond their limits. Through their actions they wound up destroying great corporations, or crippling them to the point where it will be very difficult to restore their former greatness. Examples? Look at what has happened to General Motors, Westinghouse, K-Mart, Bristol-Myers, Computer Associates, United Airlines, Boeing, and on and on. Not to mention horror stories like Enron, Arthur Andersen, WorldCom, Health South, and Tyco.

As a result, the corporate world has experienced its worst crisis since the Great Depression, and general public has lost its trust in corporations and their leaders. As we move into the 21st century, many corporations are desperately in need of a total enterprise transformation. These transformations will require a new kind of leader – a transformational leader.

TRANSFORMATIONAL LEADERS

Transformational leaders have the capacity to lead the complete transformation of the enterprise for the long-term. Their focus is on building for the future, with a clear sense of the mission and values of the organization, a vision of what the enterprise can become, and a sound strategy to transform and lead their markets (George, 2003). They are organization builders, willing to make the investments required to build a sustainable organization that will create lasting value for all its stakeholders. Finally, they produce results – for the short-term *and* the long-term – because they have the discipline and performance drive to realize their lofty goals. Let's look in greater depth at how transformation leaders go about transforming their enterprises.

Mission and Values

For transformational leaders, everything starts with their purpose and the organization's mission and values. They have a clear sense of where they want to go and what they want to accomplish. It is not a modest purpose, nor one of gradual improvement. They are bold in seeing what is possible and passionate about rallying people to their cause.

Transformational leaders have a clear sense of their own values, and are diligent and dedicated to practicing them without deviation. They seek out organizations to lead where there is a high degree of congruence between their purpose and values and those of the organization. Over time, their purpose and values becomes fused with those of the organization, and both grow together in a process called homology.

Transformational leaders call upon the desires of their employees to embrace the company's mission and use it to make a difference through their work. They are inspiring in communicating this sense of purpose throughout the organization and are able to weld the organization into a single unit with a common purpose through their leadership. This sense of mission provides the "glue" that holds the organization together and enables it to absorb difficult and even painful decisions in the long-term pursuit of the mission.

In being clear about their values, they realize that people will hold them to a very high standard, so they are dedicated to the consistent practice of their values. It is in the crucible, when they are under the greatest pressure, that their values are truly tested and everyone in their organization is closely observing whether they stay true to those values, even if they pay a price for doing so.

A year before he became CEO of Johnson & Johnson, James Burke called together the company's managers in a series of "Credo sessions." In these sessions Burke challenged his managers as to whether the famous J&J Credo written by General Bobby Johnson was still the driving force in the motivation of J&J leaders and employees. Out of these sessions came a clear commitment to the Credo and its fundamental importance to J&J.

Four years later when terrorists in Chicago killed several people by lacing Tylenol capsules with cyanide, Burke knew that all that mattered was the safety of J&J's Tylenol users.   In spite of opposition from the FBI, the FDA, and the financial markets, he took swift action to pull all Tylenol capsules from the market until they could be repackaged in tamper-resistant packaging.   He and his executive team stayed true to the mission and values of J&J, and for the past two decades the company has continued to flourish.

At Medtronic the mission is the guiding force of the company.   It was written by founder Earl Bakken in 1962 when the company was nearing bankruptcy as the cash required to commercialize Bakken's pacemaker invention far exceeded the modest revenues it generated.   He used the mission statement to garner funding from an early venture capitalist and then made it the basis of everything his young company did.

Bakken started two traditions in the early 1960s that have endured to this day and bring the mission to life for Medtronic's current 30,000 employees.   The first is a Holiday Party held in mid-December where all the employees gather in the company's atrium auditorium or watch by video conference as six patients tell their stories of how Medtronic products transformed their lives.   Employees are so moved by these stories that this session provides an incredibly high level of motivation for their work.   A second tradition initiated by Bakken is the Mission and Medallion Ceremony where all new employees meet with the founder or CEO in small groups to learn about the company's mission, its relevance to its history and to today's company and to receive from the founder a brass medallion symbolic of the company's mission of "restoring people to full life and health."

A Transformational Vision

Transformational leaders develop visions for their organizations that far exceed what anyone believes is possible, and then set out to realize them.   They have a view of the possible and of using their visions as a driving force to build the organization.   They articulate their views at every opportunity, and look forward to refining their visions as others engage it.

A transformation vision may change every five to ten years, as its goals are realized or conditions change.   Short of that, it is a constant reference point for the organization.   It is the consistency of the mission, values, and vision, and the way in which they are articulated by the leader that enable people to take on great challenges without fear of failure, and to embrace change as a way of life.   Employees can adapt to significant changes in strategy and tactics if they believe in the constancy of the vision.

In 1990 Medtronic developed a vision of transforming itself from a pacemaker company to become the world's leading medical technology company.   It foresaw the emergence of medical technology as a driving force in treating chronic ailments across a wide range of diseases.   Its leadership created a detailed plan to become the global leader in this field through technological innovations, superior customer service, and broad global reach.   In executing its vision over the past fifteen years Medtronic has grown from $800 million in revenues and a market capitalization of only $2 billion to the clear leader in medical technology with $10 billion in sales and a market capitalization of $64 billion.

Transformation Strategies

To make the vision and the mission of the enterprise a reality, transformational leaders develop bold strategies to transform their industries and attain leadership within their markets. They know that the greatest opportunities to achieve market leadership occur during periods of rapid technology or market change, and they consciously set out to create those changes in their markets. This is accomplished by technological breakthroughs, or the recognition of unique market opportunities, heretofore unrecognized by other competitors in the marketplace.

To realize its vision of becoming the world's leading medical technology company, Medtronic formulated a strategy of devising solutions for intractable medical problems using its expertise in implantable devices. It ramped up its research and development efforts, launching a number of innovative new businesses, and expanding its global organization, especially in developing countries. It complemented these organic growth strategies with the acquisition of companies that had either unique technology or market-leading positions in related fields, or both.

To introduce this strategy to its organization, Medtronic management devised a bold concept of "Reinventing Medtronic." It communicated to its employees that the company's strategy and business mix would change dramatically every five years as the company literally reinvented itself. This was highly successful in getting the organization to accept change as a way of life.

In the fifteen years since the strategy was launched in 1990 Medtronic has been reinvented from the pacemaker company of its first forty years (1949-1989) to a cardiovascular company (1990-1995), and turned into the world's leading medical technology company (1995-2000). Now with the broadened mandate of serving chronic disease, Medtronic has reinvented itself once again with innovations to meet unmet medical needs (2000-2005), and is well on its way to realizing its new vision of "providing lifelong solutions for people with chronic disease."

Organization Building

Organizational restructuring and rebuilding is the essential element of transforming the enterprise. For starters, everyone in the organization must be aligned with the company's mission, values and vision. Next, the organization must be structured to turn the transformation strategies into reality. This may mean realigning it to serve certain customer groups, to create innovative new offerings, or to launch a breakthrough product or idea.

Whatever the strategies, the imperative here is that the organization has both the capabilities to execute the new strategy and the commitment to do so. The former requires recruitment, structural changes, and assignment of key people within the organization. The latter requires intense work on the part of transformational leaders to get their entire organizations uniformly behind the strategies and believing in them. Oftentimes, reorganizations are quite healthy in that they provide leadership with the opportunity to affect change more rapidly as they shake up the complacency and inertia that exists in any organization.

When Lou Gerstner took over as IBM's CEO in 1993, he quickly realized that the very survival of one of the world's great companies was at stake. Gerstner moved quickly to eliminate layers of middle and top management, the sprawling committee system, and the bureaucratic processes that had come to dominate the IBM organization and had slowed its innovations to a trickle. He offered early retirement to many executives that could not make the transition to the dynamic, customer-focused organization required for IBM to survive, and promoted leaders capable of rebuilding the company. Now led by Sam Palmisano, Gerstner's chosen successor, IBM's transformation to a customer systems and solutions organization is virtually complete, as is its restoration.

To translate its new vision and strategies into action, Medtronic reorganized in 1990 from a functional organization to a relatively autonomous set of global strategic business units (SBUs), complemented by an independent new ventures organization and corporate development. The global SBUs reduced much of the tension between the U.S.-based product organizations and their international counterparts, and gave the organization both the motivation and the means to grow their business in new ways, without the "silo effect" of large functional groups. By operating autonomously from the established organization and without the day-to-day pressure, the ventures and corporate development teams were able to move quickly to explore and develop entirely new ideas that later matured into major businesses for the company.

Transformation Systems and Processes

Integral to the process of transformation are the systems and disciplines that enable organizations to realize their ambitious goals without significant operational difficulties, delays or shortfalls. In this regard the systems and processes must be directly related to and an essential element of the strategies, and not fall into the category of "nice to do." They must be realistic in their implementation plans and not create such difficulties in their implementation that they get in the way of the overall organization's vision and goals.

For example, when Medtronic was undertaking its goal of becoming the world's leading medical technology company, there was a conscious decision made to invest heavily in research, product development, marketing, field sales and customer support to the exclusion of information technology, organizational infrastructure, and manufacturing uniformity. The IT people complained bitterly that the company's systems were outdated and under-funded, and lacking a company-wide enterprise system that would unify all the company's data systems. Yet the investments went elsewhere, not into an ERP from SAP or Oracle. As a result, the company was able to realize breakthrough strategies in innovation, in market transformation, in competitive market shares, and in growth and profitability. Five years later the company was able to patch together a very modest IT system that met its requirements from standard operating systems without the gut-wrenching systems problems that plagued so many of its competitors.

Another example came in the quality arena. In the late 1980s Medtronic undertook a massive internal quality program offered by Philip Crosby Associates. The program involved endless motivational meetings and training sessions for its employees. All of the new measurement systems relied upon internal data. The problem was that after two years of implementation the company's quality had *not* improved, at least in the eyes of its customers, and the company's managers were more inward looking than ever. As part of the company's 1990 vision and transformation, the consultants were terminated and replaced by an externally driven quality process called "customer-focused quality." It was based entirely on customer evaluation of the company's quality. The accompanying organizational transformation required all managerial and professional employees to spend time in customer operating rooms and at medical meetings to learn about the customers' quality issues and then to return home to fix them immediately.

The new customer metrics were bold indeed, yet the organization enthusiastically embraced them when they realized that achieving them was essential to restoring the health of its patients, thus enabling them to fulfill the company's mission. Each week the company's Executive Committee opened its meeting by having the company's chief quality officer lead a discussion and review of current customer quality issues. Annually, a complete review of the company's performance in customer-focused quality was held with its board of directors.

Measurement: The Discipline of Getting Results

The old saying "you get what you measure" applies just as well in transforming businesses as it does in managing businesses for near-term results. It may be even more important as a means of communicating what is imperative in the process of transformation. The measures of transformation must be well thought out, and provide for interim measures of progress, not just long-term outcomes. These measures should represent the key strategic drivers of the business, and relate directly to the new organization structure. To have a transformative effect, they must be bold metrics, challenging the organization to reach far beyond what it believes is possible.

As CEO of General Electric, Jack Welch used to challenge his managers to take on very challenging stretch goals, even asking how they could "reduce their share of market" from forty per cent to ten per cent by a greatly expanded vision of their market. Managers that could take on and meet these goals were handsomely rewarded with promotions and incentives. In contrast, many organizations fall into the trap of letting executives play the game of setting soft operating plans and rewarding them for modest performance that severely limits the growth potential of the company.

As an integral part of Medtronic's transformation in the 1990s, the company committed itself to a very challenging set of metrics. It committed to its shareholders to grow its revenues and earnings at a minimum compound rate of 15% per annum, thus doubling every five years, and to achieve an after-tax return on net assets in excess of 20%.

To make R&D and innovation the driving force of the company, Medtronic committed to spending a minimum of ten per cent of revenues on R&D. A goal of having 70% of revenues from products introduced in the last twenty-four months was introduced, and has been achieved in each of the past eight years. To achieve this goal, the company reduced its product development lead times from forty-eight months to sixteen months. These goals were translated every year into strategic plans and annual financial plans.

The company was able to achieve these goals on a consistent basis every year. The R&D goals were especially important, as innovative new products became the sustaining factor in Medtronic's growth and expansion to new therapies and new markets. The financial metrics became a governing force. In years when the company's growth prospects were not as bright and some managers asked "to take a year off from growing earnings," the metrics served as a forcing function to cause the organization to set stretch goals and then figure out how to attain them. Over the past fifteen years it has generated compound growth of 18% in revenues, 20% in earnings, and 30% in shareholder value. As the company grew, these high rates of growth were continued on a much larger base of sales and earnings.

CONCLUSION

Leaders that have the capacity to transform great enterprises must possess both the vision to see what their companies can become and the discipline to make the transformation a reality by producing results in both the short-term and the long-term. Transformation leaders must have the *vision* to see what is possible far into the future, the *leadership* to organize and empower employees to realize such an ambitious vision, the *rigor* to put the processes and systems in place to enable their organizations to execute the vision, and the *discipline* to use basic metrics to drive the results in operational and financial terms.

The rewards for doing so are enormous as they leave behind organizations that create lasting value, and are able to sustain and renew themselves for decades.

REFERENCES

George, W. (2003). <u>Authentic Leadership: Rediscovering the Secrets to Creating Lasting Value</u>. San Francisco: Jossey-Bass.

Maccoby, M. (1977). <u>The Gamesman: The New Corporate Leaders</u>. New York: Simon & Schuster.

Whyte, W.H. (1901). <u>Organization man</u>. New York: Simon & Schuster.

CHAPTER 5

ORGANIZATION AND CULTURE CHANGE

JOYCE L. SHIELDS

ABSTRACT

This chapter provides a framework and approach to changing organizations . The importance of culture and leadership in transforming organizations is emphasized. Experiences and practices of the Hay Group that lead to successful organizational transformation are provided as illustrative examples of each of the phases of the change process. The focus is primarily on the "how to" aspects of organizational transformation with examples of specific tools and techniques.

INTRODUCTION

Changing an organization is about changing hearts and minds. It is about changing the way individuals feel, think and act. It is not a logical, analytical endeavor. And, most importantly, it is the leader's work. The leader's importance to business success has been well documented in articles and books, including the works by Jim Collins (2001, 2002). In *Built to Last* (Collins, 2001) and *From Good to Great,* (Collins, 2002) Collins provides hard evidence that a company's leadership and culture are the differentiating factors that lead to sustained, successful performance. When you boil it down, changing an organization and its culture is the work of the leader. "The single most visible factor that distinguishes major cultural changes that succeed from those that fail is competent leadership at the top." (Kotter & Heskett, 1992).

Transforming an organization and changing its culture is a complex process. Success of a transformation leads to changes in the organization's culture – changes in the norms of behavior and the shared values of the organization. However, organizational culture is slow to change and is a result of a complex series of processes. Kotter (1996) identified why many firms fail in transforming organizations and processes necessary for creating major change. It must be a process led by the leader who creates a sense of urgency and guiding coalitions, develops and communicates the vision and strategy, provides the organizational support for generating short-term gains and consolidating those gains for long-term change, and lastly anchors new approaches in the organizational culture. The change in organization culture is the result of those processes. It cannot be legislated nor delegated.

Culture refers to the relatively enduring set of values and norms that underlie a social system (Burke & Litwin, 1992). Passed from one generation to the next, a culture is slow to develop and not readily amenable to change. Culture operates on at least two levels. At the deeper and less visible level, it is constructed around a group's shared values that persist even when the group's membership changes. If a group culture emphasizes security and predictability over risk-taking and innovation, substituting new values for old may be a major effort. At a more visible level within organizations, culture represents the patterns of behavior that employees are expected to adopt for doing work. We describe this visible level of culture as "work culture." Since employees are conscious of these cultural elements, they are somewhat more malleable than their less visible counterparts (Kotter & Heskett, 1992).

IMPLEMENTING SUCCESSFUL CHANGE

To assist organizations in implementing successful change and designing the most effective organizations, the Hay Group has identified seven key levers available to leaders to achieve their overall business strategy and desired business results as seen in the Seven-Lever Model™ (Figure 1).

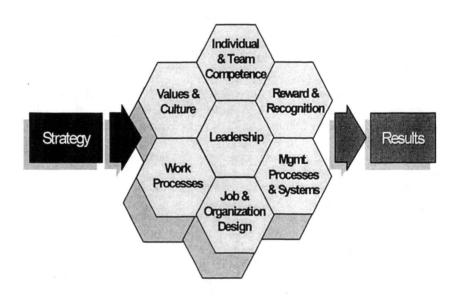

FIGURE 1. The Seven-Lever Model™

These organizational change levers include: organization values and culture; core work processes; individual and team competence; leadership; organization, team and job design; reward and recognition programs; and management processes and systems.   In brief, a description of each lever and its importance in organizational change follows:

- Values & Culture: Reassessing an organization's values and its internal culture is the foundation for building new systems and processes that ultimately create the right set of behaviors that will propel the organization forward.

- Work Processes & Business Systems: Improving the sequence of core activities through which resources are transformed to meet customer needs is an important link between the statement of a new direction and its accomplishment.

- Individual & Team Competence: Part of any change is to develop the capabilities of people - the skill sets and behaviors that will support the organization's new mission.

- Leadership: Mobilizing the organization around a new direction often requires leaders themselves to change. The leader's ultimate goal: to create a compelling vision and then embody that vision in both word and deed.

- Organization, Team & Job Design: Organizing and clarifying accountabilities effectively throughout the organization can "make or break" any major change effort.

- Rewards & Recognition: While values and culture set an organization's behavioral norms, reward and recognition programs reinforce those behaviors and the results expected from them.

- Management Processes & Systems: To achieve rapid and lasting change, management planning and measurement systems must support new performance targets.

Changing one component without aligning the other components within the system will lead to suboptimal outcomes. For instance, changing organization design without fundamentally redesigning work processes will lead to new (or fewer) people continuing to do old (inefficient) work. An integrated approach to organization transformation requires a comprehensive methodology that addresses the critical design components required to implement long-term change.

This chapter is based on experiences and practices of the Hay Group that lead to successful organizational transformation. We will focus primarily on the "how to" aspects of organizational transformation with examples of specific tools and practices.

THE CHANGE PROCESS

If we take the Seven-Lever Model^{TM} as the focus for transformation, an integrated transformation methodology should be followed that ensures all elements are properly aligned. The best action an executive team can take in transforming the organization is to take the time and expend the energy to set a clear roadmap, prescriptively preparing the organization to understand and accept their vision for the future. This entails painting a clear picture of where the organization is today, versus where it wants to be tomorrow.

For success, leadership, culture and organizational components must all be incorporated into the transformational process. The main steps that guide the change process are shown in Figure 2. This four-phase approach to an integrated change process – decide, guide, support and sustain – is prescriptive. All phases must be executed if the change is to have depth, scope and sustainability. In the sections that follow examples of techniques, tools and processes are provided for each phase. For a more in depth discussion of the four phases change, see "Leadership That Achieves Human Systems Integration" by Harris, et al, (2003).

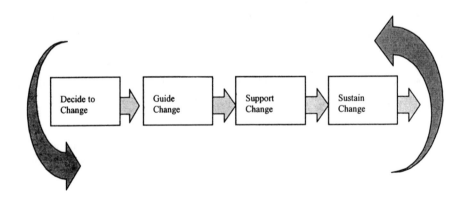

FIGURE 2. The Change Process

DECIDING TO CHANGE

Before an organization initiates a transformation effort, it must first define the context within which the transformation is pursued. Organizations contemplating significant change must have a clear understanding of the strategic issues they are trying to address, and define the critical success factors or results they are trying to achieve. If the organization fails to establish this business context, it is impossible to pursue an integrated transformation effort. The "correct" organizational design is dependent on the strategy, culture, and goals of the organization.

A well-focused business strategy must be articulated and communicated to the workforce. Clear strategic objectives are important for focusing the work transformation effort and provide the key performance goals around which the work elements are realigned. Without a clear definition of the strategic issues facing the organization, the transformation effort will deteriorate into a series of unrelated (or worse -- conflicting) change initiatives that consume resources and drain energy. The strategy must define what the organization needs to achieve within the external environment, and it must address the key performance indicators that will define success in relation to its customers, stakeholders, and competition.

Business results or critical success factors define what the organization must accomplish to achieve its strategic objectives. Operating objectives should be defined at the beginning of the transformation effort to provide change leaders and the work force with clear measures that can be used to monitor how well the transformation effort is proceeding, and to demonstrate change initiative success. Measures should incorporate multiple dimensions, including financial targets, customer satisfaction, and employee satisfaction. Once an organization establishes the business context in terms of strategic intent and operating results, critical work elements can be examined to determine their degree of alignment in support of the business strategy, and effectiveness in terms of achieving desired operating results.

Articulating the Case for Change

The most important change lever in Phase One is the role of the leader in articulating the case for change, linking the vision to core values, and building senior commitment. This process can be seen in the journey of Lou Gerstner as he led IBM from a failing organization in the 90's to a high-performing organization in 2000 and beyond. As Gerstner has said, a firm's culture isn't just important, it's "the whole game." In his 2002 book, "*Who Says Elephants Can't Dance? Inside IBM's Historic Turnaround,*" Gerstner tells the story of IBM's competitive and cultural transformation in his own words. Most of all, Gerstner provides a detailed look at the campaign he launched to rebuild the leadership team and give the work force a renewed sense of purpose.

Within days of being introduced as IBM's new CEO, Gerstner met with the company's Corporate Management Board and laid out for them the major issues he saw:

- Loss of customer trust and low customer ratings of quality

- A rush toward decentralization

- Slow response to cross-unit issues

- Tension over control of the marketing and sales processes

- A performance management system not aligned with closing sales with customers

- A vast array of alliances

Based on this assessment, Gerstner implemented several immediate initiatives including "Operation Bear Hug," which focused on IBM's biggest customers. He also disbanded the Management Committee and created an 11-member Corporate Executive Committee to help him make big-stakes decisions that cut across multiple units.

Within the first hundred days, Gerstner went public with a clear articulation of four major business initiatives, including: keeping the company together; changing the company's fundamental economic model; reengineering how the company did business; and selling nonessential assets to raise cash. At the same time, he initiated a major program to change the culture through the top leadership of IBM. As he said, "An organization is nothing more than the collective capacity of its people to create value." (Gerstner, 2002).

Linking Vision to Core Values and Building Senior Commitment

Between 1994 and 2001, the Hay Group worked with IBM to transform their organizational culture. Gerstner (2002) stated that he needed to provide support and encouragement for behavioral change among leaders. IBM's goal became to improve organizational performance through managerial and cultural change. The Hay Group worked with IBM to develop a new cadre of senior executives capable and motivated to execute IBM's new strategy of global integrated solutions. The project focused on using individual and organizational development to bring about culture change.

Hay began by developing a competency model for outstanding executives. After this, we helped articulate the new leadership behaviors that would support a culture change which, in turn, would drive a new global strategy. Over a six-year period, we created leadership programs focused on assessment and development of management and leadership capabilities.

The transformational leadership included not only the specific competencies required for success within the changing IBM, but also organizational climate created by the leaders, and their leadership styles (Fontaine, 2004). These components are described below.

Organizational Climate

Leaders create the organizational climate for success. In more than 30 years of research and practice, the Hay Group has consistently shown that organizational climate predicts up to 30 percent of the variance in organizational results, and that leadership style predicts up to 70 percent of the variance in organizational climate.

Organizations that are high performing have climates with six very specific and measurable characteristics:

- *Flexibility*: Are there unnecessary constraints in the workplace?

- *Responsibility*: Is authority delegated for task accomplishment?

- *Standards*: Does management emphasize excellence?

- *Rewards*: Are recognition and rewards tied to performance levels?

- *Clarity*: Are goals, policies and procedures clear and understandable?

- *Team Commitment*: Are there good working relationships, pride and loyalty?

Leadership Styles

Leadership styles include the types of behaviors and interactions leaders engage in with others in their work group to accomplish results. It is the extent to which the leader listens, sets goals and standards, develops action plans, directs others, gives feedback, develops employees, rewards and punishes, and establishes personal relationships with employees. Our research has shown that leadership style predicts up to 70% of the variance in organizational climate. The six different leadership styles are:

- *Directive*: Do it the way I tell you.

- *Visionary*: I'll give you the long-term direction and vision for our work.

- *Affiliative*: I want to create harmony and avoid conflict.

- *Participative*: I build commitment through consensus.

- *Pacesetting*: Do it to this standard of excellence, or I'll do it myself.

- *Coaching*: I focus on the long-term development of others.

The breadth of a leader's repertoire of styles determines his/her effectiveness in matching the appropriate style to use during a specific situation with a specific set of people.   In general, it has been found that the Visionary, Coaching, Affiliative and Participative styles in combination lead to the most positive organizational climate.   The Directive and Pacesetting styles have a negative impact on climate in most situations.

Through this process of clearly articulating and the business strategy, expected results and desired performance of his leaders, Lou Gerstner set the company on a new course that resulted in quadrupling its stock price between 1994 and 2001.

GUIDING CHANGE

The key change levers here are Values and Culture, and the ability to build a plan that links required systems, processes and actions to the new work culture.   In the early 1990s, Hay initiated research on work cultures in response to our clients' experience with attempts to change systems and processes within their organizations in order to improve business results.   Clients frequently asked us why their attempts to achieve improved results through a "hot" new approach to compensation or teamwork had failed to produce the expected ROI.   In fact, in many cases the results had been disastrous.

Hay Group research found that in many cases, leaders tried to introduce changes that did not fit their culture.   It was a misalignment.   Different cultural models require different behaviors and values, and different management systems to achieve desired business results.   It is important that the culture change initiatives align with the desired work cultures, as well as the vision and strategy.

Four Cultural Models

Hay Group's research on work cultures resulted in identifying four major "cultural models" operating in organizations today.   The cultures shown in Figure 3 are driven by the four primary areas that organizations emphasize in order to achieve their desired results: reliability, customers, flexibility and technology.

These models provide a vehicle for describing how organizations are changing from the more traditional hierarchical functional model of work to alternative models to meet changing business needs.   However, this way of describing work cultures should not be construed as being the only ones at work in organizations today, nor should they be used as organizational labels.   Of course, there are few organizations that are "culturally pure."   Most organizations are combinations or hybrids, such as a time-based/network culture.   These work culture descriptions describe the behaviors that are most important within an organization for supporting business strategy and achieving desired results.

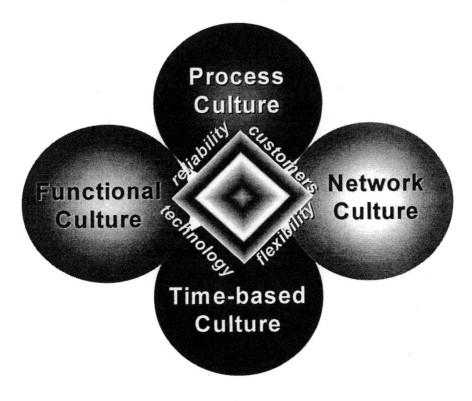

FIGURE 3. The Hay Work Culture Model

Functional Model

The most common work culture model is functional. Companies or organizational units falling within this model focus on what the organization does and how it does it consistently. These companies are driven by the need to obtain returns on investments in resources (be they equipment, financial, information or people), and to limit risks through reliability and consistency.

Work in these organizations is designed around the specialization of individuals, and is integrated through management hierarchies in which decision-making are clearly set apart from actual execution. Performance is measured in terms of size, return on equity, industry reputation and technical excellence.

During the past 50 years, the functional model has dominated organizational design. To control risk and build specialized reliability, functional hierarchies were created, and often marked by the demonstration of more sophisticated and complex technical know-how. Performance excellence meant creating results that were measured against a technical perfection standard.

Process Model

The total quality movement's emergence created a second work culture model, one driven by customer satisfaction and continuous quality improvement. Companies or organizational units demonstrating this model design work around processes for meeting obligations to customers, and execute through empowered team efforts. Planning, execution and control are integrated as close to the customer as possible. Communications – both formal and informal – are constant. The process team and customers are linked through the decision-making process with performance measured in terms of customer satisfaction and benchmark image.

The process model is most characteristic of organizations that link service and reliability, and market, and deliver constantly improving customized capabilities. Many companies are moving their organizations in this direction, reorganizing into cross-functional teams dedicated to customer segments.

Time-Based Model

Technical advances in the late 1980's – with more emphasis placed on the costs of capital and the value of being "first to market" with new products – created the time-based work culture model. Keyed to maximizing the return on fixed assets, flexibility, and technical agility, companies that operate within this model limit the levels of management hierarchy, while increasing the use of program and project work groups that cross functional boundaries.

These organizations encourage employees to develop multi-functional expertise and personal-impact competencies. Performance is measured on leadership in marshaling resources to accomplish high-payoff goals quickly, as well as in terms of traditional return on assets. Time-based organizations emphasize the ability to dominate markets in their high-profitability phases, and then move toward new opportunities as those markets reach, mature, lower-return stages.

Network Model

The network work culture model focuses on responsiveness and flexibility relative to changing customer needs. Work is designed around temporary alliances that bring together the necessary proficiencies and competencies to successfully complete a specific project. These organizations are situational and often informal in nature. "Coordinator" or "venture facilitator" roles replace the integration provided by traditional management hierarchy. This model is growing in popularity and has proven highly successful in a number of settings. Home/office construction, which requires the joint efforts of architects, contractors, electricians, plumbers and others, is an example of a network organization. Major outsourcing efforts could create a network organization.

Implications

It would be simple, of course, if every company fit cleanly into one of these four models, but reality is seldom that simple. As we stated, most organizations are hybrids. Large companies with numerous components often have several models represented. Furthermore, most organizations are changing: moving from the functional model to the process or time-based model and experimenting with a network venture. A key to successful change is having consensus among the executive leadership on the size and direction of the change required in the organization's culture.

While some senior managers take a minimalist view of change, others anticipate more drastic approaches. Without clear consensus on the goals of an organizational transformation, the leaders may run the risk of underestimating or overestimating the amount of time, resources and talent required to enact the change. Frequently, misconceptions about how various change initiatives are defined (e.g., empowerment or teamwork) lead to different responses to the question, "What will it look and feel like?" Lack of directional clarity will raise the risk that changes will be fragmented and unfocused, sending mixed signals to already anxious employees. If the leadership group can't agree, then how can they lead others or why should employees follow? Employees must have a clear, consistent and compelling picture of the goals of their changing organization. That can only occur when their leaders have reached consensus.

Targeted Cultural Modeling

How do we understand where an organization is today, and where it is going tomorrow? One of the most direct ways is through the use of an organizational "diagnostic" called the Targeted Culture Modeling (TCM) Process. The TCM is a tool that can help identify the values and behaviors that currently exist in an organization, and the values and behaviors that are desired for the future. TCM is also a process to create dialog among leadership and build alignment and consensus for organization change.

The TCM is a sophisticated assessment system that classifies organizations in general terms for the four cultural models. This modeling process offers a multi-dimensional "live picture" of the organization and how it works.

TCM Process

Hay Group research has identified 56 attributes (behaviors or activities) that define a work culture. Each culture varies depending on which attributes are encouraged and which are discouraged by the organization. To define current and desired work cultures, top executives (and/or employees at other levels) "order" these 56 attributes in seven categories that follow a normal "bell-shaped" curve.

Each individual is given two "decks of cards," each of which lists the 56 cultural attributes. The individual is asked to rank these cards -- on "pyramid" templates from the behaviors that are most supported on the left side of the pyramid to those least supported on the right side of the pyramid -- from two perspectives: the attributes/behaviors that are supported today (current culture) and the attributes and behaviors that should exist in the future (target culture).

In the card-sort (C-sort), individuals are asked to maintain a forced ranking. There is no rank or weighting within a column, only between columns.   The exercise takes about 45 minutes. The data from all the individuals are analyzed to identify gaps between the organization's current and target culture, as well as the perceptive and visionary gaps among leadership team members.

Consensus is reached on the current and desired work cultures through process consultation with senior team members. Once consensually validated models are achieved, the C-sort technique described above determines high priority behaviors or actions in the current and targeted culture. This identifies for management those cultural attributes that are most supported and rewarded in the current and target culture. This information is used to identify and understand why gaps exist, and to analyze alternative organization structures, policies, and practices. The major outcome of a culture assessment process is to identify action steps that will contribute to increasing alignment among strategy, culture, and supporting human resource processes.

A TCM Case Study

Tri-Plex Products, Inc., a fictitious company, is a billion-dollar consumer products organization with a highly "functional" work culture that traditionally placed a high priority on reliability, standardized work processes, and efficiency to capitalize on a mass market. To better compete in an increasingly complex and competitive marketplace, Tri-Plex Products is trying to become a more "time-based" organization, more opportunistic and flexible in adapting to new market demands.

As Figures 4 and 5 indicate, there are a number of significant gaps between the attributes of Tri-Plex Products' current culture and its desired culture. We see that circled attributes such as "decreasing cycle time" and "maintaining a heightened sense of urgency" move from a low-emphasis position in priority in the current culture model (Figure 4) to a priority position in the desired culture model (Figure 5). While not as extreme, we see the need for more emphasis on attributes such as "taking action despite uncertainty," "applying innovative technology," and "increasing decision making speed."

Here, the changes necessary are even more dramatic.   The attribute of "maintaining clear lines of authority and accountability" moves from the top priority position in the current culture to the lowest priority in the desired culture. We see almost the same disparity in "limiting downside risk." Other attributes calling for a relative de-emphasis include "being highly organized" and "respecting the chain of command."

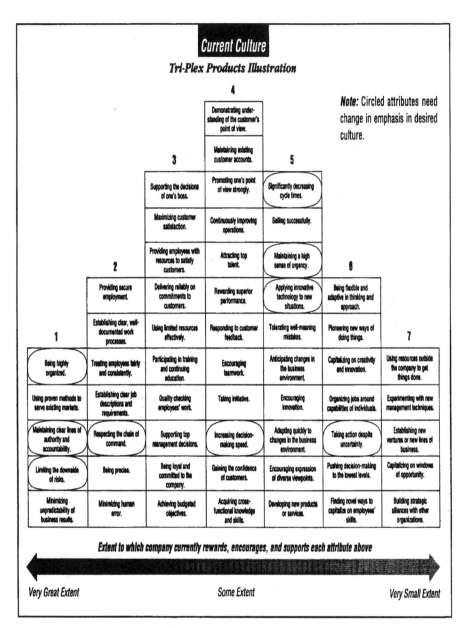

FIGURE 4. Target Culture Modeling: Current Culture

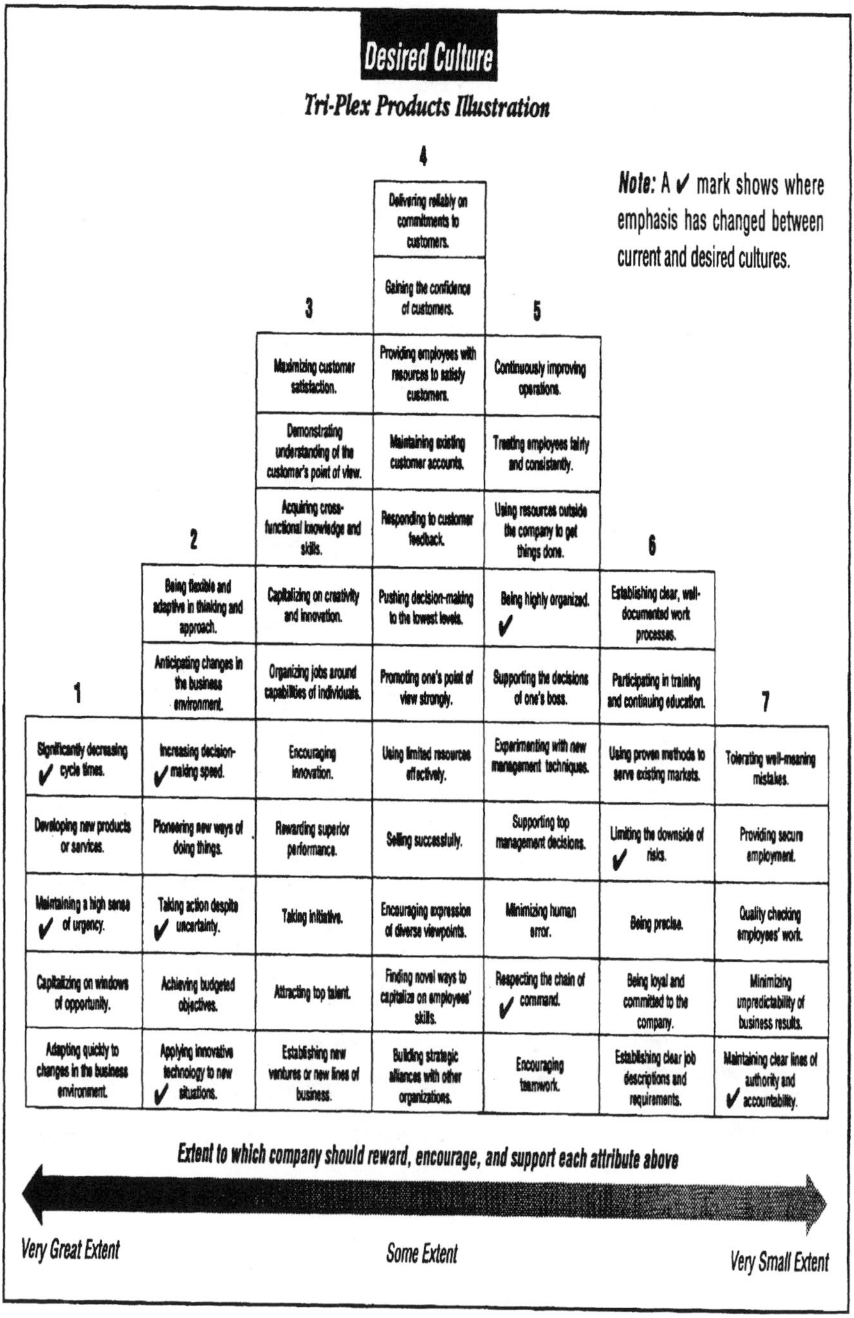

Desired Culture

Tri-Plex Products Illustration

Note: A ✔ mark shows where emphasis has changed between current and desired cultures.

Extent to which company should reward, encourage, and support each attribute above

Very Great Extent · Some Extent · Very Small Extent

4 — Delivering reliably on commitments to customers. Gaining the confidence of customers.

3 — Maximizing customer satisfaction. Demonstrating understanding of the customer's point of view. Acquiring cross-functional knowledge and skills.

5 — Providing employees with resources to satisfy customers. Maintaining existing customer accounts. Responding to customer feedback.

Continuously improving operations. Treating employees fairly and consistently. Using resources outside the company to get things done.

2 — Being flexible and adaptive in thinking and approach. Anticipating changes in the business environment.

Capitalizing on creativity and innovation. Organizing jobs around capabilities of individuals. Pushing decision-making to the lowest levels. Promoting one's point of view strongly.

Being highly organized. ✔ Supporting the decisions of one's boss.

6 — Establishing clear, well-documented work processes. Participating in training and continuing education.

1 — Significantly decreasing ✔ cycle times. Developing new products or services. Maintaining a high sense ✔ of urgency. Capitalizing on windows of opportunity. Adapting quickly to changes in the business environment.

Increasing decision- ✔ making speed. Pioneering new ways of doing things. Taking action despite ✔ uncertainty. Achieving budgeted objectives. Applying innovative technology to new ✔ situations.

Encouraging innovation. Rewarding superior performance. Taking initiative. Attracting top talent. Establishing new ventures or new lines of business.

Using limited resources effectively. Selling successfully. Encouraging expression of diverse viewpoints. Finding novel ways to capitalize on employees' skills. Building strategic alliances with other organizations.

Experimenting with new management techniques. Supporting top management decisions. Minimizing human error. Respecting the chain of ✔ command. Encouraging teamwork.

Using proven methods to serve existing markets. Limiting the downside of ✔ risks. Being precise. Being loyal and committed to the company. Establishing clear job descriptions and requirements.

7 — Tolerating well-meaning mistakes. Providing secure employment. Quality checking employees' work. Minimizing unpredictability of business results. Maintaining clear lines of authority and ✔ accountability.

FIGURE 5. Target Culture Modeling: Desired Culture

Armed with the TCM suggestions, executives used the Seven-Lever Model™ (Figure 1) to identify what other levers needed to be assessed in order to align all levers to achieve success. A number of actions to address the gaps between Tri-Plex's current and desired cultures emerged. For instance:

- Staffing, selection and development systems should be adjusted to hire and promote people with characteristics such as initiative, pragmatism, and flexibility -- rather than self-control and concern for order.

- Work should be redesigned to focus on processes rather than functions.

- Performance management systems should require appraisals from 2-4 times per year -- emphasizing short-term instead of long-term outcomes.

- Compensation policies should be flexible for key contributors, but more structured for average employees.

These action steps were incorporated into the master change plan, which included the business initiatives and success measures.

SUPPORTING CHANGE

Critical change levers in the Supporting Change Phase are Work and Business Processes; Organization, and Team and Job Design. Many organizational culture change/redesign efforts focus on jobs or functions in isolation and fail to address new complexities that adversely affect clarity and accountability. The magnitude of the change has a direct impact on the changing requirements for structure of the organization and the capabilities of individuals and teams. For example, if an organization decides to no longer manufacture products, but instead to focus on servicing others' products there is a very substantial change required in both the capabilities and functions required to implement this strategy.

As the first step to successful implementation, organizations must develop a deep understanding of both the capabilities and functions required to implement their strategies, and the capabilities they have that are truly a competitive advantage. This causes organizations to decide what core businesses and functions they should build and maintain internally, versus those that can be outsourced. As an example, many luxury automobile manufacturers contract out the car assembly, realizing that the key function that they must foster and maintain is design.

Once key functions have been identified, the challenge becomes to determine the most efficient and effective structure, so the strategy can be achieved. Historically, most organizations were simply structured -- usually in functional or geographic units -- because businesses were relatively simple. However, as businesses grew more global, consolidated through mergers and acquisitions, and required increased agility to meet new competitive threats, organizations required new structural models. Today, most organizations are complex mosaics, representing dynamic combinations of operating and support functions, business units, and alliances. However, the organizational structure's purpose remains the same: To optimally align accountabilities of jobs, functions, and business units to add value by achieving the organization's strategic goals.

For example, a domestic US insurance company acquired a European competitor to gain access to rapidly growing international markets. Prior to changing its organizational structure, there was a lack of focus and intense competition for resources. However, once reorganized into business units with product/market accountabilities, management's attention was again focused on growth and profitability. It was now clear to them why roles existed, and how they added value to the organization.

When jobs have clear and explicit accountabilities and decision-making authorities, people take initiative, appropriate risk, and innovate when necessary because they -- and the rest of the organization -- understand the scope and interrelationships of their roles. If accountabilities have been explicitly translated all the way to the job level, and there is alignment of jobs across the organization, then an organization can be successful.

Building Organizational Accountability

The Hay Group approach goes well beyond the macrostructure, deep down into the accountabilities of the individual jobs and the motives of individuals. Although the macrostructure is an essential element, the real challenge is designing the jobs and connecting them across the organizational "white space" to deliver results. This not only requires an understanding of organizational dynamics, it requires a deep understanding of people and the conditions necessary for them to be successful in a particular role. Getting the jobs, processes and people components right is significantly more challenging than determining where a particular position should report.

When all the pieces finally come together, organizations will be more resilient and more capable of adapting their structures to the changing business needs. And, they can build a culture of accountability where individual achievement directly supports organizational success.

The critical variables in organization design are capability/function identification, organization structure, and job design -- all driven by what it takes for the organization to be successful.   After determining the high-level organizational structure, all requirements are translated to job accountabilities and cascaded down throughout the organization, defined by a connection to the bigger picture. Organizations must particularly ensure that there are no accountability gaps, so no requirement is left without managerial responsibility.

For example, a retail mutual fund had a marketing organization that was traditionally responsible for generating leads, and a call center operation that was responsible for taking calls, servicing clients and ultimately selling them additional products and services.   As the financial markets struggled, the company saw a significant erosion of their asset base and customers, and their revenue. When questions surfaced over who was responsible for protecting and growing the firm's client and asset bases, marketing and operations pointed at each other.

Since accountability for a major requirement -- protecting and growing the firm's asset base — hadn't been cascaded down to the job level, there was a major accountability gap. The jobs weren't adding sufficient value to the organization because a major accountability had been overlooked. Taking a step back, it was clear that the current organizational structure was not adequate to deliver on this strategic initiative, and required reorganization and significant job redesign around the key accountabilities.

Efficiency and Value Creation

While the preceding points speak to organizational effectiveness, there also is the efficiency issue. A ruthless focus on value requires that all jobs add value. This means making sure that all jobs have a distinct and meaningful purpose, and that each organizational management layer adds commensurate value in implementing the strategy. It means ensuring that reporting relationships make sense, and jobs are not just "tucked into" a group because there is nowhere else for that position to report. New information technology and knowledge management processes have given organizations almost real-time insights into developments in their business, but some organizations have not adequately redesigned the middle management positions and professional layers to optimize the value of this information. As a result, historical structures remain unchanged and the value that these positions add is significantly reduced.

Although effective organization design requires cascading strategy into job specific accountabilities, this in itself is not sufficient. Jobs and processes must be designed to support the key interrelationships of accountabilities when they require collaboration and coordination across functions and business units. These interdependencies need to be crystal clear and connected across the organization. The key factors to consider are eliminating redundancies and gaps, and ensuring clarity of roles across functions and processes.

No Redundancies

Given the fact that most jobs are designed primarily with functional considerations in mind, it is not uncommon to find redundant accountabilities when looking across an organization. For example, a consumer products company shifted its strategy from being a low-cost provider to being much more focused on innovation to compete in a higher segment of the market. To support this objective, the head of marketing created a separate project management role specifically to coordinate the development and launch of new products. Previously, major project management responsibilities were the responsibility of the Project Management Office (PMO) that was jointly owned by the Finance and IT departments. After all, they had significant experience overseeing the implementation of complex projects and a track record of delivering on-time and on-budget -- even on projects with only a minor IT component. Predictably, the perceived overlapping responsibilities resulted in major turf wars, hostility, and frustration.

No Gaps

On the other hand, a broad view of an organization often reveals gaps in jobs and accountabilities. For example, in an effort to expand its geographic reach, a regional hotel and resort company actively acquired properties from its competitors. Although jobs existed to manage the post-acquisition transition from one brand to another, this process often took several months. However, since no jobs existed to assist in the interim property management, the service quality often declined substantially during the transition phase. As a result of this accountability gap, there was significant property value loss before its new owner could assume it. A job with the accountability to support management in the interim was established and the situation was easily rectified.

Clarity of Roles Within a Process

In many situations, work is actually done across functions as part of a process. This presents many opportunities for jobs to have accountability gaps and redundancies within a process. Where gaps exist, the process will deliver poorly, or not at all. Redundancies cause confusion and turf battles. Often forgotten in organization design is a role with accountability for process performance. This accountability can take various forms, depending on the nature of the process. Accountabilities can entail primary or shared management of each job involved in the process; they can entail integration of the jobs, or they can be limited to oversight. In any case, process performance accountabilities will have interrelationships with other accountabilities in the organization. When the interrelationships are not aligned and clear to all involved parties, confusion can reign. This is an issue of job design, as well as a significant management challenge to ensure that everyone in the process knows where one job stops and the next begins.

For example, one of our financial services clients was in the process of transforming itself from a very internally focused, process driven organization to be much more focused on the external market. Given the regulatory environment in which it operated, the legal department was traditionally required to approve any communications that would be sent to clients. In the process of reviewing for legal and regulatory compliance, staff lawyers often took the opportunity to edit the style and content of the communication. However, when a professional communications department was established to enable the organization to develop much greater customer intimacy, the legal department continued their practice of editing style and content in addition to their legal accountabilities. Understandably, this was a major source of frustration for the new communications director, who felt work quality and effectiveness was being undermined by a department that was going beyond its proper scope. The problem was solved by clearly outlining each group's accountabilities, and establishing a clear process for how they would work together to achieve the broader strategic objective.

Design Around Requirements

Designing jobs is somewhat of a lost art because it clearly goes beyond merely writing job descriptions. It requires that job-specific accountabilities be driven by the strategy and aligned with those of other jobs in the organization. And, just as importantly, it requires an understanding of what it takes for a typical incumbent to succeed. If a job is not "doable," then it is not properly designed and will become problematic as incumbent after incumbent fails.

This does not mean jobs should be designed around the talents of individuals, such as the superstar or the ultra-charismatic leader. Although the characteristics and personalities of the people will shape the roles -- particularly at the senior levels -- jobs should be designed to add value to the organization, not just to match the competencies of people who fill them. In a few specific cases, the latter situation may work, but the danger is that roles designed around incumbents do not fit together when you look at the overall organization. And, what happens if the incumbent leaves?

Job Shape Matters

The Hay Group approach to designing jobs takes into account the size and shape of the job - that is the skills, experience, problem solving and decision making required. Each job should be examined in terms of these factors. For example, if a relatively junior level job is assigned too much accountability, then there is a good chance that most people in that role will not have the skills and experience and become overwhelmed. Conversely, if too little accountability is assigned to a relatively senior role, there is a good chance that most people in that role will become bored and that the organization is spending too much and getting too little in return.

Appropriate Number of Accountabilities

Given the number of jobs that have been eliminated in the past five years without a commensurate work reduction, expectations of those remaining are such that it is difficult for these roles to be successful. In the wake of these job eliminations, job accountabilities have been assumed by remaining workers, without any rationalization of existing accountabilities. This has resulted in jobs that in many cases are not doable. To add too many and/or unrelated accountabilities creates distractions and confusion and limits effectiveness. One sign of evidence is employees who must do their "day jobs" at night, because they spend their days in meetings.

Balance of Job Requirements and Motives

Are job requirements and the motives of people doing the job consistent? While we don't believe that designing jobs around individuals is good practice, the motivational needs of typical people who would fill the jobs over time must be considered. Drawing on Hay's wealth of research on what it takes to be successful in a role, we know that asking sales people to spend more time doing administrative work, as opposed to client facing work, will result in frustration and potentially high turnover. Likewise, cross-training customer service representatives to sell provides marginal returns, not necessarily because of the job structure, but because what motivates people to excel in customer service is different than what it takes to excel in sales.

As previously discussed, a key job design dimension is the cascading through the organization of the key accountabilities necessary to execute the strategy. This is necessary for good job design, but it is not sufficient. Well-designed jobs have explicit decision-making authority, and the authority must be commensurate with the accountabilities. Without the appropriate decision-making authority, people cannot, or will not, act as required by their jobs.

Such concepts can be interpreted as restraining innovation and limiting empowerment. However, our research on effective organizations shows quite the opposite. When the scope of decision-making is unclear, or managers and employees receive mixed messages, then they will be inclined not to take risks or make even simple decisions. As with accountabilities, decision-making needs to be aligned within a function as well as across functions to ensure that gaps and redundancies do not exist. Clarity of accountability by individuals and by those who interact with them is absolutely critical for organizations to get things done without friction.

Consider Ritz-Carlton's acclaimed customer-service model. Employees can take actions without being second-guessed by their bosses because both are clear on their decision-making authority. Clearly bellhops cannot offer free weekends, but they can offer cab rides and otherwise be quite innovative within their domain.

By comparison, a fast-growing biotechnology company recognized the need to create a role for a senior-level human resource executive. They designed a position and successfully recruited a talented executive. While the SVP was expected to formulate many new HR policies, accountability for all management compensation decisions continued to rest with the company's founder. This significantly hindered the SVP's ability to implement the necessary human resource programs because the founder was continuously undermining him. Eventually, he became frustrated and resigned. Afterwards, the founder acknowledged that he had designed a role that was not balanced in terms of the level of accountability required and the commensurate decision-making authority.

Given the "white space" between business units and functions that many organizations have created through flatter structures, broader roles, and the use of teams, decision-making has become more complex and, at times, problematic. Whereas before people had sole ownership for a decision or they contributed to it, now there are many more situations where both decisions and accountabilities are shared.

Jobs can either contribute to a decision by providing input, they can be solely responsible for a decision, or they can share accountability for a decision. The role a job plays in the decision-making process needs to be explicit or there will be a lack of clarity that often results in conflict, gridlock, or decisions that might benefit a business unit or function at the expense of the broader organization. Managers in different units may not perceive the benefits of collaborating, they may have no incentive to work together, or they may simply lack the skills and resources to make the necessary cooperation happen. If the decision-making process is defined up front, then many of these conflicts can be avoided.

Interdependencies Must Be Explicit

Ideally, accountabilities are always matched with commensurate resources under direct control. There are situations where, for reasons of resource scarcity or organizational economics, resources must also be shared between functions. This creates interdependent relationships. Interdependencies exist when a manager is dependent upon the resources of another manager to deliver on his accountabilities. In such situations, the designs of both the dependent job and the resource-owning job should explicitly show the interdependency in their accountability. Service level agreements or memoranda of understanding and clear protocols should also be designed to make the relationships explicit. Without these, misunderstandings will surface, managers will compete for resources, and the next levels up will be forced to adjudicate, often too late.

To better manage large capital construction projects, a large transit authority created a small, highly skilled Program Management Organization. The operating model assumed that program managers in the new organization would have access to engineering resources residing in the operating agencies of the authority.

These assumptions were not made explicit in the accountabilities of the operating agency managers and engineers. Not surprisingly, the required engineering resources were not made available when requested by the PMO. As a result, the capital construction projects were immediately behind schedule and remained so until operating agency accountabilities were changed to reflect the resource interdependencies.

Benefit of Building Organizational Accountability

Changing the way work gets done in organizations is one of the most difficult and potentially divisive challenges. However, getting it right enables the organization to be more effective by being better able to execute strategy, respond to competitive threats, and engage employees through a positive work climate. And, it enables the organization to do so in the most cost efficient manner because it minimizes redundancies.

As a result, it is worthwhile to take a step back and apply a comprehensive framework to the process of organizing work -- one that considers jobs, processes, and organizations -- as opposed to merely reacting to bad news or unpleasant events. The real strength of our approach is that it can be applied to restructuring efforts of all sizes and scope. Whether an enterprise-wide initiative or making more local changes, the principles will help in the understanding of how these changes will affect other jobs and processes across the organization (so that solving one problem doesn't create another somewhere else). Organizations that adopt this discipline will be able to continuously evolve in a manner that drives their strategy and enables them to compete in an ever-changing and increasingly complex business environment.

SUSTAINING CHANGE

The critical change levers in this phase are Management Processes & Systems and Rewards and Recognition. To achieve lasting change, the redesign and implementation of human resource systems and policies that reinforce the new and required behaviors should be addressed at all levels within the organization. These include the functions of recruiting and staffing, development and training, performance management, compensation and benefits and communications.

Getting the Right People in the Right Roles

No change effort will be successful without the right talent. New work frequently requires people with different skills and competencies. Kotter (1966) stated that "sometimes the only way to change a culture is to change key people." This was reaffirmed by Gerstner (2002) in transforming IBM where some of the executives possessed the skills and competencies required for the transformation and others did not. Further, in Hay Group's research with Fortune Magazine and the World's Most Admired Companies (Stark, 2002) we found that the most highly correlated attribute to those companies that scored in the top three in their industry was the "attraction and retention of top talent." Critical to attracting and retaining the talent needed for success is the implementation and standardization of systems to hire, promote and develop individuals at all levels within the organization.

Performance Management and Reward Systems

Fewer activities can more strongly align employee behavior with business objectives than an effective performance management process. The inherent complexities and sensitivities of performance management systems have led many organizations to search for a "silver bullet" for addressing the challenges of managing individual, unit, and corporate performance. Through decades of consulting experience and extensive research -- including our work with *Fortune's* World's Most Admired Companies -- we have identified the essential elements of virtually all successful performance management programs (Jensen, et al, 2004).

These include:

- Creating Clarity Around Goals
- Building a Culture of Dialogue
- Establishing a System of Truly Differentiated Rewards

Effective management is the thread that ties these factors together. It is our experience that managers will comply with any ratings scale given to them. But the most capable managers can best differentiate performance and then affect the results in their people that the performance management process is intended to influence. The good news is that the skills managers need to enable an effective performance management process can be developed through formal training and ongoing coaching.

For example, after Raytheon Corp. brought a focus on dialogue and development to their performance management system, the result was greater employee buy-in and satisfaction. In addition, they built a solid foundation for improvement by enabling employees to better understand their strengths and weaknesses.

Performance management systems and processes depend on clarity and commitment from the leaders in an organization, as shown in the example from Gillette described below.

In 2001, Jim Kilts left Kraft to become the CEO at Gillette, which at the time was floundering and had lost investor confidence. Kilts developed a new Strategic Growth Plan (SGP) -- a roadmap for financial and strategic turnaround as well as functional excellence. The "functional excellence" component of the SGP surprised many employees. Gillette had a tradition of hiring the best and the brightest from top business schools and promoting from within.

Furthermore, almost 60% of Gillette employees received "exceeds" performance ratings and were paid bonuses as a percentage of their base salary -- profit sharing rather than pay for performance. Everyone thought they were high performers while the company chronically underachieved. Under these circumstances, the best and the brightest stagnated. Kilts implemented a performance management program that differentiated both performance and rewards. Corporate performance determined the overall bonus pool, which was allocated to functions and business units according to their relative performance. Finally, individual performance was measured on a five-point scale and based on achievable stretch goals clearly linked to unit and company objectives. Kilts drove the program, which he also applied to his own executive team. In the three years since implementation of this program, the number of employees "exceeding" expectations has dropped from 59% to 24%, and the stock price has grown annually by over 16%. By bringing some outside perspective and a serious commitment to paying for performance, Kilts has lived up to his reputation as a turnaround expert.

Establishing a System of Truly Differentiated Rewards

For the most part, good managers can clarify goals, create a culture of dialogue, and differentiate performers. However, if funding is not in place, they will not be able to differentiate rewards significantly enough to recognize outstanding performers. Organizations that establish funds to differentiate rewards will get significant return on their investment. If an organization is truly committed to paying for performance, then a single merit budget that adjusts for market pricing and internal equity will not work.

During periods of change, organizations often do not allocate their investment of time and resources in proportion to a program's potential return on investment. Depending on the organization, different reward programs will yield different returns, which should influence their design and efforts. For example, one of our clients recently reevaluated the various components of their executive compensation program. With the help of our objective view, they realized that their merit pay program was really a "cost of staying competitive" but not a motivating factor. In contrast, their annual incentive program touched many of their people and focused more closely on results, yielding a much higher return. This influenced the client to devote more time and effort on the incentive portion of the reward program. Figure 6 illustrates their rationale.

One might also consider "unbundling" the market competitiveness component from the performance component of merit increases. This prevents average performers from interpreting the wrong message if they received a significant increase for internal equity purposes. Given the conventional constraints of merit pay, organizations may want to consider allocating a portion of their compensation investment to reward those who have truly achieved outstanding performance. This is especially true at the executive levels.

Reward Vehicle	Investment	ROI	Rationale
Long-term Incentives (Stock Options)	Low	Medium	Rewards senior executives for building sustainable shareholder wealth, and a retention vehicle for key employees.
Annual Incentives	High	High	Touches many people in the organization, but also focuses them on results.
Annual Salary Increase (Merit Pay)	High	Low	Cost of staying competitive as an employer, but not a real motivating factor.

© 2004 Hay Group, Inc.

FIGURE 6. Reward Vehicles

Differentiate Rewards, Not Just Performance Ratings

Organizations need to ensure that performance ratings translate into differentiated rewards. Many organizations spend an agonizing amount of effort to ensure that managers "comply" with some sort of a distribution curve of performance ratings. But what value is this if the highest performer still receives only marginally more rewards -- whether it is merit pay, incentive pay, or options -- than the average performer? The ratings are merely a means to an end, and the end is higher rewards for the highest performance, not just a perfect distribution curve.

Reward Linkages

Especially during periods of change and transformation, organizations must ensure that employees understand what they are being asked to do to earn their rewards, and that their individual goals are based on a realistic view of the future and connected to what the organization needs to do to succeed. Furthermore, the reward's magnitude must be consistent with the value to the organization. For example, Fidelity's annual bonus program is based on achieving a "doable" number of predetermined goals that support the company's key strategic objectives, and are again set to reward truly outstanding performance. A portion of the annual bonus over a certain threshold is deferred as a retention vehicle. They also have a mid-term incentive program, delivered in the form of phantom shares, to drive employee behaviors toward achieving longer-term results, support retention of middle- to senior-level employees, and provide competitive total cash.

Employees at all levels are more motivated to give extra discretionary effort when they feel connected to the bigger picture and understand how their actions contribute. This is both a variable pay issue and a communications issue. Goals and measures have little value if employees are unaware of how they are progressing toward the goal, until they have either met or missed it. This means that ongoing dialogue is essential in achieving a lasting impact. Performance management becomes the way strategic change is achieved, and business drivers (e.g., customer service or quality improvement) go from being mere words to being part of each person's job. The Hay Group also recommends cascading objectives down to link individual with organizational performance measures. When narrow definitions are used exclusively as the foundation of performance goals, everyone works to meet a functional target.

Focus Program Design: Don't Pay for the Same Outcome Twice

This has been said before, but it is worth repeating: Organizations should focus their program design so they don't pay for the same outcome twice, or even three times, over. One option is to follow Fidelity's example by having merit increases be tied to achieving core elements in a job, and incentive awards tied to achieving the most critical results that enable the organization to achieve strategic and operational objectives.

Merit increases should be given to stay competitive in the labor market, which, in turn, should pay people for performing competently. Incentive pay should not be confused with profit sharing based on the organization's overall performance. Incentive pay must be tied to an individual's unique goals or it will not differentiate and reward accordingly. Organizations should determine which factors they are measuring to determine merit increases and which factors they are measuring to determine incentive pay. And, these should be distinct.

Communicate, Communicate, Communicate

Anything concerning compensation is a sensitive internal issue. For good or bad, it is the most prominent concrete measure of an employee's value to the organization. Compensation decisions and compensation changes are always highly charged. While managers overwhelmingly acknowledge this, only 23% of organizations involve employees in the actual plan design.

Some managers expect merit increases, or the lack of increases, to take the place of an active performance management process. However, merit pay increases are not significant enough to manage a poor performer out of the organization, manage the potential of a high performer, or motivate employees to acquire the skills and competencies to perform effectively. Effective communications between the organization and manager with the employee are essential to effect change. The goal is not necessarily a large volume; communications strictly by the pound generally result in overload and diminished returns. And don't be fooled, no amount of communication -- no matter how well focused or elegant -- can rescue an ill-conceived compensation program. But many sound programs flounder when employees do not get the right information in the right way and at the right time.

Organizations need to have a game plan for communications -- and content for communicating program design attributes and key principles. In addition, they should provide managers with tools and talking points about topics such as what "superior" performance looks like, how performance management and reward systems link to the business strategy, and how to deal with tough questions.

CONCLUSION

Throughout this chapter, we have explored many strategies and techniques that can be used to facilitate change and transformation within an organization. Organization transformation requires a comprehensive, integrated approach that addresses all of the critical design components required to implement long-term change. But, most importantly, as we said at the beginning, changing an organization means changing hearts and minds. No organization can succeed without that effort. And no matter what strategy you pursue or what type of organization you have, it all comes back to a single idea: Changing an organization and its culture is, above all else, the leader's work.

REFERENCES

Burke, W.W. & Litwin, G. (1992). A causal mode of organizational performance and change. Journal of Management. 18 (3), 523-545.

Collins, J. (2001) Good to Great: Why Some Companies Make the Leap...and Others Don't, New York: Harper Collins.

Collins, J. (2002) Built to Last: Successful Habits of Visionary Companies, New York: Harper Collins.

Dalziel, M., Lemaire, K., & DeVoge, S. (2003). Designing the Accountable Organization. Philadelphia: Hay Group, Inc.

Fontaine, M. (2004). Internal Communication. Hay Group, Inc.

Gerstner, L. V., Jr. (2002). Who.Says Elephants Can't Dance?. New York: Harper Business

Hackman, J.R., Wageman, R., Nunes, D., Marshall, P., Fontaine, M. & Burrus, J. (2001) Top Teams: Why Some Work and Some Do Not. Philadelphia, Hay Group, Inc.

Harris, C. S, Hart, B. K., & Shields, J. (2003). Leadership that achieves Human Systems Integration. In Harold R. Booher (Ed.), Handbook of Human Systems Integration (pp.33-60). New York: John Wiley & Sons, Inc.

Jensen, D., Lemaire, K., & McMullen, T. (2004). Bridging the Pay for Performance Gap. Philadelphia: Hay Group, Inc.

Kotter, J.P. (1996). Leading Change. Boston: Harvard Business School Press

Kotter, J.P. & Heskett, J.L. (1992). Corporate culture and performance. New York: Free Press.

Start, M.L. (2002). Five Years of Insight into the World's Most Admired Companies. Journal of Organizational Excellence. Winter 2002, 3-13.

CHAPTER 6

MANUFACTURING AND ENTERPRISE TRANSFORMATION

LEON F. MCGINNIS

ABSTRACT

At the end of the twentieth century, manufacturing enterprises were dramatically different than at the opening of the century. If we could understand the nature of the changes, and their enablers, then perhaps we could anticipate or even plan for future transformations. A number of examples of twentieth century transforming innovations and changes are described. A framework for describing the manufacturing enterprise is presented and used to generalize the nature of transformations observed. Some conjectures are given on the future of manufacturing enterprise transformation.

INTRODUCTION

In the twentieth century, manufacturing enterprises dealt with a near-constant stream of transforming innovations and changes. The nature of products transformed from mechanical to electro-mechanical to heavily electronic, and from single-function to multi-function. Manufacturing materials changed from natural metals and fibers to exotic alloys, composites, and man-made polymers. Power sources changed from steam to internal combustion and electricity. Completely new markets and products—such as telecommunications and computers—appeared and became major elements of the economy, while older technologies—such as steam engines and waterwheels—all but disappeared from view as they were transformed from ubiquitous distributed sources of mechanical power to very high-capacity centralized sources of electricity.

These were not the only transformations taking place, however. The fundamental organization of industrial processes changed, several times. From the early rise of the mega-corporation, exemplified by United States Steel (Krass 2002), to the era of the conglomerates, such as General Electric (anonymous), to the dot.com phenomenon of the end of the century, what it meant to be a manufacturing enterprise changed dramatically.

The nature of management changed. Henry Ford required a deep hierarchy of middle managers to run his manufacturing empire, but by the end of the century, middle managers were becoming an endangered species. The rise of scientific management and the engineering of labor processes in the first third of the century gave way to teamwork processes at the end of the century.

Business and marketing strategies changed. Early in the century, strategy focused on economies of scale, and competition was among a small number of brands or producers. At the end of the century, strategy focused on economies of scope and speed, in order to be successful in competing with an ever-growing number of brands and producers.

Was all this change simply the "moving hand" of the marketplace—natural evolution of the market—or is there an episodic, transformational structure to what happened? This chapter suggests that transformation in manufacturing enterprises can be viewed and understood in the context of the structure and purpose of manufacturing enterprises.

The chapter starts with an illustrative listing of a few of the major transformations in manufacturing during the twentieth century. This list certainly is not exhaustive, but will serve as a basis for discussing transformation in manufacturing enterprises. In order to make some sense of these transformations, we will need a framework, or reference model for manufacturing. A simple one will be suggested. A case will be made that successful transformations always are consistent with the purpose of the enterprise, and often represent the exploitation of either new technology or a new way to conceptualize the enterprise. The chapter ends with a few thoughts on the distinction between transformation and continuous improvement.

TWENTIETH CENTURY MANUFACTURING TRANSFORMATIONS

At the beginning of the twentieth century, electricity was just beginning to replace mechanical power for driving industrial processes, "command and control" in manufacturing was largely word-of-mouth, there was no process automation, scientific management was just beginning to emerge, and the era of large-scale mass production had not yet dawned. Manufactured products were sold predominantly in small shops, where the product selection was limited and products changed very slowly, and the competitors in manufacturing were largely domestic. One hundred years later, manufacturing is highly automated (and capitalized), labor productivities are an order of magnitude greater, "command and control" is executed through electronic networks, and the era of mass production is phasing out in favor of mass customization. Retailing has become the domain of the "big box" stores, with a wide range of products, and a broad selection that changes quickly, provided from globally sourced competitors. It seems everything about manufacturing has been changed.

If we are to make any sense of these changes, we must first begin to order them. One way to develop an ordering is to look at the focus of changes, i.e., how they affect the manufacturing enterprise. In particular, we can ask whether the change primarily addresses the manufacturing process (the physical processes of converting materials into products), the manufactured product (the embodiment of the product, including materials and technologies), or the business organization and operation (how the enterprise defines itself and interacts with its environment). We will look at each of these in turn.

Not all change is transformation. Growth, for example, is a change, but usually not a transformation. For purposes of this chapter, the term transformation will be used to reflect change that is episodic rather than gradual, and one that deviates from and disrupts the status quo. In an industry, transformation usually starts with one firm, and spreads to others.

Manufacturing Process Transformations

Manufacturing is, in essence, evolved craft work, e.g., the conversion of tin and lead into a pewter tankard. Many of the significant innovations in manufacturing processes have been focused on improving the efficiency, cost, quality, or time associated with conversion processes.

The assembly line In 1901, Ransom E. Olds invented the automobile assembly line (anonymous), which allowed him to increase the production of his factory four-fold. The assembly line fundamentally changed automobile assembly from a craft orientation to a modern factory orientation, and likewise redefined the role of automobile assembly workers, from skilled craftsmen to trained laborers. Olds was exploiting the ideas of standardized parts and mass production pioneered a century earlier by Eli Whitney in the production of cotton gins and muskets. But the assembly line innovation didn't transform automobile manufacturing until Henry Ford adopted it, refined it, and added conveyor belts that paced the assembly process. By continuously refining his mass assembly process, Ford reduced the time required to assemble a Model T from 14 hours to 1 hour 33 minutes (Pawlak 2005), and reduced the price from $1000 to $360. Ford became the dominant manufacturer of automobiles, and all his competitors soon adopted the moving conveyor approach. The reduction in price of automobiles spurred a boom in automobile ownership, and drove fundamental changes in American society. People tended to travel more, to live further from where they worked, and to move more often. They also began to demand greater public investment in infrastructure to enable automobile travel. All of these changes might have occurred eventually without Ford's innovation, but a strong argument can be made that his "perfection" of the ideas of Whitney and Olds are the key precipitating event.

Numerical control Well into the second half of the century, manufacturing machines (machine tools) required operators who configured the tools for specific operations, monitored and adjusted the tools during operation, and loaded and unloaded the parts produced. The requirement was essentially: one tool, one operator. All this changed with the advent of numerical control, or NC, a development of the Parsons Corporation and MIT in the late 1940s and early 1950s (Reintjes 1991). NC utilized servo motors to control tool paths, eliminating the "real time" involvement of machine tool operators and allowing much more complex shapes to be machined. In addition, NC made the planning of tool paths an engineering function, done off-line using a programming language (Childs 1973). With NC, once the control program was written, processing became standardized, so a part could be produced on any instance of the NC machine, either in the same factory or in a different factory, provided the necessary tooling and fixtures were available. NC improved part quality and machine tool productivity, and also allowed the use of fewer, less experienced and less knowledgeable operators.

Factory networks NC was essentially a "stand alone" solution, i.e., an NC machine tool required tooling, fixtures, and now, an NC program to be delivered physically to the tool before an operation could be performed. This changed dramatically in the 1970s, as a variety of proprietary network solutions were developed, allowing NC machine tools to be integrated with computer-based controllers in local area networks (Dwyer 1987). Networking computers was largely a theoretical idea until ARPA decided in the late 1960s to implement it (Abbate 1999). The funding for ARPANet created the basic theory and methods necessary for computer networks to become a practical reality. ARPANet's developed of networking protocols and standards ultimately influenced the emergence of a few standard protocols, such as TCP/IP (Black 1998) which further enabled factory automation. The networking of NC machine tools enabled the real-time collection of status and performance data; these data supported predictive maintenance and real-time workflow control, which were not previously possible. As a result, machine tool utilization improved, and better control of lead times was possible.

Flexible automation In parallel with the development of NC and factory networks, automated tool changing and automated part loading technologies were being developed, enabling the creation of networked, automated machine tools in systems that required no operator except in the case of breakdowns. In the 1980s, the terms "flexible automation" and "computer integrated manufacturing" described such systems, and became standard phrases in the lexicon of US manufacturing (Anonymous 1984) (Stover 1984). These systems were intended to allow the production of a variety of similar parts, in small volumes, at roughly the same cost as high-volume production of a single part type. In addition, flexible automation allowed machine setups to be done off-line, in parallel with processing operations, thus improving machine utilization, and allowing some operations to be done in a completely unattended mode.

Toyota Production System (TPS) In the aftermath of World War II, Japan's manufacturing capacity had to be completely rebuilt, but there were not ready sources of capital for acquiring manufacturing technologies from abroad. In this setting Taichi Ohno is credited with developing an approach to automobile manufacturing that became known as the "Toyota Production System" or TPS (Ohno 1988). Ohno's driving motivation was the elimination of all kinds of waste, but his innovation was to view waste as more than simply idle time on expensive machine tools. His approach differed from contemporary western manufacturing in a number of important ways: dramatically improving first pass quality ("zero defects"--ZD), dramatically reducing the time required to switch from one part type to another ("single minute exchange of dies"—SMED), eliminating unplanned downtime ("total productive maintenance"—TPM), empowering employees with multi-function skills working in teams, and carefully planning production to dramatically reduce work-in-process inventories (production "just in time"—JIT). In the 1970s, Toyota's competitive advantage in quality and cost convinced US auto makers to copy many elements of Ohno's system, but they were never able to match his overall results, partly because fully adopting TPS would require cultural transformations the US auto makers have been unwilling or unable to make.

Design for x At about the same time Ohno was developing the TPS, a number of researchers and manufacturers in the US were beginning to realize that the details of a specific product design have a great impact on the cost of manufacture, and often there are alternative designs that are equally good in terms of product functionality, but much superior in terms of manufacturing cost and yield. Their growing understanding of the relationship between design and manufacturing initially focused on assembly operations, and took the form of guidelines for designers under the name "design for assembly", or DFA (Andreasen 1983). As DFA showed opportunities for improvement, and "closed the loop" between assembly and product design, other processes were addressed, leading to a suite of "design for x" guidelines, where x could be assembly, casting, joining, etc (Boothroyd 1994).

DFx represents a transformation for most manufacturers, because it requires changing the relationship between design and manufacturing. Historically, designers designed and then "threw the design over the wall" to manufacturing. DFx requires that designers follow rules and guidelines developed from manufacturing knowledge. In other words, with DFx, design becomes constrained by manufacturing.

Manufactured Product Transformations

Consider any category of manufactured product—industrial, durable goods, soft goods, foods, transportation, communication, etc.—and contrast the products available in 1900 with the products available in 2000. The contrasts are dramatic.

Complexity One way to assess the complexity of a product is to disassemble it and count the number of pieces. For example, if you disassembled a modern automobile, you might have tens of thousands of individual pieces, compared to hundreds in a Model T. In fact, according to Mac's Antique Auto Parts, (anonymous 2005) slightly more than 2500 parts cover all Model T versions from 1909 to 1927! Similar comparisons apply to other durable goods, like washing machines or refrigerators.

Number of pieces in a given product may not fully reflect the complexity of the product family. For example, consider clothes. The range of fabrics, colors, and patterns available today is orders of magnitude greater than in 1900. To appreciate the complexity of a product type, you would need to disassemble one of each size, fabric and color/pattern option.

In many cases, complexity is hidden through integration. For example, much of the progress in modern electronics has addressed miniaturization and integration, i.e., making the electronic components smaller, and fabricating more of them on a single device. What may have required a dozen integrated circuits and two or three circuit boards only a few years ago, is available today in a single integrated circuit. That single integrated circuit is itself an extremely complex part (e.g., next generation microprocessors are expected to have a billion transistors (Hachman 2003)), but counts as only one part when you disassemble the product in which it is used.

As products become more complex, there must inevitably come a point where the old way of designing, managing design, manufacturing, or managing manufacturing simply cannot cope with the additional complexity. When that day comes, there must be a transformation to a new way of operating.

Technology In 1900, most products were simple with regard to technology. Even the automobile, one of the most complex products of the day, involved mostly mechanical technology, and relatively simple internal combustion engine technology. Today, products incorporate a much wider range of technologies. Consider for example, the ubiquitous cell phone. A contemporary cell phone includes mechanical components (hinges, slides, buttons), battery technology, visual and sound display technologies, both digital and analog microelectronic technology, and, software technology.

Whenever a new technology is introduced into a class of products, there is a transition, change, or transformation in both design and manufacture. New disciplines must be integrated, new constraints discovered and accommodated and new opportunities identified and exploited. Thus, new technologies represent not simply new technical challenges, but often new social and cultural challenges as well.

Organization and Operation Transformations

Manufacturing is a complex business, and history indicates there have almost always been significant opportunities to make it more efficient and effective. There would seem to be large rewards for the innovators in manufacturing organization and operation. The downside is that tinkering with an existing organization or way of operating, quite literally, can be a "bet the business" gamble. We hear a lot about the innovators who were successful, but rarely ever hear about those who failed.

Organization and operation transformations take place across all industry sectors, not just in manufacturing. Some of the transformations described below occurred more broadly than just manufacturing.

Integration and scale Ford didn't stop innovating with his perfection of the moving conveyor assembly line He also conceived and built the River Rouge Plant, where iron ore and coal came in one end of the site, and shiny new automobiles came out the other end (Anonymous 2005). With its own blast furnaces, coking ovens, and foundries, River Rouge was the epitome of industrial integration. It gave Ford the scale to achieve great economies in production. Integration on one site gave Ford the visibility into each production operation that was necessary to coordinate them for efficiency. A manager could view the entire supply chain in a day by walking around the site.

Ford went beyond the River Rouge Plant, to acquire raw material sources (e.g., rubber tree plantations in South America (Dempsey 2005)), producers of components, such as tires, and railways to deliver material to the plant and ship automobiles from the plant. Ultimately, the scale of integration became unmanageable with the management structure and communications technology of the day, and Ford fell from the top spot in the auto industry.

Segmentation As the auto market matured, the potential customers became more demanding. General Motors pursued a competitive strategy based on segmenting the market in terms of purchasing power, and organized itself into divisions based on specific market niches. In order to manage the diverse collection of businesses, which might have been considered competitors, GM required a highly functional management bureaucracy. Peter Drucker's famous study of GM (Drucker 1946) described GM as "the representative institution of our society" because of the corporation's management hierarchies. GM's innovation in management practices allowed them to claim the top spot in the auto industry, but their success kept them from recognizing the potential shortcomings of deep and highly structured hierarchies, and they were slow to respond to new challenges, especially those posed by Japanese auto makers in the 60's and 70's.

Flattening Hierarchies In the US, the pace of change in manufacturing began to accelerate in the 1970's as imported products captured a growing market share. This was especially true in the auto industry, and it soon was recognized that deep, rigid management hierarchies were not able to respond quickly to such challenges. Crusades were launched to "flatten the hierarchy," enabled by a combination of better (IT-based) communication technology, managers with better business educations, and willingness to distribute control to "empowered" managers (Nulty 1987). A study by Rajan and Wulf in 1997 (Rajan 2004) concluded that, in fact, over the past twenty years, hierarchies have flattened, with roughly 30% more direct reports to the CEO, and 25% fewer hierarchy layers between the CEO and managers with profit-and-loss responsibility. In addition, compensation for managers has changed as well, to better align their incentives with shareholder objectives.

Focusing In 1974, Wickham Skinner published an article in the Harvard Business Review (Skinner 1974) that was to have a significant impact on manufacturing. His thesis was that manufacturers should attempt to create a "factory within a factory" which could focus on producing a single product or product family, and achieve significant improvements in lead time, quality, and efficiency. Many companies, such as Deere, Black and Decker, Cincinnati Milacron, and 3M reported great success with the strategy. The focused factory strategy was a radical departure from then-contemporary practice, because it called for, essentially, the "de-integration" of manufacturing.

Outsourcing Another force for "de-integration" in manufacturing was the rise of contract manufacturers, or firms which had no product of their own, but produced products for OEMs. In the 1980's for example, contract assembly of printed circuit boards became a fast growing business in Silicon Valley (Arnett 1985). Contract manufacturing is attractive for an OEM in a number of situations. When the introduction of new products creates a transient capacity shortage, mature products can be given off to a contract manufacturer. When a particular manufacturing process is only available in capacity increments that significantly exceed a firm's requirements, contract manufacturing allows the firm to avoid purchasing excess capacity. Similarly, when a process requires special knowledge or skills, which are difficult to maintain under low utilization, contract manufacturing can be a cost effective alternative to in-house production. The downside of contract manufacturing is that it involves significant additional logistics. Using a contract manufacturer represents a major change for the enterprise, because it may eliminate the need for some existing capabilities, it hands over a major production responsibility to a third party, and it fundamentally changes the relationship with suppliers.

Globalization The term "globalization" is being used today to describe two quite different scenarios. In one, a manufacturing firm outsources some components, subsystems, or even complete products, but to contract manufacturers abroad. For a firm already engaged in outsourcing, this may not represent a transformation. The second use of the term is the scenario in which the firm must rationalize both product design and the sourcing of components, subsystems, and products because it is sourcing parts and selling products globally. For example, globalization may require redesigning products so a common platform can be customized in ways appropriate for different markets, and completely reconfiguring global supply chains to meet local domestic content requirements (Farrell 2004). This second use of the term can describe a transformational change.

THE MANUFACTURING ENTERPRISE

Now that we have some examples of change that might be transformational, we need to be able to discuss them in the context of manufacturing. But that begs the question, "What is it about a manufacturing enterprise that makes it different from any other enterprise?"

Any enterprise can be thought of as:

- A portfolio of resources

- Deployed through a network of activities

- To create value for customers

- By providing goods and services

- In a way that creates profit for owners

In this regard, manufacturing is no different. What sets manufacturing apart is the composition of the portfolio of resources, and the nature of some of the activities.

The environment of the manufacturing enterprise is illustrated in Figure 1 below. As with all enterprises, manufacturers have suppliers and customers with whom they exchange goods and services (G & S) for money. As with all enterprises, manufacturers have owners, and most often their ownership is traded in an equity market. As with all enterprises, manufacturers generate wastes that are absorbed in some "waste market", which may be regulated.

Like any other enterprise, a manufacturing enterprise must create economic returns for its owners. If owners are dissatisfied with their economic returns, in the form of dividends or selling shares, they will seek other investment opportunities and the value of the shares will decline. When a firm's share price declines, it becomes more difficult to raise capital through either the equity market or the debt market, because potential lenders will view the firm as a riskier investment.

Finally, like any other enterprise, a manufacturing enterprise succeeds by pleasing its customers. Customers today have very high expectations. They want high quality products, they want them to be inexpensive, and they want them right away. Product innovation is essential to remaining competitive.

Figure 1 also illustrates how manufacturing enterprises are different from other, non-manufacturing enterprises. The fundamental activities, by which manufacturing enterprises create value for their customers, are the design, realization, and marketing (including distribution) of products. Design and realization are the activities that distinguish manufacturing from other enterprises.

Both design and realization are quite complex activities, and full description of them is far beyond the scope of this chapter. Fortunately, there are only a few things we really need to understand in order to begin discussing manufacturing enterprise transformation, namely, the structure of products, the structure of realization, and the relationship between information and tangible artifacts.

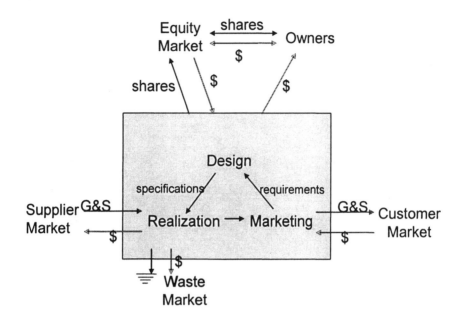

FIGURE 1. Manufacturing Enterprise Environment

Product Structure

Almost without exception, manufactured products are assembled from materials, parts, and/or systems, acquired either from suppliers or from feeder plants. A shirt, for example, may contain a dozen pieces of cloth, thread, and buttons; with different suppliers for buttons, thread, and even multiple suppliers of cloth. Even the ubiquitous no. 2 pencil contains two pieces of wood, a graphite cylinder, an eraser, a metal band, and paint, all of which may come from different suppliers. Complex manufactured products, such as an automobile or an airplane will contain many thousands of individual components, and perhaps hundreds of suppliers.

One convention in describing a product is the "bill of materials" or BOM. The BOM is a hierarchical description of the product, in terms of the parts and systems used to produce it. At the top of the hierarchy is the product itself, which has a product identification number. Consider, for example, an automobile. In the first level of the BOM hierarchy, we might find the following list: car body, engine, drive train, wheels, instrument panel, steering system, and seat systems. The car body might be further described by its components, for example: frame, front doors, rear doors, hood, trunk deck, front glass, rear glass. Doors might be further described in terms of their window glass, control systems, etc. Figure 2 illustrates an indented BOM for an automobile, where ellipses indicate additional components or systems not explicitly listed.

It is common to talk about the "levels" in the BOM, or equivalently, the number of "indents." A product with many levels is more complex than a product with fewer levels, simply because more "putting together" must take place. It also is common for there to be a product identifier associated with each item specifically called out in the BOM. In other words, this item must be designed, specified, procured or manufactured, and the associated processes must be managed in order to support the product realization process. The more specific items there are to manage, the more complex it is to manage product realization.

From this perspective, any new technology or new practice that simplifies the BOM is, *ceteris paribus*, good for manufacturing. Integrating several sheet metal parts into one, perhaps more complex sheet metal part is a good thing, because it reduces the number of parts that must be produced, handled, stored, qualified, and managed to support realization. Deciding to acquire a complex assembly from a supplier rather than to produce it in-house, for example, means that the manufacturer "shrinks" that part of the BOM from all the parts in the outsourced assembly to a single part number, namely, the assembly itself. The internal parts management problem becomes much easier.

```
Automobile
    Body
            Unibody
            Right front door system
                ...
            Left front door system
                ...
            Hood
            Trunk deck
            Front glass
            Rear glass
    Wheels
    Engine
        ...
    Drive train
        ...
    ...
```

FIGURE 2. Example of Indented BOM

Process Structure

Manufacturing activities require manufacturing processes, which have capabilities for converting material from one state to another. For example, a press, together with the proper tooling, can convert rolled steel into specific shapes, such as body panels for an automobile. A properly configured oven can convert freshly painted car bodies into car bodies with baked enamel coatings. A robotic welder can convert two separate pieces of metal into a welded assembly. Note also that moving material between two location changes the state of its location, and storing material changes the state of its age.

In conventional terminology, *process* refers to the resource used to perform a conversion, and *operation* refers to the specific conversion performed on a specific part type or set of part types. A process may perform many different operations, but a particular operation is specific to a particular process type. For example, a robotic welder is a process that can be programmed to form any weld that satisfies the constraints of the robot with respect to its workspace, and the capabilities of its welding attachments. Different assemblies can be presented to the robot, and each different assembly presented represents a specific operation.

If you imagine any single component of a finished product, e.g., a door handle on an automobile, you realize that the component has undergone a number, perhaps a great number, of operations in its conversion from raw material to finished, assembled door handle. The sequence of operations for a given part type is referred to as its *process plan* or *process route*. If you focus on any single operation in a part's process plan, it is quite likely the process used for that operation also is used by a large number of other part types requiring similar operations (i.e., their process plans also required that specific process). In other words, many different part types will cross a given process resource, and thus will create *contention* for the use of that process.

There is a process plan for each and every part type required by the final product. Corresponding to each process plan there is a flow of material, starting with the delivery from suppliers, traveling to each process, and ultimately to the final assembly operation. Now if you imagine the typical automobile, with tens of thousands of individual parts, you begin to understand what an enormous traffic control problem there can be in a contemporary factory. Much of the innovation in manufacturing over the past century was aimed at simplifying this enormous traffic control problem.

To summarize, in manufacturing, many of the resources are processes, and these processes are arranged in process networks, through which parts flow along their individual process routes. At any particular process, there is likely to be contention among the part types requiring that process, creating congestion in the process network, and requiring some form of material flow control.

Today, the process network for many products extends far beyond the walls of a single factory. The manufacture of a personal computer, for example, involves complex process networks in factories that fabricate integrated circuits, flat panel displays, and read/write heads for disc drives, factories that test and package integrated circuits, factories that assemble disc drives, factories that assemble printed circuit boards, and factories that assemble computers. These factories may be located on three continents, and require global material transport. Achieving economy, reliability, and speed in such a globally distributed process network represents a very challenging logistics problem, as well as a design and manufacturing process problem.

Information versus Tangible Products

While Figure 1 identifies the major functions of a manufacturing enterprise, it is too aggregated a view of manufacturing to be very useful in discussing transformation. Figure 3 elaborates Figure 1, and divides the manufacturing enterprise activities along two dimensions.

Key manufacturing activities can be distinguished by the nature of their products—either information or tangible artifacts. Thus, design and manufacturing planning activities work with and produce information intended for internal consumption within the enterprise; examples include design specifications, and information related to the planning or control of the manufacturing process network. Manufacturing and marketing and sales activities, in contrast, work with and produce the tangible products, intended for customers.

Another way to distinguish key manufacturing enterprise activities is by the impact of their results, i.e., do they create value or do they create costs? The claim inherent in Figure 3 is that design and marketing and sales activities create value. Design fundamentally determines the extent to which products provide to customers the functionality they desire, and the esthetic appeal they require. Marketing and sales activities are where the value is actually captured in a transaction with a customer. Manufacturing planning and production, on the other hand, create costs; unless marketing and sales can complete suitable sales transactions, these costs are not recovered.

In Figure 3, "Product Design" activities produce information that fundamentally determines the value of products. "Manufacturing Planning" produces information that fundamentally determines the cost of products. "Production" activities actually incur (or realize) the costs of manufacture. "Marketing and Sales" activities capture (or realize) value in a sales transaction.

Figure 3 also illustrates the basic nature of the interactions between the four types of activities. Note that all interactions are based on information exchange, except the delivery of (tangible) products and services from Production to Marketing and Sales.

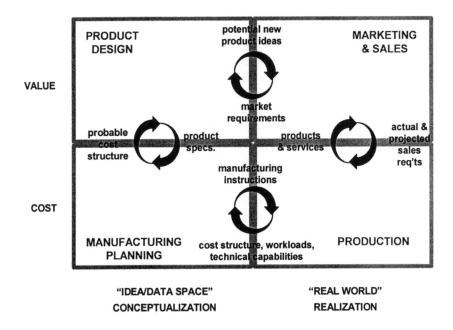

FIGURE 3. Key Manufacturing Enterprise Activities

TRANSFORMATION REVISITED

We now have a reasonable foundation from which to discuss transformation in manufacturing enterprises. Each transformation suggested earlier can be examined in light of its impact on products, on the process network, or on the four basic activities illustrated in Figure 3. If the suggested transformation doesn't impact these aspects of the enterprise, then it is a broader enterprise transformation, and not specifically a manufacturing enterprise transformation.

When Henry Ford perfected the assembly line, he transformed the production of automobiles, by dramatically improving (by an order of magnitude) labor productivity. In addition, because his assembly lines were paced, it was easier to predict the output of the factory, allowing better synchronization of the production process network and subsequent product distribution. As a result, Ford required fewer production process resources to produce automobiles than did his competitors, so his costs of production were significantly lower, giving him a powerful competitive advantage. Ford's innovation also had an impact on the marketing and sales function, although at the time, this was not as important as the cost savings in production. The economic impact on cost savings made it inevitable that Ford's competitors would copy Ford's innovation, but the advantage of the innovator lasted almost a generation.

The introduction of NC had a similar impact on resource productivity in production. Once the technology was proven effective, its adoption was inevitable. Because NC was a government-sponsored innovation, its deployment was through third party technology suppliers, i.e., through adoption by machine tool suppliers. Thus, any competitive cost advantage for the first-movers in manufacturing was temporary at best. Interestingly, the advent of NC accelerated the rise of manufacturing engineering as a function distinct from shop floor production, because NC required off-line programming to develop the NC codes from part drawings.

The impact of factory networks was felt in two ways. It continued the transformation of process resources; rather than being stand-alone and self-sufficient, processes became dependent on the factory infrastructure, and in particular, upon technical staff functions for networking, planning, and programming support. Thus, while production resource economies could be realized, additional overhead costs were created in the manufacturing planning and support functions.

General Motors was an early innovator in the area of factory networking, developing a proprietary networking standard, MAP in the early 1980's (Dwyer 1987). General Motors was able to achieve some integration of their "islands of factory automation" by deploying MAP, but absorbed most of the development costs, and any resulting net cost advantage was short-lived as a variety of vendor-supported standards emerged, and were widely adopted. While MAP itself was not a transformational technology, there is little doubt that the commitment of General Motors to factory networking had a major impact on the emergence of viable factory networking technologies, which were transformational.

The impacts of flexible automation resemble the combination of NC and networks, i.e., affecting both the network of production process resources and the associated manufacturing planning function. Interestingly, most US manufacturers used flexible automation simply to reduce the labor content of mass produced parts, rather than fully exploiting the potential for process utilization improvements (Darrow 1987). One possible explanation for this phenomenon is that in order to fully exploit flexible automation technology, a fairly sophisticated manufacturing planning function is required, and the process itself must be extremely reliable. The required levels of capability did not exist prior to the advent of flexible automation technology, thus it was much easier, and less risky, to deploy the technology to reduce labor costs rather than to achieve "flexibility". In the US, at least, one could argue that flexible automation technology was not transformational, because the same results could have been achieved with more traditional automation.

The Toyota Production System, as conceived by Ohno, impacted all four functions in Figure 3. Products had to be designed to make them easier to produce. Marketing had to provide a level schedule to manufacturing. Manufacturing planning had to determine appropriate levels of inventory, and optimize production sequences. And of course, production had to achieve low defects, high availability, fast changeovers, and "just in time" production. In other words, the TPS fundamentally impacted every key aspect of the manufacturing enterprise. To a certain extent, this also explains why US automakers were never able to match the accomplishments of Toyota; initially, they saw TPS as simply a production innovation, and tried to implement it as such (Sabatini 2000). Even transplanted Japanese automakers have been unable to achieve the same impacts in their US plants as Toyota achieved in Japan, leading many to conclude that fundamental cultural differences may inhibit the full adoption in US factories of innovations as sweeping as Ohno's. Nevertheless, there is no question that TPS has been transformational, at least in the US auto industry. Every US automaker employs some variation of "just in time" production in vehicle assembly.

It would be difficult to argue that "design for x" has been a transformational innovation. DFx is often implemented as a system of design rules that can be checked, more or less automatically, within an existing design environment. To a considerable extent, DFx institutionalizes the tacit knowledge of designers, so is of primary value either to inexperienced designers (who probably work under the supervision of more experienced designers) or in situations where the designed artifact is so complex that it has too many features for a designer to check manually. In the former case, there would have been a formal design review process that likely would uncover violated design rules. In the latter case, it is quite likely the design software vendor would supply any DFx innovation to all users for whom it would be beneficial. In either case, it is not likely that adopting DFx technology would make any significant impact on existing organizational structures or practices.

While it certainly is true that products today are much more complex and incorporate many more technologies than 100 years ago, or even 25 years ago, it is difficult to argue that either complexity or technology are transformational with regard to manufactured products. Increasing product complexity is a natural evolutionary change, as designers seek to add attractive features or improve product esthetics. Consider, for example, the addition of a CD player to the entertainment cluster in an automobile instrument panel. The added complexity may increase the number of operations in a few parts' process plans, and incrementally increase the number of parts, but it doesn't profoundly impact the structure of the process network. Thus, it doesn't profoundly impact the nature of manufacturing planning. Likewise, the addition of new technology, such as an LCD display, may add new parts, with new process routes, but doesn't fundamentally change the nature of the process network or the manufacturing planning function. Generally, increasing complexity or new technology are incremental changes in design, manufacturing planning, and production.

There is, however, a related example of transformation. Sony, in the development of the Walkman™ line of personal entertainment devices, employed a deliberate strategy of continuous rapid product evolution of a durable platform (Sanderson 1995). New features and options were added at a rate that guaranteed the Walkman products were always "fresh" in comparison to competitors. This continuous rapid product evolution required a very disciplined and integrated approach that encompassed all four functions in Figure 3. This was a transformational strategy, and propelled Sony to a leadership position in the industry and a competitive advantage that other companies found difficult to appropriate.

Henry Ford's pursuit of integration and scale at River Rouge enabled significant economies in production. Expensive processes could be used to maximum efficiency, and because the entire process network was owned, it could be carefully coordinated to achieve additional economies. By being the first auto company to achieve such size and integration, Ford created a competitive advantage that was very difficult for competitors to duplicate. History indicates that this competitive advantage in the production function was not matched by sufficiently effective transformation of the manufacturing planning function, and Ford eventually gave up its competitive advantage.

The insight represented by the General Motors strategy of segmentation was that a number of essentially independent, parallel manufacturing firms could be disciplined to design, plan, produce and market products to different segments of the consumer market. This precursor to Skinner's (Skinner 1974) focused factory concept allowed General Motors to achieve a large scale, in terms of market share, but with a simpler process network than a single monolithic enterprise. When coupled with a carefully structured management hierarchy, General Motors was able to achieve economies within the divisions through manufacturing planning, and maintain product segment discipline. This transformation of both strategy and organizational structure gave General Motors a competitive advantage that lasted until Japanese auto makers presented a new challenge in the 1970's.

The trend to reduce middle management, or "flatten the hierarchy" that began in the 1980's was in part a response to foreign competition, primarily Japanese, and in part an adoption of new information technologies. The historical role of middle managers had been to take the general direction of top management and translate it into action. This essentially "word of mouth" approach to translating intent into results necessarily meant that a single manager could cope with only a limited number of subordinate managers. Information technology fundamentally changed the situation, by enabling broader, faster communication and real-time monitoring of results. Moreover, the reduction of middle management was not just a manufacturing enterprise strategy, it was applicable more broadly. Did flattening the hierarchy fundamentally change some management practices? Without a doubt, it did. So, was it a transformational change? That is a more difficult question.

Focused factories and outsourcing represent an opportunity to rationalize the manufacturing process network, leading to simpler manufacturing planning processes, and faster, more efficient production. The first firms to adopt focused factory concepts or to outsource production were taking risks, simply because they were doing something that had not been done before. Both focused factories and outsourcing fundamentally change both the manufacturing process network and the manufacturing planning functions. They are transformational technologies. However, they are technologies easily adopted by competitors, and so provide at best a transient competitive advantage to the first movers.

Finally, globalization is a natural response to two changing aspects of the manufacturing enterprise's environment. In established markets, it is difficult for a given manufacturing enterprise to grow; as a result, growth is often achieved by entering new markets. Today, for a given firm, the new market opportunities are likely to be international rather than domestic, requiring the firm either to manufacture abroad or to export product to international markets. For US manufacturers, the domestic cost structures almost always dictate manufacture abroad. The cost and feasibility of international transportation make it possible for US manufacturers to outsource to suppliers globally and achieve significant cost reductions over domestic suppliers. For firms that sell products internationally, there are almost always substantial changes to the product design function, as products require some customization for local cultures and markets. This may lead to the development of product platforms, suitable for a global market, with variations specialized for local markets.

Globalization requires firms to develop some new functional capabilities, for example, dealing with customs, tariffs, domestic content laws, etc. For most firms, however, it is difficult to argue that globalization is a transformational change. It represents incremental change to several functions, but not a dramatic change to any one function.

SOME THOUGHTS ON TRANSFORMATION

As a dynamic entity, an enterprise's state is, by definition, changing constantly. So to be useful, "transformation" must be understood as something distinct from "change."

Change is not necessarily transformation, even if it involves changes to work processes or organizations. Continuous improvement programs can change work processes, but once in place, do not represent enterprise transformation. Wal-Mart added a store almost every three days during the 1980's, but this rapid growth did not, *per se*, represent transformation.

In both these examples, the observed changes are results of existing processes for planning and managing specific kinds of changes. Both improvement and growth are planned, expected, and routine. This leads to the following:

> Principle: Routine change is not transformational, although
> creating the processes to accommodate routine change can be.

If we can accept the principle that routine change is not transformation, then perhaps we also can accept its contrapositive, i.e., transformation is non-routine, or episodic change. Transformation occurs in response to a threat or an opportunity. Rouse (Rouse 2005) describes transformation as "driven by perceived value deficiencies relative to needs and/or expectations," where "value" typically refers to revenues or profits. The perceived value deficiency can occur because of competitors' successes (a threat) or because of an opportunity not yet recognized by competitors, e.g., the exploitation of the World Wide Web to open new markets, or enable new business models.

An episodic change that does not disrupt is not a transformation. Firing a vice-president is (one would hope) an episodic change, but not necessarily disruptive or transformational. Redefining the roles of vice-presidents, and empowering them to change business processes is disruptive, and transforming.

Transforming change is reflected in the activities of the enterprise. If the activities are not changed in some readily discernable way, then the enterprise is not transformed. Simply replicating the existing activities in more locations, or increasing the rates of existing activities is not transformational.

Finally, it is tempting to try to restrict attention to those transformations that provide the innovator with a meaningful competitive advantage, even if it is short-lived. On the other hand, consider a transformation, such as the adoption of NC, which is adopted by most competitors at almost the same time. While not necessarily giving any competitor an advantage, the innovation does provide advantages to customers in the form of better, cheaper products.

FUTURE MANUFACTURING TRANSFORMATIONS

There are at least three significant themes in the historical record of manufacturing enterprise transformations.

The first theme is the displacement by machines of jobs in which people play the role of energy sources, manipulators, and sensors. For a given technology, whether it is the steam shovel, or the assembly robot, there is a scale of deployment at which the user's cost of production using the machine is less than the user's cost of production using people. At that scale, it becomes economically preferable. We might use the term "physical automation" to describe this phenomenon.

An interesting aspect of physical automation is that as more jobs are automated, the process of further automation becomes more difficult. Subsequent physical automation technology tends to become more expensive and have greater capacity. Thus, it must be spread over more jobs. But as the number of jobs declines (due to automation!) the only way to spread a given technology over more jobs is for it to be more flexible in application.

Physical automation is fundamentally about reducing costs of production, or perhaps improving quality. An alternative to physical automation is out-sourcing physical jobs to low wage markets. Recent experience seems to indicate that low-wage markets don't stay low-wage, so this strategy has a downside, which is that the increased logistics costs are further aggravated by increasing labor costs over time.

Physical automation primarily affects the production function, but its technical support often impacts the manufacturing planning function as well.

What we can expect to see in the future is innovative physical automation that is flexible and adaptable, and can be deployed instead of wage-based outsourcing. Extrapolating from the past, such automation will either be large-scale, meaning it must replace many similar jobs in one setting, or it will be adaptable enough to replace many different jobs spread over many different settings.

The second, and related, theme is the replacement by technology of people as decision makers. Examples include NC and computers. We might use the term "intellectual automation" to describe this phenomenon. Intellectual automation requires that the decisions being automated are ones that can be reduced to a rule, a set of rules, or an algorithm. The specific decision problem must be formalized, defining the decision, the constraints, and the criteria explicitly.

Often, intellectual automation is coupled with physical automation. For example, robotic workstations may involve sensing to determine the locations and orientations of parts, and algorithms to decide how to perform a series of operations. In this case, both the decision making and the physical actions of an assembly worker have been replaced.

Intellectual automation also appears quite often in "white collar" settings. Automated call handling is one ubiquitous example. DFx is an example of intellectual automation applied to product design. Intellectual automation often has the goal of capturing both the explicit and tacit knowledge of decision makers so that it can be reused and shared with other, perhaps less experienced decision makers.

Intellectual automation primarily affects the design function and the manufacturing function. However, as the technology for intellectual automation improves, more and more of the human decision making in production is replaced by automated decision making in manufacturing planning.

Intellectual automation has been an active area of research and development since the early 1960's. Progress in artificial intelligence, data mining, optimization, knowledge representation, and computing in general are providing ever-improving technical foundations for intellectual automation. However, a case could be made that, at least in the foreseeable future, innovations in intellectual automation will come, not from replacing human decision makers, but in augmenting them. Useful innovations in intellectual automation are likely to be those which give human decision makers the ability to perceive and understand larger, more complex decision problems, and to rapidly explore a greater number and range of options, considering more criteria and the influence of uncertainty. The most likely to transform manufacturing will be innovations applicable to all enterprises, not just manufacturing, and the manufacturing enterprises that benefit most will be those who are able to most rapidly deploy intellectual automation technologies.

The third major trend observable in manufacturing enterprise transformation is the enterprise level integration of all four functions shown in Figure 3, with the goal of making the enterprise more efficient and more responsive to changes in the competitive environment. Efficiency improvements address the total enterprise lifecycle costs. Responsiveness improvements address both the speed with which the enterprise can introduce and deliver products, but also the ability to design and develop innovative products.

Enterprise integration is the most costly and riskiest of the three trends, and there are many examples of very expensive failed efforts based on software platforms. A case could be made that today the limiting factor in enterprise integration is not the information technology available; rather it is the failure to rationalize the functions in Figure 3, and to put in place the standards and practices necessary to support integration. Thus, the most likely source of transformation in enterprise integration is not software, but concepts, semantics, standards, and practices.

CONCLUSION

The goal of this chapter is to try to understand the genesis and deployment of manufacturing enterprise transformation. The framework proposed for discussing transformation consists of two key elements. The first is the description of the enterprise as a portfolio of resources, deployed through a network of activities, to produce goods and services, to meet the needs of customers, in a way that generates profits for owners. The second is the four distinguishing functions in manufacturing enterprises, illustrated in Figure 3: design, manufacturing planning, production, and marketing and sales.

What can we conclude from the manufacturing transformation examples discussed in this chapter? First, it seems clear that true transformation in manufacturing is almost always risky, and requires very strong motivation on the part of the innovator. Ford's perfection of the assembly line and Ohno's development of the Toyota Production System were responses to competitive pressures. In both cases, the firms needed to change dramatically in order to achieve a competitive advantage relative to larger established competitors. The changes they implemented might have failed, and if so, likely would have severely weakened their companies.

Second, it appears that manufacturing enterprise transformation almost always has a technological component, where technology is broadly defined to include the methods used as well as the tools. At least one of the four distinguishing functions is changed, either in the methods or the tools used, or in the basic organization of the function, e.g., the structure of the process network. In some cases, the transformation involves taking existing technologies and using them in a different way, e.g., the Toyota Production System did not require inventing anything fundamentally new. In some cases, the transformation involves being the first mover with a new technology, e.g., numerical control or factory networks. There seems to be evidence that transformation based on using existing technologies differently leads to a more sustainable competitive advantage than simply being the first mover to adopt a new technology.

Third, transformation that focuses on a single function, e.g., outsourcing one function, rather than multiple functions, appears to be easily copied by competitors, and rarely leads to a sustainable competitive advantage. In contrast, transformations that impact the entire enterprise, like TPS or the Sony design-production innovation strategy, are much more difficult to copy.

Finally, it does not appear that any manufacturing enterprise transformation leads to a permanent competitive advantage. Eventually competitors find a way to match or better the innovation, or the competitive environment changes in a way that the innovation is no longer such a large competitive advantage. Interestingly, it does appear that firms which successfully transform often fall into the trap of believing their new competitive advantage is permanent, and fail to anticipate changes in the environment or respond to moves by their competitors.

REFERENCES

Abbate, J. (1999). Inventing the Internet. Cambridge, MA, MIT Press.

Andreasen, M. M., S. Kahler, and T. Lund (1983). Design for assembly. Berlin; New York, Springer-Verlag.

Anonymous. "General Electric." Retrieved April 2, 2005, from http://en.wikipedia.org /wiki/General_Electric.

Anonymous. "History of the Assembly Line." Retrieved April 2, 2005, from http://www.aeragon.com/02/02-04.html.

Anonymous. "History of the Rouge." Retrieved April 3, 2005, from http://www.hfmgv.org/rouge/history.asp.

Anonymous (1984). Development of flexible automation systems. International Conference on the Development of Flexible Automation Systems, London, Institution of Electrical Engineers.

anonymous. (2005). "MAC's Antique Auto Parts." Retrieved March 22, 2005, from http://www.macsautoparts.com/tt.html.

Arnett, N. (1985). "Contract manufacturing gains as area firms seek market edge." San Jose Business Journal 3(32).

Black, U. D. (1998). TCP/IP and related protocols. New York, McGraw-Hill.

Boothroyd, G., P. Dewhurst, and W. A. Knight (1994). Product design for manufacture and assembly. New York, Marcel Dekker.

Childs, J. J. (1973). Numerical control part programming. New York, Industrial Press.

Darrow, W. P. (1987). "An international comparison of flexible manufacturing systems technology." Interfaces 17(6): 86-91.

Dempsey, M. A. "Fordlandia." Retrieved April 3, 2005, from http://www.michiganhistorymagazine.com/extra/fordlandia/fordlandia.html.

Drucker, P. F. (1946). Concept of the corporation. New York, New American Library.

Dwyer, J. (1987). MAP and TOP: advanced manufacturing communications. New York, Halstead Press.

Farrell, D., Pankaj Ghemawat, C. K. Prahalad, and Kenneth Lieberthal (2004). "Winning the globalization game." Harvard Business Review. Dec 1, 2004.

Hachman, M. (2003). "Intel's "Montecito" Will Be Massive." Retrieved April 3, 2005, from http://www.extremetech.com/article2/0,3973,878643,00.asp.

Krass, P. (2002). Carnegie. New York, John Wiley & Sons.

Nulty, P. (1987). "How managers will manage." Fortune 115(3): 47, 3 pgs.

Ohno, T. (1988). Toyota production system: beyond large scale production. Cambridge, MA, Productivity Press.

Pawlak, D. A. "The Tin Lizzie Life." Retrieved April 2, 2005, from http://www.themediadrome.com/content/articles/history_articles/ford.htm.

Rajan, R. G., and Julie Wulf. (2004). "The Flattening Firm: Evidence from Panel Data on the Changing Nature of Corporate Hierarchies." Retrieved March 22, 2005, from http://www-management.wharton.upenn.edu/wulfresearch/docs/ Flattening_Firm_10_04.pdf.

Reintjes, J. F. (1991). Numerical Control: Making a New Technology. New York, Oxford University Press.

Rouse, W. B. (2005). A theory of enterprise transformation, Tennenbaum Institute, Georgia Institute of Technology.

Sabatini, J. (2000). ""Old news"." Automotive Manufacturing & Production 112(9): 96, 1 pg.

Sanderson, S., and Mustafa Uzumeri (1995). "Managing product families: The case of the Sony Walkman." Research Policy 24(5): 761, 22 pgs.

Skinner, W. (1974). "The focused factory." Harvard Business Review(May-June 1974): 113-121.

Stover, R. N. (1984). An analysis of CAD/CAM applications: with an introduction to CIM. Englewood Cliffs, NJ, Prentice-Hall.

CHAPTER 7

TRANSFORMATION IN THE LOGISTICS INDUSTRY[1]

CHELSEA C. WHITE III AND DALE BELMAN

ABSTRACT

The logistics industry has fundamentally changed over several decades. This transformation has, in part, been driven by regulatory changes, including economic, coordinative, and social regulations. Customers have also driven transformation via lean manufacturing, disintermediation, the Internet, outsourcing, expanded services, off-shoring, and information technology. Consumers of logistics services have benefited substantially from these changes. In contrast, employees of the companies providing these services have not always benefited from the transformation of this industry.

INTRODUCTION

The objective of this chapter is to identify the transformations (fundamental changes), and their causes, that have occurred recently and/or are occurring in the U.S. logistics industry, where we broadly define the logistics industry as including freight transportation, warehousing, and many other services provided by logistics firms, such as supply chain management. Two fundamental forces - regulatory change and customer business practices - drive the transformations that we have identified; importantly, we note that economic regulatory change has served to enable customer driven transformations.

Regarding the impact of regulatory change on the logistics industry, federal, state and local governments have been involved in the promotion and regulation of the industry since the nation's inception. Government has provided direct and indirect financial support for transportation infrastructure and regulated transportation industries to promote their growth, efficiency, stability and public

---

[1] This chapter draws on and summarizes the research presented in <u>Trucking in the Age of Information</u>, a volume of essays on the trucking industry by members of the Alfred P. Sloan Foundation Trucking Industry Program. The authors of this chapter, who edited <u>Trucking in the Age of Information</u>, wish to express their gratitude to B. Starr McMullen, Thomas M. Corsi, Peter F. Swan and Steven V. Burks, Les Hough, Maciek Nowak, C. John Langley Jr., James Peoples, Anuradha Nagarajan, Enrique Canessa, Maciek Nowak, Will Mitchell, Francine Lafontaine, Kristen Monaco, Jennifer N. Karlin, Jeffrey K. Liker, Lee Husting, Elyce Biddle and Michael E. Conyngham for their work in advancing knowledge about trucking. We hope that our summaries do justice to their scholarship.

safety. Financial support has taken varied forms: subsidies in the form of cash and large land grants to support the extension of railroads, the development and maintenance of the system of inland waterways by the federal government, and the use of federal and state fuel taxes to raise the capital funds needed to build and maintain a national system of roads. Government regulation has, at various times, included economic regulation (the regulation of entry and of rates), social regulation (the regulation of safety, working conditions and environmental effects), and coordinative regulation (the establishment of common standards across states to facilitate the movement of freight across a national system).

Government interventions have decisively shaped the national transportation system. The physical infrastructure of transportation is most obviously an outcome of government intervention. The current system of roads, rails and waterways would be far smaller, and some services might not exist, absent the leading role of local, state and particularly the federal government in their promotion, financing and planning. Other aspects of the emerging transportation/logistics system have also been and are being shaped by government action. The information infrastructure of the transportation system has been developed on a foundation of government financed research and experiments. Again, this is most obvious in the ongoing federal funding of pilot projects to promote the application of information technology to transportation. Federal support and development of IT resources in general and the Internet and satellite location and communications systems have provided the basis for the application of IT to transportation. Finally, government has played a central role in the development of the common rules including limits on weight and length and safety rules necessary for an efficient national transportation system.

Economic deregulation has enabled the logistics industry to better respond to customer business practices, and as a result, the impact of customer business practices on the logistics industry, and vice versa, has been profound. These practices are ultimately intended to improve, in some sense, the performance of an enterprise. We view an enterprise as a network of independent companies, often located in different countries and time zones, seeking mutual business advantage, with the intent to design, manufacture, and deliver 'right-quality' and 'right price' products and/or services at the 'right-time' to customers better than the competition. Such enterprises are composed of suppliers, manufacturers, wholesalers, retailers, distribution and logistics companies, communications and information systems companies, and customers. Each company in an enterprise specializes in what it does best; ideally, the members of the enterprise cover the competencies that are critical to the goal of the enterprise and incentives are in place to insure that these companies are focused on this shared goal. No company can have world-class competencies in all areas. However, a well-designed and efficiently functioning enterprise can, thus providing formidable competitive advantage. The effective movement of goods between and within the facilities of the enterprise is inextricably linked to achieving the objectives of the enterprise.

Business practices that imply how goods are to be moved, and hence fundamentally affect how the logistics industry moves goods, include: lean manufacturing, disintermediation, globalization, outsourcing (implicit in the above description of the enterprise), and off-shoring. Impacts of these practices on the logistics industry also include an expansion of services and industry consolidation.

We now present an overview of the logistics industry and then describe the industry transformations in more detail.

OVERVIEW OF THE LOGISTICS INDUSTRY

In 2004, the U.S. logistics industry generated $936 billion, or 8.5% of national GDP. Of this amount, 33% was due to inventory (warehousing and inventory holding costs), 63% to transportation, and 4% to administration (CLM, 2004). Freight is transported by a variety of transportation modes, as indicated in Table 1, with trucking being the dominant mode for moving freight in the U.S.

The percentage of GDP generated by the movement of freight in the U.S. has decreased substantially since 1980, when the revenue generated by the logistics industry was approximately 16.3% of the U.S. GDP, till now, where this percentage is 8.5%; see Figure 1. Comparable figures for other regions of the world are presented in Table 2. Table 2 indicates that the percent of GDP generated by the logistics industry in the U.S. is at least as low as the percent of GDP generated in other parts of the world, implying that the U.S. logistics industry is one of the world's most efficient logistics industries.

Trucking Industry

Trucking is the dominant mode for the movement of freight within the U.S. The for-hire portion of the industry has for the last quarter century been segmented into package express (PX), truckload (TL), and less-than-truckload (LTL).

Package Express. The PX industry moves packages that weigh as much as 150 pounds, with an average weight of less than 50 pounds. The number of packages moved annually in the U.S. is over one billion (Swan and Burks, forthcoming).

PX companies typically have two types of fleets: (1) specialized small vans for pick up and delivery between customers and terminals and (2) tractor-trailers for inter-terminal movements. Packages in an urban area or region are picked up by the vans and taken to terminals, where the packages are consolidated and placed into the tractor-trailers. The tractor-trailers then move to other terminals in other urban areas or regions, where their loads are de-consolidated and placed on vans for delivery. Consolidation and de-consolidation at the terminals takes place using specialized material handling equipment.

Transportation Mode	Billions $	% of Total
Trucking, total	610.2	85.5
Private Trucking	273.6	38.3
Truckload	273.9	38.4
Less-than-Truckload	62.7	8.8
Railroad	35.4	5.0
Rail Intermodal	6.7	0.9
Pipeline (oil and gas)	27.2	3.8
Airfreight, package domestic	20.0	2.8
Airfreight, heavy domestic	6.0	0.8
Water (Great Lakes/rivers	8.1	1.1
Transportation Total	713.6	100.0

TABLE 1. Commercial Freight Distribution-2001 (in billions of dollars*)* *Source: Jim Corridore, "Standard and Poor's Industry Surveys", Transportation Commercial, June 19, 2003, p. 8. Sources cited by Standard and Poor's: Cass Information Systems and Standard and Poor's own estimates (T. Corsi, 2005)*

The PX industry can be divided into three segments - small parcels, overnight letters, and courier services. Small parcels and overnight letters account for the majority of packages and revenue. Prior to 1994, the maximum package size was seventy-five pounds. In 1994 UPS began taking packages of up to 150 pounds. Both UPS and FedEx now move larger package sizes that in the past typically would be associated with LTL carriers. Table 3 presents the percent of revenue by PX carrier for three submarkets – overnight letters, packages under 2 pounds, and packages from 2 to 75 pounds – and provides the names of major firms in this sector of the logistics industry and their share of the market.

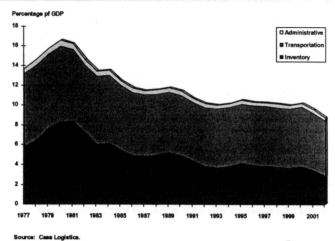

FIGURE 1. Total Logistics Expenditures and Gross Domestic Product (GDP)

	Population (billions)	GDP (trillions)	Logistics (millions)	% of GDP	Outsourced Logistics (millions)	% of Logistics (millions)	Estimated Growth of Outsourcing
USA	0.4	11	936	9%	77	8.2%	10-15%
Europe	0.5	10	900	9%	68	7.5%	10-15%
Asia – Pac (x-China)	0.6	5	600	12%	30	5.0%	15-20%
China	1.3	1	230	23%	5	2.2%	20-25%
Global	6.1	31	3,500	11%	197	5.6%	10-15%

TABLE 2. International Logistics and Outsourcing Expenditures. *Source: Armstrong & Associates, Cass Information Systems, International Monetary Fund, MercerManagement Consulting, Organization for Economic Cooperation and Development, The World Bank Group, Robert W. Baird & Co. Estimates (J. Langley, 2004).*

Sub-market	Carrier						
	Airborne*	DHL*	Emery	FedEx	United Parcel Express	USPS	All Others
Overnight Letters	10.9%	2.4%	0.1%	58.2%	15.6%	12.2%	0.5%
Packages Under 2 lbs	9.7%	0.9%	0.1%	33.8%	17.8%	17.8%	3.6%
Packages 2 to 75 lbs	4.0%	0.9%	0.2%	18.8%	63.9%	9.2%	3.1%

*Since merged

Source: From A. Robinson, Competition within the United States Parcel Delivery Market, Postcom,

TABLE 3. Percentage of Revenue by Carrier and Sub-Market in Package Express (2000). (*Hough and Nowak ,2005*)

Deutsche Post World Net (DPWN) generates the largest global revenue, $44 billion, in the small package delivery business. In 2003, DHL, now owned by DPWN, generated total global revenue of $18.6 billion. Over 90% of this revenue was earned internationally, representing approximately 40% market share in international express, which is more than the sum of international revenue from UPS and FedEx. UPS's global revenues are $33.5 billion, $5.6 billion of which is earned from international package delivery. FedEx has $24.7 billion on total revenues, $4.6 billion of which generated internationally. UPS and FedEx, however, have roughly 70 percent of the $50 billion-a-year U.S. parcel delivery business.

Truckload. In contrast to PX, the TL industry moves loads directly from an origin (typically a customer's shipping dock) to a destination (typically a customer's receiving dock) without the use of a terminal system and only uses tractor-trailers. The typical TL load weighs 10,000 to 48,000 pounds. There are approximately 150 million TL shipments annually, each shipment represents the movement of a tractor-trailer. TL carriers require little or no material handling equipment but may use specialized equipment for special commodities.

As indicated by Table 1, the TL industry is considerably larger than LTL and PX and roughly equivalent to private trucking, i.e., trucking fleets that are owned by companies not in the freight transportation business. TL generates approximately 38% of the revenue generated by the trucking industry, just slightly more than the revenue generated by private fleets.

Barriers to entry into TL are considerably lower than other segments of the for-hire trucking industry. As a result, there is a large number of TL carriers, relative to the other industry segments (Table 4), these numbers do not include the large numbers of owner-operators who own only a single tractor-trailer. In 1997, only 63 of more than 15,000 TL firms operated ten or more separate business establishments (Swan and Burkes, 2005). The four largest firms by revenue earned only 11.4% of the total revenue generated by the for-hire TL industry. The national TL carriers generating the greatest revenues (2000 revenue in parenthesis) are Schneider National ($3.1 billion), J. B. Hunt ($2.2 billion), Swift ($1.3 billion), and Werner Enterprises ($1.2 billion).

Industry Segment	2001 Revenues in billions $	Percent of Total Revenues	Number of Firms	% of Total
Building Materials	2.0	2.13	60	2.54
Bulk	2.2	2.34	98	4.15
General Freight TL	50.0	53.19	1,199	50.74
Less-than-Truckload	21.0	22.34	181	7.66
Household Goods	4.5	4.79	88	3.72
Heavy Machinery	3.1	3.30	84	3.55
Motor Vehicles	7.5	0.80	27	1.14
Other Specialized	4.8	5.11	355	15.02
Package Courier	1.9	0.20	11	0.47
Refrigerated	3.2	3.40	136	5.76
Tank	2.2	2.34	124	5.25
Total	94.0	100.0	2,363	100.0

Table 4. Distribution of Revenues and Firms Across Major Segments of the Trucking Industry, 2001. *(Corsi, 2005)*

Less-Than-Truckload. The less-than-truckload (TLT) industry specializes in loads larger than the typical loads for PX and smaller than loads for a full truckload, in the 50 to 10,000 pound range, averaging roughly 1,000 pounds a load. Similar to PX, LTL carriers have fleets for pick up and delivery, inter-terminal tractor-trailers, and a terminal system. The pick up and delivery vehicles can be straight trucks or can be tractors that pull small trailers (or 'pups'). Consolidation and de-consolidation occurs at the terminals, and the inter-terminal tractor-trailers haul consolidated loads between terminals. LTL tractor-trailers carry considerably fewer (but heavier) loads, relative to PX tractor-trailers. Inside the terminals, the LTL material handling equipment is less specialized than the material handling equipment for PX. As indicated in Table 1, the TL segment of the for-hire trucking industry generates over four times the revenue of LTL, yet the LTL industry is the second largest segment of the for-hire trucking industry and generates more revenue than does the rail and rail intermodal industries combined. Table 5 summarizes the growth of general freight carrier firms from 1984, just after deregulation, to 2000.

General Freight Carrier Firms 1984-2000	1984 Rev ($000,000)	1994 Rev ($000,000)	2000 Rev ($000,000)
United Parcel Service	6,196	14,697[b]	29,795[b]
Federal Express (now FedEx)	NA	NA	19,629[b]
Con-Way Transportation	New	1,983[b]	5,572[b]
Yellow Freight System Inc. (now Yellow Trans.)	1,344	2,197	3,588
Schneider National Carriers	193	1,325[a]	3,100
Roadway Express Inc.	1,401	2,137	3,040
USF Freightways Corp.	453	800	2,539[b]
Consolidated Freightways Corp. of De	1,284	1,847	2,352
ANR Freight System	174	1,513	Closed
J.B. Hunt Transport, Inc.	98	1,069	2,160
P*I*E Nationwide Inc	891	Closed	Closed

McLean Trucking	488	Closed	Closed
ABF Freight Systems Inc.	386	903	1,840
Landstar Ranger, Inc.	4	383	1,418
Swift Transportation Co., Inc.	NA	360	1,259
Werner Enterprises, Inc.	53	516	1,215
Overnite Transportation Co.	414	1,037	1,114
Watkins Motor Lines Inc.	115	488	944
Carolina Freight Carriers Corp.	373	624	Purchased
American Freightways Inc.	NA	466	NA
Preston Trucking Company Inc.	285	419	Closed
Total for LTL Carriers Reporting to BTS	1984	1994	2000
Total Revenue ($000,000)	15,347	15,452	19,691
Average Revenue per Carrier ($000,000)	43	231	246
Number of Carriers	353	67	80
Total for TL Gen. Frt. Carriers reporting to BTS	1984	1994	2000
Total Revenue ($000,000)	14,998	28,294	61,795
Average Revenue per Carrier ($000,000)	19	103	31
Number of Carriers	803	276	2026

TABLE 5. Growth of general freight carriers: *a = CCJ (1995) b = substantial non-trucking revenue* ▨ *= LTL Carriers. (Corsi, 2005)*

Third Party Logistics Industry

A third party logistics (3PL) provider is an external supplier of logistics services. One of the several logistics functions provided by a 3PL is to manage the movement of goods from one firm (e.g., a supplier to an OEM) to a second firm (e.g., the OEM), and hence the 3PL represents the third firm in this relationship. The majority of 3PLs are companies that expanded their services from a particular segment of an industry in logistics or a stakeholder firm in the logistics industry. The industry from which the 3PL evolved serves as a useful categorization of the 3PL industry. These industries, and examples of concomitant firms, are given below (Langley, 2005):

- Transportation-based (Ryder, Menlo Logistics, Schneider Logistics, FedEx Logistics, UPS Logistics)

- Warehouse/Distribution-based (DSC Logistics, USCO, Exel)

- Forwarder-based (UTi Worldwide, Expeditors, Kuehne & Nagle, Fritz, which has recently been acquired by UPS, Circle, C.H. Robinson, Hub Group)

- Financial-based (Cass Information, Commercial Traffic Corporation, GE Information Services, FleetBoston Financial Corporation)

- Information-based (Transplace).

REGULATION-DRIVEN TRANSFORMATIONS

We now focus on the effect of the three forms of regulation - economic, coordinative and social - on the structure and transformation of the freight system. The most dramatic change in regulatory policy toward transportation, one which was directly transformative of the industry and that laid the foundation for future transformation was the ending of economic regulation of the trucking industry in 1979 and 1980. This legislated change altered the structure of the industry, drove many incumbent firms from the industry, opened opportunities for newer firms to enter, and created an environment that has supported the rapid growth and diversification of the freight system over the last quarter century. It has had less beneficial consequences for drivers. Before discussing the effect of economic deregulation, which has helped to enable the impacts on the industry due to customer business practices, we briefly describe the origins and structure of economic regulation.

Economic Regulation[2]

National economic regulation of transportation began with the railroads in the 1880s. The impetus for regulation remains an issue of heated debate between those who believe that it was brought about to protect farmers, rural areas, and the citizenry from the rapacity of monopolistic railroads and those who contend it was supported by the railroads as a means of ending periodic disastrous price competition (Kolko, 1963). Whatever the origins, the Interstate Commerce Commission (ICC) Act of 1887 gave the ICC the power to establish prices for moving specific commodities between specific places. The ICC was also vested with the power to establish hours of work for operating employees so as to better safeguard the public.

Although trucks were used for local freight early in the last century, they only emerged as a significant factor in the movement of freight outside of metropolitan areas during the 1920s. The growth of the industry was spurred by the availability of surplus military trucks at the end of the first World War, a decrease in the size of manufactured products which allowed effective transportation by truck rather than rail and, finally, the damage to roads due to rising truck traffic that increased the public's demand for public investment in highways and other roads. Federal legislation passed in 1916 and 1921 established the current structure of shared Federal and state financing of capital road projects. Technological change, including improved road building technologies, truck tires and engines in the 1920s resulted in a trucking industry which was ever more capable of moving large amounts of freight both within and between cities. The large road building projects undertaken by the Federal government in the 1930s helped to accelerate this trend.

The trucking industry was largely unregulated in this early period of development. State regulation was limited by constitutional limits on the state's ability to regulate inter-state commerce, combined with a lack of Federal oversight. This changed with the passage of the Motor Carrier Act (MCA) of 1935, which gave the ICC regulatory powers over the industry. These powers were used to establish stricter limits on the weight and length of trucks, the working hours of truck drivers and, for the first time, regulated firm entry, routes, and prices. Trucking firms were required to obtain a permit of 'convenience and necessity' from the ICC in order to carry specific commodities between specified points. Regional rate bureaus established prices for transportation. Certain practices, such as back-hauls, were banned as they were viewed as creating a level of price competition that was destructive to firms and that retarded the development of the industry.

Economic regulation shaped the trucking industry in the period from 1935 to 1978. The ICC granted existing firms certificates of convenience. However,

---

[2] This discussion is derived from "The Evolution of the U.S. Motor Carrier Industry" by Starr McMullen (McMullen, 2005).

obtaining new entry to routes was difficult because firms had to demonstrate both a need for the new service and that incumbent carriers would not be harmed. As a result, firms often expanded through acquisition of other carriers, and the number of carriers regulated by the ICC declined from 26,000 to about 15,000 between 1935 and 1973 (McMullen, 1987). The system of economic regulation limited the types of services trucking firms could offer. Entry and routing restrictions made it difficult to develop LTL services; it took several decades for UPS to obtain the certificates needed to provide package express services throughout the United States that did not depend on other firms. Rate setting favored the industry as, by reducing competition between carriers, it made it relatively easy to pass cost increases on to customers and so provided high levels of profit to firms. These gains were shared with employees in the industry through collective bargaining by the Teamsters union.

Another effect of economic regulation was the growth of private carriage. In response to the costs and inefficiencies associated with regulation, private firms developed their own trucking fleets to move goods. As these firms only moved commodities for their parent companies, they were not subject to economic regulation and could engage in practices, such as backhauls, not allowed to for-hire carriers. Trucking firms that provided services to a small number of firms were also largely exempt from economic regulation. Both types of operations experienced considerable growth during the regulatory period.

Regulation did not hamper the rapid growth of the industry and may have favored trucking over other forms of freight transportation. The railroads had supported the regulation of trucking to reduce the increasing competition from that industry. Regulation established common rates for commodities across forms of transportation. Before, but particularly after World War II, increasing diversity in consumer products and rising concern about the quality of service caused shippers to favor truck transportation over rail except for bulk commodities. The requirement of common rates, which did not allow for differences in the quality of services between modes of transportation, favored trucks over rail. Stricter weight limits imposed by the ICC also spurred technological improvement, such as lighter weight aluminum trailers that allowed trucks to carry additional cargo. Although regulation acted to reduce the number of firms in the industry and likely increased the costs of transportation, the number of trucks used for freight transportation grew rapidly in the period from 1935 to 1978 (Table 6) and the industry grew from a small industry to the dominant provider of freight transport (Table 7).

The MCA of 1980 eliminated economic regulation of inter-state trucking. This change had its intellectual origins in the rethinking of the arguments about natural monopoly and destructive competition, which had originally under girded the move to regulation in the 1930s. Lobbying by large shippers who believed that deregulation would result in substantial savings was also an important impetus toward deregulation, as was the effort of the Carter Administration to reduce inflationary pressures in the economy by eliminating government intervention in the economy in a number of sectors, including airlines and trucking.

YEAR	NUMBER OF		
	Private Carrier	For Hire	Total Trucks
1904	---	---	700
1910	---	---	10,123
1920	---	---	1,107,639
1930	---	---	3,578,747
1940	---	---	4,590,386
1950	---	---	8,272,153
1960	10,559,300 (93%)	940,700 (8%)	11,352,618
1970	17,016,800 (96%)	783,200 (4%)	17,754,468
1980	30,692,700 (95%)	1,404,700 (5%)	32,238,223
1988	---	---	42,529,000*

TABLE 6. U.S. Truck Registrations. Figures rounded to closest thousand. "---" data not available. Note: Comparable data for subsequent years were not available. *Source: (McMullen, 2005).*

Year	Truck	Rail	Pipeline	Water	Air	Other
1948	23.2	71.1	3.2	1.6	.8	0.0
1958	38.8	53.2	4.6	2.1	1.4	0.0
1968	50.9	41.2	4.1	1.3	2.5	0.0
1978	74.1	12.8	3.0	7.1	1.3	1.7
1988	76.9	9.6	2.5	6.5	3.3	1.1
1998	80.7	11.0	2.9	2.6	3.3	N/A

TABLE 7. Percent of Total U.S. Freight Revenue by Mode (%). *Source: (McMullen, 2005).*

Economic Deregulation

Even before the passage of the MCA of 1980, the ICC had begun to reduce entry restrictions and loosen rate regulation to permit firms to compete on the basis of price. The long trend toward fewer firms in the trucking industry was reversed as new entrants obtained authorities for routes. However, many of these entrants were not new. They were either small firms, owner-operators who had worked for a firm with an authority, or firms with authorities that took advantage of the changing regulatory environment to offer new services and new routes. The MCA of 1980 removed remaining barriers to entry and ended rate setting in inter-state trucking.

Deregulation resulted in a fundamental transformation of the industry. As indicated, there was wide scale entry into the industry, but also wide scale exit. Many venerable firms were not able to operate in the new environment and went bankrupt or were absorbed by other firms. There was also structural change. Prior to deregulation, it was difficult for a single firm to provide LTL services over a large area and many trucking firms combined LTL and TL services. After deregulation TL and LTL services split off into different firms and LTL carriers restructured to provide services over larger geographic areas. LTL firms were able to restructure their networks to realize economies of scope and, by expanding their networks, avoid the problems inherent in having to inter-line freight to other carriers in order to deliver outside a regionally limited network.

The end of economic regulation also allowed firms far greater flexibility in the types of services they supplied and the speed with which new services could be introduced, thus allowing the transportation service industry to more effectively respond to customer business practices. Services, such as taking several 10,000 pound loads from different shippers to different consignees or expedited services that would have been difficult to provide under economic regulation, can now be offered subject only to the creativity of the parties and economic sustainability of the service.

Finally, private carriage declined as a result of deregulation as non-trucking firms no longer benefited economically from having their own trucking services. Although many non-trucking firms, such as Wal-Mart, have retained fleets to move goods from their warehouses and cross-docks to stores, they no longer have fleets to move goods from manufacturers to warehouses or cross-docks. Rather these services are almost universally supplied by trucking firms.

The MCA of 1980 largely ended economic regulation in interstate trucking, but the majority of states continued intra-state economic regulations into the 1990s. Although nine states had eliminated economic regulation by 1990, forty-one still regulated entry and rates for trucking within their boarders. The Airport Improvement Act of 1995 eliminated state or local regulation of trucking rates, routes or services but allowed states to continue to regulate safety, financial fitness, insurance, vehicle size and weight, and highway route controls for hazardous materials. Estimates of the effect of state regulation on trucking costs prior to this final deregulation suggested that such regulation imposed substantial costs on shippers. Comparison of data on cost per ton-mile for intra-state shipping suggests that this deregulation had modest if any effects on the growth of the industry or revenue per ton-mile (Table 8).

Year	Number of Trucking and Courier Establishments	Real Average Freight Revenue Per Ton-Mile** (1982 prices)	Nominal Average Freight Revenue Per Ton-Mile
1970	64,756	21.79	8.5
1980	69,796	20.45	11.6
1990	90,709	20.05	18.0
1994	108,971	19.84	24.4
1995	112,887	19.60	25.0
1996	116,861	19.84	25.1
1997	121,111	19.77	26.0
1998	119,572	20.00	26.2
1999	120,687	19.69	26.2
2000	122,713	19.56	27.0

TABLE 8. Market Trends in the Motor Carrier Sector. Source: (*Peoples, 2005*)

Coordinative Regulation[3]

Although economic regulation has been the focus of research on government intervention in trucking, coordinative regulation has played an equally central role in the development of the industry. The federal system of the United States has historically delegated much of the decision-making authority over truck transportation to the states. As indicated in our discussion of the Airport Improvement Act, states were allowed to retain their authority over truck safety, financial fitness, insurance, vehicle sizes and weights. Cutting against the delegation of these powers has been the increasingly national nature of the truck transportation system. Differences in state regulations about length, weight, the number of trailers that can be pulled by a tractor, insurance and safety can cause substantial problems in a national system. For example, differences in weight requirements between states could force trucking firms to limit truck weights to the minimum of the allowable rates on the shortest route, take a longer route so as to be able to load more heavily, or design loads so that there would be partial unloading before entering a state with a low weight limit. Similarly, differences in state standards with regard to length and how length was determined, some states considered only the length of the trailer, others the length of the tractor and trailer, has in the past caused problems for trucking firms and for the transportation system.

The need for common standards has moved Congress to incorporate common minimum standards for trucks into legislation that funds state highway programs. Although states may retain standards below these common minima, they can do so only by forgoing substantial federal transportation funds. As no state has chosen to follow this course, the current national standard for limits on truck weight is 80,000 pounds. The national standard for limits on trailer length is 48 feet for single trailers and 28 feet for trailers pulled in tandem. The standard for width on the interstate highway system is 102 inches. Hawaii and New Mexico permit weights beyond the national standard, twelve states permit trailers longer than the national standard. The Transportation Research Board has supported increasing the national standard for trailer weight to 90,000 pounds and increasing the length of tandem trailers to 33 feet.

Social Regulation

Although competitive markets in which there are limited external costs are efficient at allocating resources, there is no assurance that such markets promote non-economic social goals. Rather, such goals are achieved through *social regulation*. For example, we assure minimum quality standards for food and drugs

---

[3] The discussion of coordinative and social regulation is derived from the work of James Peoples (Peoples, 2005) and discussions with Kristen Monaco.

though legislated standards and the administrative rule making and enforcement of the Food and Drug Administration. Similarly, the Security and Exchange Commission (and its sister agencies) enacts and enforces administrative rules that establish and enforce rules of conduct and reporting for large parts of the financial services industry.

Social regulation of trucking is focused on protecting public safety, protecting the labor force from unsafe or unhealthy conditions or, more recently, providing adequate levels of homeland security. Public and worker safety was initially overseen by the ICC but was transferred to the Federal Highway Administration in 1966 and now resides in the Federal Motor Carrier Safety Administration (FMCSA). The Transportation Security Administration (TSA), which is now part of the Department of Homeland Security but used to be part of the Department of Transportation, oversees homeland security issues. Although social regulation of trucking includes inspection of trucks and enforcement of requirements for safe operation of equipment, the areas of social regulation which have been prominent in the last decade have been the regulation of hours of service for drivers, the requirements for obtaining commercial drivers' licenses, and new rules for reviewing the background of drivers involved in moving hazardous materials.

Transportation industries have required extended hours of work from their employees. Because of the public hazard posed by the operation of transportation equipment by sleep deprived and physically exhausted employees, urban governments began to regulate the hours of work of street railway employees in the 1870s. The ICC Act of 1887 placed the hours of work of railroad employees under the control of the ICC. Section 204(a) of the MCA of 1935 gave the ICC regulatory authority over qualifications for becoming a truck driver and over drivers working hours. Following hearings in 1936 and 1937 and after further negotiations with interested parties, the ICC enacted hours of service regulations that limited drivers to 15 hours of work in a 24-hour period. Working hours were divided into 10 hours for driving and up to 5 hours of non-driving work time, such as loading, unloading and completing paperwork prior to a mandatory break of eight hours of more (NPRM, 2000, p. 25547). A driver's weekly hours of work were limited to 60 hours in a rolling seven-day period or 70 hours in a rolling 8-day period.

The hours of service regulations were initially structured around a 24-hour work cycle, but this was abandoned in the 1962 revisions. These revisions allowed drivers to begin a new 15-hour work cycle after an eight-hour break, allowing the start time for work to be moved up each day. For example, a driver who began driving at 6 a.m. on a Monday, drove for 10 hours, spent 1 hour on other work, and then took an eight-hour break, could resume work at 1 a.m. on Tuesday. The movement away from a 24-hour cycle has been a source of chronic fatigue and long-term health problems for drivers (Belzer, et al., 2002). The practice of allowing drivers to extend their working time by not counting off-duty breaks against the 15-hour limit on total working time intensified these problems as drivers would, when possible, covert waiting and non-driving work time into off-duty breaks.

Compliance with regulations on working time has been recognized as an industry problem for many years. Drivers are motivated to work beyond the hours permitted by the regulations due to the increased income realized by driving longer hours. They are also frequently compelled to work excessive hours by the unrealistic schedules established by their firms in cooperation with shippers and consignees. A University of Michigan Trucking Industry Program survey of 1,000 drivers conducted in 1997 and 1998 found that drivers averaged 62.5 hours of work in the prior seven days, half of drivers worked at least 60 hours over that period and a quarter worked 70 hours. The survey also found that over half of the respondents reported violating the HOS regulations at least once in the past 30 days (Belman, Monaco & Brooks, 2005).

The ubiquity of these violations has several sources. One is an obsolete system of tracking a driver's work time. Drivers are required to keep paper logs of their driving, on-duty not driving and off-duty time, but these logs are easily gamed. The logs are not numbered and this makes it possible for drivers to keep multiple logs to conceal violations of the hours of service regulations. Drivers may also cover violations by not keeping their logs up to date as the penalties for not keeping the logs are lower than those for violating the hours of service regulations. Finally, the hours of service regulations are unique among labor laws in that the employee, rather than the employer, is responsible for violations. Except in extreme cases, trucking firms, shippers and consignees are shielded from the consequences of unrealistic scheduling. The lack of industry concern with drivers' hours of work has become embedded in scheduling and routing software. Prior to a recent change in the hours of service regulations, this software did not include constraints for drivers driving or working hours; a driver's time was treated as a non-binding constraint.

Preliminary efforts to revise the hours of service regulations came as early as the mid-1970s. However, despite the changes and added pressures brought about by deregulation in the 1980s, the hours of service regulations were not revised until 2003 and only went into effect in January 2004. The most important changes in the regulations have been (1) the extension of driving time to 11 hours from the prior 10 hours, (2) the reduction in total working time prior to a break from 15 to 14 hours, (3) the requirement that drivers take a mandatory 8-hour break 14 clock hours after they begin work without regard to any off-duty breaks during the 14 hours, and (4) drivers are allowed to restart with a new 60 hour 7 day cycle after 34 continuous hours off duty. The requirement for a hard shutdown 14 clock hours after beginning work is particularly important as, if enforced, it will end the practice of extending the work day by mis-recording waiting time and other on-duty non-driving time as off-duty and preventing drivers from extending their work day beyond 14 hours. The lack of an effective means of monitoring drivers working time (the Department of Transportation continues to consider, but not require, the use of electronic on-board recorders as replacements for paper logs) may undercut the advances offered by the new regulations. The new regulations have been challenged as insufficient by highway safety groups and were set aside by the U.S. Court of Appeals for the District of Columbia on July 16th, 2004. The rules were allowed to remain in effect while the Department of Transportation studied and responded to issues that the court ruled it had failed to address in its initial rule making.

Commercial Driver's Licenses

Social regulation encompasses state and federal interventions beyond the regulation of drivers' working hours. There is increasing regulation of drivers with regard to the driver's background, skills, and driving records in order to better assure public safety and security. Prior to 1986, the United States did not have a common minimum standard for being licensed to drive a truck. Although some states have extensive licensing requirements that included both written tests and skills tests in an appropriate vehicle, other states had much more limited testing and some allowed drivers with automotive licenses to drive any class of truck. It was also possible for a driver to hold licenses in several states.

Increasing truck traffic and congestion on the nations highways led to the passage of the Commercial Motor Vehicle Safety Act (CMVSA) of 1986 and the establishing of the National Commercial Drivers License program. States continue to issue drivers' licenses but must follow federal guidelines for the classification of commercial motor vehicles and meet minimum standards for testing applicants for commercial licenses. The CMVSA prohibits drivers from holding multiple licenses and requires that applicants be tested in the type of vehicle he/she plans to drive. License examinations are required to meet minimum federal standards and include both a general knowledge and a driving skills component. Applicants must also be physically qualified to attain a commercial driver's license (CDL). Vision requirements establish applicants have a distance visual acuity of at least 20/40 in each eye, with or without corrective lenses, and a field vision of at least 70 degrees in the horizontal meridian in each eye. Applicants must also be able to recognize the colors of traffic signals and devices showing standard red, green, and amber.

The Motor Carrier Safety Improvement Act (MCSIA) of 1999 further tightened the requirements to hold a CDL. The FMCSA made significant changes in the regulations for a CDL in expanding the definition of 'serious traffic violations', extending reviews of drivers' records, and the disqualification of commercial drivers for violations while driving a non-commercial motor vehicle. Regulations added in 2004 established more stringent training requirements for new commercial motor vehicle operators and required that employers share information on drivers' records and history.

Homeland Security[4]

Homeland security issues have become increasingly important to the transportation industries after September 11, 2001 and particularly since the TSA was established by the Aviation and Transportation Security Act on November 19, 2001. While issues of appropriate handling of hazardous materials, hiring of employees, and addressing the financial and public relations consequences of catastrophic accidents was once a largely a financial calculus, these issues have taken on new meaning since 9/11.

For the trucking industry, homeland security is concerned for the most part with the movement of hazardous materials (hazmat). For example, a gasoline tank truck carries about as much fuel as a wide-body airliner. The detonation of such a load in a densely populated area could cause severe devastation, albeit in a limited area. Other loads of hazardous materials, such as explosives or radioactive materials, could similarly cause substantial devastation. Public discussion of these issues has tended to focus on technological fixes, such as real time tracking of trucks with loads of hazardous materials and systems for shutting down such loads if they deviate sufficiently from pre-established routes.

The implementation of homeland security rules has, however, focused on the screening of drivers applying for and holding hazmat certification on their CDL. The TSA has, as authorized by the USA Patriot Act and the Safe Explosives Act, required the collection of background biographical information including criminal records and fingerprints of all drivers holding a hazmat certification beginning May 31, 2005. Convictions for crimes including simple possession of drugs permanently disqualify drivers from holding a hazmat certificate as does the variously defined offenses of 'dishonesty, fraud or misrepresentation'.

Although the goals of the TSA regulations are laudable, in combination with the tightening of the requirements for a CDL by the FMCSA, these new rules will create severe problems for many drivers and substantial problems for the industry. Truck driving has historically been an industry in which, in the words of the Director of Research of the Brotherhood of Teamster's:

> "Truck driving provided a stable, albeit moderate, income that was valuable to workers of ordinary educational background and opportunity. In addition, the truck cab was well suited to individuals, some of who had troubled work histories, who preferred less direct supervision and valued personal freedom and independence to a traditional office or factory setting." (Conyngham, 2005)

---

[4] This section is derived from Conyngham (2005)

As much as twenty percent of the driver labor force will be subject to TSA reviews and a substantial proportion of these individuals will be disqualified from driving hazmat. The potential impact is compounded by the legal and regulatory presumption that problems in a driver's record are disqualifying no matter how far in the past, the use of records from employers which may not be accurate and are not subject to vetting by the driver or driver representative and the lack of procedural and substantive due process in the administrative decision making. The problems are compounded because all hazmat is treated alike. Chemical waste, which does not pose homeland security hazards, and small quantities of hazmat materials such as medical radiological materials moved in LTL shipments are not distinguished from tank truck loads of gasoline or TL loads of explosives.

The new regulations will hopefully improve the security and safety of trucking operations, but it will also cause a significant portion of the trucking labor force to have to shift into less desirable positions and may cause a substantial number of drivers to leave the occupation. This will cause great hardship for a number of drivers, particularly those who have been drivers for many years, and will impede the continued growth of an industry that is already facing a shortage of labor. Greater attention to the drafting regulations to better assess the security threat posed by drivers, provide means to review any decisions and better distinguish loads that pose a security threat from those that do not, would be instrumental in reducing the negative individual and industry consequences of providing better homeland security.

TRUCK DRIVERS: TRANSFORMATION WITHOUT GAIN[5]

The last quarter century has seen a transformation of the trucking industry from a growing industry with a stable structure to one of explosive growth with dramatic changes in its structure and players. Entirely new business and sectors have arisen within trucking over this period and many firms have experienced rapid growth and evolution. The changes of the last twenty-five years have clearly benefited shippers and consignees, many firms, and much of the managerial and professional staff in the industry.

In contrast, drivers, who comprise more than a third of the nine million employees in the industry, have experienced substantial change and dislocation but little or no gain from this transformation. Data from the March, May and Outgoing Rotation files of the Current Population Survey suggest that inflation adjusted earnings have remained relatively flat for more than two decades.[6] Adjusted for inflation and reported in year 2000 dollars, the average annual earnings of drivers was $32,603 in 1975; in 2000 this figure was only $31,633,

---

[5] This section is derived from Belman, LaFontaine and Monaco (2005).
[6] Extensive information on the Current Population Survey can be found at www.bls.census.gov/cps/ and at www.unicon.com

almost $1,000 below 1975 earnings.   The latter figure represents substantial recovery from the $28,917 annual average in 1984, shortly after deregulation of the industry.

A similar pattern is found in weekly earnings (Figure 2). Employee drivers earned an average of $635 in 1975 (in year 2000 inflation adjusted dollars) and $705 in 1978. This declined to $571 in 1986 and recovered to $627 in the year 2000. For-hire drivers fared consistently better throughout this period. In 1975, for-hire drivers average $737 per week against $574 for drivers in private carriage. In 2000, the former were earning $704 weekly against $556 for the latter.

Although the year 2000 annual earnings of drivers are close to the median family income for families with a single working adult, most drivers are working close to if not well in excess of 60 hours per week. As mentioned above, data from the Sloan Foundation Trucking Industry Program survey of truck drivers suggests over-the-road drivers averaged 62 hours of work in the prior seven days, two hours more than permitted under the hours of service regulations. Outside of the organized sector, benefits such as holidays and sick leave, deferred compensation plans, pensions and health care are relatively meager. Nonunion employee drivers average 3 holidays and no sick days, 57 percent report participating in deferred compensation plan (401(k) or similar), 22 percent report participating in a traditional pension plan, 15 percent have an IRA but 88 percent have health insurance from some source. In contrast, owner-operators report no holiday or sick days, 13 percent participate in a deferred compensation plan, 13 percent participate in a pension plan, 36 percent have an IRA and 68 percent participate in a health insurance plan from some source. Putting these pieces together, drivers work about half again as many hours as the typical full time employee to earn a middle class income that lacks many of the non-wage benefits typically associated with middle class employment.

The relatively low level of compensation is somewhat puzzling given the rapid expansion in demand for drivers. Truck driving has been among the fastest growing occupations in the United States over the last quarter century (Figure 3). Employment has slightly more than doubled over this period, from 1,495,607 in 1975 to 3,013,664 in 2000.   Although the concurrent effects of the double dip recession of 1979 – 1982 and deregulation slightly reduced the total number of drivers in the early 1980s, growth in the driver labor force has been between fast and explosive almost every year since 1983. Further evidence of an ongoing demand for labor is reflected in the almost unbroken reporting of a shortage of drivers by the industry press since the late 1980s.

How might the stagnation of wages be reconciled with the rapid increase in the employment of drivers and the perception of a labor shortage? Economic theory would suggest that, all things constant, rapid increases in demand and labor shortages should be accompanied by considerable growth in wages. In this instance, several factors act to dampen such market forces. First, firm perception of a labor shortage is conditioned by their continual need to recruit new workers. Although drivers remain in the occupation for many years, movement between firms is common. The median driver has been with their firm for less than two years despite having nine years experience as a driver (Belman, Monaco & Brooks, 2005, pp 79 - 84). Firms are then continually losing their drivers to other trucking firms and having to insure the expense and trouble of recruiting replacement drivers. A second factor that has acted to dampen wage increase in the face a growing demand for drivers has been the relatively ease with which workers can enter the occupation. Although considerable on the job experience is needed to become fully fluent in the work of truck driving, the minimum skills required to work in the TL sector require about five weeks of classroom and instructed driving and several months of driving with an experienced driver. The relative ease of entry by inexperienced workers has made driving an occupation of last resort for many workers. In combination with the displacement of workers from traditional blue collar sectors in the 1980s, and the declining availability of jobs for those with less than or just a high school degree, there has been a sufficient pool of workers to maintain the rapid growth of the driver labor force.

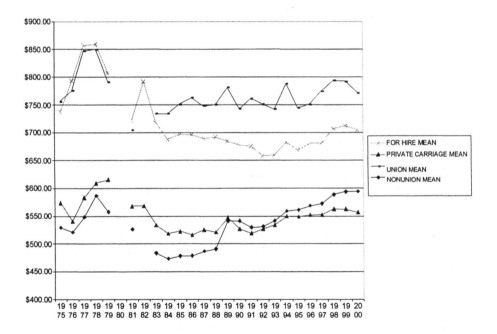

FIGURE 2. Trends in Weekly Earnings

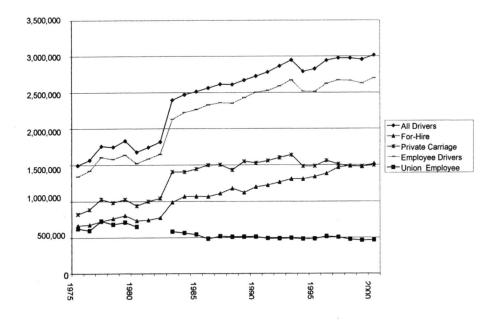

FIGURE 3. Trends in Number of Drivers

CUSTOMER-DRIVEN TRANSFORMATIONS

We now examine transformations in the freight transportation industry that are due to attempting to respond more effectively to the needs of the marketplace. The ability to so respond has been, in large part, due to economic deregulation, as indicated earlier in this chapter. We now describe how lean manufacturing, the Internet, outsourcing, expanded services, and off-shoring have affected the industry and how new forms of information technology have enabled these changes.

Lean Manufacturing

The Toyota production system - lean manufacturing, or more broadly, lean thinking – has required the logistics industry to raise its level of performance (e.g., lead times with smaller means and variances) in order to reliably meet dock time delivery windows so that inventories and their concomitant costs can be kept as low as possible. Lean manufacturing has also prompted a different type of buyer-supplier relationship, whether the supplier provides goods or services. Traditionally, particularly in the U.S. automotive industry, the original equipment manufacturer (OEM) would select a suppler from a large supplier pool on a very cost-focused basis for a short contractual period, based on a specific design developed by the OEM. A form of buyer-supplier relationship that has resulted from the lean movement is more of a partnership, based on longer contractual periods from a smaller number of potential suppliers, where the design is described functionally and hence requires supplier design, and sometimes R&D, capability. This relationship shift has tended to lead to a more efficient, agile, and consolidated supplier base for both product and service supplier industries. Further discussion can be found in (Karlin & Liker, 2005).

Disintermediation, Internet, and Expansion of PX into LTL

The ability of the package express industry to deliver goods (under 150 pounds) directly to residences, and the emerging use of the Internet for placing customer orders, has enabled certain businesses, e.g., Dell and Amazon, to move goods from the manufacturer directly to the customer at home - thus avoiding the retail store and hence reducing holding costs. This fundamental restructuring of traditional supply chains has shifted the movement of goods from TL, and perhaps to a lesser extent, LTL, to PX. In general, TL will be a loser and PX will be a winner for any business model that focuses on minimum quantities delivered expediently, particularly business-to-customer (B2C) sales. We see LTL more likely to lose, rather than win, in these restructured supply chains due to the facts that much of the movement of B2C goods is light in weight. In 2001, 43 percent of online sales were due to computer hardware, apparel and accessories, consumer electronics, and books (Corridore, 2003, p. 11). Further, PX is developing the interest and capability to effectively go head-to-head with LTL (e.g., FedEx Ground, the recent acquisition of Overnite by UPS) for what would be considered light LTL, but heavy PX, loads.

Outsourcing

Another business 'best practice' that has affected the logistics industry is outsourcing of non-core competencies. Many businesses tend to view logistics as (1) not central to their core business and (2) a business function that is often less expensive handled outside, rather than inside, the firm. Outsourcing the transportation function has lead to the examination of other functions that the transportation provider might provide, and these include the logistics function, assuming responsibility for in-plant inventory, taking components to the assembly line, and more generally helping to manage the firm's supply chain. This expansion of services has helped to enable the birth and growth of the third party logistics industry and is prevalent throughout the trucking industry.

Sometimes outsourcing the logistics function evolves organically. One of the reasons why private fleets often are not as efficient as for-hire carriers is that backhauls for for-hire carriers are not restricted to the loads of any one company. Many private fleets then look for backhauls that are not necessarily company related. If the success in attracting backhauls is high (and hence customer density is increased), efficiency is improved, then the company itself may benefit from the reduced transportation costs. A natural progression would result in spinning off the logistics function. Barriers for doing so are labor agreements and a reduction in control. Reduction in control is often considered a significant issue if company drivers have direct contact with customers.

Expanded Services

Most TL firms focus on a limited number of activities; indeed, TL firms are often characterized by their limitations: tank operations, dry vans firms, refrigerated carriers, car haulers, and flatbed haulers. However, several of the leading, larger national carriers, e.g., J.B. Hunt and Schneider National, recently have expanded their service offerings. For example, Schneider National service offerings include Dedicated, TruckRail/InterModal, Brokerage, One-Way Van Truckload, and Expedited (www.schneider.com).

In LTL, Con-Way (www.cnf.com) is an example of a transportation company that started as an LTL and recently has been expanding services significantly. Con-Way was founded in 1983 with initial focus on service-sensitive regional LTL service for the commercial and industrial business-to-business (B2B) customer. This basic business model was in response to three emerging trends in the early 1980's: the need for increased delivery reliability, the deregulation of the U.S. trucking industry, and the use of regional, rather than national, LTL service. Initial expansion was geographic. The first two Con-Way carriers, Con-Way Western Express (CWX) and Con-Way Central Express (CCX), started operations in 1983. Con-Way Southern Express (CSE) and Con-Way Southwest Express (CSW) were started in 1986 and 1989, respectively, and merged in 1994 as Con-Way Southern Express (CSE). Con-Way Intermodal (CWI) was formed in 1991 to provide service for TL shipments via rail. During the mid-1990's, the three regional LTLs (CWX, CCX, and CSE) carriers began offering inter-regional service. Con-Way Canada Express was formed in 2000 in response, in part, to the North American Free Trade Agreement. Con-Way Truckload Services (CWT) was formed in 1995 for expedited regional and inter-regional TL operations. (CWI and CWT were sold in 2000 due in large part to capital constraints at the time on the parent company, CNF.)

In 1996, Con-Way NOW was begun to provide dedicated, time-certain transportation for emergency and urgent shipments throughout North America. Con-Way NOW began air-expedited service in 2000 and now has several air options that include: same-day delivery, time-definite delivery, dedicated air charter, and next-day air delivery. Con-Way Integrated Services (CIS) was started in 1998 (later renamed Con-Way Logistics, CLI, in 2002) in response to growing customer interest in integrated transportation solutions (e.g., integrated supply chain services and complete logistics solutions) from a single source (one-stop shopping/shipping). Con-Way Air Express (CAX), an asset-light airfreight forwarder, was started in 2001. Consistent with the downturn in the economy, and at variance with the long-standing focus on service-based products, Con-Way introduced new price-sensitive offerings in 2002 under the name "Value Zone", two of which are Con-Way Full Load and Con-Way Deferred (an intermodal service).

The PX industry has seen an even greater interest in expanded services. We now describe the UPS expansion; a similar, in many ways parallel, story of service expansion exists for FedEx. UPS began in 1907 as a service that delivered by ground packages, notes, baggage, and food from restaurants. Initial expansion was geographic, domestic at first and very recently international. UPS entered the domestic overnight air delivery business in the early 1980's in order to accommodate customer demand for faster service. In 1985, UPS began international air package and document service, and in 1988, UPS received authorization to become an airline. UPSnet, a global electronic data communications network, was developed in the early 1990's to provide support for international business. Package tracking became available in 1994 via UPS.com.

In 1995, the UPS Logistics Group was formed to provide supply chain management solutions and consulting services to the international customer. At the same time, UPS began offering same-day, 'next flight out' service. In 1998 UPS Capital was founded to provide integrated financial services, completing the service offerings in moving goods, moving information, and providing capital that make up commerce. UPS Supply Chain Solutions was formed in 2000 to provide integrated logistics, global freight, financial services, mail services, and consulting services for global supply chains. UPS Supply Chain Solutions is comprised of UPS Capital, UPS Logistics Group, UPS Freight Services, UPS Mail Innovations, and UPS Consulting. In 2001, UPS acquired Mail Boxes Etc, which are now called the UPS Stores. Friedman (2005, pp. 141-150) provides an excellent illustration of how UPS has reinvented itself as a value added manager of dynamic supply chains for companies that include Toshiba, Papa John's, Nike, Jockey, HP, Segrest Farms, Plow & Hearth, and Ford.

Off-Shoring

A fundamental reason to outsource is that some other company can manufacture a subsystem or provide a service of sufficient quality less expensively that can the OEM. Often this other company is offshore, leading to more geographically distributed supply chains and requiring the logistics provider to have a global presence and contend with all the challenges of doing business internationally. International supply chains mean longer lead times, which usually means greater lead-time variability (and hence less supply chain reliability). Supply chain reliability is typically reduced further when goods cross international boarders or when the supply chain originates or goes through countries with emerging economies and developing transportation infrastructures. Such uncertainty tends to move supply chain design away from a primary focus on efficiency (and lean manufacturing) to a balance of efficiency and risk mitigation, particularly in light of major disruptions (e.g., SARS, labor disputes, terrorism and its threat, extreme weather) that geographically dispersed supply chains might experience, thus increasing logistics costs (both the transportation costs and the increase in inventory to serve as 'buffer' stock). Nevertheless, if the per unit price of a manufactured good is low enough to offset the added logistics cost, then it is good business to move off shore.

Information Technology

Advances in information technology, e.g., wireless communication, computation, and software, have had considerable impact on the logistics industry. Real-time (or near real-time) information about asset location, enabled by wireless (e.g., radio frequency identification, or RFID) and wire-line communications technologies, can have considerable value in improving the efficiency and mitigating risk (and, as an example, enhancing security) in supply chains. Further, decision support systems that address basic, important operations (e.g., routing and scheduling) are now feasible due to new algorithmic developments and more powerful and less expensive computing platforms. Further detail can be found in (Nagarajan, et al., forthcoming).

What impact have these technologies had on trucking operations? The Sloan Foundation Trucking Industry Program conducted a survey of more than 1,000 over-the-road truck drivers in the Midwest between 1997 and 1999 (Belman, Monaco & Brooks, 2005). Research with the data from the first wave of the survey found that:

> "drivers on satellite-equipped trucks realize 16.1% higher annual earnings [than otherwise similar drivers in trucks without satellite communications equipment]. The higher earnings are due to the increased mileage of such drivers, about 22,000 additional miles per year. Part of this mileage gain is explained by efficiencies provided by these systems, but drivers with satellites also work 16% more hours weekly. The increased hours would account for two-thirds of the increase in mileage, the remaining third is

associated with improved productivity and is captured entirely by firm." (Belman and Monaco, 2001)

CONCLUSIONS

This chapter has outlined how the logistics industry has fundamentally changed over several decades. This transformation has, in part, been driven by regulatory changes, including economic, coordinative, and social regulations. Customers have also driven transformation via lean manufacturing, disintermediation, the Internet, outsourcing, expanded services, off-shoring, and information technology. Consumers of logistics services have benefited substantially from these changes. In contrast, employees of the companies providing these services have not always benefited from the transformation of this industry.

REFERENCES

Belman, D., K.A. Monaco and T.J. Brooks, *Sailors of the Concrete Sea: The Work and Life of Truck Drivers*, East Lansing: MSU Press, 2005.

Belman, D. and K. A. Monaco, "The Effects of Deregulation, De-unionization, Technology, and Human Capital on the Work and Work Lives of Truck Drivers", Industrial and Labor Relations Review, March, 2001, pp. 502 - 524.

Belzer, Michael, Fulton, George, Grimes, Donald, Saltzman, Sedo, Stanley and Schmidt, Lucie, *Proposed Changes in Motor Carrier Hours of Service Regulations: An Assessment,* 2002, University of Michigan, Transportation Research Institute.

Corridore. J. Standard and Poor's Industry Surveys, Transportation: Commercial, Vol. 171, No. 25, Section 2, 19 June 2003.

Corsi, T.M., "The Truckload Carrier Industry Segment," in *Trucking in the Age of Information,* Dale Belman and Chelsea White III, eds, Ashgate, 2005.

Conyngham, M.E., "Future Truck Drivers: Where Will They Come From, Why Would They Take the Job?" in *Trucking in the Age of Information,* Dale Belman and Chelsea White III, eds, Ashgate, 2005.

Council of Logistics Management, 15th annual state of the logistics report, 7 June 2004.

Friedman, T.L., *The World Is Flat: A Brief History of the Twenty-First Century.* Farrar, Straus, and Giroux, 2005.

Hough, L., and Nowak, M., "The Package Express Industry: A Historical and Current Perspective," in *Trucking in the Age of Information,* Dale Belman and Chelsea White III, eds, Ashgate, 2005.

Karlin, J.N., and Liker, J.K., "Just-In-Time and Trucking Logistics: The Lean Learning Enterprise," in *Trucking in the Age of Information,* Dale Belman and Chelsea White III, eds, Ashgate, 2005.

Kolko, G. *The Triumph of Conservatism; A Re-interpretation of American History, 1900-1916.* Glencoe, N.Y.: Free Press , 1963.

Langley, J. C., *2004 Ninth Annual Third Party Logistics Study: Views from the Customers,* Georgia Tech, Capgemini LLC, and FedEx, 2004.

Langley, J. C., "Logistics Service Providers," in *Trucking in the Age of Information,* Dale Belman and Chelsea White III, eds, Ashgate, 2005.

McMullen, Starr, "A Preliminary Examination of the Impact of Regulatory Reform on U.S. Motor Carrier Costs," *Journal of Transportation Economics and Policy,* September: 307-319, 1987.

McMullen, Starr, "The Evolution of the U.S. Motor Carrier Industry" in *Trucking in the Age of Information,* Dale Belman and Chelsea White III, eds, Ashgate, 2005.

Nagarajan, A., Canessa, E., Nowak, M., Mitchell, W., and White, C., "Technology in Trucking" in *Trucking in the Age of Information,* Dale Belman and Chelsea White III, eds, Ashgate, 2005.

Notice of Proposed Rulemaking, U.S. Department of Transportation, 2000.

Peoples, James, "Industry Performance Following Reformation of Economic and Social Regulation in the Trucking Industry" in *Trucking in the Age of Information,* Dale Belman and Chelsea White III, eds, Ashgate, 2005.

Swan, P.F., and Burks, S. V., "Less-Than-Truckload Motor Carriers: A Story of Diversity and Change," in *Trucking in the Age of Information,* Dale Belman and Chelsea White III, eds, Ashgate, 2005.

CHAPTER 8
SERVICES MANAGEMENT

BENJAMIN SCHNEIDER[1]

ABSTRACT

This chapter describes how marketing, operations management (OM) and human resources management (HR) have confronted issues of managing firms in service industries. It describes how marketing has conceptualized service quality (especially the intangible nature of services), how operations management has seen the importance of customer contact as a key issue in the design of service delivery processes, and how HR has revealed the linkage between internal organizational processes as experienced by employees and customer experiences and satisfaction. Several contingencies are identified that relate to when service quality is likely to have maximum payoffs for organizations (high intangibility, high customer contact, service that requires people to cooperate to get the job done). Finally, a set of issues requiring simultaneous attention by management is specified for organizations wishing to achieve service quality excellence.

INTRODUCTION

Welcome to the world of services management, a multi-disciplinary field of practice and research on service quality. The field includes services marketing, services operations management, and services human resources management (HRM). A number of texts have integrated these three disciplines to increase our understanding of service quality, especially the delivery of service quality (e.g., Lovelock & Wirtz, 2004; Schneider & White, 2004; Zeithaml & Bitner, 2000). In addition there are several excellent management-focused books that simultaneously address these three interrelated facets of service delivery (Berry, 1997; Heskett, Sasser, & Schlesinger, 1997; Schneider & Bowen, 1995; Zemke & Bell, 2003). All of these books focus on the delivery of service quality rather than the "core" attributes of the service itself (e.g., the food at a restaurant, the clothing in a retail store, the safety of the rides at a theme park). Moreover, much of the services management literature has focused on consumer services rather than professional services such as law, medicine, or even higher education.

---

[1] Adapted from Schneider, B. (2004). Welcome to the world of services management. *Academy of Management Executive, 18*, 144-150. The original paper is © Copyrighted by the Academy of Management.

In this chapter, I focus heavily on the HRM piece of services management (especially on my own work on service climate). But let me begin by discussing what Marketing has been up to before moving on to describe the progress made by Operations Management (OM) as they have explored the world of services management. I explore this variety of perspectives on services because an organization interested in transforming itself into one known for service excellence must simultaneously address issues in many different domains of organizational life; there is no silver bullet.

CONTRIBUTIONS FROM MARKETING

It all began in 1977 when a young Vice President at Banker's Trust in New York, Lynn Shostack (1977), wrote that banks deliver services not things. This seemingly simple idea led many marketing researchers and practitioners to propose a conceptualization of the continua along which goods and services exist—and, as a result, the ways in which goods and services production and delivery may differ.

What marketing has shown us is that service delivery and goods production, in the extreme, anchor opposite ends of at least three continua: (1) relative intangibility, (2) relative customer participation in production, and (3) relative simultaneity of production and consumption. In brief, services tend to: (1) be less tangible (think of attending a Disney theme park or a symphony concert as extreme examples where the service is purely the intangible experience), (2) more frequently involve the customer as a co-producer (think going to the bank and using your ATM card or going to McDonalds where you get your own food and bus your own table), and (3) be more likely to be produced, delivered, and consumed simultaneously (think going to a concert or a restaurant where what is produced and delivered is consumed almost simultaneously).

In contrast, goods tend to be more tangible (think of a computer or a car), require less active participation in their production (we do not produce our car or our computer), and are less simultaneously produced and consumed (your car may have been made 6 months ago in a far away place). Marketing drew from these conceptual distinctions between goods and services a number of implications for how services might be best marketed (including considerations about pricing, advertising, customer satisfaction, and the measurement of service quality from the customer perspective). That said, the implications of these characteristics of services for the management of organizations in general and for HRM in particular have received relatively little formal attention (though there certainly have been exceptions; see Bowen & Ford, 2002 and Lengnick-Hall, 1996). Later in this article I will present some HRM implications of these attributes of services that are of potential immediate use to managers.

In addition to the conceptual work accomplished in understanding services quality, marketing scholars have also been at the forefront in assessing those experiences consumers have that define service quality for them (Parasuraman, Zeithaml, & Barry, 1994; Schneider & White, 2004). A very thorough and interesting literature on the measurement of service quality has emerged over the past 20 years. The bottom lines from this literature are that: (1) it is useful to have data on customer expectations if you want to know what to do to meet them; (2) the most important feature of service delivery is reliability—being consistent and doing what was promised when it was promised; and (3) there are strong service process and interpersonal issues associated with customer service quality (e.g., the responsiveness experienced by customers and the empathy and assurances experienced by customers as part of the service production and delivery process).

Other work emerging from the marketing perspective on service quality includes issues surrounding service recovery (how problems customers have are handled and the consequences thereof; Tax & Brown, 2000), the impact of the design of physical spaces (called "servicescapes") on customer experiences (Bitner, 1992), and understanding the nature of the long-term relationship between consumer and firm (what has come to be called Customer Relationship Management or CRM; Patterson & Ward, 2000).

While not everyone agrees that services and goods are distinguishable or that the distinctions I've presented are useful, it is clear that these are issues of degree not of kind. By that I mean services and goods are on continua and are not dichotomies; most services have goods attached to them (like food in a restaurant or clothes in a retail environment) and most goods have services attached to them (like how you are treated when purchasing a car or the way your call is handled by a customer service representative when you need help from computer company). The major point here is that *it is in the creation of the customer's service experience that the potential exists for differentiation in the marketplace.*

You might logically ask: Why would I want to apply what I learn about services to my business? The answer is that it is a possible key to competitive advantage in the marketplace. Obviously, focusing on service delivery is but one way to achieve competitive advantage. But service quality can pay rich dividends when done well. Higher levels of service quality produce higher levels of customer satisfaction which lead to increased customer loyalty and increased sales (Buzzell & Gayle, 1987; Heskett et al., 1997).[1] While a price or product strategy can also yield these outcomes, service quality if done well is more difficult to imitate and can have a more lasting competitive advantage; service quality done well can have lasting value through customer satisfaction, customer loyalty, and improved revenues. After all, it's more complicated to do service well than to change the price or to alter the inventory of goods available. So, competing on price or product may be dangerous because the price of entry is relatively cheap (Lovelock & Wirtz, 2004). Overall then, marketing has played a key role in our understanding of the potential implications of knowing when one is a service business and then taking action based on that knowledge to produce potential competitive advantage in the market place.

Management in general and HRM in particular have been slow to grasp the implications of the continua elaborated by marketing for organizational design and human resource issues. Indeed, while there are texts about services marketing and services operations management, there are no texts for the study of services HRM. Services management has been dominated by marketing and OM even though customer satisfaction is closely tied to the design and management of service organizations and the management of human resources (Bowen & Ford, 2002; Schneider & Bowen, 1995). But before we examine what we know about the management implications of these issues, let's first venture off into the world of operations management.

CONTRIBUTIONS FROM OPERATIONS MANAGEMENT (OM)

From operations management, a major insight into the world of services production and delivery has been the idea that contact with customers makes the world of service production different from the world of goods production (Chase, 1981; Kellogg & Chase, 1995; Lovelock & Wirtz, 2004). In the production of goods, the elimination of variability in production (standardization), is a given, or at least a goal to be achieved. In contrast, in the world of services, variability is something that is inherent in delivery, especially in the world of consumer services. The variability in service production is attributed to the different kinds of demands different customers make of service providers. So in the world of service production, the goal is to manage variability (McClaughlin, 1996). The implications of the degree of customer contact for the when, where, and how of service delivery have received considerable attention in OM. In contrast, the HRM literature offers little guidance about who to hire, how to train, what to pay, or how to lead as a function of the degree of customer contact employees will have as a major part of their jobs. Yet we know instinctively that there must be differences in jobs as a function of degree of customer contact. In addition, the implications of degree of customer contact for employees (e.g., levels of stress, emotional labor required, sources of job satisfaction) have received little attention. Later I will address some ways to include degree of customer contact as a variable in HRM practices and research and the importance of attention to these HRM issues for achieving organizational change.

OM has taken a much more macro perspective on service delivery than either marketing or HRM. By this I mean both marketing and HRM focus their efforts on individuals (individual customers for the former and individual employees for the latter). This stands in contrast to what managers tend to think about when making decisions--people in the aggregate. So, while HRM researchers and practitioners worry about selection of employees and equity for employees, OM researchers and practitioners worry about how *many* people to have to serve the customer base and employee pay/customer revenue tradeoffs in the aggregate. OM scholars have been at the forefront in understanding (1) the importance of demand and capacity tradeoffs versus revenue generation (Chase, Aquilano, & Jacobs, 1998), (2) the implications of waiting time for customer satisfaction and revenues (Taylor & Fullerton, 2000), and (3) the relationship between service operations (schedules of all kinds for maintenance, cleaning, safety, space allotments and so forth) and revenues (Schmenner, 1995). In brief, OM has been far more concerned with direct effects on revenues than have either marketing or HRM. Indeed, this last issue has produced interesting models for calculating the likely payoffs in revenues associated with given proposed investments in improving service quality (Rust, Zahorik, & Keiningham, 1995). Similar models and methods for such economic utility analyses exist in HRM (Boudreau, 1991) and their application to the world of services is important—but not yet attended to.

In summary, OM academics and practitioners have been action-oriented in attending to the variability customers introduce into the production mix in service organizations. When what appears before a worker is a variable customer not a standardized part, the dynamics of production change. OM, with its natural emphasis on flows of people and information into, through, and out of organizations has focused on what the design issues must be to make this throughput as efficient as possible—without sacrificing quality. An aid to making this happen is to have the human component of delivery be maximally attuned to the needs for service excellence.

CONTRIBUTIONS FROM HRM WITH A FOCUS ON SERVICE CLIMATE

Perhaps the major contribution HRM has made to understanding service quality and service delivery has been through a focus on the employees who deliver service. So while marketing has focused on the customer and service attributes, and operations management has focused on delivery processes, HRM has focused on the human service deliverer. The major work accomplished in this arena is associated with Schneider and his colleagues. They have shown that employee experiences of the service climate in which they work significantly predict customer satisfaction (Schneider & Bowen, 1985; Schneider, Parkington, & Buxton, 1980; Schneider, White, & Paul, 1998). Schneider and others have found this "linkage effect" (Wiley, 1996) to be robust across industries as diverse as banks, insurance companies, supermarkets, automobile financing offices, retail, hotels, and restaurants (Heskett et al., 1997; Schneider, Bowen, Ehrhart, & Holcombe, 2000).

In this long-term program of research, the facets of organizational life that constitute a service climate for employees have been fairly well-documented: leadership focus on goals and planning for service, recognition and rewards for service excellence, internal support from others on whom service deliverers depend, adequate tools and equipment to deliver service quality, competent co-workers, and a sense that the service delivered is of the highest quality (Lytle, Hom, & Mokwa, 1998). These facets have important implications for everything in which HRM is involved: leadership, motivation, selection and training, and in general the creation of a climate that promotes effectiveness in service delivery.

The typical "linkage" project done by Schneider and his colleagues asks employees of service units (e.g., bank branches, departments in supermarkets) to complete a survey describing the *general* management practices under which they work and the more *specific* management practices they experience with regard to the production and delivery of service quality. The basic ideas Schneider works from are that: (1) good general management practices (supportive supervision, appropriate training, necessary equipment) provide a foundation on which a service climate can be built; (2) service climate emerges by management focusing on service quality in all it does (rewards focus on service quality, planning and goal setting focus on service quality, measurement focuses on service quality, employee competencies for delivering service quality are emphasized); and (3) those who deliver service to customers must in turn be served well by those on whom they depend.

All of these issues are assessed via survey and each unit studied (bank branch, supermarket departments) is given a series of scores on the specific service climate dimensions that employees there experience as well as a summary global service climate indicator. With this diverse set of questions, Schneider is able to not only diagnose general impressions employees may have of the service climate in which they work, but the specific practices and procedures that constitute that climate.

The other important data Schneider uses in his process come from customers of the units studied. Then the employee and customer data are statistically correlated to reveal: (a) the degree of relationship that exists between what employees say they experience and what customers report; and (b) the specific facets of employee experiences that most strongly relate to customer satisfaction (these latter issues can become the targets for future interventions, a topic I deal with below).

It should be obvious from this rapid review of the service climate approach that some key drivers of customer satisfaction have been identified and it is this set of organizational design attributes that requires attention by change agents for organizational transformation to a service quality business to actually happen. The idea is that numerous HRM issues must be simultaneously addressed with the OM issues so that efficiency in the processing of customers can occur in an environment—a climate—that promotes customer satisfaction. As noted earlier, there is no silver bullet but if a company gets it right it can pay long term dividends.

Contingencies on Linkage Results

As noted earlier, there is considerable evidence that consistent relationships exist between what employees describe with regard to service quality and what customers report about their satisfaction. While these kinds of linkage appear to be robust across setting and industries, this does not mean that they always exist. My hypothesis is that this is true because the settings and industries in which the studies have been done to date tend to be characterized by high customer contact, high intangibility, and high interdependence among service deliverers. That is, it is important for us to ask how strong this linkage result is as we move away from more pure services to more pure goods production and delivery. This is a key question for managers who will want to know whether it is going to pay for them to create a positive service climate. In short, does a positive service climate always result in superior customer satisfaction?

The simple answer to the question appears to be "No it does not." Some recent projects, for example, reveal that when customer contact is high between employees and customers, then service climate is strongly linked to customer satisfaction. But when customer contact is low this linkage does not exist (Dietz, Pugh, & Wiley, 2004). A similar pattern exists for intangibility (i.e., service climate is strongly linked to customer satisfaction only when intangibility is high). Also, in a hospital setting, when service delivery must get done rapidly and employees (nurses) have to cooperate to make this happen, then service climate is strongly linked to customer (patient) satisfaction. But if the time constraints and the need to cooperate do not exist, then service climate is not linked to customer satisfaction (Gittell, 2002).

In an interesting twist, there is good evidence now that customer satisfaction is also much more predictable if the climate employees experience is a strong climate than if it is a weak climate (Schneider, Salvaggio, & Subirats, 2002). What is a strong climate? It is a climate where employees strongly agree about how service quality is attended to by what management does. When the employees in a setting can't agree about the service quality focus where they work (some think it is there while others are not sure), then customer satisfaction is much less predictable. The conclusion: If you want to achieve customer satisfaction based on a positive service climate, you better be sure you are getting the message across to everyone that service quality is the way you do business.

How does one get the message across to everyone? By achieving some uniformity of emphasis and message in the hundreds of activities and behaviors that employees experience. If service-oriented people are hired but the training focuses only on computer skills and speed, there is not consistency. If training emphasizes conflict resolution skills for dealing with customers but front-line supervisors do not permit such skills to be used ("Forget what they told you in training; I'll show you how it needs to be done") then there is inconsistency. If service quality is emphasized by the CEO in various media (e-mails; newsletters) but insufficient staff is available to serve customers then there is inconsistency. The bottom line is that employees get the message not based on speeches or vision statements but by what they actually experience.

In sum, a positive service climate is linked to higher levels of customer satisfaction when customer contact is high, when intangibility of the offering is high, when the need to do things speedily while cooperating with others is high, and when those who work in a setting can agree that service quality is the strategic imperative of interest.

THE NEED FOR STRATEGIC HRM FOR TRANSFORMATION IN THE WORLD OF SERVICES MANAGEMENT

As I noted earlier, within HRM the strategic implications of being in a service business have not received much attention, though there are some exceptions (Bowen & Ford, 2002; Lengnick-Hall, 1996; Mills, Chase, & Margulies, 1983). Some will argue with this statement, noting that HRM has become far more strategic in the past ten or so years than it was earlier. While this is true, strategic human resources management (SHRM) has developed with a focus on internal capabilities (the resource-based view of the firm; Wright, Dunford, & Snell, 2001) and not on the external demands on the firm (i.e., in the form of customers) nor on the kind of industry in which the firm operates. Consequently, SHRM seems to focus more on attempting to identify and unleash and change when necessary the generic internal human capabilities of the firm than on identifying the specific strategic goals of the firm in its industry and the implications of those goals for the development and implementation of HRM tactics.

Generic HRM will not suffice in an increasingly competitive marketplace; organizations must, to use a phrase from marketing, focus or falter. There is much to admire about organizations that have excellent HRM practices, for example high performance work practices—as they do seem to be more profitable (Huselid, Jackson, & Schuler, 1997; Lawler, Mohrman, & Ledford, 1998). And, while generically good HRM practices are more difficult to imitate or duplicate than simply changing product mix or price, it is useful to think about how much more competitive advantage might be achieved by focusing those HRM practices on superior service quality and service quality delivery—especially in a high customer contact business characterized by high intangibility and the requirement of close cooperation among employees to get the job done quickly and correctly.

I have been explicit earlier about what such a strategic focus might look like to service workers for an HRM that was an active partner in achieving customer satisfaction and revenue goals for a business. Now I want to present a bundle of efforts that I have found in my consulting work with organizations that management should implement if they want their business to be known for its service quality. Let me emphasize the phrase "bundle of efforts" because doing only one of what follows or only pieces of the broader categories I present will not raise to appropriate levels of consciousness the strategic import of service quality.

Marketing, HRM, and OM Need to Talk to Each Other

Linkage research has been difficult to do because it requires HRM survey people and marketing customer satisfaction people to share data! In addition, Marketing sometimes introduces new products and services before the OM systems are in place to deliver them and prior to the time service deliverers are fully trained to deliver them. Service deliverers feel foolish when this happens; it is not a positive service climate—and customer satisfaction suffers. Managers in different functions see the world differently—which is good because different challenges confront businesses and different perspectives are required to respond to them. Simultaneously however, people in different functions must learn to share some common perspectives, for example with regard to service quality. Project teams that are comprised of people from different functions are a good way to get people talking and linkage research could be one of those projects.

Measurement Systems Should Focus on Service Quality Indicators.

The rule here is "that which gets measured and those measurements that get used as a basis for decisions will be attended to." There are two kinds of measurements that are critical: Measures on customers and measures on employees. Measures on customers would include, but not be limited to, the following numbers: total in the customer base, new customers, lost customers, customers who have increased or deepened their relationship, customers who have narrowed or decreased their relationship, proportion of customers who rate the service quality as excellent or outstanding (not just very good), and the same data for how customers rate the competition. These numbers should be shared with everyone throughout the company and specific, difficult goals set for their achievement so that units have goals over which they have some control. Rewards and recognition should be based on achieving these goals.

Employee measurements would include but not be limited to: the immediacy with which customer contact jobs are filled when they become vacant, the proportion of employees placed on jobs who are fully trained prior to such placement, results from monitoring customer contact behavior of employees (e.g., from "mystery shopper" programs), employee absenteeism and turnover (which is directly linked to customer account turnover), and survey data with regard to role ambiguity and stress as well as service climate experienced. These numbers also should be shared with everyone throughout the company and specific, difficult goals set for their achievement such that units have goals over which they have some control. Once again, rewards and recognition can be based on achieving these goals.

These kinds of measurement programs send powerful messages to employees throughout an organization when the measurements and the goals are made public and when rewards and recognition are based on them.

Analyze the Strategic Focus Accorded all HRM Practices

How much focus does service quality really receive from HRM? Examine all HRM practices for the actual and explicit focus they give to service quality and customer satisfaction. These practices should include, but are not limited to selection procedures (competencies sought), training programs (skills taught), promotion systems (who gets promoted and why), performance management systems (is service quality there?), and mentoring and career development initiatives (including 360 degree feedback systems). A business is not in the business of service quality if its HRM practices are not suffused with a focus on service quality.

Identify What Managers at All Levels Do to Produce Positive Service Climates and High Levels of Customer Satisfaction

I have been conducting focus groups with managers and employees at all levels to identify what seems to be working for companies. I choose focus group participants based on the employee and customer survey data—and I choose the best based on these data. I ask participants to share with me the things they do to promote a service climate and to promote customer satisfaction. The results from these focus groups are very important because they particularize the actions found useful in a company. These actions can then be translated into the competencies required when people are hired, the training programs necessary for employees and managers already there, bases for performance management and promotion systems, and so forth. These data, combined with the explicit analysis of the service focus of HRM practices, can be very useful when trying to change perceptions about how important service quality really is.

Avoid the Coffee Mugs and Posters Approach to Service Quality

Posters and coffee mugs that promote a service focus for organizations are a lot cheaper than implementing the kinds of programs and approaches I have emphasized here. They should be cheaper as they will have no lasting impact.

CONCLUSIONS

In this chapter I have tried to provide a "feel" for services management, especially the role of HRM in services management. The focus on HRM is overdue. Everything that a business does is borne in the heads of employees and what is in their heads will largely determine how they behave. While this is true for any business, here I focused on service businesses and the delivery of service quality to produce customer satisfaction, something that we know is reflected in customer loyalty and revenues. I also identified the fact that service quality is not the only route to customer satisfaction and revenues. But I argued that price and product are more easily imitated as tactics for competitive advantage than a focus on service quality might be. I proceeded to illuminate some HRM approaches to building a climate in which service quality would be produced. In a real sense I showed how the management of service climate is a way to manage a service quality brand image from the inside out (Schneider, 2000). However, I cautioned that the principle of linkage—that service climate produces customer satisfaction—applies mostly to service businesses higher on customer contact, higher on intangibility, and higher on time requirements, combined with the need for cooperation to get the job done. Nevertheless, that covers a lot of businesses and the competitive advantages of inimitability might be sufficient to go beyond the coffee mugs and posters approach to service quality in transformation efforts.

REFERENCES

Berry, L. L. (1997). *Discovering the soul of service: The nine drivers of sustainable business success.* New York: Free Press.

Bitner, M. J. (1992). Servicescapes: The impact of physical surroundings on customers and employees. *Journal of Marketing, 56,* 57-71.

Boudreau, J. W. (1991). Utility analysis for decisions in human resources management. In Dunnette, M. D., & Hough, L. M. (Eds.), *Handbook of industrial and organizational psychology, 2nd ed., Vol. 2* (pp. 621-745). Palo Alto, CA: Consulting Psychologists Press.

Bowen, J., & Ford, R. C. (2002). Managing service organizations: Does having a "thing" make a difference? *Journal of Management, 28,* 447-469.

Buzzell, R., & Gayle, B. T. (1987). *The PIMS principles: Linking strategy to performance.* New York: Free Press.

Chase, R. B. (1981). The customer contact approach to services: Theoretical bases and practical extensions. *Operations Research, 4,* 698-706.

Chase, R. B., Aquilano, N. J., & Jacobs, F. R. (1998). *Production and operations management: Manufacturing and services, 8th ed.* San Francisco: Irwin/McGraw-Hill.

Dietz, J., Pugh, S. D., & Wiley, J. W. 2004. Service climate effects on customer attitudes: An examination of boundary conditions. *Academy of Management Journal, 47,* 81-92.

Gittell, J. H. (2002). Relationships between service providers and their impact on customers. *Journal of Service Research, 4,* 299-311.

Heskett, J. L., Sasser, W. E., Jr., & Schlesinger, L. A. (1997). *The service-profit chain.* New York: Free Press.

Huselid, M. A., Jackson, S. E., & Schuler, R. S. (1997). Technical and strategic human resource management effectiveness as determinants of firm performance. *Academy of Management Journal, 40,* 171-188.

Jackson, S. E., & Schuler, R. S. (2003). *Managing human resources through strategic partnerships* (8th ed.)Mason, OH: Thomson/Southwestern.

Kellogg, D. L., & Chase, R. B. (1995). Constructing an empirically derived measure for customer contact. *Management Science, 41,* 1734-1749.

Lawler, E. E., III, Mohrman, S. A., & Ledford, G. E., Jr. (1998). *Strategies for high performance organizations: Employee involvement, TQM, and reengineering programs in Fortune 1000 corporations.* San Francisco: Jossey-Bass.

Lengnick-Hall, C. A. (1996). Customer contributions to quality: A different view of the customer-oriented firm. *Academy of Management Review, 21,* 791-824.

Lovelock, C. H., & Wirtz, J. (2004). *Services marketing: People, technology, strategy* (5th ed.). Upper Saddle River, NJ: Pearson/Prentice-Hall.

Lytle, R. S., Hom, P. W., & Mokwa, M. P. (1998). SERV*OR: A managerial measure of organizational service-orientation. *Journal of Retailing, 74,* 455-489.

Mayer, D. E., Ehrhart, M. G., & Schneider, B. (2004). Contingencies on the relationship between service climate and customer satisfaction: Intangibility, customer contact, and task interdependence. Unpublished manuscript, Department of Psychology, University of Maryland.

McLaughlin, C. P. (1996). Why variation reduction is not everything: A new paradigm for service operations. *International Journal of Service Industry Management, 7,* 17-30.

Mills, P. K., Chase, R. B., & Margulies, N. (1983). Motivating the client/employee system as a service production strategy. *Academy of Management Review, 8,* 301-310.

Parasuraman, A., Zeithaml, V. A., & Berry, L. L. (1994). Alternative scales for measuring service quality: A comparative assessment based on psychometric and diagnostic criteria. *Journal of Retailing, 70,* 201-230.

Patterson, P. G., & Ward, T. (2000). Relationship marketing and management. In Swartz, T. A., & Iacobucci, D. (Eds.), *Handbook of services marketing and management* (pp. 317-142). Thousand Oaks, CA: Sage.

Rust, R. T., Zahorik, A. J., & Keiningham, T. L. (1995). Return on quality (ROQ): Making service quality financially accountable. *Journal of Marketing, 59,* 58-70.

Schmenner, R. W. (1995). *Service operations management.* Englewood Cliffs, NJ: Prentice-Hall.

Schneider, B. (2000). Brand image from the inside out. *Journal of Brand Management, 7,* 233-240.

Schneider, B., & Bowen, D. E. (1985). Employee and customer perceptions of service in banks: Replication and extension, *Journal of Applied Psychology, 70,* 423-433.

Schneider, B., & Bowen, D. E. (1995). *Winning the service game.* Boston: Harvard Business School Press.

Schneider, B., Bowen, D. E., Ehrhart, M. G., & Holcombe, K. M. (2000). The climate for service: Evolution of a construct. In Ashkanasy, N. M., Wilderom, C. P. M., & Peterson, M. F. (Eds.), *Handbook of organizational culture and climate* (pp. 21-36). Thousand Oaks, CA: Sage.

Schneider, B., Parkington, J. P., & Buxton, V. M. (1980). Employee and customer perceptions of service in banks. *Administrative Sciences Quarterly, 25,* 252-267.

Schneider, B., Salvaggio, A. N., & Subirats, M. (2002). Climate strength: A new direction for climate research. *Journal of Applied Psychology, 87,* 220-229.

Schneider, B., & White, S. S. (2004). *Service quality: Research perspectives.* Thousand Oaks, CA: Sage.

Schneider, B., White, S. S., & Paul, M. C. (1998). Linking service climate and customer perceptions of service quality in banks: Test of a causal model. *Journal of Applied Psychology, 83,* 150-163.

Shostack, G. L. (1977). Breaking free from product marketing. *Journal of Marketing, 41,* 73-80.

Tax, S. S., & Brown, S. W. (2000). Service recovery: Research insights and practices. In Swartz, T. A., & Iacobucci, D. (Eds.), *Handbook of services marketing and management* (pp. 271-286). Thousand Oaks, CA: Sage.

Taylor, S., & Fullerton, G. (2000). Waiting for service: Perceptions management of the wait experience. In Swartz, T. A., & Iacobucci, D. (Eds.), *Handbook of services marketing and management* (pp. 147-170). Thousand Oaks, CA: Sage.

Wiley, J. W. (1996). Linking survey results to customer satisfaction and business performance. In Kraut, A. I. (Ed.), *Organizational surveys: Tools for assessment and change* (pp. 330-359). San Francisco: Jossey-Bass.

Wright, P. M., Dunford, B. B., & Snell, S. A. (2001). Human resources and the resource based view of the firm. *Journal of Management, 27,* 701-721.

Zeithaml, V. A., & Bitner, M. J. 2000. *Services marketing, 2nd ed.* New York: McGraw-Hill.

Zemke, R., & Bell, C. (2003). *Service magic: The art of amazing your customers.* Chicago: Dearborn.

CHAPTER 9

VALUE-CENTERED R&D[*]

WILLIAM B. ROUSE AND KENNETH R. BOFF

ABSTRACT

The management of R&D organizations has received considerable attention in terms of the nature of the flow from research to development to deployed technology, as well as planning and managing this flow. R&D strategies, innovation funnels, and multi-stage decision processes, to name just a few constructs, have been articulated and elaborated. This chapter builds on this foundation to consider the nature of the value created by this process. An options-based approach is advocated for economic valuation of the products of R&D. Adoption and implementation of this approach is outlined in terms of ten principles for characterizing, assessing, and managing value.

INTRODUCTION

Over the past three decades, we have managed several academic, industrial, and government research organizations, ranging in size from ten or so researchers up to several hundred scientists and engineers. These organizations have served various constituencies, including the larger enterprise, technology markets, and professional disciplines. The technologies involved ranged from simulation to software, from displays to decision support.

Internal and external marketing and sales, recruiting and mentoring staff, and managing budgets and cash flow were continual issues, as they are in all enterprises. More specific to R&D organizations were the long-term uncertainties associated with the value of activities and outcomes of our organizations. Often, these activities and outcomes were not central to the overall enterprise's near-term success. This sometimes made it difficult to get the attention of key stakeholders (Rouse, 1985).

To address these challenges, we availed ourselves of the best thinking in terms of the various "generations" of R&D management (Roussel, Saad & Erickson, 1991; Matheson & Matheson, 1998; Miller & Morris, 1999), as well as articles from *Research Technology Management*, *Journal of Product Innovation*

---

[*]This chapter is based on an article titled "Value-Centered R&D Organizations: Ten Principles for Characterizing, Assessing & Managing Value," that appeared in **Systems Engineering**, Vol. 7, No. 2, 2004.

Management, and many other journals. The body of literature in this broad area is very rich.

This exploration led us to become fascinated with the specific issue of attaching value to R&D, particularly economic value. We have also been interested in non-economic attributes, especially as they tradeoff versus economic attributes. Central to the question of economic valuation is the fact that the nature, magnitude, and timing of returns from R&D investments are highly uncertain.

It is common to discount the projected financial returns from R&D due to these high uncertainties. This discounting is often severe, ranging from 20% to 50%. To lessen the effects of such severe discounting, people argue for extraordinary returns, i.e., the familiar "hockey stick" projections. This can lead to a war of attrition between discounting bean counters and wild-eyed technologists.

Participation in such conflicts caused us to argue for more explicit treatment of uncertainties rather than burying these effects in the discount rate. Further, it seemed to us that the value of R&D should increase with uncertainties. R&D provides a hedge against uncertainties. Hedges have value and this value should increase with uncertainties and, of course, consequences.

This thinking led us to real options (Amram & Kulatilaka, 1999; Boer, 1998, 1999; Luehrman, 1998), based on the options pricing theories of Black, Merton, and Scholes (1973). Adoption of an options-based framework caused us to conclude that the value of R&D is in the options created rather than the technology deployed. Deployment depends on options being exercised, decisions for which depend on a variety of factors beyond those associated with R&D. Options have value whether or not they are exercised.

This chapter describes how we formulated and operationalized an options-based framework for economic valuation of R&D. We have cast this description in terms of ten principles for characterizing, assessing, and managing value shown in Table 1. We strongly believe that these principles are more important than particular calculation procedures. As one senior executive told us, "You've got to count the numbers right, but the numbers are not all that counts."

CHARACTERIZING VALUE

In this section we address the problem of defining the value of R&D in terms of the roles it plays – or should play – in enterprises, regardless of whether they are private or public sector enterprises. Key roles include creating means for meeting contingent needs and providing means for managing uncertainty. Development of an appropriate portfolio of such means is also a central role of R&D.

No.	Focus	Principle
1	Characterizing Value	Value is created in R&D organizations by providing "technology options" for meeting contingent needs of the enterprise.
2	Characterizing Value	R&D organizations provide a primary means for enterprises to manage uncertainty by generating options for addressing contingent needs.
3	Characterizing Value	A central challenge for R&D organizations is to create a portfolio of viable options; whether or not options are exercised is an enterprise challenge.
4	Assessing Value	Value streams, or value networks, provide a means for representing value flow and assessing the value of options created.
5	Assessing Value	Valuation of R&D investments can be addressed by assessing the value of the options created in the value network.
6	Managing Value	Decision making processes -- governance – are central in managing the flow of value.
7	Managing Value	Organizational structure affects value flow, with significant differences between hierarchical vs. heterarchical structures.
8	Managing Value	Individual and team affiliations and identities affect value flow; dovetailing processes with disciplines is essential.
9	Managing Value	Champions play important, yet subtle, roles in value flow; supporting champions is necessary but not sufficient for success.
10	Managing Value	Incentives and rewards affect value flow; aligning these systems with value maximization is critical.

TABLE 1. Ten Principles for Characterizing, Assessing & Managing Value

Principle No. 1: Value is created in R&D organizations by providing "technology options" for meeting contingent needs of the enterprise.

R&D is almost always about the future. R&D organizations may occasionally become involved in today's problems, but involvement in such situations is usually focused on gaining an appreciation for the context in which the future is likely to emerge. To the extent that R&D is focused on solving today's problems, they are performing an engineering function rather than R&D.

There can be substantial pressure on R&D to provide engineering services to operational units. These units usually value this highly because it augments their technical staffs, often with very competent people. R&D also usually likes the subsequent endorsements from the field. Such services doubtlessly add value to today's operations.

Taken to an extreme, however, focusing on these services results in R&D functions, in effect, being shelved and eventually dissipated. As a consequence, the future is taken hostage by the present. Future needs, especially contingent needs, are ignored. This leaves the enterprise ill prepared for the future. Its portfolio of means for meeting future needs will be impoverished.

Even when R&D is kept firmly focused on the future, there can be difficulties assessing success. It is often perceived that success is proportional to the fraction of investments that yield technologies that transition to deployment. The goal is to transition every idea and result to providing value in the enterprise's marketplace or equivalent.

Total focus on such transitions can lead to dysfunctional behaviors. For example, solely low-risk issues may be pursued. High-risk issues, despite their importance to the enterprise, may be avoided. Creation of knowledge about why ideas failed is perceived to have little or no value. Similarly, creation of skilled people is perceived to have little or no value.

A strong desire to avoid the types of problems outlined above led us to pursue the notion of options (Rouse & Boff, 1999; Rouse, et al., 2000). An option is the right to make an investment decision in the future, contingent on the information available at that time. Put another way, an option is a chit that allows delaying a decision that one would rather not make now, but also would not like to lose the opportunity to make later.

Of course, unlike financial options, an enterprise needs much more than a piece of paper to effectively "own" an option. R&D organizations produce options in terms of knowledge and skilled people, as well as prototypes, patents, etc. Knowledge may be codified in published articles, internal technical reports, and patent disclosures. However, the "shelf life" of such things, and consequently the value of technology options, depends on frequent renewal via ongoing participation in research and professional societies, for example.

From an options perspective, the R&D "scorecard" should not be dominated by the percentage of technology options exercised. Instead, one should also count viable technology options created, some of which get exercised and some of which do not. The key point is that the enterprise needs the right portfolio of options for meeting future needs. R&D should be scored on both its demonstrated ability to provide these options and, obviously, the actual creation of the options.

The scorecard should, of course, also include some measure of options exercised. Such metrics should appear on R&D managers' scorecards as well as the scorecards of those responsible for making decisions to exercise options, e.g., managers of product lines and enterprise operations. Failure to have needed options is, by no means, simply a failure of R&D. It often represents a deficiency across the whole value stream, including overall leadership.

Assessing the value of options immediately begs the question of why options are valuable, and how to attach value to contingencies in general. We address this below. First, however, let's explore the assertion that a primary role of R&D is creation of technology options. In particular, is creation of technology options inherently a primary role of all R&D organizations?

What about universities with their focus on big R and little or no D? The problem here is not with the term "option," but with the adjective "technology." Perhaps "knowledge options" should be the phrase. Knowledge options can be exercised downstream, most likely outside academia, to create technology options. Interestingly, knowledge options, without dilution, can provide the basis for a range of technology options.

What about applied R&D organizations where problem solving is the goal, i.e., big D and little or no R? Perhaps the activities of such organizations are better characterized as engineering services rather than R&D. Hence, option creation is less relevant. On the other hand, exercising options may be very relevant. Options that are more inexpensively exercisable tend to be more valuable.

Upstream in academia the goal is knowledge creation, to a great extent for its own sake. Downstream in applications, the goal is problem solving. Midstream, where most R&D organizations operate, the goals are understanding and creating contingent value.   These goals are achieved by understanding emerging applications and drawing upon accumulating knowledge.

Within a technology-intensive enterprise, e.g., IBM or the Air Force, R&D organizations may have purview of and influence on the whole value stream. As one looks up and down the whole process, it is important to keep in mind that the meaning of "options" may differ along the stream. Nevertheless, an options-based perspective is useful for viewing the whole process.

Principle No. 2: R&D organizations provide a primary means for enterprises to manage uncertainty by generating options for addressing contingent needs.

R&D is a means of managing and often reducing uncertainty. Providing options for addressing contingent needs involves addressing various types of uncertainties beyond the uncertainty underlying the need for contingencies. One may be uncertain about whether or not something is possible, how best to do it, and what one can expect in terms of performance and cost. One also may be uncertain about what functionality will be needed, what levels of performance and cost will be required, and what competitors are likely to do.

To the extent that futures are uncertain with many possibilities, it is better to have options on alternative futures than attempt to invest in all possibilities. These investments should cover the full range of uncertainties just noted. The purpose of these investments is not to eliminate uncertainty, but to have the right portfolio of options.

The value of an option[1] increases with the magnitude of the consequences of exercising the option. This value also increases with the uncertainty associated with these consequences. Finally, value increases with time into the future when the option can be exercised. Thus, the value of an option increases with the magnitude and uncertainty of consequences, and time until these consequences can be obtained.

Balancing these relationships is the fact that the magnitude of consequences is expressed as the discounted cash flow due to exercising an option. The farther into the future one looks, the more highly discounted this cash flow. Thus, to illustrate, an option for a highly uncertain million dollars 100 years in the future will be worth its full net present value of $12. In general, the countervailing forces of increased value due to uncertainty and time and decreased value due to discounting can yield counterintuitive results.

Table 2 provides a summary of 14 selected case studies of option-based investment analysis that the authors have recently conducted – the Appendix elaborates the ways in which these valuations were formulated and calculated. It is important to note that all of these case studies involved actual investment decisions that were made based, in part, on the option-based analyses. Option "purchase" ranged in cost from $0 to over $400 million. The cost of option "exercise" ranged from $0 to almost $1.7 billion. Expected profits from exercising options ranged form $16M to almost $3.5 billion. Finally, net option values ranged from $8M to over $600M.

It is important to note that the actual investment modeling and analysis were substantially more elaborate than apparent from Table 2. The software tool employed, *Technology Investment Advisor* (Rouse, et al., 2000), enabled modeling technology maturity, production learning, and competitive positions, as well as uncertain parameter values throughout all models. The results of such analyses are probability distributions for the measures summarized in Table 2. Only expected values are shown in Table 2 to illustrate representative results.

The net option value provides a measure of the value created by owning the option beyond the cost of buying the option, e.g., investing in R&D. Thus, this provides a metric of the value or worth of R&D beyond its costs. From Table 2, it

---

[1] See the Appendix as well as Amram and Kulatilaka (1999), Boer (1998, 1999), Luehrman (1998), Luenberger (1997), and Smithson (1998) for discussions and illustrations of how option values can be calculated for a range of models.

Technology	Enterprise Type	Option Purchase			Option Exercise			Net Option Value ($M)
		Investment	Amt ($M)	Duration (Years)	Investment	Amount ($M)	NPV Profit ($M)	
Aircraft (manufacturing)	Private	R&D	0	1	Deploy Improvements	0	16	8
Aircraft (unmanned)	Public	R&D	420	10	Deploy System	72	749	137
Auto Radar	Private	Run Business	6	3	Expand Offerings	16	160	133
Batteries (lithium ion)	Private	R&D	1	2	License Technology	8	220	215
Batteries (lithium polymer)	Private	R&D	8	3	Acquire Capacity	147	581	552
Fuel Cell Components	Private	R&D	18	1	Initiate Offering	144	522	471
Microsatellites	Public	R&D	359	10	Deploy System	614	930	43
Optical Multiplexers	Private	R&D	0	2	Expand Capacity	66	568	488
Optical Switches	Private	Run Business	68	2	Expand Offerings	402	1642	619
Security Software	Private	Run Business	0	3	Add Market Channels	104	416	267
Semiconductors (amplifiers)	Private	Invest in Capacity	24	2	Expand Offerings	412	1035	431
Semiconductors (graphics)	Private	R&D	3	1	Initiate Offering	8	102	99
Semiconductors (memory)	Private	R&D	109	4	Initiate Offering	1688	3425	546
Wireless LAN	Private	Run Business	19	2	R&D	40	268	191

TABLE 2. Example Option-Based Valuations of Technology Investments

can be seen that R&D investments provide options on profits 1-4 years later for private sector enterprises and rather later for costs savings for public sector enterprises. The longer times for the public sector are due, in part, to the extended nature of their planning and acquisition processes more than the nature of the technology.

This type of thinking embodied in Table 2 tends to conflict with how large enterprises typically address and manage uncertainties. Large hierarchical and/or bureaucratic enterprises often are quite risk averse. Good decisions that yield bad outcomes are termed failures and decision makers associated with such failures find their careers thwarted. This situation is exacerbated when an enterprise has little or no real competition.

In our experience, such enterprises do not want options – they want results. Everything promised should be delivered as promised. Nothing that is delivered should be extraneous. Options that are not exercised were bad investments. Unused life insurance, in retrospect, was a poor investment. Organizations with these perspectives delude themselves about uncertainty and how best to manage it.

In contrast, strategic advantage can be gained and sustained by understanding uncertainty better than one's competitors and creating a portfolio of options that provides high-value hedges against these uncertainties. Once contingencies emerge, one can exercise those elements of the portfolio that provide the greatest competitive advantage. Organizational abilities to address uncertainty this way – enabled by R&D – makes uncertainty a factor to be leveraged rather than eliminated.

Principle No. 3: A central challenge for R&D organizations is to create a portfolio of viable options; whether or not options are exercised is an enterprise challenge.

R&D organizations can assure that options are viable – that they are exercisable. This means that knowledge is vetted, codified, and supported with "how to" models, methods, and tools. It also means that people are up to date technically and available if needed. It is also important to have a good understanding of the resources needed for these people to employ the requisite knowledge.

Whether or not viable options are exercised depends on a range of factors beyond the purview and control of a typical R&D organization. Market conditions may not be right. Resources may not be available. Of particular importance, downstream decision makers may choose to exercise other options, perhaps for technologies that now appear to provide greater competitive advantage.

This raises the question of who decides to exercise options. Other than in small new ventures, it is rare for the creator of technology options to have the discretion to decide to exercise these options. It is much more common for such decisions to be made downstream and/or higher in the enterprise. Of course, R&D should understand these stakeholders and the factors that influence their decisions.

This should provide a basis for both making investment decisions and proactively influencing perceptions of emerging technology options.

Further, the R&D management process should provide ongoing insights and opportunities for intermediate decisions to continue, redirect, or terminate investments. As indicated below, typical multi-stage decision processes also provide for involvement of downstream decision makers in review of progress towards creating viable options. This results in early "buy in" and can accelerate transitions to deployment (Rouse & Boff, 1998, Rouse, 2001).

Nevertheless, as noted earlier, technology transitions – options exercised -- should not be the dominant element of an R&D organization's "scorecard." R&D is primarily responsible for creating viable technology options. Beyond doing good technical work, this requires that R&D have a substantive understanding of the aspirations, opportunities, and uncertainties that the enterprise is facing in the future. R&D needs to provide an appropriate portfolio of options for addressing this future.

Success in addressing the challenges and opportunities of the future cannot be fully planned. The nature of what will be required, the positions of competitors, and the availability of resources are all uncertain. As a result one needs more than one idea; in fact, one often needs a fairly large number of initial ideas to yield one market success (Stevens & Burley, 1997). A recent study by the Air Force Scientific Advisory Board found multiple instances of companies needing roughly 300 initial project investments to yield one commercial success (Ballhaus, 2000).

Thus, there is typically a technology "funnel" whereby a large number of initial investments are, over time, whittled down to a few initiatives that receive sufficient investment to have a chance in the marketplace – occasionally one of them achieves market success. Managing a technology funnel is easier if one also adopts an explicit multi-stage process for managing R&D. The majority of enterprises have such processes, so this idea is by no means novel (Cooper, Edgett & Kleinschmidt. 1998a).

At the same time, however, we have both experienced large private and public sector enterprises arguing that every investment must lead to a transition to the field. With this emphasis, R&D becomes quite conservative, focused on very incremental improvements that are guaranteed to succeed and the market is guaranteed to buy. These are characteristics of a very mature industry long past its innovative stages.

Ironically, our experiences with such enterprises are that they fall far short of a 100% transition rate. However, given that the leadership and culture are so focused on the 100%, they cannot entertain serious mechanisms for managing the real transition percentages. Consequently, the pipeline becomes clogged with marginally valuable, incremental improvements, and scarce resources are spread among so many investments that critical mass is seldom achieved.

The portfolio of technology options can be portrayed as shown in Figure 1. Return is expressed in terms of NPV (net present value) or NOV (net option value). The former is used for those investments where the lion's share of the commitment occurs upstream and subsequent downstream "exercise" decisions involve small amounts compared to the upstream investments. NPV calculations are close enough in those cases.

Risk (or confidence) is expressed as the probability that returns are below (risk) or above (confidence) some desired level – zero being the common choice. Assessment of these metrics requires estimation of the probability distribution of returns, not just expected values. In some situations, this distribution can be derived analytically, but more often Monte Carlo analysis or equivalent is used to generate the needed measures.

Figure 1 provides a plot of the economic returns and risks associated with a portfolio of investments. The line connecting several of the projects (P_A, P_B, P_H, and P_Z) in this figure is termed the efficient frontier. Each project on the efficient frontier is such that no other project dominates it in terms of <u>both</u> return and confidence. In contrast, projects interior (below and/or left) to the efficient frontier are all dominated by other projects in terms of both metrics. Ideally, from an economic perspective at least, the R&D projects in which one chooses to invest – purchase options – should lie on the efficient frontier. Choices from the interior are usually justified by other, typically non-economic attributes.

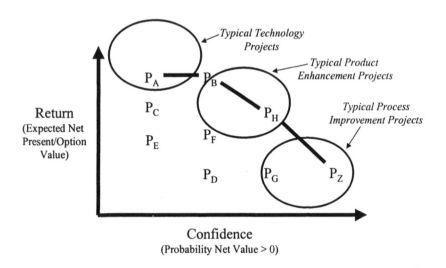

FIGURE 1. Investment Portfolio Diagram

A primary purpose of a portfolio is risk diversification. Some investments will likely yield returns below their expected values, but it is very unlikely that all of them will – unless, of course, the underlying risks are correlated. For example, if the success of all the projects depends on a common scientific breakthrough, then despite a possibly large number of projects, risk has not been diversified. Thus, one usually designs investment portfolios to avoid correlated risks.

While this makes sense, it is not always feasible – or desirable – for R&D investments. Often multiple investments are made because of potential synergies among these investments in terms of technologies, markets, people, etc. Such synergies can be quite beneficial, but must be balanced against the likely correlated risks.

It is important to note that non-economic attributes – not depicted in Figure 1 - -are also usually important. Considerations such as strategic fit, sustainability of advantage, and leveraging of core competencies are also important concerns when making R&D investments. While such multi-attribute assessments are beyond the scope of this chapter, we recognize their central importance (Rouse, Boff & Thomas, 1997; Rouse & Boff, 1999; Rouse, 2001).

Finally, it is essential to recognize that options often emerge in an evolutionary manner. Knowledge accumulates and competencies increase over time. At each decision point in a typical multi-stage R&D management process, the acceptability of progress to date is assessed. In some cases, one now knows that viable options are unlikely and investments are curtailed or redirected. In other cases, it becomes apparent that integrating multiple emerging options will both enable and enhance option value.

Occasionally, "wild card" options emerge that were never sought or envisioned, perhaps reflecting Burke's pinball effect that yields unexpected high-value options for unexpected beneficiaries (Burke, 1996). As Christensen (1997) elaborates, it is common for enterprises to encounter great difficulty taking advantage these, possibly disruptive, options.

Thus, options are not like certificates that are issued upon purchase. Considerable work is needed once "purchase" decisions are made. Options often emerge piecemeal and with varying grain size. Significant integration of the pieces may be needed before the value upon which the investment decisions were based is actually available and viable.

ASSESSING VALUE

We have characterized the value of R&D in terms of providing options for meeting contingent, uncertain needs of the enterprise. We now need to consider the processes whereby enterprises create value and how these processes result in a flow of options. This will provide a framework for discussing how value can be managed.

Principle No. 4: Value streams, or value networks, provide a means for representing value flow and assessing the value of options created.

It is useful to think of value in terms of both how technology options are created and how they are consumed. On the creation side, the focus is on R&D processes that yield viable options and the quality, productivity, and innovation associated with these processes (Rouse & Boff, 2001, 2003)[2]. On the consumption end, the concern is with how technologies make possible functionality that is embodied in products, systems, and services that provide capabilities that enable achieving the effects of interest to the marketplace or other constituencies.

R&D organizations should attempt to maximize the yield and minimize the time to create the portfolio of technology options needed by the enterprise. This affects the "purchase price" of the options. The "exercise price" and the resulting cash flows are strongly affected by how the technologies underlying the options flow to market impact. R&D often cannot directly impact the elements of the value stream subsequent to option execution. However, R&D may be able to deliver more "exercisable" options if the nature of downstream processes is understood.

Value streams can be represented as networks of connected nodes with inputs, outputs, resources, and controls (Rouse & Boff, 2003). Upstream nodes produce options for downstream nodes. Value at any node can be assessed by "rolling back" the value associated with eventual downstream outcomes in terms of cash flows due to profits and/or cost savings.

An example value network is shown in Figure 2. In this example, drawn from the authors' earlier work (Rouse & Boff, 2003), one can see repeated "kernels" associated with programmatic investments, R&D execution, and technology deployment. Programs fed each other, often in somewhat unpredictable ways. For the context of this example, namely investments in intelligent tutoring systems, two different sub-networks, one for the U.S. Air Force and another for the U.S. Navy, resulted in significant value, in this case for public high schools across the U.S.

A key distinction in such representations is between end users and next users. End users are the eventual beneficiaries of the enterprise. Next users are those immediately downstream from you who accept the options you create as inputs, add value, and then pass on options to their next users downstream from them. Your key customers are your next users rather than the end users.

When next users cross organizational boundaries, they are also referred to as transition agents. In some cases, they are explicitly tasked to transition or transfer technology. Their role is to understand both sides of the boundary. This involves, for instance, understanding the perspectives of both discipline-oriented researchers

---

[2] Rouse and Boff (2001, 2003) elaborate and operationalize the quality, productivity, and innovation attributes of value and their relationships to value strategies.

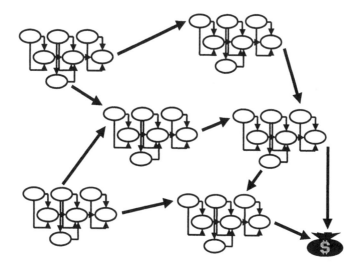

FIGURE 2. Example Value Network (Based on Rouse & Boff, 2003)

and business-focused product line managers. Often, significant translation is needed to balance the two perspectives.

As reasonable as the notion of next users seems, it conflicts with the culture of many large enterprises, in both public and private sectors. The intensity with which the defense community, for example, focuses on the "warfighter" leaves many next users very much under-served and, ultimately, undermines supporting the very end users for which so much passion is felt.

Consequently, R&D organizations may attempt to satisfy today's end users whose felt needs usually involve today's needs and deficiencies. For example, today's pilot is unlikely to envision accomplishing one of his or her current tasks without an aircraft. He or she will ask for higher thrust engines rather than a way to sight targets without moving the aircraft.

In responding to such forces, R&D organizations become engineering services organizations. This may provide significant value to operating units, at the very least in terms of staff augmentation. However, it undermines the R&D function and diminishes the possibilities for the R&D organization to create the portfolio of technology options needed for the enterprise to realize its future aspirations.

Value stream mapping can be very useful for understanding how value flows from initial R&D investment decisions to impacts in markets and for other constituencies (Rouse & Boff, 2003). It can help to assure that all the elements of a value stream are aligned with maximizing yield and minimizing time until these impacts. It also provides a means for reengineering processes that are not adding value as they should.

In terms of option values, value streams should be redesigned to:

- Decrease costs of purchasing options, decrease costs of exercising options, and/or increase returns of exercising options.

- Decrease time until options are viable, if uncertainties can also be reduced in a manner that provides sustainable competitive advantage.

- Decrease the extent to which competitors and adversaries can create and sustain options that provide them competitive advantage.

Note that redesign in pursuit of such objectives can often be enhanced by mapping and analysis of competitors' value streams.

Principle No. 5: Valuation of R&D investments can be addressed by assessing the value of the options created in the value network.

In order to appropriately allocate resources, one needs to attach value to the flows in the value streams or value network. This need for valuation has several important characteristics:

- It is multi-stage, with many contingent decisions.

- It is multi-attribute, with both economic and non-economic attributes.

- It is multi-stakeholder, with differing levels of importance of attributes

- It must address substantial uncertainties across these characteristics

We have addressed the multi-attribute, multi-stakeholder aspects of this valuation problem elsewhere, e.g., (Rouse & Boff, 1999; Rouse, Boff & Thomas, 1997). Both economic and non-economic value can be addressed using multi-stakeholder, multi-attribute utility models. The theory underlying these models and the practices for applying these models are well developed. There are issues of the relative importance of different stakeholders' perceptions. However, there is much experience in wrestling with these issues.

From an options-based perspective, a central issue concerns assessing the economic value of a network of contingent decisions over time, laced with substantial uncertainties. In the context of R&D, these decisions primarily involve purchasing options that, when exercised, yield other options. Cash flow, in terms of profit and/or cost savings, does not come until technology is deployed in products, systems, and services.

Traditionally, economic value is expressed in terms of Net Present Value (NPV) of cash flows created by an investment. These cash flows are the differences between returns and costs that, in the case of R&D, are almost always negative. Beyond the obvious fact that "money is not everything," the NPV approach presents two key difficulties.

One difficulty is that NPV calculations assume that all viable contingencies will be exercised, perhaps with associated probabilities. Yet, in reality, many alternatives are, quite rationally, not pursued once the time for their possible pursuit arrives. The returns and costs of these alternatives should not be included in the NPV calculation. The problem, of course, is that you do not know in advance which alternatives will not be pursued. Using Net Option Value (NOV) rather than NPV avoids this difficulty.

The second difficulty, particularly for public sector investments, involves defining "returns." Defense investments, for example, do not yield profits for the public that invests in these capabilities. These investments yield desired military capabilities and effects. Taking these desires as requirements or "givens," one can characterize the returns on investing in a new technology in terms of potential cost savings in meeting given requirements with this technology.

This presents difficulties when a new technology enables previously unavailable capabilities and effects. In this case, a baseline must be fabricated that provides that capability and effects without the new technology. For example, we recently used the costs of operating manned aircraft as a baseline for assessing investments in unmanned air vehicles. As might be imagined, the credibility of the baseline has a very significant impact on the credibility of the overall analysis.

Options-based framing of R&D investment decisions involves valuation of a portfolio of options, subsets of which are linked in multi-stage processes. The Black-Scholes formulation mentioned earlier, often augmented with heuristics and sensitivity analyses, enables closed-form calculation of option values. In situations where the underlying assumptions, e.g., lognormality of volatility, cannot be justified, numerical solutions of the requisite partial differential equations, binary lattice models, or Monte Carlo simulation can be employed, albeit with considerably more effort (Luenberger, 1997, Smithson, 1998).

It is important to note that options-based thinking has considerable value beyond the calculations outlined here. Elaboration of contingencies and associated uncertainties greatly improves the framing of investment decision problems. Responding to valuation in this manner, R&D organizations are often quite nimble in identifying and formalizing downstream contingencies much more broadly than typically motivated by traditional valuation methods. These conclusions are based on observations by many of the executives and senior managers involved with the assessments summarized in Table 2.

This principle – as well as these conclusions -- also applies in situations where a corporate parent or customers pay for the R&D of interest. R&D organizations in such situations are, in effect, selling options to sponsors. The key argument here would be that the R&D budget is substantially less than the value of the option provided. Hence, the Net Option Value would be attractive and the sponsor should "buy" the option.

One might argue that the costs of securing the R&D sponsorship, e.g., bid and proposal monies, can also be seen as option purchase costs. In this case, the sponsor would exercise the option by, for example, awarding the R&D contract. However, option-pricing models typically assume that options are exercisable by the purchasers of the options. A non-standard formulation would be needed to address probabilistic exercising of options by other than those purchasing the options.

MANAGING VALUE

Thus far, we have elaborated the characterization of the value of R&D in terms of option creation for the enterprise. R&D budgets are used to "purchase" options for potential cash flows (profits and/or savings) if exercised elsewhere in the enterprise. We have also discussed the methods and tools needed to assess value – value stream mapping, option pricing models, and multi-attribute models.

The first set of five principles provides the foundation for adoption of an options-based view of value. However, they are not sufficient for success. Beyond impressive foundations, an enterprise also has to execute successfully. A second set of five principles, elaborated in this section, provides the underpinnings for successful execution.

It should be noted that this second set of principles relates to the systems management elements of systems engineering. Success often requires that well-engineered systems also be well managed. To assure this, we must incorporate systems management principles into the systems engineering body of knowledge.

Principle No. 6: Decision making processes -- governance – are central in managing the flow of value.

Processes for investment decision making and investment management have a significant impact on value created and subsequent benefits to the enterprise. Good decision processes result in better decisions for two reasons. First, the right attributes and tradeoffs are considered at the right time. Second, all stakeholders understand how decisions are made, how to influence decisions, and how final decisions emerge. This greatly improves buy in.

Inadequate or inappropriate decision processes can undermine value creation by allowing poor decisions, resulting in ineffective allocations of investment resources. Misunderstood decision processes can result in a lack of individual and organizational commitment to decisions. At an extreme, a variety of dysfunctional myths can emerge (Rouse, 1998). For example, management may feel that they have consensus, the right processes, and "just" have to execute when, in fact, throughout the organization people do not know how to influence decisions, are carrying out processes that are not value-centered, and face considerable execution hurdles.

It is common for organizations to have difficulty agreeing to decision making processes, employing these processes with a degree of integrity, and communicating decisions in the context of these processes. It is also quite natural for stakeholders to attempt to work around decision processes to assure their interests are supported. To the extent that this succeeds, it undermines disciplined processes and precipitates cynicism among stakeholders.

Such difficulties are common in R&D organizations where traditions of authority and value-centered decision making are often in conflict. Strong leadership can be of great help in adopting and succeeding with a value-centered approach. However, to the extent that such leadership preempts value-based governance processes, the approach will be undermined and its benefits diminished.

An identified best practice within R&D organizations involves using multi-stage decision processes with specified criteria and objectives at each stage (Cooper, Edgett & Kleinschmidt, 1998a,b; Rouse & Boff, 2001). Early stages, when investments are relatively small, usually involve more qualitative criteria with modest target levels. Later stages, where investments can be very substantial, typically have many more quantitative criteria with challenging target levels. For such processes to be adopted and embraced, they need to be well articulated and supported. They also need to be used, both in terms of making decisions as advertised and communicating decisions in the context of this process.

More specifically, if options created is a desired outcome at each stage of the process, then arguments for continued investment should be couched in terms of net option values. If this is expected from proponents of investments, then methods and tools such as discussed earlier should be provided. Finally, investment decisions should be communicated in the context of options-oriented metrics.

If all proposals for new or continued investment are evaluated in a common manner, then portfolio plots such as shown in Figure 1 are possible and quite useful. There are, of course, always additional non-economic attributes of importance, but the ability to represent comparisons in this way, enables more focused discussion and debate of key tradeoffs across economic and non-economic attributes.

It is also important to consider the relationships of decision making processes to issues that are broader than just the attributes of alternative investments. Decision processes are needed for agreeing on organizational visions, goals, and values. The quality, productivity, and innovation of value streams are likely to affect overall satisfaction of end users, next users, and stakeholders in general. The morale and "psychic income" of researcher staff members and managers are also considerations. Investment decisions also must be made with regard to organizational processes to support R&D and other functions.

Principle No. 7: Organizational structure affects value flow, with significant differences between hierarchical vs. heterarchical structures.

Value is maximized, both in magnitude and time, when it flows through efficient organizational processes. Such processes minimize the number of steps between upstream and downstream next users, and eventually end users. It is desirable that steps with little or no value added be eliminated. However, the nature of organizations can make this difficult.

Organizations can be viewed in several ways. Organizations receive inputs and produce outputs. For R&D organizations, these inputs and outputs often are in the form of information. Structural relationships within and across organizations define the extent and content of information flows. Such flows influence the extent to which R&D organizations can deeply understand future enterprise aspirations, as well as communicate and support the options created by R&D processes.

Organizational structure also affects decision making. Hierarchical structures are useful for leadership and goal setting. Such structures, however, can impede value flow to the extent that higher levels are designed to make decisions in lower level processes. Hierarchical requests for approvals and resources add time and uncertainty while also consuming resources in themselves. In this way, the magnitude and timing of value are decreased and delayed, respectively (Rouse & Boff, 2003).

Heterarchical structures, in contrast, enable efficient horizontal flow of value. Authority for approvals and resource allocations reside at the level of the value streams. Higher levels communicate the vision and elaborate the goals but do not specify how goals are to be achieved. Value flow is monitored but intervention is rare as authority for corrective actions also resides as the level of the value streams.

Leaders in such organizations have more influence than power. They also must carefully consider and articulate the vision and goals. Design and communication of incentives and rewards are also key leadership roles. These types of leadership roles are difficult to perform well, and are not natural traits for those steeped in more authoritative models of leadership.

Organizational structure also affects the control of resources -- human, financial, and physical. This is useful in that resources usually need "homes" to be stewarded appropriately. However, it can also lead to "silos," associated with functions, disciplines, or regions. This limits the flow of resources to where value can best be added.

These tendencies can be countered by matrixing resources across organizational boundaries. The decision processes discussed above can be used to reallocate resources periodically. Such reallocations can be driven by where the greatest option values are likely to be created. This approach typically results in those who seek resources making their arguments in terms of options and their value. This is, of course, exactly what one would like them to do.

These implications of organizational structure can also be expressed in terms of who can direct what initiatives, who gets to review proposals and progress, and who determines rewards. Organizational structure and the allocation of authority should assure that execution of these managerial responsibilities is aligned with creating options for achieving enterprise aspirations.

For R&D organizations, the above considerations are manifested in terms of how information and knowledge flows, funding decisions are made, resources are allocated, and research outcomes assessed (Rouse & Boff, 1998). There is no best organizational structure for these activities. Nevertheless, structure should be derived from strategy. To this end, organizational structure needs to be designed to support the way in which options are best created and nurtured in the enterprise environment of interest.

Both descriptive and prescriptive approaches to organizational structure are needed. One must be able to understand the ways things work now in order to define the gaps between "as is" and "to be" as we discuss later. It is also important to recognize that the "best" structure may not be simply a variation within the reigning organizational paradigm. Thus, an improved hierarchy may be inferior compared to a more heterarchical structure, for example.

Kimberly (1986) suggests relationships between organizational design and innovation by considering the organization as a user, vehicle, and/or inventor of innovation. Further, the organization itself can be an innovation. This is complicated by the nature and context of R&D organizations (Miller, 1986; Jain & Triandis, 1990) and their relationships to overall enterprises. Typical R&D cultures with strong external, professional identities, as well as more inwardly directed personnel, can make organizational redesign more challenging and change difficult to sustain.

Principle No. 8: Individual and team affiliations and identities affect value flow; dovetailing processes with disciplines is essential.

R&D is often pursued by people with similar disciplinary backgrounds, e.g., scientists and engineers from particular disciplines. People in finance or marketing often work together in other aspects of enterprise value streams. The professional affiliation and identity that this encourages can be very important for professional development and knowledge sharing.

However, this affiliation and identity can also limit people's abilities to fully understand next users and end users' perspectives and needs. For this reason, it is useful to also encourage affiliation with overall value streams and associated processes. This can be fostered by providing education and training focused on enterprise value streams, as well as creating opportunities for value stream participants to meet and get to know each other.

Dovetailing processes with disciplines is important, but it can be very difficult. University education typically does a poor job at supporting cross-disciplinary perspectives. Academic faculty members are often among the most discipline-bound professionals. The best-performing students have often fully assimilated this trait.

Consequently, it is essential to be very intentional in providing value-centered education and training. This should include material on the nature and functioning of enterprise processes. Next users and end users of processes should be explicated, including the options they need and those they create. Supporting information flows should also be outlined and explained.

In addressing this principle, a balance must be managed between understanding and identification with enterprise aspirations, and affiliation and interaction with sources of disciplinary knowledge and best practices. Overemphasis on the former typically results in less then fully competent, but nevertheless enthusiastic researchers. Overemphasis on the latter tends to foster first-rate researchers, although they may at times have a somewhat cynical view of the organization.

Creating this balance is not a problem to be "solved." One should maintain awareness of how the underlying tension is evolving. If the situation evolves to either extreme and persists, it can be very difficult to reestablish a more productive balance. In this sense, perhaps unfortunately, the extremes tend to be fairly stable situations while balance takes continual effort.

Principle No. 9: Champions play important, yet subtle, roles in value flow; supporting champions is necessary but not sufficient for success.

Well-designed organizational processes can often sustain incremental value improvements. However, quantum and often disruptive improvements are frequently facilitated by champions that pursue "the cause" regardless of organizational hindrances (Christensen, 1997). Champions are noted for formulating innovation strategies, finding resources, and sustaining commitment through implementation (Rouse & Boff, 1994).

On the other hand, champions cannot convert bad ideas to good, seldom succeed without recruiting others to share responsibility and communicate the benefits of ideas more broadly. Thus, while champions may be necessary for disruptive change, they are seldom sufficient. They can be essential catalysts but rarely the sole cause of success (Markham & Griffith, 1998).

Managing value requires that champions be encouraged and supported. An explicit mentoring process can help foster champions. Recognition of champions and their contributions can also help. Once champions emerge for particular initiatives, it is also important to provide ongoing encouragement and support, ranging from visibility with leadership to additional resources.

Nevertheless, it is important that champions not be viewed as the only essential ingredient in success. Organizational processes, especially decision processes, should be designed to empower and support champions. Such processes should also be capable of sustaining initiatives when, for instance, champions depart. There are elements of succession planning that are relevant here.

Organizations seem to have natural tendencies to let champions work things out, often resulting in their having to work around current organizational processes. This is certainly better than watching initiatives fail. However, a more proactive and eventually more successful approach is to redesign and support processes based on lessons learned by champions. This will also encourage people to become champions.

More broadly, one needs to create an environment that encourages champions, while also attracting and hiring the rights kinds of people (Jain & Triandis, 1990). There needs to be the right mix of unencumbered visionaries, respected thought leaders, and competent value managers to play the roles of idea generators, gatekeepers, and coaches, as well as champions. The overall climate should encourage creative imagining and framing of options, including how they can be realized. This all must be designed in the context of typical R&D professionals and organizational cultures, including typical driving forces (Miller, 1986).

Principle No. 10: Incentives and rewards affect value flow; aligning these systems with value maximization is critical.

People respond to incentives. When incentives are aligned with maximizing value flow, people pay much more attention to providing their next users with viable options. In contrast, when incentives and rewards are not aligned – or are not realigned – with value streams, people "march to old drummers" in order to garner rewards.

It is important to balance recognition and rewards for individuals and teams associated with value processes. Individual excellence is, of course, important but excessive stress on individual disciplinary accomplishments can undermine an organization's value orientation. In an R&D organization, this could mean giving all authors full credit for a jointly-authored research paper rather than trying to assess who did what.

The key is to develop metrics that are both individually and organizationally oriented. Balanced scorecards (Kaplan & Norton, 1996), or equivalent, can be developed for both overall value processes and individual contributions to these processes. Incentives and rewards can be linked to some combination of these two types of metrics.

Whatever is measured, recognized, and rewarded will get attention. Careful design of value streams will not yield desired results without developing and implementing a measurement system that links individual and organizational performance to these value streams. A key is to relate recognition and rewards to value outcomes, e.g., options created, rather than just well intended activity.

More specifically, measures should be carefully chosen to reflect value goals and strategies, as well as the consequent nature of value streams. From this perspective, an R&D value scorecard is quite different than what one might devise for manufacturing or customer service (Rouse & Boff, 2001). It is also important to assure that personnel are educated with regard to such measurement mechanisms and trained in their use.

One particularly difficult aspect of implementing this principle involves getting seasoned middle managers to adopt new approaches. Such people are often quite skilled at succeeding in terms of the old metrics. A useful tactic is to recruit thought leaders from this population to participate in the team(s) defining new measures and scorecards. This enables early understanding of objections and use of these thought leaders to help devise countermeasures.

Enterprise strategies fall victim to two primary failures (Rouse, 2001). The first is a failure to execute – the strategy is all talk and no walk. The second is a lack of alignment between what the enterprise wants to become and how it incentivizes and rewards stakeholders. This tenth and last principle, therefore, is critical to avoiding value strategies being just a concept rather than a real way forward.

ORGANIZING FOR VALUE

Given the ten principles outlined in this chapter and summarized in Table 1, how should one go about creating a value-centered R&D organization? More specifically, how can one design or redesign such an R&D organization in a particular enterprise? This section outlines an overall design process. Some of the difficulties encountered in pursuing this process are then discussed, including a variety of best practices for addressing these difficulties. These insights are based in part on the broad literature on R&D organizations, e.g., (Rouse & Boff, 1998; Rouse, Thomas & Boff, 1998), as well as previous efforts in developing and applying methodologies for design of enterprises, organizations, systems, products, and processes (Rouse, 1991, 1992, 1993, 1994, 1996, 1998, 2001).

Overall Design Process

The design of a value-centered R&D organization can be pursued using the following general steps:

- Define desired enterprise outcomes
- Design processes for achieving these outcomes

- Design measurement system for processes

- Design structure for managing processes

- Design incentives and rewards to maximize value

These design tasks should be performed using the ten principles for generating alternatives and addressing tradeoffs.

This approach seems quite reasonable, especially if one were designing an R&D organization 'from scratch." However, most of the applications of the principles outlined here have involved existing R&D organizations that were aspiring to creating greater value for their stakeholders. In these situations, it is usually very difficult to start from scratch.

As shown in Table 3, the value principles can be applied in these cases by first assessing the "as is" organization from the perspective of these principles. The "as is" organization's strengths and weaknesses can be characterized in terms of deficiencies in satisfying principles. It is important to determine the specific nature of deficiencies rather than just their existence.

The next step is to define the "to be" organization in terms of deficiencies remedied. This should include specific programs of action to yield significantly greater conformance with the value principles. It is also important to define a time frame for accomplishing these changes and measures of success.

Defining "As Is" and "To Be"

At least conceptually, the principles as described earlier are fairly straightforward. More concretely, however, it can be difficult to map these general principles to a particular R&D organization. As surprising as it may seem, it can be somewhat difficult to determine how an R&D organization currently provides value.

This determination begins with identification and characterization of the organization's current activities, the inputs to and outputs from these activities, and how the value of these inputs and outputs are assessed. This can require significant effort, as people, especially researchers, do not necessarily think about their work this way. They just do what they do.

The typical project orientation of R&D organizations provides a means for getting started a bit easier. Beginning with a review of the portfolio of ongoing and recently completed projects, consider how the cases were made to initiate these projects and the outcomes promised in the proposals outlining these cases.

Principle	As Is	To Be
Value is created in R&D organizations by providing "technology options" for meeting contingent needs of the enterprise		
R&D organizations provide a primary means for enterprises to manage uncertainty by generating options for addressing contingent needs		
A central challenge for R&D organizations is to create a portfolio of viable options; whether or not options are exercised is an enterprise challenge		
Value streams, or value networks, provide a means for representing value flow and assessing the value of options created	Strengths, Weaknesses & Deficiencies	Programs to Remediate Deficiencies
Valuation of R&D investments can be addressed by assessing the value of the options created in the value network		
Decision making processes -- governance – are central in managing the flow of value		
Organizational structure affects value flow, with significant differences between hierarchical vs. heterarchical structures		
Individual and team affiliations and identities affect value flow; dovetailing processes with disciplines is essential		
Champions play important, yet subtle, roles in value flow; supporting champions is necessary but not sufficient for success		
Incentives and rewards affect value flow; aligning these systems with value maximization is critical		

TABLE 3. Template for Supporting Organizational Design or Redesign

The task plans associated with projects are also useful. Compile answers to the following questions:

- What problem and/or opportunity are being addressed?

- Why was this problem/opportunity thought to be important?

- What outcomes were promised in the proposal?

- What tasks were outlined for delivering these outcomes?

- How were these tasks to be performed?

- On what did performance of these tasks depend?

- What outcomes have been delivered thus far?

- Who were the recipients of these outcomes?

- What value do they attribute to these outcomes?

- What difficulties have been encountered thus far?

By focusing on proposals and progress reports, one can assess how the organization makes the case for resources and reports ongoing outcomes. For projects that have been completed, one can assess the perceived value of the final outcomes.

The key here is not to assess every project, which may be daunting in large organizations. Instead, review a large enough sample to obtain a thorough sense of how people in the organization think it functions. Reading between the lines, one can also identify or infer several other characteristics that underlie value streams:

- "Synaptic" linkages among elements of the organization in terms of information complied, created, and shared

- Transition agents that cross organizational boundaries, what specifically is transitioned, and how this is achieved

- Extent to which transitions – and value – depend on a confluence of options, stakeholders, and information

- Impacts of timing relative to broader context-specific considerations such as budget cycles, changes of leadership, etc.

- Sources of impedances that hinder transitions and affordances that foster transitions

- Means of facilitation and other organizational support for expediting and assuring the success of transitions

The results of such an analysis of ongoing and completed projects will be a set of "puzzle pieces" in an overall picture of how the organization functions, as well as several inferences regarding underlying mechanisms. These results should be viewed as hypotheses to be tested by presentation – independently -- to a sample of organization members and asking for their review, comments, and suggested corrections and refinements.

We hasten to note that this may not result in the "truth." However, it will provide an invaluable starting point. Beyond assuring that one is "in the ballpark," this process will also help to foster buy-in from important stakeholders – people in the organization. It is essential that key members of the organization perceive that the assessment and resulting characterization make sense.

Given this characterization, one next needs to assess the extent to which the organization operates according to the ten principles for value-centered R&D organizations outlined in this chapter. Such as assessment will inevitably be fairly qualitative. This will likely be sufficient, as the types of changes that are typically entertained tend to be compelling without complete quantification.

Designing Action Plans

The process just outlined usually results in identification of a variety of deficiencies. Stated as observations, examples include:

- We are so focused on helping business or operational units now, we don't know if we are doing the right things for their futures.

- Assessment of value is difficult because our "next users" have no data or projections of the impacts of what they ask us to provide.

- There are many activities dictated by the broader enterprise for which we can find no value added relative to our role in the enterprise,

- Our incentive and reward systems are not aligned with how we can best provide value, and we may be unable to unilaterally change these systems.

Such observations, as well as a typical variety of more mundane conclusions, provide a rich basis for developing action plans.

The overall process outlined earlier focuses on filling gaps to remediate deficiencies. Some changes are likely to be straightforward. However, some of the types of change illustrated in the above list cannot be initiated unilaterally. These changes require that broader stakeholders embrace an options-based view of the R&D organization.

This suggests that action plans include both overt and covert elements. Some things one can make happen immediately, e.g., require that all proposals include an options argument. There may be other changes, e.g., ceasing non-value-added activities, for which it may be much more difficult to gain approval. Nevertheless, changes that require external approval may be essential to becoming a value-centered R&D organization.

These observations beg the question of who is leading the transformation to becoming a value-centered enterprise. If R&D is the driver, there are more subtleties to negotiate. If top management is the driver, the whole process can be pursued much more directly and aggressively. This suggests, obviously, that R&D executives should focus on selling the CEO, or equivalent, rather than covertly fostering such changes despite the chief executive.

Executing Action Plans

Action plans only deliver value when plans are executed, results are measured, and remedial adaptations made. This obvious statement conflicts with the organizational reality of business as usual. Articulating project proposals and outcomes in terms of option values may be difficult for audiences accustomed to hearing of budgets and milestones. Initially at least, it may be necessary to tell the story both ways.

It is important to keep the momentum by constantly articulating the value story, explaining and advocating an options-based view. This can be facilitated by illustrating specific outcomes and the option values attached to these outcomes. It is important to keep in mind that options-based thinking is not necessarily natural. For example, the idea that options have value even when not executed can take people some time to digest.

It is essential to value-centered planning that potential outcomes be cast in terms of possible value provided. The expected outcomes of action plans need to be monetized in terms of Net Option Values. Measures of risk can be derived from probability distributions of Net Option Value. Taken together, these two metrics enable portfolio plots. Such plots will, with time, become a central element of the organization's strategic dialog.

Indeed, we have found that this impact on the dialog is more important than the numbers. Returns and risks are, of course, good topics for strategic discussions. Just as important, however, are debates about alternatives futures, the options needed to realize these futures, and how these options can be created. Being a primary provider of these options, R&D inherently plays a central role in such debates.

Implementing and managing change is a challenging undertaking in itself. There are numerous difficulties associated with gaining and maintaining momentum. Delusions that execution will be straightforward are common, as are delusions of having changed already (Rouse, 1998). For R&D organizations, recognition of having succumbed to various delusions often comes far too late to be able to remediate these problems and react to an already-changed environment.

REFERENCES

Amram, M., & Kulatilaka, N. (1999). Real options: Managing strategic investment in an uncertain world. Boston: Harvard Business School Press.

Ballhaus, W., Jr., (Ed.).(2000). Science and technology and the Air Force vision. Washington, DC: U.S. Air Force Scientific Advisory Board.

Boer, F.P. (1998). Traps, pitfalls, and snares in the valuation of technology. Research Technology Management, September-October, 45-54.

Boer, F.P. (1999). The valuation of technology: Business and financial issues in R&D. New York: Wiley.

Black, F., & Scholes, M. (1973). The pricing of options and corporate liabilities. Journal of Political Economy, 637-659.

Burke, J. (1996). The pinball effect: How Renaissance water gardens made the carburetor possible and other journeys through knowledge. Boston: Little, Brown.

Christensen, C.M. (1997). The innovator's dilemma: When new technologies cause great firms to fail. Boston: Harvard Business School Press.

Cooper, R.G., Edgett, S.J., & Kleinschmidt, E.J. (1998a). Best practices for managing R&D portfolios. Research Technology Management, 41 (4), 20-33.

Cooper, R.G., Edgett, S.J., & Kleinschmidt, E.J., (1998b). Portfolio management for new products. Reading, MA: Addison-Wesley.

Jain, R.K., & Triandis, H.C., (1990). Management of research and development organizations – Managing the unmanageable. New York: Wiley.

Kaplan, R.S., & Norton, D.P. (1996, Jan-Feb). Using the balanced scorecard as a strategic management tool. Harvard Business Review, 75-85.

Kimberly, J.R., (1986). The organizational context of technological innovation. In D.D. Davis, et al., Eds.,. Managing technological innovation. San Francisco: Jossey-Bass.

Luehrman, T.A., (1998, July-August). Investment opportunities as real options. Harvard Business Review, 51-67.

Luenberger, D.G. (1997). Investment science. Oxford, UK: Oxford University Press.

Markham, S.K., & Griffin, A. (1998). The breakfast of champions: Associations between champions and product development environments, practices, and performance. Journal of Product Innovation Management, 15 (5), 436-454.

Matheson, D., & Matheson, J. (1998). The smart organization: Creating value through strategic R&D. Boston, MA: Harvard Business School Press.

Miller, D.B., (1986). Managing professionals in research and development. San Francisco: Jossey-Bass.

Miller, W.L., & Morris, L. (1999). Fourth generation R&D: Managing knowledge, technology, and innovation. New York: Wiley.

Rouse, W.B. (1985). On better mousetraps and basic research: Getting the applied world to the laboratory door. IEEE Transactions on Systems, Man, and Cybernetics, SMC-15 (1), 2-8.

Rouse, W.B. (1991). Design for success: A human-centered approach to designing successful products and systems. New York: Wiley.

Rouse, W.B. (1992). Strategies for innovation: Creating successful products, systems, and organizations. New York: Wiley.

Rouse, W.B. (1993). Catalysts for change: Concepts and principles for enabling innovation. New York: Wiley.

Rouse, W.B. (1994). Best laid plans. New York: Prentice-Hall.

Rouse, W.B. (1996). Start where you are: Matching your strategy to your marketplace. San Francisco: Jossey-Bass.

Rouse, W.B. (1998). Don't jump to solutions: Thirteen delusions that undermine strategic thinking. San Francisco: Jossey-Bass.

Rouse, W.B. (2001). Essential challenges of strategic management. New York: Wiley.

Rouse, W.B., & Boff, K.R. (1994). Technology transfer from R&D to applications. Wright-Patterson AFB: Armstrong Research Laboratory, December.

Rouse, W.B., & Boff, K.R. (1998). R&D/technology management: A framework for putting technology to work. IEEE Transactions on Systems, Man, and Cybernetics -- Part C, 28 (4), 501-515.

Rouse, W.B., & Boff, K.R. (1999). Making the case for investments in human effectiveness. Information • Knowledge • Systems *Management*, 1 (3), 225-247.

Rouse, W.B., & Boff, K.R. (2001). Strategies for value: Quality, productivity, and innovation in R&D/technology organizations. Systems Engineering, 4 (2), 87-106.

Rouse, W.B., & Boff, K.R. (2003). Value streams in science & technology: A case study of value creation and Intelligent Tutoring Systems. Systems Engineering, 6 (2), 76-91.

Rouse, W.B., Boff, K.R., & Thomas, B.G.S. (1997). Assessing cost/benefits of R&D investments. IEEE Transactions on Systems, Man, and Cybernetics – Part A, 27 (4), 389-401.

Rouse, W.B., Howard, C.W., Carns, W.E., & Prendergast, E.J. (2000). Technology investment advisor: An options-based approach to technology strategy. Information • Knowledge • Systems *Management*, 2 (1), 63-81.

Rouse, W.B., Thomas, B.G.S., & Boff, K.R. (1998). Knowledge maps for knowledge mining: Application to R&D/technology management. IEEE Transactions on Systems, Man, and Cybernetics – Part C, 28 (3), 309-317.

Roussel, P.A., Saad, K.N., & Erickson, T.J., (1991). Third generation R&D: Managing the link to corporate strategy. Cambridge, MA: Arthur D. Little.

Smithson, C.W. (1998). Managing financial risk: A guide to derivative products, financial engineering, and value maximization. New York: McGraw-Hill.

Stevens, G.A.. & Burley, J. (1997, May-June). 3000 raw ideas = 1 commercial success! Research Technology Management, 40 (3), 16-27.

Appendix

FORMULATION AND CALCULATION FOR OPTION-BASED VALUATIONS

The option-based valuations in Table 2 were the results of a systematic process of framing downstream options, estimating input data needed, calculating option values, and performing sensitivity analyses to assess impacts of modeling and input uncertainties. This Appendix elaborates these steps of this process.

Framing Options

This step begins with consideration of the effects sought by the enterprise and the capabilities needed to provide these effects. In the private sector, desired effects are usually profits, perhaps expressed as earnings per share, and needed capabilities are typically competitive market offerings. Options can relate to which technologies are deployed and/or which market segments are targeted. Purchasing options may involve R&D investments, alliances, mergers, acquisitions, etc. Exercising options involves deciding which technologies will be deployed in which markets and investing accordingly.

In the public sector, effects are usually couched in terms of provision of some public good such as defense. More specific effects might be expressed in terms of measures of surveillance and reconnaissance coverage, for instance. Capabilities would then be defined as alternative means for providing the desired effects. Options in this example might relate to technologies that could enable the capabilities for providing these effects. Attractive options would be those that could provide given effects at lower costs of development, acquisition, and/or operations.

Estimating Input Data

Option-based valuations are economic valuations. Various financial projections are needed as input to option calculations. Projections needed include:

- Investment to "purchase" option, including timing
- Investment to "exercise" option, including timing
- Free cash flow – profits and/or cost savings – resulting from exercise
- Volatility of cash flow, typically expressed as a percentage

The analyses needed to create these projections are often substantial. For situations where cash flows are solely cost savings, it is particularly important to define credible baselines against which savings are estimated. Such baselines should be choices that would actually be made were the options of interest not available.

Calculating Option Values

The models employed for option-based valuations were initially developed for valuation of financial instruments. For example, an option might provide the right to buy shares of stock at a predetermined price some time in the future. Valuation concerns what such an option is worth. This depends, obviously, on the likelihood that the stock price will be greater than the predetermined price associated with the option.

More specifically, the value of the option equals the discounted expected value of the stock at maturity, conditional on the stock price at maturity exceeding the exercise price, minus the discounted exercise price, all times the probability that, at maturity, the stock price is greater than the exercise price (Smithson, 1998). Net Option Value equals the option value calculated in this manner minus the cost of purchasing the option.

Thus, there are Net Present Values embedded in the determination of Net Option Values. However, in addition, there is explicit representation of the fact that one will not exercise an option at maturity if the current market share price is less than or equal to the exercise price. As mentioned earlier, sources such as Amram and Kulatilaka (1999), Boer (1998, 1999), Luehrman (1998), Luenberger (1997), and Smithson (1998) provide a wealth of illustrations of how option values are calculated for a range of models.

It is important to note that the options addressed in this chapter are usually termed "real" options in the sense that the investments associated with these options are usually intended to create tangible assets rather than purely financial assets. Application of financially derived models to non-financial investments often raises the issue of the extent to which assumptions from financial markets are valid in the domains of non-financial investments. This concern is usually addressed with sensitivity analysis.

Performing Sensitivity Analyses

The assumptions underlying the option-pricing model and the estimates used as input data for the model are usually subject to much uncertainty. This uncertainty should be reflected in option valuations calculated. Therefore, what is needed is a probability distribution of valuations rather than solely a point estimate. This probability distribution can be generated using Monte Carlo simulation to systematically vary model and input variables using assumed distributions of parameter/data variations. As noted earlier, the software tool employed for the analyses summarized in Table 2 -- *Technology Investment Advisor* (Rouse, et al., 2000) -- supported these types of sensitivity analyses.

These analyses enable consideration of options in terms of both returns and risks. Interesting "What if?" scenarios can be explored. A question that we have frequently encountered when performing these analyses is, "How bad can it get and have this decision still make sense?" This question reflects a desire to thoroughly understand the decision being entertained, not just get better numbers.

Examples from Table 2

Consider the example of semiconductor memory in the second row (from the bottom) of Table 2. For $109M of R&D, this company "purchased" an option to deploy this technology in its markets four years later for an expected investment of approximately $1.7B. The expected profit was roughly $3.5B. The Net Option Value of over $0.5B reflects the fact that they bought this option for much less than it was worth.

In the second row (from the top) of Table 2, a government agency invested $420M in R&D to "purchase" an option on unmanned air vehicle technology that, when deployed 10 years later for $72M, would yield roughly $750M of operating savings when compared to manned aircraft providing the same mission effects. The Net Option Value of $137M represents the value of this option is excess of what they invested.

It is instructive to compare these two examples intuitively. For the semiconductor memory investment, the option value of over $600M (i.e., the R&D investment plus the NOV) represents roughly one third of the net present difference between the expected profit from exercising the option and the investment required to exercise it. This is due to considerable uncertainties in the 10+ year time period when most of the profits would accrue. In contrast, for the unmanned air vehicle technology investment, the option value of roughly $560M represents over two thirds of the net present difference between the expected cost savings from exercising the option and the investment required to exercise it, despite the returns occurring in a similar 10+ year time frame.

This may seem counterintuitive. However, the quotient of expected profit (or cost savings) divided by the investment required to exercise the option is quite different for these two examples. This quotient is roughly 2.0 for the semiconductor memory option and 10.0 for unmanned air vehicle technology investment. Thus, the likelihood of the option being "in the money" is significantly higher for the latter. This is why the option value is one third of the net present difference for semiconductor memory and two-thirds for unmanned air vehicle technology.

CHAPTER 10
SIX SIGMA QUALITY

TIRTHANKAR DASGUPTA AND C.F. JEFF WU

ABSTRACT

Pioneered by Motorola and popularized by GE, the Six Sigma philosophy has spread like a wildfire across the corporate world during the last decade. In this chapter, we discuss what Six Sigma means as a metric, a philosophy and as a company-wide approach for Quality Management. The road map, organizational structure and training necessary for successful deployment of Six Sigma are discussed. A case study based on an Indian manufacturing company illustrates a typical Six Sigma project leading to financial benefits.

BRIEF HISTORY OF SIX SIGMA

Six Sigma quality concepts were pioneered at Motorola during the early eighties. USA Today commented in 1989, "Motorola engineered one of the most dramatic business comebacks of the decade". Interestingly enough, the term 'Six Sigma' was coined by an engineer Bill Smith. As a Motorola employee, Smith did not share directly in the profits generated by the company's Six Sigma applications. However, over the years, he and Motorola garnered numerous awards and recognition for his vital work to improve profitability in America's manufacturing sector. He was especially proud of his role in Motorola's winning the prestigious Malcolm Baldrige National Quality Award, which the company received from President Reagan in 1988, two years after Motorola implemented Smith's Six Sigma principles.

In recent years, success with Six Sigma has been so dramatic, that it is spreading like wildfire across the corporate world. This prompted *Quality Progress, New York Times, Wall Street Journal, Business Week, USA Today, Fortune, Chicago Tribune,* etc. to take note of this and carry full-length articles on the subject summarizing the amazing results achieved by the organizations that practiced Six Sigma quality. Even the periodical *Business Today* published in India devoted one full issue to the Six Sigma quality.

Much of the credit for the widespread interest in Six Sigma quality across corporate America goes to John F. Welch, Jr., Chairman of General Electric Company. In 1995, General Electric embarked on an ambitious corporate-wide Six Sigma quality initiative in all its divisions including GE Capital, NBC, Aircraft Engines, Plastics, and Medical Systems. GE Capital and NBC are clearly non-manufacturing operations but even in the manufacturing divisions, there are manufacturing and non-manufacturing applications of Six Sigma quality as one might expect. The benefits of Six Sigma quality program implementation of GE were reported to be $1 billion in 1998 and more than $2 billion in 1999.

WHAT IS SIX SIGMA?

Six Sigma is an optimized level of performance approaching zero-defects in a process producing a product, service or transaction. It indicates achievement and maintenance of world class performance. A Six Sigma quality compliant process or transaction produces extremely few defects - 3.45 per million opportunities (99.9997% defect free). A defect is something that results in customer dissatisfaction. Customer satisfaction is the goal of Six Sigma; best bottom line performance results as a by-product. Six Sigma quality applies equally well to all enterprises, large and small, manufacturing and transactional. The current standard based on statistical process control is 3-sigma, which translate to approximately 66,800 defects per million opportunities (6.68% defective) or 93.32% good. The impact of improvement from 3-sigma quality to six-sigma quality can be enormous, as seen in Table 1.

The goals of defect reduction, yield improvement, improved customer satisfaction, lower cost, and thus higher net income, are attained by an effective use of statistical and optimization tools in analysis. Business decisions are based on factual data and not on 'gut feel'. Jack Welch aptly states, "Six Sigma quality initiatives represent a paradigm shift from fixing products so that they are perfect to fixing processes so that they produce nothing but perfection, or close to it." The root causes of problems are fixed and solutions optimized. Controls are put in place so that the problems once fixed, stay fixed.

Process Capability in Sigma Level	Defects Per Million Opportunities
2	308537
3	66807
4	6210
5	233
6	3.4

TABLE 1. Process Capability vs. PPM Defects

For an organization to embark on a Six Sigma program means delivering top quality service and product, while at the same time virtually eliminating all internal inefficiencies. In other words, it means having a common focus on excellence throughout the whole organization in everything they do. *In essence, Six Sigma means overall excellence, not only in the finished product, but in the administrative, service and the manufacturing processes throughout the whole organization.*

What makes a Six Sigma program successful is the full support of upper management and a solid phase-wise infrastructure; but as important, what makes a Six Sigma program successful is a proven methodology that standardizes the right tools and techniques, and provides the working teams with a step-wise progression to apply those tools.

THE MANY FACETS OF SIX SIGMA

According to Harry (1997), Six Sigma may be looked upon as:

- Metric (measure).

- Goal.

- Benchmark.

- Philosophy.

- Value.

As already explained in the previous section, the sigma value is a metric that indicates how well the process is performing. The higher the sigma value, the better is the process. Sigma measures the capability of the process to perform defect-free work. The Six Sigma metric and its computation for any process are described in detail in this section.

Six Sigma is a goal – because achieving Six Sigma level of performance (or equivalently 3.4 ppm defects) is the goal of any organization which desires to be a world class company.

A great thing about Six Sigma is that, it can set a benchmark for any process, irrespective of its nature. The performances of two entirely different processes may be compared with their Sigma ratings. Table 2 shows the interpretation of Sigma rating for three entirely different situations – typing, transformer manufacturing and filling of a purchase order. Note that the third activity is of a service type. Yet a Sigma rating can help us to understand the performance level of this activity on the same scale as a transformer manufacturing process.

The Six Sigma philosophy can be expressed using the following chain of causation (Harry, 1997):

- Improvement of our business means improvement of our processes.

- To improve means we must be able to predict and prevent, not detect and react.

- Prediction capability is dependent on process capability.

- Process capability is best understood and reported using statistics.

- The Sigma, a statistical measure of a process, tells us how capable it is.

- The process Sigma can be used to compare similar or dissimilar processes (benchmarking)

- Benchmarking tells us what we do well and what we do not.

- Once basic competencies and deficiencies are known, corrective action can be taken.

- Statistical tools can help in devising effective corrective actions.

- Corrective action on the process leads to process improvement (e.g., reduction of defects, cycle-time and cost).

Sigma	Typing	Transformer Mfg.	Filling of Purchase Orders
3	1.5 wrongly spelled words per page in a book	66,807 defects per million items	66,807 incorrect or unreadable entries per million boxes to be filled.
4	1 wrongly spelled word per 30 pages in a book	6210 defects per million items	6210 incorrect or unreadable entries per million boxes to be filled.
5	1 wrongly spelled word in a set of encyclopedia	233 defects per million items	233 incorrect or unreadable entries per million boxes to be filled.
6	1 wrongly spelled word in all of the books contained in a library.	3.4 defects per million items	3.4 incorrect or unreadable entries per million boxes to be filled.

TABLE 2. Six Sigma as a Benchmark for All Processes

Six Sigma may be considered as a value since the focus on various managerial and technical issues for a Six Sigma organization is entirely different from that of a classical organization (Harry, 1997). This distinction is illustrated in Table 3.

A Six Sigma organization is thus expected to use all modern concepts, tools and methodologies of quality in day-to-day activities. For details on concepts of design for producibility, see Priest (1988). An in-depth discussion of all topics related to design of experiments, including robust parameter design, can be found in Wu and Hamada (2000). A comprehensive discussion on SPC charts can be found in Montgomery (2000), and for a detailed reference on feedback and feedforward control, see Box and Luceno (1997).

Issue		Focus	
		Classical	**Six Sigma**
1	Management	Cost & time	Quality & time
2	Goal Setting	Realistic perception	Reach-out & stretch
3	Direction	Seat-of-pant	Benchmarking & metrics
4	Chain-of-command	Hierarchy	Empowered team
5	Focus	Product	Process
6	Approach	Symptomatic	Problematic
7	Problems	Fixing	Preventing
8	Reasoning	Experience based	System based
9	Problem solving	Expert based	System based
10	Analytical perspective	Point estimate	Variability
11	Design	Performance	Producibility
12	Variable search	One-factor-at-a-time	Design of experiments
13	Tolerancing	Worst case	Root-sum-of-square
14	Manufacturing	Trial and error	Robust design
15	Process monitoring	Specification limits	SPC charts
16	Process adjustment	ad hoc	Feedback/feedforward control

TABLE 3. Classical Approach vs. Six Sigma Approach

THE SIX SIGMA METRIC AND ITS COMPUTATION

We know that in order to assess the performance of any process, we need to measure its output. This output may actually be measurable (i.e. a variable); or may be qualitative, e.g. presence or absence of a defect (i.e. an attribute). We shall see that, whether the process output is a variable or an attribute, the Six Sigma metric shall help in representing it in a common form that will allow it to be compared with any similar or dissimilar process (Dasgupta 2003).

Consider a manufacturing process in which the task is to manufacture a chemical with a minimum purity of L (e.g. 99%). Corresponding to n batches of the chemical produced in a week, let x_1, x_2, .., x_n denote the purity values. Let m and s denote respectively the mean and standard deviation of x_1, x_2, .., x_n. Then the *z-value* or *sigma* value of the manufacturing process with respect to purity is defined as z=(m-L)/s. If the data pertain to a short period, this z value is termed 'short term sigma' and is denoted by z_{st}. The 'long term sigma' is computed as z_{lt} = z_{st} - 1.5, considering a probable 1.5s shift in the process setting in the long run.

The probability of manufacturing a batch with purity less than the specified value can be obtained as the area to the left of 99% in the normal curve. This may be called defects per opportunity (dpo) if manufacture of each batch is considered as an opportunity of getting a defect or defects per unit (dpu) if each batch is considered as a unit. For specification limits of the form T±Δ, the short-term sigma may be computed as (U-T)/s = (T-L)/s = Δ/s, where U and L denote the upper and lower specification limits respectively. The long-term sigma, as before, may be computed by subtracting 1.5 from the short-term sigma. Figure 1 shows a centered three-sigma process and a shifted six-sigma process (which is expected to produce 3.45 defectives per million opportunities).

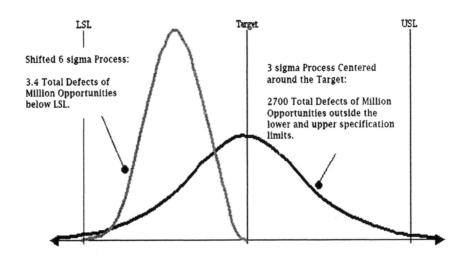

FIGURE 1. Three-Sigma and Six-Sigma Processes

If we consider the task of filling a purchase order, each entry may be considered as an opportunity for defect. Suppose there are n entries to be made in each purchase order, and during a week k such purchase orders are filled. An inspection reveals that the total number of defective entries is d. Then, the total number of opportunities is kn and defects per opportunity is given by dpo=d/kn. The yield, i.e., the probability of filling in a purchase order free of defects, is given by $(1-dpo)^n$. For large n, using the Poisson distribution, this may be approximated by e^{-dpu} where dpu=d/k denotes the defects per unit. Using the table for the standard normal distribution, the z-value or sigma-value corresponding to the yield (i.e., the value on the standard normal scale, the area to the right of which is $1- e^{-dpu}$) can be obtained.

Thus the beauty of the six-sigma measurement method is that, one can compare a chemical manufacturing process (from the point of view of output quality) and a purchasing process on the same scale. In the context of the former, a sigma level of 3 would mean producing 66,807 defective batches per million, whereas the same would mean 66,807 mistakes per million entries made while filling purchase orders in the latter case.

The concept of *rolled throughput yield* is also a very useful metric in the context of six-sigma philosophy. Pyzdek (2000) defines rolled throughput yield as the probability of being able to pass a unit of product or service through the entire process (or chain) defect free. Thus, if we consider a sequential chain of n entities, the rolled throughput yield is given by $RTY = \Pi\ Y_i$, i.e., the product of the yields $Y_1, Y_2, .., Y_n$ for the n individual entities (given by e^{-dpu} for each). The rolled throughput yield is much better correlated with other business success measures compared to the conventional notion of yield since it unearths the 'hidden factory' in terms of in-process losses, rework, increased cycle time etc.

Examples

Consider a situation where the thickness of 84 rolled gaskets have been measured to study the capability of the rolling process. A histogram constructed with the data shows a normal pattern: the average and standard deviation computed from the data are 1.55 mm and 0.02 mm respectively. The specification for rolled thickness is 1.50-1.60 mm.

Using the definitions stated before, we get

$$z_{st} = (USL-T)/s = (1.60-1.55)/0.02 = 2.5, \text{ and}$$

$$z_{lt} = z_{st} - 1.5 = 1.0.$$

Thus, the short-term sigma rating of the rolling process is 2.5. Considering the effect of shift, the long-term sigma rating is 1.0. The process can thus be called a one-sigma process.

Now, consider a case where the data is of the attribute type. Suppose 600 product items have been inspected and 50 defects have been found. Then defects per unit (dpu) = 50/600 = 0.083. Thus, the yield = e^{-dpu} = $e^{-0.083}$ = 0.920 and the percentage of defective items in the first pass will be 1-yield = 8%.

This is equivalent to 80,000 PPM and corresponds to a short-term Z-value of 2.9. This means a sigma level of 2.9. As before, subtracting 1.5, we get the long-term sigma level as 1.4, which is far from satisfactory and reflects an extremely poor level of performance.

BREAKTHROUGH STRATEGY FOR SIX SIGMA IMPLEMENTATION

Manufacturing industries are becoming increasingly aware that the practice of Six Sigma has the potential to extend many benefits to the producer, as well as to their prized asset – their customers. As we know by now that some of these benefits include, but are not limited to: (a) reduced total cost, (b) enhanced product quality and reliability, (c) lower manufacturing cycle time and (d) fewer design changes after release for production. However, such benefits can only be realized if the product design and manufacturing process can work together; i.e., the product and process are optimized relative to each other.

The breakthrough strategy for six-sigma thus addresses – how to properly **characterize** and **optimize** one or more of the product characteristics through the systematic **measurement, analysis, improvement and control** of the process. When properly done, the approach leads to all of the previously mentioned benefits.

Process characterization is concerned with the identification and benchmarking of key product characteristics. By way of a gap analysis, common success factors are identified.

- **Phase 1 (Measurement):** This phase is concerned with selecting one or more product characteristics, i.e., dependent variables, mapping the respective processes, making the necessary measurements, recording the results on process "control cards", and estimating the short and long-term process capability.

- **Phase 2 (Analysis):** This phase entails benchmarking the key product performance metrics. Following this, a gap analysis (mapping the gap between specified and implied customer requirements and the existing process) is often undertaken to identify the common factors of successful performance, i.e., what factors explain best in-class performance.

Process optimization is aimed at the identification and containment of the key process variables, which exert undue influence over the key product characteristics.

- **Phase 3 (Improvement):** This phase is usually initiated by selecting those product performance characteristics that must be improved to achieve the goal. Once this is done, the characteristics are diagnosed to reveal the major sources of variation. Next, the key process variables are identified by way of statistically designed experiments. For each process variable that proves to be important, performance specifications are established.

- **Phase 4 (Control):** This phase is related to ensuring that the new process conditions are documented and monitored via statistical process control methods. After a setting in period, the process capability would be reassessed. Depending upon the outcomes of such a follow-up analysis, it may be necessary to revisit one or more of the preceding phases.

The Measure-Analyze-Improve-Control (MAIC) cycle is something like Deming's Plan-Do-Check-Act (PDCA) cycle (Deming, 1986). Some experts prefer to characterize the breakthrough strategy as a five-step DMAIC (Define-Measure-Analyze-Improve-Control) approach rather than a four step MAIC. Table 4 lists the steps in each of the four phases of the MAIC cycle. Details of each step can be found in Pyzdek (2003) and Pande et al. (2000).

Measurement	Analysis
1. Select key product.	6. Establish performance capability.
2. Create product tree.	7. Select performance variable.
3. Define performance variables.	8. Benchmark performance variable.
4. Create process map.	9. Discover best-in-class performance.
5. Measure performance variables.	10. Conduct gap analysis.
	11. Identify success factors.
	12. Define performance goal.
Improvement	**Control**
13. Select performance variable.	19. Select causal variable.
14. Diagnose variable performance.	20. Define control system.
15. Propose causal variables.	21. Validate control system.
16. Confirm causal variables.	22. Implement control system.
17. Establish operating limits.	23. Audit control system.
18. Verify performance improvement.	24. Monitor performance metrics.

TABLE 4. The Breakthrough Roadmap

ORGANIZATION FOR SIX SIGMA

Implementation of Six Sigma in a typical organization is usually carried out by people assuming the following roles:

Senior Management: Senior Management, also known as 'C-Level Management' (CEO, CIO, CFO and peers), include the individuals that set, communicate and drive the overall business objectives. They are also the individuals that are required to incorporate Six Sigma objectives into their operational plans. Examples of objectives may include:

- X% of employees trained by a certain date.

- Y% reduction in defects for all customer visible processes by quarter end.

- $Z in back-office projects savings by the end of the year.

Champion/Sponsor: The champion or sponsor is a high level executive of the organization appointed by the chief executive to oversee the implementation of Six Sigma in the organization. The champion's responsibilities include forumlating a detailed plan for implementation of Six Sigma in the organization, benchmarking the company's performance parameters with other organizations, providing resources to complete the job and assisting black belts to select projects.

Master Black Belt: Master Black Belts provide expert guidance and coaching to leaders and members of project teams on skills and methods and help teams gather and interpret the data. They provide guidance to the project teams as and when needed. In many organizations, the master black belt is a consultant or a representative of an external agency.

Black Belts: Black belts are directly responsible for the Six Sigma projects. They select the team members, manage schedules, lead team meetings and keep records during the projects. After completion of a project, they make sure that the documentation is completed and lessons are captured and check the appropriateness of implementation.

Green Belts: They constitute the project teams, participate in meetings, carry out assignments, contribute their knowledge and expertise and learn necessary skills and methods in the process.

TRAINING AND TOOLS FOR SIX SIGMA

It is needless to say that successful implementation of Six Sigma requires rigorous training at all levels of the organization. The training needs at different levels of the organization are different, ranging from an overview of the philosophy of Six Sigma to detailed exposure to the tools necessary for specific Six Sigma projects.

Training for Senior Management should include a program overview, business and financial benefits of implementation, real-world examples of successful deployments, specific application to business/industry, and the required training and tools to ensure successful implementation. Depending on Senior Management time availability and their desire to learn the details, Black Belt training is also recommended.

Training for the Champion is more detailed than that provided to Senior Management. Topics would include the Six Sigma concept, methodology, tools and requirements to ensure successful implementation within their organization. Depending on the Champions' time availability and their desire to learn the details, Black Belt training is also recommended.

Training for Black Belts includes detailed information about the concept, methodology and tools. Depending on the instructor, the duration is usually between two and four weeks, and may include one of more weeks in between sections. Statistics is included in the agenda, but typically does not include as much detail as that provided to Quality Leaders.

Green Belts, may also take training courses developed specifically for part time Project Leaders. Training is similar to Black Belt training, but shorter in duration because less detail on complex tools and statistics is provided. Employees are instead told to ask their Black Belt for help in specific areas.

One of the major aspects of Six Sigma is to make decisions based on data, and this calls for deployment of suitable statistical tools. These tools are key elements of Six Sigma training and in several organizations like GE comprise up to half of the standard curriculum (Hahn et al. 2001). According to them, the goal of standard Six Sigma statistical training is to give Green Belts and Black Belts an appreciation of statistical thinking and a hands-on introduction to the tools needed for successful projects.

In GE, all professional employees receive training that involves eight to 15 days of instruction, given in one-week doses over a three to four month period. Topics discussed during the first week are those relevant to the 'Define and Measure' phase and include Six Sigma overview and the DMAIC roadmap, process mapping, Quality Function Deployment (QFD), Failure Mode and Effect Analysis (FMEA), basic statistical techniques, process capability analysis and measurement systems analysis. In the second week of training, the focus is on data analysis tools like hypothesis testing and confidence intervals, correlation and regression and multivariate analysis. Design of Experiments and related topics constitute the bulk of the training imparted during the third week; and the fourth week's training covers Control Plans, Mistake Proofing, etc. Those aspects of statistical training needed by Black Belts is discussed in detail by Hoerl (2001).

CASE STUDY: REDUCTION OF CRACKS IN COPPER GASKET RINGS

Define Phase

An Indian company, manufacturing gaskets and radiators for automobiles, identified this project at the initial phase of Six Sigma implementation. The company manufactures gaskets that have copper rings as one of their components. Circular discs of copper are annealed in an annealing furnace to give them their desired hardness. Next, rings cut from these annealed copper discs are fitted into gaskets. The hardness of annealed copper discs is an extremely critical characteristic as a variation in hardness results in cracking or bending of copper rings after fitting them in gaskets.

The variation in hardness of annealed copper was found to be unacceptably high. This resulted in rework on a high percentage of gaskets owing to cracked/bent copper rings. A very high percentage of gaskets had to be reworked as a consequence of this problem. The objective of the project was thus to investigate the reasons behind variation in hardness of annealed copper discs, improve the process by taking corrective actions and control the improved process appropriately.

Measure Phase

The project team collected historical data on hardness of annealed copper discs from past quality records and analyzed them using basic statistical tools including histograms, control charts and process capability indices. The process capability was found to be extremely poor and the histogram showed multiple peaks, giving indications of a mixture of various groups of discs in the output.

Analyze Phase

The project team, consisting of representatives from production, R&D and quality assurance departments, mapped and documented the current annealing process. A cause-effect diagram for the factors influencing the hardness was developed. After collecting further data on the basis of the cause-effect diagram, it was found that there was a huge variation in the hardness of the raw material purchased from three suppliers. This explained the presence of multiple peaks in the histogram. Analysis of variance, a statistical tool, was used at this stage to confirm the root cause of variation.

Improve Phase

Although a supplier-to-supplier difference in the hardness of incoming copper was obvious, owing to certain unavoidable reasons, none of them could be dropped from the approved vendors' list. It was therefore decided to conduct a parameter design experiment to make the process robust (i.e., much less sensitive to the effect of noise, which in this case, is variation in input quality).

Four control factors, i.e., temperature of the furnace (A), conveyor motor rpm (B), rate of water flow (C), and method of placing the discs on the conveyor (D) were chosen. Three levels of each of the factors A, B and C were chosen. D was, however, a two-level factor. In order to avoid "bad regions" resulting from the interacting factors A and B (see Wu and Hamada 2000, Chapter 6), the technique of *sliding levels* was used to design the experiment.

Robust settings of the four factors were obtained by analyzing the experimental data. Trial runs validated the analysis results.

Control Phase

The project team suggested implementation of statistical control charts to keep the hardness of copper discs manufactured by the improved process stable and under control. Control plans for maintaining the process variables around the suggested settings were also developed and responsibilities were clearly defined.

Documentation and Results

The study was documented by the project team leader and the master black belt and presented to all company workers to inspire similar applications. The process capability was improved three-fold as a result of this project and the instances of cracks were almost negligible after implementation.

CONCLUSIONS

Six Sigma is now the buzzword in the field of quality. Based on the principle of define-measure-analyze-improve-control, it has the potential of changing organizational performance radically. Several organizations have reported achieving dramatic improvements through Six Sigma projects.

One should, however, keep in mind the warning issued by experts like Sanders and Hild (2000) about indiscriminant use of Six Sigma metrics. According to them, a disadvantage of using measures such as dpu, sigma level, rolled throughput yield, etc., is in transporting the notion of Six Sigma processes from a management philosophy to numerical targets for individual processes. This contradicts Deming's (1986) philosophy 'eliminate slogans, targets and numerical goals'. It is top management's responsibility to disseminate this knowledge in an organization from the right perspective and ensure that measures are viewed as something that identifies opportunities for improvement and not as hardcore targets and numerical goals. If preached and practiced with purpose, the sheer motivational aspect of being a 'Six Sigma company' should be strong enough to pave the way for improvement.

ACKNOWLEDGEMENT

This research is partially supported by the National Science Foundation (NSF) grants DMS-03-05996.

REFERENCES

Box, G.E.P. and Luceno, A. (1997), *Statistical Control by Monitoring and Feedback Adjustments*, New York: Wiley.

Dasgupta, T. (2003), Using Six Sigma Metric To Measure And Improve The Performance Of Supply Chain, *Total Quality Management*, 14(3), 355-366.

Deming. W.E. (1986), *Out of the Crisis*, Cambridge, MA: MIT Press.

Hahn, G.J., Doganaksoy, N. and Stanard, C. (2001), Statistical Tools For Six Sigma, Technical Information Series 2001CRD126, GE Research and Development Center.

Harry, M. (1997), *The Vision of Six Sigma – A Roadmap for Breakthrough*, Tri Star Publishing.

Hoerl, R. (2001), Six Sigma Black Belts : What Do They Need To Know ? *Journal of Quality Technology*, 33(4), 391-406.

Montgomery, D.C. (2000), *Introduction to Statistical Quality Control*, Wiley, New York.

Pande, Peter S., Neuman, Robert P. & Cavanagh, Roland R. (2000), *The Six Sigma Way*, McGraw-Hill.

Priest, J. (1988), *Engineering Design for Producibility and Reliability*, Marcel Dekker, Inc., New York.

Pyzdek, T. (2000), Yield The Right Way, *Quality Digest*, March 2000.

Pyzdek, T. (2003), *The Six Sigma Handbook*, McGraw-Hill.

Sanders, D. and Hild, C.R. (2000), *Common Myths About Six Sigma*, Quality Engineering, 13(2), 269-276.

Wu, C.F.J., and Hamada, M. (2000), *Experiments: Planning, Analysis, and Parameter Design Optimization*, New York: Wiley.

CHAPTER 11

ENTERPRISE IT AND TRANSFORMATION

RAHUL C. BASOLE AND RICHARD A. DEMILLO

ABSTRACT

Today's enterprises are using information technology (IT) in virtually all aspects of their business. IT enables enterprises to provide seamless access to corporate data; streamline existing and create new business processes; design, improve, and deliver new products and services; and communicate and collaborate with customers, suppliers and other organizations across the globe. As enterprises undergo transformation of various kinds, IT can become a driving or inhibiting force to successful change. This chapter highlights some of the current enterprise IT trends, presents the fundamental drivers of the information economy, and suggests some basic architectural IT principles that can facilitate a smooth transformational process. The success and failure resulting from appropriately, and lack of, implementing these principles are illustrated in numerous examples and case studies throughout the chapter. The chapter concludes by introducing a novel concept of enterprise IT and transformational maturity and offering some practical guidelines.

INTRODUCTION

Information technology (IT) has been one of the key drivers of business in the twenty-first century. Enterprises in virtually all sectors of industry, commerce, and government are fundamentally dependent on information technologies. Enterprises in industries such as telecommunications, media, entertainment, healthcare, and financial services are increasingly digitizing their products, services, and offerings; often times their mere existence depends on the effective application of information technologies. Similarly, with the emergence of the Internet and electronic commerce, the use of technology is not only becoming an accepted, but also an expected way of conducting business. Consequently, enterprises are increasingly looking to use IT to improve their business operations and create new opportunities that enable them to achieve higher levels of efficiency and provide them with a source of competitive advantage.

Enterprises are using information technologies to seamlessly link their offices, factories, workers, suppliers, and customers around the globe. The use of IT has led to new business models, businesses, industries, and markets. It has become evident that business and IT are increasingly intertwined. Enterprise strategies, processes, and procedures are often dependent on IT platforms, applications, databases, and networks. A change in any one of these elements often requires a change in the other components. As enterprises pursue transformations, they must therefore take current and future capabilities of their IT systems into consideration and effectively align them with their business strategies. Continuously changing market demands and environmental pressures as well as changing technological requirements will also impact an enterprises' IT strategy throughout the transformation process. Before providing any strategic perspective, it is important to have an understanding of what constitutes enterprise IT, what underlying forces have and continue to shape enterprise IT, and have led to IT as a transformational enabler.

Information technology has become an increasingly integral component of today's enterprises. IT is ubiquitous and enables a degree of connectivity that was difficult to achieve even a decade ago. Technology has evolved so rapidly that is often the cause of enormous transformations. The growing interdependence between business and technology can be attributed to the soaring power and declining costs of information, communication, and networking technologies.

One of the most stimulating forces for businesses during the IT age has been the emergence of the Internet. The Internet provides an infrastructure that brings individuals and businesses together and enables global communication and information exchange using telecommunications and computing power. The Internet, simply stated, is a network of networks that spans the world. The Internet interconnects a myriad of different networks, systems, and computers. In an increasingly borderless world, the Internet provides its users with the tools to interact, communicate, and exchange information. The extraordinary growth of the Internet can be mainly attributed to a few phenomena that can be broadly characterized by three fundamental laws of the Internet age.

Moore's Law. The first law is the familiar Moore's Law, named after Gordon Moore, the founder of Intel Corporation. Moore's Law states that every one and half years the number of transistors on a microchip doubles while cost remains constant. In other words, Moore's Law states that computers will get faster, smaller, and cheaper over time. It has held true over the years and experts project that this phenomenon will continue for the foreseeable future as increasing supercomputing powers are being integrated into desktops, laptops, and mobile devices. Computer memory and storage capacity are two other areas that are experiencing a similar fate. This phenomenon makes it very affordable for individuals and small businesses alike to be equipped with the technological means to conduct commerce and transfer information as fast as large corporations can.

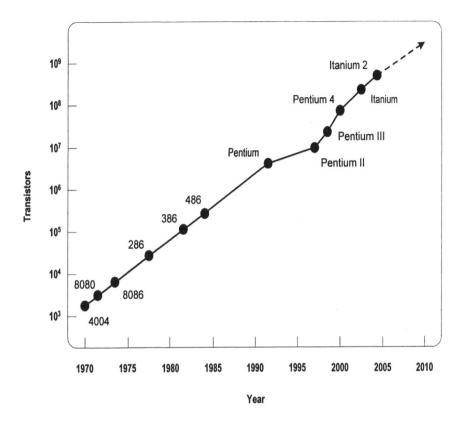

FIGURE 1. Moore's Law states the number of transistors per chip doubles every 18 months while costs remain constant (Intel, 2005).

Metcalf's Law. The second law is Metcalf's law. It states that the value of a network equals the square of the number of users, while the value to the individual user is proportional to the number of users. To illustrate this law, consider the telephone. The telephone is of very limited use if only two users have one. If a whole city is on the telephone system, it becomes much more useful. If the system expands to an entire country or the world, the value of the system grows significantly. This concept applies similarly to other technologies and has been particularly true in the case of the Internet. The value of the Internet grew dramatically as more and more computers were interconnected on the network. The combination of Moore's Law and Metcalf's Law exemplify the exponential growth of the Internet.

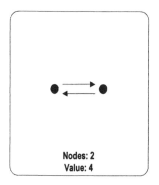
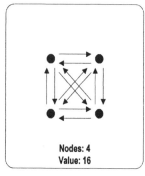
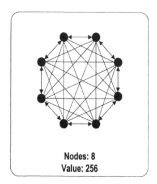

FIGURE 2. Metcalf's Law states that the value of a network scales as the square of the number of those connected to it.

Law of Bandwidth. As the demand for IT, communications, and the Internet has increased, the need for more bandwidth has also grown exponentially. Bandwidth refers to the transmission capacity of a communications channel. Similar to the progression of microprocessors defined by Moore's Law, the speed and capacity of the transmission medium has soared while bandwidth cost has dropped tremendously. This trend is further amplified by the movement of enterprises towards Internet protocol-based applications, such as telephony, videoconferencing, and streaming media, which require significant amounts of bandwidth. Today bandwidth is rapidly turning into a commodity as companies have begun trading capacity through clearinghouses.

As time has progressed, these three observations have continued to be accurate. The growth of the Internet and use of IT by businesses has largely been driven by the prophecy of these laws.

High-Performance Engineering

As enterprises increasingly embrace the use of IT, knowledge becomes a central organizational asset that needs to be managed, stored, and disseminated. Particularly in information economies, enterprise productivity often depends on the availability of knowledge. IT has indeed increased productivity in a wide-range of industries, and led to the concept of high performance engineering. Through the use of high computing power and advanced software applications, enterprises are able to develop, design, and deliver products and services at a much higher rate. While traditional physical design methodologies required designers to develop individual models and physically test their models, the use of high-performance computing systems allows designers to design their product using sophisticated graphics and simulation software, test their prototypes, and make design modifications on the computer and avoid an expensive and time-consuming development process. Boeing, for example, uses high-performance computers and computer-aided design (CAD) systems in simulations of computational fluid dynamics to dramatically shorten product development costs and time.

In the manufacturing industry, Ford Motor Company developed a product information management (PIM) system that unifies all aspects of product engineering, development, and manufacturing. This is a modern IT system that replaces many different IT tools in use at Ford's major development centers. The connection to enterprise transformation is clear: the PIM enables Ford to shift resources among its product development centers to take advantage of changing transportation, energy, and labor changes and to adapt quickly to changing global market demands.

Another prevalent example of high-performance engineering is the use of computing power to facilitate the management of the product lifecycle. Product lifecycle management (PLM) solutions help enterprises innovate new products that meet and anticipate customer demands. Based on eXtensible Markup Language (XML), PLM solutions enable a seamless exchange of data between product lifecycle processes and increase the speed and agility of product development while reducing the associated risk.

One-to-One Marketing

IT has also introduced significant changes in the way enterprises conduct business. It has decreased the cost of creating, sending, and storing information while making information more widely available. Traditional business models required customers to visit physical stores to find out information about products and services. As such, the cost of comparing prices was high as customers had to travel from store to store to find the product or service they were looking for. The advent of the Internet changed this relationship drastically. As firms provided their product and service information, customers were instantly connected and informed. In other words, physical goods were unbundled from their traditional value chain channels and changed the way firms conducted business. The Internet enabled businesses to provide their products and services online, replacing some of the traditional channels, which had become inefficient and less economical, via electronic means. For example, in pre-Internet days, consumers who wanted to purchase books had to visit their local bookstore in order to obtain information about the latest book titles, prices, and their availability. Often times, bookstores had a monopoly on this information. When Amazon.com opened its gates as an online bookstore, it provided consumers the availability to search through a vast electronic catalog to find titles, along with table of contents, reviews and information about related books. Consumers were now capable of ordering books from the convenience of their computers. Because Amazon.com did not require the cost of physical stores, inventory, and other overhead costs traditionally associated to traditional bookstores, it was capable of offering its book selection at a significantly lower cost to consumers. The attraction to consumers was undoubtedly apparent. Similar examples can be found in the financial industry, where banks now provide their services online or e-brokerages enable stock trading without the act of the middleman. The use of the Internet transformed businesses and business models as we traditionally knew them.

The attractiveness of the Internet to consumers is certainly related to the improvements in convenience it provided. However, the Internet also provided a shift in the information asymmetry that existed between the parties involved. As more and more firms offered their products and services online, consumers were now in the position to compare prices and offerings, and make a more informed decision. Similarly, businesses were now able to reach more customers with the availability of an e-presence. Geographical boundaries were not constraining enterprises to offer their products and services around the globe. As such, the Internet transformed the reach and richness of information provided to consumers and businesses.

With the use of the Internet, enterprises have also received a new weapon in obtaining more information about the customers. The Internet enables businesses to understand buying patterns, browsing behavior, and user preferences. Today's websites can collect a range of information about their customers and aid enterprises in developing appropriate strategies targeting individual consumers. Amazon.com for examples provides customers personalized information on potential items they may be interested in purchasing. These suggestions are based on the browsing patterns and user characteristics that were carefully determined through sophisticated data mining techniques.

The ability to provide personalized and customized information to consumers can also be used in the backend of enterprises. Products and services can be customized to fit the individual customers' needs before they even get created, built, or produced. The Dell Direct Model is a classic example of this type of one-to-one marketing strategy. Consumers build their desired computer online and have the ability to configure it according to their preference. As soon as they have finished "building" their system, the order to manufacturing is sent and the machine is custom built. This direct model enables Dell to minimize their inventory and provide customers real-time feedback to their computer buying experience. The Dell Direct Model has propelled Dell to the top of computer manufacturers today; the entire business has been built on the strength and advantages of IT and the Internet.

From this short list of examples it is apparent that IT has not only transformed the way enterprises conduct business but also transformed the relationships between the parties involved in the value chain. It has brought more information to the value chain participants and enabled them to communicate and transact more efficiently. In many cases, business models themselves have shifted as traditional intermediaries have now become unnecessary. Direct distribution channels have replaced traditional distribution channels. Consumers are far more involved in the product and service creation, delivery, and exchange process.

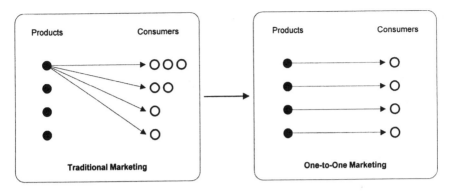

FIGURE 3. One-to-One Marketing. The use of IT has shifted traditional production of product segments for consumers to a customized one-to-one relationship.

One such trend can be found in the creation of customer self-service, where Web and other network technologies are transforming the way customer service is conducted. Using the Web, many enterprises are targeting customer service to each individual consumer often without the need of a human customer support agent. Automated self-service can conduct support services at a fraction of the cost. Examples of these services are plentiful: the ATM machine, check-in kiosks at airports, and package tracking information. These services are accessed either at the physical location of the service or from the convenience of the computer at home. While the human component within this self-service is important, many of these Web services are directly integrated with large call centers.

It has become clear that the power of the Internet changes the way business is done and the way relationships are formed and sustained. The Web has transformed not only business-to-consumer (B2C) services and products, but also business-to-business (B2B) transactions. It has been estimated that in fact B2B represents more than 85% of all online commerce and transactions. The integration of the supply chain has been largely impacted by the use of IT. Enterprises are capable of selecting their suppliers and vendors on B2B exchanges, can collaborate and communicate via electronic means, and provide their products and services on electronic exchanges. Similar to the shift in the B2C arena, the use of the Internet has transformed the relationship between businesses.

The Information Economy

Today's global economy is characterized by continuous change at an unprecedented rate. Fueled by technological innovations, we have seen a shift from the 'Industrial Economy', where manufacturing and blue-collar work dominated, to the 'Information Economy' where knowledge, data, and information play the central role. Analogies can be drawn from history. In the early 20th century, industrialists leveraged electricity and telephone network infrastructures to transform the U.S. economy; today, enterprises are leveraging computer and communications technology to transform the global economy.

The advent of the 'Information Economy' has not only impacted the way business is done, but has had significant influence on society, culture, and politics. Through the introduction of the Internet, the global market place is increasingly accessible and visible to a growing number of participants. It is this transformation that has led to the growing importance of information. The power has shifted to those parties that have information. While there is no single definition on what constitutes the Information Economy, we experience it around us on a daily basis. Information goods, such as books, football scores, stock quotes, magazines, and music, surround us. We utilize computer and communications technologies to create, extract, exchange, and manipulate information for purposes of work, leisure, and entertainment.

Every enterprise – private and public – is immersed in the Information Economy. Intelligence and defense organizations exchange information, businesses collaborate using digital supply chains, consumers and enterprises alike buy and sell products and services, financial institutions process millions of transactions, entertainment and media broadcast news stories, educational institutions provide online learning, friends and families chat using e-mail and instant messaging, all of which is done through electronic means. The age of the Information Economy has brought forward the ability to access and transfer information from anywhere to anyone at any time. 'Connectivity' has become the life force for the future. The ability to access and exchange information has a significant impact on every aspect of life (Shapiro & Varian, 1999).

INFORMATION TECHNOLOGY AS A TRANSFORMATION ENABLER

Business Value versus Cost

Over the past decade, enterprises have spent an enormous sum of money on IT. Many firms in fact have increased their overall IT expenditures by double-figure percentages annually. Despite this trend, there is still a lot of skepticism and questioning of the payoff of large IT investments. Numerous studies on the return of IT spending provide contradicting results: some studies argue IT leads to a tangible productivity improvement; others have argued that IT has mainly delivered significant strategic benefits. Undoubtedly the views on the business value of IT are divergent. Still the question what IT investments deliver in return is still a gray area. Some have called it the "productivity paradox". It is clear, however, that managers seek to measure the value of IT.

Historically, IT investments were considered an administrative expense rather than a business investment. As such costs and benefits were relatively easy to identify and measure. Today, however, IT investments are far-more than mere expenses; they present strategic choices that impact the entire enterprise and have the ability to transform business and industry structures, and change the way organizations interface with their supply chain, products, services, and markets. Understanding the business value and associated cost with such investments is therefore far more difficult than the traditional approach (Ward & Peppard, 2002).

While the cost of IT investments is often difficult to assess, understanding the flip side of the equation - assessing the value of IT investments - is often considered much tougher. For years, researchers, scholars, and managers have attempted to identify and obtain measures for the business value of IT. However, concrete measures of IT business value have not been identified. This difficulty is primarily associated with the fact that IT investments and their associated benefits often span many different organizational boundaries. IT investments furthermore do not directly create business benefits, such as cost savings or increased revenue. This is particularly the case when technology is applied to enhance the company image, customer service, or advertising effectiveness.

Another critical aspect is that the business value of IT can vary from organization to organization. This indicates that the business value of IT is not a mere function of the technology itself, but the environment it operates in, the organization that uses it, and the process by which it is implemented, adopted, and diffused. As such, organizational culture, leadership vision, and organizational practices such as learning and training, all contribute in assessing the business value of IT. Organizations in the process of adopting IT must therefore consider a wealth of factors and carefully evaluate the business value versus cost tradeoff.

Enterprises make investments in IT for a variety of reasons. The underlying purpose of these investments is to improve business performance measured in tangible aspects such as productivity and profitability. However, the use of IT brings forth a range of other, intangible benefits, such as quality, responsiveness, and coordination, which may not be immediately reflected in a tangible benefit such as profitability. Furthermore, the overall business value of IT varies significantly from organization to organization. Traditionally, many enterprises have used financial measures, such as return on investment and cost, to qualify their investments in technology. However, as IT budgets are shrinking, decision makers are increasingly looking towards the business value side of the value-cost tradeoff. Historically, IT investments too often focused on how to reduce costs rather than on the question of how IT can deliver the best value for the lowest cost. Today's economic climate, shrinking IT budgets, and increasingly competitive environment has shifted this thought of many executives. In order to address these questions, firms have turned their focus to understanding whether a firm's investment in IT is aligned with its overall strategic objectives. The alignment of IT capabilities and business strategy enables enterprises to intelligently make IT investments. Proper alignment delivers direct value as strategic aims and objectives are met with the use of IT. The tradeoff between cost and business value is therefore critical. To deliver value, the IT infrastructure must be capable of providing enterprises the opportunity to increase revenue, improve customer satisfaction, and support business strategies.

Key Processes and Transformational Events

The chapters in this book highlight the multitude of different types of enterprise transformations. Transformational events are triggered by forces that are either internal to firm, external to the organization, or a result of environmental changes. These events lead to enterprises needing to quickly adapt to the changes and transform their key processes in order to remain competitive. Enterprise-wide processes exist because organizations come to depend on a flow of documents, information, events, decisions, and outcomes. Enterprise transformations, by definition, affect systems and processes. Therefore, the extent to which an organization successfully exits from a transformational event depends in large measure on how well the dependencies that are required to deliver value have been preserved or defined. In fundamental transformations like mergers and acquisitions, for example, many business processes can be successfully carried out in parallel. Other transformational events, such as updated value chains, new products or markets, and unexpected sales demands, for example, require a rethinking of supply processes, customer relationships, and sales processes. New technology investments must therefore keep strategic objectives of the enterprise in mind when restructuring, designing, aligning, and implementing new business processes.

The Role of Architectures

The discussions above clearly highlight the need for IT. It also shows the growing interdependence between IT and business objectives. It is therefore important to build an IT infrastructure that supports the changing needs of the enterprise. This becomes even more critical during times of transformational events.

An enterprise's IT infrastructure must be capable of adapting to changes in the environment, changes to business processes, and the introduction of new products and services. Changes can also come from the emergence of new technological innovations and opportunities. When faced with new technologies, an IT infrastructure may be required to be upgraded, replacing existing infrastructure with new ones. Technological change is inevitable and hence enterprises must be continuously prepared to meet these challenges, anticipate changes, and provide an infrastructure that is both flexible and cost effective. Arguably the most critical task in developing an adaptive IT infrastructure, and one that can aid in meeting these challenges, is the development of an appropriate and flexible IT architecture.

While there is no universal definition of architecture, in general terms, an IT architecture represents a blueprint and/or roadmap for the information and technical requirements of the enterprise. The development of an IT architecture is beneficial for several reasons. As summarized in Table 1, it enables enterprise increased flexibility and a "faster adaptation to changing technological requirements and environments; it streamlines and optimizes business processes; provides enterprise-wide integration through data sharing; and enables a faster evolution to new technologies" (Cook, 1996).

At the high level of IT, an enterprise-wide IT architecture primarily provides a set of standards for the enterprise. Similarly, standards are important at the technical level of implementation, such as networking protocols, platforms, etc. Using a standards-based approach to IT architecture ensures that processes and information can be interconnected across business units enabling a seamlessly networked enterprise.

Maturity Measurement and Six-Sigma Models

The impact of transformational events requires enterprises to re-design, implement, and optimize new types of processes that integrate various back-end, legacy, and third-party applications. Processes should be designed and implemented in such a way that the broader strategic objectives of the enterprises are satisfied. This in turn should drive the overall technology strategy and investments. An understanding of current processes is therefore an important prerequisite. Many enterprises utilize IT maturity models to assess their current level of process maturity, identify a desired state of enterprise processes, and develop a gap analysis highlighting the areas of people, process and technology to invest in for better alignment with the overall strategic objectives.

- Increased Flexibility to Changing Requirements and Environments

- Streamlined and Optimized Business Processes

- Enterprise-Wide Integration through Data Sharing

- Rapid Evolution to New and Emerging Technologies

TABLE 1. Benefits of an Enterprise IT Architecture (Cook, 1996)

Enterprises must seriously consider all aspects of process maturity in order to best deliver services to the rest of the enterprise. Maturity models enable organizations to self-assess the maturity of various aspects of their processes against benchmarks and are typically constructed with five levels. Each maturity level is a plateau in which one or more processes have been transformed from a lower level to achieve a new level of capability. Each maturity level provides a new foundation of practices on which subsequent levels are built. Two common IT maturity models include the Capabilities Maturity Model (CMM) and Six Sigma.

The CMM describes the principles and practices underlying software process maturity. It is intended to help enterprises improve the maturity of their software processes in terms of an evolutionary path from ad hoc, chaotic processes to mature, disciplined software processes. The focus of CMM is to establish repeatable practices with low variability that are continuously improved to enhance process capabilities.

Another frequently used method for process analysis and design is Six Sigma, developed by Motorola engineers in the late 1980s. The Greek word "sigma" is a mathematical symbol used to denote standard deviation and – in the case of processes – measures how far it deviates from perfection. Thus, the fundamental idea behind Six Sigma is to bring a process-oriented view to enterprises in order to detect and reduce unintended outcomes. The fundamental objective of the Six Sigma methodology is the implementation of a measurement-based strategy that focuses on process improvement and variation reduction.

Maturity models and measurement practices enable enterprises to assess their current state of business processes and implement consistent policies, procedures, and practices throughout the organization. In doing so, the enterprise becomes increasingly flexible and can rapidly adjust to transformational changes. Using a quantitative approach provided by these methodologies, enterprises can assess their current practices, form a base line, and continuously improve its business processes.

IT ARCHICTECTURE AND TRANSFORMATION

Enterprise-wide processes exist because organizations come to depend on a flow of documents, information, events, decisions and outcomes. Organizations that undergo significant change rarely escape with unchanged systems and processes. Therefore, the extent to which an organization emerges successfully from a transformational process depends in large measure on whether (and, significantly, how well) key value-producing elements of enterprise-wide processes have been preserved or redefined.

There are many cases in which the right IT strategy plays a pivotal role in major transformational events. During mergers, for example, customers expect that value in the form of products and services will continue to flow. So post-merger automated systems that record customers, orders and payments must at least capture the status of the previously independent customer records. Loss of even partial customer data can lead to loss of cash that dramatically alters the viability of the merged companies. In the short run, many business activities can simply be carried out in parallel without change to operational processes, even as major new manufacturing facilities are introduced as a result. On the other hand the catastrophic loss of customer data resulting from natural or geo-political disasters, can rob even stable, healthy businesses of the capability to continue operations.

Cisco, for example (Nolan, Porter, & Akers, 2001) suffered just such a catastrophic loss of data in January, 1994. The company shut down while ERP systems for manufacturing, ordering and finance were brought back on line. Faced with a near-term continuity problem, Cisco management of course recognized that significant resources would be required to recover. It is significant; however, that the team of senior managers who were responsible for leading the recovery effort went beyond the immediate project needs to establish an architecture that solved a much more general problem. In effect, Cisco's IT and business managers realized that massive failure of business systems is only one kind of transformational event. By investing in a standards-based, scalable architecture, Cisco in essence systematized change as a core business process. This was a decision that carried Cisco through its dramatic growth in the late 1990's as it acquired companies, anticipated the changing nature of its market, and became a model for how a company can start with well-articulated business goals and build an IT infrastructure that aligns with it.

The validity of systematic approaches like Cisco's has been demonstrated many times. By 1999, Hewlett-Packard was well into a massive reorganization that led to the spinout of Agilent Technologies, its former instrument division, and, under the leadership of Carly Fiorina, HP's new, change-minded CEO, the consolidation of over 80 business units into four (with consumer-facing and business-facing sales organizations to unify the company's interface to its customers). The year 2000 fourth quarter results for HP shocked senior management and investors alike: HP had missed its own earnings estimates by nearly ten cents per share (Money, 2000). When HP closed its fiscal year 2000 books, the design of the corporate financial system that was to integrate the data from dozens of previously independent product, marketing and sales organizations (and which was being used to forecast results) was seriously behind schedule and the true status of the integration project has not yet been reported to senior management.

At virtually the same time, Cisco was relying on a standards-based, internet-enabled IT architecture to consolidate all applications (not just finance, as in the case for HP) for its far-flung R&D and marketing organizations in a massive reorganization into just three lines of business. The entire integration was carried out in 60 days at a cost of less than one million dollars.

It is very difficult to "project manage" change at the scale of an enterprise. In addition to the inherent problems in all large IT projects, enterprise transformations require transparency and predictability. Even a well-managed project can fail because critical project specifications do not take into account organizational complexities, external factors or (as in the case of HP) the tendency of line managers to resist change (Herbold, 2004) by maintaining specialized applications, shadow systems and fiercely protected local control of operational data. Just as architecture has been a competitive enabler for technology companies, IT architecture can enable capabilities that greatly increase the likelihood of successful transformation.

Transformational Events

There are a numerous events that can transform a large organization. These events can be the result of changes within organization. Other transformational events can be triggered by environmental changes. Some examples of transformation events are shown in Table 2.

- Large-scale structural change such as mergers, acquisitions and divestitures
- Internal reorganizations such as management changes and moving organizational boundaries
- New business strategies such as geographic expansion
- Updated value chains that disintermediate traditional suppliers of value
- Emerging, more agile competitors
- Cost reduction that requires focusing on a few core skills
- Unexpected sales demand that invalidates operational models, forecasts and supply chains
- New products and product cycles such as those requiring significant investment shifts for manufacturing or R&D
- New markets where existing product or service portfolios may be ill-matched to actual customer needs and preferences
- New business processes
- Regulation such as section 404 of the Sarbanes Oxley act that mandates new controls and reviews
- Geo-political events and disasters such as the terrorist attacks of September 11, 2001.

TABLE 2. Examples of Transformation Events

Structural changes such as mergers, acquisitions or divestitures are usually apparent to outsiders. These are transformations that tend to impact all enterprise systems and processes. Internal reorganizations, by contrast, may be transparent. Moving from centrally managed and funded to distributed research laboratories may have a dramatic impact on product costs and quality but customers and shareholders may not be aware that a change has taken place. Sometimes, as in the case of the formation of the Department of Homeland Security in the Executive Branch of the US Government, an internal reorganization is actually a sequence of large mergers.

Strategy changes are seldom anticipated, although companies shift business strategies all the time. Strategy shifts that are transformational and successful are relatively rare. This is in part due to business fundamentals that have little to do with technology. On the other hand, some transformations are profoundly affected by the underlying IT architecture. For example, a company that grows through geographic expansion from regional to national or international scale acquires employees, customers, suppliers and partners.

The most dramatic examples of the transformational power of changing value chains are in the communications and technology sectors. Brand value for components like microprocessors that can command premium prices has been rapidly eroded by commoditization. As a result manufacturing capabilities are decoupled from customer acquisition and product delivery. Transformations like these have had a huge effect on the personal computer industry. The internet boom of the late 1990's made it clear that incumbents have to be wary of innovation that can undercut established products with cheaper, more appealing and sometimes less capable new products. Less well understood is the role that IT plays.

However, while large enterprises rely on processes and systems to gain economies of scale, smaller, more agile competitors often rely on people rather than processes. This means that established competitors can be locked into legacy systems and ways of doing business that are ultimately harmful. Shrinking margins, international competition, increased energy costs; shareholder demands are a few of the forces that put severe pressure on costs. These pressures rarely fail to provoke large-scale transformations as companies focus on core capabilities and either eliminate or purchase capabilities that contribute to overall financial performance.

EXAMPLES OF ENTERPRISE IT TRANSFORMATION

Cisco

John Chambers joined Cisco as CEO in 1991. By 1993, the Cisco top management team had articulated a business strategy that the company adheres to even today:

- Make Cisco a one-stop shopping destination for all business network needs.

- Systematize acquisitions as an efficient business process.

- Drive networking standardization and license technology to key suppliers

- Be strategic in picking partners.

When the company began to re-architect its IT infrastructure to recover from the catastrophic failure of its central database, it adopted a hierarchical approach to technology standardization that has become a model for enterprises that want to seamlessly adapt to change in scale, structure and markets.

At the lowest layers of the hierarchy are the common computer, operating system, Internet access and productivity tools that are deployed throughout the company. On top of this base technology Cisco relies on a common suite of application packages that are used worldwide. A key element of the architecture is the ability to maintain a common Oracle database image accessible by the Internet (using the ubiquitous TCP/IP protocol). Hosting these capabilities at the enterprise level are Unix servers, the large-scale systems that are capable of high-speed transaction processing and networking. The architecture also recognizes that smaller groups need common capabilities as well. Windows™ based servers that are less expensive to acquire and operate serve these smaller groups. These capabilities are stitched together in a worldwide network supporting not only data but also voice and multimedia services.

Technology standardization has enabled an IT architecture that is designed specifically to accomplish the company's business strategy:

- Using IT infrastructure to enable key processes to operate in real time rather than according to an artificially imposed calendar.

- Providing everyone in the company the same view of data that is readily available

- Ensuring that computers and network access are universally available to Cisco employees

- Using Internet browsing as the common application and data access mechanism

- Deploying a global phone book to enable employees to reach each other and key suppliers and partners from within the browser

- Using Internet self-service websites to replace receptionists, HR specialists, and purchasing agents

Home Depot

Like Cisco, Home Depot uses open architectures and web interfaces that allow new applications and features to be added easily to implement a new business strategy (Levinson, 2004):

- Focus on dramatic improvements in the shopping experience for customers

- Gain efficiency by streamlining the stores' back office.

The scale of retail operations for Home Depot is enormous. The retail stores process over 100 million transactions daily. The infrastructure consists of 8000 servers and network capacity for 400,000 PC's that together host over 2000 applications. The underlying data warehouse contains over 4 trillion bytes of data.

Home Depot's digital architecture strategy is reflective of a continuously changing value chain. Like Cisco, Home Depot aims to replace its existing technology platform with a new one. The architecture anticipates future gains in productivity and effectiveness by new technology introduction, so the open architecture is critical to their strategy. Customers have the most intimate contact with back-office systems at point-of-sale terminals, so Home Depot chose to concentrate on that aspect of operations.

Self-checkout was one of the first new applications to be deployed. Besides the cost and competitive advantages of being first in this retail segment with such capabilities, the architectural advantages were validated because self-checkout uses the same software as the other point-of-sale functions. The new architecture also specifies a common database of transactions in an enterprise data warehouse. This enables measurement of cashier performance and an online price/code catalog. However, it also aims at improved customer experience since returns can now be made to any store.

HP/Compaq Merger

By contrast with Home Depot and Cisco the massive integration of Hewlett-Packard and Compaq systems was viewed as a series of massive IT projects which began immediately upon closing of the May 2002 merger.

The value of the HP/Compaq merger was defined by an extraordinarily contentious proxy fight as the value captured by integrating complementary businesses. It is therefore understandable that the focus of top management in both companies was on business process architecture. The goal of rationalizing the IT demands of the combined entities was capturing the economies of scale that a single company could provide. Unfortunately, the combined company's systems did not grow from a single company. Between the two companies, there were 70 or more supply chains to be migrated to an integrated ERP environment. Many of those systems were legacy infrastructure that Compaq inherited from the acquisition of DEC, a merger that failed to provide value to Compaq shareholders. In other words HP managers were trying to integrate and standardize systems from at least three large companies as well as separate supply chain and ordering systems from geographic regions such as Australia that produced their own products and therefore were not part of the US-based supply chains.

The project management approach was consistent with the overall goals of the integration teams: capture the value of synergistic businesses. From a people standpoint, significant efficiencies could be gained by winnowing multiple engineering, marketing and sales teams to a smaller number. The idea for IT was similar: reduce the 35 pre-merger ERP systems to four. Across all entities, the companies ran for 3,500 applications. To capture the synergies, this number would have to be reduced to by 60 or 70 percent.

The four ERP systems had code bases spanning all three market-facing divisions (consumer, enterprise and small-medium business), several distinct fulfillment modes and many geographic regions. The technical goal of migrating from separate legacy HP/Compaq/DEC systems to a new SAP system was frustrated by historical silos and business. This complexity proved to be too much for HP project managers when data integration complexity met an unexpected demand in orders (Bouchard, 2005). By the third quarter of 2004, $120 million worth of enterprise server order backlog had accumulated. Ultimately, these integration problems cost HP's new enterprise server division $400 million in revenue and $275 million in profits.

ENABLING CAPABILITIES

These examples really highlight two views of how IT relates to transformational events in large organizations.

Project View. The overriding principle in this view is that IT is a critical resource for enterprise-wide processes and needs to be managed. However, a project approach to IT leads to a much narrower perspective on the issues at hand. Using a project view, enterprises try to manage the transformational events and apply IT project principles. In many cases, the lack of a holistic perspective by a project approach has resulted in disconnected and inefficient silos of technology, information, and business processes. The integration of supply chain management systems at HP/Compaq is an excellent example of a project approach to large scale IT integration gone bad (Koch, 2004). Using a pure project management approach, HP's IT managers did not anticipate the complexity and uncertainty associated with the enterprise transformation. While contingency plans were in place, changes in the environment caused a significant and costly delay of system integration and rollout. A project perspective only allowed managing what had been initially planned for; in other words, the project was dependent on the parameters of the event itself, and not for change in general. In order to deliver on the larger vision of the enterprise, a more holistic approach must be taken. Particularly in times of transformation, a holistic perspective to IT enables enterprises to be agile and adapt to changing requirements caused by external events.

Architectural View. An architectural view of IT provides a more holistic perspective on enterprise IT. It approaches the role of IT from the ground-up and establishes a common blueprint for all elements within the IT infrastructure. With this view, IT is not merely managed as set of resources to meet specific project objectives, but rather is focused upon as a strategic asset that can deliver value for the long-term. In doing so, an architectural perspective on IT provides a framework that focuses not only on the technical requirements but on the overall business goals of the organization as well. The major advantage of using an architectural approach is that while change is coming and transformational events may be difficult to foresee they can be anticipated and prepared for.

Hence, the use of a well-defined and established IT architecture provides the ability to reduce the complexities of technology maintenance and development, decreases the risk of technology obsolescence, and ensure that various parts of a solution in fact integrate and work together. In other words, an IT architecture enables to deliver applications now and into the future (Morris & Ferguson, 1993).

The value of a well-defined and established IT architecture can be illustrated using a simple net present value (NPV) versus options value (OV) comparison. While the initial cost of developing and implementing a long-term oriented IT architecture may be greater than merely implementing individual enterprise systems and technologies using a project-based approach, its future, or option value, provides enterprises a range of new opportunities and offers the ability to quickly adapt to change and uncertainty. The establishment of an IT architecture hence provides enterprises the flexibility to adapt and exercise a range of critical and strategic options in the future.

Architectural principles clearly contribute to an organization's ability to navigate transformational change. Such principles can be a source of competitive advantage for corporations, but even government agencies, universities and non-profit organizations can benefit from the experience cited above. These principles include:

- Open Standards and Interfaces

- Composition and Modularity

- Data Consistency and Integration

- Network Access and Applications

- Scalability

- Service-Orientation

- Human-Centered Technology

Open Standards and Interfaces

An optimal IT architecture that is based on a well-defined standard is often visualized as an hourglass shape as shown in Figure 4. The narrow waist of the hourglass depicts a specific standard, such as the Internet Protocol (IP) for example, and enables the support of wide variety of applications above based on a range of different technologies below.

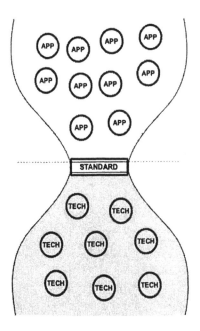

FIGURE 4. Hour-Glass Shape of IT Architecture

An enterprise that uses an hourglass shape approach to its IT architecture can quickly deploy and implement new applications and ensure the support of emerging technologies. While open standards enable the deployment of new technologies and applications, an equally important aspect is the integration of systems and applications. Using an open interfaces principle, enterprises can interconnect existing systems and avoid costly integration problems. Hence, an IT architecture based upon open standards and interfaces enables rapid integration, interconnection, and deployment.

Composition and Modularity

An important principle of IT architecture is decomposition and modularity. It has been shown that the use of a composite and modular approach enables enterprises to reduce the complexities of the overall IT architecture. A good architecture decomposes the system into modules, which can be easily maintained, upgraded, and replaced. The use of a modular approach to architecture provides enterprises the ability to group functionalities within each module, resulting in greater internal dependency, and low external dependency. Modularity also leads to reusability of components, which are highly configurable and can meet more generalized needs of the organization.

Data Consistency/Integration

A central issue facing enterprises today is the management of their growing data sources. While sophisticated data warehousing and management tools are available today, a fundamental obstacle facing IT managers is the existence of inconsistent data. Data inconsistencies occur when similar entries appear in multiple systems. When enterprises face transformational change, data from a variety of locations and sources need to be integrated. Maintaining duplicate entries of the same data leads to inefficiencies and increased maintenance costs. Keeping data up-to-date and consistent is, thus, a fundamental requirement for data management systems. Consistent data ensures a high level of data quality, reliability, and maintainability.

In large enterprises, the need for sharing and integrating data is considerable. Traditional applications are deployed as functional silos, where each application draws from its own database. While daily synchronization mechanisms can mitigate the problem, small inconsistencies can cause significant business errors. The need for integrated and consistent data is further demonstrated by the fact that enterprises demand a common and overall picture of resource status, processes, and customers and their behavior.

Network Access and Applications

Many early business applications were generally targeted to be installed on a single terminal and used by a single user. They typically shared data with other applications on the terminal through a database or file system. However, as the number of users increased, these applications become inefficient and posed problems in scaling beyond a single terminal and user. With the emergence of corporate networks and the Internet, users were now able to access applications from their personal computers. By distributing applications across a number of servers, applications could now be accessed by an increasing number of users, leading to an increase in efficiency and performance. Today's enterprises operate in a global environment without borders. Enabling access to network applications provides enterprises with a powerful means to extend their business across geographic borders. It also enables workers to access critical information and applications from remote locations. Network applications also allow businesses to collaborate and transact electronically, integrate their supply chains, and interact with customers through websites. While traditional corporate networks and the Internet limited users to fixed-terminal locations, the emergence of wireless networks and advanced mobile devices now provide the means to access applications virtually anywhere and anytime. From these observations, it is evident that as enterprises become increasingly networked, more nodes within an enterprise value system can be reached and scalability, efficiency, productivity and reach benefits can be achieved.

Scalability

A scalable IT architecture permits an enterprise to size its computer systems based on actual needs, continually add resources and users, and enhance business processes. It should be noted that scalability differs from performance as a scalable architecture does not increase performance but, rather, provides the same level of performance given a higher user or transaction load. Performance, thus, reflects system response time under a typical load while scalability refers to the ability of a system to increase that load without degrading response time. As enterprises transform it is likely that the amount of resources and users accessing the system will change. The system must therefore have the capability to accommodate the flux in resources without degrading performance and response time. A scalable IT architecture provides enterprises with this capability.

Service-Orientation

A service-oriented architecture provides a flexible and reusable framework for developing and integrating multiple applications. While several definitions of a service-oriented architecture exist, it can be broadly described as an application architecture in which all functions are defined as independent services that are connected by well-defined interfaces that can be called in defined sequences to form business processes. In other words, functions are defined as services, which are "black boxes" that function independently of each other. The resulting main benefits of a service-oriented approach are its flexibility to quickly deploy new applications and its reusability to leverage investments across multiple applications. Service-orientation enables enterprises to adapt to changing business requirements and processes and ensure efficient and effective use of system resources.

Human-Centered Technology

All too often IT system design begins with a set of technological capabilities and functions rather than the needs of human users. Early users of Microsoft Windows™ who wanted to connect personal computers to the Internet were forced to enter inscrutable parameters and codes into six or seven control panels. Worse yet, a mistake in one of those entries could cause a computer to freeze, requiring an expensive service call to restore it to a useful condition. The latest release of Windows consolidates that complexity in a single "Wizard" that guides even novice users through the process of establishing network connections for their personal computers. There is an emerging science of information systems that begins with a set of human needs and designs interfaces that shield end users from the underlying complexity of the information infrastructure.

This "human-centered" technology is well suited to changing environments because it allows architects and designers to concentrate on enterprise-wide processes. Employees need to be paid, even in the midst of a merger. A brittle information architecture would require employees of an acquired company to re-establish payroll information, either manually or by using self-service applications of their new parent, a process that might require additional training and expense. A human centered architecture would recognize that payroll is an enterprise-wide capability in both companies and absorb new employee data with minimal impact on people.

Human-centered technology is at the heart of IBM's adaptive, self-healing systems which shield system managers from the increasing complexity and costs of modern networks by building "self-management" and error tolerance into the technology (Ganek & Corbi, 2003). Human-centered technology is also driving NASA to build a new generation of pilot-oriented flight control systems that amplify the abilities of a human operator in extreme environments (NASA, 2005). By concentrating on how people work, the spaces in which work is carried out and models of communication and reasoning, designers of human-centered systems create new approaches to IT.

TRANSFORMATIONAL MATURITY

We believe there is an evolving consensus on the elements of transformational maturity in enterprise IT systems. We are not yet able to measure, in precise terms, the ability of IT infrastructure to enable transformation or its capacity to impede change, but as the examples in this chapter illustrate, there are some common threads in both successful and unsuccessful transformations:

- **Explicit process dependencies.** Even though complete documentation of key processes is unlikely to be undertaken in the course of normal operations, the successful architectures are those that take into account dependencies between processes. In mature organizations, this is accomplished by modularization and standardization. In organizations that are less mature, the dependencies multiply and, left undocumented, become brittle and the source of failures.

- **Defining information that most affects the business.** Customer data, supply chains, and financial records are clearly critical, but modern IT architectures make novel use of often humble information to accelerate decisions and processes. Therefore, Cisco's adopting of company-wide white pages and yellow pages is a key link in their collaboration infrastructure, which enables web-based access to critical data by anyone in the company.

- **Shared understanding of boundaries, roles and how they change.** Horizontal processes are not changed lightly even during massive transformations, whereas vertical process change is more likely to be subject to cost or even political decisions that are ultimately not made in strategic fashion. The existence of an IT architecture that reflects essential boundaries (e.g., internal versus external) and is indifferent to organizational labels is, as experience shows, a better predictor of transformational maturity.

- **Reduced latency of time-sensitive data.** The relevance of *when* information is recognized as being important becomes obvious during change processes. Recognizing a development *before* it has a chance to impact operations is so important that mature organizations invest heavily in infrastructure that eliminates or reduces the latency of such data.

With these concepts in mind, we can begin to see the outlines of a model of transformational maturity that IT managers can use as a tool of strategy (see Figure 5).

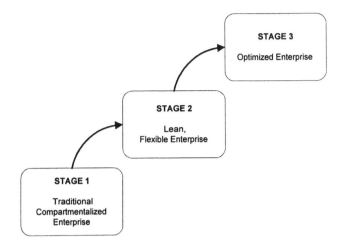

FIGURE 5. Transformational Maturity.

An enterprise at Stage 1 – for example a vertically integrated traditional manufacturing company with "stove piped" IT infrastructure – is least able to adapt (Haeckel, 1999). Few horizontal processes exist and to the extent that information dependencies are understood at all, they are understood within a set of organizational assumptions that may not be valid tomorrow. There may be great expertise about how to perform within a set of defined parameters but little knowledge about how the larger organization behaves outside those stated assumptions.

A Stage 2 enterprise, on the other hand, has adopted many of the architectural principles we have been discussing. Such a company uses horizontal processes supported by cross-company tools and methods and is not bound to a predetermined set of applications that define the current business. These companies use web-based technologies, modern software design methods, sufficient computing power and electronic marketplaces to achieve efficiency and flexibility.

A company at Stage 3 in this maturity matrix (see Table 2) is in a position to use transformation as a strategic tool (Robertson & Sribar, 2002). Such a company may have real-time data capabilities that enable predictive production, 1-to-1 business or other optimizations that a less capable company cannot achieve. Elements of Stage 3 companies can be found in some of our examples. Other aspects of Stage 3 companies await the discovery of new systems and engineering principles.

CONCLUSION

The productivity gains due to advances in information and communication technology over the past decade have been impressive. Driven by the exponential growth in capabilities summarized by Moore's Law, IT has extended the reach of enterprises beyond their premises, often beyond recognizable geographic boundaries. This has enabled not only new businesses but also new business models as global competition aided by IT marketplaces to spring up wherever value can be added to existing businesses. The growth of electronic commerce and the impact of the Internet and web-based technologies are examples that are by now familiar to all.

Maturity Stage	Description	Characteristics
1	Traditional Compartmentalized Enterprise	▪ Emphasis on vertical organizational boundaries ▪ Highly leveraged economies of scale ▪ Predictable market demands ▪ Predictable economic and competitive pressures
2	Lean, Flexible Enterprise	▪ Externally focused on customer needs ▪ Production strategy matched to markets and business needs, not to predetermined organizational roles ▪ IT is used to enhance marketing precision, understand contexts and shifts
3	Optimized	▪ Transformation is driven by strategy ▪ Quantitative understanding of external forces ▪ Predictability in execution under varying assumptions ▪ Key processes are measured and results are fed back to decision-makers

TABLE 2. Transformational Maturity Matrix

Competing in such a rapidly changing environment has required IT professionals to concentrate on the role that architecture plays in the modern IT landscape. The rush toward open interfaces, standards based solutions and platforms have been driven by a few simple economic forces. First, in a networked world, the value of IT infrastructure is measured by how many ways it can be used. Second, it is almost impossible to predict the applications and requirements of the future, so current design investments should make as few assumptions about the future as possible. Third, the cost of owning an IT system increases dramatically with the complexity of the system.

This is the attractiveness of web-based technologies. They allow organizations to deploy a common access technology (the web browser) that makes very few assumptions about the physical nature of computers and networks. Web-based technologies also make few assumptions about applications, so an IT manager is not "locked" into a large investment that is specialized to the applications of a single vendor. Finally, web-based technologies are conceptually simple and do not require the same level of maintenance as more complex integrated systems.

These are also advantages for enterprises undergoing transformation. The architectural view of IT infrastructure has proved to be a key component of IT strategy for companies that adapt and change successfully. The architectural principles that time and again are cited in studies how IT enables successful transformation include:

- Open standards and interfaces

- Composition and modularity

- Data consistency and integration

- Network access and applications

- Scalability

- Service-orientation

- Human-centered technology.

An organization that has invested in enterprise-wide deployment of systems that have these characteristics is in a better position to adapt. In fact, organizations that want to make transformation a core competency set out to explicitly build their information and communications infrastructure according to these principles.

Does that mean that a company that does not use standards based architectures and web applications cannot survive transformation? There are clearly examples to contrary. On the other hand, without an architectural basis for change, company leadership is forced to contend with change processes as a (usually complex) change "project" that has to be carefully and successfully managed. The more complex the change, the more projects there are to manage and the more complex each project becomes.

This has led us to a model of transformational maturity that classifies the inherent capability of organizations to change. The least mature enterprise has a fixed compartmentalized structure of a vertically integrated manufacturing company, i.e., a company that has been designed functionally well in a predictable competitive and economic world. A more mature enterprise is lean and flexible and makes use of IT to enhance understanding of its customers and of the large-scale forces that affect it. At the upper end of the maturity scale is the enterprise that is optimized from a transformational standpoint. An organization at this level of maturity has invested in "options" that essentially make transformation a core business competency. Not only are such companies able to accurately predict the impact of change (often with quantitative precision), they can do so under varying assumptions, can measure the effect of change on key processes and feed that data back to decision-makers who can alter the strategy accordingly.

REFERENCES

Bouchard, G. (2005). Personal communication.

Cook, M. A. (1996). Building Enterprise Information Architectures: Reengineering Information Systems. Upper Saddle River, NJ: Prentice Hall.

Ganek, A. G. and Corbi, T. A. (2003). The Dawning of an Autonomic Computing Era. *IBM Systems Journal,* 42, 1, 5-18.

Haeckel, S. H. (1999). Adaptive Enterprise: Creating and Leading Sense-And-Respond Organizations. Boston, MA: Harvard Business School Press.

Herbold, R. (2004). The Fiefdom Syndrome: The Turf Battles That Undermine Careers and Companies - And How to Overcome Them. New York: Doubleday.

Intel. (2005). from http://www.intel.com/research/silicon/mooreslaw.htm

Koch, C. (2004, December 1). When Bad Things Happen to Good Projects. *CIO Magazine,* 50-58.

Levinson, M. (2004, August 1). Home Improvement. *CIO Magazine.*

Money Magazine. (2000, November 13). HP misses 4Q forecasts, from http://money. cnn.com/2000/11/13/technology/hp/

Morris, C. & Ferguson, C. (1993). How Architecture Wins Technology Wars. *Harvard Business Review*, pp 86-96.

NASA. (2005). from http://is.arc.nasa.gov/HCC/

Nolan, R. L., Porter, K., & Akers, C. (2001). Cisco Systems Architecture: ERP and Web-enabled IT. *HBS Case # 9-301-099*, October.

Robertson, B. & Sribar, V. (2002). The Adaptive Enterprise: IT Infrastructure Strategies to Manage Change and Enable Growth (1st ed.). Reading, MA: Addison-Wesley Professional.

Shapiro, C. & Varian, H. R. (1999). Information Rules: A Strategic Guide to the Network Economy. Boston, MA: Harvard Business School Press.

Ward, J. & Peppard, J. (2002). Strategic Planning for Information Systems (3rd ed.). New York: John Wiley.

CHAPTER 12
TURNAROUND PLANNING AND EXECUTION

SCOTT AVILA AND MARK BARBEAU

ABSTRACT

The process of transforming an enterprise can be broken down into clear and logical steps. An honest assessment must be made of the situation and organization. The management team must provide leadership, and focus the organization on the problems at hand. Management must encourage prompt decision-making with the best information available, and communicate effectively both inside and outside the company. This chapter outlines four stages of enterprise transformation and discusses the elements of each stage, including key issues and success factors.

INTRODUCTION & OVERVIEW

To succeed in a dynamic economy, companies must continue to adapt and adjust to changes both inside and outside the organization (Bibeault, 1999: Collins & Porras, 1994; DiNapoli, et al., 1991; Maddi & Khoshaba, 2005; Peters, 1987). Managers who fail to address those challenges put company performance at risk, and ultimately survival of the organization. This chapter focuses on how to identify those challenges, build a turnaround plan, and then implement it using the approach and tools used by turnaround managers to achieve rapid and sustainable improvements in underperforming companies.

Drivers of Underperformance

Companies get in trouble as a result of a variety of internal and external factors. Common internal factors include a failed business initiative, failed acquisition integration, indecisive leadership, excessive financial leverage; excessive diversification or lack of focus, and poor planning and controls. External factors that can require an organization to face fundamental change in its business include, but are not limited to, competitive pricing pressure, changing market dynamics or governmental regulation, increases in raw material pricing or labor cost, poor economic conditions, and obsolescent technology.

An alert and responsive management team can normally identify these events and force the organization to evolve in response. A company led by a distracted and indecisive management team will fall behind. Over time the laggards will continue to deteriorate to the point that painful changes are required for survival. Whatever the cause, management must build a plan that is based on an honest assessment of the company's situation and identification of the drivers causing the company's problems.

The Stages of a Turnaround

Fixing broken companies requires revolutionary change to the organization, implemented through a series of small steps. This transformation of the organization comes about not from one single project, idea or concept but through many adjustments along the way. This process entails four stages:

- Organizational assessment
- Stabilizing performance
- Development of a comprehensive turnaround plan
- Execution of the turnaround plan

Key elements in a turnaround include building the leadership team, performing an honest assessment of the situation, developing a comprehensive turnaround plan, implementing daily operating meetings and metrics, decision-making and communication. The first step is taking a clear-eyed view of the organization's situation.

IDENTIFYING THE TURNAROUND CANDIDATE

Does the organization need a turnaround plan? Are the problems facing the company so severe that moderate adjustments to sales and marketing, staffing, operations and other areas are inadequate to ensure the survival of the entity? Or has the management team responded to market challenges in an appropriate way, and just needs time to show results? These questions can be answered by considering common symptoms of troubled companies.

Declining Performance

Not all profitable companies are healthy. Likewise, not all unprofitable companies are distressed. Rather, it is important to measure performance over time using a variety of financial and operational metrics to discern the true direction of the enterprise. A seriously distressed company that records a one-time gain on the sale of an asset may show a one-year profit, only to see that gain wasted away to fund operating losses. A company experiencing high sales growth may suffer operating losses in its early years as a result of one-time start-up or infrastructure expenses.

A closer look at the underlying numbers tells the story. The following is a short list of some, but certainly not all, indicators of declining performance:

- Financial metrics: declining sales or average price per unit; increasing product returns or charge-backs; deterioration of working capital (decrease in inventory turns, increase in accounts receivable as measured in days sales outstanding, increase in accounts payable); declining gross profit margins; creeping selling, general and administrative expenses as a percent of sales.

- Liquidity metrics: deterioration in cash and availability; necessity to borrow money to fund operating losses; inability to sell equity to raise cash.

- Operating metrics: deteriorating production run rates or other efficiency measures; downtime due to material shortages or similar production problems; increasing lead times for orders; increasing defect rates.

Broken Relationships

Distress and crisis can result from the performance demands placed on the enterprise by its constituents, such as lenders, suppliers, customers or shareholders. Each has a contractual arrangement with the enterprise, verbal or written, formal or informal, with various duties owed by both sides. The company's failure to perform its obligations under these agreements can trigger a cascading response by other constituents. For example, a default under a loan agreement due to poor financial performance may result in a lender reducing credit availability. In turn, the company's inability to pay vendors may result in an interruption in raw materials, and then an inability to fulfill a customer's order, further reducing cash availability to the company. This downward spiral will repeat and worsen unless dramatic action is taken. An evaluation of the company's relationships with vendors, lenders, customers and other important constituents is required. The breaking of these relationships and agreements is a sure indication of crisis in the organization.

Reacting versus Planning

Another indicator of a crisis situation is management's propensity to react to events rather than planning for events. Their companies are held hostage by events, some of them unseen, but many predictable. As a result they continuously spend time and resources dealing with the symptoms at hand but ignore longer-term causes of distress that can be managed with foresight.

An example would be the loss of a significant customer. A common response would be to quickly replace those lost sales by cutting prices to another prospective customer in the hope of gaining volume. That sales volume may be maintained, but at a lower gross profit, and will result in consequences with regard to profitability, liquidity, and setting bad precedents for future loss of customers. A longer-term response, at greater short-term cost, may entail resizing operations to maintain profitability at a lower sales volume, developing new products, or diversifying the customer base.

Breaking the cycle is important but can be costly in the short term. Supplementing a management team with fresh talent and perspective is one way to set priorities and refocus attention on the long-term viability of the organization.

Denial

The inability of management to see the world as it is ranks as another primary indicator of a turnaround situation. Denial comes in many forms: management sticking to outdated assumptions about the business despite new and contradictory information; an unwillingness to consider alternative views; shutting out subordinates who challenge assumptions, or treating them with hostility or worse; non-discussion of taboo topics at management and board meetings. Breaking through denial is essential to identifying real problems in the organization and formulating realistic strategies for improvement. There is no comfortable way to work through it. The most effective methods include confrontation with unpopular facts and open discussion of the consequences of inaction. It is crucial that the company's leaders move beyond denial and face the organization's problems. Once that is accomplished the organization can move to the next step in the turnaround process: establishing the turnaround team.

GETTING STARTED

Leadership

Turnaround situations place special demands on management. Most organizations are structured by functional areas. The CEO may have five or six direct reports each representing a functional area within the organization, and each of these direct reports has multiple individuals and related departments reporting to them. During the turnaround process the management team must let go of any inter-departmental issues and be solely focused on the tasks required to accomplish the organization-wide goals of the plan. Therefore, the team becomes the de-facto executive leadership of the organizational and their actions cuts across all departmental boundaries.

The role of the CEO during the organizational transformation process is to create and maintain an environment that allows the management team to achieve the desired results. Often the steps required for a successful turnaround are painful to the people and traditions of the company, but are necessary for survival and must be supported by the CEO. Additionally, the CEO not only provides his blessing to the turnaround plan which sets expectations for the entire organization, but also sets the tone for employees. The organizational transformation process is one of extreme urgency, high expectations and limited resources, and accordingly conflicts will arise in the organization. Indeed, if conflicts do not arise then that is a sign the turnaround team is not pushing hard or fast enough. The CEO should not act as a peacekeeper, but rather should question assumptions, agitate for change and set high expectations for performance. At the same time the CEO must maintain a positive outlook, encourage and recognize good efforts of individuals, and make sure resources are properly allocated as part of the turnaround effort. The CEO's time and energy are also limited resources and must be allocated wisely if optimal results are to be achieved.

The Team

The development and execution of a turnaround plan is best done by a select group of insightful and energetic individuals. Although the entire organization must be part of the turnaround effort, experience shows that small, dedicated teams achieve results more quickly than large teams. The team should be comprised of a small group of individuals personally and professionally dedicated to the outcome, who have the ability and foresight to marshal other resources within the organization as needed. Larger groups are more likely to conform to established organizational norms.

There are a variety of factors that should be considered when selecting the best possible individuals for the turnaround team. While most positions are filled based on function, experience, tenure, or position within the organizational hierarchy, the turnaround team should be comprised of individuals with many, if not, all of the following:

- High Energy: The turnaround process requires an extraordinary amount of mental energy. The hours will be long. Moreover, the environment in which all turnarounds operate is challenging and usually confrontational which, in turn, can be mentally and emotionally exhausting.

- Quantitative Thinking: As is discussed more fully later, the turnaround process is quantitative in nature and the turnaround team must be capable of decision-making based on the numbers. To be successful, decisions must be made promptly with the best information available. Qualitative analysis can result in unending discussion and gridlock. Setting quantitative goals and measuring results is conducive to progress.

- Entrepreneurial: Individuals must be willing to "think outside of the box," and challenge the status quo. They should always question assumptions and not accept processes and procedures out of deference to tradition. The turnaround team must be willing to challenge everything the organization has done in its past, what it is doing today, and what it should be doing in the future. Moreover, it is critical that the individuals are comfortable with uncertainty and are willing to take risks.

- Positive Attitude: Optimism is extremely motivating and contagious to the entire organization. The turnaround process will be difficult, and at times the outcome may be uncertain. Those who are focused and committed to the goal will be able to overcome the inevitable difficulties that will arise and, moreover, will be able to motivate others to do so as well. The ability to inspire performance among others in the face of uncertainty is a crucial component of leadership.

- Collaborative: The individuals on this team must be innately collaborative. The transformation process will not succeed if a strong leader dominates it and the team acts like foot solders. The team must be committed to the right solution and not how it got to the solution or who provided it. Collaboration requires one to have the ability to face issues from a variety of perspectives and be truly open to alternate views, with a commitment to the goal rather than just a commitment to one's self interest.

- Self Awareness: A high degree of self awareness directly correlates to collaboration. The team members must be aware and honest about their strengths and weakness, and those of their team members. The cost of failure is too great to let individual biases get in the way. The person responsible for assembling the turnaround team must be willing to accept, and in fact seek out, individuals whose skills and abilities are superior to theirs regardless of their title or stature within in the organization.

The team members should represent a cross section of the key operating departments: finance, sales and marketing, operations, information systems and human resources. The finance group provides the necessary analytical skills required for the detailed analysis that will be required, along with generating accurate and reliable financial and cash flow projections. The sales and marketing department provides a vital function to the turnaround team in the form of insight into the market place and redefining the company's products or services. The information systems function is another key element in the team as they provide the backbone for the information systems that the team will use to make sound business decisions. In any organizational transformation the operations group will understandably be the cornerstone of the turnaround efforts, and as such their participation is critical. In large organizations the human resource department will provide valuable support and guidance in dealing with the various employee issues that invariably arise through this process.

The turnaround team should evolve as needs changes. The organizational transformation process is dynamic and fluid, and as it changes over time, so too should the turnaround team change over time. The key is to have the right people, on the right project, at the right time. A company's turnaround efforts require various strategic and operational objectives to be achieved over the course of the process. In order to meet these various objectives the composition of the team may change to ensure that it has the appropriate skills and resources are available to achieve the desired results.

As a final comment on the selection of the turnaround team, consider the personal characteristics of the team members. The criteria for selecting the members of the team are personal attributes, and are not necessarily based on professional abilities associated with their specific function or title within the organization. It has been found that when individuals do not have the necessary abilities, and they are given an automatic slot on the team based on their title, the team is less successful or fails completely.

Many organizations assume that the President, Chief Financial Officer, and Vice President of Manufacturing should all be included on the turnaround team as they generally represent the highest ranking individuals in an organization. While it is imperative that the senior management and Board of Directors fully support and champion the organizational transformation process, their individual participation is not critical, and may in fact be detrimental, if they do not possess the necessary skills required to meet the challenges. This dilemma raises the question of whether these senior executives have a place in the organization at all if they do not have the requisite skills to fully participate in a rigorous turnaround effort. Unfortunately for them, it may be best if they move on to a new employer. The best option in that case is to bring in objective third parties with the appropriate level of expertise.

THE ASSESSMENT

At the outset of any organizational transformation process the ultimate success or failure will depend on an accurate assessment of the current operating and financial position of the organization. This requires a comprehensive review of many, if not all, elements of the business including operations, products, management, markets, financial structure and other relevant aspects of the company. Common topics in assessments are shown in Table 1.

Revenue	By product By customer By geographic region
Gross Profit	By product By customer By geographic region
Cost Structure	Fixed and variable analysis Identification of excess costs What are core operations? Outsource opportunities? Efficient operations?
Working Capital	AR, Inventory, AP Proper policies on sales/returns/etc? Inventory management Vendor payments
Fixed Assets	Plant capacity/utilization Is capital invested efficiently?
Other	Assessment of management team Sensitivity analysis and what-ifs Pricing changes Product line extension/contraction

TABLE 1. Common Assessment Topics

The turnaround team must clearly understand:

- Why the company's customers value its products or services

- How the organization creates value for its customers (the "value chain")

- Costs of generating value for customers, (the "economic drivers")

- Inherent strengths and weakness of the organization

- External and internal risks to the organization's ability to retain its current customers

- Where the company's industry is going and how the company will compete

The assessment must be comprehensive and realistic, and identify the fundamental problems and issues facing the company. Personnel doing the assessment must have full access to information within the company and access to employees for confidential interviews. Many times during the assessment phase managers will respond to probing questions with safe answers and conventional wisdom that reinforce the company line. An effective technique is to challenge those commonly held beliefs with quantitative analysis contradicting those beliefs. Managers in many organizations will blame the economy, suppliers, customers, unfair competition or commodity prices for their company's poor performance. Although these factors often have an impact on an organization, they are rarely, if ever, the primary reason for the long-term decline in performance.

Insight into the organization's problems usually can be found when talking to people below the executive management team. It should not be surprising that operational managers, supervisors, salespeople and even clerical and production line workers have hands-on knowledge of the problems afflicting the company, and solutions for those problems. Unfortunately, executive snobbery often prevents senior managers from reaching into their organizations for solutions. This is a deep well of knowledge that should not be overlooked by the turnaround team.

Preparation of the turnaround assessment is a comprehensive project that should take one to three months to complete depending on the size and complexity of the organization. It should be a full-time responsibility for the team. It should be heavy on quantitative analysis, empirical findings and graphical presentations. It should be light on common knowledge, text and unsubstantiated opinion. The best assessments consist of bullet point findings and succinct recommendations that are reasonable and practical.

DEVELOPMENT OF AN ORGANIZATIONAL TRANSFORMATION PLAN

Turnaround situations are fluid and chaotic, so the concept of a turnaround planning stage and then an execution stage is something of a fallacy. In reality, successful turnarounds employ an iterative process of assessment, planning and execution that is continuously repeated and improved. Nevertheless, the development of an initial turnaround plan provides a clear direction for the transformation process.

The goal of the planning is to develop the appropriate strategies and associated tactics that will result in a revolutionary change in the organization. The foundation for the turnaround plan is the assessment and recommendation document. Once the assessment and recommendations have been reviewed, challenged and accepted by the management team, then it is time to incorporate the recommendations into the company's turnaround plan.

The turnaround plan must be accompanied by detailed projected financial projections, consisting of an income statement, balance sheet and cash flow, with a focus on the accurate projection of cash flow. The cash flow projection is doubly important if the organization is cash constrained, as are most turnaround candidates.

Accurate cash projections can be difficult for many organizations to prepare but are crucial. The purpose of the cash projection is to accurately identify the specific cash-in and cash-out components of the turnaround plan. They must be accurate in terms of amount and timing of cash flows. Tracking the company's actual weekly performance against a weekly cash projection (along with tracking of key working capital assets and liabilities) will clearly present the actual operating performance of the business.

The balance sheet projection is also crucial to measuring the costs and effects of the turnaround plan. Identifying and correcting improper allocations of capital, whether they are in excessive accounts receivable, inventory or fixed assets, can be life-saving sources of cash to fund a turnaround.

A robust interactive financial model will have appropriate variables and assumptions that can be modified to show the results of various "what-if" scenarios. Measuring the financial impact of a set of recommendations is a prerequisite for identifying the cost of the turnaround effort, future profitability, capital requirements and capital returns.

The cash and financial projections will show the expected cost of the turnaround process and, if necessary, provide the basis for obtaining needed financing. The best plan in the world is useless if the organization cannot fund operating losses and has no means of raising the necessary capital. In many situations, approval and support from a variety of third-party stakeholders is required for debt relief, price increases, cost reductions or enhanced credit terms. These stakeholders may include trade vendors, customers, secured lenders and landlords. These stakeholders will invariably require detailed projections to justify their support of the company's actions.

The turnaround plan should include requirements for specific status reports and timelines. The status reports focus attention on progress made against goals. The plan must have short-term, mid-term and long-term goals. The short-term goals should be something the organization can accomplish in one week to three months; mid-term goals are from three to nine months and long-term goals are anything greater than nine months. The purpose of defining these various time increments is to allow for the organization to manage progress and make necessary adjustments throughout the entire time frame contemplated in the plan.

EXECUTION OF THE TURNAROUND PLAN

Turnaround plans require consistent review and adjustments as new information is generated from previous actions. This "Cycle" can best be summarized as "Plan-Act-Review". The turnaround plan should be dynamic and evolve based on the results achieved from the tactics implemented. The turnaround plan is not a static set of tasks that are to be pursued regardless of the results achieved along the way, but one that constantly adapts as new information is generated and incorporated.

Turnaround plans and the environment in which they are implemented require the team to be able to:

- Think about the specific short-term objective and the associated costs; compare and contrast the various alternatives

- Take definitive actions

- Review and compare the results to those expected

This cycle must be applied to each tactic and action defined in the turnaround plan. Moreover, the time for this cycle must be short. For many organizations operating in a normal course this cycle is usually on a quarterly basis. For an organizational transformation process this cycle is on a weekly, bi-weekly, even daily basis. As such, the team must have access to solid information on a daily basis, and must have the appropriate authority and autonomy to make the necessary changes and decisions.

The financial and operational metrics that the turnaround team uses to evaluate its short-term and long-term performance must be relevant, reliable and timely. It is preferable if the information is compiled and distributed on a daily basis where appropriate and the results are compared against goals and forecasts on a weekly basis.

The team must have ownership of the plan and the daily and weekly performance for which the plan is measured. This can be a fundamental shift from how many organizations operate. The success or failure of the plan is the responsibility of the team and everyone who can have an effect on the results. Therefore, in selecting members of the transformation team, particular emphasis must be given to selecting individuals that seek out this type of responsibility and accountability.

The organization, and more specifically the turnaround team, cannot hesitate or fear failure. Some strategies and tactics included in the turnaround plan will fail. If they do not fail, then the organization is not pushing hard enough or fast enough. Through trial and error, the planning cycle allows the transformation team and the organization the opportunity to generate confidence in themselves, the organization and the transformation process. It allows individuals to stretch the boundaries of the organization and experiment with concepts and tactics that would never have been considered previously.

This willingness to experiment and fail is important for the organization to break out of its paralyzed state created by aversion to risk. The continued unwillingness of some CEOs to act in the face of continuing losses, plummeting marketing share or competitive threats provides ample demonstration of the risks of complacency. This absence of a sense of urgency is contagious, and lethal, and will spread to the rest of the organization. Alternatively, a confident and active management team will experiment, and this willingness to take prudent risks will spread through the organization over time.

Information

The turnaround environment requires management to have up-to-date information to promptly make informed decisions. This requires the organization to develop periodic management reports that focus on the economic drivers of the business or the critical success factors of a particular project. These reports must be simple and concise, and coincide with the planning cycle. Examples include sales/shipments by day by product line, average price per unit, direct labor hours, orders per day, or quality operating metrics. The focus should be on obtaining good data to make quick decisions. Often individuals will be uncomfortable publishing information in draft or "un-audited" form that they believe may not be absolutely correct. However, this resistance must be overcome, as the goal is generate sound information to manage the direction of the business or progress of a project and take quick decisive action.

Many organizations' information systems are unable to capture the key operating information on a real time basis. In those cases it may be necessary to look outside of the company's traditional information and reporting structure to obtain this information and develop the appropriate reporting tools. The single most difficult task in developing timely, effective management reports is to determine what is truly important to the business and what is not. Burying users with extreme levels of detail data can be as counter productive as distributing meaningless or confusing information. The distribution of these critical management reports should be shared with stakeholders. The wide dissemination of information allows for everyone to see the organization's priorities, track progress and stay informed.

Organizational Transformation Environment

The turnaround team is ultimately responsible for the successful implementation of the organizational transformation plan. In many instances the execution of the plan will require to the team to significantly change the culture of the organization because the environment of the turnaround process is significantly different than the environment of the normal organization. The turnaround environment is fast paced and action oriented; it operates with a focus on short-term performance and a view towards the long-term organizational goals, and utilizes operating practices and management reports not commonly used.

Most organizations operate in a steady-state environment where they prepare an annual budget and monthly accounting statements and then compare the previous month's activity and year-to-date activity against the budget. Various departments and business units usually operate autonomously, with all inter-department issues being addressed in some form of top-down resolution process. Finally, individuals are encouraged to abide by the appropriate organizational norms. In this environment changes in organizational direction, tactics and strategy require a tremendous amount of time to plan and execute, and they require a significant amount of coordination and cooperation between departments and business units. This requires an organization to spend significant time in consensus building, communicating and organizing the various internal constituencies.

In the organizational transformation process an environment must be created that allows for the organization to

- Manage the company with up-to-the-minute information

- Implement short-term planning and execution cycles

- Provide consistent and timely feedback on a short-term basis

- Employ a revised decision making process that fosters quick effective actions across departments and business units

- Operate with a sense of urgency and purpose.

To be successful, turnaround efforts must be implemented in an environment that fosters and promotes a sense of urgency and perpetual movement in all phases of the business. The organization must learn to act quickly and decisively in all areas: operations, sales and marketing, product development, and finance and accounting. In the turnaround environment time is rarely, if ever, on the side of the management team. Many turnaround plans fail because the management team did not act fast enough, or took too many half-measures out of an aversion to risk-taking.

Communication

The turnaround team is the driving force in setting the organizational transformation process; however, the success of this process will be dependent on the entire organization. The general work force must know and believe that their actions will have material impact on the future of the organization. The depth of knowledge, analysis and capabilities found in the general workforce in struggling organizations continually surprises professional turnaround managers. Leveraging this expertise involves actively interviewing employees at all levels in the organization, letting them speak freely without fear of retribution, soliciting their observations and challenging them to suggest reasonable solutions to on-going problems. While many of these interviews may go nowhere, invariably the interviewer will uncork a flood of new ideas and evidence supporting or refuting assumptions about the business. This process is also empowering for the hard working and dedicated individuals who want to contribute to the success of the organization.

Creating an environment that fosters commitment and involvement requires two-way interaction and can only be accomplished when open communication and listening between the workforce is a core principal and nothing less will be accepted. Recognition is another driver in establishing and reinforcing the turnaround process. The recognition system must be frequent and distributed throughout the entire organization to achieve the change in attitude and behavior that will be required. Praise and public recognition must be provided for those activities that contribute to the turnaround process.

Communication is essential for the successful execution of the organizational transformation plan. Any communication program must be fact based on focused on two-way exchange of information. In a turnaround environment the communication system must be structured so that timely, accurate and relevant information can be quickly compiled from multiple sources. Once compiled the information must be distributed to the turnaround team and throughout the organization and, when appropriate, to outside stakeholders. This wide dissemination of information ensures that all parties are focused on the same financial and operational data, are fully informed of progress, and understand the goals of the organization. This communication strategy also helps the turnaround team maintain control of the discussion agenda with potentially hostile third-party stakeholders.

CONCLUSIONS

The process of transforming an enterprise can be broken down into clear and logical steps. An honest assessment must be made of the situation and organization. The management team must provide leadership, and focus the organization on the problems at hand. Management must encourage prompt decision-making with the best information available, and communicate effectively both inside and outside the company. Yet many times turnaround efforts fail. The intangibles that separate the success stories from failures include hard work, dedication and a single-minded determination to complete the job. It is inevitable that there will be setbacks, and some will be severe enough to suggest abandonment of the turnaround process. Small missteps are opportunities to adjust plans and modify behavior. A continued focus on the overall transformation goals must be maintained.

Successful turnarounds abound in today's business environment, and with the rapid development of technology, global competition, and the ever-changing competitive environment, the need for organizations to fundamentally transform the structure of their operations will be required to survive and to prosper.

REFERENCES

Bibeault, D.B. (1999). Corporate turnarounds: How managers turn losers into winners. Washington, DC: Beard Books.

Collins, J.C., & Porras, J. (1994). Built to last. New York: Harper Collins.

DiNapoli, D., Sigoloff, R.F., & Cushman, R.F. (Eds.).(1991). Workouts and turnarounds: The handbook of restructuring and investing in distressed companies. Homewood, IL: Richard Irwin.

Maddi, S.R., & Khoshaba, D.M. (2005). Resilience at work: How to succeed no matter what life throws at you. New York: American Management Association.

Peters, T. (1987). Thriving on chaos: Handbook for management revolution. New York: Harper Collins.

CHAPTER 13

FINANCING IN A CRISIS[1]

MICHAEL E. TENNENBAUM

ABSTRACT

Enterprise transformation often emerges from crises, particularly crises that threaten the financial survival of the enterprise. In such crises, cash control is often the primary, near-term goal. This chapter first considers the objectives in such crises – operate or liquidate. Selecting a capital structure, formulating a negotiating strategy, considering bankruptcy, and necessary characteristics of leaders are then discussed. Several examples of financial turnarounds are used to illustrate key points.

INTRODUCTION

Most business crises occur due to an impending shortage of cash. An immediate crisis occurs when payroll, rent, vendors, and/or interest payments and debt maturities cannot be funded. Future crises can be foreseen due to such factors as declining profitability and technological change that will affect the future availability of cash. Therefore, the degree of urgency is a primary consideration. Generally these crises relate to missed opportunities, changes in markets demand, adjustments in the competitive climate that may have evolved unrecognized over an extended period of time, or are part of an unexpected market shock.

CASH CONTROL

If the crisis is immediate, someone must become the sole controller of cash and take the necessary steps to minimize outflow and to maximize inflow. To do so properly, he/she must understand the cash inflows and outflows of the business and have the ability to project coming needs. This job requires a short-term view in conjunction with a longer-term focus on enterprise value. This type of financial manager is not always available.

After a short while, it will become apparent how long the business can survive without fresh capital. Decisions about whom to pay and how much, have

---

[1] This chapter was written with a business enterprise in mind. However, these principals apply to non-commercial enterprises as well; just some terms change (e.g., "funding," authorizations," "elections," etc.)

importance to the future of the business and must be made carefully. But, these decisions must be made quickly; lack of action (managers will tend to wait too long or are over optimistic about the upside of their organization) usually dooms the effort. Most managers are not experienced in this very unpleasant process, and would do well to bring in experts.

Whether existing management is used or the task is outsourced, tough cash control is shocking to most companies. Focus is shifted from future growth to very short-term survival; such refocusing is depressing to the typical manager. Thus, a strong leader is needed to modify company culture and to counter the inevitable gloom. Some large companies have survived mostly because a strong leader made realistic estimates about short-term liquidity and took the necessary tough measures while still preserving the business (e.g., Foster Wheeler), whereas other large companies did not (e.g., Consolidated Freightways and Read-Rite).

EXAMPLES

The following examples illustrate the key points just made regarding management of cash flow during crises. These illustrations also support several of the discussion points that follow in this chapter.

Foster Wheeler

Foster Wheeler Ltd. was about to go broke in 2003 and 2004, due to the kinds of problems that often afflict companies these days: auditing issues; trade credit reductions; too much debt. A dynamic new management team came in and developed a crisis plan. Here are some quotes from it:

"Early in the fourth quarter of 2003, a key financial officer responsible for the preparation of the nine sets of subsidiary financial statements resigned. Our remaining permanent corporate accounting staff was not structured to address this increased workload under the deadlines required so we hired temporary professional personnel to assist with the process. Because the temporary personnel were unfamiliar with our operations, this led to audit adjustments deemed material in relation to the size of the subsidiaries in the financial reporting process. The external auditors notified the audit committee of our board of directors on December 16, 2003 that they believed the insufficient staffing levels in the corporate accounting department represented a "material weakness" in the preparation of the subsidiary financial statements, but noted that this did not constitute a material weakness for our consolidated financial statements.

If we do not complete our restructuring plan, there will continue to be substantial doubt about our ability to continue as a going concern. Even if we complete our restructuring plan, we may be left with too much debt and too few assets to survive. If we are successful in our restructuring plan, we will have to continue to improve our business operations, including our contracting and execution process, to achieve our forecast and continue as a going concern. Even if we successfully complete the exchange offer, we may not be able to continue as a going concern."

The recognition just outlined was the key to this company's addressing a potential crisis quickly. As a result, after much iteration, their recapitalization plan succeeded and they were on their way to good financial health. Our firm was instrumental in the Company's out-of-court restructuring in several ways. First, we had a solid foundation in the industry and understood the fundamental value of the Company – this gave us conviction to invest and allowed us to negotiate from a position of strength. This also allowed us to build credibility with the CEO and management team, which eased negotiations. Second, as an active member of an ad hoc Creditor's Committee, we took a leadership role in negotiating a fair deal for all parties; this was a winning situation for everyone around the table. Third, after many iterations and strenuous negotiations, we bought out "hold-out" preferred at the 11th hour and immediately tendered it to ensure success in the complicated tender offer that the Company was conducting. Finally, we found a new Board member for the Company; she has deep industry experience and has become a key director in the newly constituted Company.

Consolidated Freightways

Consolidated Freightways Corporation (CFC), one of the largest less-than-truckload (LTL) transportation and logistics companies in the world, is an interesting example of managing in a distressed situation. CFC employed more than 18,500 employees and had approximately 350 owned and leased facilities across the U.S. In the late 1990's, the Company implemented an aggressive strategy to increase revenues, primarily in response to Wall Street's criticism of the company's lack of growth. This resulted in the acquisition of less desirable customers and a decline in the company's margins. In response, CFC implemented aggressive pricing policies that led to significant declines in tonnage transported. The company also suffered from increased competition from regional LTL carriers, small package carriers and private carriage and freight forwarders, high labor costs including pension and benefits, changes in supply chain management such as just-in-time inventory and growing "regionalization" of freight, and the U.S. economy's decline in 2001-2002. These factors resulted in the rapid deterioration of CFC's financial results (the company reported a net loss of $160 million during the first six months of 2002) and liquidity.

The key challenges for the business were twofold -- short-term liquidity needs driven by the company's operating losses and the need to meet insurance collateral requirements, and long-term strategic challenges posed by competition and cost structure. My firm evaluated a number of alternatives and potential structures of "rescue" financing for the company. As part of the analysis, we evaluated CFC's strategic position and the intrinsic value of its hard-to-replicate terminal network. Our analysis and experts' opinion indicated that, with the proper focus, the company could be able to return to profitability. The "downside" of a potential investment would have been well covered by the real estate value of the company's terminal network. However, the short-term liquidity needs of the company needed to be addressed immediately. As is often the case in distressed situations, management was not accustomed to managing the business in a crisis or turnaround mode and was pursuing a longer-term strategy (focused on improving operating metrics) that required more liquidity than management had anticipated.

Ultimately, the company hired a turnaround expert as the new chief executive officer, and attempted to reduce its operating losses and secure long term financing. These crisis management measures were implemented too late. In mid-2002, one of the company's surety bondholders canceled coverage and the ensuing financial crisis forced the company to seek bankruptcy protection. The company's Board reluctantly determined that the company could not continue to operate and decided to liquidate the company by selling a few divisions and a significant portion of the terminal network. Subsequently, the freight environment improved and freight rates increased significantly.

Companies in distressed situations are often faced with similar challenges where short term requirements (e.g. reducing cash burn, cost reductions, negotiations with creditors and preserving liquidity, restoring the confidence of stakeholders, etc.) are critical and must be addressed immediately before tackling long term value creation (e.g. changes in strategy, new marketing initiatives, restructuring of operations, systems implementation, etc.).

Read-Rite

One of the more distressed companies my firm invested in was Read-Rite, a publicly traded manufacturer of magnetic recording heads for the hard disk drive industry. By the time we got involved, the company had missed a major product cycle by almost a year and, as a result, revenue had dropped over 60% in one year. Furthermore, Read-Rite was out of money and still "burning" cash. If the company did not immediately raise rescue financing it would face a shut down and liquidation. We evaluated Read-Rite's business prospects, especially the strategic positioning of Read-Rite within the hard disk drive industry, focusing on its relationship with its customers, and brought in experts to evaluate Read-Rite's technology and to estimate the value of the company's assets. We then structured a highly tailored turnaround financing for Read-Rite where we captured both downside protection for our investment as well as upside potential. Our principal was invested as a senior secured loan facility with a cash "lockbox" that we controlled governing availability based on a business progress and a borrowing base concept—the facility was designed so that Read-Rite management would need to get our approval weekly in order to access cash for their business needs. We also received a significant number of warrants.

The key to rebuilding significant business value was to work closely with its key customers in getting the next generation of product technology to the market on time. We needed to reduce the cash "burn rate" to provide the time and resources to do so. We introduced operational advisors to coach the management team, who was well versed in the industry and business but inexperienced in crisis turnarounds. A number of steps were taken to reduce the cash "burn" rate of the company, including negotiations with customers and vendors to improve working capital use, rolling furloughs of the workforce, and the establishment of a central cash "task force" to bring more control and focus on eliminating or deferring unnecessary cash disbursements—including reduction of expenses and capital investments. As importantly as the operational and financial improvements, our involvement also brought a renewed sense of energy in the workforce and increased confidence in the company from the customers and vendors.

In the end the investment resulted in a reasonably successful outcome, both for us and Read-Rite -- although with a surprising twist in the end. Read-Rite had made some progress, but not enough, on its technology for us to continue to fund the company. As a result, the company filed for Chapter 7, but we continued to fund its operations in order to position it for a sale. Read-Rite was sold six weeks later -- much more quickly than could have been done otherwise -- to one of its key customers, Western Digital, who acquired the company in a bidding war for a purchase price much higher than our total investment.

OBJECTIVES — OPERATE OR LIQUIDATE

Most stakeholders seek to keep businesses going rather than to liquidate them. It is in most people's interest to do so. But it is necessary to assess the future viability of the business in order to set reasonable objectives for the stakeholders. Financial projections should incorporate all relevant factors — especially the damage done to the business' credibility with its customers, employees, vendors, regulators and the community, due to such events as a bankruptcy filing, slowing payments, reducing product offerings, laying off employees, etc. Understanding the reaction of competitors to their perception of a wounded adversary is also important; making some compromises with them could be advisable. The near-term future will be tougher than the good old days.

After developing objective financial projections, and considering both the degree of visibility of future cash flows and the major threats to them — then a range of values for the businesses and their assets can be arrived at. These values should include all scenarios including liquidation, divestitures, refinancing, joint ventures, partnerships, and licensing arrangements. Creativity in developing these alternatives is a hallmark of great restructuring advisors.

Next, a list of all financial needs must be prepared. Past due trade payables (and reduced payable terms, COD, advance payments), deferred maintenance, minimum capital expenditures, new product development and production costs, benefit plan funding, taxes, litigation and warranty reserves, etc. probably all need money for normal operations. Does the enterprise value justify funding these critical items? Can any amounts be reduced without harming the business' future? If there is sufficient value to justify the critical items, then an optimum capital structure should be selected. Alternative capital structures are worth considering, especially the amount of senior securities -- like debt and preferred stock – that can be issued.

Developing the projections is a very political process. The political variables are:

- Who hires the crisis advisors? Management and the equity owners usually want optimistic ones; senior lenders always want conservative ones; everyone wants competent ones who can deal with courtroom pressures.

- Who dominates the formulation of assumptions? If the lenders are skilled and organized, they may bias the advisor (because management teams come and go, but big lenders always are hiring crisis advisors). It's usually better to have a low case, a base case, and a high case for future operating results so that all opinions can be quantified. If divestitures are practical to consider, a big battle can erupt with management claiming the strategic importance for keeping something that the creditors want to sell in order to pay down debt. Divestiture battles are bad for employee morale and for customer loyalty, so they should be short-lived.

- How fragile is the business? Some businesses can melt down: vendors and credit card companies can refuse all credit,: key employees can walk out; major customers can transfer business; regulators can install conservators and/or cancel licenses. When a business is very fragile, the board of directors usually has the most power with the threat to file a bankruptcy proceeding being the sword of Damocles hanging over every meeting. Such crises can be very short (quick solution or rapid demise), or very long (limping along hoping for a lucky break).

SELECTING A CAPITAL STRUCTURE

The starting point should be the existing stakeholders. If large amounts are due to them, or, if they benefit greatly by the survival of the business, perhaps they will fund the recapitalization. If so, this can be the cheapest capital available and the securities they desire should be the first choices within the context of the new capital structure. Debt normally should not be maximized, because financial credibility will be vital going forward. Consequently, a common scenario is that the lenders end up becoming shareholders.

In any event, the capital structure of the peer group of companies could be the most aggressive case regarding debt. Exceptions would be if the business has much newer plant and products than the competition, and most of the future earnings before interest, taxes, depreciation and amortization ("EBITDA") is free cash flow; or if substantial funds are released from working capital because of improved future credit.

The amount of debt should be easily serviced by free cash and/or planned divestitures and should provide adequate flexibility for unanticipated events under reasonable projections. If additional senior securities are needed to satisfy claims, then straight preferred stock is the best choice. Preferred stock is a very flexible instrument and changes in its redemption price, dividend rates, and voting rights do not create the tax and legal issues that are associated with junior debt issues. Large board representation by preferred stock holders is not unusual and this could be an inducement. Lenders are concerned about having board seats due to lender liability laws and avoid such positions.

Both debt and preferred stock can be issued by either the parent company or by subsidiaries. It would be good to structure these instruments with a view to future divestitures in case they are either needed or are desirable. Review with insolvency counsel the business' projections and probable scenarios in order to avoid accounting and legal pitfalls like substantive consolidation (which can occur in bankruptcy cases), fraudulent conveyance, and piercing of corporate veils.

NEGOTIATION STRATEGY

Many participants in crisis investing do not consider the full range of issues — make sure that you do. If you are able to make both debt and equity investments, if you have patient capital, and if you are able to manage businesses, then you have great advantages over most other participants. After determining your probable exit from the investment, you can structure financing using a package of securities that provides the optimum balance between risk and reward for the investors.

Part of a recapitalization program might include purchase of existing claims, typically at discounts to par. Such transactions monetize holders who want cash today and can transfer to other holders' value in the form of critical mass, blocking positions, and/or effective control. Financial crises often trigger sales of the affected bonds and loans, in some cases because the holders cannot own distressed debt, and in some cases because the holders are embarrassed and/or tired of hearing all the bad news.

Do not accept conventional wisdom. Companies in trouble are full of people who are misinformed and who accept artificial constraints. Test assertions. See objective evidence. Utilize judgments only from sources you respect. Debunk myths. Be decisive when you have 80% of the information that you need, but take actions that have sufficient margin for error. If others are excessively optimistic, let them overpay – they'll run out of money, and you'll still be around!

Decide if you want partners. If you won't control the equity and/or the board of directors of the issuer, then you may need partners. Evaluate lenders, investors, suppliers, labor unions, customers, and managers for compatibility. Consider target holding period, hurdle rates of return, probable exits, risk tolerance, and personalities. Some people may be great economically, but you wouldn't want to count on their partnership instincts.

For debt tranches held by you, try to impose covenants that cannot be waived without your vote. Seek to have some control over the assets by collateralizing your debt balance. If your holdings aren't big enough to accomplish that, find some compatible partners who, together with you, will have blocking positions.

Distinguish between the stated and the real positions of the participants. If you think someone is bluffing, he probably is. Many "final and best" offers get made. Analyze what the real risks and opportunities are and confront your adversaries with the facts. Even if you don't prevail, it's good practice for the courtroom. Reality has a way of asserting itself over time. CAUTION: now and then, really stupid and/or reckless people destroy companies through irrational behavior. You can't negotiate with a fear of irrationality on another people's parts. Just try to protect yourself from it with a sensible legal strategy and hope that a judge will do the right things. All is not as it seems! Investors and lenders who are living through a crisis usually are afflicted with deal fatigue, recriminations, and politics. Caveat emptor!

Lender liability (a legal doctrine that weakens your claim because of actions/inactions on your part) is a grey area that can generate red ink! Always use insolvency counsel to guide you in any areas that might be management and board prerogatives. Particular care must be taken when you have both debt and equity holdings of the same issuer.

BANKRUPTCY – YES OR NO

Ironically, bankruptcy is very expensive -- many lawyers, advisors, committees, and expenses. Even worse: many months for court hearings, rulings, appeals, notice periods. It often becomes a problem to recruit and maintain talented managers, key suppliers, good customers, and credit facilities. Using the threat of bankruptcy often yields enough benefits as the vulnerable stakeholders compromise in order to avoid their worse outcomes. Even an imperfect out-of-court restructuring may be better than a thorough Chapter 11 reorganization, if it buys enough time for the enterprise.

If a relatively small number of stakeholders will be compromised by a bankruptcy, it is almost always best to do an out-of-court restructuring. The negotiations are similar, but much money can be saved if a sense of urgency can be generated. Other chapters in this book deal with bankruptcy processes.

Financiers need to predict the timing of the case and to be prepared for the key dates to protect claims and to maximize recovery. Buying blocking positions in the "fulcrum" debt securities is potentially the most profitable strategy. The fulcrum securities are the most junior ones that still have intrinsic value. Financing the Debtor-In-Possession often is a good idea as it positions one to do the exit financing when the bankruptcy case is over. Debtor-In-Possession financing is usually very safe because the court grants it the most senior status. As the term implies, this financing is given to the bankrupt company before the creditors take it over, in order for the court to consider arguments and a plan of reorganization that the stakeholders end up with.

THE LEADER[2]

The stresses of crisis and/or transformation are great. People worry about their jobs, their future, their lost opportunities, possible legal exposure, and about

---

[2] See also the chapter on leadership by Bill George, as well as the chapter on organizational culture and change by Joyce Shields.

having a cloud over their resumes. Keeping great people is tough and recruiting great people is even tougher. Furthermore, daily activities can be depressing: firing people, avoiding paying bills, eliminating business activities, begging for cash, dealing with vulture investors, and missing out on growth opportunities. Oftentimes, people work seven days a week and burn out.

In addition, most companies in crisis have culture problems. Either they don't envision external challenges that are real threats to the enterprise, or they have low metabolisms and set inadequate goals for themselves. People may not all need replacing. But, certainly, they won't change without strong leadership. A strong leader will need to construct a management team with similar goals and vision because without proper support the new leadership will fail also.

Therefore, a new strong leader is usually needed. He or she has to be willing to change everything that needs changing and to discharge everyone who needs replacing. No sacred cows. Also, he/she must have the energy to work long hours, the forcefulness to demand proper implementation, and the judgment to select a good team while under big time pressures and with (sometimes) no margin for error.

Selecting the right leader is vital. And selecting the right team is crucial. A new culture is usually needed and incentives to reinforce appropriate behavior must be installed. People are either part of the problem or part of the solution.

Often, the leader must focus the enterprise on a more limited range of activities in order to conserve both human and financial resources. Such decisions require courage. Interested parties may resist many actions and their efforts can erode even the greatest courage. Obviously, the right leader in these circumstances is a rarity and should be cherished!

One of the most effective turnaround leaders we know is Gary Sutton. In his book, "The Six-Month Fix" (2001), he outlines a prototypical series of steps for dealing with financial crises[3]. Of course, any particular engagement will never happen quite this way. No two are the same. Nevertheless, Sutton's outline provides a good sense of the flow of issues and decisions involved in leading a turnaround.

Until you've stared down bankruptcies, missed a few payrolls, kept your cool and prevailed, you cannot simply follow Sutton's script. You need the presence of mind to know when to skip a step, change the sequence, and push one that matters over another with less promise. Obviously, understanding the specific context is crucial.

Gary Sutton adds one more sage suggestion: "When business is going well, it creates a good impression if all of your key people are sophisticated Ivy League types. The carpeting gets a bit thicker, the offices a little larger, the desks fancier, and the insulation from reality unbearable. Sometimes the insulation between the executive offices and the "working troops" is so thick that obvious danger signs are ignored.

Therefore, I urge you, dear reader, to keep the eyeshaded controller, that swearing production manager, that relentless expeditor, in your employ. These

---

[3] See also Kibel (1991) and Reiss & Phelps (1991) for related guidelines and checklists.

hard-boiled individuals may be a little hard to handle when the sun is shining, but you will cry out for them when the rains begin. These tough, tenacious people may prove to be a major asset when impossible tasks have to be accomplished in short periods of time."

CONCLUSION

Investing in businesses in crisis has many pitfalls. Also, continuous pressure will be applied to all the participants in such transactions. But, because of the complexities and pressures, large profits can be earned (and they will be earned!) from this strategy. Also, great satisfactions can be derived from saving enterprises, assisting talented people in duress, and succeeding in one of the most demanding commercial endeavors.

REFERENCES

Kibel, H. (1991). How to turn around a financially troubled company. Santa Monica, CA: Kibel, Green, Inc.

Reiss, M.F., & Phelps, T.G. (1991). Identifying a troubled company. In D. Dinapoli, S. Sigoloff, & R. Cushman, Eds., Workouts and turnarounds: The handbook of restructuring and investing in distressed companies. Homewood, IL: Irwin.

Sutton, G. (2001). The six month fix: Adventures in rescuing failing companies. New York: Wiley.

LEADING A TURNAROUND

(Sutton, 2001)

- Survey the situation. As an outsider, you bring in a fresh perspective. Do this in one week, talking to trade editors, customers, employees, executives, and owners. Give the board your report the following week. If salvageable, give them a contract offer for the turnaround with your report.

- If they buy it, you're a team. Now you can execute without the distraction of explaining every move to the board. If they don't buy it, better you part ways with only a week's time lost.

  o Some businesses are terminal. If that's your feeling, the board has received the favor of this outside opinion. Anything they manage after that will feel like an accomplishment.

  o With your proposal, if you see hope, give the board less than a week to discuss and sign your contract. If they take longer, they don't feel enough pain yet, or are dysfunctional. If you were brought in by a creditor, take your fat fees. If by a shareholder, split the payments between fees and equity.

  o If the board signs your contract, delay announcing it for several days. Use those days to meet with creditors and solicit their support before publicly committing. Let only the incumbent CEO know.

- Renegotiate credit. Do this the first week. Make offers with short deadlines. Offer some warrants for debt reduction.

- Meet with the executive staff. Calculate with them the approximate date that the doors will shut, given the current cost and revenue situation. Make sure every officer is involved in this meeting; push it into the evening. Help everyone believe that change, big change, is the only option.

  o Figure out that night how to let all employees and vendors know, and do it the next day.

  o If you're a charismatic type, also use this moment to renew commitment.

  o Spend a few hours with the staff, going through your plan, changing it on the spot where they convince you, put it down in writing and ask everyone to sign it. Save that document for a celebration when cash flow reappears.

  o Plot the date for the return of cash flow. Explain to all that cash, nothing else, matters until the date that sustainable, positive cash flow returns. Look each in the eye, and explain not everybody will survive to enjoy the moment, but that your hopes are that everybody will try to stay for the fight.

- Meet with creditors and explain the plan. Unions too, if there are any. Announce times for employees who want to hear more, after hours, in the lunchroom or your office or a conference room.

- Take over the checkbook and sign checks for a few hours every week. You'll be amazed at what you see. This also keeps you angry enough to keep cutting costs.

- Blow out all inventory. Sell everything at any price you can, without plugging distribution completely. Now you know what it was really worth.

- Factor your accounts receivable. Push the collections group to knock several days off your receivables every month. Start by knocking a day off the first week. Then factor after the first two months of tighter collections.

- Find where the gross margin is. If the books reveal that, terrific. But don't trust them. Listen to customer service activity, sales effort, and returns or cancels. Find out which services or products generate more than their fair share of overhead. Sit down then with accounting and show them where the margin is, and see if they don't agree.

- Lay off people involved in the lower-margin areas. Lease or sell space and equipment related to those efforts. Allow 20% of the best employees in these spaces to transfer into the remaining areas, but terminate 20% in the businesses you'll keep, to make room without boosting expenses.

- Renegotiate the union contracts and leases. Now's the best time.

- Show the new cost basis to vendors, and get better terms.

- Cut purchases. Stand on the loading dock door and see what's coming in. Force purchasing to squeeze pricing by a targeted amount each month, and have weekly meetings to insure they're on target.

- Boost sales commissions and drop base salaries.

- Give someone, somewhere, a raise for notable effort. Publicize their accomplishment (not the raise) in the company newsletter.

- Tinker with a remaining, but marginal, product or service. Raise its price 10% and see what happens. If that fails, cut price by 20% but watch it very closely, and kill it if volume doesn't jump to recover margin.

- Eliminate two development programs. Stretch the remaining effort.

- Now start the CEO search. Six weeks have already passed; you understand the business a bit, so it's time.

- Make one more cutback. Go deep enough that this will be the last.

- Change your credit policy. Either tighten or loosen it. Make pricing and commission adjustments simultaneously, so internal effects are minimal.

- Eliminate several problem customers.

- Go back to the key creditors and try to renegotiate terms again.

- Eliminate a problem territory.

- Spend two weeks out of the second month making customer calls.

- Adjust prices and volume discounts.

- If cash is returning, offer to pay off a key vendor or creditor ahead of schedule, in exchange for a discount. Let other vendors and creditors know. Don't ask them to do the same. One or two will approach you. Deal with them.

- Launch internal competitions for best customer service and best cost savings. Personally make weekly awards of dinners or weekend trips with a plaque and photo in the company newsletter.

- Have a company picnic. Spend time cooking the burgers or being the clown in the dunk tank or competing in the three-legged race.

- Select a department or service to outsource. Do it.

- Hire the new CEO.

- Disappear. Leave the new CEO your phone number, just in case.

CHAPTER 14

TRANSFORMATION AND THE CHAPTER 11 REORGANIZATION PROCESS:

Where The "Exit" Is Just The Beginning

PAUL S. ARONZON AND THOMAS R. KRELLER

ABSTRACT

Businesses find themselves in distress and in need of restructuring for a variety of reasons. The choice of any particular restructuring strategy will be driven by the nature of the problem or problems requiring repair. One of the more drastic restructuring alternatives that a distressed company may consider is the filing of a bankruptcy case under chapter 11 of the Bankruptcy Code. While a chapter 11 filing is a dramatic step that can shake an enterprise to its core, the Bankruptcy Code recognizes that fact and, in response, affords a troubled business significant protections and powerful tools designed to facilitate management's efforts to repair the problems and right the business. The major protections and tools available to management in chapter 11, and how specific protections and tools can be used to assist in enterprise transformation efforts, are described. In addition, a broader overview of the chapter 11 environment and process, including a discussion of some of the more significant risks and burdens of chapter 11, provides meaningful context for consideration of the transformation opportunities available through the chapter 11 reorganization process.

INTRODUCTION

In a healthy going concern enterprise, transformation efforts can (and should) manifest themselves as an integral component of ongoing strategic planning. If addressed proactively and continuously, transformation efforts can be implemented incrementally as part of a coherent strategy, rather than as a more dramatic attempt to save a troubled business. Even with management's best efforts in this regard, however, businesses can find themselves in distress and in need of a significant restructuring in order to preserve the viability of the enterprise.

The need for restructuring can be prompted by a wide variety of circumstances. Fundamental operational problems, burdensome cost structures, drastic changes in competitive markets, debilitating litigation, excess financial leverage creating crippling debt service obligations – all are factors that can create or contribute to the economic distress that can drive an enterprise to consider restructuring alternatives.

The choice of any particular restructuring strategy will be driven by the nature of the problem or problems requiring repair. For example, if the problem is limited to a discrete operational issue and the enterprise has sufficient capital to invest to fix that problem, management's challenge may be limited to determining the optimal solution and most efficient and effective means to make the required investment. If the issues creating the distress are external and more far-ranging, on the other hand, the restructuring likely will require more potent tools.

One of the more drastic restructuring alternatives that a distressed company may consider is the filing of a bankruptcy case under chapter 11 of the Bankruptcy Code. Such a filing generally (and in most cases appropriately) is considered to be a strategy of last resort. Nonetheless, a chapter 11 filing affords a troubled business significant protections and powerful tools that in many instances may outweigh the costs and risks associated with the filing.

The purpose of this chapter is to provide an overview of the nature and scope of those components of the chapter 11 process that a business enterprise may be able to utilize to facilitate implementation of a more comprehensive transformation process. As discussed further below, the Bankruptcy Code can provide the distressed company with much-needed opportunities to stabilize and analyze business operations, rid itself of excess assets and burdensome contracts and leases, shed (or at least manage and mitigate) otherwise-crippling liabilities, and focus on developing a viable long-range strategy and business plan. Of course, these opportunities come at a cost, and this chapter also discusses generally some of the unique risks and challenges that the enterprise will encounter while operating in the chapter 11 environment.

In the context of exploring the process of enterprise transformation, it is important to keep in mind that a restructuring accomplished through chapter 11 does not itself accomplish the transformation, but rather is merely a tool that can be used to facilitate the broader transformation process. A chapter 11 restructuring can permit a business to leave behind historical problems, solve or mitigate presently existing problems and establish a solid platform for the business as it exits bankruptcy. But for a transforming enterprise, that exit is just the beginning. The success of the transformation will be determined not by whether the business exits from chapter 11, but by whether the enterprise successfully exploits that platform in the marketplace in the months and years following its exit. Thus, in many respects, the exit from chapter 11 is just the beginning of the transformation.

THE LANDSCAPE OF THE CHAPTER 11 REORGANIZATION PROCESS

The chapter 11 reorganization process brings together a wide variety of parties possessing a diverse array of interests in the business enterprise. Those parties interact in an environment that is equal parts business management, legal proceeding and multi-party negotiation — all under the oversight of the bankruptcy court and subject to the statutory overlay of the federal bankruptcy laws. The result is a complex, fluid and occasionally combustible process designed to accomplish two sometimes inconsistent goals — transforming a distressed company into a reorganized and viable going concern, while at the same time maximizing economic recoveries to stakeholders.

The focus of this chapter will be on the former objective — exploring the opportunities that chapter 11 presents to transform a distressed enterprise. An important backdrop to that discussion, however, is a general understanding of the chapter 11 dynamic and how the latter objective — maximizing stakeholder recoveries — may hamper efforts to achieve optimal transformation. Equally important is a general understanding of the roles played by the various participants that typically are the most active in the chapter 11 process. The following sections describe briefly the landscape of the chapter 11 process and its participants and establish the context for the ensuing discussion of the transformation opportunities that present themselves in chapter 11.

The Bankruptcy Code

The bankruptcy laws in the United States are federal laws contained in Title 11 of the United States Code (the "Bankruptcy Code"). The present version of the Bankruptcy Code is the result of the passage of the Bankruptcy Reform Act of 1978, which superseded the old Bankruptcy Act of 1898. The Bankruptcy Reform Act of 1978 has been amended from time to time, most recently by the Bankruptcy Abuse and Consumer Protection Act of 2005, Public Law No. 109-8 (the "2005 Bankruptcy Amendments"), which was enacted on April 20, 2005 and, with certain specified exceptions, will be effective in bankruptcy cases commenced on and after October 17, 2005.

Chapter 11 of the Bankruptcy Code, which is entitled "Reorganization," is the section of the Bankruptcy Code that is designed to permit business enterprises to reorganize themselves under the Bankruptcy Code, subject to the ability to satisfy all of the applicable requirements therein. In addition to chapter 11, chapters 1, 3 and 5 of the Bankruptcy Code are applicable in chapter 11 cases and contain certain important provisions that apply in the chapter 11 case of a business attempting to reorganize. Chapters 7 ("Liquidation"), chapter 9 ("Adjustment of Debts of a Municipality") and chapter 13 ("Adjustment of Debts of an Individual with Regular Income") are other chapters of the Bankruptcy Code that are not directly applicable in a chapter 11 reorganization.

As discussed in more detail below, the Bankruptcy Code creates the legal "playing field" on which the reorganization process occurs. The Bankruptcy Code identifies and empowers the players, establishes the ground rules to be followed by those players throughout the course of the process, empowers the Bankruptcy Court to oversee the parties' activities and enforce the ground rules and articulates the standards that must be met by an enterprise in order to successfully emerge from the bankruptcy case.

The Bankruptcy Court

Because the United States Constitution provides that Congress has the exclusive right to make bankruptcy law, all bankruptcy cases in the United States are administered in a United States Bankruptcy Court. Each United States Bankruptcy Court is a federal court that is a division of the United States District Court, which is the trial level court of original federal jurisdiction. Each United States District Court has a corresponding Bankruptcy Court, which means that each state has at least one Bankruptcy Court. States with larger populations may have multiple federal judicial districts, which means those states have more than one Bankruptcy Court.

The Bankruptcy Court is the trial level court for all bankruptcy cases. The Bankruptcy Court thus is the initial "trier of fact" on issues involving factual disputes during the chapter 11 case. In addition, because the chapter 11 process at its core is a judicially supervised negotiation process, the Bankruptcy Court generally has a significant degree of control over the chapter 11 process, how the parties interact with one another and the ultimate outcome of the case.

Decisions made by the Bankruptcy Court can be appealed to the corresponding United States District Court or, in certain federal circuits, the Bankruptcy Appellate Panel. Appeals from the District Court or the Bankruptcy Appellate Panel, in turn, are heard by the United States Court of Appeals, which is the last step in the process before the United States Supreme Court. Prosecuting an appeal to finality can take months and even years. Consequently, for distressed companies that do not have the luxury of time, a prolonged appeal of an unfavorable ruling simply may not be a viable option.

The Estate and the Debtor in Possession

The Bankruptcy Code provides that the commencement of a bankruptcy case creates an "estate" that generally is comprised of all of the company's assets, wherever located, as of the commencement of the case.[1] Assets are defined to include legal and equitable rights in property, contracts, causes of action (whether presently existing or contingent), and property transferred pre-bankruptcy but subject to recovery as a preference or fraudulent conveyance. Generally speaking, the "estate" concept is designed to encompass all legal and equitable rights of the company that may have value — either to the company as a component of its ongoing business operations or to its stakeholders as a potential source of recovery.

The Bankruptcy Code further provides that, unless the Bankruptcy Court orders otherwise, a debtor entity that commences a chapter 11 bankruptcy case remains in possession of the assets of the estate and in control of its business operations in the same manner those assets were possessed, controlled and operated prior to the bankruptcy filing.[2] While vested with such possession and control, the debtor entity is known as the "debtor in possession." Because the

---

[1] Bankruptcy Code §541(a).
[2] Bankruptcy Code §§1107(a) and 1108.

estate exists to capture valuable property to serve as a source of recovery to creditors and equity holders, while in possession of the assets of the estate, the debtor in possession is a fiduciary for the estate. As such, throughout the chapter 11 process, the company, in its capacity as debtor in possession, must take into account the interests of the company's economic stakeholders as parties having an interest in the estate. For ease of reference throughout this chapter, a business entity that is the subject of a chapter 11 bankruptcy case will be referred to generically as the "company" or the "enterprise."

Secured Creditors

A secured creditor is a creditor who holds an interest (e.g., a lien, security interest or mortgage) in assets of the company to secure that creditor's right to repayment from the company. Depending on the nature of the business, a company may have a variety of secured creditors or none at all. To the extent a secured creditor has a perfected lien or security interest in assets that are valuable to the enterprise, that secured creditor generally has significant bargaining leverage in the chapter 11 case. That leverage stems from the fact that, generally speaking, the Bankruptcy Code provides secured creditors with a great deal of protection for their property rights, including requiring that such a secured creditor must have its claim satisfied in full (although not necessarily by payment in cash) by the company in order for the company to retain the assets for use in the business.[3] While the Bankruptcy Code does contain several mechanisms for the company to use as part of the negotiation process with any particular secured creditor, those mechanisms are limited in nature so as not to deprive the secured creditor of the property interest that it bargained for in obtaining its collateral. Accordingly, properly perfected secured creditors are often major (and well-positioned) participants in chapter 11 cases.

The Official Unsecured Creditors Committee

Unlike secured creditors, unsecured creditors do not have any lien or security interest in any specific property to secure repayment of their claims. Generally speaking, unsecured creditors may include trade vendors and suppliers, holders of any unsecured debt securities issued by the company, parties to litigation with the company, taxing authorities and other miscellaneous creditors.

Regardless of the size or nature of their respective claims, unsecured creditors generally share a common interest in a chapter 11 case — namely, to maximize the amount of consideration distributed to the unsecured creditors under the chapter 11 plan. The Bankruptcy Code recognizes that shared interest and creates a mechanism for the formation of an "official committee" of unsecured creditors (the "Creditors Committee") designed to represent the common interests of unsecured creditors in the case. The Creditors Committee oftentimes is comprised of the company's largest unsecured creditors, but the number of creditors

---

[3] Bankruptcy Code §1129(b)(2)(A).

participating on any given Creditors Committee and the nature and size of their respective claims can vary.[4]

The Creditors Committee is recognized by the Bankruptcy Court as having standing to be heard, and to sue and be sued, in the bankruptcy case as a representative of the unsecured creditors as a group.[5] With that power comes accountability, in that the Creditors Committee and its members owe a fiduciary duty to protect the interests of all unsecured creditors. The Bankruptcy Code provides that the Creditors Committee may retain counsel and other professionals to advise it, with the fees and expenses of such professionals paid by the company.[6]

Because the Creditors Committee typically represents the interests of a significant portion of the company's creditors, Creditors Committees are very active participants in chapter 11 cases. The Creditors Committee's activities include receiving and monitoring periodic reporting from the company, reviewing and, where appropriate, objecting to requests by the company for authorization to enter into transactions that require Bankruptcy Court approval, and actively participating with the company in negotiations over the terms of any plan of reorganization.

Equity Holders

The holders of equity interests in a company that files a chapter 11 case may or may not have an economic interest in the company. If the company is clearly insolvent by the time the bankruptcy case is filed, the equity holders may be so far "out of the money" that they do not feel the need to participate in the case. There is no requirement, however, that a company be insolvent in order to obtain protection under chapter 11. Accordingly, companies that may be solvent or for which the issue of solvency is subject to dispute may seek protection under chapter 11. In those cases where value may be sufficient to satisfy all creditor claims and potentially provide a recovery to equity holders, the equity holders may be very active participants in the case. In such cases, it is not unusual for equity holders to organize and seek Bankruptcy Court approval for the appointment of a "official" equity security holders committee.[7] If such official status is granted, that committee, like the Creditors Committee, may retain professional advisors and have those advisors paid by the company.

Other Interested Parties

Other parties in interest have the right to participate in the chapter 11 case and to be heard on matters that are brought before the Bankruptcy Court.[8] Creditors holding sizeable claims may be active participants (either through participation on

---

[4] Bankruptcy Code §1102(a)(1) and (b)(1).
[5] Bankruptcy Code §1109(b).
[6] Bankruptcy Code §1103(a).
[7] Bankruptcy Code §1102(a)(2).
[8] Bankruptcy Code §1109(b).

the Creditors Committee or individually), groups of similarly situated creditors or equity holders may participate in the form of "ad hoc" or "informal" committees and regulatory authorities or taxing authorities may participate as well. As discussed below, in many ways the commencement of a chapter 11 case creates a "public forum" that accommodates the participation of a wide variety of constituents and exposes the company to a level of scrutiny that otherwise does not exist.

The public nature of the bankruptcy case and the multitude of disclosures that a company must make throughout the course of a chapter 11 case also often attract the interest of potential investors or acquirers of the company or certain of its assets. While such parties may or may not technically qualify as "parties in interest" under the Bankruptcy Code, those parties will have access to all of the public filings made in connection with the case. In addition, if either the company (acting in its fiduciary capacity), a significant secured creditor, the Creditors Committee or an equity security holders committee learns of the interest of a potential investor and believes that pursuing a transaction with the potential investor may yield value to the estate or any of its constituents, the potential investor may be welcomed into the case by one or more of those constituents. Thus, a potential investor or acquirer may see the chapter 11 environment as an opportunity to make an investment or obtain assets that might not otherwise be available to it.

TRANSFORMATION OPPORTUNITIES AFFORDED TO A CHAPTER 11 DEBTOR

A company in chapter 11 clearly faces significant challenges in operating an already distressed business under the requirements of the Bankruptcy Code, the supervision of the Bankruptcy Court and the scrutiny of various self-interested parties. Notwithstanding those challenges, the chapter 11 process provides a business enterprise with a variety of opportunities to begin the process of transformation. Those opportunities include a chance to stabilize and analyze existing business operations, the ability to dispose of "excess baggage," and the occasion to focus on and think critically about core competencies and potential new avenues for growth in developing a business plan to be implemented upon emergence. Those opportunities are discussed in turn below.

The Opportunity To Stabilize And Analyze The Business

Managers of businesses that are experiencing financial distress of any sort suffer a very common plight – too much time spent "fighting fires", resulting in too little time spent focusing on important strategic planning and other decisions necessary for successful transformation. One major benefit of the commencement of a chapter 11 case is that the Bankruptcy Code contains several provisions that interact to give an enterprise a "breathing spell" at the outset of the case designed specifically to provide management with a chance to stabilize and analyze the business in preparation for the transformation to come.

The Automatic Stay

The filing of a bankruptcy case results in the immediate and automatic stay (commonly referred to as the "automatic stay") of any actions by creditors or other parties to attempt to enforce their claims against the company or to otherwise take actions to attempt to seize or control the company's assets.[9] One primary purpose of the automatic stay is to create a protective barrier to preserve the estate that is formed at the commencement of the case (discussed above). Subject to certain enumerated exceptions, parties are prohibited from taking any enforcement or similar actions unless they obtain permission from the Bankruptcy Court to do so "for cause."[10] Thus, creditors who may have been breathing down the company's neck pre-bankruptcy in an effort to extract payments and/or other concessions are prohibited from continuing those actions unless the Bankruptcy Court permits them to proceed. In addition, the company generally will not be required to make payments on pre-petition claims, and interest ceases to accrue on unsecured obligations.

Finally, the automatic stay serves to stop litigation that is pending as of the commencement of the case. For a company besieged by significant amounts of litigation (e.g., mass tort claims, product liability claims, securities fraud actions), this protection can be an important tool that permits management to focus its attention on business, rather than legal, issues.

The automatic stay thus serves two important purposes. First, the automatic stay promotes equality among creditors by preventing a "race to the courthouse" to seize valuable assets. Second, the automatic stay provides the company with a "breathing spell" free from creditor enforcement action and other ongoing litigation. This breathing spell provides management with the opportunity to stop "fighting fires" and focus instead on the larger tasks at hand.

Ordinary Course Of Business Transactions

Once the bankruptcy case is commenced and the automatic stay has been triggered, the Bankruptcy Code expressly permits the company to continue to conduct its operations in the "ordinary course of business."[11] Again, this provision is an important tool for management, as it permits the company, with some advance planning, to continue to operate with minimal disruption to the company's daily activities. Combined with the "breathing spell" resulting from the automatic stay, the ability to continue to operate in the ordinary course can provide management with key opportunities early in the case to assess the business and

---

[9] Bankruptcy Code §362(a).
[10] Bankruptcy Code §362(d).
[11] Bankruptcy Code §363(c)(1).

engage in strategic planning and transformational thinking that may have been lacking previously.

There are two important limitations on the ability to conduct business in the ordinary course. First, the company cannot pay obligations that arose pre-bankruptcy absent Bankruptcy Court approval. For example, while the company can pay a vendor in the ordinary course for goods or services provided after the filing of the bankruptcy case, the company cannot pay that same vendor for goods and services that were provided prior to the filing. Similarly, depending on how the timing of the bankruptcy filing intersects with payroll periods, employees may find themselves with pre-bankruptcy wages that cannot be paid unless the Bankruptcy Court specifically authorizes such payments. Thus, while the ability to continue to operate in the ordinary course can greatly facilitate a company's transition into the chapter 11 case, the inability to pay pre-bankruptcy obligations of important constituents nonetheless may lead to operational disruption.

Second, to the extent the company desires to engage in transactions that are outside the ordinary course of business, the company must seek and obtain Bankruptcy Court approval to do so.[12] The process of requesting Bankruptcy Court approval generally requires that interested parties be given notice of, as well as an opportunity to object to, the company's request. Thus, while operating in chapter 11, any decision by management to pursue a transaction that falls outside the ordinary course of business will be subject to the scrutiny of the Bankruptcy Court and interested parties, as well as to delays that will result from that process. In general, this restriction on non-ordinary course transactions serves as an impediment to management's ability to pursue such transactions while in chapter 11 by adding possibly significant cost and delay to any such efforts.

Post-Petition Financing

One common symptom of financial distress is a loss of liquidity, which is often a result of a default under the distressed company's working capital credit facility. Indeed, chapter 11 filings are often precipitated by the inability of the company to obtain advances under its credit facility to fund ongoing operations as a result of defaults under that facility. Consistent with the "breathing spell" created by the automatic stay and the ability to continue to operate in the ordinary course of business, the Bankruptcy Code also provides the chapter 11 debtor with the opportunity to solve its short-term liquidity needs in a number of ways. First, the Bankruptcy Code provides that the company may incur unsecured debt in the ordinary course of business.[13] The court may also authorize the company to obtain credit or incur debt outside of the ordinary course of business on a secured or unsecured basis, subject to certain conditions. Such court-approved credit can be incurred on one of three bases: (a) as unsecured basis having priority over all other priority administrative claims; (b) as debt secured by a lien on unencumbered property or on encumbered property but subject to any valid existing liens; or (c)

---

[12] Bankruptcy Code §363(b)(1).
[13] Bankruptcy Code §364(a).

as debt secured by a lien equal or senior to existing liens (but only if the company establishes that it cannot obtain credit on any other basis and the existing lien holders are "adequately protected".[14] Financing provided under any of these scenarios is commonly referred to as "DIP financing" and is perhaps the most common source of liquidity for large companies operating complex businesses in chapter 11. In its most common form, DIP financing in essence replaces the company's pre-bankruptcy working capital facility as the company's primary source of funding for operations.

In conjunction with or as an alternative to DIP financing, under certain circumstances a chapter 11 debtor may also be able to use cash collateral to fund ongoing operations. The use of cash collateral may be a viable alternative for a company that is able to sustain its operations by utilizing cash receipts without the need for borrowings under a credit facility. In order to use cash collateral, the company must either obtain the consent of the creditor that asserts a security interest in the cash (typically, the pre-petition lender) or by obtaining court approval, which requires proof that the secured creditor whose cash collateral is being used has been "adequately protected."[15]

The ability to obtain DIP financing or use cash collateral typically is one of the most important issues confronting a company upon commencement of a chapter 11 case. While Bankruptcy Courts are reluctant to shut down a company's operations by denying approval of any such financing, they are also quite cognizant of the property interests asserted by secured creditors whose collateral may be significantly affected if such financing arrangements are approved. Accordingly, unless the DIP financing or cash collateral arrangements are done on a consensual basis, Bankruptcy Courts are likely to approve such financings only in such amounts as are absolutely necessary for the company to meet its most basic ongoing needs. While the company might like to have more funding availability, the combination of DIP financing or cash collateral use, coupled with the company being relieved of the obligation to pay pre-petition obligations, often results in the company having much greater liquidity during the chapter 11 case than it had in the weeks and perhaps months prior to the chapter 11 filing. Once again, this increased liquidity serves to provide management with an opportunity to focus less on addressing liquidity crises and more on strategic planning and transformation opportunities.

Plan Exclusivity

A company is provided with a 120-day "exclusive period" during which only the company may file a reorganization plan.[16] During this exclusive period, the company is afforded an opportunity to stabilize its operations and formulate or refine a long range business plan, which can then be used as a foundation for its reorganization plan. The exclusive period provides the company with the

---

[14] Bankruptcy Code §364(b), (c) and (d).
[15] Bankruptcy Code §363(c)(2).
[16] Bankruptcy Code §1121(b).

opportunity to engage in these efforts, unimpeded by threats that other interested parties may formulate and file plans of their own. Prior to the 2005 Bankruptcy Amendments, the initial exclusivity period could be, and routinely was, extended by the Bankruptcy Court as long as the company was making progress in its reorganization efforts, acting in good faith and not using its exclusive period for any improper purposes. The 2005 Bankruptcy Amendments, however, limit the Bankruptcy Court's ability to extend the initial exclusivity period, providing that the initial 120-day exclusivity period cannot be extended beyond a date that is eighteen months after the commencement of the bankruptcy case. The effect of this amendment will be to force some company's to formulate and file a plan earlier than they might otherwise have done so in order to avoid the risk of another party filing a different plan. In some cases, this may provide companies with a wholly appropriate incentive to formulate plans on an expedited basis; in other cases, this artificial time pressure may force an extremely troubled or unusually complex company to focus on plan formulation prematurely – and at the expense of cutting short the important step of fully analyzing the underlying business problems.

In essence, the exclusive period is designed to provide the company with the opportunity to control its own fate and devise its own exit strategy for a reasonable period of time. Combined with the stabilizing effects of the automatic stay, the ability to operate in the ordinary course and access to sufficient funding to meet ongoing needs, the plan exclusivity period is intended to provide the company with ample opportunity to carefully consider its alternatives and formulate a plan to both emerge from chapter 11 and exploit whatever transformation opportunities may accompany that emergence.

THE OPPORTUNITY TO DISPOSE OF EXCESS BAGGAGE

As discussed further below, various provisions of the Bankruptcy Code are designed to permit a business to dispose of excess or unprofitable assets, rid itself of burdensome contracts and leases and shed (or at least manage and mitigate) crippling liabilities. These provisions are powerful tools that can be used to allow a company to leave behind historical problems and dispose of non-core assets and operations that could otherwise distract management from its focus on the future.

De-Leveraging Through A Plan

The Bankruptcy Code contains a number of very important tools for reducing or eliminating balance sheet leverage that may be suffocating the business. In general, the Bankruptcy Code provides that a plan of reorganization shall, among other things, classify creditor claims against and equity interests in the subject company and provide for "treatment" of those claims and interests according to their respective priority and other legal attributes.[17] "Treatment" generally refers

---

[17] Bankruptcy Code §1123(a).

to the nature and amount of distributions to be made to creditors and equity holders on account of the claims and interests held. As discussed further below, the Bankruptcy Code contains certain requirements regarding what types of "treatment" are permissible under different circumstances.

Generally speaking, a company is much more likely to confirm a plan in a timely and efficient manner if the plan contains treatments that are acceptable to its stakeholders (i.e., a "consensual plan") for a variety of reasons. The treatment of claims and interests thus typically is the focal point of plan negotiations, as the company strives to develop a plan that is satisfactory to a variety of constituents whose interests often conflict. To aid in those negotiations, the Bankruptcy Code contains two important tools.

First, acceptance of the plan by any particular class of creditors or equity holders does not require unanimity within that class. Instead, a class of creditors voting on a plan is deemed to have accepted the plan if creditors holding at least two-thirds in dollar amount and more than one-half in number of the total claims voting in that class vote to accept the plan. For a class comprised of equity interests, holders of at least two-thirds of the equity interests that vote must vote to accept the plan.[18] Thus, as long as the company obtains the acceptance of the requisite majorities, any dissenting minority will be bound to the plan nonetheless. This power is often referred to as the ability to bind dissident, or "hold out", creditors.

Second, under certain enumerated circumstances, a plan may be confirmed even though not all classes vote to accept the plan. This power is often referred to as the ability to "cram down" the plan on a non-accepting class. The legal threshold for successfully "cramming down" a plan is significantly higher than for confirming a fully consensual plan, and cram down typically involves costly, time-consuming and uncertain litigation for both the company and the party potentially being crammed down. For this reason, a credible threat of cram down is often the company's best weapon in negotiations with a difficult class of creditors.

The threat of "cram down" to a class of secured creditors is twofold. First, in bankruptcy the amount of a secured claim is equal to the lesser of the amount of the claim or the value of the collateral. The balance of the claim, if any, is unsecured. Thus, a secured creditor may have two claims – a secured claim to the extent of the value of its collateral, and an unsecured "deficiency" claim.[19] One battleground in a cram down fight will be valuation of the collateral, with the company attempting to establish a lower value in order to reduce the amount of the secured claim. Note, however, that the potential battle over bifurcating a claim between the secured and unsecured portions is relevant only where the possibility exists that the value of the collateral securing the claim is less than the total amount of the claim. If the value of the collateral is equal to or greater than the total amount of the claim, such that the secured creditor is either fully secured or over secured, the secured creditor will not be at risk of having its claim bifurcated and the entirety of the claim (along with post-petition interest and other charges, to

---

[18] Bankruptcy Code §1126(c) and (d), respectively.
[19] Bankruptcy Code §506(a).

the extent the claim is oversecured) shall be entitled to treatment as a secured claim.

Second, once the amount of the secured claim is determined, the Bankruptcy Code provides that a cram down plan may satisfy the claim of a secured creditor by providing such creditor with deferred cash payments equal to the present value, as of the effective date of the plan, of such creditor's secured claim (and further providing for such creditor to retain its liens to secure payment of those amounts in accordance with the plan).[20] Given that payments to the secured creditor are made over time in such a scenario, whether a plan's deferred payments truly reflect the present value of the secured claim can represent an issue of paramount importance. The second battleground in cram down thus is determining the appropriate interest rate to apply when discounting the payments to present value to determine whether they in fact compute to the present value of the creditor's claim.

These two important issues — collateral valuation and applicable interest rate — permit a company to attempt to establish, through either negotiation or litigation, that: (a) a secured creditor has a significantly smaller secured claim than originally asserted (to the extent the value of the creditor's collateral has deteriorated); (b) the claim can be paid out in installments (which may exceed the original payment schedule); and (c) the restructured obligations should bear interest at a rate that may be materially lower than the rate on the original debt. In the right circumstances, the ability to "stretch out" secured creditors and to reduce interest rates non-consensually represent powerful tools that permit a company to achieve significant de-leveraging by lowering the principal amount of its secured debt and/or reducing its debt service obligations by lowering interest rates.

The threat of cram down to unsecured creditors is equally daunting. While secured creditors at a minimum generally are assured of retaining their lien rights in the company's assets (albeit to secure modified obligations), unsecured creditors have no such protection. For unsecured claims, the Bankruptcy Code requires that a cram down plan must either (1) provide payments representing the present value of such unsecured claims, or (2) make no distribution to any claim or interest junior in priority to that of such unsecured claim.[21] Using the latter of these two alternatives, a company can convert significant amounts of unsecured claims to equity by distributing equity in the reorganized company to unsecured creditors in satisfaction of their claims. While the creation of an entirely new group of shareholders obviously gives rise to an array of corporate control and governance issues, the ability to convert debt to equity in this fashion is a very powerful de-leveraging tool.

The ability to stretch out existing secured debt, the potential for ratcheting down above-market interest rates and the ability to convert debt into equity are at the heart of the financial component of most complex restructurings. Many investors actively search for companies that may have valuable core operations but are burdened with excess debt, acquire control positions in the debt and then seek to prompt a restructuring whereby that debt is converted into the equity in the reorganized, and now de-leveraged, company. That type of financial restructuring

---

[20] Bankruptcy Code §1129(b)(2)(A).
[21] Bankruptcy Code §1129(b)(2)(B).

often goes hand-in-hand with an operational restructuring designed to create additional value out of the core businesses. When implemented properly, the investor finds itself with a controlling equity interest in a reorganized, de-leveraged and therefore hopefully much more valuable enterprise.

Selling Assets "Free And Clear"

Under certain enumerated circumstances and subject to Bankruptcy Court approval, the Bankruptcy Code permits the sale of a company's assets "free and clear" of property interests (including liens of secured creditors) asserted by third parties and notwithstanding contractual provisions that might otherwise prevent such sale.[22] Outside of chapter 11, any such sale might be delayed or prevented by creditors or others asserting rights in the assets, and potential buyers might be discouraged from pursuing the assets for fear of not being able to obtain clear title. In chapter 11, the Bankruptcy Code gives the Bankruptcy Court the power to approve such sales (after crafting appropriate protections for objecting third parties) and providing buyers with the comfort of a federal court order evidencing their clear title to the assets.

From the company's perspective, these provisions facilitate the company's ability to dispose of a variety of assets that may no longer be desirable to the enterprise – whether due to non-profitable or deteriorating performance, lack of strategic fit, or otherwise.

Rejecting Burdensome Contracts And Leases

Similarly, subject to Bankruptcy Court approval, a company may reject executory contracts and unexpired leases that management determines to be overly burdensome to the enterprise.[23] The most common example of the strategic use of lease rejections is the company operating a large number of retail locations that files for chapter 11 with a view towards either downsizing generally or exiting specific geographic markets by closing stores and rejecting a large number of leases. The Bankruptcy Code also permits the rejection of other contracts that may constitute significant components of a company's cost structure, such as management contracts, collective bargaining agreements, and retiree benefits (in the latter two cases, subject to fairly rigorous standards designed to protect the interests of present and former employees).

Rejection of a contract or lease gives rise to a claim for damages arising from the rejection. Generally, such rejection damage claims are treated as unsecured claims having no priority over any other claims. In addition, damage claims resulting from the rejection of certain types of contracts are expressly limited under the Bankruptcy Code. For example, damage claims for the rejection of nonresidential real property leases and long-term employment contracts are subject to specific limitations. Thus, the Bankruptcy Code can be used not only to reject

---

[22] Bankruptcy Code §363.
[23] Bankruptcy Code §365.

burdensome contracts and leases, but also to limit, in some cases significantly, the claims arising from such rejection.

Leaving Behind Legacy Liabilities

For an enterprise whose source of distress is the existence of massive, protracted litigation that threatens to drain company resources indefinitely, a chapter 11 filing can provide the company with a means for managing that litigation in a manner that is significantly less harmful to the ongoing business. The Bankruptcy Code contains a number of provisions that can be helpful to a company struggling to address unliquidated, contingent claims that, if left in the civil litigation forum, may take many years to resolve.

First and foremost, the Bankruptcy Code provides that the Bankruptcy Court may estimate any "contingent or unliquidated claim, the fixing or liquidation of which . . . would unduly delay the administration of the estate."[24] Although estimation proceedings can be quite complex and may require the submission of substantial amounts of evidence, they can also be significantly less time consuming and costly than a full trial to liquidate the claims. Estimation of large numbers of claims for purposes of classifying and treating those claims appropriately under a plan of reorganization can be an incredibly powerful tool for a company facing what would otherwise be crippling litigation.

Perhaps the best examples of the use of this tool are the chapter 11 cases of companies faced with thousands of potential mass tort or product liability claims. In such cases, an effective mechanism for dealing with those claims has been established whereby: (1) the Bankruptcy Court estimates the aggregate amount of actual claims (typically using expert reports and extrapolating from statistical data about actual claims experience of similar pools of claimants); (2) the company formulates a plan of reorganization that places those claimants in a class and allocates a certain amount of funding to be set aside in a "trust" for that class; (3) the plan contains a "channeling injunction" that provides that each claimant's recourse is limited to seeking its recovery from the trust and that the claimants are precluded from pursuing any recovery from the reorganized company[25]; and (4) once the plan becomes effective, the litigation vehicle is carved off and essentially operates separate and apart from the company's ongoing business. While the diversion of funds to fund the trust and the ongoing expenses of the trust in defending against claims obviously has an economic impact on the company, the estimation proceeding, coupled with the channeling injunction, in effect permits the company to isolate the massive litigation in a separate vehicle and allows management to focus its attention on operating the business going forward. In this fashion, an enterprise can take advantage of chapter 11 to leave behind potentially very large legacy liabilities.

Securities fraud claims can also generate crippling litigation that can significantly drain corporate resources. The Bankruptcy Code provides a very straightforward mechanism for dealing with such claims, providing that any claim

---

[24] Bankruptcy Code §502(c)(1).
[25] Bankruptcy Code §524(g).

for damages arising from the sale or purchase of a security "shall be subordinated to all claims or interests that are senior to or equal to the claim or interest represented by such security."[26] Thus, where securities fraud claims are based on the purchase or sale of debt securities, those securities fraud claims will not be entitled to any recovery under a plan unless and until the debt securities themselves are paid in full. Where securities fraud claims are based on the purchase or sale of common stock, the securities fraud claims will be on parity with (and therefore will be entitled to the same treatment as) the common stock itself.

Depending upon the terms of the company's plan and how much value is being distributed on account of claims and equity interests, the subordination of securities fraud claims can permit the company to leave behind substantial securities fraud claims and the attendant litigation entirely. For example, if the company is insolvent and the plan of reorganization provides for no distribution whatsoever to common stock holders, any holders of securities fraud claims in connection with the purchase or sale of common stock likewise will receive no distribution. Those claims will be extinguished under the plan, and the reorganized company will be permitted to move forward without the need to litigate those claims any further.

THE OPPORTUNITY TO FOCUS ON THE FUTURE

Having stabilized and analyzed the existing business, disposed of excess or unprofitable assets, rid the company of burdensome contracts and leases and created vehicles for dealing with legacy liabilities that will not drain or distract from the company's future operations, management should find itself in the position of focusing on the future prospects of the enterprise. Herein lies the proverbial "fresh start" that chapter 11 is designed to provide.

Most management teams relish the prospect of focusing their attention on a going forward business plan for the enterprise. In many cases, management has been distracted for months, if not years, dealing with the various crises faced by a troubled business. The opportunity to put those crises in the past and focus on the company's core competencies and transformation opportunities comes as a welcome new challenge. Not surprisingly, however, the chapter 11 environment imposes some specific requirements in this regard that make this business planning process a particularly (and perhaps appropriately) rigorous one in the chapter 11 environment.

One of the prerequisites for the Bankruptcy Court to approve a plan of reorganization is that the Bankruptcy Court must find that the business plan underlying the plan of reorganization is "feasible."[27] While satisfying the feasibility test does not require that the company prove that its business plan is certain to succeed, that test does require the company to establish, as part of the plan confirmation hearing, that, following emergence, the reorganized company

---

[26] Bankruptcy Code §510(b).
[27] Bankruptcy Code §1129(a)(11).

has a reasonable prospect of success. Thus, it is not sufficient that the company merely formulate a business plan that is acceptable internally, but that the company justify that business plan to the Bankruptcy Court.

In addition, the company's business plan will be subject to review and challenge by all of the various interested parties who are active participants in the chapter 11 process — any significant secured creditors, the Creditors Committee and significant individual creditors, equity security holders, either individually or in the form of a committee, and others having a stake in the business. As part of the plan confirmation process, each of these interested parties will have the opportunity to review the material aspects of the company's business plan and raise issues and objections regarding its feasibility. In many instances, this scrutiny by interested third parties that often are extremely knowledgeable about the company's business can subject the company's business plan to very rigorous challenge.

While management may not necessarily be enamored with exposing its business plan to such scrutiny, the accountability to the Bankruptcy Court and interested parties that comes with attempting to satisfy the feasibility standard should serve as an appropriate motivating force that propels management to develop a sound and well-substantiated business plan. Indeed, the exercise of preparing a business plan that will be subject to public consumption and criticism is an exercise that a good management team should welcome.

THE CHALLENGES OF OPERATING IN CHAPTER 11

As discussed in detail above, the Bankruptcy Code provides a variety of protections and benefits that can be very useful to a troubled company as it attempts to stabilize and restructure itself. Those protections and benefits, however, come at a cost to the business. As an economic matter, a chapter 11 case can prove to be an expensive undertaking. The administrative and disclosure requirements imposed upon a chapter 11 debtor in possession can consume significant company time and resources. In addition, the company bears the expense of professional advisors who are experts in the restructuring field not only for the company itself, but also for the Creditors Committee and any other official committees that may be appointed in the case. In addition, the toll of operating in chapter 11 is not measured only as an economic cost. Operating in the chapter 11 environment gives rise to other significant challenges that can drain management of its time and energy and thereby create a significant drag on the company's business.

As discussed above, the filing of a chapter 11 case places the company in a very public forum, subject to significant disclosure requirements and the scrutiny of the Bankruptcy Court and interested parties. Any decisions to engage in transactions outside the ordinary course of business are subject to Bankruptcy Court approval, with interested parties having an opportunity to question or object to the proposed course of action. Thus, management will need to be prepared to have its decisions criticized and second-guessed by a variety of constituents. While imposing this additional level of accountability on management decision-making is not necessarily a bad thing (after all, management should be able to justify its decisions with sound rationales), the public nature of the chapter 11 case is a new and unusual environment that management can find to be challenging and intrusive.

The chapter 11 environment also imposes upon management a certain degree of loss of control in a number of respects. Decisions of the Bankruptcy Court can have a significant impact on how the company must conduct itself during the case. Other interested parties can influence the company's ability to take certain actions by interposing objections to requests that the company makes to the Bankruptcy Court. Even more extreme, under certain circumstances the Bankruptcy Court can order the appointment of an examiner (to investigate certain aspects of the company's conduct) or a trustee (to take over management of the business). The loss of control inherent in the chapter 11 process, coupled with the threat of even more drastic remedies available to the Bankruptcy Court, can be extremely disconcerting and distracting to a management team struggling to navigate a troubled business through the chapter 11 process.

Needless to say, the risks and uncertainties inherent in the chapter 11 process can take a significant toll on company management – at a time when optimal management performance is perhaps most critical. There are a number of measures that a company can take to attempt to mitigate the negative affects created by these additional levels of pressure placed on management.

First, the retention of experienced legal and financial advisors who are trusted experts in the restructuring field can provide management with a tremendous degree of comfort. In many chapter 11 cases, management finds itself in a completely unfamiliar environment. The presence of experts who know the terrain and can carefully guide management through the process can be an invaluable stabilizing influence for the company.

Second, in many large chapter 11 cases, the company requests early in the case that the Bankruptcy Court approve some form of "retention plan" for senior management and other key personnel. While Bankruptcy Courts and creditors scrutinize these requests carefully, reasonable retention plans are generally recognized as an important and appropriate means to avoid the harmful attrition that a company might otherwise experience as a result of the uncertainties faced by company personnel upon a chapter 11 filing.

Finally, management and its professional advisors should work diligently to keep company personnel appropriately informed about developments (and anticipated developments) in the case. A chapter 11 filing generates rampant speculation and a fear of the unknown among even the most senior and knowledgeable personnel. The best way to combat those negative influences is to establish reliable and informative lines of communication to impart accurate information throughout the organization.

ALTERNATIVE PATHS TO EMERGENCE FROM CHAPTER 11

Successfully exiting a chapter 11 case in most cases requires that the company confirm (i.e., obtain Bankruptcy Court approval of) a plan of reorganization that provides for the company, as reorganized, to emerge from the chapter 11 process and begin operating and competing in the marketplace without the protections and free of the burdens of the Bankruptcy Code. The path to plan confirmation varies – sometimes driven by planning and strategy, many times determined by circumstances and negotiation. Set forth below is a brief description of three alternative paths to confirmation and some of the major costs and benefits associated with each.

Pre-Packaged Chapter 11 Plans

A "pre-packaged" chapter 11 plan refers to a chapter 11 plan with respect to which the company solicits and obtains all necessary votes in favor of the plan before the company actually commences its chapter 11 case. Under this scenario, the company typically engages in plan negotiations with its significant stakeholders, formulates a plan that is acceptable to a significant number of those stakeholders, prepares a disclosure statement describing the proposed plan and solicits votes on the plan from all stakeholders that are "impaired" by the plan. This type of solicitation, which takes place prior to any chapter 11 case being filed, must be conducted in accordance with all applicable non-bankruptcy laws governing the adequacy of disclosure in connection with any such solicitation. Many pre-packaged plans involve the restructuring of publicly held debt and equity securities. Consequently, the out of court solicitation must be done in accordance with all applicable securities laws. If the solicitation yields a sufficient number of acceptances in the affected classes, the company can proceed to file its chapter 11 case, schedule a prompt hearing with the Bankruptcy Court to approve the solicitation process (after the fact) and confirm the plan.

Because the negotiations with stakeholders and solicitation of votes occurs prior to the chapter 11 filing, the duration of a chapter 11 case involving a pre-packaged plan can be very short. If all goes as planned, the plan can be confirmed by the Bankruptcy Court and the company can emerge in as little as thirty to forty-five days. It is possible, however, that interested parties may attack the adequacy of the pre-petition disclosure, the propriety of the solicitation process, substantive provisions of the plan or other issues. If any such challenge is successful, the "pre-packaged" plan can unravel, and the company can find itself starting from ground zero in what becomes a more traditional chapter 11 case.

The pre-packaged chapter 11 plan has the significant advantage of greatly limiting the duration of the company's stay in bankruptcy. Where the company's sole restructuring objective is to restructure its balance sheet by exchanging existing debt or equity securities for new debt or equity securities, the pre-packaged chapter 11 plan can be a very effective tool. Given the short duration of a case involving a pre-packaged chapter 11 plan, however, a company's ability to utilize the other protections and benefits of chapter 11 is very limited. While the company pursuing a pre-packaged chapter 11 plan has access to all of the benefits of chapter 11 while its case is pending, the limited duration of the case simply does not permit the company to utilize any of those provisions in a meaningful way.

Indeed, to try to sell assets, reject contracts or leases, or engage in other transactions that might otherwise be beneficial in fact would likely impede efforts to confirm the pre-packaged chapter 11 plan quickly by provoking disputes with interested parties that might well serve to delay implementation of the pre-packaged plan. Viewed purely from an enterprise transformation perspective, then, the prepackaged chapter 11 plan is of limited utility.

Pre-Negotiated Chapter 11 Plans

An alternative to the pre-packaged chapter 11 plan is what is commonly referred to as a "pre-negotiated" chapter 11 plan. Similar to the prepackaged plan scenario, in a pre-negotiated plan scenario the company negotiates the terms of the plan of reorganization prior to commencing the chapter 11 case. In the typical pre-negotiated case, the company commences the chapter 11 case once it has agreed on the terms of the plan with one or more of its significant creditor constituents, but prior to conducting any formal solicitation. Often times the pre-negotiated plan is filed with the Bankruptcy Court on the same day the chapter 11 case is commenced, along with a request that the Bankruptcy Court set a prompt hearing to consider a proposed disclosure statement and to establish procedures to be used by the company in connection with soliciting votes upon its plan. The actual solicitation of votes on the plan will not occur until the Bankruptcy Court has approved the disclosure statement and established appropriate solicitation procedures.

Even in the best of cases, pursuing a pre-negotiated plan to confirmation typically will require several months. Accordingly, a company filing a pre-negotiated plan must assume that it will be operating in the chapter 11 case for at least a few months prior to emergence. In addition, pre-negotiated cases typically involve more issues than the straightforward exchange of old securities for new securities that is involved in a pre-packaged plan. If those issues are more complex or problematic than originally anticipated, the pre-negotiated plan can be delayed for several additional months.

Because a company pursuing a pre-negotiated plan is likely to spend at least several months in chapter 11, its opportunities to utilize the benefits of chapter 11 are much greater than those available to a company pursuing a pre-packaged plan. The longer stay in chapter 11 may permit the company to obtain and utilize post-petition financing in favorable ways, dispose of excess or unproductive assets, reject burdensome contracts and leases and implement other operational initiatives during the course of the case to better position the company for success upon emergence. Because the timeframe for the chapter 11 case is still relatively short, however, planning for any such activities must occur prior to the bankruptcy filing in order to be effectively implemented during the case. Thus, a company pursuing a pre-negotiated plan will need to be conducting its "stabilizing and analyzing" functions pre-filing, without the benefit of the automatic stay and any post-petition financing.

"Traditional" Chapter 11 Cases

A traditional chapter 11 case is commenced by the company's filing of a chapter 11 petition, usually as a direct result of either an impending threat to the company's viability (e.g., a foreclosure on significant assets) or by a lack of liquidity that can only be alleviated by obtaining DIP financing. As opposed to the pre-packaged or pre-negotiated scenarios described above, the traditional chapter 11 case often times is commenced by the company for the principal purpose of taking advantage of the "stabilizing and analyzing" opportunities provided under the Bankruptcy Code. Thus, while the pre-packaged and pre-negotiated scenarios forgo much of the "stabilizing and analyzing" opportunities in exchange for limiting the duration of the chapter 11 case, a company filing a traditional chapter 11 case does so in large part to exploit those opportunities.

The duration of a traditional chapter 11 case depends on many factors. First, much depends on how long it takes the company to stabilize, analyze and shed its excess baggage, and formulate its plan for emergence. From the legal perspective, the duration of the case will be dependent on many factors, among them the Bankruptcy Court's willingness to extend the company's plan exclusivity period and thereby shelter the company from threats of alternative plans, along with the extent to which creditors and other interested parties are willing to permit the company to continue to operate in chapter 11 without taking aggressive action to pursue their own self interest. Given the interplay of these various factors, it is not unusual for large, traditional chapter 11 cases to have durations of 18 to 30 months.

CONCLUSION

The need for restructuring – whether operational, financial or a combination of both – presents both a challenge and an opportunity. The challenge is to find effective solutions for whatever specific problems have necessitated the restructuring. The opportunity is to incorporate into the restructuring process broader concepts of enterprise transformation by focusing not only on narrow problem-solving but also on seizing the chance to implement more comprehensive strategic plans.

Restructuring through the chapter 11 process is no exception. While extremely challenging in a variety of respects, the chapter 11 process also provides a business remarkable opportunities, as well as considerable protections and powerful tools, to facilitate significant transformation. Most notable among those opportunities are the chances to stabilize and analyze business operations, dispose of excess assets and burdensome contracts and leases, shed (or at least manage and mitigate) otherwise-crippling liabilities, and focus on developing a viable long-range strategy and business plan.

The chapter 11 process does not itself represent the transformation of the enterprise, however. Rather, the chapter 11 process is merely a tool that can be used to facilitate the broader transformation process by allowing a business to leave behind historical problems, solve or mitigate presently existing problems and establish a solid platform for the business as it exits bankruptcy. For an enterprise in need of real transformation, that exit is just the beginning. The success of the transformation efforts will depend on whether the enterprise successfully exploits that platform in the marketplace in the months and years following its exit.

CHAPTER 15

TAX ISSUES IN CRISES

JEROME M. SCHWARTZMAN AND STEVEN J. JOFFE

ABSTRACT

Managing taxes is critical to the success of a business. This is even truer for companies in crisis. The tax consequences of restructuring are addressed. Restructuring in bankruptcy versus out of bankruptcy is discussed. These issues are considered from the perspectives of several key stakeholders. General limitations on the use of net operating losses and taxes on pre-bankruptcy operations, as well as partnership bankruptcies, are discussed.

INTRODUCTION

This chapter focuses on the tax consequences of the financial restructuring of companies in crisis. Specifically, this chapter addresses the role of tax issues in planning the financial restructuring of a company, provides an overview of the tax consequences of restructuring a company in and outside of bankruptcy, and provides a comparison of the two restructuring alternatives. This chapter also briefly addresses special issues, such as partnership bankruptcies, income tax audits, state and local taxes and liquidating/settlement trusts.

Overall, this chapter is intended to provide non-tax professionals with an appreciation of the importance of tax issues in financial restructurings, as well as the tools necessary to understand the critical tax decisions that must be made in connection with financial restructurings. For the convenience of the reader, we have added a flow chart at the end of the chapter that depicts the tax impact of restructuring in or out of bankruptcy in graphic form.

Tax Issues for Companies in Crisis

Since they often represent a material cash cost for businesses, properly managing taxes is critical to the success of a business. This is even truer for companies in crisis.[1] That is because, in addition to the usual tax costs of running a business, debt modifications and financial restructurings raise tax issues that can materially

---

[1] For a definition of companies "in crisis" see Chapter 13.

impact the tax posture of a business, its available cash and its value.[2] As will be explained in this chapter, actions taken by a company in crisis without proper tax advice can result in the CEO's and CFO's personal liability for trust fund taxes, as well as the triggering of taxable cancellation of indebtedness ("cancellation of indebtedness" or "cancellation of debt" are referred to in the tax community as "COD") income, among many other unintended and unfortunate tax results. Accordingly, the CEO and CFO of companies in crisis should seek appropriate tax advice as soon as possible and certainly before any actions are taken.

Primary Tax Considerations for CEOs and CFOs of Companies in Crisis

The most important thing for CEOs and CFOs of companies in crisis to do is to preserve the value of the company's tax attributes to the greatest extent possible. Management should consult with legal and tax advisors as soon as possible to understand the various options available to the company and the tax implications of the options.[3] Usually, preserving the value of the company's tax attributes means preserving the company's net operating losses ("NOLs"). The primary threats to the NOLs are the inadvertent triggering of COD income, or triggering an "ownership change" that would limit the company's ability to use the NOLs in the future.[4] Another threat to the NOLs is shareholder and creditor sales of their interests shortly before filing for bankruptcy.

An equally important thing for CEOs and CFOs of companies in crisis to remember is that, while companies in crisis are often tempted not to pay "trust fund" taxes, such as payroll taxes, in an effort to prioritize the use of its limited cash, this can result in the CEO's and CFO's personal liability for such taxes.[5] Thus, it is recommended that companies in crisis continue to pay these trust fund taxes and, if bankruptcy protection is sought, that the first day orders provide that the company can continue to pay such taxes (Jenks, Ridgway & Purnell, 2004).

Things CEOs and CFOs Should and Should Not Do

The most important thing management should do when a company is in crisis is to obtain tax advice before taking any action. Good tax advice will include an overview of the options available to the company and the tax implications of those options. As will be discussed in detail below, a final decision regarding

---

[2] Even when a corporation generates a net operating loss for a year, there are other tax costs, such as Alternative Minimum Tax, property tax and payroll taxes.

[3] Generally, the exact tax implications cannot be calculated until a detailed analysis of the company's NOLs, tax basis of assets, debt posture, and corporate structure is completed.

[4] Under Section 382 of the Internal Revenue Code, a more than 50 percentage point change in the ownership of the stock of a company (over a rolling three-year period) results in a limit on the future use of historical NOLs. The Section 382 limitation rules play a significant role for companies in crisis and will be explained in detail below.

[5] Under Section 6672 of the Internal Revenue Code, certain responsible officers have personal liability for payroll taxes that the company has failed to pay over to the government (the so-called "100% penalty"). There are similar provisions under state law regarding payroll, sales and other trust fund taxes.

restructuring debt should be made only after understanding the details of the various options, such as the amount of remaining NOLs, remaining tax basis, and estimated future regular and Alternative Minimum Tax ("AMT") tax costs. Calculating these amounts will likely take time and require significant analysis by the incumbent tax accountants, as well as other tax advisors. The tax advisors may also advise management to initiate discussions with large shareholders and creditors to preserve certain options.[6] Management should also request its tax advisors to determine whether there are any tax refund opportunities available that would provide desperately needed cash to the company. Refunds may be available, for example, from the carryback of NOLs under special 10-year carryback provisions for certain specified liability losses, or from property taxes if property values have declined (particularly if there has been an impairment of assets for financial statement purposes).

Unfortunately, the list of things management <u>should not do</u> is probably longer than the list of things management <u>should do</u>. Based on experience, it appears very easy to fall into traps for the uninformed. A few of the things that management should <u>not</u> do when their company is in crisis are:

- Renegotiate the terms of debt (which could trigger COD income) before consulting with a tax advisor;

- Fail to consider the cash cost of AMT because, while the company may have sufficient NOLs to offset taxable income, there may still be an AMT cost to pay, and AMT may also become a significant cash tax cost if one of the special bankruptcy tax rules applies;

- Fail to prevent shareholder and creditor actions that could severely impact the value of the company's NOLs;

- Fail to take into account the tax cost of being a built-in loss company or the tax benefit of being a built-in gain company;

- Fail to time certain actions, such as the sale of non-core assets, appropriately to maximize tax benefits;

- Fail to do the math to determine the tax costs of various restructuring proposals;

- Fail to take into account the property tax costs of continued operations or failing to obtain a property tax refund for prior years;

---

[6] If a shareholder owning 50% or more of the stock of a company takes a worthless stock deduction, the NOLs may essentially become worthless. Similarly, if there is too much trading by the creditors, an extremely favorable tax rule for bankrupt companies may not be available. These rules will be discussed later in this chapter under the discussion of the Section 382 loss limitation rules.

- Fail to critically analyze whether all of the company's NOLs will be respected by the tax authorities;

- Fail to take into account the state tax impact of various proposals; and

- Rely on a financial model that uses estimated tax rates (such as 35% or 40%) rather than the actual tax position of the company.

These are just a few of the examples in which uninformed decisions can steal value from companies in crisis (Schwartzman & Joffe, 2005).

TAX CONSEQUENCES OF RESTRUCTURINGS

In general, a company pays tax on its taxable income that is determined by subtracting its expenses from its revenue. For asset intensive companies, depreciation and amortization of the company's tangible and intangible assets may be a significant tax deduction. For most companies, taxable income for a specific tax year may be reduced by using NOLs incurred in prior tax years. Accordingly, in reviewing a company's tax posture in connection with a restructuring it is important to determine the amount of its NOLs and the tax basis of its assets. This may or may not be a simple exercise, depending on the quality of the company's books and records, and whether the company is part of a group of corporations filing consolidated federal income tax returns (a "consolidated group"). When the company is a member of a consolidated group, complex rules apply.

The most significant tax implications of restructurings are:

- When corporate debt is reduced or cancelled, the company has COD;

- When COD occurs outside bankruptcy, tax attributes (NOLs and tax basis) are reduced by the COD to the extent the company is insolvent (the "attribute reduction" rule). COD generated outside bankruptcy is taxable if the company is solvent;

- To the extent a debtor company has taxable COD when it restructures out of court, the taxable COD is treated as "built-in gain" which could increase the availability of its NOLs;

- When COD occurs in bankruptcy (whether under a pre-pack or under a regular bankruptcy plan of reorganization), tax attributes are reduced under the attribute reduction rule and generally does not result in current tax;

- Generally, in a restructuring (whether in or out of bankruptcy), the debtor company undergoes an "ownership change" for tax purposes because more than 50 percentage points of its stock (by value) changes hands. As a result of the ownership change, any NOLs remaining after attribute reduction will be subject to an annual limitation;

- The annual limitation equals the product obtained by multiplying 1) the net equity value of the company by 2) an interest rate published monthly by the IRS (which has generally ranged between 4% and 5% during 2004 - 2005);[7]

- When an ownership change occurs outside of bankruptcy, the equity value will be the value of the company's stock on the day <u>before</u> the ownership change (usually zero if the debtor is insolvent) for purposes of determining the annual limitation. When an ownership change occurs in bankruptcy, the equity value for annual limitation purposes is generally the equity value <u>after</u> debt forgiveness (i.e., the pre-change equity value is increased by the amount of debt forgiven) or, in certain circumstances, the company may be able to use its NOLs without limitation; and

- The annual limitation may be increased in the first five years after an ownership change if the company is a "built-in gain" company (i.e., the value of its assets exceeds their tax basis) but post-change losses and depreciation deductions may be severely limited if the company is a "built-in loss" company (i.e., the value of its assets is less than tax basis).

Importance of Information Gathering

A principal job of the tax advisor in a restructuring is to determine the most effective way to minimize taxable income in the restructuring and to preserve the tax attributes of the company for use in post-emergence tax years. By preserving tax attributes, the company can minimize its cash taxes post-emergence, thereby allowing for a greater portion of its cash flow to be used in the business and/or to repay indebtedness.

Determining the best way to preserve tax attributes, however, is not a simple exercise and may entail an in-depth analysis of the application of the attribute reduction and loss limitation rules. This exercise would involve the calculation of any COD generated by the restructuring, any reduction of tax attributes, and the determination of any limitations on the use of NOLs if the restructuring results in a significant change in the ownership of the company's stock. Consequently, it is critical to gather the basic information required for the analysis. Among the critical pieces of information required are:

- Amount of the debtor's NOLs;

- Amount of debt to be exchanged/retired and basic terms of the old and new debt;

---

[7] For example, if a company with $1 billion of NOLs and a $100 million net equity value had an ownership change, it would only be allowed to use $5 million of its NOLs in each year after the ownership change (assuming a 5% IRS interest rate).

- Value of consideration to be paid for the debt to be exchanged/retired;

- Amount of debt to remain outstanding;

- For the debt to be exchanged/retired, who the creditors are and how long they have held the debt;

- Whether the debtor is part of a consolidated group and, if so, what is the legal structure of the group;

- Tax basis of assets (best by entity, but at least in aggregate);

- Whether the book value of the debtor company's assets been impaired under GAAP;

- Whether the value of the debtor company's assets increased relative to their tax bases; and

- In what states does the debtor operate?

The value of a company's tax attributes cannot be over emphasized. In one recent matter, a majority shareholder of a mail order retailing company in bankruptcy offered to buy out the creditors. However, the offer provided no value for the company's substantial NOLs. Although the majority shareholder was adamant in its refusal to offer value for the NOLs, an analysis of the present value cash benefit of the use of the company's NOLs under various exit strategies proved that the NOLs were worth between $50 million and $150 million. When provided with the analysis, the majority shareholder's tax advisors could not rebut any portion of the analysis or its conclusions. Although the analysis was not simple and was costly, the value it provided was clear.

Parties to Restructurings

For companies in crisis, it is important to identify the parties in interest. The primary interested parties include the creditors (which are interested in the amount of value they can receive for their debt and which may ultimately own the equity of the company), the shareholders (which may or may not receive value in a restructuring) and the company itself (which is looking to survive a critical stage in its corporate life). Each of the parties has differing tax consequences associated with the various restructuring alternatives available to companies in crisis and each party should seek their own tax advice.[8]

While this chapter primarily discusses the tax consequences to regular corporations, other entities, such as S corporations and partnerships, may also be in crisis and face their own tax issues in restructurings (Joffe & Schwartzman, Partnerships, June 2004; Joffe & Schwartzman, August 2004).

RESTRUCTURINGS IN BANKRUPTCY VS. OUT OF BANKRUPTCY

As noted above, we have added a flow chart at the end of the chapter that depicts the tax impact of restructuring in or out of bankruptcy in graphic form for the convenience of the reader.

Companies in crisis often face the question whether to restructure in bankruptcy or out of court (Henderson & Goldring, 2004). From a tax perspective, restructuring under the protection of the bankruptcy court often provides a more tax efficient result. Restructuring in court offers the advantages of avoiding taxable COD and a current AMT cost, more favorable loss limitation rules, as well as the stay of collection of taxes by government authorities. The benefits of restructuring out of court are usually strategic, such as avoiding the impact on customer and supplier relationships, and the expense of bankruptcy proceedings.

In a recent situation, the CEO of a telecom company was faced with the decision whether to restructure the company's debt in bankruptcy or out of court. The CEO's preference was to restructure out of court for fear that a bankruptcy would damage the company's reputation. After analyzing the tax impact of restructuring in or out of court, it appeared that restructuring out of court would cost the company an additional $10 - $20 million in cash tax on a present value basis.[9] If the company restructured out of court, it would have a zero annual limitation on the future use of its NOLs because its net equity value would be zero on the day immediately before the restructuring. As a result, it would not have been able to use any of its historic NOLs after the restructuring (unless the built-in gain rule applied). If the company restructured under the protection of the bankruptcy court, it would be able to use between $5 million and $10 million of its NOLs per year, resulting in substantial present value benefit. Based on this analysis and the recommendations of its legal and tax advisors, the CEO concluded that it was in the best interests of the company and it owners to restructure in bankruptcy.

When a company would like to take advantage of the tax benefits of restructuring in court, but wants to avoid the potentially negative impact of a bankruptcy, a prepack should be considered. In a prepack, the new financial

---

[8] For example, the creditors may or may not have taxable gain or loss on the exchange of their debt for cash, new debt and/or equity. Similarly, shareholders may seek to claim losses on their stock.

[9] The $10 million to $20 million numbers were based on differing value assumptions and included value for only the first five years after emergence. The present value cost would have been much higher if utilization of the NOLs were calculated out to their full 20-year life.

structure of the company is already determined when the company files, thereby substantially reducing the amount of time in bankruptcy (Kirschner, et al., 1991).

Out-of-Bankruptcy Restructurings/Corporate Debtor

As briefly discussed above, the tax consequences of financial restructurings outside of bankruptcy differ significantly from restructurings in bankruptcy. If a company settles its existing debt out of bankruptcy by exchanging new debt, equity and/or cash worth less than the face amount of the existing debt, COD is generated. Generally, such COD is currently taxable to the company. Although it may have sufficient current or historical NOLs to offset the COD income, the company may nonetheless have to pay cash taxes under the AMT regime (generally equal to 2% of the COD).

When a company settles its existing debt out of bankruptcy, it may avoid current taxation of the COD if it is "insolvent," but only to the extent of its insolvency. This is known as the insolvency exception to COD. While the calculation of insolvency for this purpose starts with the company's balance sheet (i.e., the excess of liabilities over the fair market value of assets), items not reflected on the balance sheet (such as unrecorded goodwill or contingent liabilities) may also be taken into account for this purpose.

Tax on COD may also be avoided if payment of the liability would have created a tax deduction. Moreover, tax on COD may be avoided where the liability is in dispute. Finally, tax on COD may be avoided if the reduction in the amount of the indebtedness results from an agreement between a buyer and seller of corporate property to reduce the amount owed on purchase money debt. This so-called "purchase price adjustment" exception only applies where the debtor is solvent and not in bankruptcy.

The purchase price adjustment exception was critical in resolving the tax treatment of COD in a recent bankruptcy matter that was being negotiated with the IRS. In that case, a retailer that had been acquired from a conglomerate negotiated a reduction in the purchase money indebtedness issued to the conglomerate in the original sale transaction. Since the retailer was insolvent at the time, it was able to take the position that any COD resulting from the reduction in purchase money indebtedness was not taxable under the insolvency exception to the extent it was insolvent and that any additional COD was not taxable under the purchase price adjustment exception.

Bankruptcy Restructurings/Corporate Debtor

From a tax perspective, restructuring under bankruptcy court protection is much more advantageous than restructuring out of bankruptcy. In addition to enabling a company to avoid current taxation on COD, a company may also be able to protect its valuable tax attributes from creditor and shareholder actions that can destroy the value of those attributes. Under the Prudential Lines case, the bankruptcy court may be called upon to prohibit or void such actions in order to preserve or protect the value of the tax assets to the estate (Prudential Lines, 1989).

As noted above, COD is generally not taxable when a company is in bankruptcy (or insolvent). When COD is not taxable because a company is in bankruptcy, its tax attributes are reduced. Under the ordering rules applicable to attribute reductions, the company's NOLs are reduced first, and then the tax basis in its property is reduced. For this purpose, property includes fixed assets, stock in subsidiaries, inventory and accounts receivable. This reduction in basis may create "phantom income," and result in an immediate cash tax liability, where the tax bases of accounts receivable and/or inventory are reduced and the inventory is sold or the receivables are collected following the reduction.

It is important to note that a company's tax attributes are reduced on the first day of the tax year <u>following</u> the COD event. This means that the company's tax attributes remain available in determining its tax liability for the tax year in which the COD event occurs. This nuance of the tax law may enable a company to dispose of assets in a tax efficient manner <u>during</u> the year in which the COD event occurs and use tax attributes <u>before</u> they would otherwise be reduced by COD.

The importance of tax planning for attribute reduction was emphasized in the case of a manufacturing client. There, the manufacturer had completed its negotiations with its creditors under the protection of the bankruptcy court and was preparing to emerge from bankruptcy. The negotiated plan of reorganization contemplated a reduction of indebtedness that would result in COD and, consequently, a material reduction in the company's NOLs under the attribute reduction rule. The plan also contemplated the sale of non-strategic assets, which would have resulted in the recognition of significant gain. By delaying confirmation of the plan of reorganization until the beginning of the next tax year, the company was able to use its available NOLs to offset the gain on the sale during that year before its NOLs were reduced under the attribute reduction rule, thereby increasing the amount of cash available to its creditors under the plan.

The IRS recently issued new regulations that determine how tax attributes are reduced when a company is a member of a consolidated group for federal income tax purposes (Joffe, 2005; Joffe & Schwartzman, June 2004). Very briefly, where a company is a member of a consolidated group and has its debt cancelled, it recognizes COD and suffers a reduction of its tax attributes (NOLs and tax basis of assets, including the tax basis in stock of its subsidiaries) under the general attribute reduction rules discussed above. If the company reduces its tax basis in the stock of its consolidated subsidiaries under the attribute reduction rule, the subsidiaries' own tax attributes are reduced to the extent of the reduction in their stock basis (the so-called "tier-down" of "deemed COD"). Finally, NOLs of other members of the consolidated group (but not tax basis of assets) are reduced to the extent of any remaining COD generated by the member with actual debt cancellation (the so-called "fan-out" rule). If a subsidiary has more "deemed COD" than attributes, however, the excess cannot be used to reduce attributes of any other members of the consolidated group under the "fan out" rule.

Thus, it is imperative in the context of the restructuring of a company that is a member of a consolidated group, to analyze the tax attribute reduction rules in order to understand the tax consequences of various exit strategies, as well as to assess cash tax liabilities upon emergence from bankruptcy. This analysis may also enable the company to determine if the basis of assets will be reduced, to determine whether any phantom income would be created after application of the attribute reduction rules, and to determine whether it is possible to avoid the phantom income.

The importance of understanding the impact of the consolidated attribute reduction rules was underscored in a matter involving a mail order retail client. The analysis of the effect of attribute reduction on a consolidated subsidiary revealed that the tier down of deemed COD to a particular subsidiary would require a $300 million write down to the subsidiary's accounts receivable and inventory. The accounts receivable and inventory would be collected and sold, respectively, within months after emergence from bankruptcy. As a result, the subsidiary would have recognized $300 million of taxable income (so-called phantom income) in its first year after emergence. Fortunately, because the analysis revealed this impending tax landmine, a strategy was adopted in advance to avoid the write down to these assets. Had the analysis not been done, the issue would not have been raised and the company may have wound up with $120 million less cash ($300 million times 40% tax rate) because it would have had to pay an unexpected tax bill related to the phantom income.

Similarly, in another bankruptcy matter involving a power generation and transmission company, the investment bankers advising the company recommended that all of its assets be sold to maximize the cash that would be payable to the creditors. The secured creditors wanted to obtain the power generation plants that served as their collateral before the sale of other assets, but were told that the company would suffer adverse tax consequences. After creating a sophisticated tax model applying the IRS regulations to the situation at hand, the company and its creditors were able to agree on a tax efficient transfer of the collateral and the proper timing of the asset sales relative to the confirmation of the plan of reorganization of the company so as to maximize the use of NOLs.

Impacts of Shareholder and Creditor Actions on Use of NOLs

As noted above, a company's NOLs may represent a valuable asset. Under the loss limitation rules briefly discussed above, a company's NOLs effectively become worthless if a shareholder holding 50% or more of a company's stock takes a worthless stock deduction with respect to its stock. In addition, under these rules, creditors' sales of their positions in the company's indebtedness may prevent the company from taking advantage of a favorable exception that would permit it to exit bankruptcy without being subject to the loss limitation rules. Since these actions by shareholders and creditors can negatively impact the value of the NOLs, the bankruptcy court has the authority to prohibit or even void such actions under the Prudential Lines case. Thus, it is imperative to monitor the ownership of the company's stock and debt from the beginning of the road to bankruptcy to determine if it is possible to prevent actions that could impair the value of the NOLs.

The importance of monitoring shareholder activity was shown in a recent matter. At the proverbial 11th hour, after many months and hundreds of thousands of dollars had been spent in analyzing the attribute reduction a healthcare company would suffer under a proposed plan of reorganization, it was determined that a 75% shareholder had taken a worthless stock deduction with respect to its holdings in the company. This deduction would result in the reduction of available NOLs from $100 million to zero. Only by immediate court action to require the shareholder to reverse the worthless stock deduction could the company reclaim the value of the NOLs for its creditors.[10]

Similarly, in another matter, a consolidated group claimed a deduction for the abandonment of partnership interests owned by a subsidiary member of the group. The partnerships held power generation facilities and the deductions were based on the theory that the company had "abandoned" these interests for tax purposes. This deduction deprived the subsidiary of hundreds of millions of dollars of losses that could have been used to offset gains on the anticipated sale of its assets and to increase cash available to pay creditors. Again, only by immediate court action to require the corporate parent to reverse the abandonment loss deduction or to compensate the subsidiary for the deduction claimed by the corporate parent could the company reclaim these deductions for itself or realize their economic value.

Utilization of NOLs and Sale of Assets in Bankruptcy

A restructuring may often involve the issuance of new stock of the company. If so, the company remains in existence and its tax attributes will be retained (i.e., historical tax basis will carry over and NOLs will be retained, though likely subject to limitation). Alternatively, the company may sell its assets in a Section 363 sale under the Bankruptcy Code and utilize NOLs that would otherwise be reduced or subject to limitation post-emergence. When assets are sold, the buyer would obtain a fair market value tax basis in the assets and would not inherit any of the debtor's NOLs. The buyer might, however, be able to "freshen" or generate NOLs through increased depreciation or amortization deductions on the purchased assets if the value of the assets is greater than their tax basis. A taxable sale, however, may be subject to recast by the IRS where the shareholders and/or creditors of the company own the purchaser. Where a taxable sale would result in a higher tax basis in the assets because the assets are worth more than their current tax bases, proper tax planning could enable the company to avoid a recast by the IRS (i.e., a "Bruno's" type transaction).

---

[10] The present value benefit of $100 million of NOLs is approximately $20 million (assuming $5 million of NOL use per year over 20 years, with an 8% discount rate and a 40% tax rate) or approximately $27 million (assuming $10 million of NOL use per year over 10 years, with an 8% discount rate and a 40% tax rate). Thus, the majority shareholder's worthless stock deduction would have cost the creditors between $20 million to $27 million in cash if immediate court intervention were not sought on these facts.

A company in crisis often needs cash. One method for maximizing cash is to determine whether there are any tax refund opportunities, including federal or state income tax, or property tax. In this regard, there are special rules allowing for a 10-year carryback of specified liability losses, such as deductions for amounts paid to satisfy product liabilities. In addition, there may be special state NOL provisions allowing for carrybacks that may have been overlooked. In addition, if property values have declined, a company may be able to recover refunds of property taxes (Schwartzman & Joffe, 2004).[11]

In two recent matters, clients were able to generate substantial cash for creditors by carrying back specified liability losses to earlier years and obtaining tax refunds. In the first matter, a retail chain had obtained insurance to fund its workmen's compensation claims in excess of a self-insurance layer of liability. To assure that the amount of workmen's compensation claims that were to be self-insured would be paid, the insurance provider required the company to post letters of credit to assure payment of claims by the company. When the company declared bankruptcy, the insurance company seized the letters of credit which under the plan of reorganization had to be used to satisfy claims and could not otherwise be claimed by the company. On advice from its tax advisors, the company was able to take a deduction for the amount of the letters of credit and carry the resultant loss back under the specified liability loss provisions, thereby obtaining substantial cash for its creditors.

Similarly, in a matter involving a multi-national corporation restructuring its asbestos claims under the protection of the bankruptcy law, the company will be able to claim a deduction when it transfers its stock to a Section 524(g) trust formed to settle asbestos claims. Any such deduction claimed may be carried back under the specified liability loss provisions and will produce substantial cash for its creditors. In short, when cash is critical, no refund stone should remain unturned.

Tax Impact to Holders/Corporate Debtor

Under the tax law, an exchange of property for other property is generally taxable. Thus, when a creditor exchanges its debt for new debt, equity or cash, it is generally taxable. Thus, the creditor will have a taxable gain or loss with respect to the debt. Gain or loss is determined by comparing the creditor's tax basis in the debt with the value of the property received in the exchange. Usually, if a creditor has held its debt position for some time, it will recognize a loss on the exchange. On the other hand, if the creditor had recently purchased its debt position (for example, a purchase by a vulture fund), it may recognize a gain. Finally, it is important for the creditor to allocate the property received between principal and

---

[11] Schwartzman & Joffe discuss a case where a telecom company attempted to have a bankruptcy court determine the value of its assets for property tax purposes, which would have been binding on the state and local taxing jurisdictions. Unfortunately for the taxpayer, the bankruptcy court declined to allow itself to be used to resolve the taxpayer's daunting task of negotiating the value of its property with each of the jurisdictions. Perhaps the court would have been more willing to assist the taxpayer had it requested the court to determine its property tax liability for each jurisdiction.

accrued interest, since the creditor will either be taxable on interest paid (to the extent not already accrued into income) or the creditor will be entitled to a loss on interest accrued but not paid in the exchange.

If the debt held by the creditor qualifies as a "security" under the tax law, an exchange of a debt instrument for another debt instrument or stock of the same issuer may be tax free. The tax law does not have a clear definition of "security," but a good rule of thumb is that a debt instrument with a term of five years or more is a security. Where securities or stock are received, the creditor will not have taxable gain or loss, although there may be ways to structure the transaction to enable the creditor to claim a tax loss. Any property received by the creditor that is neither a security or equity may be taxable as "boot."

Post Emergence Tax Consequences

The structure of an emergence plan will have material tax consequences. For example, in a recent matter, a company restructured its debt and equity, but managed to have historical shareholders retain sufficient equity to avoid an ownership change. As a result, the company's NOLs were not subject to limitation. In another case, the company negotiated a plan that would be acceptable to the secured and unsecured creditors to allow it to satisfy Section 382(l)(5), a very favorable bankruptcy tax provision discussed below, thereby avoiding a limitation on the use of its NOLs after emergence.

Structuring a plan can also involve creating a new vehicle for the business. For example, a group of secured creditors which will obtain 100% of the equity of a bankrupt entity may wish to operate the business in a pass-through form (LLC or partnership) even though it was historically operated in corporate form. The attorneys can easily structure this, although in most circumstances the new entity will take a fair market value tax basis in the assets, which may be less than the historical basis of the assets.[12] In one situation, the assets of a partnership were being transferred to the creditors in satisfaction of their claims. The deal was structured in a manner that preserved the historically high tax basis in the assets, thereby preserving a higher current tax shield for the creditors/partners, although this result is no longer possible under the American Jobs Creation Act of 2004.

In another matter, a consolidated group in bankruptcy had two sets of creditors that were to each take the stock of different subsidiary groups in settlement of their claims. One set of creditors ("C-1") offered a structure that involved a "G" reorganization (a tax free reorganization for bankrupt companies). The other set of creditors ("C-2") considered the G reorganization implausible and countered with a structure of its own. C-1 agreed to C-2's proposal but demanded a $20 million payment because it claimed that C-2's proposal would utilize a significant amount of the NOLs available to the C-1 subsidiary group. An analysis of the various plans revealed that C-2's proposal would use substantially less of the NOLs of the C-1 subsidiary group. Based on the analysis, C-1 was persuaded to accept C-2's

---

[12] It is preferable to retain higher tax basis because a higher tax basis generates higher tax depreciation, thereby reducing taxable income (and thus reducing cash taxes).

proposal with only a $3 million payment. Without the analysis of the attribute reduction and the tax impact of breaking up the consolidated group, C-2's negotiating team would not have known how to evaluate C-1's $20 million payment demand.

To summarize, there are various ways to structure a company in crisis and a number of factors should be reviewed to find the most tax efficient structure.

GENERAL LIMITATIONS ON UTILIZATION OF NOLs

Generally, NOLs can be carried back two years and carried forward 20 years. If not used within that period, the NOLs expire. Special rules allow certain types of NOLs to be carried back for ten years (e.g., specified liability losses such as asbestos liabilities and product liabilities).

Regarding the carry back of NOLs, it is critical to ensure that NOLs have been carried back to the maximum extent possible to take advantage of all refund opportunities to produce immediate cash for the company in crisis. Considering the carry forward of NOLs, a company's NOLs may be reduced by the amount of the COD that is not taxable where it is insolvent or in bankruptcy. To the extent they are not reduced, the NOLs can be carried forward to post-emergence years to reduce taxable income. However, the Section 382 loss limitation rules may apply to limit the amount used in each year.

If the ownership of the stock of the company changes by more than 50 percentage points (an "ownership change"), Section 382 generally applies to limit the amount of NOLs that can be used to offset taxable income in each year after the ownership change. This "ownership change" test is based on changes in stock ownership of shareholders (or shareholder groups) that own at least 5% of the stock and takes into account all such changes within a rolling three-year period. In addition, complicated "constructive" ownership, aggregation and segregation rules apply when determining whether a company undergoes an ownership change.

If an ownership change occurs, the amount of NOL that can be used in each year after the ownership change is generally determined by multiplying the equity value of the company by the "long-term tax-exempt rate" published monthly by the IRS. For example, if a debtor company with a net equity value of $50 million has an ownership change as a result of a restructuring plan, it would only be able to use $2.375 million of its NOLs each year (the Section 382 annual limitation), assuming a 4.75% long term tax exempt rate. Consequently, if it had $10 million of taxable income after emergence and $250 million of NOLs, the amount of NOLs that could be used to offset its $10 million of taxable income would be limited to the $2.375 million Section 382 annual limitation. As a result, it would owe approximately $3 million in cash taxes (assuming a 40% effective tax rate), even though it has $250 million of NOLs.

If the debtor's assets are worth more than their current tax basis (e.g., if they have appreciated in value relative to their depreciated tax cost), there may be an opportunity to increase the Section 382 annual limitation, thereby reducing the debtor's post-emergence cash taxes (the "Built-In Gain" rule). Conversely, if the debtor's assets have declined in value, depreciation and amortization deductions may become subject to the Section 382 annual limitation, thereby increasing the debtor's post-emergence cash taxes (the "Built-In Loss" rule). The Built-In Gain and Built-In Loss rules apply to the first five years after the ownership change.

When a company emerges from bankruptcy, there are generally three possible Section 382 scenarios:

- Section 382 does not apply because current shareholders retain at least 50% of the company's stock and any issuance of stock in the restructuring does not cause an ownership change;

- Section 382 does not apply because the historical creditors and shareholders own at least 50% of the company's stock following the restructuring (Section 382(l)(5)); and

- Section 382 applies and the special Section 382 bankruptcy rule applies to increase the value of the company for purposes of determining the Section 382 annual limitation (Section 382(l)(6)).

Section 382(l)(5) applies if the company's shareholders and historical creditors own at least 50% of the company (by vote and value) following the restructuring (Joffe & Schwartzman, December 2004). For this purpose, historical creditors include creditors that have held their debt for at least 18 months prior to the filing of the bankruptcy petition (so-called "old and cold debt") and ordinary course creditors.[13] When Section 382(l)(5) applies, the company's NOLs must generally be reduced by the amount of the interest expense deductions taken on the company's debt that is converted to equity under the plan of reorganization that were paid or accrued during (i) the three-year period preceding the year in which the ownership change occurs and (ii) any short tax year in which the ownership change occurs.

Where Section 382(l)(5) would be advantageous, it is critical to determine who the creditors were or are before filing a bankruptcy petition to prevent dispositions of debt that might prevent Section 382(l)(5) from applying. Similarly, since Section 382(l)(5) provides that any "ownership change" within the subsequent two years causes the Section 382 annual limitation to be reduced to zero, it is critical to consider a "lock-up" or similar agreement and to monitor post-emergence sales of equity by the former creditors. This rule limits creditor exit strategies and must be taken into account when considering the issuance of equity to creditors and creditor discretion regarding the sale of stock post-emergence.

---

[13] For this purpose, advances from revolvers and lines of credit used to fund ordinary course deductible expenses should qualify as "ordinary course." Further, a position may be taken that ordinary course debt includes DIP financing if the DIP financing is used for ordinary course liabilities, such as payroll, although this position is not free from doubt. Certain creditors that become less than 5% shareholders in the bankruptcy reorganization may also be considered to meet the holding period requirements.

The application of these special bankruptcy rules can best be illustrated by some examples. In one recent matter, a multi-national company restructuring its asbestos claims under the protection of the bankruptcy law proposed to restructure by issuing stock to a Section 524(g) trust to be established to settle the asbestos claims. Of critical importance, the stock issued to the trust would count toward the Section 382(l)(5) ownership test since asserted and contingent asbestos claims would qualify as "ordinary course" debt, notwithstanding the transfer of the claims to the Section 524(g) trust, the issuance of stock to the Section 524(g) trust, and by the trust to the claimants.[14]

In another recent matter, a rust-belt manufacturer proposed to exchange some of its outstanding indebtedness for stock. The principal shareholder of the company was an historic creditor and also had provided debtor in possession ("DIP") financing to the company. The principal shareholder wanted to maintain control of the company while qualifying under the Section 382(l)(5) special bankruptcy rule. Since the principal shareholder's stock would be cancelled in any restructuring, the critical issue was whether the indebtedness held by the shareholder would qualify as old and cold debt, whether the DIP financing would qualify as ordinary course debt and how the principal shareholder might retain control of the company as a consequence of exchanging debt for equity. Although an argument could have been made that the DIP financing could be counted as ordinary course debt for purposes of Section 382(l)(5), the tax advisors proposed that all of the historic creditors be offered the opportunity to exchange their debt for stock (with the right to elect a majority of the board of directors of the company) or new debt. The expectation of the tax advisors was that only the principal shareholder would exchange debt for stock and would thereby retain control of the company.

TAXES ON PRE-BANKRUPTCY OPERATIONS

Sarbanes Oxley and managing a company in crisis are enough of a headache. As the CEO or CFO of the company, you don't want to add personal liability for the company's trust fund taxes to your headache.

Normally, a corporation is required to withhold employment taxes from its employees' wages and must remit these taxes to the federal and state governments. When a company fails to withhold and/or pay over such taxes, "responsible" officers become personally liable for these taxes. Accordingly, the first day orders requested during the bankruptcy process should provide the debtor with the authority to pay all trust fund taxes (contrary to the general rule prohibiting the payment of pre-petition taxes after filing for bankruptcy protection) to avoid personal liability of the officers. Similarly, if a creditor pays the wages of debtor employees directly or provides additional financing to the debtor that is specifically earmarked for the payment of wages knowing that the debtor will not

---

[14] Under the complex and highly mechanical ownership change rules of Section 382, the Section 524(g) trust's transfer of the stock to the claimants could be viewed as a separate transfer that should be taken into account in determining qualification for Section 382(l)(5).

properly withhold and remit employment taxes, the creditor can become liable for such taxes.

Once a company files for bankruptcy protection, the federal and state governments become creditors and must file proofs of claim prior to the bar date in order to be entitled to collect pre-petition taxes. The IRS and the state tax authorities usually receive notification of the bankruptcy soon after the filing. Determining which taxes are pre- versus post-petition becomes important because pre-petition taxes may generally not be paid (other than pursuant to an approved proof of claim), whereas the debtor must timely file tax returns and pay taxes while it is in bankruptcy.

Although the bankruptcy rules bar a government from collecting pre-petition taxes during pendency of the bankruptcy, the rules do not prohibit governments from auditing or assessing the debtor. Accordingly, the IRS and/or the state tax authorities may conduct income or other tax audits while the debtor is in bankruptcy. If the IRS successfully asserts a deficiency against the debtor, most state laws require it to amend its state income tax returns to reflect the changes made by the IRS. If a state failed to file a proof of claim, arguably it may not be able to collect any additional tax resulting from these changes. However, states are starting to challenge this position and state assessments of deficiencies resulting from IRS audits may become prevalent (Joffe & Schwartzman States' Collection of Pre-Petition Taxes).

PARTNERSHIP BANKRUPTCIES

Partnerships in bankruptcy raise a host of tax issues that differ from the issues dealt with in typical corporate debtor work (Joffe & Schwartzman, Partnerships, June, 2004). A partnership is not a tax paying entity. Rather, it reports its income on an informational return and this income flows through to its partners in accordance with the partnership agreement. The partners are liable for the tax on their allocable share of income from the partnership. Often, partnership agreements provide that cash may be distributed to the partners to enable them to pay the tax liability associated with their allocable share of partnership income.

Briefly, in a partnership workout, COD is determined at the partnership level, while the taxability of the COD is determined at the partner level. For example, if a partnership has two partners, one bankrupt and one not, and the partnership recognizes COD, the bankrupt partner will be able to exclude its share of the COD from income, while the non-bankrupt partner will be currently taxable on its share of the COD. A partner may also be required to report capital gain to the extent the partner is relieved of partnership debt in an amount greater than its tax basis in its partnership interest.

A common issue in partnership workouts is whether a contribution of partnership debt to the partnership in exchange for a partnership interest creates COD income. Historically, one view was that no COD is created because the contribution qualifies as a tax-free contribution of property to the partnership under the general partnership tax rules allowing for tax-free contributions of property. However, another view was that COD is generated to the extent the value of the partnership interest received is less than the face amount of the debt contributed. The American Jobs Creation Act of 2004 provides that when a partnership issues a partnership interest to a creditor in satisfaction of partnership debt, the partnership recognizes COD income in an amount equal to the difference between the amount of the debt and the fair market value of the partnership interest issued (American Jobs Creation Act, 2004). Thus, as is often the case, where the partnership interest received has little or no value, COD will be generated.

Procedurally, when a partnership files for bankruptcy protection, no new taxable entity is created for federal income tax purposes, no new federal taxpayer identification number is required and the partnership's tax year does not close.[15] Any taxable income generated by the partnership is passed through and taxed to the partners in accordance with the partnership agreement, provided that, the allocation has economic substance. Under the Bankruptcy Code, however, the partnership is not permitted to distribute cash or other assets to enable the partners to satisfy their tax liabilities.

Finally, the state law dissolution of a partnership does not terminate the partnership for tax purposes. Rather, a partnership remains in existence for federal income tax purposes until all of its affairs have been wound up. Thus, if partners attempt to abandon their partnership interests in a bankrupt partnership to avoid being taxed on COD income, it is unlikely that such abandonment would be respected for federal income tax purposes. In a recent matter, a law partnership in bankruptcy had to prepare its tax returns. Prior to the year in which it entered bankruptcy, a number of partners left for other opportunities. If the partners had left because they knew of the partnership's precarious financial condition, the IRS could potentially assert that they remained partners for tax purposes until all of the partnership activities were wound up. Thus, in filing returns, the facts will have to be examined to determine whether or not the partners who resigned from the firm should nevertheless be considered partners despite their formal resignations. Along similar lines, the Supreme Court recently held that the IRS's timely assessment of employment taxes against a partnership kept the statute of limitations open to collect the taxes from the partners.

OTHER ISSUES

State & Local Tax Impact

The state tax treatment of COD varies by state. In addition, the state tax treatment of attribute reduction where affiliated corporations file consolidated federal tax

---

[15] Amazingly, it remains unclear whether a trustee appointed by the court in connection with a partnership bankruptcy must sign and file the return or whether the partners retain that responsibility. In informal pronouncements, the IRS has held that the trustee must file as "agent" for the partnership. On the question of whether a trustee must sign the partnership tax return, the instructions to the partnership tax return indicate that a trustee must sign the return, notwithstanding the fact that Section 6063 of the Code requires that the partnership return be signed by a partner.

returns is unclear. Moreover, the state tax treatment of state NOLs differs by jurisdiction. Consequently, it is critical to assessing the tax consequences of a restructuring plan to understand the potential state tax implications.

Liquidating Trusts

Liquidating trusts can be used to isolate a company's assets for the benefit of creditors until they can be efficiently sold or can be used to set aside assets to satisfy contingent claims. Legally, assets can be set aside for this purpose in trusts, limited partnerships, LLCs or escrow accounts. Trusts or other vehicles are particularly useful where the debtor has illiquid assets that can only be converted into cash over an extended period of time.

Generally, liquidating trusts are taxed as grantor trusts (rather than as partnerships or corporations) if they qualify under IRS guidelines. As such, the income of the grantor trusts is taxable to the beneficiaries of the trusts. A trust qualifies under the guidelines if, among other things, it is formed for the primary purpose of liquidating the contributed assets, it is not formed with the intention of conducting a business, has a fixed term (the IRS requires three years, but the courts are more generous – with five years being generally acceptable), any proceeds from the sale of assets transferred to it are invested only in short term investments, and the trust distributes sales proceeds at least annually. If the trust qualifies, contributions to the trust will be treated as a taxable disposition of assets transferred to the trust by the debtor's estate to the creditors/beneficiaries, followed by the beneficiaries' contribution of the assets to the trust. As a consequence, the beneficiaries of the trust will have a fair market value basis in their trust interests and the trust will have a fair market value basis in its assets. Care must be taken, however, to provide for the payment of any taxes that might be due on the estate's (deemed) sale of the assets because the trust could be held liable for such taxes.

Qualified/Designated Settlement Funds

Trusts established under Section 524(g) of the Bankruptcy Code may qualify as "Qualified Settlement Funds." Qualified Settlement Funds ("QSFs") are funds established to resolve or satisfy a claim under environmental laws (CERCLA) or a tort, breach of contract or violation of other law. QSFs are similar to Designated Settlement Funds ("DSFs") and are subject to similar although not identical, qualification requirements. QSFs, unlike DSFs, may be used to satisfy disputed claims or to make partial payments. Also, stock of the transferor is a qualified contribution to a QSF, but not to a DSF.

Establishing a QSF or DSF allows a company to take a tax deduction for the amount of cash or the value of assets contributed to the trust when the contribution is made, rather when the claims are actually paid which may, if the liabilities assumed by the trust qualify as specified liability losses, enable the company to obtain tax refunds. QSFs are generally separate taxable entities and are taxed at the highest marginal tax rate applicable to trusts and estates. The state tax treatment of DSFs and QSFs, however, remains somewhat unclear.

Property Taxes

A company's property tax liability may be significant, depending on the nature of its business. The post-emergence property tax liability may be a material cash cost that must be considered in determining whether a company can be effectively restructured and in determining the economic recovery of the creditors. In addition, there may be a potential to claim a refund for prior years' property taxes (or to reduce future property tax liability) where the value of the property was (or is) less than its cost or assessed value as a consequence of economic obsolescence or asset impairments for GAAP purposes (Schwartzman & Joffe, September 2004).

Pension Issues

A debtor company may be required to make significant cash contributions post-emergence to meet minimum funding standards if it has an unfunded pension liability. Minimum Plan funding requirements must be considered in determining whether a company can be effectively restructured and in determining the economic recovery of the creditors.

CONCLUSIONS

In considering the tax impact of financial restructurings, management's objective should be to preserve the value of the tax attributes to the fullest extent possible. As this chapter has revealed, the decision making process can be difficult and full of traps for the uninformed. Accordingly, it is critical for management to obtain tax advice as soon as possible in the process of financial restructuring.

REFERENCES

American Jobs Creation Act, (2004), House Resolution 4520.

Henderson, G. & Goldring, S. (2004) Tax Planning for Troubled Corporations. Aspen.

Jenks, C., Ridgway, C. & Purnell, E. (2004) Corporate Bankruptcy, BNA Tax Management Portfolio, 790, Tax Management, Inc..

Joffe, S. & Schwartzman, J. (2004, June) Partnership Taxation in Bankruptcy, The Bankruptcy Strategist, pp. 1 – 7.

Joffe, S. & Schwartzman, J. (2004, June) Recent Guidance on the Effects Upon Tax Attributes of Debtor's Reorganization, The Bankruptcy Law Reporter, 16, (23), 515 – 516.

Joffe, S. & Schwartzman, J. (2004, July) Lowering the Bar: States Collecting Pre-Petition Income Taxes Post-Emergence Where a Proof of Claim Was Not Timely Filed, Norton Bankruptcy Law Adviser, pp. 12 - 14.

Joffe, S. & Schwartzman, J. (2004, August) S Corporation Bankruptcies: Not all Pass-Through Entities are Created Equal, The Bankruptcy Law Reporter, 16, (34), 766 – 767.

Joffe, S. & Schwartzman, J. (2004, December), In Search of the Holy Grail: Musings on Section 382(l)(5), The Bankruptcy Strategist.

Joffe, S. & Schwartzman, J. (2005, January), In Search of the Holy Grail: Model Bankruptcy Order Released, The Bankruptcy Strategist.

Joffe, S. (2005, May), Final IRS Regulations Hurt Consolidated Groups – Restructuring Financially Troubled Groups Now Even More Complex, The Bankruptcy Strategist.

Kirschner, Kusnetz, Solarsh & Gatarz, (1991) Prepackaged Bankruptcy Plans: The Deleveraging Tool of the '90s in the Wake of OID and Tax Concerns, 21 Seton Hall Law Review, 21, 643.

Prudential Lines, Inc., 107 B.R. 832 (Bankr. D.N.Y. 1989), aff'd, 119 B.R. 430 (S.D.N.Y. 1990), aff'd, 928 F.2d 565 (2d Cir. 1991), cert. denied, 112 S. Ct. 82 (1992).

Schwartzman, J. & Joffe, S. (2005, January) Ten Common Tax Mistakes to Avoid During Workouts, Journal of Corporate Renewal.

Schwartzman, J., & Joffe, S. (2004, September). Order in the Court: Limits on the Court's Preservation of Debtor Assets (or How I Should Have Saved Millions of Dollars in Property Taxes), The Bankruptcy Strategist, pp. 3 – 4.

Appendix

TAX FLOW CHART

The tax implications of restructuring out of court differ significantly from the implications of restructuring in bankruptcy. The purpose of the following chart is to visually present an overview of the two primary tax issues in restructurings (COD and loss limitation). However, we caution that the actual tax implications of restructurings will be much more complex and will involve issues not presented in this chart. The chart is divided into two parts, restructuring out of court (Figure 1a) and restructuring in bankruptcy (Figure 1b). Both charts are divided into two issues, COD and loss limitation.

RESTRUCTURING OUT OF COURT

Issue I – COD. COD in restructurings out of court is a function of whether the debtor is solvent or insolvent. Accordingly, the COD issue is divided into two parts, one for solvent debtors and one for insolvent debtors. As discussed at length in the text, COD is taxable to a solvent debtor and the taxable amount may be offset by any NOLs, although the debtor may have an AMT liability. COD is *not* taxable to a solvent debtor if 1) the debt would be deductible when paid, 2) the debt is contingent or 3) the debt is reduced as a purchase price adjustment.

For an insolvent debtor, COD is not taxable to the extent of its insolvency. Any COD amount that is not taxable under this rule, would serve to reduce the debtor's NOLs and/or tax basis of assets under the Attribute Reduction rules. COD is taxable to the extent it exceeds the amount by which the debtor is insolvent and the taxable COD may be offset by any NOLs, although the debtor may have an AMT liability.

Issue II – Loss Limitation. If there is a less than 50 percentage point change in the ownership of the debtor's equity as part of the restructuring, the debtor's NOLs will not become subject to the loss limitation rules and, therefore, the NOLs can be used to offset future income without limitation.

If the ownership of the debtor's equity changes by at least 50 percentage points, the loss limitation rules will apply. Accordingly, there will be an annual limitation on the use of the debtor's NOLs that remain after reduction under the Attribute Reduction rules. In general, the annual limitation equals the net equity value of the debtor immediately *before* the restructuring, multiplied by an interest rate published monthly by the IRS. In addition, if the debtor is a built-in gain company (i.e., the value of its assets exceeds their tax basis), the annual limitation may be increased in each of the first five years after the restructuring. However, if the debtor is a built-in loss company (i.e., the value of the debtor's assets is less than their tax basis), built-in losses such as depreciation and amortization may be limited in the first five years after the restructuring, thereby increasing the likelihood that the debtor will be a taxpayer soon after emergence.

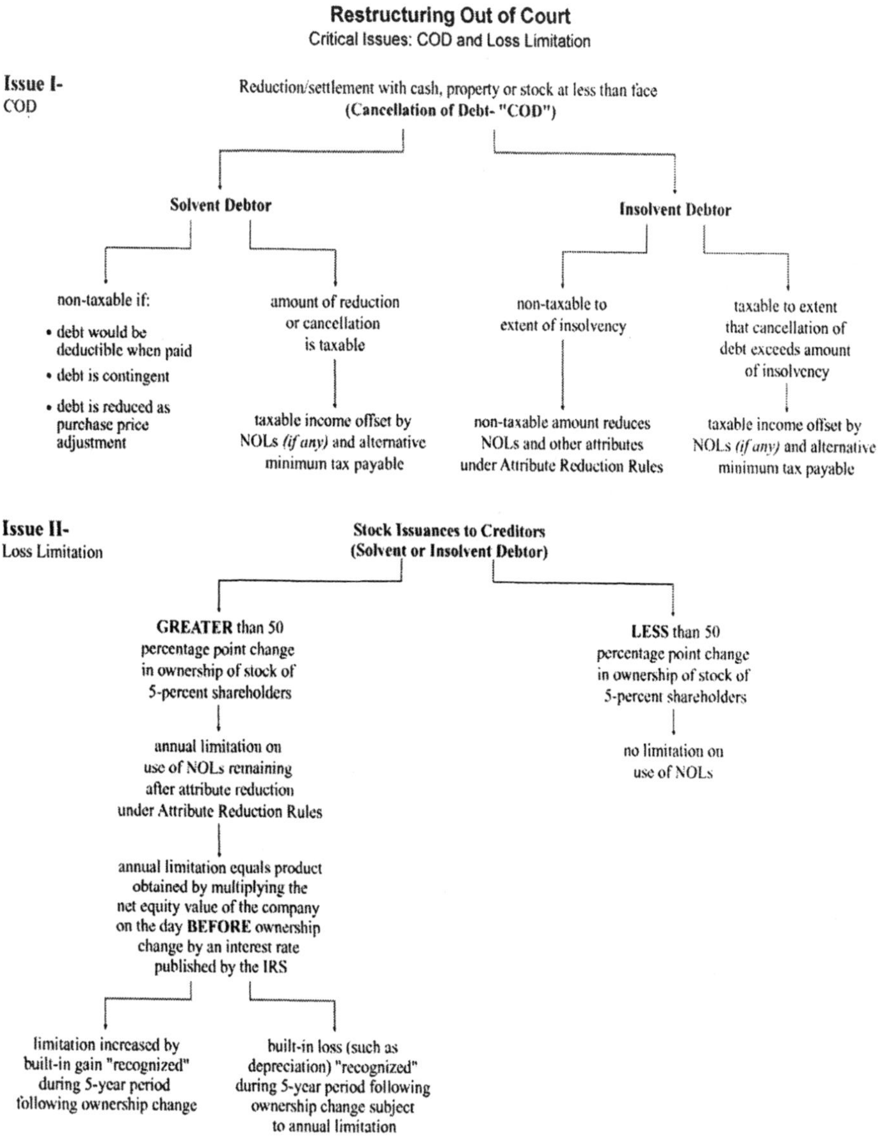

Restructuring Out of Court
Critical Issues: COD and Loss Limitation

Issue I-
COD

Reduction/settlement with cash, property or stock at less than face
(Cancellation of Debt- "COD")

Solvent Debtor

non-taxable if:

- debt would be
  deductible when paid
- debt is contingent
- debt is reduced as
  purchase price
  adjustment

amount of reduction
or cancellation
is taxable

taxable income offset by
NOLs *(if any)* and alternative
minimum tax payable

Insolvent Debtor

non-taxable to
extent of insolvency

non-taxable amount reduces
NOLs and other attributes
under Attribute Reduction Rules

taxable to extent
that cancellation of
debt exceeds amount
of insolvency

taxable income offset by
NOLs *(if any)* and alternative
minimum tax payable

Issue II-
Loss Limitation

**Stock Issuances to Creditors
(Solvent or Insolvent Debtor)**

GREATER than 50
percentage point change
in ownership of stock of
5-percent shareholders

annual limitation on
use of NOLs remaining
after attribute reduction
under Attribute Reduction Rules

annual limitation equals product
obtained by multiplying the
net equity value of the company
on the day **BEFORE** ownership
change by an interest rate
published by the IRS

limitation increased by
built-in gain "recognized"
during 5-year period
following ownership change

built-in loss (such as
depreciation) "recognized"
during 5-year period following
ownership change subject
to annual limitation

LESS than 50
percentage point change
in ownership of stock of
5-percent shareholders

no limitation on
use of NOLs

FIGURE 1a. Restructuring Out of Court

RESTRUCTURING IN BANKRUPTCY

Issue I – COD. As discussed in the text, COD is not taxable to a debtor in bankruptcy. Rather, the COD would reduce the debtor's NOLs and/or tax basis of assets under the Attribute Reduction rules.

Issue II – Loss Limitation. If there is a less than 50 percentage point change in the ownership of the debtor's equity as part of the restructuring, the debtor's NOLs will not become subject to the loss limitation rules and, therefore, the NOLs can be used to offset future income without limitation.

If the ownership of the debtor's equity changes by at least 50 percentage points, the loss limitation rules will apply. For bankrupt debtors, there are two possible loss limitation rules, Section 382(l)(6) and Section 382(l)(5). In most situations, Section 382(l)(6) will apply. If so, the annual limitation on the use of the debtor's remaining NOLs will equal the debtor's net equity value immediately *after* the restructuring, multiplied by an interest rate published monthly by the IRS. In addition, the built-in gain and built-in loss rules will apply.

If the debtor qualifies for Section 382(l)(5), there will be no limitation on the use of its NOLs as a result of the restructuring and the built-in gain and loss rules will not apply. To qualify for Section 382(l)(5), the debtor's "old and cold" and "ordinary course" creditors, and its historic shareholders, must own at least 50 percent of the debtor's equity (by vote and value) after the restructuring.

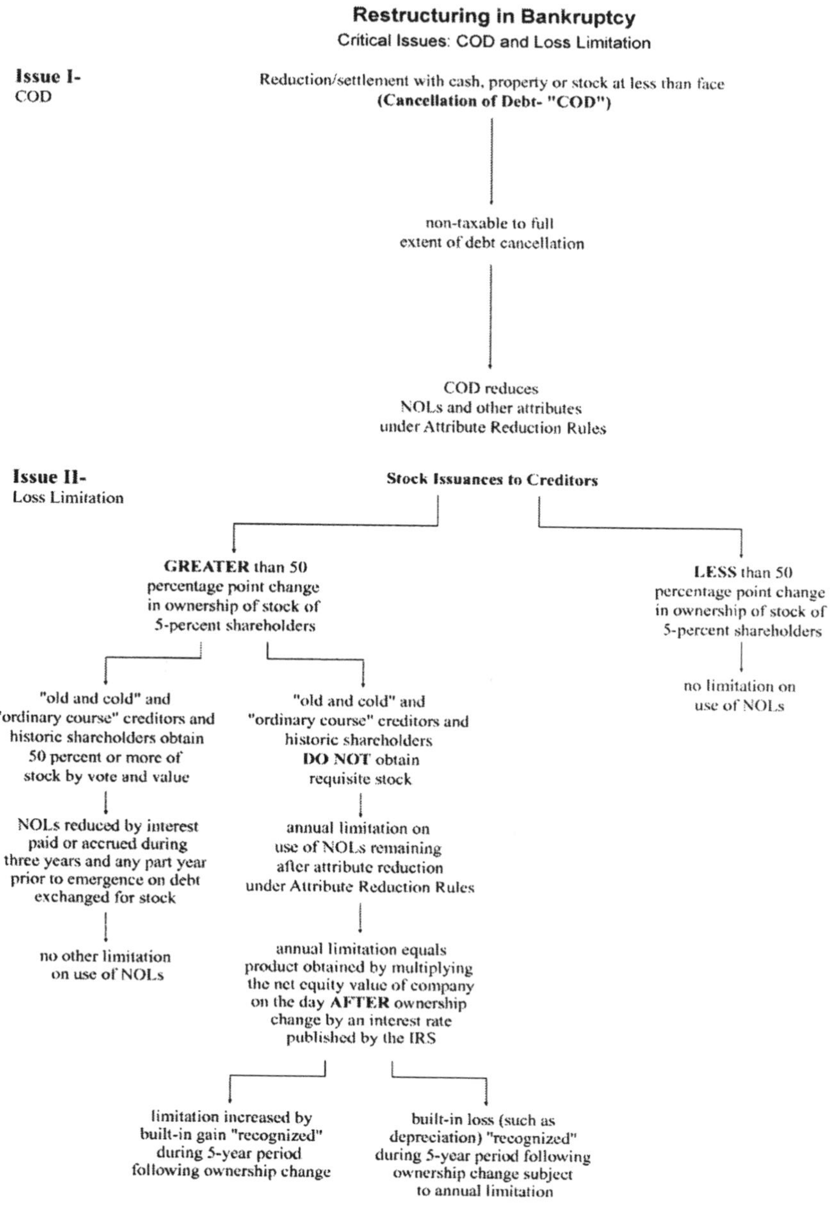

Restructuring in Bankruptcy

Critical Issues: COD and Loss Limitation

Issue I-
COD

Reduction/settlement with cash, property or stock at less than face
(Cancellation of Debt- "COD")

non-taxable to full
extent of debt cancellation

COD reduces
NOLs and other attributes
under Attribute Reduction Rules

Issue II-
Loss Limitation

Stock Issuances to Creditors

GREATER than 50
percentage point change
in ownership of stock of
5-percent shareholders

LESS than 50
percentage point change
in ownership of stock of
5-percent shareholders

no limitation on
use of NOLs

"old and cold" and
"ordinary course" creditors and
historic shareholders obtain
50 percent or more of
stock by vote and value

"old and cold" and
"ordinary course" creditors and
historic shareholders
DO NOT obtain
requisite stock

NOLs reduced by interest
paid or accrued during
three years and any part year
prior to emergence on debt
exchanged for stock

annual limitation on
use of NOLs remaining
after attribute reduction
under Attribute Reduction Rules

no other limitation
on use of NOLs

annual limitation equals
product obtained by multiplying
the net equity value of company
on the day **AFTER** ownership
change by an interest rate
published by the IRS

limitation increased by
built-in gain "recognized"
during 5-year period
following ownership change

built-in loss (such as
depreciation) "recognized"
during 5-year period following
ownership change subject
to annual limitation

FIGURE 1b. Restructuring in Bankruptcy

CHAPTER 16

PUBLIC RELATIONS IN CRISES

MICHAEL SITRICK

ABSTRACT

This chapter addresses communications in times of crises. Several principles are outlined and illustrated. These principles include telling the truth, organizing the facts, focusing of messages, using irrefutable sources of facts, taking control of communications, getting help for communicating, and maintaining consistent messages. Extensive vignettes and case studies are used to illustrate these principles.

PROLOGUE

I had just come back into the office from a meeting when my intercom rang.

"Mr. Sitrick, Mr. McNealy would like to see you right away," my assistant said. Mr. McNealy was the Chairman of the Board and Chief Executive Officer of Wickes Companies, an organization I had joined just nine months earlier as head of communications. When I got to Mac's office, he asked me to close the door and join him at his conference table.

"Mike, you are one of only three people in the company outside of the Board who knows this at this point, but I have decided to resign as Chairman and CEO. This is, as you might expect, a very difficult decision for me. But with the economy and housing market as it is, our high debt level and all of the other pressures on the company, Wickes needs someone who can shrink and restructure the company and I am a CEO who grows companies. So the Board has decided to bring a man in who has expertise in this area. A man named Sanford Sigoloff. You, Art Kirchheimer (then the general counsel of Wickes) and a handful of other senior people will be meeting with him this weekend in Los Angeles."

Great, I thought to myself. I have just moved my family across the country, given up a job I would have had for life and now the man who hired me – in fact, likely much of the management team I had joined – is leaving or will be replaced. My first thought was, "I wonder if and how long I will have a job."

Wickes had grown from a small lumber company in Saginaw, Michigan to one of the 50 largest companies in the United States. Through a series of very aggressive acquisitions, it now had 3,200 retail stores, 100 manufacturing locations and something like 60,000 employees. Its businesses included supermarkets, drug stores, home improvement stores, lumber stores, and women's clothing stores – to name just a few – as well as automotive parts, manufacturing plants and tool and die operations. It had $4 billion in sales. That was the good news. It also had a crushing amount of debt, was heavily dependent on the housing market which was in a horrendous depression at the time and was losing millions of dollars a year.

Having gone through one transformation – growing from a small regional lumber company into a massive conglomerate – Wickes now had to go through another, more painful transformation: it had to find a way to reduce costs, turn losses into profits and shed its debt.

After three weeks of intensively reviewing financial and other data, flying across the country to tour facilities and meet with employees and managers of the various operations and digesting all the information, it was concluded that the only way to preserve the assets and save the company was to put it in Chapter 11, a bankruptcy reorganization.

It was clear that change was needed – not only in the structure of the business, but in the way in which it was run. People had to change the way they thought, as well as the way they acted. This is true in the major transformation of any enterprise. Unfortunately, getting people to discard former behaviors can be difficult – especially when the old way of doing things is well-engrained, comfortable, secure, and convenient.

INTRODUCTION

Welcome to the world of enterprise transformation (DiNapoli, 1991, 1999). As Niccolo Machiavelli pointedly observed in his book, *The Prince,* "There is nothing more difficult to undertake, more perilous to conduct, or uncertain of success, than to lead in the introduction of a new order of things." The difference between success and failure in the introduction of a "new order of things" is often the presence or lack of effective communication by the leader seeking to affect the transformation of the enterprise.

In its simplest form, such change can be broken down into three sentences:

- I want you to *do something.*

- I want you *not to do something (*or *stop doing something).*

- I want you to *let me do something.*

The problem is, of course, that these kinds of behavioral changes cannot readily be effectively achieved through coercion in a free society (which any enterprise is, since people can choose to depart at any time) – but only through effective persuasion. Successfully influencing behavioral change requires appeal to both intellect and emotion – and the establishment of *credibility*.

How do you get someone to believe the truth of what you are saying, especially if credibility of the enterprise has been eroded through prior actions or circumstances (as is so often the case in situations where an enterprise must transform itself)? If you are working from a position of diminished credibility, there are seven ways to get your messages accepted. They are:

- *Tell the truth.* This is obvious, yet essential, even when the facts are unfavorable or unpleasant. Lies and deception are almost always ultimately exposed; once your credibility is destroyed, it is difficult if not impossible to repair.

- *Organize the facts.* Tell the truth, but organize the facts in a way that supports the message you are trying to get across. Select and focus on the facts that support your goals. Caveat: if negative facts are likely to get out, you should be the first to disclose them, to put them in the best possible light.

- *Focus your messages*: Address your constituents' needs, hopes and fears. Put yourself in their shoes, rather than asking them to stand in yours. Answer their two most important questions: "So what?" and "How is this going to affect me?" Successful persuasion requires that you address both the intellect and the emotion. These two avenues into the mind are mutually supportive. If you emotionally *want* to believe something, you are more likely to accept factual evidence. If information seems factual, it is more likely to stimulate emotional trust. To succeed, both kinds of appeals to the mind require *credibility*.

- *Use sources of facts that cannot be rebuffed.* Some *sources of information* carry more credibility than others; rely on those that cannot be assailed as biased, inaccurate or inauthentic.

- *Take control.* Tell your own story, on your own terms, rather than waiting for others to tell it for you. Opponents of change will invariably characterize things in the way least favorable to your goals. The rumor mill will almost always get it wrong. Silence is the enemy of success.

- *Get help.* Where possible, identify and use *credible third parties* to tell your story for you. It is often helpful to have a politician, prominent businessman or even, where appropriate, a former employee or executive provide support for the message you are trying to impart. Where appropriate, you might want to utilize the media as an additional means to tell your story. A story in your local newspaper, or, if your organization is large enough, in The *Wall Street*

Journal, that no management changes are planned will add significant credibility to that same statement in a meeting, press release or email. Conversely, a story in The *Wall Street Journal* that significant management changes are planned at your company when you have put out an email to the contrary will create serious credibility problems for you and your email.

- *Be consistent.* A common mistake in communications is telling one audience one thing and another audience something else. It is important to be consistent – not only to your various audiences, but from one day to the next. Having said that, facts change. People understand that fact of life. However, if the facts of the situation change, explain what the changes are and why they have changed. This is key to maintaining credibility. You also should be consistent in lines of communication: you need to communicate regularly – with both the good news and the bad.

This chapter discusses each of these seven rules in more detail, and then shows how they apply to the challenge of enterprise transformation.

TELL THE TRUTH

You learned this rule in elementary school and it still applies. Although telling the truth has a moral aspect, our focus here is on practical considerations. Lies are almost always found out. Once discovered, your credibility is almost always irreparably harmed.

Mark Twain observed, "If you always tell the truth, you don't have to remember anything." He was right. It's much more complicated if you have to remember which version of which story you told to which person. This is even more true today than in the past, because there will be overlaps between constituencies. Employees are also shareholders. Customers read newspapers, major business publications, and probably your annual report. Securities analysts read everything about you, and look for inconsistencies. And then, of course, there is the Internet. There are no more secrets.

Computers may have version control, but people don't. Telling conflicting stories to different constituents just doesn't work. Lying doesn't work. You can find examples in most successful legal prosecutions, not to mention many political scandals. And lying to cover up lies just makes things worse. We saw that in the Watergate case, which was less about the initial crime than about the cover-up. Bill Clinton wasn't impeached for his sexual activity in the White House, but for lying under oath about what he did, or didn't do, with a White House intern. Martha Stewart went to jail for lying to federal agents about trading on insider information more than for the "insider" trade itself.

The Internet has made it much more difficult to foist false information on the public than in the past. A classic example is the furor created when CBS News infamously reported that they had a letter that proved that George W. Bush had received poor performance evaluations while he was in the National Guard during the Vietnam era. Exposure of documents on the Internet quickly led to the demonstration that they were forged. CBS, after initially defending the authenticity of the story, was forced to issue an embarrassing retraction. CBS didn't lie, but its source did, and CBS was trapped into defending the lie.

This example leads to an important point: when you're communicating – especially in sensitive situations – you need to *be sure of your facts*. If you accept and use a statement as true and it turns out not to be, the effect is the same as if you'd told a lie. At Sitrick And Company, when we first start to work with a client, we research that client and its executives extensively on the Internet and through other sources that provide access to anything published in any newspaper anywhere in the world, legal proceedings, and other sources. We do this even with clients whom we fully trust, because we want to know what facts are available to a diligent reporter who might conduct the same sort of search.

This is critical when undertaking an enterprise transformation. If new management is coming into a situation, they need to know what has previously been said, what has been promised, which promises have been kept and which have been broken, what people view as the strengths of the organization and what they view as the weaknesses.

Similarly, if there is false information "out there" you need to take action to correct those inaccuracies, particularly if they are harmful to the organization and your efforts to transform it. This is exactly the situation we found when we were called to assist the New York clothing store chain Barneys New York, shortly after it filed for protection under Chapter 11 of the federal bankruptcy laws.

Barneys, which at the time was owned by the Pressman family and run by two brothers, Gene and Robert Pressman, sons of the firm's founder, found itself in bankruptcy court as a result of a dispute with Isetan, the Japanese company that had financed the transformation of their family-owned business "from a single store in an out-of-the-way Manhattan location," as one magazine put it, "to the ritziest specialty chain in America." Perhaps understandably, but definitely mistakenly, Bob and Gene thought they could get by with merely announcing the bankruptcy filing and then toughing it out. To call that a miscalculation is to put it mildly indeed.

Taking advantage of the Pressmans' silence, Isetan's representatives were able to feed the media a decidedly jaundiced account of what was going on – and to persuade more than a few reporters that Barneys had lied to them, both in explaining why it had filed for bankruptcy protection, and in announcing its financial results over the previous years.

As a result, the press turned on Barneys and the Pressmans like an angry beast. Not only did their side of the story remain untold, but the once adored clothing chain and the family that owned it suddenly found themselves pilloried in the local and national media. Even worse, their silence was taken by employees, vendors, creditors, and customers as a tacit confirmation that the appalling accusations being spread by Isetan had to be true. It was negatively affecting their business both on the inside, from morale to productivity, and on the outside, impacting both the volume of business they were doing and the way they were able to do business with all of their critical partners.

By the time Sitrick And Company got involved in the case nearly three months after the bankruptcy filing, the company's public image was in tatters. Only a year earlier, Barneys had been generally regarded as the smartest and most cutting-edge fashion retailer in the country. Now the business press was holding it up as an example of everything that was wrong with trendy fashion marketing. And the mainstream press was piling it on. Newsweek accused Barneys of racism. The *New York Times* reproached it for hubris. Vanity Fair described the Pressman family as a latter-day House of Atreus.

Through the 1980s, the Barneys empire consisted of a single (though highly regarded) clothing emporium on the not terribly fashionable corner of Seventh Avenue and 17th Street on Manhattan's lower west side. Founded in 1923 by Barney Pressman as a haberdashery for bargain-hunters, Barneys became something of a New York institution after World War II, when the elder Pressman turned the business over to his son Fred. While retaining Barneys' emphasis on value, Fred Pressman took the store up-market, offering a wider range of more stylish clothing and accessories. Before long, it was *the* place to shop in New York for quality-conscious businessmen, not to mention several generations of bar-mitzvah boys.

Following his father's lead, Fred eventually brought his own two sons, Bob and Gene, into the business. In 1976, Gene convinced Fred to expand into women's wear, and by the early eighties Barneys had mushroomed into a seven-story, 70,000-square-foot temple of chic that was considered the trendiest clothing store in New York, and one of the most successful anywhere.

The logical next step, of course, was to expand Barneys beyond its downtown birthplace. To that end, in 1988 the Pressmans' bankers introduced them to Isetan, a $4-billion-a-year behemoth that was Japan's sixth-largest retailer. Though Isetan was publicly traded, it was (like Barneys) family run, and its president at the time, a cosmopolitan 43-year-old named Kuniyasu Kosuge, was every bit as brash and expansive as Bob and Gene Pressman.

Hitting it off, Kosuge and the Pressmans quickly sketched out an ambitious if somewhat intricate alliance whose aim was to link the two companies in what both parties agreed would be a "global retailing partnership." A new subsidiary, called Barneys America, was formed; 55-percent owned by Isetan, it proceeded to open Barneys mall outlets in nine upscale U.S. markets such as Manhasset, Long Island; Short Hills, New Jersey; and Dallas, Texas. Isetan also got the right to open Barneys stores (20-percent owned by Barneys Inc.) in Tokyo and Yokohama, a plum the Pressmans said would be worth more than $200 million over the next thirty years. (Indeed, the Japanese stores were hugely successful right out of the box; originally projected to take eleven years to become profitable, they were both making money within four.)

At the same time, Isetan agreed to finance the construction of three new full-size Barneys branches in Beverly Hills, Chicago and midtown Manhattan. The terms of this part of the deal were particularly complicated; under the arrangement worked out by the partners, Isetan would pay all the land and construction costs for the three stores, in return for which it would receive a monthly rent based on a combination of the property value and sales volume at each location.

Amid champagne and sake toasts in New York and Tokyo, Barneys and Isetan sealed their pact in the spring of 1989. Both sides were so enthusiastic about the deal that the final agreement called for the partnership to endure for 499 years. As things turned out, it lasted barely half a decade.

What happened was that, for a variety of reasons, the Beverly Hills and midtown Manhattan stores turned out to be much larger – and hence more expensive – than first planned. As New York magazine later reported, "In Beverly Hills, the city unexpectedly required Barneys to build a five-story underground parking garage and the store had to be built from the ground up rather than moved into an existing building." Similarly, the cost of the midtown Manhattan outlet wound up ballooning after Metropolitan Life, which was supposed to occupy the office space above the store, unexpectedly pulled out at the last minute.

As a result, what Isetan had initially thought would be a $250 million investment wound up soaring to $600 million. Quickly, it became clear that the original idea of Barneys paying Isetan a rent based on the value of the new stores no longer made sense. (Given the larger size of the stores, the rent would have been prohibitively high.) Thus, as early as 1991, Bob Pressman began suggesting that they renegotiate the alliance into a more straightforward equity partnership. Among other things, he offered to convert the original Barneys branch at Seventh Avenue and 17th Street into the "flagship store" of Barneys America, the chain of mall outlets that Isetan partly owned. The following year he wrote a letter to Isetan pointing out that "since the investment amount and corresponding store sizes, etc., are much different than originally contemplated," an "overall restructuring" of their alliance would seem to make eminent sense. To that end, he approvingly quoted an Isetan executive's suggestion that Barneys and the Japanese company put all our interests into one big pot.

Unfortunately, by then the atmosphere at Isetan was no longer nearly as warm as it had been when the deal with Barneys was first struck. Battered by the Japanese recession, reeling from the effects of a currency-trading debacle and a raid on its stock, Isetan had changed. Among other things, the ebullient Kosuge was no longer in charge. Kicked upstairs, he was replaced by a cadre of bottom-line types who were far less excited by the strategic potential of long-term growth -- and far more concerned with the immediate burden of escalating short-term costs. By the end of 1993, they had cut off the flow of funds to Barneys. As a result, Barneys found itself forced to use its own money (some $63 million in all) to complete construction of the new stores and get them properly furnished. Strapped for cash, the Pressmans appealed to Isetan for help, and in March 1994, the Japanese company agreed to provide an emergency loan. As a condition, however, it insisted the Pressmans sign an agreement promising to work out a deal under which Isetan could convert the loan, along with the Barneys real-estate it owned, into an equity stake in Barneys Inc. Since this was precisely what the Pressmans had been suggesting since 1991, they had no trouble accepting the provision.

The negotiations, however, went nowhere. Though the Pressmans were willing, Isetan dragged its feet. As a result, Barneys soon found itself once again running out of money. By the end of 1995, its cash on hand, which usually totaled around $25 million, had dwindled to barely $4 million. Ironically, the business itself was doing fine. The nine mall stores, along with the two big New York stores and their counterparts in Beverly Hills and Chicago, were all making money on an operating basis. It was the cost of seeing through the expansion without sufficient help from Isetan that had brought Barneys to the brink.

On January 11, 1996, after efforts to force Isetan to come around had failed, Barneys filed for Chapter 11 bankruptcy protection. The move stunned customers and competitors alike -- no one more so than Barneys' 7,000 or so suppliers, who suddenly had no idea when, or if, they'd ever be paid for the goods they'd shipped to the chain or its once proud employees. While refusing to speak publicly themselves, the Pressmans issued a press release insisting the bankruptcy was nothing for anyone to worry about, that their business was healthy and Barneys' debts would be paid. The filing, people were told, was merely a tactic in what was described as a "lease dispute" with a joint-venture partner.

To outsiders, who knew little of Isetan and had no idea of the complicated back-story, this cryptic explanation was of limited effectiveness -- all the more so because right up to the filing, the company had been insisting that business was better than ever. In that, Barneys had been reacting to insolvency rumors arising from complaints from vendors that it had been slower than usual in paying its bills. Now the tactic seemed to backfire. As one skeptical observer told The *Wall Street Journal*, "When a privately held company makes grandiose statements about how good business is and then suddenly goes into bankruptcy court, you begin to wonder what is truth and what is fiction."

To add to the growing suspicions, Isetan reacted to the bankruptcy filing by unleashing a barrage of PR that accused the Pressmans of playing fast and loose with both the facts and its money. The Pressmans, it insisted, were lying to the press when they claimed their business was healthy; in fact, the giant Japanese retailer insisted, Barneys was nearly insolvent – a predicament of its own making that the Pressmans were now trying to blame on the too trusting Japanese.

Isetan followed up its accusations with a lawsuit in which it claimed the Pressmans had failed to disclose that Barneys had been piling up "significant losses" even as Isetan was financing its ambitious expansion plans. Equally damaging, Isetan insisted that its involvement with Barneys was never "an open-ended partnership," but merely consisted of some "limited real-estate investments by Isetan." Without any information to the contrary, the press accepted Isetan's version of events, and turned on Barneys and the Pressmans with a vengeance.

If there was ever a time for someone to stand up and explain their situation, this was it. Unfortunately, with court papers flying back and forth, the Pressmans' advisers counseled silence, and the brothers took their advice. Thus unchallenged, Isetan's spokesmen were able to spin to their hearts' content without fear of interruption, distraction, or contradiction. Not only had the Pressmans misled their Japanese backers by concealing huge operating losses at Barneys, they told the press, but they had lied to reporters as well. What's more, they had gone on a wild spending spree in building the new stores, outfitting them in the most extravagant and irresponsible manner imaginable – then concealing the massive budget overruns from Isetan until it was too late.

Now *that* was a story. The arrogant trendsetters of the eighties overreach themselves in the nineties, taking merciless advantage of the generous but naive Japanese, and when their dishonesty is exposed for what it is, they try to escape the consequences of their misdeeds by declaring bankruptcy, heedless of the impact on the thousands of small businesses that depend on them. Given that the Pressmans' only response to Isetan's lurid account was a series of easily discounted routine denials, who could blame the press for clutching such a wonderfully simplistic melodrama to its collective bosom and running with it?

The same press that had celebrated the rise of Barneys through the seventies and eighties, cheering on the Pressmans' brash ambition and imaginative marketing skills, now turned with gusto to its dismemberment. And by holding their tongues, the Pressmans accelerated their own execution.

It was towards the end of March 1996 that the Pressmans brought in Sitrick And Company to try to turn the situation around. The company was in disarray. Its employees were embarrassed and demoralized by the press accounts. Its vendors, customers and other constituents were obviously dismayed. By the time we got involved, Barneys was widely perceived to be the villain of the story, and the press accounts of its woes were appropriately merciless. For the most part, the media (and much of Barneys' other publics) had bought into Isetan's claim that not only had Barneys lied to its Japanese benefactors, but worse – *much* worse – it had lied to them as well.

Thus propelled as much by moral outrage as by the lust for a good story, virtually every media outlet from the smallest trade paper to The *Wall Street Journal* ran stories about how Barneys, for all its cool insolence and outward glossiness, was in fact a financial shambles – how the Pressmans' arrogance and self-regard was finally getting the comeuppance it deserved. Newsweek devoted a full page to an African-American staffer's angry account of how, six years earlier, he had been unjustly accused of shoplifting at Barneys – and how he now hoped to "dance on its grave." *New York Times* op-ed columnist Maureen Dowd devoted no fewer than three separate columns to savaging Barneys, which she seemed to regard as a symbol of everything that was wrong with contemporary popular culture.

The press was so bad that its dark predictions of Barneys' imminent demise were in danger of becoming self-fulfilling prophecy. After all, who would extend credit or ship goods to a company that everyone was saying not only might be going down the tubes, but *deserved* to go down the tubes?

In short, the situation was dire, and at my first meeting with the Pressmans and their senior management, I laid out the strategy I felt we needed to follow. "What we've got to do first," I said, "is get our side of the story told…first to the media and then to each of our other key constituencies."[1] That, of course, would be easier said than done. Still, we had a few things going for us. For one, the facts were on our side. Contrary to Isetan's assertions and the media's repetitions, Barneys was *not* losing money on an operating basis, nor had the Pressmans lied to the Japanese or anyone else. For another, the Pressmans had assured me there was plenty of hard evidence to back up their claims.

This last point was crucial, for as I told the Barneys team, "If we go to the media with our side of the story, we're going to have to be able to document it. Otherwise, they're going to say, 'Look, you say this, while Isetan says that. How do we know who we should believe?'"

To that end, I spent days with Bob Pressman (the number-cruncher of the two brothers) going through huge stacks of letters, memos, and financial reports, assembling our case like a lawyer preparing to go into court. Given the uniformly negative coverage from even the most usually reliable of media, what I found astonished me. There it all was in black and white: proof that Barneys' business *was* operating in the black, and that the Pressmans had never misrepresented anything to Isetan (or anyone else, for that matter) – not their company's financial condition nor the fact that from the start it had been clear that the cost of their ambitious expansion project would be much higher than both they and their Japanese partners had originally anticipated.

Thus girded, I now had to figure out the best way to use this powerful ammunition. Clearly, it wouldn't make much sense to announce it in a press release. For one thing, no one would believe it. For another, even if someone did, chances are they wouldn't give it very much play, and a story as complicated as ours desperately needed sufficient space if it was to be both coherent and persuasive. (Space was also important because the length of a story is generally taken as a measure of its importance. A long story is a major story, one that has impact. A small story about Barneys – even if it had somehow managed to tell the tale accurately and understandably – would have gotten lost in the back-and-forth of the publicity battle.)

No, the way to get a complicated story like the Barneys tale fully and fairly told is to offer it on an exclusive basis to an established, respected editor or reporter at an established, respected news outlet. There are few motivations more powerful in the journalistic personality than the desire to score an exclusive – to "own" a story by coming up with information or access no rival can hope to match. In this case, what I had to offer was pretty potent stuff – an exclusive, inside look

---

[1] Without correcting the widespread media accounts, it was clear that the chance was slim of convincing the company's other key constituents that what had been said about Barneys was untrue.

at one of the hottest business stories of the day: the Pressman brothers' own account, backed up by all the documentation a reporter could hope for, of what was really going on between Barneys and Isetan.

The question was, who should I take it to? Ordinarily, I would have gone to the most prestigious and influential publications available – in this case, The *Wall Street Journal* or the *New York Times*. Unfortunately, the reporters covering the Barneys bankruptcy for both of those eminent newspapers already had equity in the other side's story – which is to say, what they'd written up to that point had pretty much reflected the Isetan party line. In order to present our account, therefore, they'd in effect have to tell their readers, "You know, for the last few weeks we've been reporting how Barneys had fooled both us and Isetan. Well, now it turns out that Barneys was really telling the truth and it was Isetan that was lying to us." I doubted either of them would be willing to do that – at least not readily.

The thing to do, obviously, was find a respected reporter and a respectable publication, neither of which had already staked out a position on Barneys. A little research quickly yielded the answer. New York magazine, I discovered, had yet to publish any major pieces on the controversy. I was delighted, for New York was the perfect vehicle for our story. Highly regarded by journalists, it was also widely read in both the financial and fashion communities. Adding to its allure, I happened to have worked with one of its senior editors, Rich Turner,[2] whom I'd gotten to know when he was a reporter in The *Wall Street Journal*'s Los Angeles bureau.

For a story like this, you couldn't ask for a better journalist than Turner. To begin with, he was highly thought of in his profession, a tough reporter, not one you could easily spin, but a guy with integrity who was willing to consider all sides of a story. Beyond that, he had a business background (courtesy of The *Journal*) and he was very smart – which was crucial in this case. We were, after all, dealing with a fairly complicated situation. Without an experienced financial reporter who knew how to read a balance sheet and could understand the intricacies of the Barneys-Isetan relationship, we would all be in trouble.

So I went to the Pressmans and recommended they not only sit down with Turner but that they open their files to him. I also gave them a speech that I often give clients in their situation. "Understand," I told them, "we are not talking about a puff piece here. Assuming Rich and New York decide to do the article, there's a very good chance – in fact, you can depend on it – that parts of it are going to make you wince. Not everything he says about you and your business is going to be complimentary. But you can't let that bother you. What we're concerned about is the overall tone, the overall message. If we do our job right, the story as a whole should completely change perceptions among both the media and the public."

The Pressmans agreed to give it a shot. With their OK in hand, I immediately phoned Turner. As expected, he was more than intrigued when I asked him if he

---

[2] Rich Turner is once again a reporter with The *Wall Street Journal*

thought his magazine might be interested in an exclusive interview with the Pressmans and the first account of their version of the inside story of the battle between Barneys and Isetan.

Over the next few weeks, Bob and Gene Pressman and I spent countless hours working with Turner, taking him through the numbers, explaining the history, laying out our case. We documented everything. Each time Bob or Gene would mention a letter he'd sent Isetan, I'd insist that he go through his correspondence file and dig out a copy to show Turner. "Here's the time-and-date stamp," he'd say. "See the telltale on top – it shows exactly when we faxed it." We presented our story to him precisely the way you would present a case to a judge and jury.

At the same time that we were working with Turner, Sandi Sternberg, one of my firm's managing directors, and I were also looking for an opportunity to expose our side of the story to the regular beat reporters at the newspapers that really mattered to Barneys – in particular, The *New York Times*, The *Wall Street Journal*, and *Women's Wear Daily*. We got our opportunity when Barneys was ready to announce its latest quarterly earnings. At that point, we invited each of the reporters in for a private briefing – in effect, a mini-version of what we were doing with Turner. Not that we were pitching anyone a story. All we wanted was the chance to walk each of the beat reporters through the numbers, to show them (literally) that Barneys was operating comfortably in the black and had been for some time. Needless to say, this fact invariably surprised them, which gave us the opportunity to explain how they had been misled by Isetan.

Now, none of the reporters actually wound up writing that he or she had been deceived by Isetan. But overall the tone of their coverage began to change. Not only did they all report Barneys' positive quarterly results, they all noted that the company had been operating profitably for some time – in effect, putting the lie to Isetan's assertions without saying so in so many words. As a result, by the time Rich Turner's story came out in New York magazine early that May, the atmosphere was just right: both the press and public were ready for a wholesale reevaluation of Barneys' situation.

Turner's story, which sprawled across seven full pages of the magazine, turned out to be everything we'd hoped for and more. Though it announced in an early paragraph that "we're not here to restore Barneys' trashed image," that's pretty much what it did. Making full use of the information we'd made available to him, plus the extensive reporting he did on his own, Rich produced a warts-and-all portrait of the Pressmans' frustrating relationship with Isetan that portrayed them, not as amoral exploiters, but as sympathetic strivers, victimized in part by their own ambition, but more by Isetan's inconstancy.

The piece's impact was both immediate and profound. Combined with the background work we'd done with the beat reporters, it transformed Barneys' relationship with the media and its other constituents virtually overnight. Having once been held in high esteem, and then vehemently despised, the Pressmans were now regarded once again in a positive light. With their reputations restored, the brothers not only were able to manage the delicate business of operating a company under Chapter 11 protection without any major problems from suppliers or creditors, they were also able to put Barneys on the road back to solvency by negotiating a new partnership with Hong Kong-based Dickson Concepts. Neither of these accomplishments would have been possible had they not followed the first rule of spin – and recognized the importance of making sure their story got told.

DETERMINE AND THEN ORGANIZE THE FACTS

It is important to learn the history of the organization, what has happened, what has been said by whom and to whom, what promises have been made and which of those promises have been kept. Once that is accomplished, you then have to decide what to say and to whom to say it. In most situations, there is a range of facts available. What you choose to impart and how you organize that information is not only critical to the success of your communications effort, but to maintaining your credibility as well.

Of course, it is important that you choose those facts that best buttress your case and then organize them in a clear and concise fashion. Just stating the facts, however, is not sufficient. You need to give some perspective and put yourself in the shoes of the people with whom you are trying to communicate. It is just as important to address what they are looking to hear as it is what it is you are trying to communicate. And when putting together this information, you need to look at the situation from all sides. What are the facts that someone taking the other side might point to? We call it addressing the "yes, but" questions. Identify those facts and preemptively address them in your initial remarks.

And don't forget the bad or negative news. Putting on a happy face might be nice for a Broadway musical, but in communicating to important constituencies you must tell the full and complete story. If you want to maintain your credibility, you must disclose the bad with the good. If you are closing a facility or laying off 10% of your workforce, for example, address that action and explain the reasons why you have taken it. A good rule of thumb is, when in doubt, err on the side of disclosure. Having said this, of course there will be situations where this approach will be overruled by the lawyers, but in general we have found this practice to be very effective and successful.

When there are no good facts, you may have to create new facts to make the transformation of the enterprise possible. This does not mean creating falsehoods. It means making strategic decisions at the enterprise level that become significant facts in and of themselves. Has your enterprise just been caught up in a financial reporting scandal? Don't just report that you're the subject of a federal investigation. Create new programs to "make certain that something like this can never happen again." Announce those programs as part of your very first steps into the public arena. The facts that you are undertaking steps A, B and C become very much part of the story. You can *change the story by changing the available facts.*

Imagine you're the CEO of a national retail chain who has just been informed that, according to government investigators, the subcontractor who manufactures your house brand of leisure-wear has been producing the stuff in illegal sweatshops with child labor. The news will almost certainly be featured that evening on each of the nightly network news shows, and again the next morning on the front pages of most of the nation's newspapers. Your company's reputation, in other words, is about to be shredded. The subtleties of spin may seem to offer precious little comfort at such a time, but the fact is, if properly applied, spin can help salvage your good name. Indeed, as horrified as both the public and press will no doubt be, there is no question that an appropriately crafted response on your part can put the embarrassing incident behind you quickly and cleanly.

What kind of response could possibly be appropriate in the aftermath of such a potentially disastrous revelation? In a nutshell, one that anticipates the needs of both the public and the press in these sorts of situations. Pundits often stress how important it is for a company that has dropped the ball in one way or another to take responsibility for its actions and apologize to the public. In part, this approach reflects an understandable impatience with the traditional corporate practice of stonewalling when things go awry – and indeed, it is crucial that wayward companies (and individuals too, for that matter) freely admit when they've done something wrong, that they show some genuine remorse for their misdeeds. But while such responses may be necessary if public trust is to be maintained, confessions of guilt and expressions of sorrow alone are hardly sufficient.

That's because, as a rule, people don't care nearly as much about what happened in the past as they do about what's going to happen in the future. It's the same with the media. Some elements of the press may love to spend time finger-pointing and assessing blame in the aftermath of a disaster (PR or otherwise), but most news people quickly grow tired of rehashing the same old information. What excites them far more than stirring the ashes of a dying fire is the prospect of being offered some new development they can use to freshen a story that may be growing stale.

For anyone who finds himself called to account by the media for some mishap or misbehavior, the implications of these realities ought to be clear. Going on about how sorry you are for whatever it was that you did wrong is nice, but it will only get you so far. Without a doubt, the most important thing you can do to recover from your misstep is to emphasize to the public exactly what actions you intend to take going forward to ensure nothing like it ever happens again.

In the case of our embarrassed retail chain that would mean undertaking an aggressive and very public series of actions. First, the company would announce it was immediately suspending the contractor caught using child labor. At the same time, it would publicize the launch of an intensive internal investigation of the labor practices at all its other subcontractors as well as a review of the procedures it normally employs to monitor them. Needless to say, the results of both these inquiries would be released to the media, and based on what was found, the company would then devise and implement – and once again announce to the public – an array of new corporate practices designed to ensure to the greatest extent possible that none of its subcontractors could violate U.S. labor law.

Assuming the company was sincere in its efforts – and its new safeguards made sense to the public – this kind of open, forward-looking response would likely have enormous impact. At the very least, the sight of the company dealing with its problems, rather than denying their existence, would be bound to mollify concerned customers. And the new procedures would give the press something else to write about besides the heart-breaking plight of underage workers. More quickly than one would have thought possible, the public outrage generated by the initial headlines would evaporate, and before very long the crisis would have passed.

This may strike you as an overly ambitious claim. In point of fact, however, I have used this technique of spinning a story forward in order to put bad news behind you for years – helping both individuals and institutions rebound from what might otherwise be fatal transgressions. One of my favorite examples of this approach involves a remarkable business recovery in which Sitrick And Company played a role. The case concerned a product far more sensitive than leisure-wear -- namely, health care -- and a company that had been accused of lapses that bordered on the macabre. Even so, by holding out the prospect of a better future, rather than trying to defend an indefensible past, we were able to contribute to what I think may have been *the* corporate enterprise transformation of the nineties.

Since confidentiality issues preclude the identification of the company in this example by name, we will refer to it as "XYZ." Founded by an erstwhile tax attorney with just six hospitals and a $25 million public stock offering in 1969, XYZ had ridden the revolution in employee and taxpayer health-care programs in the 1970s and 1980s to become one of the fastest-growing and most profitable hospital chains in the nation. By 1991, with well over 100 acute-care and psychiatric facilities on four continents, it was earning close to $600 million a year on annual revenues of nearly $4 billion. But storm clouds were gathering. For one thing, the double-digit growth rates that had propelled the company through the previous two decades were proving impossible to sustain. For another, the billing and patient-admissions practices that had produced those growth rates were themselves becoming the subject of both government and insurance-company investigations – as well as fodder for lawyers representing countless former patients, scores of whom were suing the company on a wide range of charges, including some alleging that patients had been held against their will in XYZ psychiatric facilities until their hospitalization coverage had been exhausted.

Things really started to unravel at the beginning of 1993, when The *Wall Street Journal* published a devastating front-page report on the company's woes. At the time, XYZ was facing more than 100 lawsuits brought by former patients. In addition, some nineteen insurance companies were accusing XYZ of over-billing them by as much as $1 billion, and no fewer than fourteen separate federal and state investigations were underway against it. The rap on the company was straightforward – and ugly. As The *Journal* described it, XYZ represented a classic example of the tendency of commercial hospital operators "to place profits above the needs of patients." A few months later, *Business Week* elaborated further, detailing insurance-company charges that the pressure to keep earnings up at XYZ was so great that the company's "top management instructed hospital administrators to adopt intake goals designed to lure patients into XYZ hospitals for lengthy and unnecessary treatments."

The crisis seemed to come to a head at the end of April 1993, when the company's founder, William B. Smith[3], resigned as chief executive. Two months later, he gave up his post as chairman as well. He was replaced in both jobs by a 49-year-old investment banker named John L. Simons.[4] Simons had been a member of XYZ's board of directors for a number of years, but otherwise he had no experience in the health-care business. Still, he was very, very smart and unflappable – and he was determined to get the company back on the right track. In the weeks following his appointment as CEO, he shook up the top management, announced a restructuring of the company, and began settling some of the suits brought by former patients.

But XYZ was not yet out of the woods – not by a long shot. On a Thursday morning late in August 1993, upwards of 600 FBI and other federal agents (as estimated by the media) descended without warning on XYZ offices and hospitals in more than twenty cities from Washington to San Diego – among them, the company's Santa Monica, California, headquarters, where some forty agents swarmed through the corridors, brandishing search warrants and seizing files. In all, investigators carted off hundreds of boxes of documents, further bolstering the media's belief that XYZ had been guilty of criminal acts ranging from widespread overbilling to concocting fraudulent diagnoses in order to keep healthy patients from checking out of its lucrative psychiatric facilities. Coming as they did immediately after a White House announcement that the Clinton administration was going to make the fight against fraud a significant part of its embattled health-care reform package, the dramatic raids not only made headlines in virtually every major newspaper in the nation, they also generated extensive coverage on radio and TV, including each of the nightly network news shows. In one fell swoop, the complicated charges against XYZ had been elevated beyond mere business-section boiler plate; now the company's woes were front-page news, and its continued existence was suddenly in doubt.

It was against this backdrop that I got a telephone call the next afternoon from John Simons . (I have yet to figure out why these sorts of calls always seem to come on Friday afternoons.)

"I don't know if you've been following what's been happening with our company," John said to me, but we had a visit from the FBI yesterday."

---

[3] William B. Smith is a pseudonym.
[4] John L. Simons is a pseudonym.

"I'd have to have been on Mars to have missed it," I replied.

John continued without missing a beat. "I asked my people a number of times to phone you – to get your firm involved," he continued. "Well, now I have *told* them. You'll be getting a call shortly from one of my executive vice presidents. If you're free, I'd be grateful if you could come over to our offices and speak with a group of our management people."

Thirty minutes later, Mike Kolbenschlag, a managing director of my firm and I, were sitting in the XYZ boardroom with a number of the company's top executives and a bevy of attorneys.

After receiving a briefing on where matters stood, it was clear to me what needed to be done. "Look," I said, "from the media reports I've seen, there's no question that your company must act immediately to assure your various constituents that whether or not you're guilty of what's been alleged, those things will not happen in the future. Your key constituents have all lost confidence in you. The insurance companies you do business with are all suing you. Your patients have all heard about your troubles by now, and hundreds of them are also suing you. The government – well, let's just say they don't send 600 FBI agents to make a social call. As for your employees, they've been reading about the company's problems for months, and at the very least, they've got to be very demoralized."

No one at the table disputed my assessment. But it left at least one person unmoved. Certainly, he didn't seem particularly seized with any sense of urgency. "The thing is," this executive said, "we're really bushed. I think we should take a break and reconvene on Monday. After all, the media have already done their stories."

Another executive echoed agreement. "We've had an exhausting 24 hours here," he said. "The press has written all they're going to write about this. I mean, what else are they going to say?"

"Look," I replied, "this is not going to be a one-day story. It is a major news event that will be generating headlines for days, if not weeks, to come. My God, the media reported that you had 600 government agents swarming all over your facilities yesterday. I promise you, come Monday morning there will be a whole slew of follow-up stories – and most of them are being written right now. If you don't give the reporters writing those stories something new to talk about, they are simply going to wind up rehashing all the old allegations, making guesses about what else might go wrong, and speculating about whether the company can survive."

"Oh come on," the same person said. "There's no way that's going to happen."

"I disagree," I responded. "What we need to do is reconvene not on Monday but at seven-thirty tomorrow morning to figure out exactly what sort of actions we can announce to the press that will convince all of XYZ's different constituencies that what this company has been accused of cannot and will not happen in the future."

That suggestion prompted another round of side discussions – followed by a polite request that Mike Kolbenschlag and I leave the room for a few minutes. "Well," I said to Mike as the doors closed behind us, "that might have been the shortest assignment we've ever had."

As it turned out, of course, it wasn't. We did, however, have to agree to one compromise: our proposed Saturday morning meeting was pushed back to eight A.M.

Even so, it wound up yielding excellent results. Working through the weekend, the crisis-management team came up with a five-point plan that John Simons was able to unveil on Sunday during interviews we scheduled with The *Wall Street Journal*, the *New York Times*, and the *Los Angeles Times*. Among other things, the plan included the appointment of an independent task force to monitor company practices regarding patient admissions and referrals, the establishment of local governing boards in all XYZ hospitals, enhanced quality-management audits, tighter billing and documentation procedures, and the installation of a toll-free "patient satisfaction line" over which patients and their relatives could report any problems or improprieties.

The plan was specific, well-reasoned, and credible, and the media responded to it just as we had hoped they would. Instead of focusing yet again on what had happened the previous week – and fostering speculation that the FBI raids might have marked the beginning of the end for XYZ – the second-day coverage took its cue from John's forward-looking announcement, depicting the company as acting decisively to restore confidence among its various constituencies. The *Los Angeles Times* headline said it all: "XYZ Promises to Beef Up Oversight of Its Hospitals," it declared. After nearly a year of almost completely negative stories, the positive action implied in that headline marked a radical departure in the press's view of the company. The same attitude was reflected in a follow-up profile of John that ran in The *Wall Street Journal* a few days later. "Simon's Mission at XYZ: Resolve Litigation, Strengthen Business," it proclaimed, noting approvingly both John's "ability to appear calm and reassuring in a crisis" and his efforts to "restore confidence and send a message that any past illegal or unethical practices won't be tolerated."

Interestingly enough, as the media tide turned, so did the government's attitude (helped along by a lot of hard and brilliant work by XYZ's lawyers). According to the company's lawyers, Justice Department investigators seemed pleased by the fact that rather than hunkering down and refusing to admit any wrongdoing, XYZ was taking measures to correct what it openly conceded had been areas of abuse.

Over the next few months, we spent many hours working on ways to get the word out to patients, doctors, and staff – not to mention Wall Street and government regulators – about what the company was doing. We talked about how Simons had set up two separate management groups within XYZ: one to concentrate on cleaning up all the old messes, the other to make sure the company's ongoing businesses didn't suffer in the process. We also began to promote the positive things going on at XYZ, including various profit-improvement, debt-reduction, and re-positioning programs.

At the same time, the company undertook an aggressive effort to put its myriad legal problems behind it. And indeed, by the following summer, it had resolved virtually all of the cases that had been brought against it – including, most significantly, the huge government fraud investigation that had prompted the embarrassing FBI raid. In June 1994, XYZ reached a landmark $380 million settlement with the federal government and 28 states, under which the two-year-old probe was dropped, allowing the company to face the future unencumbered by the consequences of its long-ago misdeeds.

Its troubles finally behind it, XYZ – which eventually moved its headquarters and changed its name – went from weakness to strength. By 1997, its stock had quintupled in value from its 1993 low, and the company had come to be widely regarded as the very model of a modern major health-care company. Indeed, the best indication of the firm's total rehabilitation was the fact that when the nation's largest hospital chain, Columbia/HCA, found itself the target of federal investigators in the summer of 1997, the old XYZ Company was held up as an example of how the for-profit hospital business should be practiced – and was widely touted as a potential rescuer of its embattled rival. As The *New York Times* noted, "That XYZ even has a good name to bestow on a huge combined entity is evidence of its recovery from its own scandals."

At bottom, what made the recovery effort at XYZ so successful wasn't spin, of course, but the fact that its management was extremely competent and completely sincere. Simon and his people really were genuinely determined to reform the company. That was crucial, for as I warned everyone at the beginning of the process, while cleverly-phrased announcements of 30-, 60-, and 90-day improvement timetables can buy you a little breathing room, the public has an annoying habit of remembering self-imposed deadlines. So while you may get a bit of a break at the beginning, if you don't actually get your corrective programs up and running in earnest, you're going to be in big trouble 30 or 60 or 90 days hence when the press comes back to check up on how it's all going.[5]

FOCUS AND FRAME YOUR MESSAGES

As we've observed, you need to tell a consistent story to every constituency. But you also need to recognize that various constituents will approach the same set of facts with differing biases, understandings, hopes, and fears. You need to put yourself into the shoes of your audience. Address the "me" questions: "What's going to happen to me?" or "What's in this for me?"

A classic need to frame the story arises in bankruptcy cases. When employees first learn that a company is filing for protection under Chapter 11, their first reaction is that they will soon be out of work. The financial and legal professionals who are advising a company know otherwise, and take it for granted that most employees will not be affected by a bankruptcy filing *per se*. Financial reporters may or may not understand that fact. But you absolutely need to give assurance to your employees in a situation like this that their paychecks will continue to come out at the normal time, that banks are required by law to honor those checks, that benefits will continue (in most cases), etc.

The story that you're filing under Chapter 11 must be communicated to all your constituents – customers, vendors, employees, investors, lenders, and community leaders at your factory locations, just to name a few. But each constituency will need to have that information framed and focused with particular details in order for it to make sense. For your employees, it's a job security question. For the president of the local school board in your factory town, it's a question of what's going to happen to property tax payments that she needs to keep the school running.

You also need to explain to your constituents why certain facts are important, even if they don't seem so...what we call the "so what?" factor. People will pay a lot more attention to factual information if they understand its significance.

USE FACTUAL SOURCES OF UNIMPEACHABLE VERACITY

Some facts are more believable than others. When you have a choice, lean on facts that others are more likely to believe. What sort of sources do people tend to believe more? The following constitutes an approximate, informal relative ranking

---

[5] Our job completed, we ceased work for XYZ in the late 1990s. In April 2005, a newspaper article reported that the federal government intended to sue the company, formerly known as XYZ, its former CEO and five other former executives over the hospital chain's Medicare billing payments. The article said that the company abandoned its controversial billing practice in early 2003, a few months after they came to light. Lawyers for both the former CEO and the named executives denied any wrongdoing.

of trust of various sources of information, synthesized from our experience and a variety of public opinion polls.

1. Any fact that is published in a nationally prominent newspaper or magazine. "According to an article in The *Wall Street Journal*[6]...." is a phrase that will almost always heighten the credibility of any factual claim, even if the *Journal* article itself is quoting a source whose veracity might be suspect if he states a fact directly. Why is this so? Because there is an assumption – not always accurate, but nevertheless widely held – that publications like The *Journal* and the *New York Times* will verify the factual accuracy of any statement that they use, even in a quote. For this reason alone, media placements should be a major factor in any rational communication strategy related to enterprise transformation. What's written about your enterprise in the media is more likely to be believed than almost any other source.

2. Evaluations and statements made by Non Governmental Organizations (NGOs), especially "watchdog" groups, consumer advocacy groups, and the like. They're perceived as having the interests of "the little guy" at heart, and now are generally regarded as more trustworthy than governments themselves.

3. Studies, reports and proclamations by academic institutions – especially major research universities – and statements by individual faculty members of such universities. Academics have a high "trust" factor because people think they are pure seekers of truth. Again, the facts are often otherwise. Professors hire themselves out as consultants and advisors to businesses all the time, and essentially lease their credibility to the client. Some journalists are becoming skeptical of "hired gun" professors, but in general they maintain high believability.

4. "Independent" think tank organizations, even when privately funded, such as RAND Corp. have high credibility. Politically focused think tanks like the Reason Institute are still respected, but likely to be perceived as coming from a particular point of view.

5. Trusted individuals – a pastor, a doctor, a respected community volunteer, etc.

6. Any facts obtained from *any* independent third party or source who doesn't have a dog in your fight.

7. Facts obtained from "non partisan" government sources. People generally place high credence in reports and facts issued by the Government Accounting Office (GAO), for example, and by other agencies that do not have a history of political controversy, such as the Centers for Disease Control (CDC) or the Securities and Exchange Commission (SEC). Government proclamations

---

[6] You could substitute any major media outlet: The *New York Times*, *Los Angeles Times*, Newsweek, CBS News, etc.

tinged with political partisan overtones have less credibility, though they still fare better than statements by for-profit corporations.

8. Reports filed by corporations and institutions to government agencies like the SEC – especially when there are stiff penalties for lying in such reports. People are a lot more likely to believe what a company says in its Form 10-K than in an advertisement.

9. Almost anything asserted as a factual statement in a legal filing. Of course, legal proceedings are often riddled with mis-statements, factual distortions, and even outright lies, but the public presumption is that if you say something in a document that's filed with the court, it must be true. Would anyone lie to the court system? Yes, of course! But that's not the general perception.

10. Similarly, any testimony given either in person or in writing while the party is under oath and faces legal or financial sanctions for lying.

11. The Internet. Yes, that same place filled with emails offering variations of the Nigerian Scam, reports of abductions by UFOs, bizarre theories about the creation of the universe, spam, pornography, endless pop-up ads selling low-cost drugs, performance enhancement aids, low-cost mortgages, and the job opportunity of a lifetime. *That* Internet. How has the Internet gained credibility? Because of Blogs (a shortened form of Web Log, an online diary or commentary). Blogs have changed the nature of journalism, and the nature of communication on almost any subject that people care about. Well-established Blogs have real credibility, because every day they put themselves in front of Internet readers and critics who are all too ready, willing, and able to challenge statements made on a Blog. The Blog-o-sphere has become incredibly effective at ferreting out factual inaccuracies, lies, misrepresentations, and general baloney. The Internet also holds an incredible trove of information about you, your opponents, your issues, your constituents, and everything else that will come into play as you communicate regarding enterprise transformation. It's impossible today to discount the Internet, despite the weirdness, misinformation, and general lack of organization that characterizes much of its content.

When faced with a variety of potential sources of information, take the time and make the effort to establish the relative veracity of various sources. Publicly available research can often guide you usefully. For example, in a report issued in New Jersey regarding health care issues (http://www.njabr.org/media/research america), attitudes toward various sources of information were ranked as follows: "New Jersey residents consider the most trustworthy sources of information about health and medical research issues to be personal physicians, nurses, medical schools, and dentists. In fact, about 94% consider their personal physician to be very or somewhat credible, and 92% express this general sentiment about nurses. Additionally, 91% find medical schools credible, and doctors garner credibility from 90% of state residents. Pharmaceutical companies are considered significantly less credible, with less than three-fourths saying they are either very or somewhat credible, followed distantly by Health Maintenance Organizations (HMOs)." Data in the survey report tellingly show that as "very trusted" sources, personal physicians got a 66% rating, while pharmaceutical companies got only a 20% "very trusted" rating and HMOs got only 7%! All other ranked sources had a "very trusted" rating of at least 42% in this survey, which illustrates the uphill battle that for-profit corporations face in almost any public dispute where facts are at issue.

This sort of evaluation can be very valuable to anyone planning a communications campaign. For example, if you are an advocate for more drug research funding, would you rather have the backing of family physicians or HMOs? If you're an HMO, what would you do to establish credibility if you were on one side of a fight and a government agency were on the other? One thing you might consider is using data obtained from private physicians and their organizations, such as medical societies, or from medical schools.

TAKE CONTROL

If you don't take control and tell your own story, someone else will. (The Barneys New York example cited earlier is a perfect example.) You need to fill the void or someone else will do it for you. If you don't there is a real possibility that the media and others could frame the story in a way that is not favorable to you or your organization.

It is essential to understand a related issue about public reputations. While you may be innocent until proven guilty in a court of law, in the court of public opinion the burden of proof with respect to innocence is on the accused. Sometimes by taking control, by acting strategically and preemptively, you can significantly change the facts and alter the fate of the enterprise transformation. We did exactly this for a client in Colorado.

A lawyer with whom we had worked on a previous case was phoning from Denver to ask us to help out with some damage control. "We're going to liquidate the Purgatory Ski Resort," he explained bluntly. The shutdown, he added, would throw several hundred people out of work and devastate the economy of the southwestern Colorado town of Durango.

"Why are they liquidating it?" I asked.

"The bank is refusing to renew their line of credit," he said.

"Why? Is Purgatory losing money?"

"Not at all. In fact, it's moderately profitable."

"So what's going on?"

With a discouraged sigh, the lawyer explained that the United Bank of Denver, which had been providing Purgatory with financing for more than a decade, had recently been sold to a larger, out-of-state bank. Though nothing about Purgatory's financial health had changed -- indeed, it had just come off of one of its most successful seasons ever -- the new management had abruptly decided to cut off the resort's credit line. Ski resorts generally depend on such lines to get them through the moribund summer months, when revenues are almost non-existent but expenses – which include advertising and marketing for the upcoming winter – are high. Purgatory was typical: each summer it would meet its cash needs by drawing $2 million or so from its credit line, which it would pay back with interest when business picked up again at the end of the year. Without its credit line, there would be no way for Purgatory to meet its payroll, no less afford the promotional efforts necessary to make the next ski season a success.

"We're still talking to the bank, hoping to change its mind," the lawyer concluded, "but it doesn't look good."

I thought about all this for a moment. "How recently was the bank sold?" I asked.

"Not that long ago," the lawyer replied. "The deal was just finalized within the last few weeks."

"In that case," I said, "I don't believe you're going to have to close the place after all."

"Why?" the lawyer asked with disbelief. "Do you know some arcane Colorado banking law that we don't?" "No," I said, "I have enough trouble practicing public relations, without trying to practice law. But tell me this: what do you think the governor of Colorado is going to say when the *Denver Post* asks him if he considered the impact on the state's most important industry, the ski industry, when he approved the sale of Purgatory's bank to an out-of-state institution? What is he going to say when they ask him if he bothered to inquire whether the bank intended to continue supporting businesses within Colorado? What is he going to say when they ask him if he was aware that one of the new management's first acts would be to devastate an entire town of 2,500 people? What do you think the state banking commissioner is going to say?"

There was dead silence on the other end of a line. After a long moment, the lawyer finally spoke up. "How soon can you guys be here?" he asked. My colleague David McAdam was on a 6:30 A.M. flight to Denver the next morning.

Determining just what the objective happens to be – and then tailoring your actions accordingly – is one of the most important elements to enterprise transformation. Business school professors call this management by objective, and I happen to be a great believer in it. Whenever I take on a new client, the first thing I do is try to determine exactly what his objective is. More often than you might think, the client is as in the dark about his real aims as I am. He thinks he knows why he called me – to get his name in the papers, he might insist, or to keep it out – but after a bit of discussion he may come to realize that what he's actually seeking to achieve is something else entirely.

The lawyer for Purgatory, for example, thought he was calling Sitrick And Company in order to get some help containing the bad publicity he correctly assumed would accompany an announcement that the resort was going out of business. And had he phoned a regular public relations firm there's a good chance that's precisely what he would have gotten. A traditional PR man would have gone promptly to work doing just what the lawyer had asked – drafting a press release, drawing up a list of media contacts, fashioning a damage-control plan. The liquidation of Purgatory would have proceeded apace, and within a few days or weeks the resort would have been history – along with all those jobs and a good-sized chunk of the local economy.

But that's not really what the lawyer was hoping to accomplish. What he really wanted more than anything else was to keep the resort open – to find a way to restore the credit line that the bank had canceled. By questioning him closely I was not only able to uncover this more fundamental objective, I was also able to discern the elements of a solution to his problem.

In the end, what I wound up doing was actually rather simple. Over the weekend, I phoned up the business editor of the Denver Post.

"I've got a story that will knock your socks off," I told him. "But before I say another word, here's the deal. My clients still think there's a chance they'll be able to negotiate their way out of this. So I'll give you this information on two conditions: one, that it's off the record until I say otherwise; and two, that if my clients are successful in their negotiations, this conversation never happened – meaning that nothing of what I'm going to tell you can ever appear in your paper."

The editor didn't hesitate. "Deal," he said.

"Oh, and one more thing," I added. "I'm going to give you this story exclusively, but in return I want major play."

"Mike," he responded, "you know I can't guarantee anything. But if the story is as good as you say, there shouldn't be any problem."

That was good enough for me, and I proceeded to lay out for him the story of Purgatory and its cancelled credit line.

"God," the editor said when I'd finished, "I sure hope your clients' negotiations aren't successful."

As it turned out, they weren't. The following Monday, representatives of Purgatory met with bank officials for three hours – at the end of which the bank told them to take a hike.

We phoned the *Denver Post* late in the afternoon to let them know what had happened. After we'd finished briefing the reporter who'd been assigned to the story, she put in calls to the new bank owner and the governor's office. By then, however, it was early evening, and no one was available in either place to offer an immediate comment.

The next morning, her story appeared on the front page of the *Post*'s business section, under the ominous headline, "Resort Faces Closure." Noting that the bank's inexplicable decision seemed to leave Purgatory with no choice but to shut down, the story pointed out that the resort provided more than 700 jobs at the height of the ski season (making it La Plata County's biggest employer) and poured more than $45 million in gross revenues into the local economy.

Not surprisingly, no sooner had the *Post* hit the newsstands with its Purgatory story then all hell broke loose. Both the governor and the state's chief banking regulator labeled the bank's actions outrageous, and a state senator called for an investigation. The bank itself, apparently having gotten a call from the governor's office (or so we were told), issued a statement from its out-of-state headquarters insisting there must have been some sort of misunderstanding.

More stories followed. More politicians got into the act. By Wednesday, the bank and Purgatory were in negotiations. By the end of the week, the bank had not only agreed to restore Purgatory's credit line, but also to make a significant reduction in the interest rate it charged. The resort's future was once again secure. And there was no longer any need to do any damage control.

BE CONSISTENT

As indicated earlier, it is critical that you be consistent both in what you say and how often you say it. Having said that, things do change.

What do you do then? Communicate what happened and why. If you say there are not going to be any layoffs, but then find two weeks later that you have lost a major order and, as a result, now have to cut costs – including staff – make sure this fact is communicated to your key constituents. Employees may not like it, but they will understand it and respect you for being honest with them. On the other hand, if you just affect the layoffs and other cost cutting measures without any explanation, there is a good chance that the "grapevine" will assume you knew it all the time and purposely misled them for some unknown reason.

It is also important for a variety of reasons that you communicate regularly in an enterprise transformation. To make repeated communication possible, you need to establish, maintain, and nurture the communications channels through which you can reach your constituencies. In an enterprise transformation situation, for example, you need to communicate regularly with employees. You need to tell them your goals, your vision, and your strategy. You need to tell them what it will look like when the enterprise has been transformed. You need to describe the signposts they will see on the road from where they are to the place you want to lead them.

All that requires a continuous flow of communication. We often recommend that during difficult situations – and most enterprise transformations are difficult by nature – that leaders use the mode of communication that their audience is most accustomed to using. But this is far from a hard and fast rule. Suppose that the old form of communication (say, a weekly printed newsletter) hasn't been working well because you can't get it distributed in a timely manner. You don't want to keep using it. Consider alternatives: emails or an Intranet (if most employees have access to the Internet on a daily basis). Blast faxes that are posted on bulletin boards. "Tailgate" remarks by managers to address employees before they jump into their trucks and head out for a day's work in the field. You need to do some research to find out how your constituents (such as employees) would prefer to receive information, whom they most trust as sources (the CEO, or first line supervisor?) and how often they would like to get information. Crank all that data into your decision about communications channels. And remember that in a transformational situation, the mere fact that you are establishing a new means of communication sends a positive signal that you are serious about transformation.

Make sure you establish methods of feedback from your constituents back to the top of the enterprise. This serves three purposes. First, it lets your constituents know that you care about their opinions. Second, it provides a good way to find out whether your messages are getting through, are held as credible, and are affecting the way people act. Third, it provides a natural opportunity for repetition of key messages. For example, a CEO could set up a weekly email system to all employees. In it, he could say, "Joe Jones of Nashville wrote and asked if our new growth strategy means we will be dumping older product lines. Good question, Joe! The answer is that we will evaluate each product along the lines I mentioned a couple of weeks ago – are we in a dominant position in the marketplace with this product? Does it have good growth potential? Do we have good margins? We don't care whether a product is brand new or has been around for decades. If it meets our key tests to sustain growth, we'll keep it. If it doesn't, we'll either fix the problems or get out of that line of business."

CLOSING THOUGHTS

Many people characterize what we do as communications professionals: reviewing the facts, determining which are the most relevant and presenting them in a concise, persuasive fashion as "Spin." While I would not dispute that characterization, I would dispute most people's understanding of that term.

As I stated in the last chapter of my book (Sitrick & Mayer, 1998), which not coincidentally is entitled, "Spin," popular impressions to the contrary, our notion of spin has nothing to do with obfuscation and misdirection. (Or as Harry Truman once put it, "If you can't convince 'em, confuse 'em.") Rather, it's built on the recognition that while you're not likely to win in the long run if the facts are against you, simply having the facts on your side is not enough. In order to carry the day, you must also know how to present them effectively. That, in a nutshell, is all spin is -- effective presentation.

Regardless of the circumstances, (however,) there is one tool no spin doctor can do without -- credibility. The ability to persuade, after all, depends almost entirely on one's credibility. Eloquence, technical expertise, and a sense of drama -- all these qualities can help. Without credibility, however, they are so much empty wind.

Credibility, of course, is not a technique. It is an empirical characteristic; a quality that derives from nothing else but consistently demonstrated truthfulness -- which is to say that it is as fragile as it is powerful. Once it has been called into question, it can take years to restore. The implications of this fact of public life are obvious (or should be): the smart (executive should never do) anything that could damage his credibility..."

The classical Greek tragedian Sophocles had it right some five centuries before Christ. "The truth, he noted, is always the strongest argument. Nearly 2,500 years later, would-be executives attempting enterprise transformation ignore his advice at their peril.[7]

REFERENCES

DiNapoli, D. (Ed.).(1999). Workouts and turnarounds II: Global restructuring strategies for the next century. New York: Wiley.

DiNapoli, D., Sigoloff, S.C., & Cushman, R.F. (Eds.).(1991). Workouts and turnarounds: The handbook of restructuring and investing in distressed companies. Burr Ridge, IL: Irwin Professional.

Sitrick, M., & Mayer, A. (1998). Spin: How to turn the power of the press to your advantage. Washington, DC: Regnery Publishing.

---

[7] Several of the examples in this book, as well as the conclusion are from the book, Spin," published by Regnery in 1998and written by Michael Sitrick, with Allan Mayer.

CHAPTER 17

LESSONS FROM THE TRANSFORMATION FRONT

WALLACE P. BURAN AND W. BRUCE CHEW

ABTRACT

This chapter summarizes the "lessons learned" from both successful and unsuccessful enterprise transformation initiatives. The goal is to arm the reader with successful practices and warn of potential pitfalls and fatal moves drawn from years of direct transformation involvement and research by the authors and The Monitor Group. Two major types of enterprise transformation are identified and defined. This chapter compares and contrasts the two types of transformation and the different aspirations and business challenges they address. Type I transformations are centered on *focus* and *performance*; they are built on breakthroughs in control. Type II transformations are centered on *capabilities* and *advantage*; they are built on breakthroughs in integration. Perhaps the single most striking insight for practitioners is the crucial role a well-chosen and well-defined "pivot point" plays in successful transformations. An initiative's "pivot point" is defined and the manner in which it provides both guidance and leverage for the organization is illustrated and explored. Finally, the relationship of enterprise transformation to strategy is considered.

INTRODUCTION: LESSONS FROM THE "FRONT"

Over the last twenty years the authors have performed, identified, initiated, motivated, trained, led, sometimes forced, (and in some cases, cleaned-up-after) enterprise transformations. For that reason, we were asked to reflect on the hard-won wisdom -- such as it is --of our experience; wisdom dubbed "Lessons From the Front." We like to think the title conjures up images of intrepid war correspondents broadcasting from "Somewhere Behind Enemy Lines." A trip to Merriam-Webster's Online Dictionary, however, suggests a different, richer, albeit less dramatic picture. There are many potential meanings for "The Front"; all of them surprisingly apt.

Initially, we had in mind "Front" as in "Vanguard" ("the troops moving ahead of an army (or) the forefront of an action or movement") with "forefront" and "moving ahead" both central to enterprise transformation. The military's use regarding "a line of battle (or) a zone of conflict between armies" also seems to fit, though the "armies" are typically *within* the enterprise with the "line of battle" typically drawn between tradition and transformation.

But the non-military definitions fit equally well. The "Front" can be "a stand on an issue (or) an area of activity (as study or debate)." Enterprise transformation certainly involves all of those elements. It can be, appropriately enough, "a position of leadership or superiority." And in far too many situations we have seen the "Front" prove to be a "feigned appearance especially in the face of danger or adversity" or "a boundary between two dissimilar air masses" (leading all too often to violent storms).

Perhaps the most appropriate definition derives from the political sense of a "Front"; namely "a movement linking divergent elements to achieve common objectives." For discussion here we will focus less on the challenge of "winning the battle" or even "weathering the storm." We will try to draw lessons from our experience and research in trying to identify and communicate "common objectives" and drawing together those "divergent elements" to achieve enterprise transformation. Though to put that challenge in perspective, we will try to hold onto one more definition of "the Front." Enterprise transformation is not "a process" or a "one-time event." When most successful, it meets the archaic definition of "Front": "a <u>Beginning</u>".

TWO TYPES OF TRANSFORMATION

Like it or not, every organization has and/or will face the need for transformation. The need arises from the dynamics inherent in the competitive landscape. Success, i.e., longevity in the marketplace, guarantees that eventually enterprise transformation will be called for. Whether it is opportunistic (in pursuit of the potential inherent in a new market or technology), prudent (in response to a competitor's move, emerging regulations or evolving customer tastes) or desperate (to countermand falling profits or market share) it is above all inevitable.

The different drivers of the need for transformation provide one frame for investigation. Another would be the tools/methodologies used by managers in the transformation process. But our point-of-view centers on value creation and value capture. Ultimately all enterprise transformations are about value; and one critical test of a "true" transformation is the Value Creation Test. True enterprise transformations create new value; and successful ones capture a significant portion of the new value created. Enterprise initiatives that merely deploy new mechanisms to capture existing value are not what we consider here as enterprise transformations (great initiatives, yes; transformations, no).

With a focus on the link to value we find two types of enterprise transformation. These are not derived from theory or the result of a clever taxonomy. They are based on our observance of a pattern in the work we've done with firms. There are two different situations under which we've seen firms realize a *major* increase in value (measured as shareholder return, positive cash-flow, return on capital, profitable sales growth or whatever metric is preferred). The distinction between the two is important because it impacts management challenges, and should impact management actions and expectations. Furthermore it highlights an often-misunderstood connection between performance improvement and enterprise transformation.

Linking Performance Improvement and Value Creation

Successful improvement programs tend to follow a predictable path. After some initial floundering, they show dramatic early improvement with diminishing absolute gains over time (although the percentage improvement may be more constant). Operating performance metrics, then, tend to follow one of the patterns shown in Figure 1; rising with diminishing gains (e.g., on-time product launches, sales-call-conversion-to-sales rate) or falling with diminishing reductions (e.g., defects, order-fulfillment-time). The performance value approached may be established by a world-class or best-in-class benchmark or an absolute limit (like zero inventory). How does management's widespread experience with operating improvements relate to enterprise transformation?

Naive observers might expect the company that experiences the gains shown in Figure 1 to have its financial returns mirror the operating performance profile. Such a direct-drive relationship is shown in Figure 2. "Since a firm is a collection of processes," this logic goes, "process improvement should translate directly into enhanced financial performance."

There are a number of problems with this plausible but false logic. First, there are competitive and marketplace forces that shape financial returns independently of internal operating performance. Second, the gains shown are examined through a narrow window; performance improvements here might be offset by falling performance elsewhere creating potentially offsetting competitive impacts (e.g., inventories may go to zero while our on-time deliveries deteriorate dramatically).

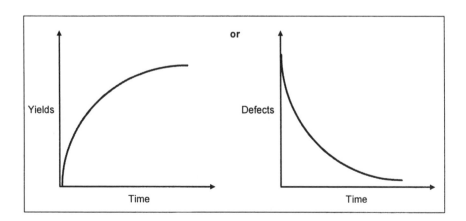

FIGURE 1. Patterns of Performance Improvement

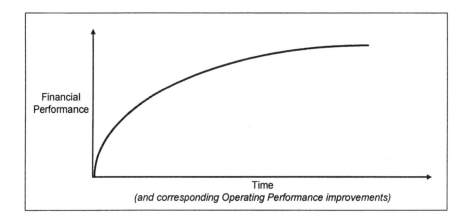

FIGURE 2. Hypothetical (but generally not realized) Financial Performance Expected From Operating Improvements

But our interest here is in a more basic problem with the logic. Operating performance, when examined metric by metric, is driven by the effectiveness and efficiency of processes. Financial performance, on the other hand, is driven by the effectiveness of the enterprise's business model relative to those of its competitors. While an enterprise's operations may usefully be thought of as a collection of processes, *an enterprise's business model is an interdependent system*. The performance of the whole is not the simple sum of the parts. System effects like feedback, delays, bottlenecks, critical paths, thresholds, non-linearities, tipping points, etc. overwhelm the simple one-to-one mapping of added improvements to additional dollars.

But in a strange way this is good news for the manager. If competition were simply a never ending race among operating metrics, we would all become Lewis Carrol's Red Queen exclaiming that "here, you see, it takes all the running you can do, to keep in the same place. If you want to get somewhere else, you must run at least twice as fast as that!" But the actual patterns we have observed in breakthrough financial performance are not one-to-one maps of operating performance. Instead we see two distinct opportunities for breakthroughs; both of which are enterprise transformation with common as well as differing characteristics. The timing and the value impact of the two are shown in Figure 3.

Improvements in financial performance do not slowly accrue; rather they occur as breakthrough changes, the hallmark of enterprise transformation. *Type I transformations are associated with increasing levels of control and focus.* Waste in a variety of forms is eliminated and an enterprise-wide focus on where and how to make money is achieved. In a quality-driven transformation this occurs when processes are now "capable" and "in control" in a technical sense. In a customer-portfolio-driven transformation this occurs when "target customers" are identified and pursued (while others receive less or no attention). In both cases, however, to enjoy the significant financial gains shown the changes must ripple through the organization well beyond the relatively narrow focus areas described above. These focus areas can be thought of as pivot points on which the transformation turns (more on the critical role of pivot points is discussed below).

In Figure 3 the Type I transformation gains bring a step change in value which typically lays the ground work for continual incremental improvement going forward. For the industry's performance leader, this step change should lead to short-run superior returns. For the process improvement followers it will cause them to "catch-up" to the leader's returns (and may bring down the leader's return in the process). For the very late followers, the Type I transformation will bring them up close to industry average performance (assuming they still have the resources available to successfully transform). In all cases there is a step up in returns in absolute terms, though timing impacts the nature of relative returns. While this is obviously important,, it is not the determinant of whether a Transformation is Type I or Type II.

Type I transformations have a primarily internal, performance focus, though often the stated reasons and drivers have an external root. In effect, these efforts can best be characterized as "doing more -- and more valuable things --with less". That is not to imply these transformations are less challenging, less dramatic or less valuable to the companies and owners involved. They are among the highest short-term value-creating activities a firm can undertake and represent some of the most publicized enterprise transformations. They are generally focused, however, on improving the organization's relative performance level within the current constraints of their industry, competitive structure and customer channels. In effect, Type I transformation programs seek to play the game at a fundamentally higher level, not change the game.

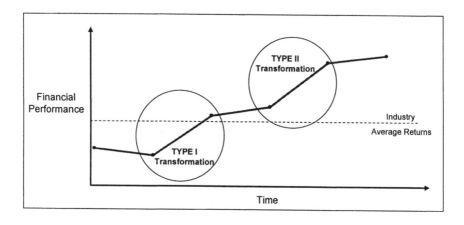

FIGURE 3. Two Types of Enterprise Transformation

Table 1 provides a "short-hand" summary of some of the typical distinguishing characteristics of transformation Types I and II. Type II transformations pursue a fundamentally different game in order to forego the Red Queen's race. While Type I involves a breakthrough in performance, *Type II transformations require a breakthrough in meeting customer needs and the economics to do so*. Alignment and focus are critical to both, but Type II transformations will align and focus *uniquely* in their industry. Type II is about aligning distinctive capabilities to create defensible market and/or economic advantage.

Are Type I gains greater than Type II gains? They can be, but generally are not over the long term. Much depends on how great is the distinctive value of the Type II transformation, how sustainable is the advantage and, ironically, on how "out of control" things have become prior to a Type I Transformation. The more impaired current operations are, the greater will be the benefit of gaining control and focus (that is, if it's not too late). Is Type II more defensible than Type I? It can be, but much depends on the nature of the transformation. Ironically, all else being equal, the harder the transformation was to achieve (especially with regard to integrated system effects) the more defensible it is likely to be!

Differentiating Characteristics	Type I Transformations *playing the game better*	Type II Transformations *playing by different rules*
Goal	Creating Greater Value	Creating Unique Value
Customers	*Who* best to Serve?	*How* best to serve?
Focus	Breakthrough performance	Breakthrough Business Model
Parties Involved	Entire Organization: achieve control and a common purpose throughout the organization	Extended Enterprise: reach out to customers / partners / suppliers to transform along with us
Behavior and Rewards	Select and reward behaviors that are competitive	Select and reward behaviors that can be leveraged in the marketplace
Execution	It's all about execution	It's all about what we are executing toward
Alignment	Align the organization's operations to achieve targeted results	Align the organization's capabilities to achieve advantage

TABLE 1. Distinctions Between Types of Transformations

Both Types can yield dramatic financial gains. But those gains are not automatic. In Type I transformations, greater operating control (in either a technical statistical sense or a broader managerial sense) enables less fire-fighting and greater reliability, which make a focus on profitable activities possible. Greater control and focus make the enterprise manageable, but they do not automatically bring the changes in management that lead to financial breakthroughs. In Type II transformations, it is often the achievement of new performance levels that make unique value creation possible. But it requires a redirection of the enterprise to take advantage of that opportunity and retain the value created for their shareholders. Both types thus require strong leadership and entail risks; not least because they both mandate disruptive, broad-based and discontinuous change.

A brief (and somewhat disguised) experience the authors had at "DrillCo" may help to make the distinction between enterprise transformation Types I and II more concrete:

A Tale of Two Transformations

Baseline at DrillCo: At roughly $400 million in sales, DrillCo was one of the three major full-line competitors in the industrial drill bit market (industry disguised). To paraphrase <u>A Tale of Two Cities</u> to fit the situation at DrillCo when we first became involved: "It was the worst of times and it was the worst of times." DrillCo was one of the higher cost producers of industrial drill bits selling to customers who seemed to care only about price.

Drill bits are sold to a wide variety of machining customers who typically operate in industries sustained on very narrow margins. These customers worry obsessively about their costs. Drill bits – while a small yet highly visible element of total customer costs -- were not thought of as "value-added" items by customers. Drill bits were classed as "consumables", i.e., they were worn out and replaced as part of the manufacturing process. As such, purchasing agents were instructed to minimize the cost of drill bits. This would seem to open the door for "longer-lived" drill bits, but over time customers had increasingly determined their optimal drill bit configurations (taking into account issues such as hardness of material, machining speed, bit hardness, number of passes, cutting angle and so on) and demanded every supplier to meet these specifications exactly. Worse, any higher performance drill bits that allowed customers to get longer tool life (and therefore generate higher prices and margins) required most customers to restudy work standards and renegotiate incentives and piece work rates. Few companies were willing to take on this effort in union environments. This meant both little ability to differentiate product in terms of the (customer controlled) specification and an enormous proliferation of bits of every shape and size to precisely meet the needs of a particular customer's specific application.

As if this marketplace challenge weren't enough, DrillCo had its own set of internal challenges. The plant had historically been run on a piece rate system with the established rates varying widely (and sometimes wildly) across bits. This led to a scheduling system driven by "worker preferences" rather than market demand. The result was overproduction (and lots of inventory) of drill bits where the piece rate was set higher than reasonable; and underproduction and long lead times where the piece rate was considered "unattractive". To further complicate what some considered an "out of control" workforce, materials flows were also out of control. The combination of recalcitrant workers, mushrooming product variety, complex set-ups, proliferating rush orders, traveling bottlenecks, and inventory's shop floor overflow meant that simply finding orders and forcing them through the process consumed most of management's time that was not devoted to handling irate customers.

Type I: Speed as a Transformer: Here clearly was a candidate for change, sweeping change. They had fallen behind in the process improvement race and needed to enhance performance significantly just to reach average industry returns. One prominent option was to sell off the DrillCo name and assets to a recent foreign entrant into the North American market. That option's financial consequences were clearly superior to continuing with business as usual, and there were those that argued for it. The alternative was to try to transform the enterprise. This would entail a massive amount of change in the individual worker on the floor, in management effort (both focus and frankly quantity), in the culture, and in customers' perceptions. There were those who felt that such a dramatic change was unlikely to succeed and, specifically, the union would strike which could sound a death knell for the business and hurt the sell-off value of DrillCo's name and assets.

The decision was made to transform the enterprise and a number of managers chose early retirement rather than participate in the effort (some self-selected this option, some of the strongest opponents of the transformation program had it suggested to them). The initial focus was not on forcing new union contract terms, but on gaining control of the materials flow. Specifically the focus was squarely on customer lead-times (and hence minimizing work-in-process and process predictability). Lead time was an excellent choice for this enterprise's transformation because it:

- Was (after senior management's data-driven communication) recognized as a critical competitive problem by all constituencies,

- Served as a high leverage, long term focal point (see pivot points discussion below) for the organization

- Impacted virtually every function within the company

- Required a system-wide approach (only insignificant gains could be made at any one point)

- Could not be solved by "buying something" (new inventory-tracking-and-scheduling systems might make it easier to find orders among the chaos, but the shop-floor reality has to change before the advantages IT offered could really be exploited)

- Lent itself to clear, concrete observable measurement (both in terms of external and internal metrics and customer anger and the "piles of stuff" clogging the shop)

- Increased the overall visibility and timely recognition of a host of other issues

Significantly, as a result of the above, as lead times and inventories were reduced, the increased visibility of operations made the dysfunctional nature of some worker practices transparent. This, coupled with management's clear commitment to the operations future, led to a new approach to setting piece rates and managing production without a strike.

Roughly nine months after the initiative was launched the organization had seen its economics transformed. DrillCo was now a well-controlled, smooth flow, lower inventory, customer-responsive organization. Focused factory concepts were implemented and customer orders were segmented to match specific focused factory capabilities, and team based incentives based on order specific asset utilization within a focused factory were implemented. Workers produced what was needed at more reasonable cost. Scheduling was no longer fire-fighting. Marketers could talk with customers about the true positives of buying from DrillCo and focus on those customers that were most attractive. Product engineering could now talk with customers about their future needs without the caveat the DrillCo bits are likely to delay your product launch. In concert these changes led to a classic Type I transformation of the enterprise and a step function change in financial performance (see Figure 4).

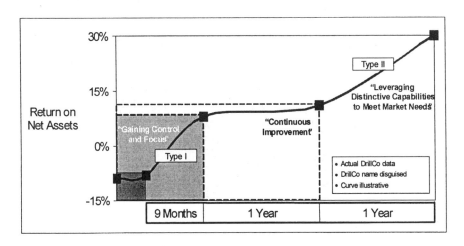

FIGURE 4. Enterprise Transformations at DrillCo

This situation went on, continuously improving and reinforcing itself in a virtuous cycle for another 12 months. The story might have ended there but for the realization that the plant had achieved one-day production cycle time on most products. By itself this simply added incrementally to the gains that had accrued when DrillCo's order cycle reached one week, then three days, then two days, then three shifts and finally one day. DrillCo's second transformation built on the speed resulting from its Type I transformation, but it was triggered not by this ongoing improvement in cycle time, but by discussions that began with a lunch shared between the operations and marketing managers.

Type II: Leveraging Distinctive Capabilities: Over lunch, the operations manager, having received the congratulations of the marketing manager for the recent gains, noted that DrillCo now had the fastest turnaround time in the industry, having delivered emergency customer orders from scratch over night in virtually all cases. The marketing manager had two initial thoughts. The first ("I don't believe you") he kept to himself. The second thought was that, if true, this distinctive capability could create a very powerful selling proposition for DrillCo.

Using close personal customer relationships, the marketing manager tested the operations manager's claim. Sure enough DrillCo could make and deliver (through FedEx) a drill bit order in 24 hours. The marketing manager then championed DrillCo's second transformation. He recognized that customers concerned about minimizing drill bit costs would value not having to inventory the dozens and dozens of types of bits they used. Overnight order fulfillment, while costing slightly more in delivery charges, would reduce overall customer costs by eliminating customer inventories. The customer would achieve their cost-focused goals, while DrillCo could use their 'Availability Guarantee" to win new customers and lock in more of their existing customer's business. The "overnight position" was defensible because while other firms could match the overnight *promise* they couldn't currently match the overnight *capability*. In order for them to offer overnight drill bits they would have to hold extensive finished parts in inventory – making their internal overnight economics highly unattractive.

Of course realizing those potential financial gains called for more than simply recognition of the opportunity. To make the new business model work, operations had to move from the ability to fill some orders overnight to the ability to reliably serve large numbers of overnight customers. DrillCo management needed to figure out how much "cushion" capacity to have and which types of drill bits (and how many) should still be made to inventory regardless of how they were ordered. Marketing had to identify and target those customers and bits that "fit" with their distinctive capabilities (e.g., customers with predictable drill bit usage patterns are easier to serve overnight than customers with sudden spikes in unexpected demand; if we're making to order, seasonal demand may create problems great enough that we should avoid those customers, and so on). Even product engineering had to take into account the impact new technologies would potentially have on overall process flows.

Once again, DrillCo found itself engaged in an enterprise transformation. Significant and disruptive changes throughout the organization were required for this classic Type II transformation. This time, however, the transformation was not driven by the desire to survive but by the desire to seize an opportunity. As such, it brought with it new leadership challenges. It's easy to persuade people to jump out of a plane when it's on fire. It's much harder when people are comfortably enjoying their flight.

As Drillco moved through its service-driven Type II Transformation and close working relationships with customers grew, several customers suggested new ideas for Drillco to develop new products. Drillco had developed the capability to extend tool life, remove more metal and hold tighter tolerances, but it cost more. Because most of it's customers were unwilling to renegotiate their labor standards to take advantage of Drillco's new product, sales were very disappointing. But working with several important customers, Drillco redefined and repackaged it's new product as a quality improvement innovation. This allowed customers to eliminate some previous manufacturing steps, because they could remove more metal and still achieve tight tolerances. The results were dramatic. Within nine months this "quality" enabling product was over 30% of total revenue at a 50% increase in margin. As the Division Manager stated, "if we had not been their delivery partner based on our "next day" service, we might never have seen the opportunity. We have gained over 13 points of market share from this product!"

This is a surprisingly common pattern in Type II transformations. As the leaders change the "rules of the game", they find new and unanticipated ways to play often initiated by their delighted customers. And the "frontier player" earns the right to capitalize on these new opportunities and their associated share and profit gains. Followers generally get only the new costs not the new business.

DrillCo: A Final Note: DrillCo experienced a Type I transformation, then after a "time out" from discontinuous change, initiated a successful Type II transformation. We find this to be the dominant pattern. Type I enterprise transformations seem to be a necessary prerequisite for troubled, underperforming organizations even if their long run goal is to change the game through a Type II transformation. Regardless of the opportunity to change the game, if the organization is not already well-controlled, focused and performing at a high level, attempting a Type II transformation virtually never works. Generally, all they accomplish is to prove out the transformational value to a competitor who is better able to take advantage of the opportunity, or worse, the failed transformation significantly hurts the organization's ability to compete at all due their demonstrated inability to deliver the promised new value.

Managers also tell us that the "time out" in between transformations is also a necessary step for the organization. As one manager vividly framed it "(during the Type I transformation) it was like we woke up every morning having to remember how to breathe all over again. That's how different the new world was. We needed breathing to become second nature again before we tackled another significant challenge." In this sense a "breather" between transformations is both a literal and figurative requirement.

While the "Type I – Breather –Type II" Transformation pattern is common, it is not universal. Many firms never recognize that the opportunity for Type II

Transformation exists. They fall into a pattern of Type I Transformation followed by a sense of "Good, now we've got it right!" followed by a slide into sub-average performance followed, if they're lucky, by another Type I Transformation (and in all likelihood another sigh of relief because "now we've got it right.").

This leaves the potential pattern of Type II alone. While launching a Type II transformation when a Type I is needed is a recipe for disaster, this does not mean that managers always recount Type I transformations prior to successful Type II transformations. We have seen Type II transformations without a prior Type I transformation identified. But careful scrutiny reliably uncovers one of three situations:

- *There was an earlier Type I Transformation but it wasn't identified as such.* Instead it was known as the "New Management Regime", the "Major Acquisition", "Going Global" or the "Big Asset Write-Off". But rarely does a single event (no matter how dramatic) turn around an enterprise's fortunes on its own. Often these are Type I transformations under another name.

- *There was no transformation "event" but incremental changes have led to substantive change.* Over time an enterprise can incrementally build up competitive levels of focus, control and execution. But the caveat is that the opportunity to build capabilities at this relatively leisurely pace requires a number of supporting marketplace and competitive characteristics to be in place.

- Finally, and perhaps most exciting among the "No-Priors" transformations, we find transformation-oriented firms aggressively pursuing new opportunities or proactively responding to new technologies and competitive moves. By pursuing change in the natural course of business, they rarely find themselves behind the industry's performance frontier and requiring a Type I transformation. *Through a series of Type II transformations, leading enterprises are continually pushing the frontier outward.*

Summary

We have identified two types of enterprise transformations and compared and contrasted them. What we have not done is identify the determinants of successful or unsuccessful transformations of either type. As we will we show, they share some determinants while other determinants differ between the two types of transformation. Further, the challenges of conducting one successful transformation differs from the challenge faced by the leading enterprises just discussed, i.e., the firms who consistently push the frontier through enterprise transformation. These determinants and challenges, as well as false impressions, necessary conditions, tricks-of-the-trade and potential traps, are all described below as we turn to the lessons from the leaders.

LESSONS FROM THE LEADERS

When searching for "best practices", "lessons learned" and "benchmarks" from successful enterprise transformations, care must be taken to validate the identification of successful transformations and the actual practices and efforts used to achieve them. Many pundits and observers have written extensively about enterprise transformations and the practices used, but unfortunately the vast majority of these writings fall into the realm of anecdotes and opinions. In extensively researching and working in this area over the last 20 years, we have found very little fact-based, objective findings upon which to base an assessment of either successful transformations or "best practices".

Beginning in 1988, we started taking a data driven approach to identifying "Top Performing Companies", and studying other organizations that had achieved step function changes in financial performance. We used a data and research intensive approach to spot Top Performing Companies based on publicly available financial data for the largest 6000 public companies that have consistently grown shareholder value, capital productivity, labor productivity and market position over the previous ten years. We call them simply Leaders. We then researched what they do differently function by function, what works, why it works, what does not work and what concepts and learning other companies can apply. The result is a body of knowledge we call "Frontier Practices".

So how well did these leaders perform? On average, the top 100 from our research generated between three and four times the total return to shareholders (stock price appreciation plus dividends) than did the Standard and Poors 500 companies did over any 10-year period for the last 15 years. Further, the top 100 grew capital productivity and their markets at a rate more than double the S&P 500 and the entire largest 6000 public companies. They are truly leaders for their owners, stakeholders and customers.

More recently, we built upon our own enterprise transformation experience and the extensive experience of our Monitor Group colleagues to assess the successful Enterprise Transformation Practices of these Leaders. The Monitor Group also studied a set of "No-Growth Transformers", firms that have substantially increased their market value (beyond that of others in their industry) without significant revenue growth. By definition (after accounting for announcements of forthcoming new technologies, acquisitions and so on) these No-Growth Transformers must have radically altered their economics for the better. The exciting findings from our research are that the leaders and other companies who have achieved measurable, successful financial results do approach enterprise transformation very differently from their less successful counterparts. The result is our "Frontier Practices in Enterprise Transformation". Over the last 5 plus years, we have been field testing, refining and applying these Frontier Practices in a number of client environments and in a range of different industries. The results have been encouraging and dramatic, with all clients obtaining at least the projected benefits anticipated, and most achieving multiples of the returns they expected.

Dispelling Some Myths

Before proceeding, however, it is important to dispel several myths and misconceptions that have grown up, and even been published, about leaders and how they achieve superior results. In fact, several widely held "everyone knows that" beliefs appear to be consistently wrong.

- **Myth: Superior performance goes to firms lucky enough to be in attractive industries or markets**. This may well be true, but leaders also exist in most industries even when the industry structure is unattractive and average industry performance is negative verses the S&P 500. Companies such as Nucor Steel and Cooper Tires have consistently outperformed the S&P 500 average in industries that in aggregate have significantly underperformed. Similarly, many companies have underperformed the average in high performing industries. It is about how you manage not just where you play.

- **Myth: Leaders have to be in growth markets.** They may be in growth markets, but leaders also emerge in declining markets. In fact, high growth markets often require such investment levels and deferral of value, some or most of which never occurs, that they under-perform the market. With regard to enterprise transformation, it is not the case that successful transformers are more likely to be in growing firms. Rather it is that in order to grow consistently, firms must be successful transformers.

- **Myth: Leadership goes to the firm that's willing to spend the most to buy it.** We found no technology or service offering that generated enterprise transformation type results, and purchased technology solutions were not correlated with successes. There was even some indication of a negative correlation with information technology based solutions. While many leaders and successful enterprise transformation companies used purchased technologies, including information systems solutions, we found no cases where purchased solutions drove or were even the major factor in transformation. We also found a number of failed transformations where information technology solutions were the driver. The clear message is that purchased technologies and capabilities can support and perhaps enhance transformation, but clear thinking and effective execution by the organization will be the driver of success.

- **Myth: Leadership results from world-class "*fill in function name here*"** One area or function cannot achieve breakthrough competitive performance results on its own (although it may achieve breakthrough levels on a given operating metric, as discussed earlier) While this may sound obvious from the term "enterprise transformation", it is clearly not obvious to many executives who in fact try to make step function changes along a narrow, functional front. All the successful enterprise transformations we have either studied or supported involved and required coordinated changes by multiple functions and these changes were highly integrated. Conversely, one function lagging behind could and did prevent a number of well-founded transformations from reaching their goals.

- **Myth: New directions call for new leaders.** While it is true that this type of discontinuous change calls for *new leadership* that does not necessarily require *new leaders*. This myth results from two common phenomena. First, moving from the original entrepreneur to a transformation necessitated by dramatic organizational growth and rising industry maturity is often seen to call for new managers. Whether this is because the original entrepreneur cannot do the task or simply would rather not do the task, the track record is fairly clear. But the majority of transformation efforts do not involve the management transition from enterprise creator to business managers. Second, and more to the point, it is common to see some managers step down leaving the firm or retiring early rather than be involved with a major transformation. In our experience, this is often a realistic reflection of how much effort is going to be required. Some managers simply do not feel they want to put forth that amount of effort at this point in their careers. But when the existing management team *does* embrace the new ideas and effort required for transformation it provides enormous credibility to the initiative.

- **Myth: The CEO must drive it personally.** In rare, yet highly publicized cases, CEO's do drive transformations personally. Cases like Microsoft's embracing the internet in the 1990's, Chrysler's return from the brink of bankruptcy, and IBM's shift to a leading information services company were led by very visible, visionary and personally engaged CEO's. But even in these companies where the business press lauded the role of the CEO, all of these talented executives were primarily the visionary and cheerleader who empowered others to drive change far more directly. Normally transformations have been organizationally driven and led by a broad cadre of talented executives, supported and often coached by a CEO. Perhaps the best historical analogy would be the role of George Marshal in the Second World War rather than that of Eisenhower or Patton. This is not to say that the role of the CEO is unimportant; the support and encouragement of the CEO is vital. But a personally led CEO driven program is not necessary and sometimes even counterproductive if the CEO is too forceful.

- **Myth: Good leaders avoid the need for enterprise transformation.** Many, if not most of our identified leaders aggressively pursue enterprise transformation regularly and many do so more often than their less successful industry counterparts. Some as a result of acquisitions, some from rapid shifts in their industry structure and/or competitive dynamics, and most from seeking to take advantage of opportunities to change their marketplace for their own benefit. Thus, studying leaders yields very useful insights into transformation and they are a rich source of Frontier Practices, particularly regarding Type II transformations. While leaders do their share of Type I transformations, they do the majority of the Type II transformations.

- **Myth: Leaders lead in the application of "Best Practices."** Our use of "Frontier Practices" is intended to highlight the importance of thinking about leading practices not as a list of "Best" ones to apply, but as a set that is appropriate to a particular firm in a particular industry at a particular time. There is no single formula or process, nor is there a universal set. Each leader selects, adapts and develops the required Frontier Practices to fit the internal and external situation it is facing. No leader uses every Frontier Practice. But there are common patterns and themes.

- **Myth: Leaders have followed the newest path or paradigm to success.** No matter how many times "experts" claim that they have identified the new right and best path to victory (and to be honest some of our consulting brethren are notorious for this), there is no single path to superior profits. After all, if everyone followed the same path, the one certainty is that the resulting identical competitors would compete away the industry's profits. Product mix, industry structure, technology requirements, customer needs and competitive dynamics all demand a wide variety of approaches. Leaders follow many paths to achieve superior performance. There is no one path or model to leadership or success in enterprise transformation. But there are patterns of success and principals which top performing organizations use in effectively pursuing enterprise transformation.

FRONTIER PRACTICES OF SUCCESSFUL ENTERPRISE TRANSFORMATIONS

As discussed earlier, enterprise transformation efforts can be broadly divided into two fundamentally different types. But there are some common themes and Frontier Practices that occur broadly across both types of transformation.

- **Clear goals and objectives continually communicated.** All successful enterprises transformations start with both clear thinking and a clear articulation of the goals and specific objectives involved. Individuals can lead major change, but only directed organizations can marshal the resources and efforts required for broad-based enterprise transformation. Yet often mobilizing the organization toward a common goal proves difficult and elusive. Successful transformations of all types have a common denominator in a clear and compelling reason for change that is effectively communicated and widely understood. In most successful initiatives, employees at all levels can readily articulate the transformation being pursued and their own individual contribution toward it.

- **External goals, threats or opportunities are used to drive transformation.** Seldom are the effective drivers of an enterprise transformation not based on external goals – "delighting customers", "beating the competition", "dominating markets", are all common drivers. Only in the case of a financial crisis is the driver an internal one, though often even this extreme Type I transformation has a "save the company from the outsiders (banks, unwanted takeover, bankruptcy court)" theme. As one executive stated, "ROI and profit are the focus of the executive suite, but it is a poor motivator of the organization." Almost all successful enterprise transformation programs have an external catalyst and external goals.

- **Blueprint the path to value.** This is a concept made popular by the major private equity players, but it accurately describes a core element common to successful enterprise transformations. In every case we have studied, developing a clear "blueprint" or plan for how specifically targeted value will be achieved, internally and for customers, along with the required actions and resources to enable it is key. The blueprint clearly defines the actions needed, their sequence, how they fit together, alternatives, expected progress and clear responsibilities. While plans may evolve, the blueprint is the master plan and it is continually updated and a source of control.

- **Rationalize activities, investments and projects.** A key learning of leaders is that in order to initiate a major transformation program it is as important to stop doing activities, as it is to initiate activities. Putting an end to existing projects is essential in order to execute the transformation blueprint. This means rationalizing projects and improvement efforts against the demands of the transformation program, aligning the various activities and resource allocations against priorities and integrating all efforts into an effective, time phased program. Interestingly, leaders also evaluate very well the capacity of their organization to absorb and leverage improvements to meet targeted results. Very often, they restrict or limit the pace of programs to the execution capacity of the affected groups long before they exhaust the physical resources available to drive change. In effect, they recognize that while money and talented manpower are in short supply, so is management energy and attention.

- **Targeted, specific performance measures integrated across the company.** Another universal characteristic of successful transformation programs is a clear, understanding of the financial and operational measures that matter. The key is a detailed focus on the few critical measures that drive performance. At the financial level these might include cash on hand and/or ROI; at the market level market share and/or customer satisfaction might be critical; for operations the metrics could focus on capacity utilization and/or delivery time. Normally, performance against these measures is directly tied to compensation and a critical few are identified for each manager. What separates the approach of leaders, however, is not simply a better choice of metrics. It is a better integration of metrics. In leading transformation efforts, managers not only know the metrics they are responsible for, but they have a clear line of sight on how their metrics impact other measures and ultimately link to customer and financial success. This line of sight makes it possible for managers across functions to work together effectively and enables managers throughout the organization to make independent trade-offs that produce a consistent whole.

- **Respected leaders in the company publicly drive and direct efforts.** As one recent client stated, "You can only win with the first string". Successful transformation programs are characterized by placing top performing and well-respected managers in charge of leading, guiding and directing major program elements. Unsuccessful transformations, generally staff their change efforts with whoever the organization can spare, rather than who can best deliver success.

- **Intolerance of laggards and resistors.** Successful enterprise transformation companies are unwilling to allow key executives to resist or "sit on the sidelines". They work very hard to enlist support and commitment across the executive ranks and below, but then are steadfast in their demand for active contributions from every manager. Managers who will not support the transformation goals and efforts are not permitted in positions of influence or typically even to remain on the payroll. As one CEO stated, "We are going on a great journey. We will carry the wounded and shoot the stragglers". This is most hard, but most critical, with top talent players and past heroes, but it is highly correlated with success.

- **Opportunistic responses to the unexpected results of progress.** The US Army has a saying "no plan of battle ever survives the first shot". Leaders in the transformation world clearly understand this, and continually adapt their programs to the needs and opportunities they discover; yet they do so without constant changes in direction or focus. While this at first sounds contradictory, it is achieved by evaluating new opportunities against the goals and blueprint for value to upgrade and enhance the program not chase every new idea with a priority of the month effect. The result is a flexible yet focused effort over time that allows effective mobilization and focus across the organization.

In our research and work, with few exceptions, all major, successful enterprise transformations leveraged the above Frontier Practices. While some practices appear to be basic common sense, it is sometimes surprising how uncommon these common sense approaches can be.

Type I Enterprise Transformations – *Playing the game better.*

In addition to the shared "Frontier Practices" discussed above, we have also observed a number of "Frontier Practices" specific to Type I transformations. It should be remembered that Type I transformers are learning to "do more -- and more valuable -- things with less". They are generally focused on improving the organization's relative performance level within the current constraints of their industry, competitive structure and customer channels.

- **Leadership and resolve.** – Type I enterprise transformations do not just happen, they are made to happen by dedicated and committed leaders. While not necessarily the CEO, a core cadre of senior executives must share the vision and sustain the resolve to make changes happen. As one client stated, "everyone likes progress, but nobody likes change, especially to them!" Leaders of Type I changes get a multitude of reasons why the plans will not work or cannot be done now. Their resolve to fight through the resistance quickly and with positive guidance to the organization is a key driver of success.

- **Continual focus on the goal.** – Very often the urgent tends to overwhelm the important. This is particularly true during Type I transformations. Generally the organization faces a number of problems and challenges. Determining which urgent problems must be addressed and which ones can wait is key to remaining focused on the program's goals and allocating the resources and thinking needed to develop solutions to longer-term issues. Effective Type I transformations are characterized by continual, unremitting emphasis on the plans and efforts in their correct order needed to achieve the objectives in the time established. As one executive stated, "We are mono-maniacs on a mission."

- **Communicate, but only what the organization needs to hear.** – This is made infinitely more difficult by the fact that what the organization *needs* to hear should not be confused with what the organization *wants* to hear or what executives *feel good about* saying. The leaders of successful Type I transformations are very focused on communicating and over-communicating what the organization needs to hear and in ways they can best hear it. Written, oral, e-mail and casual conversations all carry a consistent message. When done well, it appears quite simple, but executives are careful to evaluate their decisions and control their behavior to reflect and reinforce their message. It is neither easy nor simple, and it requires continual focus. It is a universal hallmark of successful transformations.

- **New metrics and performance measures.** – If the enterprise had the right metrics in place, it would probably not find itself in serious need of a Type I transformation. New outcomes call for new behaviors. New behaviors call for new metrics. In Type I transformations it is usually not enough to add new metrics to the existing set of performance measures. Given a "portfolio" of metrics to perform against managers will cling to the familiar; providing a built-in set of excuses for performance failure. "I know we didn't hit the new customer satisfaction number," they will explain, "but our on-time percentage is up 8 percent!" A cynic might suggest that the above quote could easily result from dysfunctional actions, e.g., operations simply added an extra week to promised delivery times, thus reducing satisfaction and raising on-time rates simultaneously. Managers do not necessarily cling to old measures simply out of habit or stubbornness. There is real anxiety associated with new performance standards, especially when they are not just new targets for old metrics, but fundamentally different metrics. When pressed, one manager in the midst of a transformation admitted, "I know the old numbers are screwed up, but I know *how* they're screwed up."

- **Hard and timely choices.** – All transformation programs face difficult and uncertain choices at some point. A major differentiator between successful and unsuccessful programs is the way and style with which managers address choices. Unsuccessful transformations typically delay choices as long as possible, make decisions without fully exploring alternatives and choose the options that are perceived best in the short term by the organization and the power players in it. Successful transformations make choices when they can best be made with a bias toward early resolution and clear messages supporting long-term goals. Yet they are not so quick to pull the trigger on a decision that they fail to recognize that a given performance "symptom" may have a variety of potential root causes and each root cause may have multiple solution options. They are quick to confront problems yet careful to understand the root causes and viable alternatives. Because they avoid the "I've-seen-that-symptom-before-and-the-correct-answer-is-X" syndrome common to unsuccessful transformations, they are able to evaluate a number of choices against the defined goals of the transformation and choose the option that both addresses root cause and promotes the long term interests of the organization. To the people involved, the decision process appears very consistent, timely and even predictable

- **Internal alignment.** – Enterprise transformation programs involve a number of functions, processes and activities across the company. Aligning all these activities to the desired goals is an obvious challenge. Transformation efforts also involve a number of specific projects that change over time and interact in non-obvious ways to change the current and future capabilities and performance of the enterprise. Aligning each project with all other projects and maintaining that alignment over time as projects, people and conditions change is an even greater internal alignment challenge. Yet this is precisely the enterprise transformation challenge and a key differentiator between successs and failure. While companies use a wide range of tools and approaches to accomplish this feat, all of the winners find a way to do an excellent job in managing projects and in the quite different task of managing the project portfolio. We have found virtually all successful programs are able to achieve and then consistently maintain internal alignment very well. Less successful programs typically stumble on this challenge. Their failing is seldom due to the failure of individual project managers. Rather it is in the arena of dynamic management of the project portfolio. In fact, many failed transformation efforts do not evem recognize that the management of the projects portfolio calls for something more than good independent management of the individual projects.

- **Rigid execution of flexible plans and progress tracking.** – A critical conflict facing all Type I transformations is how to evolve and adapt efforts over time as learning and new performance levels are achieved and unanticipated problems occur. As stated earlier, maintaining focus on overall goals and consistency in the eyes of the organization is required for success; yet flexibility to take advantage of unexpected opportunities and challenges is also required. This apparent conflict initially seems quite difficult to resolve and many programs founder on this problem. Yet the key lies in defining the problem and thus the solution correctly. Successful programs are laser focused on their goals and generally adjust them only upward and in response to external changes and opportunities. Any changes are as carefully communicated as the original goals and drivers. However, the transformation "blueprint" defining the actions required to achieving their goals is viewed as an evolving path from which change and deviation is expected and normal as long as it improves the organization's ability to succeed. Progress milestones are frequently employed and changed periodically, usually as a reaffirmation of progress and adaptability. Management is viewed as open to considering changes as long as they further progress, but course corrections are not made casually or without a clear cost benefit assessment. It is a powerful combination – focused goals supported by flexible and evolving projects.

Type II Enterprise Transformation – *Playing by a different set of rules*

Type I and Type II transformations share many similarities. However, they are very different in their approach, focus, goals and challenges. Table 1 summarized several of the key differences earlier. Many of the Frontier Practices of Type I successes, are also applied by successful Type II transformers. Type II transformers also have more options and can and do utilize additional Frontier Practices in how they manage and transform their operations to lead their competitors. They operate in an exciting and very proactive world.

- **Change is normal and expected.** – Successful Type II companies view change as an opportunity to excel not a threat or problem. While embracing change might be too strong a statement, these companies look at changes externally as an opportunity to make a breakthrough or extend their lead. They are organizationally confident of their ability to capitalize on change without the arrogance of believing that change cannot affect them or their markets. As one client stated, "dramatic progress can only be made in times of change and uncertainty, we want to own that moment of truth".

- **Early recognition / early detection.** – Successful Type II companies search carefully for "weak" and "soft" signals from customers and market partners. They look for unmet needs, often those not stated or even yet recognized. Yet they are careful not to invest or even meet those needs until they are prepared and they are ready to deliver on new promises and capabilities. The early awareness and close touch with customer and their markets "buys" them the time and provides focus to their efforts.

- **Keep dry powder.** – A somewhat related core hallmark of Type II leaders is the maintenance of a "tactical reserve" of both capital and talent. This allows them to meet and leverage unexpected opportunities and react effectively to problems. Panic is not a part of their culture; tough fast action is. These companies are not really that much better at predicting and forecasting -- though they are faster to realize needed course corrections -- but they are dramatically faster at marshalling the resources and focusing the required parts of the organization on reacting and leveraging the unplanned. They work hard at having the capacity to be agile. Contractors, suppliers and consultants may be a part of their reserve, but it is by design, not necessity. From the outside they look smarter and more visionary, and they are, just not in the way most observers think. They simply accept that they are unlikely to anticipate and predict everything, but they can prepare, recognize and react faster than their competitors.

- **Purchase options and experiment.** – A very striking characteristic that separates leaders from laggards, is their willingness to "purchase" options on emerging technologies, markets, channels and customer needs. They, like others, try to understand and predict likely future events, but they are careful to also understand the potential of early insight even when accurate forecasting is not yet practical. They are very likely to selectively invest both people and assets to learn, evaluate potential and preserve their ability to move fast. They are by no means quick to throw money at a portfolio of simply interesting ideas, but they readily partner with customers, suppliers, universities, consultants and even competitors to be ahead in their knowledge of relevant, disruptive change drivers. They also internally invest in carefully selected technologies and capabilities at an early stage if they believe them capable of altering their business model. These experiments may be small, but they are viewed as critical to long run success. In some cases, these early stage experiments have built a foundation for achieving a "stealth" transformation, one that surprises customers and competitors by changing market structure or the basis of competition.

- **Not afraid to fail.** – Successful Type II companies are not able to succeed at everything they try, nor do they expect success in every venture. In business, an R&D manager in an under performing company once remarked, "we have a term for experiments that prove a commercial hypothesis to be false. We call them career-ending failures." Not so among Type II Leaders. The "failure" of a business concept may be rewarded providing the attempt was well executed and the learning valuable. In fact, enterprises that excel at Type II transformations have a different definition of "failure" altogether: "An experiment doesn't fail when it shows you were wrong," we've been told, "an experiment fails when you don't learn anything." The Type II culture is much more risk tolerant, but much more judicious in managing risk in total. The portfolio of risks is what is considered most critical to manage, not the avoidance of risk in any one project. Type II change managers are also recognized and rewarded for stopping or redirecting established projects that can no longer contribute appropriately to the company's goals. This frees up not only manpower and cash, but also the far more scarce resource of management attention.

- **Capital deployment and productivity as critical drivers.** – Over the last 20 years, the S&P 500 companies in aggregate have seen a decline in capital productivity (sales or EBITDA divided by total assets) of over 50%. Successful Type II companies have generally increased their capital productivity against the same measures over the same time. This is not a coincidence. These companies are careful with how and where they make investments, what activities and functions they have inside their organization that can consume capital and how they can quickly earn a return on capital in an uncertain environment. They are quick to invest in people but slow to deploy capital. They are clear on the returns they seek, and it is seldom just a financial return. Yet when capital investment is crucial to transformation they readily deploy capital. They do so fully, unstintingly, and they generally buy future options to extend the leverage of their investments. They make a distinction between capital invested in commoditized markets and investments in commoditized capital. There are opportunities to leverage distinctive capital-associated capabilities through transformation in the former (e.g., through scale, scope or learning advantages). But in the latter scenario, commoditized capital investment is discouraged because it represents resources tied up without contributing to competitive position. As a result, they are often partnering with product and service providers in areas where they choose not to invest. These are not "capital light" companies, they simply "sweat their capital investments hard" to ensure that current investments will create value in their changing competitive context and additional resources are available for the next transformation.

- **Cannibalize existing products, technologies and channels before others can attack.** – Prior investments are treated as sunk costs. They are protected and leveraged fully, but these companies own their investments, their investments do not own them. Type II transformers are quick to adopt new technologies, adapt products and abandon positions and channels as better options are available. As one client stated, "change is inevitable, growth is optional". These companies strongly reflect this belief in how and when they invest in transformation. Many firms look at attacking their own business model and transforming their own job and organization and ask if the transformation is worth the effort in dollars, energy, bodies and so on. "Aren't there easier investments with higher ROIs?" they ask. Leaders frame the question differently. They recognize that transformation is inevitable. The question is not *if* the enterprise will transform but *when*. "Should we rapidly embrace a new business model now," they ask, "when we have both the management and capital reserves to make the difficult transition, or should we wait until performance deteriorates and resources are less available? Or perhaps we should wait so long that what would have been a Type II transformation bringing superior financial returns will by default become a Type I transformation trying to rally, control and focus the scarce resources available?" Framed this way, the question hardly seems worth asking. But keep in mind the willingness and ability to attack one's own position is not just a matter of attitude. It is the Type II leader's early recognition of opportunities, focused investments in capital and learning, maintenance of "dry powder" and so on that has created the opportunity for the leader to even consider transformation at this potentially attractive juncture.

- **Early to market but not always first.** – Type II transformers are careful not to invest too early, or too late. Many are not first to market, but they generally are fast followers when they are not leaders. Their goal is to be early to the market and the first in the market with the enterprise configured so that it can achieve both market and financial success. They may allow others to lead or even be surprised by a competitor, but they are quick to respond or follow and have the resources and focus to quickly take the lead. This positioning is cognizant of the true drivers of financial returns. A great innovation may create the opportunity for great value creation, but it often takes a transformation of the enterprise to exploit that opportunity. The true "first mover" may not be the firm that first builds and delivers the "new product." It may be the firm that first builds an enterprise that effectively delivers the new product's full value to customers.

- **Look beyond products and marketplace transactions.** – Over the last ten years, most companies have increased the service offerings they provide customers – some profitably, many not. Type II transformers have been among the pioneers in moving beyond products sold at arm's length to deploying capabilities (in the form of products and/or services) to create distinctive value for targeted customers profitably. They view services, products, activities and assets (regardless of current ownership), and information as integral parts of both their value proposition and their potential offering portfolio. For example, a recent packaging materials client transformed its value proposition for its large customers from a "provider of purchased packaging materials" to an "integrated packaging solutions outsourcer". They now have their employees deployed at the customer's facility where they remove finished products from the end of their customer's finishing operations, package them to customer specifications, handle all finished goods inventory management, shipping and in some cases even delivering products to their customer's customer. The result has been a 40% gain in their share of the targeted large customer market, a dramatic increase in sole-source customers, a value-based (not price-based) purchasing conversation with their customers and a new revenue stream for the company that now exceeds 30% of the original revenues of the entire division. Their customers have also reduced their packaging and shipping costs by over 30%. Our research shows this type of example is not uncommon and is growing. The critical element here, however, is not the insight that imagined the innovative new value proposition. It is the dramatic transformation the enterprise had to go through to profitably deliver the innovative new value proposition. Success called for transforming marketing (we're no longer who we said we were), the workforce (who are now offsite and not under direct control and supervision), the salesperson's role (they now have to understand their customers system economics not just their own product's economics), product development (*our own* profits are now impacted directly by factors like the frequency with which plastic rolls have to be changed) and more. Failure on any *one* of these fronts would have destroyed the ventures market success and/or profitability. Firms that are failing in this new beyond-the-product market space are those who think they can transform the customer's value proposition without transforming their own organization.

- **Fluid Organizations.** – Type II transformers have a very different approach to managing the organization of their company. They view organization structure as a convenient and temporary tool for structuring the growth and development of the company. Change is expected and occurs frequently. They have found that any structure incorporates tradeoffs and compromises that need to adjust over time as both the competitive landscape and the executives in the organization change. For example, should process development report to product development, production or independently of both. A strong case could be made for any of these three structures depending on the managers involved, capabilities of the organization, the activities and programs occurring at the time, challenges faced by the business, development needs within each function, etc. While many companies struggle to resolve this conflict, Type II transformers generally accept the inherent conflicts and tradeoffs and seek to leverage them specific to a point in time, and are quick to change the structure as needed to optimize for the situation they face. Their expectations and those they build into the organization are that organization changes are expected and normal. They use fluid organization structures to facilitate agility, not stability. This not only reduces the disruptive impact of transformation (a dangerous risk for a successful firm serving old customers under the old paradigm while transforming to meet new needs) but also permits more "evolutionary" change across time permitting adaptation or transformations smaller in scale and scope than other firms might have required in the same situation. (Transformation scale and scope are addressed in more detail in our closing discussions).

- **Escaping "The Tyranny of 'OR.'"** – Perhaps the most striking difference between successful Type I and Type II transformation organizations is in their approach to industry-recognized, fundamental tradeoffs. Type I transformers force clear choices and execute aggressively on those choices; Type II transformers often find new choices and in doing so open new competitive space and positions. The auto industry of the late 1960's and 1970's provides a good example. The dominant players offered a bewildering variety of options, colors and interiors. Ford proudly estimated it would take several months to make all permutations and combinations of product configurations for the Thunderbird alone. Smaller European and Japanese producers could not afford to offer this variety given their supply chain length and thus offered only a few options, colors and interiors. Toyota and others then leveraged this "inherent conflict" of variety versus cost by offering standardized packages including most of the options then available. Radios were AM/FM only, not a choice between the two. Suspension and drive train options were integrated into one or two packages, not individually selected. The typical range of packages was under 5 with limited colors. By combining options into packages that included most if not all of what a large mass of customers wanted, supply chain, manufacturing and parts complexity was dramatically reduced and costs were actually lowered while offering customers more for their purchase dollars. The rest, as they say, is history. Escaping the *Tyranny of "OR"* by building distinctive capabilities is almost always a successful approach because it relieves customers of the need to compromise. Today's personal computer buyer would like a system tailored to his or her personal needs. But they also want it cheap and right now. Dell is a modern example of a firm that was built on a new "OR-escaping" business model. Just how difficult it is to transform an enterprise to wipe out a historically prominent trade-off is illustrated by the enormous difficulty large, resource rich, well-run firms are having in competing with Dell. Successfully solving *The Tyranny of "OR"* is often at the core of powerful and sustainable Type II transformations.

AN OVERARCHING CONCEPT – *THE PIVOT POINT*

One of the most consistent and compelling findings in our work and research on both successful and unsuccessful transformation efforts is the use of "pivot points" to drive and focus transformation initiatives. Our use of the "pivot points" concept has analogs in physics, geometry, history and even great literature. But the basic concept of a pivot point is second nature to anyone who has ever remodeled a kitchen. Just as a refrigerator can be "walked" across a kitchen by pivoting its bulk on opposing corners, so an organization can be "walked" to its new position by leveraging its own pivot point -- see the discussion: "Refrigerator" Transformation."

"Refrigerator" Transformation

At some point in the remodeling process the time comes to move the refrigerator. In most cases due to time pressure, a lack of manpower, unbridled optimism or sheer laziness, the decision is made to move the refrigerator without first emptying its contents. The challenges now facing the refrigerator mover are (in order of occurrence):

- Moving the refrigerator at all

- Moving the refrigerator to its desired new location

- Moving it to its new location without destroying everything inside en route

The parallels to managing an enterprise transformation should be obvious to anyone who has ever been through the process.

Going It Alone: The homeowner now gets their first lesson in Refrigerator Transformation. He or she finds that you can push and push on the side of the refrigerator and nothing will happen. Nothing at all. You can, however, throw your weight violently into the refrigerator and it will move; in fact it will tip over and land on the floor ruining its contents and making it impossible for you to ever right it again on your own. This is much akin to the problems resulting from the isolated, independent, heroic efforts of the overly forceful CEO discussed earlier.

Building a Team: The homeowner reaches out to his or her friends, recognizing that Refrigerator Transformation is a neighborhood-wide effort. It quickly becomes clear that pushing on the side of the refrigerator as a team sends it crashing to the floor much more quickly and violently than pushing on it as an individual. Alternatively, the team could gather round the refrigerator and lift it in unison. This democratic, unified approach is tricky – there are no handles on a refrigerator just as there are none readily visible on an organization – and if any individual's palms become sweaty the refrigerator will crash down on someone's toe (perhaps many someone's toes). Assuming the unified, democratic team *is* able to lift and move the refrigerator, they will soon find another problem thwarting their best efforts and intentions. No matter where they want to place the refrigerator, one of the hard-working team members surrounding the refrigerator will be in the way. The many parallels to enterprise transformation should again be self-evident.

Finding and Using the Pivot Point: The homeowner, if they have not yet forsaken the whole endeavor, will discover that there is in fact one effective way to perform Refrigerator Transformation. The refrigerator can be "walked" across the kitchen by taking advantage of its natural pivot points, i.e., the corners of the base. By tipping the refrigerator onto its pivot point a small amount of force can overcome the weight, inertia and friction encountered when pushing. Further, once the refrigerator begins to move, exerting effort and attention to the pivot point can control its direction and forward motion. The fundamental task has not changed. But it has been made manageable by the leverage created through the use of the pivot point.

Managing the Process: As in any transformation, there are some salient management warnings that accompany the leverage available through the use of pivot points:

- This should not be attempted alone as once in motion the refrigerator is unstable and many hands are needed to safely control its advance.

- A shared understanding of the ultimate desired position must be clearly communicated to and understood by team members before they begin.

- Participants must also agree on *which* elements are to be the pivot points. While any two corners will serve as pivot points, there must be agreement over which two will be used in the current situation.

- More than two pivot points will not be effective; three or more simply leads to going round and round in circles.

- A strong, energetic, unflappable team member should be stationed at/responsible for each pivot point.

- With these elements in place the refrigerator can be easily, quickly and safely moved.

- An absence of these clear agreed upon goals and process decisions will lead to non-aligned forces working against each other, at best, and the whole thing crashing to the ground ruining everything inside at worst.

- One last point of similarity between refrigerator and enterprise Transformations, neighbors who do not want to exert themselves and would prefer to sit at the table, drink your beer and criticize your efforts should be removed from the kitchen as quickly as possible.

All successful enterprise transformations we have examined used a key focal point around which all aspects of the program are integrated and driven. We've dubbed these critical core integrating and guiding themes "Pivot Points" to emphasize their focus and the leverage they provide for moving the enterprise. For example, DrillCo used "customer lead-times" as the focal point of its Type I transformation. As described earlier "customer lead-time" served as a motivating, high-leverage, long-term pivot point that lent itself to clear metrics and required system-wide changes impacting virtually every function.

As at DrillCo the pivot point is often communicated in a pithy theme, goal or doctrine statement (e.g., Quality is Job 1, Moments of Truth, Six Sigma, "F.A.S.T.", Run To Target, etc.). But it is not the catchiness of the slogan that matters, it is the relevance of the pivot point it emphasizes. The catchy slogan (or in some cases picture) serves as an in-house shorthand for the richer understanding of the pivot point and its role in the transformation initiative. "Quality is Job 1" was used as a popular ad line, but its meaning within Ford was much richer. Ford wasn't just saying "Quality is the top priority." In the auto industry "Job 1" is the all-important first vehicle off the line in a new model launch. Within Ford "Quality is Job 1," conveyed a sense of re-launching a whole new business model, i.e., a pivot point for enterprise transformation. (We have occasionally seen successful programs with two pivot points but the two were always related and that relationship was clearly articulated).

Failed or low success enterprise transformations typically either did not identify and use a pivot point or used far too many. In the case of no pivot point, the various efforts of the program were managed as a collection of projects with no clear, integrated outcome defined for the organization. Similarly, those programs that used too many pivot points seemed to confuse the organization, creating conflicts and offering no clear means of resolution, let alone a vision of how efforts could be integrated to achieve breakthrough results. The result with none or too many pivot points is the same: lots of ineffective action.

The reason a pivot point is critical is straightforward, but not initially obvious. For enterprise transformations to be successful, multiple projects and efforts must be integrated in order to fundamentally change the capabilities of an organization. And it is changes in capabilities that are the goal not just changing a business process or function. Further, changes in capability generally do not occur until all the required elements of the change are in place. The whole really is greater than the sum of its parts. Partial completion, if not carefully managed, cannot only yield disappointing results; it can even give negative results, and often does. Pivot points create the ability to integrate multiple projects across multiple functions, and facilitate conflict resolution between projects. Finally, using a clear and compelling pivot point also allows the company to reinforce consistent goals even as the specific projects change over time. An effective pivot point provides guidance and goals throughout the transformation. It must therefore be framed in a way that its message will not lose value as the actions advance the firm's position. A pivot point like "Launch the XK10 on time" loses its leverage once the XK10 is launched.

Pivot points serve as integrating and guiding mechanisms, but when used effectively they also motivate and energize the organization. For this reason, pivot points are generally driven by goals or outcomes external to the company. Mechanistic internal goals like "improve ROI" or "grow the bottom line" will not galvanize the organization however important such a goal might be to the executive suite and the board. These internal goals may well be the driving reason *for* an enterprise transformation, but that does not imply that they will serve as effective pivot points. To be motivating, the transformation needs to be directed toward an external goal relevant to the stakeholders in the organization and be relevant to their business life. Such pivot points as "take back our market", "delight the customer", "surround the competition", and "own the internet" have been highly successful. But to drive the efforts of the organization long term, the message must be more than inspirational. The value of the message must be real and be something the organization can rally around. As one client said recently, "In the Army we learned solders do not get out of their foxholes and charge the machine guns for their commander, they do it for their squad mates and their country". In business, employees do not take on the exhausting, tough and risky tasks of transformation for the investors or management, they do it to win customers, dominate markets and beat the competition.

An effective pivot point provides unique leverage on the organization. To do so it must be clear enough to guide choices and its value real and relevant enough to motivate employees to focus on something larger than their self-interest. A strong, targeted, clearly articulated pivot point is a hallmark of successful enterprise transformations.

FATAL MOVES

One of the most striking findings of our enterprise transformation research and work is the consistent pattern of errors made in unsuccessful enterprise transformations. There are many points at which a transformation effort might go awry but we find a disproportionate number of initiatives foundering on the same few key fatal moves that successful programs routinely avoid. When discussing these "fatal moves" with executives, the general reaction is "of course that would be a bad move, we would never do that". Yet these errors continue to haunt the world of enterprise transformations. Why? We have several hypotheses.

First, these are easy errors to make even with the best of intentions. Often the lack of clearly thought through targets and goals allows companies to gradually let one or more of these errors to slip into their programs, typically disguised as a temporary, urgent decision, or a deferred decision. This is one of the reasons that unambiguous and granular statements of purpose, goals and milestones are so critical to successful efforts.

It also seems that there is an inherent tension in managing transformation. It appears that it is dangerously easy for leaders to get caught up in issues of the moment and thus loose the larger perspective needed to make the tough choices in a way that produces an integrated effective whole. There is so much going on and so many choices to be made that it is difficult to retain a view of the forest while toiling among the trees. This is doubly true when so many of the changes and choices are emotionally charged because of their ties to the past.

Yet at the same time we find managers who have difficulty remaining focused on completing plans and programs even though they are effective at developing and initiating them. As a result, day-to-day management of transformation programs tends to get further and further from key decision makers and their rich understanding of goals and challenges. As decisions are delegated downward, the clarity of decisions and their implications are often lost and the ability to surface hard choices and confront them in a timely fashion falls.

This simultaneous challenge to avoid getting lost in either the trees or the clouds is not a reflection of management style, as one might suspect. Indeed, it is common for a single manager to wrestle with both problems at different stages in the transformation effort. This is another area where a clear pivot point can help. It provides the manager with a focus that should connect future competitive position to today's actions, helping him or her to come up from the trees or down from the clouds. For others in the organization the pivot point can provide guidance and motivation should the relevant managers find themselves less able to balance this trees and clouds tension than they need to be.

Finally, these "fatal moves" do not announce themselves in practice. Initially they do not appear to hurt a transformation effort too badly. But their result over time should not be underestimated. While a compromise or two may not kill an effort, a consistent pattern over time will. It sends a powerful message across the organization and calls into question the commitment of the company to real and sustainable transformation.

Below is a brief summary of the most common fatal moves we repeatedly see. We share them in hopes that more organizations can avoid them. Hopefully forewarned is forearmed.

- **Relying on outsiders to drive change.** – You cannot buy enterprise transformation from anyone. It is not a technology that can be purchased, a resource that can be hired or a project that outsiders can lead regardless of what some consultants and information technology companies claim. Enterprise transformation is hard work an organization must do for itself. Skilled consultants can guide and tools can help, but enterprise transformation must be driven by strong leaders who can motivate and sustain the effort required to change a company.

- **Planning is not execution.** – In too many less successful initiatives, management focuses heavily on identifying solutions and putting plans in motion. Execution is then delegated to line executives to implement. This seldom if ever works. It is a tempting idea, but the "implementation phase" is the very time an organization most needs tight focus, visible leadership and hands on problem solving. This is when challenges from the status quo and the politically threatened emerge to delay, stall and divert major change efforts. Transformation leaders need to be active in identifying problems, making course corrections and motivating from the front on an ongoing basis. Effort usually needs to be increased and outside advisors need to be available to help fit the last pieces together and evolve plans as required. As one executive put it, quoting Yogi Berra, "It ain't over 'til it's over".

- **Failing to rationalize initiatives.** – Perhaps the most common and deadly fatal move is overwhelming the company with initiatives. Adding the 101st initiative to the organization agenda not only dilutes effort and focus; it usually detracts and de-motivates managers involved. Activity is not progress. More initiatives will accomplish less not more. As a recent manager put it, "Nothing is more demoralizing than perceiving you are risking your personal capital to take on a random objective." Executives must resist the temptation to add "just one more thing" to the transformation agenda, regardless of the intrinsic virtue of the "one more thing." Equally important, almost all successful enterprise transformations rationalized existing initiatives into the overall agenda or eliminated them. This is the key signal to the organization that this time it truly will be different.

- **Leading and managing transformation as a part-time job.** – It is very tempting to approach transformation as a part time role for several key executives. After all, the existing customers, products and ways of doing business all still require attention while the new world is being created. Approaching transformation as a part-time job is a critical mistake. Transformations need to be led by a key executive or group of executives respected in the company. Often with the best of intent, leadership can easily become a part time role spread across several executives many of whom also play a key functional role. But the data shows it does not work. The urgent will generally overwhelm the important. Further, functional bias can easily be perceived even if it is not real. Leading a major transformation effort requires full time effort and focus. If leadership is not willing to fully commit to a transformation, line managers tend not commit either. Part time efforts can be effective from executive supporters and even from individual project team members, but leaders must be dedicated and focused on the transformation goals and undistracted by functional bias or general management work.

- **Not making the hard choices.** – The essence of enterprise transformation is choice and focus. At the core of every successful program is the ability to understand the choices confronting the company and the ability to make critical decisions even when the choices are difficult. Typically, difficult choices involve people, organization structure and priorities. In fact, the single most common failing in this area is not confronting or replacing key players in the organization who are not aligned with the needs of the transformation. This can be particularly difficult for managers if the recalcitrant individuals have been critical contributors previously. Other problems include not focusing efforts on the most important markets and customers, not selecting between positioning alternatives and not abandoning markets and products when their value and importance has declined. It is tempting to look for compromises or an acceptable path that avoids conflict, particularly if it involves talented individuals. It is a core mistake that hurts many transformation programs. If leadership will not concentrate efforts on the key issues, progress is slowed or lost. If leaders will not make tough, painful choices when required, take calculated risks and confront obstructions, the organization cannot be expected to either.

- **Believing in scale as "the answer."** – A number of transformation efforts have failed because they started with the wrong goals driven by fundamental misperceptions of the problems and imperatives facing the company. A surprisingly common error is the belief that greater scale is the answer and then acting to scale up through acquisitions (typically poorly integrated) or making "home run" level investments. History shows it seldom works, and it generally makes a bad situation worse. But it is seductively attractive to the executive suite, and it is dramatic. In contrast, successful transformation efforts start by carefully identifying and focusing on the fundamental drivers of cost and value by market. Investment and major business moves are delayed until the root causes are understood and the path is clear. From this the correct levers of change can be selected and the right pivot point can be established.

- **Driving choice and action from existing data.** – A closely associated fatal move to relying on scale, is rushing into action based on existing data and current understandings of problems. All too often, firmly held beliefs, known facts and organizational wisdom are built on nothing more than anecdotal evidence and untested perceptions from the past. Seldom are they right, and often they doom a transformation effort early; making subsequent efforts even more difficult. Enterprise transformation is a big effort under often tremendous pressure. It is tempting to "get moving" right away but initiatives cannot and should not be launched too quickly. There are too many moving parts and people involved to "shoot first and ask questions later". Redirecting a hastily launched, misguided initiative may call into doubt the credibility of the entire transformation. Nothing de-motivates an organization more than the belief they are heading in the wrong direction or working on efforts that are not truly valuable. Successful transformation programs need a firm fact base, a thorough understanding of root causes, and a creative exploration of options and alternatives. This does not imply transformation programs should not have a bias for action and experimentation or that Type I transformation may not require immediate actions. But *urgent* actions should not be confused in either the mind of executives or the organization with actions *required* to drive enterprise transformation. Immediate actions should be thought of as a part of the investigation phase and a tool to provide time to plan. The organization's sense of urgency needs to be channeled first or in parallel into a sound blueprint to value. Creating this blueprint does not have to take long, but we found every successful enterprise transformation program started with a clear fact base and well-defined goals. Any up-front delay was more than made up by more effective actions and greater results once the plan was in place.

- **Relying on the "Magic Bullet" solution.** – Simple answers to complex problems are generally for simple minds. Simple problems seldom drive the need for enterprise transformation. Yet many companies continue to search for and pursue simple, "magic bullet" solutions. The desires to "buy" transformation from the outside or to "solve" the problem through scale are simply two of the most common manifestations of the "magic bullet" mindset.

- **Hero syndrome.** – A single individual cannot do the difficult and complex work of transforming an organization of any major size. If it could, there would be many more success stories. Enterprise transformation is about new strategies, new operating methods and behavior throughout the organization. Charismatic leaders are clearly an asset in any organization, but they must be able to extend their leadership across a broad based team. Only a focused, aligned and motivated team can exert the leverage needed to execute a complex set of integrated plans. Remember, a single point specific change led by an outstanding leader may help, but it cannot be fully leveraged without appropriate change elsewhere in the organization. This is the differentiator between enterprise transformation programs and on-going business improvements.

- **Confusing reengineering with transformation.** – A number of companies pursued reengineering programs as a means to transform their company over the last 15 years. While many obtained operating performance improvement, few achieved enterprise transformation. This is not to say reengineering is a bad tool; it in fact has been one of the more successful business concepts deployed in the 1980's and 1990's and has been used as a tool in many successful enterprise transformations. But reengineering focuses on process level performance changes, generally on a process-by-process basis. Enterprise transformation requires that multiple processes and sometimes technologies be combined and aligned to change an organization's capabilities. Reengineering supports but does not drive enterprise transformation.

- **Getting back to basics.** – While getting fundamental performance drivers back to a high level is always appropriate, this is almost never why an organization is facing a transformation imperative. It is certainly a worthy effort, but getting "back to basics" seldom results in effective transformation. The flaw in the "back to basics" approach is the implicit assumption that current challenges arose because the organization has lost its way with regard to the market, its customers and its roots. Generally, it is not the case that the company has "fallen away from what made us great". Usually the world *moved* away. The market, customer expectations and competitors have moved the needs of the business beyond the capabilities of the company and the design of its operations. Simply reinstating the way we used to do things might provide a short term "bump" in performance simply by getting everyone in the organization focused on *something*, but it does not generate real and sustainable value. Like reengineering, a "back to basics" approach is at best a tool, not a transformation solution.

WHEN IS ENTERPRISE TRANSFORMATION STRATEGIC?

We have come this far without once using the words "strategy" or "strategic." But as we close out these lessons from the front, "strategy" deserves to be addressed. In our work we find wide spread confusion about how enterprise transformation relates to strategy and vice versa.

The Transformation Framework (Figure 5) introduced in Chapter 2 suggests that enterprise transformations can be positioned in a space defined by three dimensions: the **Scope** of the transformation (from work activities, to business functions, to organizational units, to the enterprise as a whole), the **Ends** the transformation seeks to achieve (from increased cost efficiencies, to enhanced market perceptions, to new products and services, to fundamental changes of markets) and the **Means** it uses to achieve them (from upgrading people's skills, to redesigning business practices, to significant infusion of technology, to fundamental changes of strategy). "Strategy" in the context of this framework refers to the enterprise's fundamental approach to competition, i.e. its value proposition and economic model.

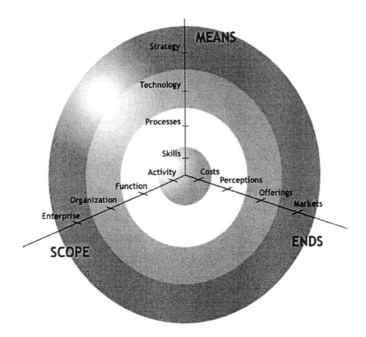

FIGURE 5. Enterprise Transformation Framework

This framing lets us map the wide array of transformation initiatives that have been launched in recent years (the frame allows the mapping of failed attempts due to its use of "Ends" as opposed to "Outcomes"). The smaller, lighter spheres near the axes intersection typically locate initiatives that are relatively focused, e.g., upgrading worker skills at critical activities to reduce costs. The outer, darker rings involve more broad-based changes, e.g., directing an entire cost-focused enterprise into a new market where success is built on innovation. The extremes of both positions blur the boundaries of our transformation domain. Are inner circle changes so limited in focus that they are really discrete improvement projects rather than an enterprise transformation? Are the outer circles built on such a new set of assets, people and activities that they represent new business ventures rather than transformative efforts?

While a problem in the abstract, these definitional issues do not pose serious stumbling blocks to practitioners. Transformations seem to fall readily into the "I know'em when I see'em" category. Most real world transformations are not positioned within a single "ring level" in our mapping framework. The Ends may be narrow (cost reduction) while the Scope may be enterprise-wide. Alternatively, the Scope could involve entry into a whole new marketplace through enhancing the skills and activities of a small number of salespeople.

As a broad rule-of-thumb, inner-ring initiatives are typically narrower, better understood a priori and require less overall investment than outer-ring initiatives. But this masks the huge determinate impact of the enterprise's current situation. "How much investment is required? Is the change well defined and understood? How big a change in behaviors/thinking/systems will be required? Do we have the requisite skills for the new environment? Do we have the requisite skill to get from here *to* the new environment? Are sufficient resources available? In short, how big, risky and hard will the transformation be?" These questions depend as much or more on the enterprise's current situation as they do on the nature of the transformation initiative.

The insight provided through the Enterprise Transformation Framework is not found in a "degree of difficulty" metric. That measure will be dependent on many factors including the current situation and the leadership provided. Rather the value of the Enterprise Transformation Framework is that it allows:

- **A vehicle for discussing and defining the initiative's charter.** "Is that too much? Too little?"

- **Clear communication of the nature, focus and limits of the initiative.** "When you say everyone, do you mean *everyone*?"

- **Assessment of this transformation initiative relative to the enterprise's past programs/efforts/initiatives.** "How is this different from the turn-around effort three years ago?"

- **A basis for comparison of a given initiative to the *relevant* experience others have had in transforming their enterprises.** "ACME did Y and Z in the first three months. Should we?

- **Easier categorization of Type I and Type II transformations.** "What kind of benefits should we expect? When? Which of the lessons described here will apply most to my initiative?"

Type I transformations tend to be more inner-circle focused, while Type II require at least some degree of outer-ring focus. This is especially true for the Ends and Means elements of the Framework. As demonstrated in our DrillCo example the broad value realization that comes from a Type II transformation can be tapped by changing certain narrower elements of the organization to exploit capabilities that exist elsewhere in the enterprise.

But this does not imply that Type I enterprise transformations are not "strategic" while Type II transformations are. "Strategy," we say at The Monitor Group, "is about *informed choice* and *timely action*." It is more than a plan, it is an integrated set of choices and actions that create and capture value in a defensible way even in the face of industry and technology uncertainty and competitive moves. There are those who categorize Type I transformations as exercises in non-strategic "operational improvement" regardless of how sweeping the initiative or dramatic the change in performance. These observers fail to note two important facts. First, Type I changes often are the source of new capabilities that enable Type II transformations (even if not the origin of that value creation they may be a necessary prerequisite). Second, in choosing a Means, Scope and Ends for a Type I transformation initiative, irreversible actions are taken and future options are enabled or foreclosed. The need to dramatically transform a company's product designs may be achieved through in-house creation of new design capabilities or through an outside alliance (which calls for a different set of capabilities around working with outside partners, protecting IP and exploiting new designs developed elsewhere, etc.). Both approaches may generate a breakthrough in value creation and capture. Both approaches will call for new capabilities. *But the two paths will produce very different enterprises in a strategic sense going forward.* One of the critical elements of long term success (returning to our lessons from leaders for the moment) is to take *not* the first recognized or even necessarily the fastest transformational path but take the path that positions the enterprise most effectively for the future. The challenge of *tomorrow's* inevitable next transformation depends in many ways on the choices made in initiating *today's*.

CONCLUDING THOUGHTS

We have tried to provide practical advice "from the front" for managers about to embark on or already caught up in an enterprise transformation. If you are not among those ranks you soon will be through an optimistic effort to capture more value than ever before, a nostalgic attempt to recapture old value or a desperate scramble to grab enough value to stay in business. Whatever the setting for your journey, we hope these lessons will serve as a "checklist" before launch and a set of "warning gauges" while in flight.

First and foremost, remember that there is no "formula" for success. Perhaps the most important lesson from our leaders is their diversity. They represent diverse industries, initiatives, and individuals. What they have in common is an ongoing commitment to clarity, communication and change.

We identified two types of enterprise transformation and the way in which they drive value. Type I transformations are centered on *focus* and *performance*; they are built on breakthroughs in control and application. Type II transformations are centered on *capabilities* and *advantage*; they are built on breakthroughs in integration and alignment. The lessons from successful transformation initiatives identified shared and differing keys to success for the two types. They both call for strong leadership, a clear blueprint to value, clearly prioritized investments in time and dollars, individual commitment and adaptability. Type I transformations also place a premium on making the difficult (and often unpopular) decisions and sticking to them. Successful Type I transformers clearly understand the organization's current limits. Type II transformations call for a balance between commitment and uncertainty. They seek to clearly understand how the organization can break free of the industry's current limits. No one organizational effort we've explored scored 100 points on every one of the lessons we pointed to. They represent a collective experience and each enterprise may find itself assembling its own unique set. But while no success required 100% of the lessons, there were no successes that failed to achieve at least a "passing score" on most of the list.

The exception is the pivot point. All of our success stories effectively used a pivot point in their transformation. They used it for leverage, for communication, for clarity, for focus, for a shared guide to decision making, and for a goal that could be personally relevant and timely throughout the initiative. If readers take nothing else from these lessons we hope they will remember the central role of the pivot point in effective enterprise transformation.

In closing, we looked at "Fatal Moves" and "Strategy." As you transform your enterprise, look back to the list of fatal moves to help guarantee that your initiative will be successful. Look also to the strategic implications of your initiatives to help guarantee that your initiative will lay the groundwork for future successes in an ever-changing economic landscape. Perhaps the key question in today's competitive world is not "Is your transformation strategic?" but "Is your strategy transformative?"

CHAPTER 18

NEWELL RUBBERMAID

WILLIAM PIERRE SOVEY

ABSTRACT

The formation and evolution of the Newell Company from 1902 to 2000 is chronicled. Changes of the retail marketplace in the period are discussed and Newell's adaptations are explained. The lessons learned from almost 80 acquisitions in the 1967-2000 period are summarized. This experience base gained from these acquisitions led to the construct of "Newellization," which is introduced and elaborated.

INTRODUCTION

It is instructive to learn the principles one company employed to grow a modest business investment of $1,000, made over a century ago by a man who had no experience in the businesses that he purchased, into a highly successful multi-billion dollar international enterprise. This achievement resulted from many factors that came together in such a way that unusual success was achieved. The efforts of countless people were focused and directed over many years by successive management teams that continued to follow the path that led the company to the successful achievement of its objectives. The methods the company employed were all just common sense, but they accomplished uncommon results. Their success helped to transform the consumer products industry as it positioned itself to serve the needs of the revolution that was occurring in the marketplace. Mass marketing was redefining the face of retailing throughout the world and the Newell Company was well positioned to take advantage of the changes that were occurring.

In the 1980's a new word was coined that continues to be used today. The word cannot be found in dictionaries, but nonetheless has become well known in the business community. That word is "Newellization" and it has come to stand for the process of taking underperforming companies and, by applying the principles of Newellization, reshaping them into outstanding performers producing exceptional financial results. The process was repeated time and time again during the 1980's and the 1990's as The Newell Company acquired companies with unrealized profit potential. By implementing the profit improvement and productivity enhancement process, Newell brought newly acquired companies and product lines up to their high standards of profitability. That process became known as "Newellization" and proved to be a transforming method for enhancing the performance of acquisitions the company made. This insured profitable growth for the parent company and, as a result, increased returns for stockholders year after year.

NEWELL HISTORY

The Newell Company was founded in 1902 in Odgensburg, New York. This was during the period when many towns and cities across the country were vying for new businesses, seeking to take part in the industrial expansion that was occurring throughout North America. Edgar A. Newell owned a wholesale firm selling books, stationary and notions in Odgensburg and was President of Odgensburg's Board of Trade, the forerunner of the Chamber of Commerce. In that role, he signed a note advancing $1,000 to the Linton Manufacturing Company of Providence, Rhode Island, a manufacturer of brass curtain rods, to entice the company to move to Odgensburg. Although he had no understanding of manufacturing himself, when the company floundered soon after the move, Edgar Newell felt obligated to take it over. Fortunately, this was a time when manufacturing was beginning to boom and new methods produced new products that found many uses as the economy expanded and the country's population grew.

The manufacture of large plate glass became a reality during that period enabling retailers like F.W. Woolworth to display their products in the front of their stores. People could now see a variety of goods as they walked the sidewalk and the term "window shopping" was born. (Cuthbert, 1983). Larger glass windows in homes soon followed and curtains and draperies and the hardware required to support them became in increasing demand. Edgar Newell had purchased a company with a future potential that was very promising.

Newell's business initially centered around selling to hardware stores and specialty retailers but soon gained national distribution by obtaining listings with F.W. Woolworth's growing national retail chain. The company expanded into Canada and into the middle west and later to the west coast as the country grew westward. F.W. Woolworth became Newell's largest customer on the eastern market and Kresge – later to become K-Mart – became the predominant retailer and Newell's largest customer in the mid-west.

In 1907 Edgar Newell hired his son Allan, a recent graduate of Williams College, to run the business. With the help of several men who came with the acquisition of Linton, Allan Newell was able to get the business under control and started producing brass extension curtain rods for the expanding market. The purchase of the Linton Company was Newell's first acquisition. Many more would follow.

Newell soon expanded into Canada forming Newell Manufacturing Company Ltd. in Prescott, Ontario to service the Montreal and Toronto markets. Ben Cuthbert, working as an accountant in the Odgensburg operation, became the general manager and eventually made the business very successful. Later when Allan Newell retired, Ben Cuthbert was asked to run the entire company. By 1909 total employment had reached almost 20 people and annual sales approached $50,000.

In 1921, Newell opened the Western Newell Manufacturing Company in Freeport, Illinois. It was an immediate profit maker thanks largely to the skill of the general manager, Leonard Ferguson, who had joined the company that year. Western Newell prospered and grew under Ferguson's leadership and became the largest and most profitable of the Newell companies. Later when the businesses were all combined, including The drapery hardware business Newell started in California, Leonard Ferguson became the president of the entire Newell Company and ran it very successfully until he turned the presidency over to his son, Dan Ferguson, in 1966.

Newell realized early that the future of the company would best be served by supplying products to the large "mass retailers". That policy later became central to the successful strategy the company employed. The company's main focus for many years continued to be on curtain rods and drapery hardware and later on window shades. By the mid 1960's sales had reached almost $15 million and, while still a very small family business, the foundation had been laid that would permit the company to enjoy continued success. What was missing was an effective growth strategy and that came in 1967.

Strategy

Dan Ferguson succeeded his father Leonard as President and CEO of Newell in 1966. The company was sound and profitable with a limited product line but had no defined strategy for the future. Soon after taking over, Dan, a recent graduate of Stanford's MBA program, attended a Young President's Organization meeting on strategy led by Stanford professor Bob Katz. Dan was young and looking for guidance and direction as Katz explained how important a proper strategy is to the success of a business enterprise. The two connected and Katz was asked to join the Newell Board of Directors, the first non-family member to be invited on the board. Together the two conceived the strategy that enabled the company to achieve the success it enjoyed in subsequent years.

In analyzing the company's strengths, it was clear that manufacturing, merchandising and selling low cost products in quantity to large volume purchasers was what the company did best. They also knew how to relate with and sell to large national retail chains and this became the basis for establishing a very simple and basic strategy that would become the road map to Newell's success.

Newell defined itself as a manufacturer and full service marketer of high volume consumer products serving the needs of volume purchasers. Newell's primary business strategy was to merchandise a multi-product offering of brand name staple products while emphasizing outstanding customer service. Newell's products were to be non-seasonal and available on retailer's shelves year round - products that were low in fashion and technology content, low in price but high in volume and value – products that would sell well in good times and bad and ones that would be useful in every household.

Mission

The mission was to build a Fortune 500 company with above average earnings growth and return on investment and with a reputation for excellence in performance and management.

July 1, 1967

STATEMENT OF NEWELL COMPANIES

Newell defines its basic business as that of manufacturing and distributing volume merchandise lines to the volume merchandisers. A combination or package of lines going to the large retailers carries more marketing impact than each line separately, and Newell intends to build its growth through performance and the marketing leverage of this package. This package will also have more economic impact on the financial community both for the securing of financing for future expansion and for the establishment of a market for the Companies' equity securities.

Newell is in a financial position to build the desired package. It has a net worth of approximately 10 million dollars with no long term debt and earnings are substantial and growing.

Newell management is professional, young, aggressive, and in excellent control of the basic hardware and shade business. We are aware of the tremendous marketing base, good will, and expertise we have in dealing with large merchandisers, and we are dedicated to building growth in earnings for Newell on this solid base.

Daniel C. Ferguson
es

Source: Newell Company

FIGURE 1. Newell Strategy Statement, 1967

Financial Objectives

Newell's financial objectives were to maintain returns on equity of 20% or above, achieve sales and earnings per share growth averaging 15% per year, to increase dividends consistent with earnings growth and to maintain a prudent degree of leverage with debt not to exceed one half of equity.

JANUARY 1, 1985

TOTAL NEWELL STRATEGY

DEFINITION

NEWELL IS A MARKETER OF STAPLE VOLUME LINES OF CONSUMER GOODS TO THE VOLUME PURCHASER.

MISSION

TO BUILD A FORTUNE 500 COMPANY WITH ABOVE AVERAGE EARNINGS GROWTH AND RETURN ON INVESTMENT AND WITH A REPUTATION FOR EXCELLENCE IN PERFORMANCE AND MANAGEMENT.

BASIC STRATEGY

TO MERCHANDISE TO THE CONSUMER GOODS MARKET A MULTI-PRODUCT OFFERING FOR MAXIMUM PENETRATION AND PROFIT LEVERAGE.

FINANCIAL GOALS

RETURN ON INVESTMENT (ROI)   20% PLUS

OPERATING TURNOVER $\left(\dfrac{\text{SALES}}{\text{TANGIBLE ASSETS}}\right)$ 2

DEBT   1/2 OF EQUITY (1:2)

EARNINGS GROWTH   15% OR GNP + 5% MINIMUM

FIGURE 2. Total Newell Strategy

Culture

The magic in the strategy that Newell embraced was in its simplicity. What set the company apart from its competitors and allowed it to make outstanding returns was its focus on a basic strategy, on performance for Newell's customers and on profitability and return for the company's stockholders. Those precepts were all woven into the fabric of the company and became part of the company's culture.

The company's headquarters moved from Odgensburg, New York to its larger operation in Freeport, Illinois and later to a farmhouse set amid cornfields on the border of Illinois and Wisconsin. (Collis & Montgomery, 1977). The corporate headquarters were modest and reflected that the growing company favored a lean approach to business. Its mid-western values and family owned entrepreneurial spirit created a culture where people and the company thrived.

CHANGING RETAILING MARKET PLACE

Newell recognized very early the shift in retailing away from the smaller mom and pop stores to the larger retailers that became the mass merchants that we know today and positioned itself to serve that changing marketplace. The company believed that during times of change great opportunities presented themselves to those who recognized what was necessary to support that change. The company was one of the first with value added marketing programs that offered computer-to-computer information systems thereby simplifying the ordering process for their customers. They tailored sales programs to meet individual customer requirements so that competing retailers could offer similar products displayed and merchandised differently so that price comparisons were difficult to make. They also provided unparalleled on-time delivery and line fill, coupled with innovative in-store merchandising support. Newell established the first modem connection for Electronic Data Interchange (EDI) transfer with Wal-Mart in the mid 1970's and followed with Quick Response inventory supply systems. (Collis & Montgomery, 1977). Newell was more advanced in its computer systems than their competitors were and even ahead of the retailers. This advantage made Newell a valued supplier.

Newell's strategy for growth was focused on providing outstanding products and service to their customers while achieving above average returns for their stockholders. The growth strategy supported this goal through a structure that included new products, innovative merchandising, above average returns to investors, internal growth, acquisitions and Newellization. Newell sought to achieve balanced growth fueled by a combination of internal growth and acquisitions. (Newell Annual Report, 1987).

NEWELL GOES PUBLIC

The company went public in 1971 and joined the New York Stock Exchange in 1978. With its strategy, culture, discipline and finances in place, the company started its cycle of growth seeking to acquire companies that had products that were number one or number two in market share and that fit the company's strategy of staple products that could be sold to volume purchasers.

Company Organization

Initially, the company was centrally organized with all business functions performed by the corporate organization. As the company grew, it became apparent that the company should be broken up into discrete divisions responsible for their own performance. Divisions were charged with designing, manufacturing or procuring their own products, merchandising and marketing them and supporting their customers with outstanding service. The administrative functions were retained at corporate where customer orders were received by computer and transmitted to the various divisions for shipment. Corporate was also responsible for accounts receivable, payables, insurance, cash management, information systems, accounting, taxes, employee benefits and the financial and legal functions.

Each division was led by a President who also served as the principal marketing officer and was expected to be in constant contact with customers. Each division had its own unique strategy that supported the corporate strategy. Divisional strategies were reviewed semi-annually in conjunction with corporate to insure that the divisions were following their very narrowly focused strategy and not becoming involved with supplying products or services that did not fit with the overall corporate plan.

Each division had its own budget and compensation plan that included both stock options and incentives that enabled the participants to significantly increase their total compensation by achieving stated objectives. While the divisions helped one another in gaining new business with customers by sharing their knowledge, there was healthy competition between divisions to turn in the best performance and to be recognized as outstanding contributors to the company's success.

Budgeting at the divisional and corporate levels was considered to be a "contract" to achieve the financial objectives established. (Collis & Montgomery, 1977). The variable budgeting process was strictly monitored monthly and negative variations to budgets prompted divisions to be called in to corporate for dreaded "bracket" meetings to explain discrepancies. If business conditions changed significantly resulting in large gains or losses in business during the year, budgets were adjusted so as to reflect current operating conditions. Adherence to budget was strictly controlled and competition between the divisions for performance recognition was keen.

Newell's objectives and culture permeated throughout the organization. Managers attended Newell University, which was conducted quarterly, as well as annual management meetings and conferences for sales and marketing, controllers, customer service and operations. Division presidents' meetings were held every other month and quarterly operation reviews were conducted at each division.

Recognition and awards were made to worthy individuals and divisional achievers at the annual management meeting award ceremonies.

Start of Growth Cycle

From a small manufacturer of drapery hardware with sales approaching $15 million in the late 1960's, Newell started its dramatic growth. By 1985, sales had reached nearly $350 million with net income of $20 million. This growth resulted from integrating acquisitions supported by internal growth from existing product lines as the vehicle to execute the company's multi-product offering. People thought that Newell was in the acquisition business, but they were not. They were building a package for the mass retailers and acquisitions were but one of the tools to create that package. (Casey, 1988).

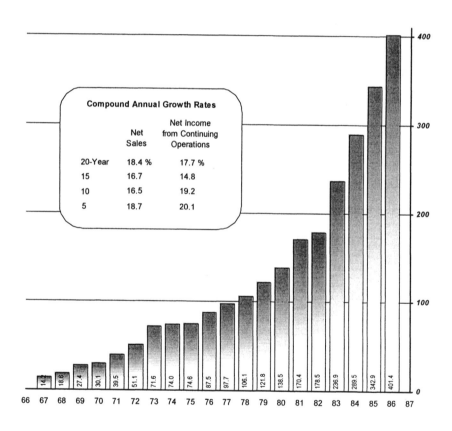

FIGURE 3. Newell Twenty Years of Growth

By 1990, sales had exceeded $1.2 billion with net income of over $126 million. By 1995, sales had reached $2.5 billion with net income surpassing $226 million. The company had acquired more than 50 companies in the prior 25 years and, in the past 5 years alone, Newell had completed over 10 major acquisitions representing nearly $2 billion in additional sales.

	Newell Acquisitions **1967 – 2000** **(Partial List)**
1967	Joint venture with Breneman, Inc. – window shades
1968	Newell Manufacturing Company Canada – drapery hardware
1969	E.H. Tate Company –home hardware Mirra-Cote – bathroom hardware Dorfile Manufacturing Company – shelving systems
1971	Boye Needle Company – art needlework
1973	EZ Paintr Corporation – paint applicators Jordan Industries – home hardware
1978	Red Devil Canada – paint applicators Edgecraft Corporation – shelving systems Baker Brush Company – paint applicators
1980	Brearly Company – bath scales (Counselor)
1981	Jiffy Enterprises – home hardware Judd Drapery Hardware – drapery hardware
1982	Bernzomatic Corporation – handheld torches Handi-Man Corportation – home hardware
1983	Mirro Corporation – cookware and bakeware
1984	Foley-ASC Inc. – cookware and bakeware Lilo-Rail of Canada – drapery hardware
1985	William E. Wright Corporation – ribbon, lace and trimmings Androck Inc. Canada – paint applicators and hardware Ignitor Products International Incorporated – handheld torches 39% of American Tool – Vise Grip - locking tools
1986	Enterprise Aluminum Company – cookware

1987	Borg Company – bath scales
	Anchor Hocking including:
	    - Anchor Hocking Glass
	    - Anchor Hocking Plastics
	    - Anchor Hocking Packaging
	    - Plastics Incorporated
	    - Anchor Hocking Industrial Glass
	    - Amerock

1988	Thomas Industries – paint applicators division

	Vermont American – tool accessories division
	REMA Corporation – bakeware
1989	Wearever – cookware
1990	15% equity of Black and Decker – tools
	Keene Manufacturing – office products \
	W.T. Rogers – office products
1992	Intercraft – picture frames
	Stuart Hall – office products
	Sanford Corporation – writing instruments
1993	Levolor – window covering
	Systems Works – cabinet hardware
	Lee Rowan – hardware
	Goody Products – hair care and accessories
1994	Home Fashions Incorporated – window coverings
	Louver Drape – drapery hardware
	Faber-Castell Corporation – writing instruments
	Corning Incorporated European Consumer Products – Pyrex-glassware
1995	Decorel Incorporated – picture frames
	Berol Corporation – writing instruments
1996	Holson Burnes Group – picture frames
1997	Rolodex Corporation – office products
	Kirsch – drapery hardware
	Eldon, Rubbermaid Office Products Division – office products
	Acme Frame Product – picture frames
	Wilhold – picture frames
1998	Calphalon – cookware
	Swish U.K. – drapery hardware
	Panex Brazil – cookware
	Gardinia Germany – drapery hardware
	Rotring Germany – writing instruments
	Cosmolab – writing technical products
1999	Rubbermaid including:
	- Rubbermaid Home Products
	- Rubbermaid Commercial Products
	- Rubbermaid Cleaning Products
	- Curver Europe
	- Graco
	- Little Tykes
	- Century
	- Carex
	Regal – cookware
	Spur U.K. – shelving systems
	Reynolds France – writing instruments
2000	PaperMate – writing instruments
	Parker – writing instruments
	Waterman – writing instruments

FIGURE 4. Newell Acquisitions 1967 - 2000

As part of its acquisition planning, Newell looked for branded, staple consumer products with long product life cycles, products that had the potential to reach the company's high standards of profitability. Unrealized profit potential was one of the primary factors that attracted Newell to the companies it acquired and "Newellization" was the improvement process that was applied to the newly acquired product line to bring them up the Newell's standards. Newell quickly redirected acquired businesses to focus on their more profitable core products while pruning away unprofitable ones and aligning themselves with the corporate core strategy. The hope was that 2+2 would equal more than 4 and that the "power of the package". (Newell Annual Report, 1993) would become stronger and more desirable to their customers. It was profit growth, not sales growth, that was important. (Newell Annual Report, 1995).

ELEMENTS OF NEWELLIZATION

Elements of the "Newellization" process included:

- Establishing a focused divisional business strategy consistent with the corporate strategy,

- Improving customer service dramatically including on-time delivery and line fill,

- Building partnerships with customers,

- Eliminating corporate overhead through centralization of administrative functions,

- Trimming excess costs,

- Tightening financial controls,

- Improving manufacturing efficiencies,

- Pruning non-profitable product lines,

- Reducing inventories,

- Increasing trade receivable turnover, and

- Improving sales mix profitability through application of program merchandising techniques.

None of the individual elements of Newellization were unique or unusual, just the common sense application of proven principles of management.

Potentially lucrative incentive plans helped to motivate the newly acquired divisions to reach their objectives. As part of "Newellization", sales often declined as unprofitable product lines were reduced or eliminated. In the Newell growth strategy, once an acquired company had been Newellized – a process that usually took about 2 years – it was expected to increase its sales profitably and contribute to Newell's internal growth initiative.

New acquisitions were staffed with a veteran President and Controller brought in from another Newell division. This enabled the culture, discipline, systems, controls and focus on profitability to be put into place ensuring an early start toward Newellization. Teams of corporate managers and executives, acting in addition to their regular jobs, quickly moved in to assist in the Newellization process. (Collis & Montgomery, 1977). These teams had experienced this many times, knew exactly what to do and how to do it and never tired of the challenge.
Newell's culture empowered people to take on responsibility knowing that they would be recognized and rewarded. Managers were motivated and skilled and turnover was very low.

MAJOR ACQUISITIONS

Some acquisitions proved to be defining moments in the company history. In 1973, Newell acquired the EZ Paintr Company which became the largest paint applicator company in the world as Newell made other acquisitions of companies that produced paint brushes and rollers. While it was not Newell's first acquisition, it was the first significant one and provided another product line to market in addition to drapery hardware and window shades.

The next major acquisition for Newell brought the company into the cookware and bakeware product category with the purchase of the Mirro Corporation in 1983. Many cookware acquisitions followed including Foley, Enterprise Aluminum, Wearever and REMA with its bakeware brands of Cushionaire and Airbake. Newell later acquired the upscale cookware manufacturer, Calphalon.

The acquisition that propelled Newell into prominence and that grabbed Wall Street's attention was the 1987 acquisition of the Anchor Hocking Company, the maker of glassware and hardware products that brought Newell the Anchor Hocking and Amerock brand names.

In 1985 Anchor Hocking's sales totaled $720 million compared to Newell's $350 million, however, Newell was substantially more profitable. Newell's profit margins of 11% vastly exceeded Anchor Hocking's 0.5% margin. (Collis & Montgomery, 1977). Newell saw a strategic fit plus unrealized profit potential and succeeded in taking over the company. The combination pushed Newell's sales to over $1 billion in 1988 and gave the company the opportunity to see Newellization transform the newly acquired company into a valuable contributor to Newell's total profitability.

Every element of Newellization helped contribute to the turnaround. Unprofitable segments were either sold of discontinued. Segments that did not fit Newell's strategy were Newellized too, made more profitable, and sold. The remaining businesses were broken into seven separate divisions, each with its own management and narrowly focused strategy. The remaining business segments then gave the company expanded housewares and hardware offerings that made Newell a more important source for branded consumer products for retailers. The later acquisition of Corning's Pyrex operations in Europe provided access to international markets which resulted in increased sales of more products to Europe's mass merchants.

Not every company that Newell acquired underwent the complete Newellization process. One company in particular, Sanford, the writing instrument company acquired in 1992, was clearly an exception and unlike most did not require a refocus on profitability. Sanford, the maker of the Sharpie permanent ink marker, EXPO dry erase markers, Accent highlighters and Uniball rollerball pens was the most profitable and, up until Rubbermaid, the most expensive acquisition the company had ever made. Their already high level of profitability was enhanced even more as all administrative functions were taken over by Newell. Corporate overhead was cut, inventories reduced, marginal product lines eliminated, a focused strategy defined and strict financial controls were employed.

Prior to the acquisition of Sanford, Newell had purchased several small office products businesses realizing that the office products retail marketplace was drastically changing just as the mass merchandise market had changed. The corner stationery store was giving way to the office superstores – Office Depot, Office Max and Staples. Newell saw opportunity with this changing retail environment and wanted to participate in the growth it represented.

The smaller acquisitions of Keene, Stuart Hall and W.T. Rogers were opportunities to understand the business and the Sanford acquisition signaled to the marketplace that Newell intended to be a serious participant in the growth of the office products category. Many acquisitions followed to strengthen Newell's position including Rubbermaid's office products division Eldon, Berol, Faber-Castell, Rotring, Reynolds, Rolodex and Gillette's writing instruments businesses including PaperMate, Parker, and Waterman.

All were Newellized, improving profitability, and the office products segment became the most profitable part of the company. Newell became the largest writing instrument manufacturer and supplier in the world, producing products that were easily sold without modification to both domestic markets and markets throughout the world.

INTERNATIONAL GROWTH

Newell's growth strategy was initially focused solely on the North American marketplace. While an export division was created that supplied limited products to foreign markets, it wasn't until the mid-1980's that Newell began to turn its sights toward international markets. While the primary growth opportunity was still centered in the United States, Canada and Mexico, the company began to look for acquisition opportunities abroad. Europe represented an area of both familiarity and opportunity so the company began to make acquisitions overseas that complemented the businesses in North America and that were a fit with the company's overall strategy.

As the company grew both domestically and internationally, the product lines offered expanded to include housewares, hardware and tools, office products and home furnishing. Newell's customer base expanded as well to include such notable retailers as Wal-Mart, Home Depot, Lowes, Target, Ace Hardware and European retailers such as Carrefor and Metro.

By 1995, Newell was truly a global company with exciting opportunities both at home and abroad and progress continued. Growth from internal sources and acquisitions, sales to a diversified domestic and international customer base and a well-defined, focused business strategy had enabled Newell to attain its aggressive financial objectives.

CONCLUSIONS

Since going public in 1971, Newell's common stock had split two-for-one four times and had doubled the total return of the S&P index. The company consistently achieved returns on equity exceeding 20%. For many years during this period Newell was considered to be among the top 100 stocks to own on The New York Stock Exchange and in 1992 was ranked 24th on the Fortune 500 list for highest total return to investors over a 10 year period (Walden, 1989).

The last half of the decade of the 1990's saw Newell's growth continue with acquisitions followed by Newellization fueling the company's growth. At the end of the century, Newell' sales reached almost $7 billion as more companies with brand name products were acquired by the company. In 1999 Newell acquired Rubbermaid and changed its name to Newell Rubbermaid. Today the company employs over 33,000 people in its worldwide operations with products that service markets for consumers all over the world.

Newell Rubbermaid is an example of what can be achieved in business when a simple, basic strategy is executed in a way that benefits all the constituents of the company – its customers, employees and stockholders. Sticking to principles that are well tested and proven, while adding the common sense process of Newellization, helped to transform the company and make it into a highly successful business enterprise.

REFERENCES

Casey, Lisa Ann, (1988). <u>Newell Accesses Acquisitions – The Weekly Home Furnishing Newsletter.</u>

Collis, D.J., & Montgomery, C.A. (1977). <u>Corporate Strategy – Resources and the Scope of the Firm.</u>

Cuthbert, W. (1983). <u>Newell Companies – A Corporate History – The First 40 Years.</u>

Newell Annual Reports   1987, 1993, 1995

Walden, Gene, (1989), <u>The 100 Best Stocks to Own in America.</u>

CHAPTER 19

THE TRANSFORMATION OF REEBOK

DOMINIE GARCIA WITH DAVID PERDUE

ABSTRACT

Corporate transformation can take many forms and be instigated by a diverse set of forces. In the case of Reebok, a prolonged period of losing to the competition and not foreseeing market changes precipitated the need for major change. David Perdue, one of the leading executives during the transformation, tells the story of how the company was able to pull itself out of danger, and reorient itself both internally and externally. Reebok, for at least the second time in its history, was able to reinvent important aspects of the footwear business while at the same time infusing its corporate culture with renewed energy and focus.

INTRODUCTION

In 1895, Mr. J.W. Foster, a runner in England, put roofing tacks through the bottom of his street shoes and the first track shoe was born. Mr. Foster and his family built a footwear business around this concept and in 1958, two of Mr. Foster's grandsons founded a sister company named Reebok, after an African gazelle.

In 1979, Mr. Paul Fireman purchased the license to distribute Reebok products in the United States. Only a couple of years later, he bought the entire company. With the introduction of Reebok sneakers into the United States, the company rocketed to success throughout the 1980s. The brand was recognized and coveted by buyers of many age groups and had innovated many areas of fitness and exercising, playing a pivotal role in opening the public's eyes to women's involvement in sports and fitness. Nike was its major competitor throughout this period, and the two vied for top market share position.

However, something happened in the mid 1990s that resulted in a quick decline of the financial success of Reebok. By 1998, the company's sales and profits were the lowest they had been in almost a decade. There seemed to be little hope for a turnaround or revitalization. Just two years later, however, the company was on its way up again. In the year 2000, Reebok was the best performing stock on the S&P 500 index. Since then the true depth of the turnaround effort has become apparent and the company continues to improve.

This chapter will tell the story of this rapid turnaround, what led initially to the need for transformation, and the factors that brought the company out of its downward spiral. The story comes from one of the key players in the transformation, David Perdue, who was a fundamental part of this era of change at Reebok, serving first as Senior Vice President of Operations and later as President and CEO of the Reebok brand during the transformation.

The chapter will briefly review the history of Reebok, setting up the context and background of the decline in the 1990s as well as the transformation leading to revitalization and success. The forces that combined, both externally and internally, to create the need for large-scale change will be discussed. Chairman and CEO, Paul Fireman, and his executive management team implemented a five-pillar strategy to focus the company on the goals that would bring Reebok out of its slump. These five fundamental pillars related directly to the nature of the industry, the state of competition and customers' needs.

The environment that the Reebok leadership team created fostered a new energy for all within the company and directly translated to the execution of the transformation process, which subsequently translated into clear recognition by customers, investors, and competitors of the strength and drive of the company. Leadership techniques that were applied will be explained and illustrated in order to fully convey the different aspects of the transformation process that allowed for such a strong turnaround. Under Mr. Fireman's leadership, the firm's entrepreneurial legacy was reborn and the turnaround was achieved largely because many people within the company took risks and succeeded.

Lastly, we will discuss the lessons that can be learned from the Reebok transformation story. As part of a larger volume on enterprise transformation, this story can lend much insight into how the leadership of a company in need of transformation recognizes the need for change, implements the transformation, and keeps the focus on financial success throughout. These lessons can be applied to not only the industry in which Reebok operates but to many large organizations operating in mature industries that find themselves facing a critical situation and contemplating failure if transformation is not undertaken.

HISTORY OF REEBOK

Reebok was brought to the United States by a licensing agreement negotiated by Paul Fireman in 1979, to distribute the British-made running shoe in the US. The product quickly garnered much attention and success and two years later, the company realized revenues in excess of $1.5 million. In order to keep the upward momentum going, Fireman and his management team realized that there was a large market that had not been addressed by the initial running shoes sold in the U.S. by Reebok – women. At the same time, as the country was coming out of the '70s, and many of the women's movement's goals had been met, a new exercise program was gaining traction. Aerobics, embraced by women, was becoming a hot exercise regimen. Reebok combined its sports technology knowledge and its existing brand name to develop a shoe that addressed this market niche.

The development and introduction of the "aerobic shoe" was inspired by the experience of one of the company's top executives, Angel Martinez, who in the early 1980s observed his wife's exercise class working out barefooted because there were no appropriate shoes. Together with the product development and technology teams, Martinez and Fireman developed a first-of-its-kind shoe targeted at a growing segment of women who were exercising with new aerobic techniques.

Once the first aerobic shoe, Freestyle, was introduced, it quickly gained acceptance and success in the market, and Reebok was on an upward trajectory. The company increased its product offerings, inspired by the success of its first line extension. The first half of the '80s was marked by constant growth in sales and profits, as well as brand name recognition in the U.S. In 1985, the initial public offering of Reebok was completed successfully, and on July 26 the first public issue of Reebok stock was sold at $17 a share and increased 53.7% by year-end. The latter half of the decade saw expansion into international markets and the expansion of distribution networks – both independent and Reebok-owned. In addition, much of the company's efforts at this time were focused on product development and increased technological differentiation, birthing among others the Pump Technology, which garnered huge attention and success in the market. Throughout this period, Reebok maintained its reputation and connection with the female market, constantly innovating products for running, walking, and other sports women enjoyed.

Much like the company that helped shape an exercise platform, with the advent of the aerobic shoe, so did Reebok create a new exercise market with the invention of the Step system of exercise. Scientific and biomechanical research showed this new exercise system to be very effective with low impact. As a result, Reebok launched Step Reebok in 1989, to much acclaim, helping to revitalize the health club market in the US. Soon thereafter, Step Reebok became an international success as well, and today is an integral part of health club offerings around the world.

EXPANDING THE LINE

The 1980s saw Reebok expand its offerings by acquiring Rockport in 1986, a company that realized sales in 1985 of $64 million. By buying Rockport, yet keeping its new acquisition as a wholly owned subsidiary operating independently of the Reebok brand, the company added a line of footwear that was outside of its traditional athletic shoe product lines. Rockport makes a line of footwear and related apparel marketed to professional men and women that are engineered for comfort. These products include both causal and dress shoes. By buying the company, Reebok extended its reach in the same market segments that it was already targeting with athletic footwear.

In the early 1990s the firm developed a relationship with Greg Norman. This led to an agreement in 1991 for Reebok to license the "shark" logo that Norman had developed for his company, Great White Shark Enterprises, on golf apparel, shoes and golf gloves under a licensing agreement. The Greg Norman Collection produces golf-related apparel and accessories, as well as related athletic and fitness apparel targeted to the leisure segment, and is still structured as a separate division.

In 1996, Polo Ralph Lauren entered into a long-term exclusive licensing arrangement with Reebok to design, develop, manufacture, market and distribute footwear under prestigious Ralph Lauren brands. This included the Polo and Polo Sport brands and all segments of the market – children's, men's and women's shoes. The licensing deal allowed Reebok to also acquire the existing licensees in the US and Canada. The new operations were placed under the Rockport division of the company and managed as part of that brand. However, growth of the Ralph Lauren Footwear division was rapid, as the market quickly reacted to an increased offering of fashionable and comfortable shoes. By 1998, the division was changed to operate as a wholly owned subsidiary. Today, Reebok International Corporation operates Rockport, Greg Norman, and the Ralph Lauren Polo Footwear division in addition to the flagship Reebok brand.

THE NEED FOR CHANGE

During the 1980s, Reebok's success in the fitness and exercise arenas continued and its reputation with its core customers remained strong. Female fitness buffs, exercise leaders, and women who exercised regularly were the brand's strongest and most loyal customers, recognizing the value and quality of the products and the fact that the designs were specific to women's bodies and needs. At the same time, buoyed by its tremendous success, the company began to look beyond the traditional fitness and exercise markets towards the professional sports world as its next area of customer focus.

As late as the early 1990s, Reebok and Nike, the firm's largest competitor, were very close in terms of global market share. By 1997, Nike had grown to be considerably larger than Reebok, particularly in the US market, where it had grown a 47% market share. Reebok's share in the US had dropped to 15% in 1997. This occurred primarily as a result of Nike's sports marketing efforts centered around marquee athletes such as Bo Jackson ("Let Bo Do It") and Michael Jordan. Figure 1 shows a chart of the market shares for both companies. (Note market share numbers vary according to source, and comparable figures for 1999 were not available.)

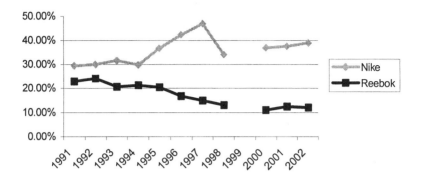

FIGURE 1. American Market Shares

Furthermore, Nike had focused much of its efforts on securing strong relationships with the large retail chains that began to gain in strength during the 1990s. By the end of the decade, Reebok's market share, profits and other financial measures were well below its previous record of success, and the company was fast losing ground to its competitors. Figures 2 and 3 show the yearly profit and global sales numbers for Reebok.

Internally, although Reebok's organizational structure was stable, there was a high rate of turnover with the middle management staff, which caused a constant state of uncertainty.

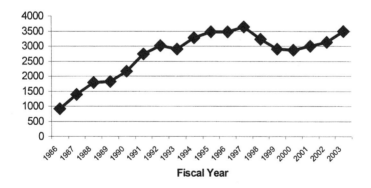

FIGURE 2. Net Sales (MM$)

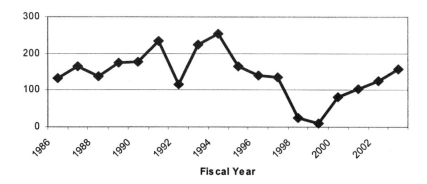

FIGURE 3. Net Income (Loss) (MM$)

One other external factor that contributed to Reebok's financial situation in the later 1990s was that throughout that decade consumers in general were becoming much more discerning about their choices. As choices in the market increased, consumer demands became much more specific. The company had been losing its focus on quality and innovation in terms of consumer products and their relevance, just as consumers were learning more about how to choose between products and brands.

While Reebok continued to develop new technologies and to make significant marketing investments, it somehow lost its edge in the '90s regarding product quality and the specific needs of different customer groups. By 1998, Reebok was in a much different position than it had been five or ten years earlier. Its financials were suffering greatly, and Wall Street had lost much confidence in the company. Its core customers were faltering in their loyalty and market share had been severely lost to its largest rival. Its relationships with the distributors and retailers had deteriorated. It was time for a major transformation.

Paul Fireman, the Chairman and CEO of the company since its inception in the US and the architect of all that had been accomplished so quickly, recognized the need for this change.

THE FIVE PILLARS OF THE TRANSFORMATION

In 1998, the situation at Reebok was troubling for several reasons. The internal financial measures were not healthy as evidenced by large debt, large overhead (SG&A), and low margins on reduced sales numbers. The market share numbers had been decreasing for several years, and the customer base seemed to be waning.

Paul Fireman, with the help of his executive team, developed a five-fold strategy to address the major issues and turn the company around. The timeline was short, given the huge debt burden and the mature and competitive nature of the business. These five pillars were executed under a broader segmentation strategy that served as a major driving principle of the company. In addition, a renewed focus on product was instituted. The five pillars identified were:

1. Clean up the balance sheet

2. Fix the income statement

3. Reconnect with the customer

4. Segment product development and marketing strategy

5. Partner effectively with retailers

Pillars 3 and 4 were the most important aspects of the transformation, and all of the five pillars needed to be implemented simultaneously. The overall strategy for the transformation evolved out of management discussions about the current state of the company, the market, competitors and customers' expectations. Paul Fireman realized that the company had lost its focus on quality and product, and decided that a "back to basics" approach was needed to focus the operations, marketing, and product development of the company.

One example of this was the Princess shoe – one of the first aerobic shoes for women. Originally, the shoe was the first in the industry to be made of "garment leather", which made it light and very comfortable. As the years went by, the specifications for the leather were changed marginally but several times to reduce cost. The resulting shoe was not as light or as comfortable. Sales were declining rapidly. Mr. Fireman knew something was wrong and when it was discovered that the leather spec had been changed, he immediately changed it back to the original (higher cost & quality) specification. Sales of the Princess rebounded nicely and it remains in the line today.

Based on insight and knowledge of market, economic and demographic factors, the management team understood that this focus on quality and product could best be implemented and executed by an overall segmentation strategy, both in the product development and the marketing functions. These ideas required operational excellence, organizational discipline and a streamlined structure in order to be executed quickly and effectively. Thus, the segmentation strategy drove the focus of the management team, as well as the functional groups that executed the strategy and structural changes on a daily basis.

The segmentation strategy was a derivative of the commitment to product and quality that drove the executive vision of the transformation. Fireman believed that in order for the transformation to effectively take place, the company had to change perceptions of itself, both internally and externally. In addition, one of the most effective aspects of this transformation strategy and process was that none of the areas of focus were seen as being independent of the others. All were connected, with overlaps everywhere. This implied that communication needed to be open and the different groups within the company needed to understand what others were doing. As mentioned, people were being encouraged to take risks to improve their work product quickly.

Cleaning Up the Balance Sheet and Fixing the Income Statement

Market forces affecting Reebok in the late 1990s affected its financial statistics as well. Revenues had been steadily declining as the company lost market share to its competitors, while at the same time, net income was declining at a much more rapid rate, due to increased costs within the company. (See Figures 2 & 3). As the executive team developed a strategy of focusing on product and quality through a targeted segmentation strategy, they also realized that the financial situation of the company had to be stabilized quickly in order to free up resources to pursue such a transformation.

Needed attention was given to reducing internal costs of operations and reducing long-term debt that had been accumulating. (Figure 4 shows the long term debt figures.) The internal financial strategy was focused around two fundamental goals. The first was to increase communications among the management team to raise the level of information and knowledge that the decision makers had about the current state of business operations. The second goal was to simultaneously heighten awareness among senior executives to manage to internally-set estimates and goals. This increased emphasis on financial discipline and connecting it with the long-term strategy was an important piece of freeing up resources to pursue many of the changes.

Several of the items that increased financial and operational efficiencies were connected to the shared services capability that Reebok had begun to develop and implement in 1998. Because over 80% of Reebok International Ltd. sales had always been generated by the Reebok brand, it made sense to aggregate many of the support functions under the structure and operations of the Reebok brand for the three other divisions – Greg Norman, Rockport and Ralph Lauren Footwear. In addition, with the consolidation of shared services across the four brands, management also eliminated other general and administrative expenses, cutting up to $200M (or close to 20%) of the overall company expenses. These disciplined financial moves released resources to shift many of the company's investments, thereby freeing up more capital and setting the stage for the change of strategy that was at the heart of the transformation.

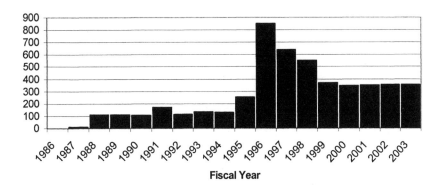

FIGURE 4. Long Term Debt (MM$)

At the same time, the firm's significant marketing investments were redirected. The company's sports marketing was dramatically refocused and decisions were made to connect with the customers the brand aspired to attract in new and different ways. Key team members, focusing on the financial situation of the company, were closely tied into the segmentation strategy and encouraged the product development and marketing operations to take more risks for long-term success. Internal financial operations began to include a more focused strategy about where the majority of the resources were allocated, assuring they would be completely in line with product development priorities.

Reconnecting with the Customer

In thinking about the question of how Reebok got into trouble in the late 1990s, after having enjoyed such rapid success, the issues of authenticity and identifiability came to light. Reebok had been trying to send the same message and sell similar products to all of its consumers. However, these were all very different groups and could not relate to the same marketing messages, nor did they have the same product demands or needs.

Reebok had lost much of its brand equity with women that it had originally developed in the early 1990s. Nike had always owned the young male athletes' market segment, and had been seen as aggressive in its tactics and marketing. Reebok was seen as a more responsive presence, focused on engagement with and loyalty to the customer. As a result, the young, mostly male, black athletes and those consumers that looked up to them did not see Reebok as relevant, hip, or cool. Overall, the company did not have a clear message targeted to any particular consumer group, nor were its product offerings focused on these individual segments.

Once these issues had been identified, and the need for transformation became clear, a focus and overriding theme for the change was envisioned by the CEO – re-focus on product and quality. Company executives realized that the connection with customers was so vital to the revitalization that it could only be achieved through an appropriate segmentation strategy. Through market research and the inherent understanding of the consumers that management had developed over the years, the company segmented the customers into three general classes – young women, the "authentic athlete", and boomers. Each group of consumers was then analyzed, in terms of its characteristics, its demands, and its opportunities for future growth and direction. These segments were then appropriately connected to the product development and marketing strategies.

Reebok had lost some resonance with female customers and the "true" female athlete. This was the core and loyal group of customers upon which the company had originally built its reputation and success. Women involved in fitness began looking at other brands to fulfill their needs. For addressing the needs and demands of the female customer, including girls, young mothers and other young, active women, the company first created a small team of women to work on analyzing the needs and desires of these customers by conducting extensive market research.

For the "authentic athletes," who were mostly males, and were the earliest fashion adapters and leaders, Reebok realized the key was to connect with the community. The brand had not been seen as relevant to the authentic athletic community. The idea of combining sports, music, and entertainment as a way to reach and connect with this segment was one of the elements that helped the company gain a stronger foothold with the authentic athlete market segment.

For the "boomers", walking was a predominant activity. This group was the strongest for Reebok but there was still a need to revitalize product offerings and connect with these consumers. Reebok has developed an image as the white shoemaker for older people.

Segmentation of Product Development and Marketing

Based on market research and the identification of three main consumer groups, Reebok developed a matrix to focus its product development operations. The product development team began to develop specific footwear in each sport for each consumer segment. A matrix oriented effort resulted. This helped reduce the number of SKUs, thereby reducing inventory, while at the same time broadening the reach of the product lines. This also helped to differentiate price points along consumer dimensions. Figure 5 shows a representation of the product development matrix.

Sport/functional class	Women	Authentic athlete	Boomers/older consumers
Basketball			
Football			
Cleated			
Tennis			
Walking			
Running			
Fitness/exercise			
Classics			

FIGURE 5. Product Development Matrix

Previously, the functional/sport specialist would focus primarily on whatever consumer group appealed to those managers/developers. Under the new system, specific technologies, styles and designs were developed according to what made sense to each consumer segment and the particular sport. This allowed the company to regain the high ground on quality – quality was designed into the shoe from the beginning of the process. Technology was forced to become more applicable to the particular combination of sport and consumer on the matrix. For example, DMX, or moving air support, was always a great technology, and had been extremely successful for Reebok. It was, however, a very high-end technology and therefore did not need to be included in all shoes. There were other high-quality technologies that were more applicable to certain consumer segments, the application of which was discovered during the segmentation of the product development process.

One example of the dedication of the employees to this turnaround and the focus on segmentation is the development of a women's group focused on development of women's specific products. Many of the female employees at the company had critiqued the female products as being "me too" of the men's shoes. When given the chance during the transformation, this group of women dedicated themselves to developing female-focused products that addressed women's needs and desires for both shoes and apparel. They created an integrated approach across footwear and apparel products as well as fashion and functional need.

In addition to segmenting product development efforts to line up with the consumer groups, portions of the product development operation were moved out of the U.S. and into development centers in Asia. This greatly reduced the time to get product to market because product development was closer to manufacturers.

Just as the consumer segmentation strategy drove product development, it also drove the marketing strategy. Not only had Reebok fallen short of developing focused products for different groups of customers, but it had also been sending similar messages to these different customer groups. Once the research indicated what the needs and interests of the segments were, specific marketing strategies were developed.

For female consumers, marketing was specifically targeted to print media because research had shown that this was a more effective channel for reaching women. Rather than condescending to the female consumer, the marketing campaigns tried to relate to the female and her specific level of need. In terms of branding, Reebok made the decision to use the vector logo for this sector. Based on all these activities, the company revitalized brand identity with the original core customers. Female designers were put in charge of this effort.

For the authentic athlete, the most lucrative and growing consumer segment, Reebok had its lowest market share. Getting into the community and listening to customers revealed the need to innovate in terms of its strategy as well as the need to secure relationships with top professional athletes. As a starting point to connect with this consumer segment, Reebok began its focus on basketball. A relationship with Allen Iverson began in 1996, when he was drafted from Georgetown into the National Basketball Association (NBA). In November of 2001, after five years of a positive working relationship with Reebok, and being awarded NBA MVP in 2000, he was signed for a lifetime commitment with Reebok.

The branding strategy here was to develop the Rbk brand, which appealed more to the street-wise attitude of this segment. At the same time, Reebok utilized the vector logo surrounded by a parallelogram for this segment.

During this transformation, Reebok hired the Arnell Group, an outside marketing firm that became a consultant to the company on this issue. The key players in the marketing firm were Peter Arnell and Steve Stoute, who were very connected to the urban music scene. They developed the idea to tie together music, entertainment and sports. This represented a way for Reebok to develop grass roots marketing, connect with the community, and get involved with young athletes. Reebok developed relationships with top hip-hop artists, such as Jay-Z and 50 Cent, and began to sponsor these entertainers on annual tours in urban communities that combined street basketball and music. These tours continue today and have grown in size and popularity and attract a broad market segment to the Rbk brand of footwear and apparel. Increasing the connection and relevance in the urban communities and with popular athletes also allowed the company to get more shelf space in major distribution channels.

In order to fund these new marketing efforts, a strategic decision was made to focus on sports at the highest level. That meant the company needed to focus its sports marketing investments on professional sports. Because of that, sports marketing with colleges was greatly reduced. Many endorsement contracts with professional athletes were also not renewed to allow the firm to focus its investments on top athletes. The firm called these top athletes "aspirational" because they could drive sales in a product group. Athletes such as Allen Iverson, Venus Williams and Andy Roddick were chosen for this focus.

In addition to focusing only on top athletes, an all out effort was made to change the way Reebok partnered with professional teams it sponsored. In 2001, Reebok secured exclusive licensing agreements with both the National Basketball Association (NBA) and the National Football League (NFL), a first for any footwear or sports apparel company. Both licensing agreements secured exclusive rights for Reebok to provide all warm up, sideline and coaches' apparel, as well as uniforms for all of the NBA and NFL teams. In addition, Reebok has been granted the exclusive licenses to manufacture and distribute official replica NFL and NBA branded apparel for certain channels of retail distribution in many countries around the world. (The specific countries in the licensing agreements differ for the two professional leagues, but generally encompass the largest markets internationally.) The NBA deal includes the same licensing and distribution agreements for WNBA teams as well.

In February 2002, Reebok secured a partnership deal with the Indy Racing League (IRL). The company will design apparel for IRL officials and selected teams. With the acquisition of Hockey Co. Holdings in June 2004, Reebok has also secured a licensing deal with the National Hockey League. In addition, Reebok also has negotiated several licensing deals for many high-profile football (soccer) teams in Europe and Canada.

All of these marketing strategies are very long-term propositions and execution and branding is still in process. At the time of writing this chapter (Fall 2004) Nike is still on top in terms of market share in this segment, but Reebok has gained a lot of ground and continues to increase its visibility and reach to the authentic male athlete.

For the boomer segment, walking shoes and retro look shoes were determined to be appropriate. Reebok had the largest market share in walking but was losing shelf space to new players. New designs with adapted technologies were introduced and revitalized this area. Also, the firm's very popular line of shoes and apparel called "classics" was updated and focused for this segment of consumers.

Partnering with Retailers

As Reebok refocused on product and quality, it also began to reexamine its relationships with retailers. In order to change what had traditionally been a somewhat unhealthy and competitive relationship, the company first began to revamp its distribution strategy by segmenting the retailers along the same lines as the consumers. There were particular retailing channels that were more suited to the buying patterns of the different groups of consumers. Women, for example, were more apt to buy in smaller boutiques and specialty stores in certain geographical areas. The young male athletes were more likely to buy in the larger chains, such as FootLocker. The older group was more comfortable buying in department stores. Reebok focused on these different channels and established close relationships with retailers to better understand their customers and to gain more targeted shelf space.

In addition, the company had to increase its level of communication and information flow with the retailers, and it did so by focusing on the marketing segmentation strategy. The new products and parallel new marketing messages were communicated to retailers and partners in a way that had never before been done. This was a very laborious process, as the company changed the relationship with retailers from a traditionally transactional one to more of a long-term partnership. This included a targeted marketing strategy and process. The deal with the retailers became one where they pushed the product while Reebok backed up the product on the shelves with targeted marketing in order to help move the shoes quickly. This in-store marketing effort supplemented the overarching brand marketing strategy.

Much of this partnership mentality with retailers was reflected in a new relationship established with FootLocker. Throughout most of the 1980s and 1990s, Nike had controlled a dominant market share in FootLocker stores. Because Reebok was not seen as terribly relevant to many of Footlocker's customers, the retailer saw little need to carry many Reebok styles. As the combination of music and athletic footwear and apparel evolved through Reebok's marketing efforts, the company began serious negotiations with FootLocker to increase the level of Reebok exposure. A pivotal meeting at the Universal Studios offices in New York city with Reebok and FootLocker displayed innovative ways of marketing and displaying the shoes in the stores and introduced a dynamic new way for both companies to increase their sales by increasing their relevancy and credibility with the young, urban crowd that was driving so much of the market.

This marriage of music and sports was brought to life not only with advertising and displays in traditional shoe retailers, but also with focused sneaker displays in over 1200 music stores. This was the first time ever that products such as shoes or apparel were featured in music and entertainment stores, and it served as a breakthrough idea. Reebok was more quickly noticed by the young kids who generate so much of the sales of certain market segments, especially those targeted by the Rbk brand.

STRUCTURE AND ORGANIZATION

One key to the success of this turnaround was a total reorganization within the company. A shared services structure was adapted and layers of management were eliminated. This made the company more flexible, closer to the customer and quicker at getting new product to market. Paul Fireman, as he had always been, was the visionary that set the tone for product and quality. A leaner management team that included several new players supported him.

As part of a new organizational structure that aligned focus on the customer and product quality, much emphasis was placed on implementing more disciplined processes, such as the use of strict calendars and deadlines to help speed the product development process. Several months were taken out of the product development process, which allowed Reebok to bring new and more relevant products to market much faster.

Leadership and Management

Throughout the sometimes confusing and often-difficult transformation process, CEO and Chairman Paul Fireman was a great energy driver and continuously focused on quality. Fireman has always been the ultimate authority on quality and instilled this characteristic and focus throughout the company. However, as the company became more successful during the 1980s and '90s, high quality at a high price point for a small number of products was not a feasible strategy and management neglected other markets and price points that were needed.

Fortunately, the cultural aspects that allowed for transformation and renewed focus on product development and segmentation were already in place within the company. Employees instinctively understood the segmentation strategy and buy-in was almost immediate.

The evolution of the strategy involved collaboration between Paul Fireman and his executive team. Paul wanted to get the company back to basics and focused on product. Operationally focused managers understood this meant the need for segmentation in product development and marketing. These ideas implied the need for execution, operational excellence, and speed of product development, with high quality standards and retailer segmentation. As these ideas developed, top management was in the trenches with the rest of the company, working in small teams focusing on the goals at each step. Operational silos were eliminated. Prior to the transformation, one of the driving ideas had been to seek one large win – a "grand slam". The transformation shifted the focus to lots of small wins on all levels – customers, retailers and product.

Fireman has described one of the key cultural success factors of the transformation: "It is the essence of the behind the scenes workings that make the turnaround possible. One of the key elements is the quality of thinking and the championing of ideas that does not come from the top. The courage and sometimes blind faith in one's opinion that, without reasonable predicted results, are the course that is steered while fear and concern ride on your shoulder during your journey." (Fireman, 2004) This perspective fueled the financial turnaround at the turn of the century (see Figures 2 & 3), and the changes in net sales and income were a direct result of all the efforts of Reebok employees.

LESSONS LEARNED AND FUTURE DIRECTION

One of the fundamental lessons that the entire Reebok organization has been able to take away from the recent transformation is the need for constant attention to both short term and long-term strategies and outcomes. There is a fine balance to strike between paying attention to the daily activities, results and financial situation, and keeping some focus on longer term growth strategies that may not produce immediate results, but yet create a much more sustainable position for the company.

This is not a lesson specific to Reebok or even to the footwear and apparel industry – this is the story and the driving success factor for many organizations in varied industries. There is a realization that emerges once an organization experiences a crisis and subsequent emergence from that situation – transformation, or change on a regular basis is needed so as to avoid a subsequent need for massive strategic, structural, and operational transformation such as the one that Reebok had to execute. Perhaps the difference is in the scope of change – if an organization can continuously attend to the factors that will require it to change, maybe it can avoid situations where it must substantially reinvent itself. Maybe, though, sometimes one has to reinvent, realign, and implement a total shift of strategy and all that supports it to maintain a fresh perspective in an increasingly mature market.

Reebok's turnaround was certainly successful in its original goals – to interrupt a downward decline that the company was experiencing, revitalize the brands in several relevant consumer groups, and support the brand with focused marketing, sales and retail partnerships. The company sales have increased, as has its market share, and costs have been controlled and reduced so as to significantly impact margin. Nonetheless, many opportunities and challenges face the company as it continues to grow.

Certainly within the United States the athletic footwear market is mature. Opportunities for innovation and differentiation still exist. However, strategies in the athletic footwear and apparel sector are focused on gaining market share since the overall sector is not growing rapidly. This is compounded domestically by the fact that younger generations of Americans are increasingly less active than previous generations.

At the same time, the retailer base has shrunk in numbers, as the number of big box discount retailers, such as Wal-Mart and Target, has grown. Smaller numbers of retailers imply larger power bases for vendors of athletic shoes, thus concentrating much of the industry power with retailers, away from brands.

These market conditions do not allow for much strategic change, though they also do not allow for complacency. Transformation has become a constant need. Although Reebok was fairly quick to recognize its losing position in the late 1990s, and radically change much of its strategy, structure and operations to pull itself out of the situation, new challenges already exist. Some of the changes made during the recent transformation may in fact lead to the need for other changes down the road.

There are several areas that may provide needed growth and innovation opportunities for Reebok, which it has already begun to exploit. There is tremendous growth potential for the athletic footwear and apparel market in Asia, and with the majority of its manufacturing and product development operations already established in several Asian countries, the company is well positioned to increase its placement and share. Its replica NFL and NBA product lines have great potential in Asia.

Because of the singular attention of the CEO on quality and design, and therefore technology and product development, Reebok is well positioned to take advantage of another potential area for growth – technological innovation and performance-enhancing products. The company must include the abilities it proved so well to possess during the transformation – agility, adaptability, and discipline – to continue to adapt to the changing needs of the marketplace and different segments. These competencies, coupled with the structural opportunity to gain efficiencies through new and innovative ways of delivering the products to the customers and branding the products worldwide, will allow Reebok to continue to transform as necessary, growing and avoiding serious crises.

CONCLUSIONS

The study of transformation is intimately tied to the stories of enterprises that have successfully completed such a massive change. Transformation, by definition, includes shifting and redefining operations, structure, and/or strategy most often catalyzed by forces that the enterprise in question has not been able to control. Reebok's story is a perfect example of many transformational forces. The company realized tremendous and rapid growth from its inception in the U.S. market and subsequently, like so many of its peers in retail, realized a decline and potential failure. Due to the actions of its leadership and a focused strategy, Reebok was able to stave off potential disaster and begin its path to future success and growth.

As with most corporate transformations, the evolution of Reebok continues. Change really has no defined end point. What is most critical is that a dynamic process of change is embraced and woven into the fabric of daily strategic and tactical decision-making. This may be the most important outcome of Reebok's latest transformation.

REFERENCES

Fireman, Paul. (2004). Personal communication.

Lazich, R. S. (1993-2004). Market Share Reporter. Farmington Mills, IL: Gale Group.

Reebok. (2003). Annual Report. Boston, MA: Reebok.

CHAPTER 20

LOCKHEED MARTIN AERONAUTICS
Restructure and Transformation

WILLIAM C. KESSLER AND RALPH D. HEATH

ABSTRACT

Lockheed Martin Aeronautics Company (Lockheed Martin Aeronautics) was established in January 2000 from three existing Lockheed Martin business units that had operated for decades as separate entities. Each designed, developed and manufactured military aircraft. Each of the heritage companies had enjoyed success and contributed significantly to America's defense in the Cold War era, with products such as the F-117 Stealth Fighter, C-130 Hercules and F-16 Fighting Falcon.

Consolidation in the aerospace industry in the 1990s had placed the California, Texas and Georgia-based operating units under a single corporate flag – Lockheed Martin – but did not truly unite their cultures or end their long tradition of competing with one another for military aircraft business. By 1999 it was apparent that duplication in their operating structures was financially burdensome to the corporation, strategic alignment was lacking and, most alarmingly, customers were becoming increasingly dissatisfied with performance at each of the sites. Leadership recognized that restructuring and transformation were necessary to re-establish a viable aeronautics company for customers, shareholders and employees. Underlining the urgency of the action, a major objective was to improve Lockheed Martin's chances of winning important new business such as the lucrative Joint Strike Fighter® contract – which is potentially the largest defense program in history.

The transformation approach was built around setting clear intents, supporting the deployment of operating capability to meet those intents, and then executing with the capability to achieve outcomes equal to the intents. The outcomes to date, as compared to the transformation intents, are impressive:

- Formed a new company, Lockheed Martin Aeronautics, on the foundation of "one company, one team and one strategy" and based on the principles of customer focus and financial soundness.

- Rapidly "laid the keel" for the new company by restructure and right-sizing to provide a near term operating cost reduction of about 5% of year 2000 sales. Employment was reduced from 23,000 to about 18,000 in this initial restructure phase. Primary savings was from the reduction of excess infrastructure and overhead. Additionally, hard decisions were also required to adjust staffing to align with a more realistic business operating plan.

- All company aircraft programs were maintained ("kept sold") through the 5-year transformation process. Of special note are:

  o The Joint Strike Fighter® program – now designated as the F-35 – was won in a hard-fought competition with Boeing and the Lockheed Martin Aeronautics restructure and transformation played an important role.

  o The F/A-22 Raptor program was able to restructure and transform itself in a two year span to achieve rate production capability and to achieve lot-to-lot significant cost reductions.

- All financial metrics and other growth measures have dramatically improved from 2000 to 2005:

  o Moved from three companies with revenues of $3 billion (2000 sales) to a single $11 billion company (2004 sales).

  o Driven by increased business requirements, employment has bounced back from the early-transformation reductions to the current level of nearly 28,000.

  o Company backlog of orders has doubled.

  o Double-digit, compounded annual growth in sales sustained.

  o Significant capital investments, important to profitable growth, have established the world's most advanced facilities for military aircraft production at the Georgia and Fort Worth sites

Five years into the initiative, Lockheed Martin Aeronautics has achieved all its principal transformation intents. Efforts are continuing to ensure the company is capable of perpetuating the gains while also strengthening its ability to adapt to new and unforeseen challenges that could emerge in the dynamic (continuously changing) military aircraft business.

The authors have two intents for this chapter: 1) to chronicle the key elements of the restructure and transformation that led to the successful outcomes outlined above, and 2) to outline, based on real lessons, a more capable approach for addressing future change. The primary structure of this chapter will follow the key steps of transformation: 1) deciding to transform, 2) designing the transformation, 3) deploying the capability to transform, and 4) executing to achieve transformation expectations.

LOCKHEED MARTIN AERONAUTICS RESTRUCTURE AND TRANSFORMATION

Making the Decision to Restructure and Transform

The realities of the defense business in the post-cold war era converged for the Lockheed Martin Corporation in 1998-99. Defense Department acquisition budgets had already dropped by about 60% compared to the peak during the 1980's. The primary strategy of the surviving aerospace and defense corporations had been to grow their business by mergers and acquisitions.

Lockheed Martin Corporation's aeronautics business provided more than 30% of the overall corporate revenues and was comprised of three separate companies – Tactical Aircraft Systems in Fort Worth, Texas, Aeronautical Systems in Marietta, Georgia, and the Skunk Works® in Palmdale, California. Each of the three aeronautics companies had their own president, executive staff and their own responsibility for company profit and loss. With the decline in military acquisition, each of these separate aeronautics companies had excess capacity, a dwindling backlog of business orders, and high overhead costs. Additionally, the three Lockheed Martin aeronautics companies each had unique capabilities and they were all pursuing significant and individual roles within the largest-ever Defense Department procurement – the Joint Strike Fighter® Program.

Although all three aeronautics companies were in the same business, all three had vastly different views, expectations and orientations of leadership. Differences in company culture, information technology and systems, major processes, accounting approaches, and business criteria had created barriers for years. Figure 1 illustrates the wide variety of products from the previous separate three companies that made up the new Lockheed Martin Aeronautics. The culture, approaches, skills, methods and tools supporting this range of products across the three sites was vastly different and had been honed over a long period of time.

In an attempt to more effectively link the three aeronautics companies, an aggressive enterprise resource planning initiative had been launched from Lockheed Martin Corporate. As time progressed, it was clear that a focus on process and business system consistency alone did not address the larger issues of duplicative, costly infrastructures and competing business views.

With this backdrop, Lockheed Martin Corporate approved the following actions:

- Consolidate the three stand-alone, full service aeronautics companies into a single company, Lockheed Martin Aeronautics, having one president, Mr. Dain Hancock. Mr. Hancock was the president of Tactical Aircraft Systems in Fort Worth and he accepted the position of corporate executive vice president and president of Lockheed Martin Aeronautics contingent upon strong corporate support for consolidating the three separate aeronautics companies.

- Mr. Hancock, the new president, would lead Lockheed Martin Aeronautics to:

      o   Establish high customer confidence – keep current programs sold, align strategies, grow business, and work toward achieving double digit margins.

      o   Establish a higher standard; a better, more effective, more competitive way of running the business than any of the three heritage aeronautics companies had used in the past.

      o   Invest in the required change from the savings of dismantling the heritage companies.

      o   Win the Joint Strike Fighter® competition.

In the late fall of 1999, Mr. Hancock was named president of Lockheed Martin Aeronautics. A comparison of the three, formerly separate, business units that made up the new single business unit is provided by Figure 2 and clearly delineates the redundant infrastructure at the time as well as the different business systems.

FIGURE 1. Range of Products within New Lockheed Martin Aeronautics

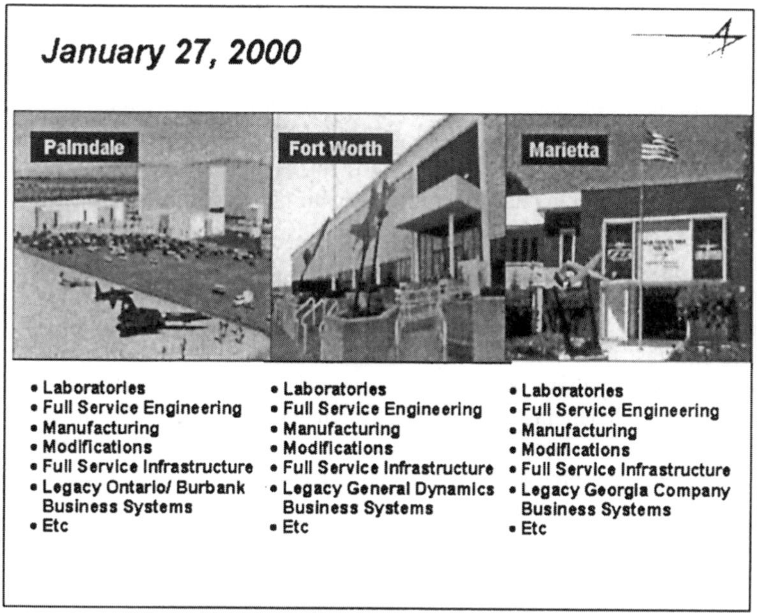

January 27, 2000

Palmdale
- Laboratories
- Full Service Engineering
- Manufacturing
- Modifications
- Full Service Infrastructure
- Legacy Ontario/ Burbank Business Systems
- Etc

Fort Worth
- Laboratories
- Full Service Engineering
- Manufacturing
- Modifications
- Full Service Infrastructure
- Legacy General Dynamics Business Systems
- Etc

Marietta
- Laboratories
- Full Service Engineering
- Manufacturing
- Modifications
- Full Service Infrastructure
- Legacy Georgia Company Business Systems
- Etc

FIGURE 2. Lockheed Martin's Three Former Aeronautics Companies

Leadership Realities of Large Scale Transformation

As separate companies, each deployed (with varying degrees of success) enterprise resource planning, process reengineering, balanced scorecards, theory of constraints, lean principles and tools, six-sigma black belt training and projects, and a host of quality initiatives.

When the Lockheed Martin Aeronautics restructure and transformation began in 2000; the leadership found no proven, available change methodology and tool set that focused on the full scope of transforming a large-scale enterprise. Several helpful references spanned a variety of principles, approaches, methods and tools – none addressing a total enterprise, but all addressing important aspects within an enterprise (Hammer, 1997, 2001; Kessler, 2002, Murman, et al., 2002, Paul, 1999; Rouse, 2001; Womack & Jones, 1996).

The transformation task was further complicated by the fact that the pre-existing separate companies had unique cultures and pre-existing businesses to run and grow. Over the five-year restructure and transformation, these realities affected how resources could be allocated and how fast transformation progress was achieved. Restructuring to a single company and transforming to a new concept of operations resulted in three on-going initiatives that were often competing for resources:

- Rapidly restructure from three independent companies to one company positioned for effective transformation.

- Successfully perform the current business and aggressively solve any "pop-up" problem that is critical to the new, single company's business survival.

- Transform to the new operating capability prescribed by the one company concept of operations.

In the case of Lockheed Martin Aeronautics, the President placed the highest, earliest intensity on the "right sizing, or restructuring." This topic had a very specific and fast time line. The outcome was a significant cut in total operating costs and the ability to present a "single face and strategy" to our customers.

Continually balancing emphasis between the three on-going initiatives is a reality for any large-scale change activity. In many cases, the most scarce resource to be balanced is the time of the leaders and managers.

Setting Intents -- First Step In Restructure & Transformation

The Lockheed Martin Aeronautics consolidation, announced and made effective January 27, 2000, established one company with one profit and loss statement (instead of three), and one president (instead of three) who was accountable for the overall profit and loss of the new company. Mr. Hancock, the new Lockheed Martin Aeronautics president, kicked-off the company transformation process in March 2000 at a two-day workshop in Fort Worth, Texas. Here are a few of the transformation relevant facts from that workshop:

- To set the stage for change, only the "senior leadership" of the new company was invited to participate. This represented about 40% of the previous, combined senior leadership of the three legacy aeronautics companies.

- Mr. Hancock laid out his intents and reasons for the transformation.

- A structured "concept of operations" for the new Lockheed Martin Aeronautics was presented. Ralph Heath, the Chief Operating Officer for the new company, prepared and presented the concept. The ability of the leadership to articulate how Lockheed Martin Aeronautics would operate in the future (and why) provided an important foundation for the restructure and transformation.

- A time span and schedule for the envisioned company transformation was provided. The first year focus was to be on the "physical transformation (restructure)" of three companies to one company and the establishment, consistent with the concept of operations, of the organizations needed to run the business.

- Visible and important roles of the President, Chief Financial Officer, Chief Operating Officer and Executive Vice President for Programs projected to the entire leadership team that the top executives were "on the same page" in their commitment to transformation and to the urgency for implementing the changes.

- Time was spent in small groups so the new leadership team, drawn from across the three sites, could get to know each other by discussing the LM Aeronautics concept of operations and the behaviors required to make the company successful. This time spent was important in building trust and collective accountability among the leadership team.

The Lockheed Martin Aeronautics restructure and transformation was to be centered on three specific intents:

- Intent 1: Restructure into one company with a single vision and with exactly the right capabilities for the business of the new organization.

- Intent 2: Establish an organizational structure that aligns with the efficient and effective conduct of work, assures clear accountability, and has no unneeded redundancies.

- Intent 3: Deploy the Lockheed Martin Aeronautics concept of operations that is driven by the principles of customer focus and financial strength.

The new Lockheed Martin Aeronautics concept of operations included:

- An executive leadership team (President and Executive Vice Presidents) to set the strategic direction and the overarching resource allocations for the company.

- A Lockheed Martin Aeronautics principle core value process that starts with customer needs and ends with customer solutions. Solution invention, campaign pursuit, and program execution (design, build and support) are part of this core value process

- A set of functional and staff capabilities that enable the principle core value process by providing capability via people, processes and tools.

Leadership established four imperatives to be used in measuring transformation progress:

- Imperative 1: Business – Achieve year-over-year sales growth and sustainable, increasing profit margins.

- <u>Imperative 2</u>: Customer – Be the supplier of choice, meet commitments, develop positive relationships, provide innovative solutions, build relationships and consistently integrate objectives.

- <u>Imperative 3</u>: Process – Operate with company-wide capable and affordable processes in all discriminating areas.

- <u>Imperative 4</u>: Workforce – Be the employer of choice: attract, motivate, and retain skilled employees; establish an open work environment with a diverse workforce and a range of work/life options; have capable, productive and engaged employees.

For the LM Aeronautics transformation, the early directives were to:

1. In one year, achieve the required Lockheed Martin Aeronautics restructure to one company with the capability to conduct current business in alignment with the new concept of operations.

2. Deploy transformation action plans and directives via the yearly company objectives.

3. Over a five-year horizon, design and incrementally deploy the new concept of operations; execute to meet the defined transformation intents and imperatives.

Figure 3 provides the Lockheed Martin Aeronautics approach and time line for transformation responsive to the intents and imperatives

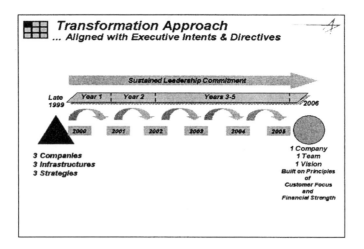

FIGURE 3. Designing the Transformation Program

Launching the Restructure and Transformation – The Foundation and Design Phase

Establishing a foundation of trust and collaboration across the three sites of Lockheed Martin Aeronautics was the prime focus of leadership. The approach to this early physical transformation had to be familiar, logical, interactive, fast and transparent. The approach had to cause the structural change and also begin the culture and behavior transformation.

Laying the Keel for the New Company (Directive 1). Figure 4 illustrates leadership's approach for rapidly restructuring while also shaping the "to be" mission of Lockheed Martin Aeronautics' organizations. The President called this the "physical transformation" of the new company and its approach was announced at the March 2000 workshop. The intent was to move quickly to get all organizations in place to conduct the day-to-day business of the company while also "laying the keel" for future changes. The restructure had to be consistent with the "one company concept of operations" and not add any barriers that impeded the 5-year transformation process to the "to be" state.

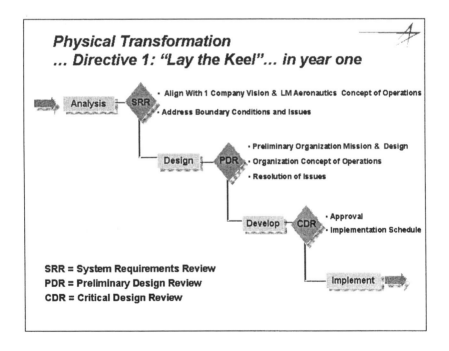

FIGURE 4. Physical Transformation of Lockheed Martin Aeronautics

The process for quickly "laying the keel" was a key to Lockheed Martin Aeronautics' success. A three-step approach and terminology were used that were familiar to the senior leadership, managers and employees adopted from familiar terms in the aircraft development business – system requirements review, preliminary design review and critical design review.

Inputs to the process were the selected organizational executives, existing organization designs and missions at the three heritage companies, and the new concept of operations. The outputs were a set of organizational missions and designs aligned to the Lockheed Martin Aeronautics operating concept, approval of all proposed senior-level management positions, and a plan to be fully operational within six months.

The basic intents of the three milestones in the selected approach were as follows:

- System Requirements Review: Collectively baseline each organizational leader on the restructure expectations of the company and their organizations. Make a preliminary assessment if leader is addressing the full expectations.

- Preliminary Design Review: Collectively agree that expectations are being addressed and confirm that the organization leader is designing a capable structure to meet all objectives.

- Critical Design Review: Approve structure, document remaining interface issues, and approve six-month implementation action plans.

This rapid (about 3 months) organization design approval, followed by 6 months of implementation and early execution, provided the foundation for the longer term Lockheed Martin Aeronautics transformation process. The approach was very successful in "laying the keel" for the new company and is expected to be part of the preferred transformation methodology in the future. Highlights follow:

- Use of a familiar, structured company organization design process that allowed interaction of the collective leadership team and which rapidly converged to organizational designs consistent with the company concept of operations.

- Use of common information and data templates so the same type information was obtained from each "organizational designer."

- Participation by the entire leadership team, led by the Chief Operating Officer, to ensure human centered issues and organizational interface boundary conditions could be quickly resolved with all points of view considered in the "organizational design meetings."

- A supporting organizational integration design team that maintained a design room and focus on the overall integrated company design. This assured that the result was an integrated design and not just a collection of individually designed parts.

The three-step approach assured that all organizational leaders understood the implications of the "new Lockheed Martin Aeronautics intents and imperatives" on their organization's mission and needed capability.

Of paramount importance was the effort of leadership to establish a fair and transparent processes for filling each of the approved leadership and management positions. The number of positions was decreased about 50% by the restructure and each position being filled would have candidates who were peers and who might come from any of the three heritage sites. All deserved, and were provided, a "fair shot at the position".

Defining the "To-Be" Enterprise Capability Architecture (Directive 2). The Chief Operating Officer established a design team for creating the *capability architecture* and deployment plan based upon the operating concept presented at the March 2000 meeting. These early efforts were needed to support the "laying of the keel" for the new Lockheed Martin Aeronautics and the more detailed deployment plans that would be needed to support capability deployment priorities.

In this design effort the design team used the Institute of Electrical and Electronic Engineers Standard for the architecture: "... the structure of components, their relationships, and the principles and guidelines governing their design and evolution over time". The resulting Lockheed Martin Aeronautics "to-be" design capability architecture (Figure 5) consists of three principal processes: leadership, core value, and enabling. These three principal processes, in turn, are supported by a total of 13 enterprise wide processes.

The next step in creating the capability architecture involved developing the right level of content for each of the 13 enterprise processes included in the design. Developing the content required company-wide subject matter experts who understood the company-wide processes.

Discussions quickly focused on "what is Lockheed Martin Aeronautic's current capability, what is world class, and where does the company really need to be in 5-years." The design group and executives converged on the business reality that: for the aerospace and defense business sector, it did not make sense to target being "world class" in all aspects of the business – even if resources were available to pursue this. Instead, Lockheed Martin Aeronautics targeted specific capabilities in certain discriminating areas.

In the "cold war era," defense companies had focused primarily on the performance of weapon systems. The primary discriminators in competition for new business were technology and innovation. This long cold war era provided numerous technological breakthroughs; but also left a legacy of "arms length relationships" between customers and suppliers, a "stove pipe" mind-set for disciplines and activities within companies, and an enterprise-wide mentality of cost justification instead of total cost understanding, management and reduction.

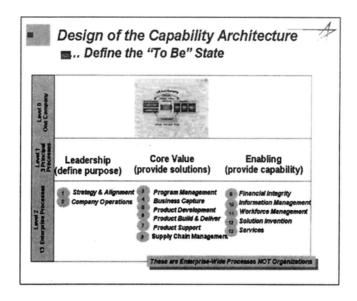

FIGURE 5. Design of the Capability Architecture

The "post cold war era" of the 90's began to change the characteristics of most defense companies as the Office of the Secretary of Defense and the military services placed more emphasis on "weapon system affordability." Today's defense business is focusing on "performance based capabilities and total life cycle affordability."

Lockheed Martin Aeronautics leadership's focus, as restructure began in 2000, was on gaining customer confidence in the company's ability to manage affordable, complex, weapon systems programs. Reducing costs, providing technology and manufacturing innovation, and meeting all customer commitments would be fundamental to winning the Joint Strike Fighter competition. These requirements dictated the capability architecture content and the priorities for early deployment.

A secondary focus was placed on "positioning Lockheed Martin Aeronautics to be responsive and competitive" in the rapidly changing post-cold war era. The new concept of operations was intended to result in a company that is agile and possesses exactly the capability needed – no more and no less! A few examples provide clarification and insight to how these decisions set architecture design requirements:

- Total Solutions: In a world-class environment the intent would be to provide total solutions to all stakeholders. Moving from the "as-is" capability at Lockheed Martin Aeronautics to such a world-class capability would be a long term and expensive journey. In the near-term, emphasis was placed on providing affordable products and services to the Corporation and the paying customers, per commitments. Basic design and development processes were upgraded to incorporate a much-needed robust systems engineering capability across the aircraft systems life cycle. Recent efforts at Lockheed Martin Aeronautics focused on another element of providing total solutions – performance-based sustainment of aircraft products. Lockheed Martin Aeronautics continues to adapt and re-examine the "front end of the business" – the solution innovation capability – to assure it is capable, integrated and aligned to be responsive to new customer needs.

- Multilateral Partnerships: A world-class capability would include global, working partnerships with all customers, suppliers, peers and even competitors. Such a capability would allow rapid formation of teams with exactly the right skills to provide solutions needed. Lockheed Martin Aeronautics executive direction recognized the importance of multilateral partnerships where such partnerships were required. Immediately this placed the Joint Strike Fighter® Program emphasis on teaming in new ways (not just "dividing up the airplane" like would have been done in the past). The new partnering approach used by Lockheed Martin, BAE Systems and Northrop Grumman on the JSF was a significant discriminator in winning the Joint Strike Fighter® System Development and Demonstration contract in October 2001 Program. The Joint Strike Fighter® approach and experience to global partnering allows the rest of the company to use a proven model.

- Unparalleled Integration: This capability would be world-class and certainly would provide a competitive edge in the aerospace and defense business. It is also a pursuit that is expensive, requires large shifts in culture and behavioral norms, and is disruptive to conducting current business. Immediately, Lockheed Martin Aeronautics placed an emphasis on deploying a "common" set of organizational policies, processes, and procedures across the new company (recall that each of the three former companies previously had their own). The highest priority of all was to quickly have one common accounting system for Lockheed Martin Aeronautics. A single portal into a company information system (AeroCode) was established to help manage the convergence of command media and ensure easy access by employees. A heightened focus on functional and program organizations working together to provide customer solutions was embraced. In the longer term, unparalleled integration is a competitive edge for being responsive to external environmental change, meeting customer commitments, and managing total costs. Lockheed Martin Aeronautics progress has been real but progress is paced by over-coming past cold-war era cultural norms, resource (skills, time and dollars) investment, and behavioral norms of the past.

The operating systems' 13 enterprise-wide processes include interfaces with customers and suppliers. The architecture design team examined the content required within each of the 13 company-wide processes from a perspective of "as is" and "to be." The design team identified the gaps in company operating capability as well as in organization capability. The team developed the following content for each of the 13 company-wide processes:

- Requirements (primary focus and secondary focus) for the company-wide capability.

- Inputs and who provides them.

- Outcomes and who receives them.

- Supplier – Input – Process –Outcome – Customer (SIPOC) diagram.

- Characteristics of good inputs and good outcomes.

- Measures of effectiveness for good inputs and good outcomes.

- Key commitments for assuring performance capability.

- Three-year deployment plans.

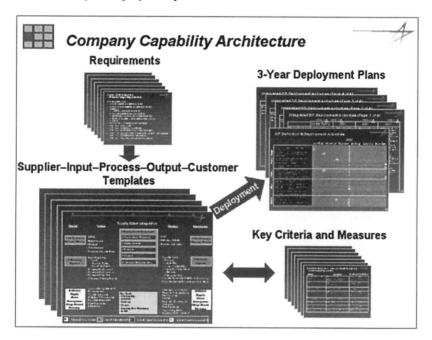

FIGURE 6. Lockheed Martin Aeronautics Capability Architecture

Although the top-level architecture design (Figure 5) was available in year 1 of the Lockheed Martin Aero transformation, the capability architecture (Figure 6) became available late in year 2. The design and the resulting capability architecture were helpful in clarifying company objectives, identifying discriminating topics, and defining an overall structure for documenting company-wide processes and procedures. The capability architecture provides a "north star" for setting transformation priorities and approving actions; as related to the operating performance needs of the company.

The design team also developed an execution framework to aid programs in the most effective use of the information in the capability architecture. The design team analyzed the inter-relationships (inputs and outputs) between processes within the capability architecture as well as their measures of effectiveness. This "cause and effect" information available from the capability architecture led to an ability to establish a program execution approach in terms of defined "toll gates" and the exit/entrance criteria for phase transition required in defense contracting. Figure 7 illustrates the toll gates, transitions, and the management roles and responsibilities. Examples of the "toll gates" where specific information is required would be: requirements freeze, line freeze, build-to-package release, first article manufacturing schedule, first flight, etc.

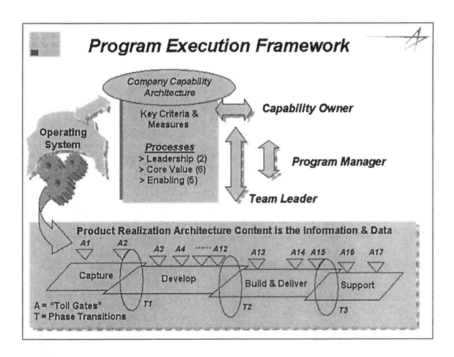

FIGURE 7. Lockheed Martin Aeronautics Program Execution Framework

Note that successful program execution, using the new capability architecture also requires changes in behaviors, roles, responsibilities and accountability of Program Managers, Integrated Product Team Leads, and Capability Owners.

Establish Capability to Restructure & Transform – The Deployment Phase

A company like Lockheed Martin Aeronautics realizes that the <u>only</u> option is to successfully conduct current business while also deploying the capability to achieve the overall restructuring and transformation intents. The total resources (time, people skills, material and dollars) available within an enterprise in transformation are in most cases limited or, as was the case with Lockheed Martin Aeronautics, come from the restructuring itself. The total set of resources that can be applied to deploying major change is constrained by the consumption of resources required to operate the current business and to attack unexpected "pop up" issues. Lockheed Martin Aeronautics accomplished the resource allocation balance via yearly action programming in conjunction with setting and deploying the yearly company-level objectives.

When launching a transformation one realizes quickly that: "we can't do everything at once, so what do we do first?" The answer to this question depends on the "as-is" state within the enterprise, the capability within discriminating areas, resources, and the readiness of the culture to assimilate the required changes.

The rubber meets the ramp in this deployment phase when leadership moves from talking about the intents to funding the actions to create new capability. A few examples are discussed below to illustrate action plans and directives that were approved.

Specific directives were provided related to the first year restructuring:

- In three months, have the Lockheed Martin Aeronautics' top leadership in place and reduce executive positions by over 50%.

- By the end of the year (8 months), have the next three levels of management in place and realize a 30% reduction in company-wide overhead staff.

- By the one-year point, have critical organization design issues all resolved and declare the completion of the physical transformation. At this juncture, turn attention to performing in the new company.

Operating capability action plans were approved and some examples follow:

- Conduct structured three-step approach to set the Lockheed Martin Aeronautics initial organizational design. Depopulate the previous organizational structures and populate the approved organizational design. Eliminate 50% of the existing management positions and 60% of the executive positions. It is imperative to design a fair, legal and robust enabling process to eliminate identified executive and management positions; and competitively fill the remaining and resultant positions.

- Launch immediate consolidation/restructuring cost savings initiatives focused on eliminating excess and duplicative capabilities from the three-company consolidation – capture the year-over-year savings. Outsource "non-core" work to reduce costs in all organizations.

- Establish the "to-be" capability architecture of Lockheed Martin Aeronautics: Base the design on "negotiated executive intents" and use the capability architecture to prioritize implementation actions.

- Establish, deploy and manage a company objectives process that is rooted in the company strategy and transformation intents.

- Launch and monitor a critical behaviors initiative; including employee engagement, collective accountability, and fact based decision making as behaviors to be advocated, modeled, and rewarded in the organization.

- Establish common accounting/finance methods and systems across Lockheed Martin Aeronautics.

- Establish common Program Management methods, tools and measures for Programs.

Program execution action plans were also resourced and approved; some examples follow:

- Apply all capabilities to proposing and winning the Joint Strike Fighter.

- Apply all capabilities for effectively moving F/A-22 and C-130J from development to full rate production and successful operations.

- Apply all capabilities to re-establish a predictable and capable production system for the production, delivery and support of the F-16 following the introduction of two advanced versions.

These executive-approved directives and action plans were based on company priorities, resources, and the reality of the culture to assimilate the change. This is exactly the way a serious transformation of an existing enterprise should progress – understanding the total enterprise architecture but metering out specific changes based on criticality, impact, affordability and readiness.

The efforts to enhance capability of operations and program execution were linked to the "to-be" capability architecture, yearly company-wide objectives, available resources, and realistic executive intents as illustrated by Figure 8.

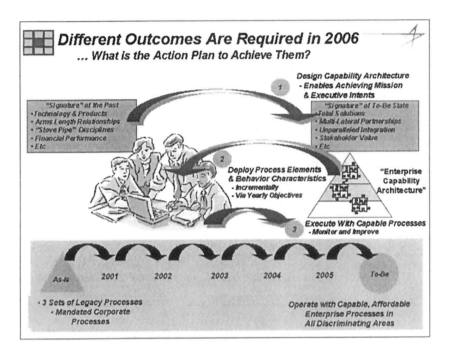

FIGURE 8. Approach to Deployment of Capability Architecture

Some examples of operating capability deployment within the construct of the architecture design (refer back to Figure 5) are:

Leadership. The following capabilities were designed and deployed:

- Enterprise Process of "Strategy & Alignment"

  o Create, based on environment and opportunity, the strategic direction for the company and adjusting yearly.

  o Establish and deploy yearly company-wide objectives that are rooted in the strategic direction.

- Enterprise Process of "Company Operations"

  o Evaluate progress toward the company-wide objectives and drive corrective actions.

  o Combine, eliminate or defer organization processes, procedures and policies providing "common-across-the-organization" approaches. Capture all appropriate command media in a single portal information system called AeroCode.

Core Value. The following capabilities were designed and deployed:

- Enterprise Process of "Program Management" – Designs, builds and deploys common methods, tools and metrics across all Programs based on the program execution framework.

- Enterprise Process of "Product Build and Deliver" – Executes with a closed-loop quality system that immediately identifies quality escapes and findings of paying and operating customers and drives them back into corrective actions and prevention within flight testing, production, supply chain, and engineering.

- Enterprise Process of "Supply Chain Management" – Designs and deploys a supply chain integration approach that reduces the number of suppliers in our supply base by an order of magnitude, allows point of use integration of kits, minimizes shortages, and integrates sub-assemblies effectively in our assembly lines.

Enabling. The following capabilities were designed and deployed:

- Enterprise Process of "Financial Integrity" – Establishes, deploys and uses common finance and accounting methods across the company.

- Enterprise Process of "Workforce Management" – Integrates the behaviors of work force engagement, collective accountability of leadership, and fact-based decision making in all we do.

- Enterprise Process of "Services" – Documents, communicates and reinforces the new concept of operations throughout the workforce.

As part of the initiative to "document and communicate the new concept of operations," a 40 page reference guide was developed (Lockheed Martin, 2002) – see Figure 9 -- and distributed in hard copy and on the company intranet. The concept of operations provides a frame of reference for employees on how the company is intended to operate. The Lockheed Martin Aeronautics policies, procedures, and processes documented in the company's single portal for command media, the AeroCode, relate back to the concept of operations.

Successfully transforming to a new operating concept requires leadership, management and the workforce to embrace different ways of doing work. Communication, via documents such as shown in Figure 9, is helpful but certainly not sufficient to assure success. Real culture and behavior changes at individual and group levels are also critical to any transformation. It is worth covering the Lockheed Martin Aeronautics approach to this difficult topic.

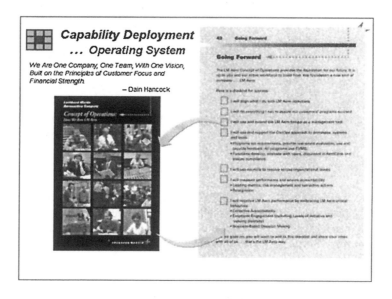

FIGURE 9. Communicating the Concept of Operations

The most fundamental culture and behavior change that the new concept of operations was introducing was to move from a past hierarchical "command and control" approach to a "principle-centered" approach, i.e., "one company built on the principles of customer focus and financial strength."

After review of many external approaches and ideas for enabling behavior change; the decision was made to focus on a small set of critical behavior changes required to operate with the principles of customer focus and financial soundness.

- First, Collective Accountability: "Work across organizational boundaries, clearly define and agree upon actions you will take to support co-workers and other organizations. We are mutually responsible for the success of Lockheed Martin Aeronautics".

- Second, Employee Engagement: "To achieve the highest levels of productivity possible, leaders are responsible for providing employees with the information, resources, freedom and clear expectations to act with their own abilities and knowledge to achieve team objectives. Meaningful employee engagement requires diversity."

- Third, Business-Based Decision Making: "Performance… running the business like a business… requires fact based decision making in which each leader consciously considers the impact of each decision on the overall competitiveness of the company."

Progress toward these behaviors is measured by periodic workforce vitality surveys.

To provide some perspective on the capability deployed via the restructure and transformation, consider Lockheed Martin Aeronautics operating capability outcomes in the timeframe from 2000-2005:

- Tripled the production rate on the Fighting Falcon F-16 aircraft.

- Doubled the production rate on the Raptor F/A-22 aircraft and received Department of Defense approval for "full rate production" following a successful flight operational test phase.

- Increased production rate on the Hercules C-130J with vast improvements on delivered-to-operating-customer quality.

- Initiated production on the multi-role Joint Strike Fighter® (F-35).

- Met delivery commitments on all products over past two years with measurable gains in quality.

Such impressive operating capability (meeting required timelines with the required quality) has also led to outstanding financial performance in terms of sales, margins and free cash flow. The free cash flow has provided needed investment funds for continued enhanced capability. Sales increasing over the period by double digit percentages compounded per year. Employment has increased from 18,000 in 2001 to 28,000 in 2005. The increase is based on business requirements and a realistic operating plan.

As Lockheed Martin Aeronautics evaluates its operating capability, it always notes that significant work remains to fully transform to a "principle-based company". Clearly, measurable improvement of the over all capability of core value processes (capture business, development, build, deliver and support) have been achieved, but more must be done. For example, the capabilities of the leadership engagement process, the systems engineering process, the company-wide quality process, and the integrated product support process are being enhanced as the new Lockheed Martin Aeronautics president, Ralph Heath, assumed this position in January 2005.

Restructure & Transformation Results -- The Execution Phase

Once intents have been defined and capabilities to achieve these intents are deployed; the next task is to execute with the upgraded, restructured, transformed capability to provide new, better outcomes. The ultimate measure of success is for the outcomes to meet or exceed the intents. Two specific program examples illustrate how the Lockheed Martin Aeronautics restructuring and transformation achieved the intended outcomes.

Example 1: The F-35 Joint Strike Fighter®

A key intent for the restructure and transformation was to execute with the required capability to win the Joint Strike Fighter® competition. Winning the Joint Strike Fighter® competition and having the capability to execute the program were required Lockheed Martin Aeronautics transformation outcomes.

The F-35 Joint Strike Fighter®, in the eyes of the government sponsors and the defense aerospace community, is itself a transformational system <u>and</u> program. A different approach was needed to design, build, deliver, and support the weapon system – with a key emphasis on efficiency and affordability. A new digital environment was required to provide data and information to realize the weapon system and to achieve total program management. A new business approach was mandatory for the global acquisition and maintenance of the aircraft system. The system itself was to be integrated in a future battle space.

In its successful quest to win the Joint Strike Fighter® Program, Lockheed Martin Aeronautics is generally credited with three distinct and innovative winning strategies – all are elements that emerged from the company restructuring and transformation.

<u>First, Achieving Demonstrated Breakthrough Technology and Product Styling.</u> The short takeoff and landing variant of the F-35 requires a total vertical thrust of 39,800 pounds to achieve lift off. There were only a few proven ways to solve this problem and each carried adverse affects on the flexibility to style the aircraft design. Lockheed Martin Aeronautics, through research and development at its Skunk Works® (Advanced Development Program), embraced a new and innovative approach. The Lockheed Martin Aeronautics F-35 Short Take Off and Vertical Landing (STOVL) design relies on a gimbaled nozzle in the aft of the aircraft to provide 17,600 pounds of thrust *plus* an ambient air fan right over the aircraft center of gravity to provide an additional lift of 18,500 pounds. The wing-ground effects from the nozzle and fan provide an additional 3,700 pounds of thrust. A closed loop, autopilot system is incorporated to guide the vertical lift off. This innovative, breakthrough and validated propulsion system won the aerospace industry's most prestigious technical achievement award, the Collier Trophy. A major outcome of this breakthrough was the flexibility it allowed the team to style the product design. The result was a significant competitive edge in product performance and style. This outcome was enabled by the consolidation of the capabilities within the three separate companies plus an effective integration of the front end of the Lockheed Martin Aeronautics business (Business Development, Engineering and the Skunk Works®).

<u>Second: Fielding an Experienced Team Via Multi-Lateral Partnerships.</u> A second strategy involved demonstrating that the Program team could be established that would provide the capability to assure overall Program technical and management success. The team of Lockheed Martin Aeronautics Company (with sites in Texas, Georgia, and California), Northrop Grumman in California, and BAE Systems in the United Kingdom represented an unparalleled, worldwide experience base in military aircraft technology, performance and management. The experience level

of the team was impressive, but the Program strategy had to center on how this experience would be brought together differently to enable success.

On past military fighter aircraft programs, the approach often involved "dividing up" the airplane between the "partner companies". One company would design and build a wing; another would design and build the tail, etc. This way the individual "partner companies" design rules, tools, and manufacturing methods were kept separate and not shared. Joint Strike Fighter® Program leadership took a totally different approach. The decision was to integrate the three partners' teams into a single Program team using the "best athlete approach." The result was a single Program team that is totally focused on the overall design, manufacture, and support of the F-35 aircraft.

Third: Proving the Credibility of the Lockheed Martin Aeronautics Management Team. The third major factor in winning the Joint Strike Fighter® Program related to the restructuring and transformation of Lockheed Martin Aeronautics itself. During the early phase of the competition, Lockheed Martin consisted of three aeronautics companies. From a customer perspective, these three separate Lockheed Martin companies were often viewed as having separate business and technical strategies – and sometimes seemed like competitors with each other. The restructure and transformation of Lockheed Martin Aeronautics quickly resulted in a single strategy, the ability to leverage company-wide capabilities for addressing the Program challenges, a common company-wide accounting system, integrated processes in core capability areas, and a very significant reduction in overhead costs. The outcome of this swift restructuring and the tangible results provided a significant indication to the government customer that Lockheed Martin Aeronautics management was committed to the Joint Strike Fighter® and was a very capable management team.

These three strategies combined to provide a major, competitive win for Lockheed Martin Aeronautics (Figure 10) in October of 2001.

FIGURE 10. Delivered Solution – "Joint Strike Fighter® Win!"

The most challenging part of the Joint Strike Fighter® Program may *not* be the technology that is involved in the aircraft, but how the total Program is managed and how the program executes the required multilateral partnerships. The first Monday after the program award, the Secretary of the Navy, Gordon England, visited the plant in Fort Worth. His words had a major impact on all in attendance: "OK, fine, you have had a day to celebrate. Now you have got to meet every wicket, every day. Everyone will be watching you. You are a huge target. Any slips in this program and you are going to be under attack."

During the competition, Lockheed Martin Aeronautics had to establish and demonstrate the capability to execute the customer's transformational program post-award. The following four examples provide powerful illustration of the capability put in place by Lockheed Martin Aeronautics for the Joint Strike Fighter program. The examples were chosen to illustrate the capabilities in F-35 digital product data management, storage, and use.

- Products and Technology: F-35 focus is on total solutions. F-35 has one production line that produces three variants of the aircraft system that meet the battle space requirements of all the military services. Program Management requires digital product data for the lifecycle of the F-35 products. E-Management must be linked to the digital product data and its maturity. Modeling and simulation are required across the product lifecycle and the battle space of the system.

- Business Relationships: F-35 focus is on global multilateral partnerships to provide the experience and capability to achieve the total solution. Program Management requires Integrated Product Teams with representatives from all the stakeholder groups. These team members must have a total loyalty to the JSF Program objectives and yet be able to protect any flow of sensitive or proprietary information. There is common Program training for all as they come on-board. A global secure network with near real-time access has been established. Eight countries are now participating in F-35 development.

- Disciplines: F-35 focus must be on unparalleled integration (development, production, support, supply chain, information technology, people management, etc.) to provide full capability across the product lifecycle. Program Management requires processes that align with the product lifecycle and not the functional disciplines. Methods, tools, and databases must enable programs and companies to focus their efforts on the value stream that provides each customer their required product.

- Financial: F-35 is to focus on providing value to all the key stakeholders that enable the total solution. Program Management requires cost benefit analysis for deployment of the enabling methods, tools, and databases to be addressed. For example, commercial off the shelf technology is used wherever it can be leveraged."

Example 2: The F/A-22 Raptor

When the Lockheed Martin Aeronautics transformation was launched in 2000, the Air Force's F/A-22 Program was in its development phase at the company site in Marietta, Georgia. This program was critical to the newly formed Lockheed Martin Aeronautics Company. The executive intent in March 2000 for the F/A-22 was simply "keep the program sold".

By January 2002, two years into the company transformation and a few months after winning the F-35; serious cost, schedule and performance issues surfaced on the F/A-22. Such a "pop up" or unexpected issue immediately focused leadership time and energy on the F/A-22. From a transformation program perspective, such unexpected "pop-ups" that refocus leadership attention must be considered as "the norm" for planning.

In 2003, Ralph Heath (Lockheed Martin Aeronautics Chief Operating Officer since the company inception in 2000 and the company lead for restructure and transformation) was assigned as executive vice president and general manager for the F/A-22 and began the task of solving the F/A-22 capability shortfalls by establishing clear executive intents. The challenge would be to rapidly assure that the Program established the capabilities required to achieve the intents and then would execute with the deployed capability to deliver the required solutions.

From a transformation perspective, the solution approaches for the F-35 and the F/A-22 were very different. The F-35 was practically a "green field" solution approach since it was a brand new competition. The F/A-22, on the other hand, had been in development for 20 years by the Air Force. Subsequently, all three of the Lockheed Martin Aeronautics heritage sites (Marietta, Palmdale and Fort Worth) had significant emotional investment in, and work investment on, the F/A-22 over the years. The F/A-22 solution approach would be a real test of the new Lockheed Martin Aeronautics ability to operate as a single, integrated company in solving a company-level survival issue.

In short order, the new General Manager established a set of leadership intents to align the F/A-22 team:

1. Successfully conclude the Air Force's contractual "Engineering and Manufacturing Development" phase.

2. Rapidly transition from development-oriented production to required rate production.

3. Keep a team focus on the customer's "Initial Operational Test and Evaluation" phase that provides the Department of Defense information required for making a full rate production decision.

4. Regain the U.S. Government confidence in the team's ability to execute as well as the airplane's performance.

As an enabling step to achieve the intents, an F/A-22 organizational mission and design change was made. The design change was not a "rearrangement of the deck chairs." The new organizational design was aligned with executing the work required by the customer – the new organization design made it clear where accountability resided and where resources were to be focused.

The organization design changes integrated Lockheed Martin's partners, Boeing and the Air Force, into the leadership structure. The design included three organizational elements that aligned with the product value stream, each organization consisting of an "integrated product team." First, the F/A-22 Development Organization was tasked to bring the development efforts to an end, support the move to rate production, and structure future modernization needs incorporating robust system engineering practices. Second, the F/A-22 Build & Delivery Organization was tasked to finalize the lean production system, establish an experienced manufacturing staff for achieving rate production, and relentlessly move from development to rate production to provide the customer high confidence in a quality, on-time aircraft. Third, the F/A-22 Product Support Organization was tasked to assure ease-of-maintenance for the military maintenance officers, achieve maintenance hours per flying hour to meet requirements at initial operations & test evaluation, and establish a program approach to the Department of Defense's performance based logistics.

In less than two years, the F/A-22 has demonstrated delivery of quality products (Figure 11) per commitment, performed magnificently in initial operational testing, reduced year-over-year unit cost as measured by the Air Force's yearly purchases, achieved Defense Department approval for full rate production, and made great strides in regaining government customer confidence.

FIGURE 11. Delivered Solutions – Production Ready F/A-22

The F/A-22 can be viewed as a Program restructure and transformation within the on-going company-level restructure and transformation. The F/A-22 used the same general approach as leadership did at the company-level: set clear intents, support deploying the capability to achieve the intents, and execute with the capability and accountability. However, the span time for achieving change within the F/A-22 has been remarkably faster than what is being achieved at a company-level. The following summarizes the leadership intents set by the F/A-22 General Manager as well as the capability deployed to achieve those intents.

Intent 1: Conclude the Contractual "Engineering and Manufacturing Development" Phase. Implementing the new organizational design and placing clear responsibility and accountability, within the Development Organization, for concluding all contractual tasks in the development phase was a key step to stabilizing the product design and enabling the movement to rate production. Military weapon systems require very high performance and require the latest technology, materials and innovation. However, the concept and development phases for these systems often span decades due to many factors involved in the government's acquisition process itself. This environment spawns numerous engineering change requirements. The F/A-22 concept and development phase had stretched out for nearly 20 years and had been faced with all the issues associated with avionics technology advances and material suppliers who had left the business. These factors resulted in engineering changes that affected the production planning and implementation.

Two significant capabilities were deployed immediately to enhance stability in the factory to allow systematic production ramp up:

- Production Avionics Laboratory. The challenges of integrating modern, complex avionics into the world's most high technology weapon system required real time and continual engineering involvement. The production line was upgraded to include an integrated Production Avionics Laboratory expressly for the purpose of moving quickly to a rate production system by providing short span responses to any avionics integration issue.

- Modification Line. With the high number of engineering changes, every aircraft coming down the production line had enormous traveling work. A separate modification line was established to work these engineering changes aircraft-by-aircraft instead of at the production line. The separate modification line capability is temporary and is being phased out as the rate production system capability is being established.

Additionally, the new Development Organization worked with the Air Force customer to develop and execute a "burn down plan" for all work tasks on the development contract. The work and associated staff reductions were quickly implemented.

<u>Intent 2: Transition Rapidly to Required Rate Production</u>. With the Modification Line and Production Avionics Laboratory capabilities deployed and providing improved stability for the production line, Production Operations deployed the additional capabilities needed to achieve full rate production.

- Validate the F/A-22's lean, pulsed production line. This effort was fully staffed and the needed skills and management were added to the team. The major elements of the rail-centered pulsed moving assembly line were already in place. Investments had been made to move all the utilities beneath the factory floor and to provide kitted parts and tools "point of use" along the line. With the Production Avionics Laboratory and the engine staging integrated within the line, the need was to achieve the capability of the overall integrated system. The most significant barrier to achieving the production capability became maintaining alignment of the structural assembly as it progressed down the line. Requirements on alignment were very stringent due to the tolerances demanded for a stealth capability in the aircraft. The production operations team was able to resolve this challenge, provide the contractually required production rates, and validate high confidence to the customer of the production rate capability.

- Integrate the supply chain with the production line. The nagging issue of part shortages was also a barrier to achieving capable production. Disciplined "return to green" plans were developed with each of the problem suppliers. As of mid-2005, there is confidence that all the issues are being resolved and supplier shortages and quality breaches have been significantly reduced. However, with other production issues now resolved, the issue of parts shortages remains a focus topic.

- Deploy a capable, closed-loop, advanced quality system. A single quality escape on a fighter aircraft delivered to the operating user is one too many. Moving from development to rate production demands an unyielding focus on quality. Production operations deployed their advanced Raptor quality system that allowed no traveling work to the flight line, had company and government representatives deliver the aircraft to the operator and resolve issues at point of delivery, and received real-time feedback from operators in the field. All quality breaches within assembly were documented, analyzed for root cause, corrective action taken, and then tracked to assure no repeats going forward. Support teams have been integrated within the production line flow to provide rapid response to issues and assure corrective actions. Nonconforming hours per 1000 earned hours dropped dramatically as the capable quality system "came alive".

Intent 3: Keep Focus on the Customer's "Initial Operational Test and Evaluation" Phase. Initial operational test and evaluation is totally a Department of Defense activity but the company needed to be prepared to support the event as appropriate and as requested. The government proclaimed the F/A-22 "suitable for operations" after exhaustive flight and maintenance testing. The government stated that the F/A-22 is "overwhelmingly effective, demonstrated by the Raptor's ability to operate against adversary ground and air defenses with impunity. Ground defenses could not engage the F/A-22, nor could adversary aircraft survive."

Intent 4: Regain the U.S. Government Confidence. As a customer, the government understandably expects performance to their contractual requirements, that all commitments will be met, and that a superior product will be provided by the contractor. To those directly involved in the F/A-22 program, there was never a serious question regarding the superior performance of the F/A-22. However, the company and program had to regain the government customer's confidence in their ability to complete development, validate the rate production capability required, deliver the Raptor on schedule, and aggressively attack production costs.

With the capabilities in place addressing Intents 1 and 2, the major "confidence concerns" of the customer were: is the production system capable of quality on-time deliveries, and can unit cost reductions be achieved?

The production operations team was outstanding in providing the capable lean production system that could achieve the production rates required. Within 18 months, the team was able to validate to the customer a loaded production line, a year's worth of met commitments in deliveries to the operating customers, and a second year's worth of Raptors in the production pipeline. This was an awesome and visual validation for customers visiting the Raptor production line. The outcome was that the Defense Acquisition Board approved the Raptor to move from development to production in April 2005.

Remaining was the challenge to validate a capable solution to achieving unit cost reduction (beyond the "normal learning curve") of the F/A-22. Past efforts on cost reduction had been continual and invested in by the customer and the company. However, it was nearly impossible to trace actual cost reductions caused by the investment due to a variety of "cost uppers" such as requirements changes and engineering changes.

To place the highest focus on the topic of cost reduction, the General Manager surprised most by assigning himself as the lead of the F/A-22 Cost Reduction Task Force that had as its purpose to make cost reduction "job 1" on the Raptor and to achieve predictable cost reduction capability in the year-to-year negotiations of the unit cost of the Raptor.

The Cost Reduction Task Force provided a capable approach for tracking cost reduction to negotiated unit costs in recent lot buys. Cost reduction is now being institutionalized within the F/A-22 program structure and the "aperture of ideas" for cost reduction has been opened. Much more needs to be done in this area but a capable and proven approach is in place.

Conclusions

By all measures, the Lockheed Martin Aeronautics restructuring and transformation is a success. The "keel for the new company" was put in place in the first year by eliminating redundant infrastructure, deploying a common accounting system, providing sustainable savings, and establishing each organization's mission and structure to align with the new operating concept.

The next four years involved deploying discriminating capabilities to allow the winning of the Joint Strike Fighter Program and to move all existing Programs to a much-improved state of predictability and reliability. The F/A-22 and F-35 restructure and transformation intents, capability deployment and outcomes are worthy of separate case studies.

Although more remains to be done at a company-level, Program-level, organizational-level and enterprise process capability level, Lockheed Martin Aeronautics is now one company with one vision and one strategy – built on the principles of customer focus and financial strength.

RESTRUCTURE AND TRANSFORMATION LESSONS AND NEW APPROACH

Lessons From Restructure and Transformation

After five years of solid outcomes and continued progress in the Lockheed Martin Aeronautics restructure and transformation, some experienced-based observations and lessons have been identified that will help guide Lockheed Martin Aeronautics future change efforts:

1. Leadership sets the intent and the seriousness of the transformation. The leader and the leadership team must "walk the talk". Real operating change in any enterprise requires changes in behaviors and actions by all employees. Gaining such a realignment of the employees to the new or different intents is impossible if leadership sends mixed messages

2. Immediately get started with the restructure portion of the transformation. Leadership must act quickly to "lay the keel" and complete the "physical transformation". Move quickly on any required staffing changes and the chartering of organizations to keep the current business on track as well as systematically deploy the capability needed for the future.

3. Address the totality of the transformation in the design phase. Once the intents of a transformation are decided, have a company-wide team design the "to-be" operating capability architecture that is capable of meeting the transformation intents. The design will be a "North Star" for setting deployment and resource priorities.

4. Treat transformation as a program. In the military aeronautics industry, a program is usually defined as an integrated set of separate projects that are orchestrated to achieve an overarching goal. It is important to set clear transformation objectives. It is most effective to set these objectives on a yearly basis in conjunction with the yearly resource allocation process. Leadership must assure the transformation objectives are actionable and that past approaches are dismantled. Deploy action plans with metrics and a corrective action process. Revisit the transformation objectives periodically for progress and also for their reality in terms of applied resources and workforce ability to assimilate the changes.

5. Achieving total workforce alignment on the change objectives is a powerful lever for success. Concise and understandable objectives, communication, engagement, clear accountability, and workforce feedback are all important to achieving the critical employee behaviors needed. This can't be done without the alignment of the total leadership and management teams.

An Emerging Framework Supporting Large Scale Transformation

A large-scale transformation requires a system, or enterprise, design perspective – anything less provides a sub-optimal solution that may not achieve the transformation intents or be sustainable over time.

In March 2000, Lockheed Martin Aeronautics had a concept of operations defined for the new company. Lockheed Martin Aeronautics also had a familiar and interactive approach for rapidly and decisively "laying the keel" for the longer term large-scale transformation. However, the company did not have a proven approach for the longer-term transformation from the three heritage companies to one company capable of executing with the new concept of operations.

A transformation framework and approach emerged over time, with experience, trial and error, and learning. The transformation framework became quite helpful in assuring completeness of scope and approach during the five-year transformation.

The greatest value of this framework and approach may well be found in the future as Lockheed Martin Aeronautics faces the reality and challenge of additional change. In today's global business world, the ability to recognize the need for change and to rapidly adapt to the new environment and leadership's intents will be a powerful capability.

The framework and approach are based on previously sponsored Lockheed Martin Aeronautics efforts (Dement, 2004) and depicted by Figure 12. The framework consists of three major enterprise transformation processes – establishing transformative intents, providing capability to achieve the intents, and producing solutions that meet the intents:

1. Purpose process: starts with leadership intents and environmental intelligence; ends with transformation directives and time frames.

2. Capability process: starts with identified shortfalls in the operating capability required to meet leadership intents; ends with a deployed enterprise operating capability that is matched to the leadership intents.

3. Solutions (products and services) process: starts with identified shortfalls in the enterprises' solution (e.g. life cycle product realization) process; ends with execution of the operating capability that provides required, intended solutions (products and support) for operation by the customers.

This framework and its processes, Figure 12, are useful to assure that all the important elements of a complex large-scale transformation are considered and that all phases (design, deploy and execute) of a transformation are addressed. Conducting an actual transformation is complicated by the fact that there is concurrent and significant work progressing in all three transformation processes and the three phases. Each of the "9 blocks" are active themselves and interactive with the other 8 blocks. These complexities are in addition to the "competing priorities" for resources for operating the existing business, addressing unexpected "pop up" issues, and overcoming the inertia involved in change of people behaviors and culture.

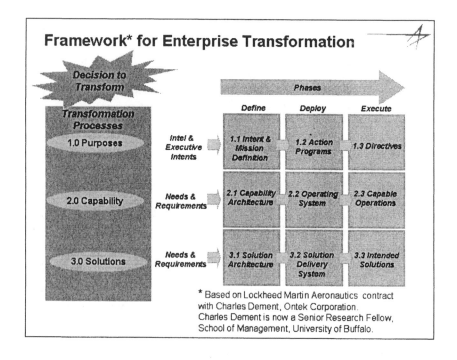

FIGURE 12. Enterprise Transformation Framework

In the transformation framework; there is a strong linkage on the diagonal that moves from establishing leadership intents (1.1), to deploying a capable operating concept (2.2), to producing solutions for meeting the transformation intents (3.3). The transformation team must address all 9 blocks and their inter-relationships and different time spans. Most others in the enterprise are only interested in the diagonal. The graphic of the nine blocks that compose the matrix of the three transformation processes and their three phases, provides an "icon" that has been applied on each of the figures (3–11). These chart "icons" were highlighted so the reader can track which of the Figure 12 processes and phases were being addressed by the transformation work described in the text.

Applying the framework (Figure 12) to transformation also highlights that successful change requires leadership's direct and disciplined involvement – at certain times, within each of the 9 blocks. Too often leadership engages in setting the intents (1.1) and then places their attention on "the outcomes" (3.2 and 3.3). Such a tactic misses the needed role of leadership in deciding on the critical capability discriminators and assuring they are properly resourced and deployed. It is action programming (1.2) where the rubber really meets the ramp since this is where resources are allocated to deploy capabilities and assure results.

In the case of Lockheed Martin Aeronautics, the design phase of the capability architecture was iterative and resulted in adjusting some of the original executive intents and "spiked out" discriminating elements for early deployment -- like the company-level objectives setting and deployment process. The yearly establishment of action plans (1.2) for discriminating elements of the capability architecture (2.1) assured that leadership deployed the most important topics in achieving their intents.

The reader should note that the transformation framework (Figure 12) applies at any scale of a transformation. It is applicable to an enterprise such as Lockheed Martin Aeronautics, a program such as F/A-22, or an Organization such as F/A-22's Build and Deliver Organization.

When drilled down to the appropriate levels of detail, this transformation framework yields a more formalized approach to large-scale enterprise transformation than previously available. The importance of a more formalized approach is that a shorter time-span for change is possible and a significant amount of wasteful and low priority actions can be avoided. This is a very important contribution in these days where transformation and radical change have become the norm. The transformation framework is an important contribution within the developing field of enterprise engineering and enterprise transformation (Keyworth, 2005; LAI, 2005; Tennenbaum Institute, 2005). It is based on a more formal approach to enterprise engineering and it has been "test driven" within an on-going five-year large-scale transformation.

REFERENCES

Dement, C. (2004). *Final Technical Report, LM Aero Engineering Support*, Purchase Order RQ 87273; Orange County California: Ontek Corporation.

Hammer, M. (1997). *Beyond Reengineering: How Processes-Centered Organization is Changing Our Work and Our Lives*, New York: HarperCollins.

Hammer, M. (2001). *The Super Efficient Company, Harvard Business Review*, 77(6), 108-118.

Institute of Electrical and Electronic Engineers (IEEE) Standard 610.12. *Architecture*.

Kessler, W.C. (2002). Company Transformation: A Case Study of Lockheed Martin Aeronautics, Information Knowledge Systems Management. 3 (1), 5-14.

Keyworth Institute at Leeds University, UK. *Enterprise Engineering*. http://www.keyworth.leeds.ac.uk.

Lean Aerospace Initiative at MIT. *Lean Enterprise Value*. http://www.lai.mit.edu.

Lockheed Martin (2002). *Concept of Operations: How We Will Run LM Aero*, Fort Worth: Texas. Lockheed Martin Aeronautics Company.

Murman, E. et al (2002). Lean Enterprise Value: Insights from MIT's Lean Enterprise Initiative. New York: Palgrave.

Paul, G. A. (1999). *The Process-Centered Enterprise: The Power of Commitment*, New York: St. Lucie Press.

Rouse, W.B. (2001). *Essential Management of Strategic Management*, New York: John Wily and Sons.

Tennenbaum Institute at Georgia Institute of Technology. *Enterprise Transformation*. http://www.ti.gatech.edu.

Womack, J.P. & Jones, D.T. (1996). Lean Thinking: Banishing Waste and Creating Wealth in Your Corporation, New York: Simon and Schuster.

CHAPTER 21

DOING WELL BY DOING GOOD

Interface's Vision of Becoming the First Industrial Company in the World to Attain Environmental Sustainability

L. BERIL TOKTAY AND LYNN SELHAT WITH RAY ANDERSON

ABSTRACT

One of the most challenging transformations a company can undertake is towards sustainability. The raw materials used in production are often not recyclable, technologies to close the loop are often not available, and most importantly, legislation and market economics are not strong enough reasons to completely overhaul the way the company designs, manufactures and distributes its products. Consequently, there seldom is a pressing need to undertake such a transformation. Interface Inc. is one company that initiated such a transformation ten years ago, and has made significant progress towards its goal of being not only sustainable, but restorative. In this chapter, we trace its journey, analyze its transformation in the context of Kotter's eight steps on leading change, and discuss key challenges and learnings of interest to top-level managers who wish to lead such a transformation in their own organization.

INTRODUCTION

If you want to get an audience to pay attention, say something they do not expect to hear. Ray Anderson, chairman of the board of Interface, the world's largest producer of commercial floor coverings, does this a lot. Ever since his self-described "epiphany" about the futility of our current take-make-waste industrial process, he has brought a message of warning and hope to audiences around the world. In 1986, during one of his first public speeches on the topic, he told a national convention of 500 interior designers in Boston, "Someday, people like me may be put in jail" (Anderson, 1998, p.8). Anyone dozing off at that point would have woken up. And that's Anderson's goal: to wake up anyone who will listen to the fact that we simply can not continue to take from the earth, pollute our air and waterways, and dump our waste into giant holes in the ground.

Ironically, says Anderson, by current environmental standards, he and Interface, a publicly traded company with annual sales of roughly $1 billion, are guilty of nothing. "No one is accusing me," Anderson said in this now landmark speech, "I stand convicted by me, myself, alone, and not by anyone else, as a plunderer of the earth" (Anderson, 1998, p.5). This gets to the heart of Anderson's argument: that politicians and lawmakers are far behind in structuring policy that recognizes the real cost of goods. This includes the kinds of line items not typically found on an accounting spreadsheet, for example, the cost of military operations to safeguard oil in the Middle East or the costs of industrial spills. Until companies like his do something, says Anderson, no one else will take the lead. Politicians will gladly jump in front of a parade, he observes, but someone has to get the parade started. So why not Interface?

THE INTERFACE STORY

The Awakening

To understand where Interface is headed, it's important to understand its past. Ray Anderson, a hard-working young manager with 17 years work experience and a degree in industrial engineering from Georgia Tech, founded Compact Carpets, Inc., the predecessor of Interface, in 1973. Anderson had worked in the flooring industry most of his career and left a secure job to partner with a British firm that manufactured carpet tiles, the square pieces of carpet now routinely found in hospitals, schools, and offices. This was a fairly new concept in the U.S. at the time, and Anderson saw an opportunity to build his own company around the idea. Fast forward to 1994. The company, by this time known as Interface, had 29 manufacturing sites, annual sales of $725 million and a hold on roughly 40 percent of the world's carpet tile market. By all accounts Interface was the great American success story and Anderson a role model for any aspiring entrepreneur. It's hard to imagine that a day would come when Anderson might sit back and completely rethink the company he had spent 20 years building. But that day did come, and was precipitated by the words of entrepreneur and environmentalist Paul Hawken, author of *The Ecology of Commerce*. The book was given to Anderson in 1994 as he prepared for a speech to a new task force launched by Interface Research Corporation, Interface's research arm, to address questions posed by more and more customers about Interface's environmental record. Until then, admits Anderson, his only real message to company managers was "comply, comply, comply." He was therefore stunned to read Hawken's cry for help on the part of silent Earth. Among the many abuses our planet is sustaining in our lifetime, Hawken outlined:

- The depletion of the Ogallala aquifer, the great underground body of fresh water under the American Midwest, and the implications of that, namely famine in the U.S.

- The worldwide loss of 25 billion tons of topsoil every year (equivalent to all the wheat fields in Australia disappearing, and a hungry world population increasing by 90 million a year).

- The usurpation of a disproportionate share of Net Primary Production, the usable product of photosynthesis, by the human species – one species among millions of species taking nearly half for itself – and pushing the ecosystem toward overshoot and collapse for thousands, maybe millions, of species.

- An alarming increase in the rate of species extinction, now between 1,000 and 10,000 times the average rate since the mass extinction of the dinosaurs 65 million years ago.

- The cutting of vast areas of natural forests in Brazil, a critical lobe of Earth's lungs, to clear land to raise soybeans to feed cows in Germany to produce surplus butter and cheese that pile up in warehouses.

- Illness from pesticide poisoning numbering in the millions each year, with uncounted deaths resulting.

Anderson says, bluntly, "I read it, and it changed my life" (Anderson, 1998, p.39). Hawken's central point is in three parts: 1) The living systems and life support systems of Earth – the biosphere – is in decline; it is a crisis, 2) The biggest culprit in this decline is the industrial system – the take-make-waste system, fossil-fuel driven – of which we are each a part, and 3) The only institution on Earth that is large enough, powerful enough, pervasive enough, wealthy enough and influential enough to lead humankind out of this crisis is the same one that is doing the greatest damage, the institution of business and industry (Anderson, 2004a). He says he wasn't halfway through the book before he had the vision he was looking for, not only for the speech, but for his company. "Hawken's message was a spear in my chest that is still there," said Anderson (Anderson, 1998, p.39).

In that speech, Anderson offered the task force a vision: Interface, the first name in industrial ecology, worldwide, through substance, not words. Then he offered a mission: to convert Interface into a restorative enterprise, first to reach sustainability, then to become restorative, putting back more than it takes and doing good to Earth, not just no harm – by helping or influencing others to reach toward sustainability. Finally, he offered a strategy: Reduce, reuse, reclaim, recycle (Interface later added redesign), adopt best practices, advance and share them. The Interface journey toward sustainability, and a massive enterprise transformation, was just beginning.

The Journey

Anderson had laid out a roadmap toward sustainability in his 1994 speech to Interface's research group. But getting 7,000 employees worldwide, plus customers and suppliers to begin climbing "Mount Sustainability" was no small challenge. First and foremost is that the carpet industry is a highly polluting industry, heavy in its usage of petrochemicals. But it is not so much *what* they make that is the problem, but *how* they make it. As explained in Interface's 1997 Sustainability Report:

> "Our current system of industrialism developed in a different world from the one we live in today: fewer people, less material well-being, plentiful natural resources. What emerged was a highly productive, take-make-waste industrial system that assumed indefinite supplies of resources and infinite sinks in which to place our industrial wastes. Industry moves, mines, extracts, shovels, burns, wastes, pumps and disposes of four million pounds of material in order to provide one average, middle-class American family their needs for a year. In order to reduce the amount of material we take and the waste we create, we first need to analyze all of our material flow—everything that comes in and goes out. Only then can we begin to address the task at hand."

Analyzing its material flow, as well as the material flow of its suppliers, is at the heart of Interface's transformation. In presenting what has taken place over the past 10 years at Interface, we borrow from John P. Kotter, professor of leadership at Harvard Business School, who in 1995 penned "Leading Change: Why Transformation Efforts Fail" (Kotter, 1995). In it he addresses the process of leading change. He says that only leadership can blast through the many sources of corporate inertia. Only leadership can motivate the actions needed to alter behavior in any significant way. Only leadership can get change to stick, by anchoring it in the very culture of the organization.

According to Kotter, the first four steps are required to break through the hardened status quo:

1. Establish a sense of urgency

2. Create the guiding coalition

3. Develop a vision and strategy

4. Communicate the change vision

The next three steps introduce new practices:

5. Empower a broad base of people to take action

6. Generate short-term wins

7. Consolidate gains and produce even more change

The final stage grounds the changes in the corporate culture, and helps make them stick:

8. Institutionalize new approaches in the culture

Establish a Sense of Urgency

We hear bad news about the environment every day. So how does a business leader establish a sense of urgency amidst the noise swirling around an already hot topic? Anderson first used the range of his own emotions – anger, fear, sadness, disgust, guilt, and even hope – to couch his messages. Throughout his book, *Mid-Course Correction,* and in his speeches, he speaks candidly and quite emotionally about his personal reaction to lifting the veil off of our current industrial processes.

- In the dedication to his book, he thanks "those who have shaped my new-found attitude toward Earth, its fragile ecology, and my haunting role in its devastation."

- During his speech to the Boston interior designers, he sites the 1.2 billion pounds of material extracted from the earth so the company could produce $800 million worth of products. He goes on to say that the number "made me want to throw up."

- When reading Hawken's warnings about species extinction, Anderson is struck by Hawken's phrase, "The Death of Birth," a phrase that Anderson admits "brought tears to my eyes the first time I read it."

Beyond sharing his own feelings about this crusade, Anderson creates a sense of urgency by personalizing the fight. For example, rather than spouting emotionless facts and figures, Anderson brings his argument to any everyday level. A typical example is his 2004 speech to the Western Governors' Association North American Energy Summit (Anderson, 2004a). He talks about the need to save the biosphere that supports all of life on Earth. He then asks rhetorically, "How does one lose a biosphere?" He proceeds to paint a picture we can all relate to:

- One silted or polluted stream at a time

- One collapsing fish stock at a time

- One dying coral reef at a time

- One eroded ton of topsoil at a time

- One developed wetland at a time

- One butchered tree at a time

- One songbird at a time

- One lost habitat at a time

- One-tenth of a degree of global warming at a time

- One choking or leaching landfill at a time

- One belching smokestack or tailpipe at a time

- One depleted or polluted aquifer at a time

His audience does not need to be scientists to understand the world he is describing. Choking, belching, butchered, eroded, dying, polluted: these are powerful words that speak to ordinary people. Later on in this chapter we will talk further about Anderson's style of communication and his effectiveness at bringing so many people on board with him through his "Power of One" message. For now, we can see how his style works to ensure the first step in creating lasting change: establishing a sense of urgency.

Create the Guiding Coalition

Early on, after reading Hawken's book, Anderson went on to devour similar books. Many of these authors, activists, and scientists went on to become friends of Anderson and later joined Interface's journey to sustainability as part of its "Eco Dream Team," a collection of experts Anderson invited to help remake Interface into a leader in sustainability. One or two meetings a year were organized to update the Dream Team on the progress Interface was making. The team would help Interface stay focused while bringing in the latest thinking in their particular area of expertise. Recently Interface engages them more on a one on one basis with particular projects they are working on.

In addition, Interface charged its R&D arm, Interface Research Corporation (IRC), with providing the intelligence for the myriad efforts toward sustainability. IRC, led by Dr. Michael Bertolucci, is now at the disposal of every Interface business unit, to create product and process solutions. IRC helps businesses examine every step of their manufacturing processes, from procurement to outbound logistics, even *inbound* logistics to feed recycling processes, analyzing and understanding the impact of each step on product quality, process efficiency, and the environment. Bertolucci is also part of Interface's eight-person management team, ensuring that sustainability issues are a constant presence at the highest levels of the company. In addition, Bertolucci chairs the Sustainability Council (made up of representatives from different business units across the globe), which is charged with "backcasting" from its 2020 goal of "zero footprint," and charting the progress made.

Create a Vision

After establishing a sense of urgency and creating the guiding coalition (including R&D support), Anderson set out to create a vision for the company – one that would make sense to employees, suppliers, and customers. The first vision, mentioned earlier in the chapter, was expanded to offer more specifics. It now reads:

> "To be the first company that, by its deeds, shows the entire industrial world what sustainability is in all its dimensions: People, process, product, place and profits — by 2020 — and in doing so we will become restorative through the power of influence."

Of course a vision is only as good as the road map for getting there. Early in the journey, Anderson and his advisors laid out an ambitious plan for climbing Mount Sustainability – the seven faces of "Mount Sustainability."

1. Eliminate Waste – not just incrementally reducing waste but eliminating completely the concept of waste.

2. Benign Emissions – focusing on eliminating molecular waste emitted to natural systems that have negative or toxic effects.

3. Renewable Energy – reducing the energy demands of Interface processes while replacing non-renewable sources with sustainable ones.

4. Closing the Loop – redesigning Interface processes and products into cyclical material flows.

5. Resource Efficient Transportation – exploring methods to reduce the transportation molecules (products and people) in favor of moving information. This includes plant location, logistics, information technology, video conferencing, e-mail, and telecommuting.

6. Sensitivity Hookup – creating a community within and around Interface (customers, suppliers, communities) that understands the functioning of natural systems and the firm's impact on them.

7. Redesign Commerce – focusing on the delivery of service and value instead of the delivery of material. Engaging external organizations to create policies and market incentives that encourage sustainable practices.

Interface developed this roadmap in part through its work with The Natural Step, an international non-profit advisory and research organization working to accelerate global sustainability. Founded in 1989 under the leadership of Dr. Karl-Henrik Robèrt of Sweden, The Natural Step offers a frame of reference to define the system conditions of ecological sustainability. Anderson did not simply want to "go green," taking the superficial steps that many companies take to reduce and reuse. Rather he wanted to make a major shift in how the company worked – from linear industrial processes to cyclical ones. The Natural Step offered the rationale for making such a radical step, and defined the goal, zero footprint.

Communicate the Vision

Interface's enterprise transformation story, interestingly, owes its success to "a story." Anderson understood early on that the mammoth task he was proposing could not be forced on employees. Rather, he sought to make the task something everyone would embrace. How did he accomplish this? By telling a story. In speech after speech, Anderson crystallized a story most of us know, but rarely reflect on. "We are living on spaceship Earth," he would say. "We have only one spaceship. It's in trouble. We're in this together and need each other." Subtext: This is all there is. Once we lose this planet, there's no going someplace else. When we talk about throwing something "away", there is no *away*. Earth is finite, and so are her resources. Screenwriting coach Robert McKee, who consults to CEOs, believes that stories, not PowerPoint slides, are the way to engage listeners and encourage change. In a *Harvard Business Review* interview, McKee explains (McKee & Fryer, 2003):

> "Essentially, a story expresses how and why life changes. It begins with a situation in which life is relatively in balance. You come to work day after day, week after week, and everything's fine. But then there's an event – in screenwriting, we call it the 'inciting event' – that throws life out of balance. You get a new job, or the boss dies of a heart attack, or a big customer threatens to leave. The story goes on to describe how, in an effort to restore balance, the protagonist's subjective expectations crash into an uncooperative objective reality. A good storyteller describes what it's like to deal with these opposing forces, calling on the protagonist to dig deeper, work with scarce resources, make difficult decisions, take action despite risks, and ultimately discover the truth."

In Anderson's story the "inciting event" is an abrupt awareness of Earth's decline and our role in it. The opposing forces to restoring balance: ignorance, tax and trade laws that don't reflect the real costs of goods, companies that take-make-waste, companies like Interface *if* it chooses to do nothing. His case is made: if we will not be part of the solution, we will remain part of the problem. Anderson anticipates the next logical question: "But how can we be part of the solution?" In response he presents yet another story: The "Power of One," one person can make a difference. In this story, Anderson talks about the seven steps to climbing Mount Sustainability mentioned earlier. "It is daunting," he explains. "It's a mountain to climb that is higher that Everest."

He reinforces that the company can do well by doing good, again by telling a story. He explains that the Chinese symbol for crisis is a combination of two characters: danger and opportunity. The danger is clear, and the list is limitless – the loss of the rainforests, disappearing wetlands, global warming, toxic landfills. "You want a business case for sustainability," he asks in his book. "How about, for starters: survival?" Balancing out danger is the vision for opportunity that Anderson communicates. In his book and in speeches, Anderson reinforces that the company can do well by doing good in three ways: First, by earning customers' goodwill, and their predisposition to work with Interface; second, by achieving resource efficiency; and third, by setting an example that other companies cannot ignore. Says Anderson: "If we do well enough through creating goodwill and becoming resource-efficient, to the point that we are kicking tail in the marketplace, then that is the example other companies will see and want to emulate. Maybe they will become converts *and*, hopefully, customers, too."

Empower Others to Act on the Vision

In their quest toward sustainability, Anderson and his team introduced a process that all employees could rally around: QUEST™ (Quality Utilizing Employee Suggestions and Teamwork), a process developed by Interface. QUEST teams are active in every plant and division worldwide, helping to localize sustainability solutions. QUEST focuses mainly on waste, the "low hanging fruit" that is easier to realize than some of the other steps in the process. QUEST succeeds on a number of levels. First, "employee" is in the title, clearly communicating that employees are encouraged, expected, and empowered to be part of the waste-reduction solution. Second, QUEST is a broad mandate that can be applied at the local level, allowing employees the world over – who know their site best – to seek out opportunities to reduce waste.

In a recent interview, Anderson explained one of the many benefits of QUEST: creating standards across all sites for measuring waste.

> "When you look at a manufacturing operation, you know there is going to be a certain amount of off-quality, so you build in cost allowances for these, and you have a standard cost system that allows so much expected waste and so much off-quality and so forth. Interface has manufacturing operations all over the world, and everyone had a different idea of what was standard. You couldn't compare one operation with another without getting into the question of, 'How did you establish your standard?' So one day we said, 'Let's just measure everybody against perfection. Let's take all the waste out of the cost, and see what our cost would be if we had no waste and no off-quality. If we did it right the first time, every time.' We found that 10 percent of the sales dollar was going to waste, most of it allowable under the standard cost systems. During the nine years we've been measuring it, the elimination of waste – the savings – represents 28 percent of our operating income, and we still have 60% of it yet to go. We've already captured about 40%. It gets close to doubling your profit if you can eliminate waste." (Anderson, 2004c)

Supporting QUEST is a set of suggestions for how to go about waste reduction. Practices Leading Toward Sustainability (PLETSUS) offers very specific, highly detailed directives that can be localized to the circumstances of a specific manufacturing location or plant. PLETSUS offers directives around: people (customers, employees, suppliers, community, and management), product (design, packaging, manufacturing, marketing and purchasing), and place (facility, maintenance, landscape, and transportation).

Suggestions range from the obvious:

- Make copies on request; otherwise, route material

- Maximize use of bulletin boards

- Eliminate cover sheets on faxes

To the creative:

- Start an employee vegetable garden

- Plant a butterfly garden near an area that employees use often

- Mulch lawn clippings

To the less obvious:

- Use excess plant heat to heat offices

- Have a "dumpster diving" activity to understand the makeup of your waste stream

- Create internal "green taxes" to highlight the most profitable enterprise from total cost perspective

To the downright courageous:

- Create an atmosphere that encourages employees to question the status quo and take risks

- Provide honest information about the known environmental impacts of your company and product

- Invite customers to audit and critique your efforts

A message of "the sky is falling, we need to do something," simply doesn't work if employees are not empowered to do something about the problem. In offering solutions such as QUEST and PLETSUS, and applying a very strict measuring system, employees were, and continue to be, empowered to act.

Generate Short-term Wins

QUEST's success in generating quick wins, plus Interface's system for measuring environmental progress – EcoSense™, a program managed by Interface Research – allowed Interface's efforts to push forward quickly. But as Anderson explained, it took some 50 speeches and two long years before the effort really gained traction (Anderson, 2004c). Early wins, generated through QUEST, were key to keeping the energy moving. Between 1994 and 1997, when net income totaled about $84 million during the same period, Interface saved $50 million in reduced materials costs, reduced energy costs, and reduced waste: hard cash that went toward paying for the rest of the "revolution." These savings were communicated to the entire company through their first-ever Sustainability Report, published in 1997. The report shows the ever-present face of Mount Sustainability, and QUEST savings working their way up the mountain. The report then revisits all seven fronts, with each page containing a problem statement and the Interface solution, along with specific results attained by different Interface business units. By communicating real and tangible results, the report instills a bit of competition between the various business units, and continues to encourage long-term employees, while inculcating new hires to the culture of sustainability.

The Sustainability Report shows how progress occurred across all business units and was attained through creativity and innovation. This is a sampling from the report:

No. 1: Eliminate Waste

- *Recycling Internal Waste*

  o Guilford of Maine has an extensive recycling program, diverting from landfills 1,028 tons of waste fiber as well as over 300 tons of other materials in 1996.

  o Interface Europe has created teams to find ways to reuse or recycle 25 types of waste streams.

- *Product Change*

  o Interface Flooring Systems converted to a metric tile sizing system that reduced trim waste (20,000 square yards) and energy consumption (enough to power 140 homes).

o Interface Flooring Systems in the U.S. and Canada have reduced the standard tile backing weight by up to 15%, saving both materials and energy, and improving quality.

- *Process Change*

  o Interface Architectural Resources and Interface Flooring Systems Canada installed more efficient water chillers, reducing water use by over 65% and 40%, respectively.

  o Re:Source Americas offers seminars to train their carpet installers on practices to minimize waste.

No.2: Benign Emissions

- *Benign Air Emissions*

  o Bentley Mills replaced their flat goods dryer with a low NOx, high-efficiency dryer, reducing NOx emissions by approximately 50%.

- *Benign Water Effluent*

  o Prince Street reduced chemicals by 40% and water consumption by 800,000 gallons per month through dye-bath water reuse.

  o Guilford of Maine built a state-of-the-art waste treatment plant to reduce water effluent by at least 50 million gallons annually.

- *Toxics Elimination*

  o Interface Europe has reduced or completely eliminated dyestuffs containing heavy metals.

  o Bentley Mills' backing facility has eliminated all four of their hazardous waste sources through substitution of cleaning agents.

No. 3: Renewable Energy

- *Reducing Demand by Increasing Efficiency*

  o Interface Europe/Asia-Pacific achieved enormous energy savings through smart engineering design in the layout of the new facility in Shanghai. By reducing friction using large pipes and small motors, instead of small pipes and large motors, and laying out pipes before setting up equipment, they cut the necessary pumping power from 95 to 7 horsepower.

o   Bentley Mills and Interface Europe installed high-efficiency dryers, reducing gas consumption by 25% and 30%, respectively.

- *Renewable Energy Supply*

  o   Interface Flooring Systems Canada has reduced its dependence on nonrenewable fossil fuel/unit of production by 74% since 1996. It is the first customer of wind-generated, certified "Green Power" from Ontario Hydro.

No. 4: Closing the Loop

- *In the Technosphere*

  o   Interface Research is working extensively with the flooring companies to create technologies for recycling post-consumer carpet, re-extruding post-industrial PVC backing, and developing new, low-energy processes for PVC-free backing systems.

- *In the Ecosphere*

  o   Interface's ultimate vision is to create completely benign and renewable products that do not depend on nonrenewable petrochemicals, and to minimize its footprint on the Earth due to its facilities' locations.

No.5: Resource Efficient Transportation

- *People*

  o   Interface joined the "Trees for Travel" program, which plants one tree for every 1,500 miles traveled by an Interface employee.

- *Product*

  o   Interface is actively increasing the efficiency of product transportation by shipping via transcontinental rail, by locating manufacturing facilities closer to global customers, and by reducing packaging (and therefore, product weight) and material requirements.

- *Information*

  o Interface is maximizing the efficiency of communication and learning through use of new information technologies. A global network of shared software, electronic messaging, and Internet access is being installed as all Interface Internet sites are updated and expanded.

No. 6: Sensitivity Hook-up

- *Employees*

  o Interface Flooring Systems Canada encourages employees to take environmental conservation attitudes home by implementing a Home Energy Savings Plan and subsidizes energy conservation audits and retrofits.

- *Customers and Suppliers*

  o Interface sponsors a number of events to develop strong relationships with customers and suppliers that combine concepts of "Play to Win" and sustainability. "Power of One" events focus on the environment and the power of individual action multiplied by many.

- *Community*

  o Interface Research Corporation administers the Interface Environmental Foundation that funds small grants to local teachers for the education of K through 12 students in areas of environmental sustainability.

No. 7: Redesign Commerce

- *Service*

  o Interface established the Evergreen™ Lease, a shift from selling a product to selling a service.

- *Business Methods*

  o Environmental Management Systems are critical to the ongoing management of global operations. Interface has set a goal for each facility to become registered to a globally recognized environmental management system, such as ISO14001 (International Standards Organization) or BS7750 (British Standards).

- *Organizations*

  o Interface and its subsidiaries are involved in a large number of external organizations promoting social or environmental sustainability issues. The common thread in these organizations is their mission to re-invent how business conducts its affairs. Interface is drawn toward these organizations to influence their vision of sustainability and to learn best practices from others.

These results crystallize the idea of the Power of One; that every gesture matters, even one that may at first appear to be insignificant. Anderson points out, for example, that Interface realized a 1 oz per sq yard (4%) reduction in face weight across the entire product line. This may not seem like a lot, and you certainly can't miss it in the carpet, says Anderson, but the energy saved in upstream processes due to not using the nylon is enough to run the entire modular flooring factory in Lagrange, GA for two years. "This finding produced an amazing recognition of the upstream impact of our actions," says Anderson.

Consolidate Gains and Produce Even More Change

All of the advances outlined above took place in the first four years of Interface's transformation (1994 – 1998). From there, Interface was able to consolidate gains and use the momentum to produce even more change. Eventually, QUEST and EcoSense merged to form teams with representatives from all businesses worldwide, each team with an assigned scope of investigation and implementation. The teams have created some 400 sustainability initiatives throughout the company, initiatives that reduce costs and Interface's footprint on the Earth. To date, QUEST savings are $262M cumulative in ten years.

With the "low-hanging fruit" addressed, Interface set out to address some of the harder issues. One effort involves completely redesigning how we think of commerce. This effort gets back to one of Paul Hawken's original observations – that our current economic system does not allow markets to recognize the true cost of what they produce. A major goal of Interface, thus, is to work toward shifting taxation away from economic and social benefits – such as labor, income and investment – to detriments, including pollution, waste, and the detriment of primary resources. Interface has joined many sustainable development organizations in order to compare progress, learn from others, and influence the debate. These organizations include the President's Council on Sustainable Development (U.S.), the World Business Council for Sustainable Development, the U.S. Green Building Council, Business for Social Responsibility, World Resources Institute, the PEW Center on Global Climate Change, and the Wildlife Habitat Council.

The Evergreen™ Lease, mentioned earlier, is one of the developments to have come out of this goal of redesigning business. The idea was to create a shift from thinking of products as *things* to thinking of products as a means to deliver a *service* to a customer. Instead of buying carpet, Interface needed to convince customers to lease it, much like one would lease a car. Interface would therefore own and maintain the carpet throughout the life of the carpet, including taking over the responsibility for the "end of life" process, which ideally would lead to Interface "closing the loop." Later in the chapter we will talk about some of the challenges Interface encountered when trying to develop the Evergreen concept.

Institutionalize New Approaches in the Culture

In his book, Ray Anderson talks about wanting to give employees "a higher cause," referring to Maslow's hierarchy of needs. "When compensation is sufficient and growth opportunity is satisfied," he says, "people want to work for a company that makes a difference, that serves a higher cause" (Anderson, 1998, p.97). According to Interface's online sustainability report, which has replaced the paper version, the sustainability effort has had a major impact on employees:

> "We have created a global corporation made up of companies that were formerly independent, and in some cases competitors. We've created a common goal and language – an immediate bond between employees from distant locations. Our employees have a common sense of purpose, broader than selling a particular product. We've bred what we term 'ferocious cooperation.'"

Sustainability training is a major part of Interface's efforts to institutionalize its sustainability efforts. The company wants every associate to understand what sustainability is and what it means to Interface, as well as how they can contribute to the realization of the vision. An ongoing learning initiative called Sustainability Learning began in November 2000 when representatives of each of Interface's key business units met with a representative of The Natural Step to develop content for the classes and redefine the Train the Trainer process. The classes use interactive exercises and easily understood metaphors to provide a basic definition of sustainability and explain the scientific concepts behind The Natural Step and how it relates to Interface's vision. The Train the Trainer process involves preparing internal associates to lead classes in their department and/or location.

Beginning in 2001, the company moved toward online training through a program called Learn2.com. The theory is that online training gives associates access to a variety of courses when and where it is most convenient for them, assuring that more associates have the opportunity for more training than ever before. Some of the courses available are Listening to Lead, Being a Team Player, Problem Solving and many others. Interface found that delivering training through the web expands the breadth of learning initiatives at 10% of the cost of traditional training methods. No travel or logistical expenses are incurred – thus reducing air pollution – and because associates are not required to be away from their jobs, productivity is not affected.

Another important process for cultivating a culture of sustainability is Interface's EcoSense Points System, which educates associates about sustainability and helps them discover things they can do to work sustainably. Essentially, it provides associates with a road map to sustainability and furnishes the necessary metrics for Interface to determine how sustainable it is. Interface awards EcoSense Points for those who successfully complete activities that fall within specific categories (Environmental Management Systems, Quality Management Systems, Sustainability Training, Sensitivity Hookup, Employee Safety and Education, Resource Efficient Transportation, Ecometrics, Purchasing, and Eco-efficiency). For example, associates who participate as mentors in a school with which an Interface company is partnered are awarded points under Sensitivity Hookup. The Interface facilities that are ISO 14001 certified receive points under Environmental Management Systems. EcoSense Points for each facility are forecasted each year based on the cumulative state of environmental and quality programs to date.

In addition, the related EcoSense Bonus Supplement Program is incorporated into a bonus system that gives employees financial incentives for progress on sustainability goals. For example, Interface Flooring Systems has tied hourly employees' bonuses to the annual goals set by the QUEST and EcoSense task forces. In some businesses, factory floor associates are awarded salary bonuses based on percentage QUEST savings.

KEY LEARNINGS/OPPORTUNITIES

We have traced the Interface journey. We've seen how Ray Anderson and the leadership team guided Interface up "Mount Sustainability." Now we examine how these key learnings can be applied to other enterprises starting their own transformations towards creating a sustainable company.

Creating a Sense of Urgency

Regardless of the industry, neither market forces nor legislation are currently enough to compel companies to significantly overhaul the way they use natural resources, or review their waste stream and impact on the environment. Yet one of the key elements of leading change is getting employees to buy in to the urgent need to go from point A to point B. Most significant enterprise transformations are undertaken in the face of major distress, such as loss of market share, threat of competitor entry, threat of bankruptcy, etc. In the absence of a compelling profit- or even survival-based argument, getting a large organization to move towards becoming a sustainable enterprise is a major challenge. The sense of urgency needs to come from a shared understanding that it's our long-term survival that's at stake. The power of words in personalizing the fight, the power of images that evoke visions of a dying planet cannot be underestimated, and this is how Ray Anderson successfully communicated the urgency of the need.

There is a strong emotional component to the call for sustainability that has the power of rallying people around this goal. But if the rallying cry is "Let's save the Earth," it is possible to run into defeatism (what can one employee, one division, one company do?), cynicism (this is a passing fad, is it our job to save the earth?) or alarm (this is going to be a black hole where our profits go). Interface coped with these responses in ways that can be adopted by other companies. First, they emphasized that every step, each action by each employee, each division helps (the power of one); the mountain can be climbed only one step at a time. QUEST was instrumental in ensuring the participation of all employees in identifying ways to reduce the environmental impact of Interface. Second, they stayed on message year after year in a consistent way, with a clearly articulated roadmap. Third, they made sure that initial savings were visible to all, fuelling internal and external buy in. Fourth, they encouraged design and R&D to innovate with sustainability in mind. By underlining the power of influence, they gave all employees a vision bigger than the company's internal processes. As Anderson said in a recent interview, "Saving the Earth is too big. We said: 'Let's just lead the industrial world. Let's do more than be sustainable, be restorative. Do more than doing no harm. Do good.' How do you do that? It's not only through what we do, but through the power of influence" (Anderson, 2004b).

Value Creation – Doing Well by Doing Good

There are several ways in which sustainability initiatives can create value for the firm.

- Reducing internal waste

- Encouraging, even stimulating, innovation

- Closing the loop so that the value of any innovation (product design, easier recycling or disassembly) can be reaped by the company

- Creating customer good will and capitalizing on productivity gains and customer goodwill to grow in the market

The specific industry or product will influence the relative value of each of these approaches. We discuss the specific challenges relating to each of these items below.

Reducing internal waste

Interface defines waste as anything that does not add value to its customers. This includes the traditional definition of waste such as scrap and byproducts of the production process, but also non-traditional aspects like a misdirected shipment, a defective product, and an incorrect invoice. Reducing waste can be the low-hanging fruit for most companies, and an excellent way of ensuring the participation and buy-in of a large employee base early on in a sustainability initiative.

Interface set the complete elimination of waste as a goal, and developed a process called QUEST (Quality Utilizing Employee Suggestions and Teamwork) to attain it. QUEST is a process to elicit and implement employee suggestions in identifying, measuring and eliminating waste. It is reminiscent of the Quality Circles of the Total Quality Management (TQM) movement, but with zero-waste as the ultimate goal, which parallels the zero-defect concept of TQM. Is zero waste a goal that can contribute to "doing well by doing good"? For answers, we turn to our knowledge of TQM, a now well-studied, well-understood concept.

The zero-defect concept of the TQM movement was initially met by skepticism, based on arguments such as in Juran and Gryna (1980), who considered inspection versus failure costs to conclude that the most profitable approach is to allow a positive defect rate. The authors based their analysis on the concept of achieving quality by inspecting the output of an existing process. In contrast, Deming (1982) argued that defective items are a result of material and process problems, and that quality should be built into the process. According to this view, quality and cost are inversely related, so the optimal quality level is to have zero defects. In time, the second view prevailed, and TQM became a widespread practice. Due to its emphasis on employee suggestions, many TQM initiatives have resulted in product and process innovations that improve productivity, paying amply for themselves in the process and moving the firm to a new capability frontier. Hendricks and Singhal (1997) hypothesized that effective TQM implementations will improve profitability. They compared the operating performance of a sample of 463 quality award winning firms to a control sample over a 10-year period and concluded that (i) the mean change in the operating income was 107% higher, and (ii) changes in the ratios of operating income to assets, sales and employees was 20% higher in the test sample compared to the control sample.

Corbett and Klassen (2004) argue that the same skepticism that surrounded TQM in its early days surrounds sustainability initiatives today, namely that they are seen as too costly, so that the most profitable level of environmental impact (from the firm's perspective) is positive. They argue that this view ignores the capability shift and productivity jump that can come out of sustainability initiatives due to process and product innovations, and predict that as the urgency of reducing the environmental footprint of industry grows, more and more firms will undertake serious sustainability initiatives that take them to a new capability (and profitability) frontier.

QUEST, as applied at Interface, is a good example of an employee-centered process that ends up not only paying for itself, but also generating hard cash that can fuel other sustainability initiatives. It is not the only thing a firm can do, but it is a concrete way of getting started. And it is universally applicable.

Encouraging and Stimulating Innovation

According to Hargadon and Sutton (2000), the best innovators are "knowledge brokers" who use old ideas as raw materials to generate new ideas. These companies systematically bring ideas together from different contexts, put existing technologies to use for new applications, and borrow knowledge from one industry to innovate in another. According to the authors, the four practices of good knowledge brokers are (i) capturing new ideas, (ii) keeping ideas alive, (iii) imagining new uses for old ideas and (iv) putting promising concepts to the test.

Participating in industry forums, benchmarking across industries, collecting related products and writings, and observing users are some of the ways in which companies can capture ideas (Hargadon & Sutton, 2000). Initially, books on both sides of the sustainability debate, and later, the "Eco Dream Team" consisting of experts on various facets of sustainability, provided Interface access to the knowledge base on the topic. Interface continues to engage these experts on a project-by-project basis. It also works with a number of NGOs. Employee participation at all levels ensures that a large number of people of different backgrounds are called on to contribute ideas. As outlined earlier, this practice has resulted in a diverse set of sustainability initiatives across Interface companies.

Interface has succeeded in encouraging not only its employees, but also its suppliers and business partners to stimulate innovation by capturing existing ideas. When lead designer David Oakey of David Oakey Designs read about biomimicry for example, it changed his whole way of approaching the design process. Explains Anderson: "He sent his designers into the forest and said: 'Go and see how nature designs floor coverings. And don't come back with leaf designs. That's not what I'm looking for. Come back with nature's design principles. How does nature do it?' It dawned on them, when you look on the forest floor you don't see anything alike. No two sticks, no two stones, no two leaves, no two anything alike. Nature's passion is diversity. Nature's design principle is chaos. So they came back into the studio and they designed a carpet tile where the face design is such that no two tiles are alike. Because you can't see where the design starts or ends, there is very little waste when laying the carpet. It has quickly become a best-selling product."

Keeping ideas alive, especially when they are not embedded in tangible objects, and propagating them throughout the corporation is a big challenge according to Hargadon and Sutton (2000). They propose spreading information about who knows what as a powerful way of keeping ideas alive. Some steps Interface took towards this goal were to charge Interface Research Corporation with providing sustainability-related intelligence to every Interface business unit, to institute a Sustainability Council made up of representatives from different business units across the globe, to publish a Sustainability Report, and to launch the Sustainability Learning initiative.

Imagining new uses for old ideas is particularly relevant in a sustainability initiative. According to Dr. Bertolucci, "It's not that the technologies are not taught in school, it's how you put them together with sustainability in mind that's not taught. It would be very easy for example to put together a machine that would cut carpet tile from a length of broadloom and do it very fast, but to do the same job with the objective of leaving zero waste is a lot more complicated. It requires a completely different concept of the design of the cutting operation than you would normally do." According to Dr. Bertolucci, the fundamentals of how R&D thinks need to be different in a company that tries to be sustainable and competitive than in one that just tries to be competitive. This can be achieved by setting the right targets and metrics. The technologists then make the transformation themselves as they look towards the goals: They start using existing technologies differently, or adopting different technologies and ideas in an ongoing learning process. Says Dr. Bertolucci, "When we started, we weren't really sure where the answers might be. For example, we've recently discovered that biomimicry has a lot of areas where the answers lie, which we didn't know early on."

Putting promising concepts to the test is a crucial step in innovation. Externally, Interface is willing to act as a test bed for demonstration projects of new technologies. For example, Interface is tapping methane gas from a landfill and installing a solar array. According to Thomke (2001), rapid experimentation, and failing early and often, are key to breakthrough innovation. Incremental learning in this manner is one of the characteristics of Interface's internal R&D strategy. Says Dr. Bertolucci, "I would like people to understand that the goals can be quite lofty. For example, eliminating dependence on nonrenewable fossil fuels. That's a very scary goal. People think it's just not possible; it scares them to death. What people should understand is that you can approach bodacious goals one step at a time. You can start first by reducing your demand to the absolute minimum, and then look at the nature of the challenge, starting to offset it step by step. And as you do it, it becomes easier and easier."

Closing the Loop

To close the loop, Interface developed the Evergreen Services Agreement (ESA) concept whereby they would offer operating leases to their customers and retain ownership of the carpet. Interface would install the carpet and reclaim it at the end of its life. For a monthly service fee, Interface would also maintain the carpet (deep professional cleaning) and selectively replace carpet tiles, guaranteeing the function and appearance of the carpet for the term of the lease. Reclaimed carpet would be reprocessed so as to divert it from landfills, where it would otherwise sit for 20,000 years (Oliva & Quinn, 2003).

Leasing is currently widespread in the U.S. when it comes to equipment. Of the $668 billion spent by business on productive assets in 2003, $208 billion, or 31 percent, was acquired by American businesses through leasing. In 2004, projected leasing volume is estimated at $218 billion (ELA, 2004). The most frequent reason given is the need for equipment flexibility related to either changes in the business or protection against technological obsolescence. In response, many manufacturers offer leasing programs, and provide a wide range of services related to equipment. This allows a company to focus on its core business as opposed to managing equipment. To give but a few examples, Xerox was one of the first to offer copier leases (which included maintenance) instead of ownership. General Electric has moved from selling products (e.g. aircraft engines) to providing leases that include financing and maintenance services. Leasing is a $10 billion business for GE today. Caterpillar also has changed its strategy to "selling miles and use" rather than selling machines (Gutowski, et al., 2001).

In addition to the conventional convenience and financial advantages of leasing, there have been recent claims that leasing is beneficial for the environment. The practice of leasing products, rather than selling them, is viewed by many as a strategy for increasing resource productivity, particularly by preventing waste generation and moving to a pattern of closed-loop materials use (Fishbein, et al., 2000). This school of thought argues that by maintaining ownership of the product, the manufacturer can successfully put in place a product recovery strategy consisting of reuse, remanufacturing, and recycling. Most argue that the greatest environmental benefits arise from closing the material loop through reuse and the "dematerialization" of products (and the economy), i.e., reducing material flows in production and consumption, while creating products and services that provide customers with the same level of performance (Robert, et al., 2002; Mont, 2003). In addition, higher efficiencies through better maintenance are seen as advantageous.

These are the arguments that led Interface to propose leasing as an environmentally friendly option. Despite the financial advantages of an operating lease, however, it never took off. The basic reason is the lack of technologies to recover the materials in used carpet. The current U.S. tax regulations for operating leases require that the lease term be at most 75% of the product's expected lifetime. Unfortunately, there is little residual value in the product at that point because it can neither be sold on the secondary market nor can the material yet be reclaimed in a cost-effective way, regardless of the quality of the maintenance. Yet U.S. tax regulations stipulate that the cost of the lease cannot exceed 90% of the value of the product. Thus, Interface essentially needs to price the lease at a discount. In addition, service is a small fraction of the total cost of ownership of the product for the buyer, and basic custodial services are cheap, so margins on servicing are low. Interface proposed deep cleaning services that are more expensive than the basic custodial services that most firms would choose. This is of value to Interface, since it extends the life of the product and reduces the need for replacement tiles, but not to the customer since carpet tiles are quite durable so that basic custodial services are mostly sufficient, and extending the life of the product has no value to the customer. Finally, the reverse logistics of collecting used carpet are complex and costly. This is a problem that needs to be addressed at an industry-wide level, through an industrial consortium for example, which has not happened to date.

Nevertheless, Interface took steps to improve the viability of leasing in the long run by developing a way of reclaiming the PVC backing of modular carpet tiles and using it in new products, a technology that has been commercialized. They have diverted 60M pounds of used carpets[1] from landfills since they began the effort. The technology to reclaim the face of the carpet does not yet exist, so it goes into energy, the step before landfilling in terms of environmentally desirable options.

The bottom line is that there must be a net economic benefit from closing the loop for leasing to take off. This benefit can then be shared between the lessor and the lessee, generating a win-win scenario. Benefits from closing the loop can come from (i) the manufacturer having easier access to existing second-hand markets; (ii) the manufacturer having the technology to recover used products in a profitable way; or (iii) the manufacturer increasing the residual value of the product in cost-effective ways through the servicing agreement. Once a critical mass of leases is reached in the market, return flows would be larger and more stable, and the reverse logistics challenges could be handled by the manufacturer or outsourced to a third party logistics provider. In addition, the manufacturer would have a strong incentive to invest in innovation to further increase recovery efficiency by redesigning products and processes.

In the case of carpet, these three conditions are not satisfied. Nevertheless closing the loop remains a sound environmental concept and Interface continues to pursue the necessary technologies. In addition, this concept has the potential to already generate value in other industries where recovery possibilities are more developed.

Creating Customer Goodwill

If a firm can go beyond mere green-washing and show a sustained commitment to the environment, this will easily translate into customer good will. It's difficult to

---

[1] The industry discards 4.7 billion pounds of carpet annually, of which 96% ends up in landfills (Oliva & Quinn, 2003).

know just how much business Interface has won because of its sustainability efforts, says Anderson. "There is no question that we've gained market share across all our businesses. Sometimes the sustainability initiative is one of many factors. Sometimes it's the main factor. Sometimes it's the factor that breaks the tie in our favor." In 2001, the commercial market in the floor covering industry experienced one of its worst slumps in forty years, with commercial flooring sales down more than 15% compared to the year prior (O'Neill, 2002, 2003). In this environment, Anderson believes that customer goodwill generated by the sustainability initiative has been their salvation. He offers an example of how goodwill can work:

> "One day, our Japanese sales manager called us, and said, 'We're about to get the order for the headquarters building of Daiwa House, a housing company in Japan that manufactures prefabricated houses.' Because Ms. Honda had heard me speak a year ago she went back and convinced the CEO that they had to have Interface carpet tile, that it was the only company in the world they could deal with. It was a huge order, well over $1M."

Whether customer goodwill can be converted into increased sales depends on the sensitivity of customers to environmental issues and to the level at which the products are priced relative to competitors. The Cone/Roper Cause Related Marketing Trends Report notes that if price and quality are equal, more than three quarters of consumers are likely to switch to environmentally friendly brands (Arellano, 1999). Clearly, if sufficient productivity gains are obtained as a result of sustainability initiatives, pricing can be very competitive. Coupled with increased customer goodwill, this is a win-win situation for growing market share.

An important point here, says Anderson, is that value is perceived as a quality/price ratio from the customer's point of view. "Quality is a very qualitative thing," he says. "Green is becoming a qualitative aspect of quality. And people value it." Thus customers will pay more if they value green more. But is green a sustainable trend? From a purely anecdotal perspective, Anderson believes it is. He points to the fact that in 1995 he spoke to a conference sponsored by the U.S. Green Building Council. "There were 135 people in the audience. Last year, there were 9,000 people. In addition, the LEED certification system[2] has been developed and applications for LEED certification are growing exponentially. And it's an amazing phenomenon. People are not saying, 'It costs more, let's not do it'; they just do it. It's the value proposition. It's more valuable to them, even if it only

---

[2] "The LEED (Leadership in Energy and Environmental Design) Green Building Rating System® is a voluntary, consensus-based national standard for developing high-performance, sustainable buildings. Members of the U.S. Green Building Council representing all segments of the building industry developed LEED and continue to contribute to its evolution." (http://www.usgbc.org/LEED/LEED_main.asp)

means sleeping better at night. That's part of the value equation. It's a bit like aesthetics. It's not cut and dried, like it's a pound of meat. It's so subjective, and there is so much included in this value equation."

The Interface "sustainability story," now more than 10 years in the making, has much to teach other companies wishing to take the same path. We conclude with Ray Anderson's personal insights into the process and his hopes for the future.

A CONVERSATION WITH RAY ANDERSON

How is the sustainability transformation different than other enterprise transformations, like restructuring the business?

Restructuring, downsizing, shutting down factories – this is very conventional, companies do it all the time. We've done it recently ourselves because of a 40% decline in the commercial segment – we went from 8,500 people to 5,000. These types of activities have a "We've got to do this *now*" quality, while sustainability is more of a "We've got to do this to survive for 20 years, 30 years" approach. It requires a much longer view. And maybe a sense of legacy, too. "What's this company going to be when it grows up? What does this company really stand for?" I don't expect any CEO thinks he or she will stand before his or her maker one day and talk about shareholder value. But the higher purpose has a huge beneficial effect, it gives a company a reason for being, it gives people working for the company something to work for, it has a galvanizing effect. If you go to any Interface factory, you'll find an amazing attitude. They know they're there for something other than just making a living.

Do you think that sustainability is ingrained in the company culture? Do you believe the company would continue in the same path if you decided to retire?

I believe it's in the DNA of Interface now. My confirmation of that first occurred in 2001. We brought our top 125 managers from around the world for a three-day vision-mission-strategy exercise. Unsolicited, they were almost unanimous in saying, "This is the core value of Interface." And today, I tell you, it is an inextricable part of the brand. So if it's in the DNA and inextricably linked with the brand, it's probably safe for the foreseeable future. And the reason is, the advantage is obvious and manifest. Our QUEST teams will tell you to look at our savings; our sales people will tell you that we're winning business because of it. It is a better way to make a bigger profit and it is a new paradigm for business, "Doing well by doing good."

Do you find competitors jumping on board with sustainability initiatives in response?

Everybody is doing something now. We've moved an industry. Every competitor has his green effort. But I don't think there is anybody who has the broad frontal approach we've taken, who has shown the overall footprint reduction we've shown, which carries into every product we make. What you see from competitors is a green product here, and a green product there.

Floor Focus magazine does a survey of interior designers that goes back several years. The environment did not even appear in earlier versions, now it does. You see more and more companies appearing on the radar screen; it shows that other people are trying. So, maybe Interface is head-and-shoulders above everybody, but here is the thing: If you move the entire carpet industry worldwide, you've moved a $21-22B industry in a $40 trillion economy; it's a drop in the bucket. But if you attract other industries to the model, and I would dare say that Interface, a $1B company, is having a greater impact in terms of influence than the rest of the carpet industry together, this is the transformation we really want to see – the transformation of many industries.

Your vision is "Doing Well by Doing Good." Has Interface done well or has the sustainability initiative come at a cost?

It's been our salvation, through the market shrinking by approximately 40% over the last six years. We have survived. I attribute that largely to the sustainability initiative. You picture revenues in any organization declining that much, that's a recipe for going out of business. Financials, on the face of it, have been miserable. We've had a huge restructuring to deal with the shrinking marketplace; we have gone from 8,500 people to 5,000 people. Profitability is just now coming back. But there has not been one thought of turning back on this initiative. It has been too valuable to us in the marketplace. The proof is that we've survived, and there is no doubt that we've gained market share across all our businesses, though we cannot quantify it exactly because many competitors are private or subsidiaries of large companies. The resource efficiency is there and that undergirds the credibility, which translates into goodwill. Our costs are down, not up. Our products are the best they've ever been. Our people are motivated.

Customer goodwill has been an amazing fact for us. We don't know how much business we've won because of the sustainability commitment. But the goodwill is palpable. You just know it; it's there. You can capitalize on it. You ask the accountant, "Can we afford photovoltaics?" He says "No way." You ask marketing people, "Can you sell solar made carpet?" And they say, "Bring it on." So you ignore the accountant, you go and make the investment, and your top line benefits in ways that you never imagined from customer goodwill, and from the appeal of "solar made." Our Bentley facility is generating enough photovoltaic electricity to tuft about a million square yards a year of solar made carpet. The goodwill from that? It's big. It sells.

What was the hardest part of Interface's transformation, from the perspective of preventing your vision from being realized within the company?

People and technology. There is always the human element, keeping everybody moving, getting everybody on board. You never get everybody on board, but you need critical mass. It took years, literally. And then you come to the part of doing it and the technologies are very, very difficult; they don't yet exist in many cases, particularly technologies to close the loop. Renewable energy is expensive, so you need to justify it on the basis of market acceptance.

What counsel would you give a CEO or manager leading a major enterprise transformation, specifically on sustainability?

You have to deal with inertia – it's a fact of life. The way to overcome it is to get on message and stay on message, year after year after year. We've been on the message for 10 years now.

ACKNOWLEDGEMENTS

We would like to thank Dr. Michael Bertolucci and Dr. Stylianos Kavadias for their valuable input.

REFERENCES

Anderson, R. C. (1998). Mid-Course Correction. White River Junction, VT: Chelsea Green Publishing Company.

Anderson, R. C. (2004a). The Business Case for Sustainability, speech delivered to the Western Governors' Association North American Energy Summit.

Anderson, R. C. (2004b). Interview with L. Beril Toktay, November 17, 2004.

Anderson, R. C. (2004c). Nature and the Industrial Enterprise, an interview with Ray C. Anderson. Engineering Enterprise, Spring 2004.

Arellano, K. (1999). Is green good for business? The Denver Business Journal. 50.

Deming, E.W. (1982). Quality, Productivity and Competition Position. MIT Center for Advanced Engineering, Cambridge, MA.

ELA (2004). Industry Research: Overview of the Equipment Leasing & Finance Industry. Equipment Leasing Association, http://www.elaonline.com/industryData/overview.cfm

Fishbein, B. K., L. S. McGarry & P. S. Dillon (2000). Leasing: A Step Toward Producer Responsibility. New York: Inform, Inc.

Gutowski, T. G., C. F. Murphy, D. T. Allen, D. J. Bauer, B. Bras, T. S. Piwonka, P. S. Sheng, J. W. Sutherland, D. L. Thurston & E. E. Wolff (2001). Environmentally Benign Manufacturing. Baltimore, MD, International Technology Research Institute, World Technology (WTEC) Division.

Hargadon, A. & R. I. Sutton (2000). Building an Innovation Factory. Harvard Business Review. May-June, 157-166.

Hawken, P. (1993). The Ecology of Commerce: A Declaration of Sustainability, New York: HarperCollins Publishers, Inc.

Hendricks, K. & V. Singhal (1997). Does Implementing an Effective TQM Program Actually Improve Operating Performance? Empirical Evidence from Firms that Have Won Quality Awards. Management Science. 43(9), 1258-1274.

Juran, J.M & F.M. Gryna (1980). Quality Planning and Analysis. New York: McGraw Hill.

Kotter, J. P. (1995). Leading Change: Why Transformation Efforts Fail. Harvard Business Review. March-April, 59-67.

McKee, R. & B. Fryer (2003). Storytelling That Moves People: A Conversation with Screenwriting Coach Robert McKee. Harvard Business Review. 81(6), 5-8.

Mont, O. K. (2003). Editorial for the special issue of the Journal of Cleaner Production on Product Service Systems. Journal of Cleaner Production. 11(8), 815-817.

Oliva, R. & J. Quinn (2003). Interface's Evergreen Services Agreement. Harvard Business School Case 9-603-112.

O'Neill, F. (2002). Focus 100 Manufacturers. Floor Focus Magazine. May 2002.

O'Neill, F. (2003). Focus 100 Manufacturers. Floor Focus Magazine. May 2003.

Robert, K.-H., B. Schmidt-Bleek, J. Aloisi de Larderel, G. Basile, J. L. Jansen, R. Kuehr, P. Price Thomas, M. Suzuki, P. Hawken & M. Wackernagel (2002). Strategic Sustainable Development - Selection, Design, and Synergies of Applied Tools. Journal of Cleaner Production. 10(3), 197-214.

Thomke, S. (2001). Enlightened Experimentation. Harvard Business Review. February, 67-75.

CHAPTER 22

TRANSFORMATION IN ACADEMIA[*]

WILLIAM B. ROUSE AND DOMINIE GARCIA

ABSTRACT

The globalization of university-based engineering education and research is associated with the creation of national and international "brands" by leading research universities. Such branding is reflected in rankings of universities and their programs. High brand visibility appears to lead to high rankings and vice versa. This chapter explores this phenomenon for university-based engineering programs. Attributes associated with ranking systems are discussed and universities' abilities to influence these attributes are considered. Both moving up in the rankings and sustaining highly ranked positions are discussed. These issues are addressed both in general and for the specific case of Georgia Tech. Three fundamental conclusions are reached: research and education continue to be the key to universities achieving world class status and economic development for key stakeholders; size provides universities with the resources and abilities to pursue strategies that lead to increasing recognition; and vision and leadership both attract resources and enable the focus needed to achieve the highest levels of recognition.

INTRODUCTION

The pre-World War II 20th century provided a hotbed of research in physical sciences and mathematics. Physics and computing are of particular note. However, the modern research university, particularly in the U.S., emerged following World War II. Vannevar Bush, a 20th century leader in engineering and science, was instrumental in defining the vision.

Bush articulated the central principles in <u>Science: The Endless Frontier</u> (1946):

- The federal government shoulders the principal responsibility for the financial support of basic scientific research.

---

[*]This chapter is based on an article titled "Moving up in the Rankings: Creating and Sustaining a World-Class Research University" that appeared in **Information • Knowledge • Systems** *Management*, Vol. 4, No. 3, 2004.

- Universities – rather than government laboratories, non-teaching research institutes, or private industry – are the primary institutions in which this government-funded research is undertaken.

- Although the federal budgetary process determines the total amount available to support research in various fields of science, most funds are allocated not according to commercial or political considerations but through an intensely competitive process of review conducted by independent scientific experts who judge the quality of proposals according to their scientific merits alone.

Perhaps not surprisingly, Bush's home university, the Massachusetts Institute of Technology (MIT), was very successful in adopting these principles. James Killian, MIT president from 1949 to 1959, notes that "From MIT's founding, the central mission had been to work with things and ideas that were immediately useful and in the public interest. This commitment was reinforced by the fact that many faculty members had had during the war direct and personal experience in public services." (Killian, 1985, p. 399).

He reports that MIT's relationship with the federal government reached new heights with World War II:

- MIT took on critical challenges, e.g., the Sage missile defense system and the Whirlwind computing project

- Faculty and alumni served in important advisory roles in the federal government

- Faculty, including two MIT presidents, served in senior executive positions, on leave from MIT

As a consequence, MIT became and remains a national resource, perhaps the key player in "big science." In the process, MIT was transformed into a university. This was facilitated by several factors (Killian, 1985):

- A single, unfragmented faculty in consort with one central administration

- Close articulation of research and teaching, of basic science and applied science

- Continuous spectrum of undergraduate and graduate studies

- Mobility of ideas resulting from the high permeability of the boundaries of both departments and centers

- The extensive interconnection of its buildings

MIT, and a handful of other leading institutions such as The University of California at Berkeley, California Institute of Technology, University of Illinois, and Stanford University, led the way defining the nature and "rules of the games" for research universities. In the process, science and technology has become central to our economy. As Richard Levin, former president of Yale University, indicates, "Competitive advantage based on the innovative application of new scientific knowledge – this has been the key to American economic success for at least the past quarter century." (p. 88). He asserts that the success of this system is evident: The U.S. accounts for 33% of all scientific publications, has won 60% of Nobel Prizes, and its universities account for 73% of papers cited in U.S. patents (Levin, 2003).

However, it is not clear that this traditional model is sustainable. James Duderstat (2000), former president of the University of Michigan, summarizes several areas of concern identified in a National Science Foundation study:

- Public support has eroded with continual decline throughout the1990s

- Limits on indirect costs have resulted in cost shifting

- The focus on research funding has changed the role of the faculty

- Increased specialization has changed the intellectual makeup of academia

He argues that the real issue is a shifting paradigm for universities. National priorities have changed, although recent security concerns have moderated this trend. The disciplines have been deified, yielding a dominance of reductionism. This presents a challenge for interdisciplinary scholarship, particularly in terms of valuing a diversity of approaches and more flexible visions of faculty career paths. At the same time, undergraduate education is receiving increased attention, as have cultural considerations that, he cautions, tend to encourage "belongers" rather than "doers."

Ruminating on the roles of publicly supported research universities, Duderstat suggests several possibilities for strategies that universities can pursue as a response to current challenges:

- Isolation: Stick with prestige and prosperity, e.g., MIT, Caltech, Princeton, Chicago

- Pathfinders: Participate in experiments creating possible futures for higher education

- Alliances: Allying with other types of educational institutions

- Core-in-Cloud Models: Elite education and basic research departments surrounded by broader array of entities

Derek Bok, recent president of Harvard University, addresses the future of universities in light of many recent trends (Bok, 2003). He is particularly concerned with the commercialization of the university in response to a plethora of "business opportunities" for universities. He notes "Increasingly, success in university administration came to mean being more resourceful than one's competitors in finding funds to achieve new goals. Enterprising leaders seeking to improve their institution felt impelled to take full advantage of any legitimate opportunities that the commercial world had to offer." (p. 15). He argues that this increased focus on commercialization may jeopardize the focus on education and learning.

Bok recognizes that this shift is nevertheless taking place. He cautions, however, that universities typically face several challenges that can hinder entrepreneurial aspirations. Bok summarizes these challenges, "On three important counts, the environment in most research universities does not do enough to encourage the behaviors needed for the sake of the students, the society, and the well-being of the institution itself." (pp. 23-24).

- Efficiency: "University administrators do not have as strong incentives as most business executives to lower costs and achieve greater efficiency." (p. 24)

- Improvement: "A second important lesson universities can learn from business is the value of striving continuously to improve the quality of what they do." (p. 25)

- Incentives: "Left to itself, the contemporary research university does not contain sufficient incentives to elicit all the behaviors that society has a right to expect." (p. 28)

These seem like reasonable challenges, at least for businesses. However, Bok argues "Leading a university is also a much more uncertain and ambiguous enterprise than managing a company because the market for higher education lacks tangible measurable goals by which to measure success." (p. 30). Further, he asserts "Presidents and deans are ultimately responsible for upholding basic academic values but they are exposed to strong conflicting pressures that make it hard for them to carry out this duty effectively." (p. 185).

We would expect that market forces would resolve these pressures. However, Bok reasons "Neither the profit motive nor the traditional methods of the research university guarantee that faculties will make a serious, sustained effort to improve their methods of instruction and enhance the quality of learning on their campuses." (p. 179). In other words, we cannot expect an organically based transformation of academia, despite financial and social forces for fundamental changes. There is a fundamental tension between what is naturally happening in research institutions (i.e., increased focus on the external viability of research), and the way in which this is being managed, or not managed, within the same universities. The lack of attention and process in the midst of this evolution could halt the progress and risk the outcomes of the changes.

However, successful transformation is possible. In the past 10-15 years, Georgia Tech has leaped ahead of what one would expect of incremental change and improvement. Tech has, without doubt, moved up to the "inner circle" of top five engineering programs, as reported by the most followed ranking system, *US News and World Report* (USN&WR). To put this example in context, we first need to explain the nature of how academic programs are ranked in the U.S. The remainder of this chapter then addresses how Georgia Tech accomplished its transformation and suggests how we can best understand such a leap.

RANKINGS OF ACADEMIC PROGRAMS

There are two ranking systems that receive most attention. The annual USN&WR (2003) system has become a key source for high school juniors deciding where to apply for college, and college juniors and graduates deciding where to apply for graduate study. The National Research Council (1995) performs more in-depth evaluations, roughly every ten tears. While academics tend to give more credence to the NRC rankings, the general public is much more aware of the USN&WR rankings.

For establishing the rankings of undergraduate and graduate engineering programs, there are two major views offered by USN&WR -- one ranking for overall university programs, e.g., engineering, and rankings for the different disciplines within these programs. For the overall program ranking, several variables are measured and the means are standardized, scaled and weighted so as to produce an overall score. Rankings are based on these scores. For the individual programs, the ranks are based solely on judgments of deans, chairs, and other faculty. For each of the schools surveyed in each discipline, based on the overall, quantitative ranks, the deans are asked to name the ones they feel achieve excellence in the particular disciplines. The votes are tallied and the ranks are reported.

In addition, USN&WR differentiates between those schools whose terminal degrees are masters versus doctoral. The disciplines surveyed in the engineering field are: aerospace/aeronautical/astronautical, bioengineering/ biomedical, chemical, civil, computer, electrical/electronic/communications, environmental/ environmental health, industrial/manufacturing, materials, mechanical, nuclear, and petroleum. As indicated later, Georgia Tech, for many years, has been ranked in the top 5 overall, and in the top 10 for at least 7 of the 12 disciplinary categories. Specifically, as discussed more in depth below, Georgia Tech has achieved the number 1 rank in the industrial/manufacturing engineering category for 14 of the past 15 years. This has been a tremendous change in the status quo, and the story of this change can provide insights to other institutions, as to how to change their ranks and reputations in a domain that seems to be characterized by much inertia.

Although there is much discussion and debate in the academic community concerning the relevance and validity of methods used to arrive at the USN&WR

rankings, these rankings are certainly the most well-known and recognized of the ranking systems. Despite misgivings or beliefs of over-emphasis on this particular set of university rankings, there is still widespread recognition of the public's acceptance of these rankings as important in guiding education decisions, and therefore universities continue to spend much energy and resources on increasing their ranks in this scheme.

The 1995 National Research Council report included its findings from a four-year study on the rankings of research-doctorate programs in the U.S. The study was conducted as an update of the first such publication in 1982. The NRC conducted both reputational surveys and rankings of objective characteristics in order to arrive at compound measures of university rankings. Different disciplines were researched, providing separate ranks for humanities, sciences, and engineering, and the sub-disciplines within these broader categories. Based on both the reputational and objective characteristic surveys and ratings, Georgia Tech's Industrial and Systems Engineering program was ranked number 1 in this report. This provides some credence to the annual USN&WR rankings, but is, of course, far from a definitive assessment of the parallels between the two sources.

CASE STUDY OF TRANSFORMATION

The Georgia Institute of Technology was founded in 1885. Up until the early 1970s, Tech's reputation was as an excellent undergraduate engineering school. Larger aspirations emerged with the presidency of Joseph Pettit (1972-1987), who arrived from having served as Dean of Engineering at Stanford University. Pettit's emphasis on Ph.D. research began the Institute's remarkable climb from being ranked a top 20 engineering program in the 1980s, to top 10 in the early 1990s, and top 5 since 1997. As later national data indicates, this is indeed quite an accomplishment.

During the last 15 years, enrollment has grown only modestly, slowing shifting the balance towards graduate education. The number of faculty has also only grown modestly. However, almost 80% of the current faculty has been hired in the past 10-12 years. This is an amazing level of turnover, especially given the tenure system in academia. Much of this change can be attributed to a progressive leadership that emphasized the need for a constant influx of new ideas and directions.

Almost 5% of faculty members have been elected to the prestigious national academies. Roughly one-eighth hold endowed chairs or professorships. Over one eighth have won coveted career awards from the National Science Foundation. Thus, the turnover has resulted in greatly increased excellence among the faculty, in addition to infusing the university with new and fresh perspectives.

During this time, annual awards of research grants and contracts have doubled, as has the Institute's overall budget. The percentage of the budget coming from the State of Georgia has continually declined, currently at roughly 25%. Decreasing state support of public institutions is a nationwide phenomenon, and all research universities have actively pursued several other funding sources so as not to suffer as a result of reduced state university budgets. Tech has been able to maintain its size, and thus access to necessary resources, despite this decrease in support. As discussed below, maintaining access to important resources is a critical factor in achieving and sustaining top rated status for universities.

The quality of incoming students has continued to rise during this period. Average scores on Scholastic Achievement Tests are approaching 1400 on a 1600-point scale. The mean high school Grade Point Average is 3.80 on a 4.0 scale. Undergraduate degrees now account for only 60% of degrees granted.

Although much of the emphasis has been on increasing quality of graduate education and research, the undergraduate student body still acts as the foundation of the school. Because of this, there has also been much attention placed on improving quality of undergraduate education, thus attracting students of the highest caliber. The prime focus of the undergraduate initiatives is creating an environment where the students can supplement their academic education through study abroad, undergraduate research, leadership studies, and volunteer activities. In addition, the university offers first year orientation and extensive tutoring services for all.

The changes initiated by Pettit and enhanced by his successors, John P. Crecine (1987-1994) and Wayne Clough (1995-present), can be summarized as follows:

- Greatly increased emphasis on PhD programs and sponsored research

  o Plus increased emphasis on multi-disciplinary research & education

  o Plus substantial increase of endowment, e.g., faculty chairs

  o Plus substantial expansion and upgrade of research & education facilities

  o Plus increased emphasis on university's role in economic development

- Top-down vision and leadership with bottom-up strategy and execution

  o Plus clear institutional direction

  o Plus prioritization of opportunities

  o Plus embracing pursuit of innovative strategies

  o Plus support of strong entrepreneurial institutional culture

Also of note is the 1996 Olympics hosted by Atlanta. This resulted in substantial investments in the Institute's infrastructure, ranging from new dormitories and athletic venues, to greatly enhanced landscaping across campus. In parallel, a Capital Campaign targeted to raise $300 million dollars during this period yielded almost $800 million, and safely concluded before the Internet "bubble" burst. One of the primary uses of these resources was a dramatic increase in the number of chaired positions, thereby enabling the attraction of the "best and brightest." This relates directly to our conclusions about size elaborated below.

DETERMINANTS OF RANKINGS

It is natural for an engineer or scientist to wonder what actually affects rankings of educational programs. The influences just summarized for Georgia Tech represent a consensus of current and past leaders of the Institute. However, these conclusions are far from scientifically rigorous. What do we really know about the determinants of rankings?

This question caused us to explore in depth the available data for one field – industrial engineering and manufacturing. The School of Industrial and Systems Engineering (ISyE) at Georgia Tech has enjoyed the top ranking in this field for many years, in fact for all the years that these rankings have been reported, save one over ten years ago.

As chair of this school, the first author was interested in why the *U.S. News & World Report*, and other well-reputed ranking systems, awards ISyE this ranking, as well as what we should do to preserve this position. Based on the different methods of ranking overall university programs and disciplines within these programs, it is clear that the latter are rather subjective. Therefore, we wanted to explore whether the subjective rankings could be predicted by or correlated with more quantitative, objective measures. We had the good fortune to be able to address this question in some depth due to the availability of data from a long-standing annual benchmarking study performed among all the leading programs in this field.

The a priori expectation is that certain variables, such as those that measure size of school and research dollars, will be correlated and/or able to predict changes in rankings, after a certain time period. Deans are generally aware of major changes within their peer group of schools, and although it may take a few years for the changes to reflect in the rankings, we believe that there should be some predictability in the changes of school rankings based on previous changes in benchmark data.

Each year, we email all the top programs a spreadsheet that includes entries for the following items:

- Degrees Awarded – number and type

- Enrollment – for undergraduate, masters and doctoral programs

- Student Information – SAT scores, etc.

- Teaching Loads

- Sections Taught

- Number of faculty – full, associate and assistant professors

- Faculty Honors & Awards – National Academies membership, etc.

- Faculty Salaries

- Research Support

- Staff

- Space

There are also a variety of sub items within each of the categories. These data were available for all the top-ranked programs for roughly the same 15-year period for which rankings have been published.

Statistical analysis of these data via time series analysis and non-parametric, rank-order correlation metrics indicated several interesting conclusions. First, over 95% of the variance in any university's ranking is explained by their ranking the previous year. Thus, year-to-year, there is a very high level of inertia in the system. This suggests that Georgia Tech's climb during the past 10-15 years is truly unusual.

Second, over many years, the best predictors of a university's ranking are:

- Number of faculty – rank-order correlation of 0.3-0.5, with a typical lag of 4-5 years

- Number of graduate degrees awarded – rank-order correlation of 0.5-0.6 with a typical lag of 1-2 years

- Number of undergraduate degrees awarded – rank-order correlation of 0.5-0.6 with a typical lag of 1-2 years

Clearly, size matters[1]. We explore possible interpretations of this conclusion below. The fundamental implication of size is that it provides the resources that enable cultivation of characteristics that help universities achieve world-class status.

Third, contrary to the NRC findings, level of research support per faculty member was negatively correlated, albeit weakly (0.1-0.2), with a university's ranking, particularly for the less recent years. This was due to two lower-ranked

---

[1] With one exception, the NRC report found similar correlations and associations as did we in our analyses of benchmark versus rank data. Both size – as measured by the number of faculty and graduate students – and involvement in research were found to be highly correlated with the quality assessment and rank of a program.

programs – but still top ten – having once had much higher levels of support than the other highly ranked programs. This illustrates the problems of small data sets – 15 years of data for 10 universities.

Interestingly, our data set was rather unusual. These types of data are seldom available for such a long period of time. In other words, this data set was about as good as it gets, but still insufficient to avoid possibly anomalous results. Of course, lack of data has not deterred various pundits from articulating "truths" about rankings. Our experience is that expertise in one particular science or engineering discipline appears to enable experts in that discipline to reach conclusions about social and organizational phenomena without any data to support these assertions.

Returning to the issue of size, we have developed several hypotheses about the underlying phenomena. Faculty size, for example, predicts rankings because, we think, having more faculty members increases the likelihood of having more well known "stars." These stars, we hypothesize, provide the impetus for higher rankings rather than the simple number of faculty members, especially given the subjective and reputational bases of these rankings.

Similarly, number of graduates is not the underlying predictor. We hypothesize that the larger number of graduates increases the probability of outstanding leaders in academia, industry, and government who provide perceived evidence of the excellence of the university. Size matters because it provides more opportunities for excellence.

In other words, size provides more opportunities for "tipping points" where big differences suddenly happen (Gladwell, 2000). Hoards of faculty and graduates are not the driver of rankings. However, these hoards provide increased opportunities for the people who make big differences in the world to be associated with your university.

Of course, talent also counts. So, what you want is hoards of very talented people. This almost guarantees excellence. The question then becomes one of how to get the most talent into your university. MIT, for example, has known how to do this for 50 years or more. Georgia Tech has figured this out over the past 10-20 years. Given that talent is not unlimited, the determining competency is the ability to get the talent to choose you.

It is also important to emphasize that excellence comes in many forms, many of them not academic. Large numbers of talented graduates that pursue industry and government careers will tend to yield large numbers of leaders who create strong economic impacts, both for their enterprises and themselves. Both forms of economic success provide sources of increased resources for their alma mater.

Finally, it is essential to note that the characteristics of success seldom emerge on their own. Vision and leadership are needed to recognize and foster intellectual synergies that transform a collection of talented faculty and resources into a coherent set if initiatives with high potential impact. Of course, as noted above, vision and leadership are also needed to attract the resources to attract the talent.

CONCLUSIONS

It is clear that research and education continue to be the keys to world-class status for a university and economic growth for its key stakeholders. World-class status provides a wealth of opportunities for the university to serve the public. Economic development has long been a central element of such service. Universities' international initiatives are also becoming increasingly important in their quest for broader impacts as well as the resources to fuel these initiatives.

Achieving world-class status requires excellent faculty and students, innovative programs, enormous resources, and lots of friends. Size tends to provide more opportunities, but not guarantees, for realizing these characteristics. The heterogeneity of research universities' constituencies makes it difficult to balance and satisfy competing interests. Consequently, Bok (2003) indicates that, even at Harvard, "There is never enough money to satisfy their desires." (p. 9).

This argues for the importance of vision and leadership in building a great university. World-class status is now much less likely to slowly emerge from intelligent people independently doing good work over many decades. This status is more likely to be attained when university leaders articulate focused strategies and cultivate the resources to attract the best people to pursue these initiatives.

REFERENCES

Bok, D. (2003). Universities in the marketplace: The commercialization of higher education. Princeton, NJ: Princeton University Press.

Bush, V. (1945). Science-The Endless Frontier: A report to the President on a program for postwar scientific research.. Washington, D.C. National Science Foundation.

Duderstadt, J.J. (2000). A university for the 21st century. Ann Arbor, MI: University of Michigan Press.

Gladwell, M. (2000). The tipping point: How little things can make a big difference. Boston: Little Brown.

Killian, J.R., Jr. (1985). The education of a college president: A memoir. Cambridge, MA: MIT Press.

Levin, R.C. (2003). The work of the university. New Haven, CT: Yale University Press.

National Research Council. (1995) Research-Doctorate Programs in the United States: Continuity and Change. Washington, D.C. National Academy of Sciences.

US News & World Report. (2003). Best Graduate Schools. Corporate Website: www.usnews.com

ORGANIZATION INDEX

AUTHOR INDEX

SUBJECT INDEX